The Hrvard Conference on

The Internet & Society

The Harvard Conference on

The Internet
& Society

Edited by
O'Reilly & Associates
Cambridge • Köln • Paris • Sebastopol • Tokyo

Distributed by
Harvard University Press
Cambridge • London

The Harvard Conference on The Internet and Society

Published by O'Reilly & Associates, Inc.
101 Morris Street, Sebastopol, CA 95472

Distributed by Harvard University Press
79 Garden Street, Cambridge, MA 02138

Project Manager:	Donna Woonteiler
Production Editor:	David Futato
Copyeditor:	Patti Polisar
Cover Design:	Edie Freedman
Technical Illustrations:	Chris Reilley
Tools Specialists:	Mike Sierra
	Norm Walsh
Interior Design:	Mary Jane Walsh
Printing History:	March 1997: First printing

ISBN: 0-674-45931-8 (paperback)
0-674-45932-6 (paperback with CD)

Sponsors & Organizers

BENEFACTORS

Apple Computer, Inc.

Microsoft Corporation

ASSOCIATES

Bay Networks, Inc.

Beneficial Corporation

Coopers & Lybrand, LLP

Digital Equipment Corporation

IBM Corporation

Intel Corporation

KPMG Peat Marwick, LLP

The McKinley Group, Inc.

NYNEX Corporation

RCN/Liberty Cable

Xerox Corporation

CONFERENCE ADVISORY BOARD

Kim B. Clarke
Dean, Harvard Business School

Robert C. Clark
Dean, Harvard Business School

Harvey V. Fineberg
Dean, Harvard School of Public Health

Jeremy R. Knowles
Dean, Harvard Faculty of Arts and Sciences

Paul C. Martin
Dean, Harvard Division of Engineering and
Applied Sciences

CONFERENCE CHAIR

H. T. Kung
Gordon McKay Professor of Electrical
Engineering and Computer Science, Harvard
Division of Engineering and Applied Sciences

CONFERENCE ADMINISTRATION

David A. Shore
Director, Center for Continuing Professional
Education, Harvard School of Public Health

A Note from the Editor

This volume is an edited transcription of the Harvard Conference on the Internet and Society, which took place on May 28–31, 1996. Our goal in editing this work was to keep the integrity of the spoken word while making the speeches clear. As with all transcribed material, in spite of our best efforts, there may be errors and omissions.

Those cases where we were unable to identify the speaker—for instance, when audience members spoke in a discussion—are indicated like this:

___: [*text follows*]

You will notice that three panels are formatted a little differently: "Intellectual Property Online," "The Wireless Internet," and "Life and Politics on the Net." Because of a bomb scare immediately preceding these sessions, they were not taped. In all three cases we have included session notes taken either by panelists or Harvard University students during the conference. These session notes, as well as the news stories that preface each session, were originally published online at *http://www.harvnet.harvard.edu/online/*.

Many changes have taken place in the world of the Internet since the Spring of 1996. Our goal in publishing this work was not to update the material, but to archive a vitally important piece of Internet history. You will, however, find comments, descriptions of acronyms, and references to World Wide Web addresses throughout this volume that were not in the original transcriptions. Added information is either surrounded by square brackets ([ ]) or is footnoted. (Some authors contributed their own footnotes after editing the original transcriptions. We have not distinguished these from our footnoted comments.)

We have published two versions of the proceedings, one with CD-ROM and one without, in order to suit the needs of the range of audiences. The CD version contains Microsoft's Internet Explorer 3.0, linked indexes, and all of the material in this book in an easily navigable format.

Many people have worked on the book and CD-ROM. Thanks to Mulberry Studio, Inc. for transcribing speeches; Patti Polisar for spending long hours copyediting and contacting authors; David Futato for heading up production; Edie Freedman for designing the book cover and the CD-ROM; Jennifer Niederst for graciously inheriting the CD-ROM design and implementation; Mary Jane Walsh for designing the interior text; Seth Maislin for writing the indexes; Norm Walsh for overseeing the CD-ROM process; Mike Sierra for lending technical support; Brian LaMacchia for guiding us through the nether reaches of ATM; Frank Willison for his vision; our friends H.T. Kung and Vera Groper at Harvard University for their support; Chris Palma at Harvard University Press for his ability to see the Big Picture; and the dozens of speakers who answered technical questions, contributed graphics, and worked with the O'Reilly team along the way.

Donna Woonteiler
January, 1997

Introduction: Personal Internet and Common Societal Vision

The impact of the Internet on society lies in its extraordinary potential for being all things to all people. Using a Web browser one can read, listen to others, research, communicate, and pursue virtually any interest over the Net. The Web's consistent user interface, with its wide range of applications, represents a major advance in interface design.

End users expect the Internet to keep up with their demands. Unlike many other technologies, information technology fuels itself. As soon as a faster computer is built, plans for the next fastest machine are established, using the capabilities of the existing machine. Similarly, as soon as a new network is deployed, designers collaborate on next-generation network tools. The "self-improving" nature of this technology will inevitably lead to the age of the personal Internet.

The Internet brings unprecedented power to individuals and organizations. For the first time in history, access to the population at large is no longer limited to the rich and powerful. People can use their home pages on the World Wide Web to publish fact and fiction, and companies can advertise product information that has the potential of reaching millions of people instantaneously.

The fact that the Internet will exert a major influence on society is already clear. However, we must not fail to recognize the warning signs. I am troubled, for instance, by the lack of popular understanding about this technology. This lack of understanding clouds vision and blocks the way to consensus for necessary ground rules. That such rules are needed is clear from debates on security, freedom of expression, censorship, junk email, privacy, and more. As the technology moves forward, our capacity for handling its societal impacts has been put to the test. Now society, in turn, must affect the evolution of the Internet.

Harvard's goal in sponsoring the Harvard Internet and Society conference was to provide understanding by bringing together some of the most thoughtful and articulate leaders in important fields—business, education, medicine, law, and government, as well as technology—7to discuss the potent effects of the Internet on modern life. For three days, the participants looked at the potential the Internet provides for their disciplines and the problems that lurk behind the scenes. The result was three days of lively exchanges, debates, speculations, and predictions. Technology leaders heard from doctors; lawyers listened to librarians; teachers talked to politicians; and we gained a better understanding of the global impact of Internet technology. I am pleased to have been a part of this epochal event.

H.T. Kung
Cambridge, Massachusetts
December 1996

Contents

Rudenstine Says Universities Should Lead Internet's Intellectual Development

By Esther Vegh

Calling the emergence of the Internet a "moment of real transformation" for higher education, Neil Rudenstine, President of Harvard University, yesterday reached back to the 19th-century creation of the modern research university to emphasize the magnitude of changes, and to exhort higher education to take a leading role in shaping the medium.

"I believe that universities have a special responsibility to exert real leadership in this sphere," said Rudenstine, "not in the development of the technology itself, but in the imaginative and thoughtful uses of the technology for learning."

Among the Internet faithful—a full house yesterday in Sanders Theater of conference participants still enthusiastic after a long day of panels and presentations—Rudenstine noted that such leadership would include defining values for the vast potential of the Internet for the good of general society.

"The Internet will not tell us what to do about individuals and societies that cannot afford to be on the Net. It will not tell us how to pay attention to those who are left out of the race. It will not show us—any more than our libraries full of books—how to create a just society."

While not announcing new initiatives, the speech—like the multidisciplinary Internet Conference itself—is a step in defining the role that liberal arts universities can play in guiding the rapidly changing technology and a firm acknowledgment that the Internet is here to stay as an integral part of higher education.

Still the role of Harvard and other liberal arts colleges may be less one of providing leading-edge software or hardware development than of exerting moral influence on how the technology is used. Rudenstine asked participants to question the effect they want to have on society and to proceed thoughtfully, particularly in considering how the Internet will change the lives of individuals.

The message hit a chord with some participants.

"I taught at Dorchester High School in Boston," said attendee John Scollins, Jr., of *Financial Times*. "What they need is the fundamentals of using computers, never mind the advanced functions. He tied it to something very relevant."

Rudenstine described how he believes the Internet will qualitatively change education in a way that earlier technology did not, while cautioning that the expenditures required—at least $125 million at Harvard over the next five years alone, at a time of close scrutiny of educational costs—mean that investments must reap a real return.

"The stakes are high and so are the costs," said Rudenstine.

"The last time universities experienced such far-reaching change in information processing, along with exponential expenditure growth, was [when] the huge information systems that we call university research libraries reached their point of take-off," said Rudenstine. "When that moment arrived, universities were forced to confront problems, including information overload, similar to problems we now face."

Despite the costs, Rudenstine emphasized the investment must be made. "There is a close fit between the Internet and university teaching and learning. Students can carry forward their work in ways that are tightly intertwined with the traditional ways they study and learn in libraries, classrooms, lecture halls, informal discussion groups, and laboratories."

As an educational tool, Rudenstine focused on several critical uses: the Internet as a source of unlimited information, an electronic library with a worldwide collection. The Internet as a provider of infinitely detailed, interactive course materials. The Internet as a facilitator of dialogue between teachers and students and between groups of students, even across international borders.

And the Internet as the supporter of Socratic learning, educational inquiry propelled by the student.

"The emerging theories of education have stressed not so much the authority of the faculty member as teacher, but the role of the student as an active agent, someone who searches for information," said Rudenstine. "The Internet virtually requires or even demands that the user be an engaged agent, solving problems, buttressing arguments, and exploring unknown terrain. The Internet has distinctive powers to complement many of our most powerful traditional approaches to learning."

Special Address
May 29, 1996

Neil L. Rudenstine
Harvard University

Good afternoon, and welcome once again. I'm very glad to be with you.

I want to talk about the Internet and higher education: what changes are taking place in universities as a result of this recent advance in information technology? Are the changes significant and are they likely to be long-lasting, as I believe they are? If so, why?

The questions are obviously important, because our conclusions will determine whether Harvard and other institutions should make very large financial investments in the next five to ten years, at a time when flexible resources are clearly constrained already.

But more important than the financial issues are those of substance. Any deep transformation in communications—in our ability to gain access to data, information, and ultimately knowledge—affects higher education. So as we assess the new information technology—the Internet—we have to make the right bet, because the stakes are high.

When I refer to the Internet, I use the term as shorthand for a cluster of technologies that includes networked personal computers, hypertext and hypermedia, the World Wide Web, and other adjuncts. This cluster has, during the past few years, already begun to have a dramatic effect on the ways that many students and faculty are approaching the whole activity of teaching and learning. In the context of Harvard and at least some other universities, these changes are more dynamic and pervasive than any previous breakthrough in information technology during this century—including the introduction of the personal computer itself. The effects are visible in nearly every part of our own campus, as well as elsewhere in higher education.

From one point of view, the Internet marks just one more point on a long continuum of inventions—in the course of the last century and a half—from the telegraph and cablegram, through the telephone, radio, recorded sound, film, television, early calculating machines, and then the earliest computers.

But we know that certain events along a continuum can represent much more than another simple step in a natural, gradual progression. There are moments of real transformation, and the rapid emergence of the Internet is one them.

Many inventions (such as radio, film, and television) have, of course, had a massive effect on *society*—on how people spend their time, entertain themselves, and even gain information. But, in spite of many predictions, these particular inventions have had little effect on formal, serious, advanced education. Why should the Internet be any different? Is there any evidence—or a reasoned explanation—for betting on the Internet, when so many earlier inventions have fallen short of expectations?

Let me start by mentioning a few facts.

In our Faculty of Arts and Sciences, as well as nearly all of our nine professional schools, teachers and students—including freshmen—are online, with easy access to the network. Email is commonplace. Activity on the Net is heavy at nearly all times of day and night, with the only major slowdown occurring between 3 o'clock a.m. and 6 o'clock a.m.

In 1992, we began a retrospective conversion of Harvard's entire library catalogue system—the largest university library system in the world—at a projected cost of $22 million. By next year, full catalogue entries for the approximately 12 million volumes in our 92 libraries will be online and "searchable" in any number of ways. In addition, there are more and more actual texts, images, and other materials online.

The rate of change and growth is exceptionally fast. A year ago, the Arts and Sciences Web site (which includes many subsites) experienced about 150,000 hits in the month of March. This March, just one year later, the number of hits increased to 2.3 million. There is no sign of a slowdown.

A year ago, the volume of email traffic on the Arts and Sciences network was about 80,000 transactions per day. Twelve months later, the number had grown by about 170 percent, from 80,000 to about 215,000 per day—or about 6.5 million per month.

These figures, let me stress, are only for Arts and Sciences. They do not include our Schools of Business, Design, Dentistry, Education, Government, Law, Medicine, Public Health, or our central administration and various other units.

So if I am asked whether something very unusual—something qualitatively and quantitatively different—is under way, the answer is a clear "yes." And we are only at the beginning.

In purely economic terms, Harvard has recently committed itself to spend approximately $50 million on new administrative data systems in the next five years. In addition, we expect to spend something in the range of $75 million to $100 million on academic-related information technology—above and beyond the substantial investments made since the early 1990s.

The last time universities experienced such far-reaching change in information processing, along with exponential expenditure growth, was during the last quarter of the 19th century and the first quarter of the 20th. It was then that the huge information systems that we call university research libraries reached their point of "takeoff" in accelerated development.

At Harvard, the moment of takeoff came during the 1870s and 1880s. When that moment arrived, universities were forced to confront many problems—including that of information overload—similar to several of the "electronic" problems we now face.

In 1876, for instance, Harvard President Charles Eliot reported that the main library building had become completely inadequate to accommodate the sharp rise in acquisitions. Books, he said, "are piled upon the floors....Alcoves are blocked up....Thousands of [volumes]...have been placed in temporary positions." He noted that large numbers of books were being stored haphazardly: "42,000 volumes scattered among twenty-nine [locations]...in sixteen different buildings."

The real challenges, however, were not those of space and money. They were organizational and conceptual. How should books be arranged for optimal use? What kind of cataloguing system could be invented to allow rapid access to the huge number of volumes that were now being acquired? How could convenient linkages be created among books and articles in different but related fields? How should library books be integrated into the university's programs of instruction—especially if the library owned only one or two copies of a book which fifty or sixty students were asked to read for class discussion?

Finally, what was to prevent students (and even faculty) from disappearing into the stacks for days on end, pursuing a subject from book to book, shelf to shelf, unable to discriminate easily among the unlimited number of volumes, or to absorb more than a small fraction of the information available on a given topic? And what could possibly prevent less industrious students from simply browsing their lives away in sweet procrastination?

Some of these fears were not completely new. Anxieties had been building for some time. As early as the 18th century, Diderot remarked that "a time will come when it will be almost as difficult to learn anything from books as from the direct study of the whole of the universe.... The printing press, which never rests, [will fill] huge buildings with books [in which readers] will not do very much reading.... [Eventually] the world of learning—our world—will drown in books."

Meanwhile, a treatise on public health, published in Germany in 1795, warned that excessive reading induced "a susceptibility to colds, headaches, weakening of the eyes, heat rashes, gout, arthritis, asthma, apoplexy, pulmonary disease, indigestion, nervous disorders, migraines, epilepsy, hypochondria, and melancholy."

People were warned not to read immediately after eating, and only to read when standing up, for the sake of good digestion. Fresh air, frequent walks, and washing one's face periodically in cold water were also prescribed for habitual solitary readers. Most of all, it was feared that excessive reading would make people socially dysfunctional, would take the place of direct human contact, and could well lead to a society composed of certified misfits.

Historical parallels are never exact, but the story of university research libraries, and of the habit of solitary reading, has some obvious relevance to modern information technology—especially to the Internet's ability to give individuals unbounded access to a new universe of information that they do not yet know how to manage at all well.

There is also the serious problem of the very mixed quality of the information available. How do we sort it? How do we gain maximum return on the time and energy invested in searching?

More recently, another concern has surfaced: the problem of electronic addiction. A *Washington Post* article reported that, at MIT, students unable to break the Internet habit, riveting themselves to their computers for days on end, can request that the university simply deny them access, cold turkey, whenever they try to sign on. At Columbia, the university's Center for Research on Information Access noted that there is an increasing number of students who "really drift off into [the Internet]…world, at the expense of…everything else." Several students have already flunked out, purely electronically.

Given this situation, it is not surprising that many people are now asking some of the same questions that were raised in the early days of research libraries—and expressing some of the same fears. The Internet is in fact not easy to navigate, much of its available information is trivial, it appears to be hazardous to the health of at least some peo-

ple, and it also has the capacity to distract many people from following what others regard as more serious pursuits.

Some of these concerns can be alleviated by recalling the evolution of our research libraries. Other concerns—such as the worry that the Internet may turn out to be no more educationally useful than radio or television—need to be answered differently.

Why is the Internet likely to succeed as a vehicle for real education, when so many other inventions have faltered? Why isn't it simply one more in a long train of distractions? Doesn't it, ultimately, take students and faculty further and further away from books, from the hard work of sustained study and thought, and from direct human contact with other students and faculty?

There is a very close fit between the structures and processes of the Internet, and the main structures and processes of university teaching and learning.

Let me suggest some of the main reasons why I believe that the Internet is fundamentally different from those earlier electronic inventions, and why I believe it is already having—and it will continue to have—such a major effect on higher education.

To begin with, there is the steadily mounting evidence of dramatic change and intensity of use, as I mentioned just a few moments ago. All of this is certainly not a mirage.

More fundamentally, there is in fact a very close fit—a critical interlock—between the structures and processes of the Internet, and the main structures and processes of university teaching and learning. That same fit simply did not, and does not, exist with radio, film, or television. This point is in many respects a remarkably simple one, but—in the field of education, at least—it makes absolutely all the difference.

By critical fit, I simply mean that students can carry forward their work on the Internet in ways that are similar to—and tightly intertwined with—the traditional ways that they study and learn in libraries, classrooms, lecture halls, seminars, informal discussion groups, laboratories, and in the writing and editing of papers or reports.

Some of these activities are more cumbersome and less successful when transplanted to the Internet environment. Others are substantially improved. In most cases, however, the new technology acts primarily as a powerful supplement to—and reinforcement of—the major methods that faculty and students have discovered, over the course of a very long period of time, to be unusually effective forms of teaching and learning in higher education.

Specific examples can help us see more clearly how the capacities and processes of the Internet relate so closely to the university's traditional forms of education.

For instance, the Internet, as we know, can provide access to essentially unlimited sources of information not conveniently obtainable through other means. Let's assume that most of the technical and other problems of the Internet will, in time, be solved: that there will be, as there are now in the research library system, efficient ways to help users find what they want; that there will be procedures for information quality control, and for creating more effective linkages among different bodies of knowledge in different media.

At that point, the Internet and its successor technologies will have the essential features of a massive library system, where people can roam through the electronic equivalent of book stacks with assistance from the electronic equivalent of reference librarians. In short, one major reason why the characteristics of the Internet are so compatible with those of universities is that some of the Internet's most significant capabilities resemble, and dovetail with, the capabilities of university research libraries. Just as the research library is a very powerful instrument for learning, so too is the Internet—and for much of the same reasons.

In fact, the library and the Internet are being viewed increasingly as a versatile, unified system, providing an enormous variety of materials in different formats—so that data, texts, images, and other forms of information can be readily accessed by students and faculty alike. Indeed, we are already well along this path.

If we now shift for a minute from libraries to the formal curriculum, we can see that the Internet has another set of highly relevant capabilities: it can provide unusually rich course materials online.

For instance, traditional text-based Business School "cases" are already being transformed. I recently reviewed one of the new generation of multimedia cases, which focused on a small sock-manufacturing plant in China—an American-owned plant plagued by serious production and delivery problems, and losing money much faster than it could make toes or heels.

The materials for this case began with a video tour of the plant, close-up moving pictures of the workers operating their machines—or not operating them—followed by interviews with several managers at different levels in the company's hierarchy. Interviews with the workers were also available. Detailed production and supply data, financial spreadsheets, and a company report containing an official analysis of what was wrong with the plant—all of this and more was obtainable in the electronic course-pack.

What one saw, of course, was that the interviews with different people revealed totally different theories about the plant's problems, and the data was anything but conclusive. The company's official report, meanwhile, only served to complicate the picture further. Students taking this course had to analyze not just a text and statistics, but also the whole range of attitudes, expressions, and behavior—recorded on video—of the different executives, as well as the workers.

How many of the plant's problems were basically cultural—since the key American manager spoke no Chinese, and had to communicate with the workers through interpreters? How many problems were the result of a more general human systems failure, given the fact that the plant was embedded in a larger bureaucracy? How much of the difficulty stemmed from internal inefficiency, bad organization, and managerial blundering?

What is so effective about cases presented in this way is that far more of the entire human and social—as well as operational and financial—situation can be revealed, and this requires students to deal with a vivid dramatization that is much closer to the complicated reality of an actual company that is functioning in a particular culture. Suddenly, the case becomes three-dimensional or multidimensional when the viewer brings to bear all the skills of a careful observer of human nature, along with those of an operations analyst, a financial analyst, and a scholar of organizational behavior.

In short, the Internet turns out to be an exceptionally fine tool for the creation of densely woven, multilayered, and highly demanding new course materials, that are superior to traditional case studies in several respects. Once again, an important component of university learning, the course and its texts, can now be reinforced—even enhanced—by the introduction of Internet technology.

Another point of compatibility between the processes of the Internet and those of the university concerns the basic activity of communication. We know that the constant exchange of ideas and opinions among students—as well as faculty—is one of the oldest and most important forms of education. People learn by talking with one another, in classrooms, laboratories, dining halls, seminars, and dormitories. They test propositions, they argue and debate, they challenge one another, and they sometimes even discover common solutions to difficult problems.

The Internet allows this process of dialogue—of conversational learning—to be transferred easily and flexibly into electronic form. Communication can be carried on at all hours, across distances, to people who are on-campus or off-campus. Student study groups can work together online; faculty members can hold electronic office hours, in addition to their "real" office hours; and teaching fellows can make themselves available for after-class electronic discussions.

In all these ways, the Internet works to create a significant new forum—a limitless number of electronic rooms and spaces, where one of the most fundamental educational processes—energetic discussion and debate—can be carried on continuously.

It's also worth noting that recent experience suggests that student participation levels tend to rise in the electronic forum. Students who are consistently reticent in actual classrooms are more likely to speak out, regularly and confidently, on the network.

No one should believe that electronic communication can be—or should be—a substitute for direct human contact. But the electronic process has some features that do permit an actual extension of the scope, continuity, and even the quality of certain forms of interaction, even though communication over the network lacks other absolutely essential aspects of "real" conversations in the presence of "real" people.

Finally, the Internet may well be having—it's not altogether easy to tell—a subtle but significant effect on the relationships among students, faculty members, and the subject or materials that are being studied in a course.

Let me oversimplify for a moment. The direction of movement in teaching and learning has, for more than a century, been shifting away from a previously established model that viewed the faculty member (or an authoritative text, or a canon of text) as the dominant presence—as the transmitter—with the student as a kind of receiver.

Since at least the 1870s, the emerging theories of education have stressed not so much the authority of the faculty member as a teacher, but the role of the student as an active agent, an energetic learner: someone who asks questions, searches for information, discusses ideas with others, and generally moves ahead as if he were an investigator, discoverer, or adventurous scholar-in-the-making.

In this model, the faculty member retains "residual" authority; but the faculty role, more and more, is to draw students out, to steer but not actually direct the discussion, unless it becomes necessary to do so. The faculty also organizes the structure of the curriculum, courses, and class assignments. But the course materials are not likely to be treated as "authoritative texts" that offer definitive solutions. They're intended to be approached critically, and they are usually arranged in a point/counterpoint way. This arrangement inevitably suggests that many—or even most—of the important questions in a course are still open and unresolved, waiting to be discussed and addressed and answered.

As a result, it's perfectly natural for us now, in the 1990s, to assume something that would have been quite radical just a little more than a century ago—that students should conduct much of their education on their own: with constant guidance and the right kind of Socratic teaching from the faculty, but with a very large part of the positive charge coming from the students themselves.

We don't have to agree fully with this theory of education to see that it has in fact produced very potent results in colleges and universities. We can also see why the structure and basic processes of the Internet technology appear to be so closely linked to—so compatible with—the approach to education I've described.

The Internet virtually requires—even demands—that the user be an engaged agent, searching for information and then managing or manipulating whatever is found: solving problems, buttressing arguments with evidence, and exploring new, unknown terrain. Students are beguiled into tracing linkages from one source to another. They can easily share ideas with others on email. They ask for comments and criticisms. Their posture or attitude, seated in front of the computer, is to make something happen. And they generally act or pursue, rather than merely react and absorb.

So, if we step back and look at the full picture I've tried to sketch, we can start to understand why the Internet and its successor technologies will not only have a profound effect on society in general—as radio, film, and television previously did—but why it has so quickly and dramatically begun to transform significant aspects of higher education, in a way that previous inventions simply did not.

As I've tried to suggest, the cluster of technologies we call the Internet has very distinctive powers: a unique ability to complement, to reinforce, and to enhance many of our most powerful traditional approaches to university teaching and the process of learning.

The Internet is new, it is different, and there is always reason for caution when things are changing so quickly. We need to find the right pace to achieve the best possible results for education, and those results will require an intense focus on the substance of what the new technology can deliver, as much as on the process.

It takes time and money to create superior course materials. It also takes considerable faculty expertise—technical as well as scholarly. It will take time before the Internet and the Web are easily navigable, and before they possess a large enough store of rich material to rival our greatest research libraries.

But these things will happen, and as they do, education will be enriched. Meanwhile, I believe that universities have a special responsibility to exert real leadership in this sphere: not so much in the development of the technology itself, but in the imaginative and thoughtful *uses* of the best technology for the purposes of better teaching and learning.

We must be prepared to do now—over the course of the next ten to twenty years—what our predecessors achieved during the late 19th century, when they made a conscious decision to create unrivaled university research libraries, new curricula, and new teaching methods. It can be done, and now is the time to begin.

Is there a cautionary note on which to end? Only one: good data, new information, and excellent communications are all critical to virtually everything that we do, in universities and in life. But they are not self-justifying, and they obviously do not in themselves constitute the essential stuff of education.

All the information in the world will be of no avail unless we can use it intelligently and wisely. In the end, as we know, education is a fundamentally human process. It is a matter of values and significant action, not simply information or even knowledge. The Internet will not tell us what to do about individuals and societies that cannot afford to be on the Net. It will not tell us how to pay attention to those who are left out of the race—or who appear to have already lost the race. It will not show us—any more than our libraries full of books will show us—how to create a humane and just society.

So, as we think about the effects of the Internet on society, let us not forget what we mean by a "society": what it is that we want to have an effect *on*—and what kind of an effect we want to have. It is how we address these questions—of values, of aspirations, of the consequences of our choices on real human lives, all lives—that will finally determine the effectiveness of our new technologies for education, and for people and communities around the world.

About the Speaker

NEIL L. RUDENSTINE is the President of Harvard University. He is also Professor of English and American Literature and Language. Before assuming the Presidency of Harvard on July 1, 1991, he served for three years as Executive Vice President of the Andrew W. Mellon Foundation. During the two preceding decades, he was on the faculty and administrative staff at Princeton University, where he served both as a Professor of English and as Dean of Students (1968–72), Dean of the College (1972–77), and Provost (1977–88). He received the B.A. from Princeton in 1956, the B.A. from Oxford University as a Rhodes Scholar in 1959, the M.A. from Oxford in 1963, and the Ph.D. from Harvard in 1964. He is the author of *Sidney's Poetic Development* (1967); co-editor of *English Poetic Satire: Wyatt to Byron* (1972); and co-author of a study of graduate education in the arts and sciences, entitled *In Pursuit of the Ph.D.* (1992).

Keynote Addresses

LARRY TESLER

Apple Computer

BILL GATES

Microsoft Corporation

DIANA LADY DOUGAN

Global Information Infrastructure
Commission

SCOTT McNEALY

Sun Microsystems

STEVEN McGEADY

Intel Corporation

ENRICO PESATORI

Digital Equipment Corporation

Apple's Tesler Promises to Make Internet "As Easy to Use as Macintosh"

By Katrina Roberts

The first Apple Macintoshes made computers easy to use. The next goal, says Larry Tesler, Apple's chief scientist, is "making the Internet as easy to use as a Macintosh."

Tesler, the opening speaker at the Harvard University Conference on the Internet and Society, told a packed Sanders Theatre that Apple would extend its leadership in the multimedia arena to the Internet, taking on a formative role in the development of content for the Net. "The Internet is mostly about content," he said, "and Apple's intent is to make that a shared partnership."

Introduced as the "prince of user friendliness" by Jeremy Knowles, Dean of the Faculty of Arts and Sciences, Tesler described Apple's own strategy for the Internet and discussed where Internet technology is headed in the future. Apple computers are second only to Unix as Web servers, he asserted. He proceeded to demonstrate several Apple products from the QuickTime family which can contain several data types, including animation, audio, and video. The QuickTime modality can increase the amount of useful time on the Web, Tesler said; for example, a user can start viewing a video as soon as the link begins downloading the data.

Noting that Internet access is now a primary reason for computer purchase—25 percent of computer buyers purchase them in order to get online—

he said all new Apples will come web-ready, with boosted memory, increased speed of connection, and bundling of up to three ways of getting online. He said Apple was incorporating Sun Microsystems much-talked about Java programming language into all its systems.

Speaking of hardware, Tesler addressed a much-abused Apple product, the Newton hand-held computer, which has been perceived as a beleaguered, failed enterprise. He acknowledged that a significant amount of Newton's negative reception was "our fault," but was upbeat about its future. The Newton, he said, is "a hand-held Internet tunnel. It puts the Internet in the palm of your hand."

Tesler described the Message Pad 130, a new Newton scheduled for June 1996 release, as an Internet enabler that opens up new powerful applications because it offers "wireless Internet solutions." For example, a foreman on a large construction site where the work crew is equipped with such Newtons will not have to walk around the physical site to deliver updated instructions to his crew, or to receive progress reports from them. Workers will be able to download details from blueprints or lists of tasks onto their own Newtons. To move beyond such local wireless systems to metropolitan, regional, or national or international connections, however, successful linkages require low-flying satellites. But since such satellites orbit the globe, they can raise new challenges, since, as Tesler noted, operating them entails getting frequency approvals from various nations or international organizations. However, he predicted that most Newton Internet traffic would be local. With respect to global media events, Tesler outlined some of the ways in which Apple intends to create Webcasting possibilities.

"We will go to the Olympics in Atlanta just as we went to the Grammy Awards a couple of months ago," he said. "On the Web, people can see live video of events taking place, while participating in online chats."

When Tesler turned to the question of where the Internet is headed in the future, his answer was, in brief, "It's under construction." And to him, the entity under construction is a bridge. He described Macintosh and Windows as creating "parallel platforms, with a huge chasm between them. It's hard to stop that from happening, but the Internet creates a bridge.

"What's being bridged is not just hardware; the bridge is more than connecting machines," he continued. "It's connecting individuals, organizations, nations, cultures, interest groups." He said the Internet is the final frontier in the history of communication, "until we go to another planet."

Keynote Address
May 28, 1996

Larry Tesler
Apple Computer, Inc.

Apple's Internet Strategy

Apple's Internet strategy has four parts. The first part has to do with authoring. The Macintosh is the most popular platform for desktop publishing and desktop presentation. Most media authors work on the Macintosh and produce a large number of CD-ROMs, even if they are producing those for other platforms. Apple's plans are to take the leadership we have in publishing and presentation with multimedia, and extend that into the Internet space and build a very strong role in the creation of content for the Internet.

We also are working on both the client and the server side. On the client side, we're going to take our operating system, which is very easy to use for working on personal types of applications, and make it very easy to use on network types of applications. We're also going to bring all the multimedia capability that we have on the Mac into the Internet.

On the server side, we have a couple of the most popular servers for the Web that are in the market today. Our plan is to boost that business and do a lot more work on providing people with low-cost web servers. Because authors are creating content for servers, it's very natural for the people who are creating the content to use servers that run the same operating system they're used to. The fourth part of the strategy has to do with content. Really, the Internet is mostly about content, especially with the advent of the World Wide Web. But even in terms of newsgroups, email, and so on, the Internet is really a way to get at and share content. Apple is working with a lot of other companies that are content providers, as well as providing our own content. Our goal is to set new standards in the quality of content on the Internet, using multimedia and our knowledge of ease of use.

So to sum up, our idea is to make the Internet as easy to use as we made the Macintosh. We're going to do that by taking some of our technologies—our multimedia technologies and our user experience technologies—and giving that to the Internet. The Internet is a set of standards that have been created by donations from universities, from individuals, from standards bodies, and from corporations, and Apple feels an obligation to contribute some of our standards as well. We're also going to take Internet standards that other people have defined and integrate those into all our platforms, so that the Apple operating systems and computers become first class Internet clients. We have already done most of that, but it's a constant process. We will be working a lot with third party developers. We have a record number of third party developers now working on the Mac platform. And we're also going to be working with all the other players in the Internet communities—standards bodies, universities, and other companies.

Now, overall, Macintosh has less than ten percent of the world market in desktop computers. However, in terms of Internet access, we're much stronger. Because we have had Internet access built into our operating system now for years, and a single standard way to do it, because of the authoring issue I talked about, and because of our strength in the higher education market and engineering, about 20 percent of Internet access in the world is from Macintoshes—which is still second place, but it's obviously a lot stronger (see Figure 1).

In terms of the creation of the content, using multimedia, we're number one, with something over probably 40 percent. We also are the number two web server—not after NT, as many people think, but after Unix. Unix is number one and MacOS is number two for web servers.

In Japan the number is even higher. In Japan, almost 40 percent of Internet access is on Macintosh. Part of that is because we have very good

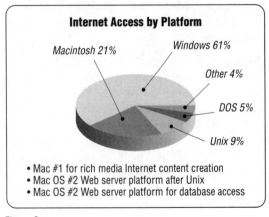

Internet Access by Platform

Macintosh 21%

Windows 61%

Other 4%

DOS 5%

Unix 9%

- Mac #1 for rich media Internet content creation
- Mac OS #2 Web server platform after Unix
- Mac OS #2 Web server platform for database access

Figure 1

support for international languages, using our WorldScript technology.

Now, I said we would be contributing technologies to the Internet, primarily the QuickTime technologies. QuickTime is not just a way to do movies, which a lot of people think: it's a way to contain data types that have to be synchronized with each other as they play over time. So for example, animations, videos, audio, title tracks, 3D, and so on, can all be contained within a QuickTime file.

We also have QuickDraw 3D, a three-dimensional package for the Mac. It has a file format called the 3D metafile format, which has been adopted by SGI [Silicon Graphics] and Netscape as part of the VRML [virtual reality modeling language] 2.0 moving world standard.

We also have an agreement with Adobe and Netscape to work together on fonts for the Web. Adobe recently made a deal with Microsoft so that we can make sure that these standards are the same on all platforms. That involves both True-Type, which was developed by Apple, as well as Adobe's Type 1.

Now, I started to tell you before about web authors using the Macintosh. Most people who create media use the Mac. They used it originally to publish documents; now they're using it to author web pages. And lately, with the interest in creating dynamic web pages with some action,

that's also becoming very popular, including pages based on Java.

QuickTime, as I mentioned, is very popular. Over 50 percent of all multimedia objects on the Web are in QuickTime format, and another 33 percent or so are in MPEG format, which is also a very important standard. The QuickTime 2.5 release, which is coming out soon, can actually access both QuickTime and MPEG files. And because the Mac is strong in this area, that's one of the reasons Harvard Business School just adopted the Mac as the sole platform for video on demand. I think they got 400 machines to do video on demand for their executive program.

I'd now like to show you our latest QuickTime work. One of the issues with attempting to do a media-rich user experience on the Internet is that people say, "It takes a long time to download big video files to your computer to play them. Isn't that a problem?" So we've made a new plug-in for Netscape, which will be shipped as part of Netscape 3.0 (I've got a beta of Netscape 3.0 here, so cross your fingers).

There's a site in San Francisco, the Blue Water site, which has an Apple QuickTime plug-in demo. In the past, if you wanted to use Quick-Time from the Web, you had to download it to your machine. It would launch a helper application and run it in a separate application. Amazingly, there are 100,000 or so sites that have QuickTime anyway, even though this is pretty inconvenient.

Let me go to the Apple QuickTime rock clip. If you look at the blue moving bar at the bottom, you can see where it's downloading the movie. But while it's downloading, it's already started to play. So you no longer have to wait.

So the idea is, you don't have to download a large video file to get multimedia. You can start playing it immediately, as soon as a little bit of it is downloaded. On a slower link, it would wait longer, maybe five or ten seconds, before playing. On a faster link, it will start playing pretty quickly. So we expect this to increase the amount of QuickTime on the Web even more. Not only that, the movie actually appears in the web page; you no longer have to launch a helper application.

Another important standard we are adopting from Sun is Java. Java is a very important language, and Scott McNealy will address that in more detail. But we are taking Java and embedding it in all our operating systems—not just into the Mac operating system, but into our Pippin multimedia player, and into the Newton operating system. We're also going to be putting it into OpenDoc, our component architecture, and in the QuickTime media layer. We're going to put Java in our servers, we're going to make our tools generate Java, and we will be working with Java-Soft as they extend the APIs [application program interfaces], along with the rest of the computer industry. We're trying to get all our developers to develop really great Java applets.

To summarize what we're trying to do on the client side, we assume that only a small percentage of the people who have a Macintosh are currently accessing the Internet. But that's changing very fast, as you've heard before. So what we're going to do is change the notion of Internet from being optional to standard. It's not that you're going to *have* to get at the Internet, but we're going to expect that people will want to do that. Twenty-five percent of those buying computers today list getting online as their primary reason for purchase.

By the end of this year, we will be boosting the memory in all our computers, so that we can run some of these larger existing web applications. We're going to increase the speed of connections, depending on the type of model, and we will also be bundling one or two or sometimes three different ways of getting at the Internet: America Online for beginners; Apple Internet Connection Kit for people who like the current suite of applications (Netscape, Emailer Light, Fetch, and all the other standard kind of applications); and CyberDog, which is a more integrated suite.

I want to talk a bit about Pippin, which I mentioned a minute ago. You've heard a lot of talk lately about network computers. Last year Apple announced Pippin as a multimedia player. It takes

CD-ROMs, which are basically developed for the Mac operating system with some slight restrictions, and plays in this low-cost box that just sits on a television set. You can take that same CD and play it on the Mac, and also make a cross-platform CD that plays Pippin, Mac, and Windows. This means that there's a very strong economic model for multimedia developers for Pippin, because they can make a CD that will play on multiple platforms, even while the Pippin market is relatively small.

The first licensee of Pippin is Bandai. (Apple currently is not making any Pippin machines ourselves.) Bandai introduced something called the "AtMark" in Japan recently, and announced a couple weeks ago that they're going to be introducing it in the United States this year.

Last week, Apple teamed up with Oracle, Netscape, IBM, and Sun to announce an agreement on a set of standards called the "Network Computer Platform." The idea of this platform is that we're all going to be making these appliance-like devices, and we want to make sure that there is some degree of compatibility between them, to make the target platform for software developers as large as possible. So rather than going off in all different directions, we agreed we would have machines that would comply with this set of standards. Now, each of us is going to differentiate from those in various ways. For example, we have our CD-ROM capability, running Mac titles, and so on. But there will be titles designed to be Network computer compliant, and there will be web sites that are Network computer friendly. All these companies will have machines that can do that. The Pippin, or something derived from it, is one machine from Apple that will do that.

Another thing I want to talk about is the Newton. Now, you read in the press that Newton is beleaguered, failed, all sorts of other negative words. It's hard to find an article about the Newton that doesn't have some big negative term associated with it. And that's our fault, because when we first announced it, we made quite a lot of to-do about how it was going to be the next consumer product, and that turned out not to be the case. But actually, it has been a very successful product in vertical business markets. With the Internet, we have now added more capability to the Newton so that it can be used as a hand-held Internet terminal. Now you not only can do Internet mail, which we've had for quite a while, but using a couple of different available web browsers, you can do wireless web browsing as well. This is currently limited to text, but in the future, as the wireless links get faster and some other changes are in place, we will be able to support graphics as well.

This is kind of interesting because you can have something that will fit in your coat pocket or your purse, take it with you, and just get on the Web from anywhere. This is very important for intranet solutions, where you take a sales force or a service force and equip them all with Newtons that have wireless capability. Or, say, people working at a construction site, where they are contacting a central computer on the construction site. In any case, a Newton allows you to stay in touch with your Internet or intranet applications, so we think that's going to be very important.

Before I move to the vision part of the talk, I want to mention our server family. We have a series of AIX servers. As I said before, Unix are the most popular servers for the Web right now; and they are very good for very fast real-time processing. We have hot-swappable power supplies, hot-swappable disks. You can even change the RAM, if you need to, in about a minute. So it's a 24-hours-a-day, round-the-clock type of server.

We also have our Apple Internet server solution, based on the Mac operating system, which is a higher volume solution: very, very easy to use, and also can support quite a high number of hits per day. In fact, there are a lot of sites out on the Web that do a lot of transactions off MacOS servers. Here are a few examples.

In the future we will be taking server capability and putting it into the client operating system. That means that anybody can go into an application, create web pages, and then save it to their own disk. You can already save it to another disk on a server on the network today, without using FTP or anything like that, just by doing a "save as." But in the future you'll be able to save it to your own disk, and just run web service right out of the Mac on your desk.

We're also going to take all our AppleTalk services on our old proprietary network and keep that network going, and make the same services available on IP [Internet protocol]. So basically, IP is now a peer to AppleTalk on the Mac. In the future, most of our work is going to be in that space.

The last thing I want to say about our strategy, again, is that content is very important as a key component of the user experience of the Internet. And at Apple, in addition to the web sites we use for our employees, for our customers, and for our third-party developers, we also have something we call "web casting." The idea of web casting is, we go to an event like the Olympics this summer [1996], where we will do the City of Atlanta at the Olympics. Or as we covered the Grammy Awards a couple months ago: we have video, we have interviews with people, online chats, and so on, all broadcast through a web site. People can get up there and actually see live video on the Web of events that are going on, listen to delayed audio, participate in chats, and so on. We're learning a lot about that. And as we learn, we're going to be helping our customers to do the same things in their own businesses.

We have many content partners we're working with, who are using our QuickTime technology and have various alliances with us, so that we can learn together how to best make effective use of the World Wide Web.

Future Directions for the Internet

The Internet is pretty much still under construction. You see a lot of web sites that say "under construction." But frankly, the entire Internet phenomenon is still under development, and it is very hard to predict where it's going to go.

The metaphor I want to use today is to think of the Internet as a bridge. Of course, the Internet is made up of lots of bridges and routers and so on, but I'm not talking about the hardware of the Internet here. I'm talking about the Internet as a bridge that connects people together, that connects organizations, vendors and customers, suppliers, and so on; that also connects different nations. The Internet is a worldwide phenomenon. It gives a way for people in various cultures to communicate. It lets people who have common interests work together at a distance.

Another element, which isn't perhaps what we think about so much, is that the Internet is causing a very interesting phenomenon in the computer business: different computing platforms—Unix, Macintosh, Windows—are being bridged by the Internet, as well as various component architectures.

So I thought, well, I'm going to be at Harvard, and you can go to Harvard and take a four-year course in history from the best history professors in the world. Or you can listen to me give the one-minute version of the history of the universe from a computer scientist's point of view. We'll start with hunters and gatherers.

Hunters and gatherers, maybe 250,000 years ago, developed something called speech. That worked pretty well. We still use it. Then we went into an agrarian kind of society some time later, 40,000 years ago, or something. And writing started appearing. And because of that, instead of just being able to talk with maybe a few dozen people or through trading networks, gradually having cultures mix together across a continent, now you could communicate over time and you could communicate with a lot of people. And this really expanded the number of people in the community with which you had contact during your life.

The Industrial Revolution brought telegraphs, telephones, televisions, and so on. And suddenly things blew up by a factor of 1,000. And the kind of community with which we work—the things we read, the people we know things about and get things from and share things with—gets up into the millions. So from the computer scientist's point of view, the end of history is the Internet. That's the Information Age, where everybody is connected to everybody else. And it's sort of the ultimate, until we discover life on other planets, or something like that. So that's it—your history lesson for the day. Glad you came to Harvard today.

Now, instead of going back to the beginning of time, let me just go back 150 years, and think about communication since we have had electricity. It's interesting to see. The telegraph originally was just something that only people with specialized skills could use. You didn't send your own telegrams. You gave your message to an agent who would send it to somebody. Around 100 years ago, we gained the ability to talk directly between people. (These aren't the dates of the inventions. This is when they started becoming popular.) Then about 50 years ago, we started getting television, there was this new idea that somebody could broadcast to an audience all at once—all over the country and eventually all over the world—through satellites. And now we have the Internet, which lets anybody communicate with anybody else. But unlike the telephone, you can also communicate one to many, many to many; any combination is possible.

If we go back just 40 years and look at the history of computing, it's characterized by four different paradigms (see Figure 2). I'm going to give a three-minute summary of a model that we developed at Apple about eight years ago. In the end of the '80s, we were wondering what the '90s would be like. So we looked at the '60s, '70s, and '80s, and tried to project the '90s from that. The decision we made was that, just like there was batch [processing] in the '60s, time-sharing in the '70s, and personal computing in the '80s, in the '90s we would have something called *network computing*—which is pretty much what people are calling it now.

The differences among them are:

Location. The people doing batch computing were in the computer room with decks of cards; the people doing time-sharing sat in terminal rooms and typed; the people in the personal computer era were able to do computing at their own desktop; and in the network era,

Four Paradigms of Computing	Batch 1960s	Time Shared 1970s	Personal 1980s	Network 1990s
Location	Computer Room	Terminal Room	Desktop	Mobile
Users	Experts	Specialists	Individuals	Groups
User Objective	Calculate	Access	Present	Communicate
Data	Alpha-numeric	Text Vectors	Fonts Bitmaps	Speech, 3-D, A/V
Interconnect	Peripherals	Terminals	LANs	WANs
Applications	Custom	Standard	Generic	Component
Languages	FORTRAN COBOL	PL/1 Basic	C Scripting	C++ Java

Figure 2

people use laptop computers, even PDAs [personal digital assistants], and can be mobile.

Users. You had to be an expert to use batch processors, and a specialist to use time-sharing systems, for data entry or whatever, whereas anybody can use a personal computer. The interesting thing about network computing is that it enables groups to work together.

Objectives. Now, what do we want computers to do? Originally, computers were for calculating. That's why we call them computers. Time-sharing systems allowed people to get access to a big computer from someplace else. Personal computers let people do publishing, presentation, modeling, and so on, that they could do themselves, at their desk, and then print and show it to somebody. Network computing is more an online kind of communication. Instead of communicating through offline media (like paper), you communicate directly through the computer, screen to screen.

Data. The kinds of data people started using were alpha-numeric, and then text, and then we added fonts. In the '90s, we're beginning to use speech. Graphics didn't really even exist in the '60s, except in a very experimental way. But by the '70s, we were doing vector graphics, bit-map graphics in the '80s, and now we're doing 3D. Also, audio and video are becoming very important in the network era. And all this has to work over networks.

Interconnection. In the '60s, "interconnect" meant connecting peripherals to computers, and time sharing was terminals. Personal computers had LANs [local area networks]. And now we have WANs [wide area networks] in the Internet.

Applications. Applications used to be custom in the batch era, and became more and more standardized through time. But in the '90s we're beginning to see component architectures, because instead of increasingly bigger applications, people want to be able to mix and match little pieces. Also, if you want to download software through the Internet, the smaller the better. And components—Java applets, Netscape plug-ins, and so on—are very nice for expediting that.

> *The Internet is about ubiquity and interoperability. It's about everybody, everywhere, being able to communicate through standards, which is essential.*

Languages. Batch computers used FORTRAN, COBOL—for experts and for people who wanted a little less technical language. In the '70s, that turned into PL1 and BASIC, languages like that. In the '80s, there was C and then various kinds of scripting languages: Visual Basic, HyperTalk, things like that, for personal computers. And we predicted that the '90s would be characterized by object-oriented dynamic languages. C++ is the nondynamic object-oriented language that is very popular today for developing applications on almost all platforms. But finally, our prediction of object-oriented *dynamic* languages came true just last year, with Sun coming out with Java as a big hit. It's the same kind of language as SmallTalk and some of the others around, but it has become very widely accepted in a very short time. And sure enough, it's associated with networking. So we were on the mark on that prediction.

So what's going on? We have here a number of trends that are intersecting. There is the Internet. There's multimedia, which has been around for a few years. There is component software, which has also been around. And these are coming together, interacting in very interesting ways. Multimedia demands bandwidth and has a lot to do with enhancing the user experience. The Internet is about ubiquity and interoperability. It's about everybody, everywhere, being able to communicate through standards, which is essential. When you have separate online services that can't talk with each other, it's tough to build a community, if some people in the community are on one network and some are on another. You need the networks to be interconnected. And finally, component software is important because it provides reusability. It allows users to configure their software any way they want. And because components are small, you can distribute them electronically.

So what have we been doing in the industry? Well, in addition to the standard operating system platforms—Windows, of course, Macintosh, Unix, OS/2—there is a new platform being created that Netscape calls the "Internet Application Platform," or the "Internet Application Framework." I call it the Platform. The idea here is that you take a lot of the Internet standards that are out there, all the ones that have been developed by the Internet community over the years, originally by universities and government agencies. Plus, now companies are beginning to donate standards—for example, Sun Java. Netscape has taken HTML [HyperText Markup Language] further than the original definitions developed at CERN [Centre Européen pour la Recherche Nucléaire] and NCSA [National Center for Supercomputing Applications]. Adobe has been defining type standards for the Web. Silicon Graphics has been involved with other companies on VRML. Apple has been working on Open-Doc with IBM and some other companies, and also on the QuickTime media layer I mentioned. As shown in Figure 3, all these things come together and form a platform on which you can base development.

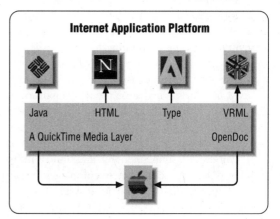

Figure 3

So what is the significance of this? I think this is very significant. In the past what we had was different platforms that basically ran on whatever hardware they ran on, had an operating system, had some kind of application toolbox for developing applications for the desktop. Then we started getting component architectures. On the Mac side, we are pushing OpenDoc. On the Windows side, they're pushing OLE [object linking and embedding]. Of course, both Apple and Microsoft have announced plans that these will run on each other. IBM is putting OpenDoc on Windows and OS/2, and Microsoft is putting ActiveX on the Macintosh, and already has OLE there, after a fashion. Then there are frameworks built up on top of this. So again we're getting this creation of parallel platforms, with a huge chasm between them, which is always a quandary for everybody. Well, it's very hard to stop this from happening.

But what is interesting is that the Internet framework has come along, the Internet platform has come along, and created a kind of bridge between these. We now have standards being created not just by Apple and by Microsoft, but by the industry. Anyone in the industry can create these. And with these new technologies, you can create network applications. There are also plug-ins that you can use inside the various OSs—in your OpenDoc framework, for example.

So I think this provides a bridge between the platforms. And it's very important, because when you do a network application like an enterprise, finance, or human resources system, it's too expensive and time consuming to have to deploy it on every different operating system platform you have (and most companies have three or four or five). By developing those types of applications for this common Internet platform, using Java as a language that will run on any computer and any operating system, you avoid that problem. And you can deploy simultaneously and much more quickly. Also, it means that if companies merge and were using different operating systems or different client/server architectures, as long as everybody is using IP, you simplify the job of merging organizations or reorganizing companies.

Now we see a new kind of computer being defined: a network computer is being built as hardware that will run this Internet platform. And this will be very important for the development of very, very low cost devices, the consumer-level devices and presentation players for business, hand-held demos, and so on. We're also taking the desktop operating systems and getting them to support these. As I showed you, the Pippin is an example of our taking parts of the Macintosh and porting them over, underneath the Internet platform. That gives you a hybrid of a network computer and a desktop computer.

Well, a lot of phenomena have transpired very quickly in the world of computing, like the adoption of PCs in the '80s. But the fastest thing I've ever seen happen is people rushing to intranets. In the past, everybody used proprietary client/server platforms, and everybody saw the advantages of client/server architectures, but it really took a long time to get them deployed. At Apple, we have been moving our corporate information systems over to intranet. What we're finding is that instead of running over schedule, we're running under, and running under budget, because it's just a lot less expensive. With all the tools that are available, with the simple protocols out there (like HTML), it's just a lot cheaper to develop enterprise systems on the Web.

So here are several sites we use to communicate with our internal employees, with our customers,

and with developers. And everybody all around the company can develop their own material. There's one significant benefit—and the reason it's simple—is that individual groups can address their customers directly, instead of having to go through IS all the time. IS just provides the infrastructure.

I think this is a profound change. Because it's often easier to develop a brand new version of an application on the intranet platform than it is to revise something on an old proprietary client/server system, it's one reason, I think, that people are moving very, very quickly to intranets. And everybody in the computer industry is keenly aware of that and trying to respond very quickly. We think that's very important because companies that have had difficulty managing multiple client platforms in their organizations are now finding that it's less of a problem. As they start developing for the intranet platform, everything can be deployed simultaneously on all clients.

Now, one of the issues is, what do you do about all your legacy systems? You spent a lot of money on your mainframe systems and so on, big databases. You're not going to throw those away and start over. What you're really trying to do is use the intranet as a way to address the end user in a uniform way. And you still want to have all those back-end systems accessible.

So I'll talk about one way that's done. One of the problems is that people have all kinds of different data spread around the intranet. And we'd like to be able to present a uniform view to the user. To do that, we need some way to describe all the different databases. Some of them are relational; some of them are full text; some of them are non-relational databases, hierarchical databases; and so on. So what we need is some kind of format to do that. Some people call that a meta-data format. We call it a meta-content format. There's actually a W3C [World Wide Web Consortium] meeting today, that is going to begin trying to standardize on some kind of meta-data format.

So what is the idea of this? Well, I'm going to give you a kind of futuristic application. Say you have a client that wants to access corporate data that is stored on all sorts of different servers, mainframes, and so on. Today, what's necessary is for the client to send a query to one and get a response, and then send another query to another one and get a response, and then a third query, get a different response. These are three different queries to three different databases that have three different schemas. The user then has to integrate all the results together manually on their personal computer—or in this case, even tougher, on a PDA, where it's very hard to do. So what we need instead is some way to mediate that. And so the concept we have is a virtual database agent. The idea is that you send a message to the agent. It sends messages simultaneously to all the servers, gets the query results, integrates all the results, and presents them to the user in a form the user can understand.

How does that work? From the server's point of view, there is a schema or a description of a schema using the meta-content format for each of the different servers, each of the different databases, no matter what kind or what format they are. The client sees a virtual schema that is simplified and is in its terms. So for example, this might be census data here; purchase patterns over here; demographic data over there. And the client will see something very simple about name and age and income and so on. What goes on in the middle is a schema mapper, which is an intelligent technology that takes the queries and maps them to each different type of actual schema, and then takes the results that come back and translates them all back into the client view. So that's all enabled by the meta-content format.

Last, I want to talk about how the Internet bridges component architectures. Netscape plug-ins and Java applets are being created in large quantities. I think of these as universal components. They can play in web browsers, they can play in applications, etc. And a lot of things are being done as Netscape plug-ins. OpenDoc is a universal container that can contain any kind of component. So the idea here is that you can develop a part for OpenDoc. You can develop a Netscape plug-in, or a Java applet, and they will all run in an OpenDoc container. And since

OpenDoc will be supported on many, many platforms, you have a very nice combination here. This allows you to mix and match components.

Conclusion

Earlier I talked about people accessing the Internet, people who author for the Internet, and people who run servers. In the past, these have been three different kinds of people. But the Internet is now serving to bridge these different roles, because when we have personal servers, everybody who can author can also be a web master and can also access the Internet. So I think we'll see a big change there.

To recap, the Internet is a bridge. It bridges not just wires, it bridges people, organizations. It bridges people of common interests. It even bridges competing platforms with the new Internet Application Platform. And it now allows the bridging of component architectures by encouraging companies to work together so all their different types of plug-ins work together.

Thanks very much.

About the Speaker

In March 1996, Gil Amelio, Chairman and CEO of Apple Computer, appointed **LARRY TESLER** to the position of Vice President, Internet Platforms. As Apple Computer's chief scientist, Mr. Tesler advises the corporation on its product technology strategy, serves as a representative of Apple's technical community, and manages certain technology alliances. His current focus is on the Internet.

Mr. Tesler has held numerous positions at Apple, including Vice President of Engineering for the Personal Interactive Electronics Division, Vice President of the Newton Group, Vice President of the Advanced Technology Group, and manager of Object-Oriented Systems. Prior to Apple Mr. Tesler was at Xerox Palo Alto Research Center, where he was a researcher at Stanford University's Artificial Intelligence Laboratories.

Mr. Tesler is published in the fields of computer science, software, engineering, and scientific applications. He earned his bachelor's degree in mathematics from Stanford University. He has one daughter and lives with his wife in Portola Valley, California.

HARVARD NEWS

CONFERENCE ON THE INTERNET AND SOCIETY

May 29-31, 1996   Cambridge, MA

Gates Insists Microsoft Will Dominate Internet

By David Bank

The new Bill Gates may seem kinder, gentler, and even funnier, but his keynote address yesterday at Harvard's Conference on the Internet and Society made clear that the goal of Microsoft's chief remains the complete domination of the world of computing.

And he's taking—or at least naming—names as he kicks butt.

Computer operating systems, for example, are becoming increasingly homogenous, Gates said. He said the 80 percent market share held by Microsoft's Windows has created a "positive feedback" phenomenon that is driving out competing systems.

"You heard yesterday from one of the minority representatives," Gates said. "One of them is even quite humorous and we'll keep him around, as long as his jokes are good."

Gates was referring to Scott McNealy, head of Sun Microsystems, who aimed several barbs at Gates during his own speech. The sparring between Gates and McNealy is part of a long-standing feud within the computer industry. For the moment, Gates may have bested McNealy, who had said he would be "bummed" if Gates filled the 600-seat Sanders auditorium. A standing-room only crowd turned out for Gates' early morning speech.

The two corporate leaders shared a talent for using their speeches as extended promotions for their companies' Internet products and strategies.

Only in passing and in general terms did they touch on the other topic on the conference agenda: society.

In his comments, Gates did go a small distance further than McNealy, who described himself as a radical libertarian and called for "as little government intervention as possible."

Gates spent about five of his 45 minutes laying out "issues for society" that he said "industry can't address." But on problems such as invasion of privacy, unequal access to information, and censorship, Gates declined to take any firm positions.

"People don't realize how many bits of information about them are being collected," Gates said. "With these toochat many people would see as an overly invasive view of their activities."

He said that protection of privacy was not a technology issue. "Once the rules are known, the computers can enforce them."

He acknowledged that divisions between "haves and have-nots" existed in access to computer technology, and that the most troubling division was between developed and developing countries.

Gates concluded on a note of vague, sunny optimism. The way we interact, work, and play are destined to change, he said, "on the whole in very positive ways."

Gates' attempt to address issues of wider concern is part of an attempt to soften his cutthroat image, said Denise Caruso, a new media columnist for the *New York Times* and writer of a cover story on Microsoft's media strategy in the current issue of *Wired* Magazine.

"It's really clear Bill's handlers are trying to make him seem more statesmanlike as Microsoft becomes more dominant in the marketplace," Caruso said. "It's not seemly for someone who owns 80 percent of the market and is hellbent on owning 100 percent to always seem like they have a stiletto in hand, going after the competition."

Gates did not directly address the increasing presence of Microsoft at all levels of the computer-communication-entertainment industry food chain, but the message was clear between the lines and in his overhead slides. A chart showing "Internet Building Blocks," for example, featured exclusively Microsoft products.

In fact it may be Microsoft's commanding position that gave Gates the confidence to poke fun at Internet hype in a video that mocked IBM's "Solutions for a Small Planet" and AT&T's "You Will" ad campaigns. A mock infomercial for the "Web of Wealth" get-rich-quick scheme featured a clip from Bill saying, "It's so easy to get into the online service provider business. If I can do it, you can, too."

That may not be true for long. Caruso said Microsoft is poised to dominate the Internet in the same way it did the desktop era of computing.

"In all likelihood, Microsoft wins this," she said. "There's no reason to think Netscape or Sun will have any long term impact on this. Microsoft has the money to iterate until they get it right. You've got to admire that at some level."

Keynote Address

May 29, 1996

Bill Gates
Microsoft Corporation

Good morning. It's great to be back [to Harvard]. One of the few classes I actually attended was held here, and it was Professor Finley telling us about the *Odyssey* and the *Iliad*. What we are going to talk about today is a little bit different than that, but it is an epic tale of massive changes.

The personal computer revolution has been an amazing thing. It started 20 years ago with the invention of the microprocessor, and it's swept its way not only through businesses, but now more and more into homes as well. And it certainly has changed the way people think about creating documents. Over 90 percent of all documents are now created electronically. But in a certain sense it hasn't changed all that much. Despite the fact that you create the documents electronically, the way you transmit them and distribute them is still overwhelmingly to print them out and deliver them, just as you would if they had been hand-written.

So we really can't say the PC until now has been a communications tool. Now, there are a lot of reasons for that. The cost of communications has been high. And it's also very important that communications technologies are all subject to critical mass phenomenon; that is, as long as only a few people, say, have a telephone, then the telephone has no utility. It's only if you get a substantial percentage of the people that you want to stay in touch with, who understand it, own it, and use it regularly, that you get any value out of it as a communications tool.

In the last couple of years, with several factors coming together, we're now seeing the PC emerge as the latest communications device. This all has to do with the Internet and the number of users that have gotten connected. We're now experiencing the positive spiral effect. Since we've passed critical mass, the more people that get connected, the more people want to create content, and the more people are willing to send mail. And that is a powerful positive feedback phenomenon. The amount of content we have today is fantastic. But it's nothing compared to what we'll have a year or two from now.

People are being drawn in. I have a lot of friends who swore they would never buy a personal computer. But if I ask them, "What are your hobbies, what are you interested in?" and then sit them down and help them browse through some of the web pages on those topics, I can see that they're starting to break down. They're starting to think that maybe it's a relevant tool for them, even though they're not fascinated by the technology itself.

So it's fair to say what's going on today is like the arrival of the printing press, or the telephone, or the radio. And these communications tools did have pervasive effects. They made the world a smaller place. They allowed science to be done more efficiently. They allowed politics to be done a new way. They had a modest impact on how people were educated, but people were optimistic that they would make a very big change.

Now, the personal computer connected to the Internet is far more powerful in many ways than any of these other communications devices (see Figure 1). It's not a broadcast medium where you have to have millions of people interested in something. If only a few people are interested, it works just fine. Even if they don't know each other, there's a way to connect to each other. The marginal cost of publishing in this environment is close to zero. If you have a PC with a little bit of software and a communications line, you're as empowered as Time Warner or any other media conglomerate. Now, that doesn't mean anybody will ever visit your home page; it just means that it's there. A lot of people have very lonely home pages nowadays—and they're just dying to have their mother or their relatives get out there and visit them.

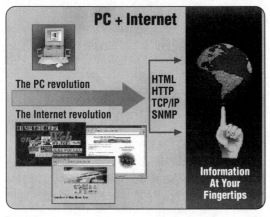

PC + Internet

The PC revolution

The Internet revolution

HTML
HTTP
TCP/IP
SNMP

Information
At Your
Fingertips

Figure 1

There are really two miracle technologies that have brought about these changes. The first is the microprocessor itself. It's subject to what Gordon Moore coined and is now called "Moore's law": Every 18 months the power of the chip more than doubles, and without any increase in cost. The second is communications technology—in particular, optic fiber connected to digital switches. The rate of improvement of the speed we can get for a certain cost in switching technology is actually improving even faster than the microprocessor. And you can contrast that with other technologies, such as improvements in car fuel efficiency and work productivity.

You know, there is nothing like exponential improvement. And it makes it very hard to predict things. The easiest way to predict things that are improving that rapidly is to simply say to yourself, "What if computing was free?" What if you could have an infinite amount for every person? What would you do? Likewise for communications. What if there was infinite bandwidth connected to every point on the globe? How would people use that? How would they reach out and think of the world differently?

Now, by some time scales this revolution is going to be very, very rapid—something like the telephone. There was a whole generation of people who grew up thinking it was a strange device, and they didn't have to incorporate it into their lifestyle. And then the generation that came afterwards took it for granted, just never even thought

about it. Computers and the Internet will be the same way. At some point they'll be so much a part of everyday life that, like piped water or electricity in your home, you'll just take them for granted. You'll think it was quaint that people once had to read the same newspaper, that it wasn't customized for individual preferences. You'll think it was quaint that if you had a curiosity about a subject you weren't able to reach out and explore that subject in very individualized fashion.

But this may take something like 20 years. And the main reason is that to get these high-speed connections to be pervasive, particularly getting them into homes around the world, will take a long time. We are in a kind of frenzy right now, almost a gold rush, where people are in some cases even going overboard, being a little bit over optimistic about how quickly it will take place. But even though they're wrong, to have something like this happen in 20 years is really unprecedented.

People often ask, "What was the very first day that this happened?" Well, the technology and protocols involved actually go back over 20 years ago. When I was a student here, in 1973, TCP/IP, the basic protocol that drives all this stuff, was in widespread use. In fact, it was kind of fun. There was a data computer down at Carnegie Mellon, where they had a big disk and they'd let you just FTP files down there and keep them. And that seemed rather fantastic, because the cost of this storage was very high. The fact that you could randomly send files down there and they would just sit there and be available, seemed fantastic.

There are two things that have brought this into the mainstream. Certainly you can't ignore the fact that having a lot of PCs out there was part of it. But another important recent event was the arrival of hypertext capabilities, or web capabilities, that have an ease of use that goes way beyond file transfer, such as FTP or even Gopher, which were intermediate steps that allowed you to have various types of menus.

The idea of hypertext has been around since the early '60s. People like Doug Engelbart (at Stanford Research) or Ted Nelson actually talked about sophisticated forms of hypertext that still don't exist in the Internet today. In the Internet today, for example, if you have an article, it's very hard to annotate that article and have people come in and see your annotations. Ted Nelson talks a lot about that. Certainly we will have that with software over the next couple of years.

I think the key factor in all of this is the arrival of low-cost communications. To somebody who's involved in this business, none of the individual pieces are all that amazing. The way a name is resolved, the way a page comes up—it's all pretty straightforward. But the fact that it all works at the scale that it does today—with an economic model where you don't pay extra for additional usage or for connections to the person next door or around the world, with traffic jams that are rather modest, with technology staying ahead of that with ever-faster switches and faster optic fiber—that is an impressive thing.

It's very different from the phone system, where one company had all the factors under their control and made it come together. Here you have literally hundreds of companies who provide the backbone, the software, the computers, and yet it all works extremely well.

When the PC was first becoming popular it was a lonely cause. There were a few people who believed in it. We'd get together and say, "Aren't we right about this? Aren't we going to overthrow those big computers? You know, we'll show everybody." We felt like people weren't paying enough attention. Well, this revolution is the opposite of that. People are almost paying too much attention. You can't get away from it. You go to watch TV, and the next thing you know there's just URLs on your TV set. And all the arcane things are there for everybody to look at. Well, I think it's fantastic, given the impact of all this attention.

It's the biggest gold rush that has ever taken place: new companies, big investments. And this almost overinvesting is a wonderful thing for

moving this system ahead very, very rapidly. The competition is quite incredible. All these protocols are being worked on in companies and committees, and so even for something like security that just six months ago was a major issue, now we have a protocol for using credit cards across the Internet. In some ways it's actually more secure than simply giving your credit card out on the phone, because the actual merchant that you buy from doesn't even get the credit card number, they just get a bunch of bits that only the bank is able to access. This is just one example of how rapidly things are advancing.

People are almost paying too much attention. You can't get away from it. You go to watch TV, and the next thing you know there's just URLs on your TV set.

The authoring tools are also a big part of this. It's a lot easier to create pages now than ever before. It's important to remember that the machines involved here are going to continue to improve. We haven't reached any limits in terms of Moore's law or the other elements in the system. And some of these improvements change the character of what it is like to be browsing.

For example, if you have large storage capabilities on your machine, all the parts of the Internet that you are particularly interested in can be downloaded to your machine in advance. So you just set aside some of the storage and say, "I'd like to look at The Journal and Sports Zone." Say you have 20 or 30 sites, by the time you walk up to your machine it will have retrieved and posted the latest updates, so you won't have any speed issue there.

With the PC of the future, you won't even have to turn it on and off. It will essentially be on all the time, so there will be no waiting. The extra speed will be used to make it more engaging, delivering better graphics and sharper multimedia.

Higher-speed connectivity is fundamental here. In a sense, the speed of the network today is too slow for the mainstream. Waiting four or five seconds for a page to come up just doesn't cut it.

We will have new ways of interacting with the system, not just through the keyboard, but also with voice and handwriting—even what I call video. With a camera that you use for video conferencing, watch what's going on, and it can see who's sitting down in front of the computer. You can even make gestures indicating, "Scroll that document," or "Throw that document away," and it will see that on camera and do those things for you. So we're going to be driving the ease of use very rapidly.

One thing I think is important for video is getting very high quality screens. The computer screen today is a terrible limitation versus reading the newspaper. The amount we can get up on the screen is far smaller. Now, the investment levels, say, in flat-screen technology promise that sometime in the next decade large screens will be quite affordable. And so the surface of your desk can be entirely a flat screen. A lot of the walls in your office or your home will also be flat screens with very, very high resolution. And that greatly shifts which documents you'd like to see on paper versus on screen.

At Microsoft, we use electronic mail to send everything. But when you get a large document, it's very typical to print it out on your local printer and then read it on paper. Many people do this because anything more than about four or five screensful is just easier to read that way. But with new screen technology, that won't be necessary.

When you think of the Internet as it evolves, there will actually be quite a variety of devices connected to it. There will be the device that you sit close to, which I think will continue to be called the PC. It will be so much better than today's PC that it almost stretches the term. But you'll have both desktop and portable machines. You'll have the screen you sit further away from, which will be the successor to the TV. This will evolve by building electronics into the TV, or by

using what's called the "set-top box" that connects the TV to the cable system, or by having a game machine with a modem that connects you to the Internet.

Today that's not happening because the communications charges so high that pages aren't authored that way (along with other limitations). But over time, taking advantage of the TV certainly will make sense. Even the phone will be connected to the Internet. Now, it won't be much different than today's phone. It may have some voice recognition to do directory for you or the long-distance charges may be cheaper, but the fact that it's all hooked together will be seamless to you. You'll certainly have a small device that you can carry around and put in your pocket. It will connect to a wireless digital network, and we call that the Wallet PC.

There are a lot of early, almost prototype machines in this space, but they're too expensive and they don't really connect up to the Internet. Digital wireless networks are still not pervasive today. It will be three or four years before all the pieces are in place. But the ability to see a map of where you are because the device will contain a global positioning sensor, the idea of being able to receive messages, track your charges, use digital tickets and digital money—all of this will be so much more convenient with the small devices everyone will have. And there will be a companion device for the large machine. Whenever you add something to your schedule, for example, it will automatically appear on both machines.

Finally, just to give you a sense of the variety there will be, you will have a computer in your car that, once again, uses a map, shows you traffic conditions, lets you find the nearest restaurant— whatever your particular tastes are. And this will be commonplace, with all of these machines hooked up and working together.

There are two main things that really hold back the Internet. Why doesn't it happen overnight?

1. The rate at which people can absorb new technology. How quickly are people drawn in to this? How quickly does the content get up

there? That just takes time. The fastest that any new communications technology has been broadly adapted so far has been about 20 years. Now, if it were just the suffusion rate holding back, it would probably be less than a decade.

2. The speed of these networks (see Figure 2). Unlike PC performance or storage, which improve exponentially, communications networks—especially when it comes to the local part of the connection—are much harder to improve because there is a fixed cost of going in and putting in new wires.

So there are three different generations of communications bandwidth. First, there's today's phone system, which is called narrowband, and uses a modem that connects to 28.8 Kbps [kilobits per second]. In that world, text comes up super-fast, but images take maybe five or ten seconds to appear, so it is quite limiting.

Internet Speed Generations

Generation (kbaud/sec.)	Speed	Technology	Application
Narrowband (today)	14.4 28.8	Modem	Text great, Pictures OK
Midband (1-2 years)	100-400	ISDN, PC cable modem	Pictures great, video OK
Broadband (2+ years)	1500+	ATM	Video great

Figure 2

Then there is the next generation that's called midband. There are many examples of this: ISDN, ADSL, PC cable modems. We're just at the very start of this phase. They are all fairly expensive today and they're not all hooked up. And in the case of things like the cable system, there's a pretty significant rebuild required on parts of the system before it has two-way capability. It certainly will happen, but by the year 2000, of all the homes in the U.S., at most three or four million will have these midband connections. Most, if they're connected to the Internet, will

still be narrowband and we will still be trying anything we can to reduce the bottleneck this lower speed creates. With midband, the still images are very, very fast and you can start to do fairly low-quality video, probably good enough resolution for a video conference but not good enough to watch a two-hour movie through that kind of resolution.

The holy grail is broadband. That's where you get data rates over a couple of megabits. And the beauty of that is you can start to do very high-quality video. So as you track how this spreads out, it's very important to watch communications speeds. Those are the key holdbacks.

The U.S. is in the best shape of any country, because now with our telecommunications deregulation bill, we have a very strong cable industry that has an incentive to compete with the phone companies for the most difficult piece of the business, local access. But having two companies in competition is not as good as having ten or twenty. And assuming there's no radical breakthrough in wireless technology, with the kind of data rates we have now, the only way for urban areas to become connected is through wires running into the home.

As I said, there's a lot of competition, and that leads to great industry issues. There are many different operating systems. You heard from what I might call some of the "minority representatives" in that area yesterday. And they're very articulate. They do wonderful work. One of them is even quite humorous. And, you know, we'll keep him around as long as his jokes are good.

The world of operating systems becomes more and more homogeneous over time. Today something like 85 percent of the computers on the planet run the same operating system. There's sort of a positive feedback cycle here! If you get more applications, it gets more popular; if it gets more popular, it gets more applications.

Historically PCs were very low-end computers. And it's only because of Moore's law that they're now moving up into the more demanding tasks: scientific visualization, business databases, and so on. There are still some pieces being put into place to make that all happen. And the competition is very healthy. The only thing to take away from the industry issues is that we're going to keep each other honest, and no one's going to get something that's completely proprietary.

There will be a variety of machines that hook up to the Internet. And the software that does all this is going to be fantastically inexpensive. In fact, it's Microsoft's position that this software will just be built into every operating system. So, if you get Windows, you'll get your browser and everything you need. If you get a Mac, you'll get your browser and everything you need. You won't even have to buy add-on pieces. The history of computing is like that. Things that you first had to get separately are increasingly built into the system.

So you have this dynamic of deciding when you use a PC versus a more expensive machine. And more and more, that moves to the PC. There is at least a paper battle about a PC versus something less, something whose virtue is its incompatibility or that somehow something has been taken away. This is the so-called *network computer*. And, you know, it's a great debate that will be raging for a long time. There's going to be a key milestone, though, when they actually make one. And at that point you'll be able to look at it and ask, "What did they take away? What is left?"

I think PCs will get less expensive. They've got to get less expensive. They've got to get down to even $500 for all of this to be pervasive. Absolutely, that can be done. When you have so much innovation, the market's always making a tradeoff, between using the innovation just to get a more powerful machine at the same price or using the same machine at a lower price. And many people have offered inexpensive PCs. They haven't sold that well because the market to date has opted for more power at the same price.

But as the absolute level of power gets to a certain level, as we get the ability to do advanced 3D graphics, motion video, and all of that, then eventually the marketplace will move a lot of that innovation into lower prices. In fact, just recently the price of memory has come down a lot, a very

positive thing. So certainly there will be a variety of devices. What's a PC and what's not will be a tough call.

When we think of the Internet, there are so many different scenarios that are important to consider. It is not just messages, it's also a replacement for paper forms. Think about bills today and how much overhead there is when you mail out a bill. You've got to print it and then mail it. Somebody's got to look at it, figure out if it's wrong, and they call somebody. They mail something back that then goes into a system. Compare that to simply having an electronic bill arrive in your mailbox. If you don't think it's right, you send back a mail message saying, "Why is this this way?" You get a quick response. The overhead you can take out and the convenience you can bring to this is very dramatic.

Companies like to get the data out there. Clients like to share information. Every night the new DNA sequencing information goes up onto the Net and the biotech companies look to see if anything that fits the patterns they're trying to find is there. So it's advancing the progress in science.

We'll have a lot of software to allow for conferencing across the Internet. If you want to negotiate a contract, you'll be able to both talk about and edit the contract at the same time. If you're confused about what's going on with your PC, you won't just have the phone connection, you'll be able to share what's on your screen and have somebody step you through exactly how to do something. So support will be greatly improved.

The very mechanism of capitalism is greatly improved by the electronic market. Some large markets like currency are well mediated today. But most markets, like finding a good lawyer, a doctor, a consultant with particular capabilities, or even a babysitter, are not well mediated markets, in the sense that matching all the buyers and sellers with the right characteristics is hard to do. Well, electronically, that's immensely easy to do. So you'll see things like classified advertising and the Yellow Pages move over to electronic form as the system becomes more and more pervasive.

One of the key areas that people haven't figured out yet is, how does this impact learning? Clearly there is a lot of potential here, but universities really haven't decided how to redesign themselves when all of this expertise is out there on the Net and easy to browse. What does that mean for the way they function?

One of the flavors of the Internet that will catch on very quickly is the intranet. That's where you share things internally. You could do this previously with PCs networked together, but knowing server and filenames and when the file was last updated was just too much work. So now you have pages that are completely self-explanatory, and if you want to do something, you just click on a link to do it. People are now sharing documents this way. And it just uses today's software, perhaps new versions of it at very low incremental costs, because the PC and the network are already in place.

One of the practical applications is to reduce the cost of PC ownership, using the intranet to transmit software updates and any information that people want. Companies today maintain all the human resource data, all the financial data, sales tracking information, and all the project status information on pages that people just navigate. It's an incredible thing. I doubt there's a company represented here who couldn't go further using this type of sharing and getting more value out of the PC investments that have been made.

There are a lot of software pieces that go into this, including enhancing the operating system and having server software that makes sure the data is dished up very quickly, even from structured databases that have very good protection and clear capability. You'll have actual code in these applications—BASIC code, C++ code, and Java code—and you'll have the normal sort of text and images. All those things have to be brought together to get very rich information sharing.

One of the things that's hard today is navigation. The way you move around the Internet is very different than the way you move around your local storage files. So we're going to unify that so

you use the good things about the Web when you're working with your local information. Then you only need to learn one metaphor. Instead of files and pages, you have it brought together so every time you look at a directory, it's like a web page. You can think of a directory today as a degenerate web page where all you have is the link; the individual filenames for each link can take you to that file. Here you can have lots of explanatory text, and, whether something's local or remote, it becomes transparent to you (except for the speed).

We also need to take these pages and make them active, so that you can get sound, or a movie, or a ticker with news and stock data. That's starting to be a big thing. Now we need a little technology to do this, and we're pushing an approach called Active Controls and Active Documents (Figure 3) to achieve this.

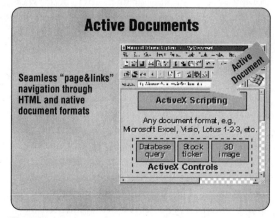

Figure 3

The quality is going to be there. Don't let anybody confuse you or question if security will always be broken or traffic will be overwhelming. The industry will solve those issues. The broader challenges and things that the industry can't address alone are some of the things I have said here.

People probably don't realize today how much information about them is stored electronically. It's pretty phenomenal. And with these tools, you can gather the little bits of information together and create what most people would view as an invasive profile of somebody's activities.

So the question is, if you buy a product from a company, what right do they have to take your name and give it to other people and make that information public? This will be hotly debated. And it has nothing to do with technology. I mean, once the rules are known, the computers can enforce them. But it is a deep problem There are people who think that, politically, we should go to the extreme and have ultra-privacy. That, too, has some real drawbacks: you're not able to use information on behalf of a person, to let them know about sales or to guide their navigation in a richer fashion.

One of the bigger issues is the haves versus the have-nots, if you actually believe that this is great technology. If you think it's all just a bunch of computer guys goofing around, then don't waste any money worrying about pervasive availability. On the other hand, if you think this is like books, where everybody as part of their learning experience or throughout their life should have access, then we have to figure this out: How do we use schools? How do we use libraries? How do we allocate resources to make these things available? There are a lot of great pilot programs in these areas, but it's a tough problem. And the issue of the haves versus the have-nots has many dimensions: rich versus poor, urban versus rural, young versus old, and perhaps most dramatically, developing countries versus developed countries.

We have a lot of security technology in the network. I said that's going to work very well, but from time to time that security technology will break down. And so having ways that you can fix that and bind the difficulties this creates is very, very important. Recently, in Japan, they had electronic cards for playing Pachinko. Somebody broke the code on those cards and made fake pachinko cards. So a couple of large companies in Japan lost $100 million because of all that essentially counterfeit currency generated from playing Pachinko.

There's a huge political issue with security, which is that the U.S. government makes it impossible for software companies here to export decent security technology. That's because the spy agencies still want to be able to tap into mail that's sent around the world by different people. Unfortunately for them, this technology is fairly pervasive, so there's this debate about whether they should let software companies, like Microsoft and others, actually have decent security.

Another security scheme is for you to give the keys to the government. So, if the government wants to look at what you're doing, they can do that. The problem is that the people who the government might want to look at are the very ones who won't turn the keys over. So this whole key escrow debate is a big issue that has a political element to it.

A final issue centers on what should be allowed on the Internet. There are some idealists who think the Internet should be a lawless environment. That is, that you can libel somebody, you can promote securities that are fraudulent, you can steal software, you can do anything out on the Internet. It seems kind of neat to think, "Oh, this is something that no government will touch." Well, that's not likely to take place. The Federal Trade Commission has started to look into scams here. The Securities Exchange Commision is starting to look into problems that have come up here. Certainly companies that sell copyrighted software or people with intellectual property are very interested in rules being enforced.

There are some tricky issues, because the fact that the network is global means that a national government has a hard time reaching out to various Internet sites. And telling all the communications providers in a country to block an Internet site is very difficult, because it can move very quickly. So censorship becomes very difficult, and yet there are going to be some rules about what's out there on the network.

My belief is that there are some very deep implications. It's great to see early debate about what all this means. The way we learn, the way we elect politicians, the way we spend money, even the way we entertain ourselves, is destined to change, and on the whole in a very, very positive way.

About the Speaker

WILLIAM H. GATES, 40, is chairman and chief executive officer of Microsoft Corporation, the leading provider of software for personal computers worldwide.

Gates began his career in personal computer software when he started programming at age 13. In 1974, while an undergraduate at Harvard University, he developed BASIC for the first microcomputer, the MITS Altair. Led by the belief that the personal computer would ultimately be a valuable tool on every office desktop and in every home, Gates formed Microsoft with Paul Allen in 1975 to develop software for personal computers.

Gates's early foresight about personal computing and his continuing vision have been central to Microsoft and the software industry. With Gates's leadership, Microsoft's mission is to continually advance and improve software technology, to make it easier and more enjoyable for people to use software. The company is committed to the long term by investing in new technology, state-of-the art projects, and new products for the further expansion of personal computing.

HARVARD NEWS

CONFERENCE ON THE INTERNET AND SOCIETY
May 29-31, 1996   Cambridge, MA

Dougan: Net Technology Has Global Impact

By Debra Bradley Ruder

A group of Peruvian cab drivers knew a good thing when they saw it. Their government had decided that cellular phones should be for wealthy people only and boosted the prices, but the cabbies felt they needed the phones to help promote their services.

"After a few weeks, some of these cabs started parking on the side of the road," Diana Lady Dougan recalled yesterday afternoon in a keynote speech to the Harvard Conference on the Internet and Society. "What were they doing? They were turning themselves into pay telephones."

Dougan used the example to illustrate the different ways that technology can be used, especially when entrepreneurship and competition enter the fray—and when governments miscalculate in their regulations.

She also used it to underscore the importance of looking beyond the Internet to a variety of communications tools being used around the world in different and creative ways to approach problems.

"The Internet is dependent on a variety of infrastructure," she told a crowded Sanders Theatre. "The growth of the Internet is going to depend upon the growth and diversity of infrastructure in the future." She noted, for example, that more than 50 countries are currently restructuring to attract private-sector financing to build up their telecommunications networks.

Dougan, who has held senior policy and management positions in the telecommunications and broadcast field for more than two decades, is senior adviser and chair of the international communications studies program at the Center for Strategic and International Studies in Washington, D.C.

She is particularly active in Asia, and she was recently appointed to co-chair the new Center for Information, Infrastructure, and Economic Development in Beijing, which is under the auspices of the Chinese Academy of Social Sciences.

China is going to be "the proving ground for the future of the Internet," she said. "I believe how China is going to deal with access and use of information will have more to do with our grandchildren's lives than anything else I know."

Dougan sought to downplay some of the hype about the Internet, noting that less than five percent of the U.S. population currently has access to the Internet, and less than half the world has yet to make its first telephone call.

"To hear most people talk, the Internet is going to do everything except solve world hunger and do our laundry," she said. "I think we've got to be careful about that…. For all the talk about how the Internet is changing our lives and having an impact on society, we have a long way to go."

As new actors step onto the Internet stage, industry must take an aggressive lead in regulating the Internet, according to Dougan. Although she does not want to see a government body like the F.C.C. assume that role, she believes government should play a part. "Industry can do it, but it can't do it by saying, 'Government, stay out,'" she warned.

Dougan serves on a global infrastructure commission, which aims over the next three years to strengthen the role of private-sector leadership, bring developing countries into the process, and focus on applications and models that work.

"We need to continually share ideas and information," she said. One of the biggest challenges many countries face, Dougan concluded, "is turning data into information, information into knowledge, and knowledge into wisdom. Together, I think we can do it."

Keynote Address
May 29, 1996

Diana Lady Dougan
Global Information Infrastructure Commission

Benchmarking the Internet: Reaching Beyond the Bell Curve

Having had the opportunity to hear my fellow keynoters, Scott McNealy and Bill Gates, I realize they have established an obligatory ritual whereby as a keynote speaker, I must begin my remarks by confessing my past association with Harvard. OK, I admit it, even I did a little stint at Harvard, but it was only one of those Harvard Advanced Management Programs and a few guest lectures. I am not foolish enough to comment on how past involvement with Harvard extrapolates into this conference on the "Internet and Society." We have plenty to talk about focusing on the present and the future.

This year, as software becomes more friendly, bandwidth more capacious, and phone lines more accessible, we are being inundated with growth statistics that are spewing out faster than microwave popcorn on "high." Despite the epidemic of corporate and regulatory restructuring, the growth velocity of industries driven by information technologies, in addition to the communications industries themselves, has been breathtaking.

This growth is not without pain. Just this morning, for example, National Public Radio did a wistful feature on AT&T's announcement that this week will mark the end of live telephone operators for their New England service. So there go another hundred or more jobs lost to technology. But amazingly, save for the Unabomber, even Luddites are captivated by the economic horizons of information technology and service. The vortex of this excitement is the Internet.

It is easy to get carried away with the Internet as the seemingly endless frontier for new jobs, new ideas, and new commerce. In theory, every man, woman, and child on the planet could settle in this "electronic frontier" by early in the next century. According to the Internet Society, over a thousand new Internet domain names—and heaven knows how many addresses—are being added daily. In most countries, access to the Internet is doubling monthly. In some of the least developed countries, where only a few dozen people could tap into the Internet a year ago, the statistical growth percentages are ten- and twenty-fold. Experts who scoffed last year at estimates of 300 million people on the Internet by the end of this century as outrageously high, now think those projections may be conservative.

> *More than half the people on earth have yet to make their first phone call. Touching a keyboard is not even a vision.*

To hear some people talk, the Internet will do everything short of solving world hunger and washing our laundry.

We must be careful about getting swept up in all the "hype." There are clouds gathering on the horizon, clouds which can cast dark shadows on the Internet as a positive force in society. Today I want to bring you more than just a weather report on some of the issues.

A few sobering thoughts will put things in focus. Even here in the U.S., where the Internet started, less than five percent of the population actually uses it. More than half the people on earth have yet to make their first phone call. Touching a keyboard is not even a vision.

These statistics are more than factoids. They are stark reminders of a reality which must not be ignored. We have a long way to go before we can share a vision of "Internet and society."

Hype, Metaphors, and Reality

There is little doubt that the Internet is creating whole new industries and job categories. How many employment agencies could have told you even a year ago that "Web site managers" were anything other than exotic jobs for spider lovers? The number of new jobs and businesses directly attributable to the Internet is impossible to assess. By my calculations, the fastest growing job categories may be "Hyperbole Harvesters" and "Metaphor Managers."

I confess to helping turn them into full-fledged professions. Starting with my first presentation explaining the potential of interactive cable TV to a city council almost three decades ago as Cable TV Marketing Director for Time, Inc., to keynoting the Electronic Commerce Summit in Beijing last month, I have found it difficult to avoid hyperbole and metaphors. While I have the good grace to blush at some of my own past over-ripe rhetoric, I do believe it is important to help people think beyond the mind-numbing statistics of economists or mind-boggling terms of technocrats. Indeed, I was amused to see this month's *Wired* magazine quotes one of my early attempts at "metaphor murder." But it may be even more on point than when I first asserted over a decade ago: "If there ever was an Information Revolution, it is over. Information won!"

But it is time to move on to new realities as well as new metaphors.

Instead of linear images of Information Highways and high drama of "Revolution," new concepts are needed. For example, in terms of impact on electronic commerce, it is more useful to describe the Internet as an immeasurable number of electronic, multimedia shopping carts whizzing down the aisles and across the malls of commerce and ideas. These electronic shopping carts are not weapons of revolution, nor are they limited to the highway imagery of traditional networks. But they are knocking down clerks and cashiers and picking up customers and consumers. They are also tipping over tidy shelves of inventory where "country of origin," content, and price were once clearly labeled. Moreover, while electronic fund transfers are now well accepted between financial institutions, consumer transactions still find problems of security, reliability, and liability languishing at the "virtual" check-out counters.

I use this extended metaphor and imagery to introduce the idea that we must change the way we think about electronic communications if we are to understand its effect on society. It is not enough to talk about updated software and expanded networks. The policies which enable or thwart services are equally important.

It is not enough to have information infrastructure. One must be smart about its use and the policies and practices which make it accessible and useful. For this reason I am spearheading a special new initiative called the IIQ—Information Intelligence Quotient. The IIQ will provide a much needed framework for measurement, analysis, and benchmarking of the impact and interrelationship between information infrastructure, its accessibility and use. I will detail this later in my remarks.

First, let us take a look at some of the infrastructure, access, and use factors which will be critical to the future of the Internet.

The Internet Depends on More than Networks

While the Internet uses networks, it is not itself a network. It is dependent on a diversity of infrastructure. Furthermore, that infrastructure is of little use if it is not affordable as well as accessible. Why is this important? Global growth and diversity in infrastructure are critical to growth of the Internet.

The competitive factors which led to more accessible and affordable telecom services in the U.S. are well known. A high watermark was the breakup of AT&T in 1984. The AT&T break-up did a lot more than fuel domestic growth and competition. It unwittingly was a major propellant internationally as well. Ironically because the Regional Bell Operating Companies [RBOCs] were precluded from providing long distance services at home until this year's telecom reforms, they became major investors and operators of telephone systems abroad. Moreover, the RBOCs often rode investments in alternative networks such as cellular and cable as Trojan horses to invade the borders of entrenched monopolies. As an aside, now that competition is finally opening up in earnest here in the U.S., I predict that most RBOCs will default their international opportunities to major foreign carriers and new telecom consortiums. While this shift back to a domestic focus is understandable, it is short-sighted. But I'll come back to that point later.

The diversity of technology as well as expansion of infrastructure become increasingly important as new applications are developed and as new customers come online. In my view the increased portability and mobility of wireless services is the biggest growth area. A surgeon in a field hospital or a geologist on an oil platform currently has little use for Internet services which are tethered by limits of traditional wires and cables or even the high capacity of fiber. Indeed, in my judgment, if the last Internet explosion came with the World Wide Web, the next one will come when the flexibility and portability of wireless access to the Net become commonplace.

Meanwhile, we must not ignore humble services such as voice mailboxes and paging networks as strategic infrastructure. Too often we forget that customers don't always need real-time high speed, much less interactive communication. While I won't elaborate on it now, I predict that an "Internet voice" connection, while not as fast, efficient, or clear as regular telephone service, will start sounding better and better to anyone with friends far away. I wonder if my old friend Sir Arthur Clarke had this in mind when he grandly declared in one of his science fiction books that "all phone calls will become local by the year 2020."

Bill Gates asserted this morning that short of a radical breakthrough in wireless technology the Internet will remain on wire. I respectfully disagree. Technological "breakthroughs" have been sitting on laboratory shelves for years.

It is customers, applications, and enabling policies which push the market.

In this context, wireless may have gotten an unexpected boost with this spring's PCS [Personal Communications Services] auction. The $10.2 billion feeding frenzy over the "C-block" licenses (which were considered the least attractive) looks like an invitation to financial indigestion for the winning bidders. But it may also be an inspiration. Simple mobile phone service won't be enough to pay the bill to compete with cellular and offset auction costs; other features must be developed. Even the benefits of immediate digitization won't be sufficient to attract enough customers to compete with already well-entrenched cellular services. Thus it is logical that applications other than voice service will get serious attention.

I predict wireless Internet access for electronic commerce, electronic data interchange, and other revenue generating applications will be early targets for PCS. This is already happening with cellular outside the U.S. For example, wireless Internet access is now available in Hong Kong, whose market includes several competing networks and the world's second highest per-capita cellular use.

Meanwhile, cable and broadcast industries are wasting no time in positioning themselves in the Internet picture. In this morning's newspaper, the cable industry reported a 92 percent increase in set-top modem sales this year. Broadcast networks are talking about "information skyways" and eyeing the HDTV [high definition television] spectrum bonanza with the Internet in mind. Even the humble radio is getting into the act. For example, Progressive Networks plans to download radio news, information, and music programs to your computer by early summer. The unveiling of a "Direct PC" satellite service and "turbo-Internet" downloading capabilities by Hughes is already raising the ante on the high-stakes face-off between more entertaining computers and smarter TVs.

All of these multimedia advances sire bandwidth "hogs." The increasing bandwidth appetites combined with exponential growth of general Internet use for less exotic services such as email and file transfer are raising dire predictions of Internet "choke." Add in Internet voice and you have a scenario which should not be left to science fiction scriptwriters.

I repeat: growth and diversity in infrastructure are critical to growth of the Internet.

New Players and Cultures Are Taking Over

Like it or not, electronic commerce and entertainment services are now paying for, if not dominating, the Internet. Gone forever are the early Internet days of a cozy community of scientists and academics who exchanged dense data and clever email.

The libertarian culture of the Internet has given way to market reality. Industry must take aggressive leadership and responsibility to offset increasing government controls.

As this audience knows well, it was the U.S. Government (and the Defense Department to boot) that created and ran ARPAnet, which in turn spawned the Internet. It is more than ironic that they parented the world's most collegial, uncontrolled, and unhierarchical entity. While the Defense Advanced Research Project Agency is long forgotten, Vint Cerf and other Internet pioneers in our audience today are still charting a future of creativity, flexibility, and individual empowerment. We owe them a great debt of gratitude.

Indeed, I believe the Internet provides the "template" for 21st century communications.

Meanwhile, for all the hoopla over the merging of technologies, the corporate cultures have not. Computer hardware and software companies were born competitive and entrepreneurial. While phone, broadcast, and cable companies all say they want to compete, the blood and money shed over the Telecom Act of 1996 demonstrated that their "regulatory relief" cultures are hard to shed. I have no doubt that if the computer industry had grown up in a highly regulated environment like telecom and broadcast, we would not be where we are today.

The Internet's unhierarchical, "nobody controls it" structure has been key to its growth and success. To many this is an elegant curse. But it's like the old Chinese curse: "May you live in interesting times." Many of us wouldn't want it any other way. There is a libertarian streak in most Americans; I count myself among them. It is no accident that the Internet reflects our common law heritage of belief in free speech and rights belonging to people instead of governments. Because academic and research communities in most countries pride themselves on independence and collegiality in pursuit of knowledge, the early spread of the Internet maintained this culture. But it is sadly naive to believe it can prevail in today's environment.

A recent interview in *Computerworld* with Don Heath, the new President of the Internet Society, is emblematic of the old Internet culture. When asked if there is any role for government to ensure openness and universal access to the Internet, his answer was an unequivocal "No!" Scott McNealy struck much the same note in his speech yesterday.

Unfortunately, the world is not so simple. Many customers, not just countries, are demanding that governments play a role in insuring standards and practices, especially in areas which are already regulated or arbitrated in other contexts. While Internet veterans rightfully groan at proposals calling for a global FCC [Federal Communications Commission], they ignore ideas like this at their peril!

The absence of sovereign jurisdiction or "cyber laws" has benefits. However, there is a long list of issues which industry as well as government needs to address in "cyberspace": theft, pornography, rights of privacy, liability, currency controls, taxation, and tariffs are only a few of the concerns which are even more complex in an electronic environment seeping beyond traditional borders, to say nothing of nation states.

The old line is true: "With more use comes more abuse." For example, hackers have always been part of the Internet culture. More and more, however, they are criminals, not "egos at play."

The National Computer Security Association estimates that on average, one computer on the Internet is broken into every 20 seconds, and that just accounts for the detected break-ins. The large majority of computer break-ins go undetected. The *Financial Times* reports there are now more than 20,000 aggressive, deliberately destructive hackers in the U.S., and the number is growing over five percent per month.

As the Internet universe expands and more money is at stake, criminality will increase.

Piracy and intellectual property rights are some of the high visibility areas where industry needs government help. According to the Business Software Alliance, copyright theft costs U.S. industry over $15 billion annually. USTR's "copyright alert" list includes China and several European countries where, they assert, more than half the software in use is illegally procured. Meanwhile here at home, the picture is only a little less grim. The Business Software Alliance calculates that 35 percent of all the software in the U.S. is illegally used. Enforcement is difficult at best. In my view, the tradition of community respect and ethics, which most societies feel about traditional mailboxes and libraries, must be targeted in schools and offices to expand to include electronic communications. Criminal and trade penalties will only scratch the surface.

In the U.S., computer security has been primarily a matter of individual and industry responsibility. Indeed, one of the fastest growing information technology industries is computer firewall construction. The Yankee Group predicts, at a 66 percent annual growth rate, that firewall construction will be a $1 billion business by 1999. The private-public sector relationship in this area is an uneasy one. The Clinton Administration found that out when it tried to invoke the "Clipper chip" initiative to deal with government concerns over crime, terrorism, and national security. It ended up in a buzz-saw of well-orchestrated opposition.

Unlike the U.S., governments in most of the world feel a paternalistic need to play caretaker, if not outright gatekeeper, of national culture, politics, and currency, reaching far beyond issues of national security. This mentality is not limited to the few remaining totalitarian regimes. In Europe, for example, where memories of Nazi persecution of Jews still haunt the continent, most European Union governments, including modern Germany, put privacy protection of records and data on a higher plane than the right of access.

France takes the well-publicized position that cultural preservation requires restrictions and quotas. Whether that will effectively extend from televisions to computers is still in debate. Meanwhile, in Asia, a number of countries are considering Singapore's policy of "protecting" the public from unbridled access to the Internet.

Surprisingly, the notion that industry rather than government should take lead responsibility in electronic commerce got a boost recently from an unexpected supporter: China.

Last month, a Call for Action and Principles for Globalizing Electronic Commerce was adopted in China at the Electronic Commerce Summit, which I had the honor of co-chairing with the head of the People's Bank of China and the Coordinator of China's "Golden Projects." Since China has installed more phone lines in the last year than the rest of the world combined, their hosting of this summit was more than symbolic.

It is noteworthy that the Chinese not only hosted the forum, but the seminal "Beijing Declaration" identified a concise four-point set of principles and a fast-paced timetable to advance globalization of electronic commerce. It was an unprecedented agreement for many reasons, not the least of which was the very first principle adopted, which states:

> A dynamic electronic marketplace depends on the ability to tap the benefits of fast changing technologies and new service offerings. Governments should facilitate a favorable environment, but industry has lead responsibility for developing the cooperative frameworks for global electronic commerce.

Because I also co-chair the permanent Center for Information Infrastructure and Economic Development [CIIED] based in Beijing under the Chinese Academy of Social Sciences, I see China as much more than a major market. I am often asked whether China will become a superpower. From my perspective, the answer is not "whether" but "what kind" of superpower China will be in the years ahead. In my view, how China deals with the issue of access and use of information may have more to do with how our global grandchildren will live than any other single issue.

During an in-depth meeting I had earlier this month in Beijing with China's Vice Premier Zou Jiahua, we discussed the Internet at length. As the visionary of China's informatization initiative, Zou has more than a layman's understanding of firewalls, computer viruses, and terabytes. While he agreed with my assertion that the Internet and electronic information access in general are important to China's development, he also reminded me of the old Chinese saying: "Even a good stew can be ruined by a single mouse." I could not resist pointing out the double entendre meaning of "mouse." It amused him mightily. He listened soberly, however, when I explained that many international companies have begun to self-regulate with "red light" districts to proscribe objectionable material. The Vice Premier responded that if markets don't self-regulate, the government may overregulate.

Traditional Institutions and Influences Under Siege

The Internet has two overriding and unusual characteristics. First, it bypasses traditional institutions which have long served as gatekeepers and distributors of information. Second, it erodes traditional influences of time, distance, sovereignty, and even identity.

The strength of the Internet depends on maintaining the ability to bypass barriers and circumvent hierarchies.

As most of you know, the Internet was purposely designed to get around gatekeepers and to self-heal when anyone attempts to damage it. Therefore it is designed to be accessible through an ever expanding variety of infrastructure.

Problems of access are critical, but they will not be solved by subsidies or even the artificial promise of "universal service." Public policy makers must avoid the arrogance of predetermining what people need or will pay for. It may surprise you to learn that it is a communist, not a capitalist country, that makes people pay through the nose for telephone installation. The Chinese Ministry of Post and Telecom charges of more than $800 for a basic residential phone connection are among the highest in the world. I was not surprised, however, when MPT Minister Wu recently explained to me that many provinces are now doing promotional discounts to attract new customers. Communist market economics is alive and well.

All governments are guilty of regulations and laws which second-guess the market. One of my favorite examples is cellular phones in Peru. It is a wonderful dramatization of how much conventional wisdom can be wrong, how governments can miscalculate, and why the marketplace often knows best.

As in many countries, the Peruvian government made the assumption that cellular phones would only be marketable to the rich. Accordingly they reasoned: we'll charge a great deal of money and make a big profit off of these rich people.

Only a few signed up for this high priced cellular phone service. And not surprisingly, they were indeed limited to wealthy people, with one exception: a bunch of cab drivers. These cab drivers decided that they needed cellular phones to help promote their cab service since there were problems with their trunk radio systems. But a very strange thing happened. After a few weeks, some of these cabs started parking on the side of the road. What were they doing? They were turning themselves into pay telephones.

Since traditional phone service was limited and unreliable, people were being creative in meeting market demands. Indeed, a number of the cab drivers started making more money as pay telephone operators than they did as taxis: strong tribute to what can happen when customers and entrepreneurs, rather than governments or regulators, are allowed to flourish.

Developing Countries are the Customers of Tomorrow

My anecdote about Peru also highlights another important point with which I want to leave you. It is critical that developing countries be brought into the process. Indeed, a major dimension of the Global Information Infrastructure Commission, which I had the honor of founding, is to involve developing, not just industrialized, countries in globalizing electronic communications. The mission of the GIIC is to foster private sector leadership and private-public sector cooperation in the development of information networks and services to advance global economic growth, education, and quality of life. The GIIC is an independent, non-governmental initiative involving diverse communications industry leaders from around the world. At their inaugural meeting, hosted last year by the World Bank, these leaders identified the involvement of developing countries in the building and utilization of a truly global and open information infrastructure as one of three essential steps in accomplishing that mission.

This is strategically important. It is not just nice or humanitarian. The facts of the matter are that the developing world will become the markets of tomorrow. The newly industrialized are already the markets of today. According to World Bank analysis, 20 percent of global GDP and 41 percent of global growth is generated already by developing countries.

If we are to expand global economic growth, it is critical that we reach beyond the G-7 and highly industrialized world. For the first time, less developed countries are asking, "How can we play?" not, "How can you pay?"

Today over 50 countries are in the process of restructuring their telecom sectors and adopting regulatory reforms to attract private sector investment to expand and upgrade their information infrastructure. These countries recognize that telecommunications and information technologies have become critical to economic growth and development. Most have determined that government resources can no longer maintain the level of investment required, much less keep up with market demands. Thus, the focus is on privatization. Within varying political limits, competition and external investment are also encouraged to speed up the process.

However, the reforms needed to continue expanding infrastructure and services are neither politically easy nor economically graceful. Very powerful and entrenched interests are under siege. For example, government-owned phone companies are among the largest employers in over half the world. International phone call revenues remain the single largest source of foreign currency in over a dozen countries.

The collapse this spring of the World Trade Organization negotiations on liberalization of basic telecom services further illustrates this is not an easy process. The negotiations have been put on warm ice until next February. Internet users cannot afford to be innocent bystanders. The U.S. predicts that customer cost savings brought on by opening basic telecom markets will save phone customers more than $1 trillion between now and 2010. Phone customers are increasingly Internet customers.

Countries large and small are putting telecommunications high on their agendas. Most of them think their problems are somehow different or unique. In reality I have found that all countries are wrestling with many of the same issues and questions.

Asking the Right Questions Is Not Enough

The Internet, and electronic communications in general, is fast outpacing traditional networks, constituencies, and applications. Not only is there no single "correct" model for communications development, but the models that are working now may soon be outdated or overtaken by technology and market forces. There are few measurements or benchmarks countries can utilize in assessing what is really working in practice, not just theory.

While there is no single set of "right" answers, countries as well as companies should be answering a lot of the same questions. I might add, in one way or another they are relevant to the Internet's future as well.

- How do we make electronic communications more accessible? more affordable? more applicable?

- Whose policies are working and why?

- What can we learn from other countries and companies?

- How do we measure effectiveness and impact?

Measuring Impact: The Information Intelligence Quotient—The IIQ

If we are to effectively address these shared questions and concerns, I believe we must develop new and different ways to measure and benchmark critical dimensions of electronic communications. Current definitions and measurements of infrastructure, accessibility, and use are inadequate and misleading. For example, despite the importance of other versatile and competitive delivery systems such as cellular, VSAT, and cable, not to mention computers and TVs themselves, the only widely accepted measure of electronic communications deployment remains the "teledensity"—the number of phone lines per capita.

Teledensity is useful but outdated. We must consider other factors, many of which I have outlined here, if we are to effectively measure or benchmark what's working and why. At this critical time, when countries as well as companies are restructuring to take advantage of new technologies and services, both government and industry need better tools to measure impact and define success. They must reach beyond traditional definitions of infrastructure and look at the "who," the "how," and the "why" information infrastructure is used or needed. In the process, the policies and practices which enable as well as thwart need to be assessed. As I mentioned earlier, I am spearheading the concept of an Information Intelligence Quotient—IIQ—to develop more effective ways to assess impact.

Like IQ tests themselves, my proposed IIQ approach is not without controversy. Indeed it is tempting to indulge in the pun of talking about *Beyond the Bell Curve*. But to be "intelligent" in our policy reforms and resource deployments, we must reach beyond quantification of today's telephones as the focal point for development.

The IIQ will provide a much needed framework for strategic resource and policy planning as well as benchmarking. This benchmarking approach will be designed for use in specific application areas such as education and health care, not just economic productivity. In the process, the IIQ can be a catalyst for new ideas and approaches to old problems.

During the coming months, working with the program I chair at CSIS in Washington and with affiliate organizations in Asia, Africa, Europe, and Latin America, we will be developing criteria for benchmarking. While we will draw on existing data banks and traditional measurements of the ITU [International Telecommunications Union], World Bank, OECD, and our partnering institutions, we will also utilize case studies targeting success stories in specific regions and applications.

Like concepts such as "total quality management," I see the IIQ as a tool for planning and strategy, not just for comparative analysis. Benchmarking the Internet and other elements of electronic communications will be neither easy nor static. But it is important. We must test hype against reality.

I applaud Harvard for providing this forum for us to share ideas and perspectives. While we each may see things differently, we clearly share many common challenges. For all of us, I believe that the greatest common challenge is "turning data into information, information into knowledge, and knowledge into wisdom." Together we can do it.

Thank you.

About the Speaker

AMBASSADOR DIANA LADY DOUGAN has served in senior communications, foreign policy, and management positions for more than two decades, including appointments by both Republican and Democratic Presidents in Senate-confirmed positions. She is currently Senior Advisor to the Center for Strategic and International Studies and Chair of the International Communications Studies Program, where she oversees a diversity of initiatives and strategic analysis involving government and industry leaders from developed and developing countries. She is especially active in Asia, including co-chairing the Governing Board of the Center for Information Infrastructure and Economic Development (CIIED), based in Beijing, under the auspices of the prestigious Chinese Academy of Social Sciences (CASS).

Ambassador Dougan writes extensively and lectures internationally on a wide range of information technology, media, and foreign policy issues. She has authored numerous articles and is active in a diversity of educational, cultural, civic, and public policy endeavors including the Council on Foreign Relations, the Fighting Blindness Foundation, the Council of American Ambassadors, and the Academic Technology Foundation. She also chaired the Editorial Advisory Board of The Christian Science Monitor TV. Her public service and professional leadership accomplishments have been recognized by a number of awards, including the Distinguished Service to Journalism Award (University of Utah), National Security Agency Medal, the Outstanding Women in Communications Award, AAUW's Utah Women of the Year, Outstanding Young Women in America, and Distinguished Citizen of Maryland (Governor's Award). In 1965 she was given the Key to the City of Seoul and made an honorary citizen of Korea.

Sun's McNealy Says Java Will Challenge Microsoft

By Margie Kelley

Consider the gauntlet thrown.

In his keynote address to attendees at Harvard's Conference on the Internet and Society, Sun Microsystems head Scott McNealy made it clear that the guy from Microsoft had better be on his toes now that Java is here.

"I want you to know I graduated from here. I didn't drop out and I'm still trying to make up for his two and a half year head start," McNealy mused to a near-capacity but sometimes skeptical crowd in the Sanders Theatre.

In between quips about his Harvard necktie and his hopes that he drew more of a crowd than Gates—who will deliver his keynote address today—McNealy revealed Sun's intentions to boost worldwide Internet access via its hot product, the programming language called Java. He also cautioned the government to stay out of the Internet's development.

Statues of early Americans James Otis and Josiah Quincy seemed to look on in fascination as McNealy used high tech multimedia technology to present his case for a single computing language—one developed cooperatively by competing computer manufacturers and untouched by government regulation. Known for its Unix workstations, servers, and related software, and the maxim, "the network is the computer," Sun Microsystems has, of late, been experiencing a huge burst in the popularity of Java, which acts as a universal interpreter of computer program languages.

"This is a very different model of computing," said McNealy. "Computers will be faster. They won't be driving some big operating system—they will just be driving applications."

Looking more like Bill Gates than Bill Gates in chino slacks and loafers, McNealy spoke in the same technologically visionary terms. His talk—alternately jocular and technical—was a fast-paced romp that captivated listeners.

Citing Java's potential to improve Internet access, networking, communications, business, and education, McNealy said Sun is going to "go like crazy" to drive the technology forward.

"We're seeing two fundamental changes," McNealy said. "We're no longer talking about multiple dialects and multiple operating systems. It used to be that nobody could communicate across these different systems. Now, we have one dialect. The network sets the standard. Until recently, nobody had even heard of Java or Mosaic, and now Java obsoletes every programmer."

While Java is currently offered to users through the Internet browser, Netscape, it has yet to be adapted for use across all operating systems. However, according to McNealy, every manufacturer of operating systems has agreed to work "to be able to run the Java language across environments."

"We want to create an opportunity where everybody can get on the Internet," he said. "This conference is no good if we can't get everyone on the Internet."

Quipping that PCs are "like fingerprints, no two are alike," McNealy described Java as a simplifying and cost-saving approach to computing and networking.

"You just turn on your computer, and click, and it would immediately download your applications," he said. "You could check in to your dorm room and there would be a Java client, not just a desk. It would be part of the furniture and would allow you to register for class, turn in your homework, look up reference books, all online. It would re-engineer the whole learning process."

McNealy blamed government regulation for spoken language barriers and re-emphasized his view that government should not regulate the Internet too closely. "The biggest problem between nations has been that there's not one language," he said. "There's no government mandating computer language, but a fixed operating language is a better answer. And you'll never get sued if you write in Java. It gives us the ability to innovate.

"Most computers are veritable petri dishes of applications—an ugly science experiment," he quipped. "Java is like a prophylactic—can I say that here?—layer which enables safe computing."

Clicking a remote control to change the enlarged computer screen images on stage, McNealy showed a variety of diagrams supporting Java's attributes of "write once, run anywhere, on anything, safely."

Not surprisingly, McNealy sees Java as having significant implications for the computing industry. "There's a new model, a new paradigm. To launch, we give it away for free." On screen, flash a progression of words on a grid: "Ubiquity, Mind Share, Brand Equity, and Profits."

Too good to be true?

"I'm sure it will happen," said conference attendee Dr. Ing Steffen Leistner, of Booz-Allen & Hamilton in Dusseldorf. "The whole idea of the Internet has reached critical mass, beyond which it is self-propelling. I think a singular language would come about sooner or later anyway. Also I think Microsoft understood a year ago that if they don't sign on, they will stand alone, because it's going to happen."

"I think Java has lots of value in some systems," says Ron Evans, of Mitel Corporation, Kanata, Ontario. "It will help ubiquity and reduce devices."

"I'm not sure," said attendee Ian Munns, also of Mitel. "It's a matter of building a better mousetrap. It will force more competitiveness. A single operating system would be positive, but I don't think Java has found its proper place. Also, I don't like that, with Java, someone else is controlling me."

Munns' colleague, Ken Anderson, is not convinced by McNealy either. "With 250 million PCs on the planet, I'm a bit skeptical. Where's the money in it? What's his angle?"

Keynote Address

May 30, 1996

Scott McNealy
Sun Microsystems, Inc.

Oh, dear, I almost filled the place. I'll be really bummed if Gates fills it tomorrow. But I'm sure his ears will be burning before this one's done.

It's kind of amazing when you think about this kind of an event happening and that people would actually show up. A year or two ago it would have been funny to think about holding a conference, getting people to show up, and talking about this issue and it's impact on society. It seems to us that it's not such a big deal. We've been on the Internet since we started the company in 1982 and it's kind of fun to see people discover email.

But it's happening and stuff is happening. We've had this strategy for a long time. People come to me and say, "Did you really say 'The network is a computer' back in the '80s?" Well, yeah, we did. That was our slogan for a while, and then we hired some new marketeers who hired consultants. We spent lots of money to come up with new slogans and finally figured this one was actually better so we went back to it.

There have really only been two styles of computing. The first is post-based computing—that's the model where you have either a mainframe in the server room or a mainframe on your desktop called a PC. It basically has a file system, a disk storage system, backup and software distribution mechanisms, and it's 32 megabytes. We believe in this network-centric computing model and that's what we've invested in—that's really what's created the Internet, an intranet. (I love how we've renamed corporate networks "intranets." It sells more. Our stock price tripled so I guess we'll keep calling them intranets. So maybe the intranet is the computer. I hear our stock price going up right now. Go buy quick.)

The other major change is open interface. These are really the two fundamental changes in the computer industry. No longer are we talking multiple dialects. Fifteen years ago, everybody spoke a different computer language. Some people spoke Wang OS, other people spoke VMS, others spoke DOS, and nobody could communicate or interoperate; nobody could share information. Everything had to be reported or reengineered, or whatever.

What happened was the world said, we can't deal with that, we're going to have to consolidate to a few dialects. Hopefully, we'll consolidate to one open dialect that everybody can implement. That's what open interfaces have done. And the thing that really made all of this happen was the Internet. The Internet sets the standards now. It's not computer companies that set standards anymore. It's not a big Fortune 500 organization that says, "This is going to be the interface." The network sets the interface.

There's obviously something at work here when Microsoft is actually OEMing software without buying the company. It's because the Net is setting the standards. I think this was appropriate with the movie *Twister*. The marketing department's always right on there. But it really is changing. Today is within a day or two of the birthday of the announcement of Java. Think about it. A year ago, Java didn't exist. Now everybody's doing it. It's a bigger brand than Sun. Three, four years ago, nobody had heard of Mosaic. Some kid at the University of Illinois was off inventing it, and just look at how fast things have happened.

We used to say there was 20 percent skills obsolescence per year per employee at our company. I think that's conservative, very conservative. Right now Java basically obsoletes every programmer on the planet unless they learn it. And though making their skills obsolete is not exactly why we invented it, it is a fallout of the pace of change we're all dealing with. I'm not going to linger on this, but everybody sees what's happening: your Nintendo game kind of melds into your TV and your TV kind of becomes a computer. Then you start doing telephone calls and video telephone calls over the Internet, using your cable modem, and you see that these worlds of telecommunications, data communications, and entertainment all come together.

If you think about it, the computer companies have been providing datatone, the cable companies videotone, and the telephone companies dialtone. All of these are coming together into one environment, coming in over one wire, coming in wireless, and coming at us everywhere. We're all going to be wired in very strange ways. Does anybody here *not* have an email address? I see. No one. Two years ago, I'd ask who has an email address and three people would raise their hands. Today, you can't get anybody to raise their hands to the other question. Everybody has an IP address today.

Down the road, very shortly, we're all going to have multiple IP addresses. Your car will be an IP address, your TV will be an IP address, your phone will be an IP address, your cellular phone. All the GSM [global system for mobile communications] phones now are basically IP addresses in Europe. They're all digital. This is the way the world is going. You need to think about the world as converging. It is happening. Television companies are embedding. NorTel announced they're putting Java in their telephone handsets. This stuff is happening and it's happening faster than we all know how to deal with.

Now I'm not sure I believe this but I think it's probably the politically correct way to present what the Internet's all about. I don't think it's equal opportunity. It's equal opportunity if you're online, but if you're not, it isn't. Despite my education (and I'd like it to be known that I graduated from here, I didn't drop out early. I'm still trying to make up for that two and a half year headstart he got), I am a raving market economist capitalist. I am an absolute (at least from an economic perspective) raging libertarian, and I don't believe that the government has more than just a couple of tasks that should be probably less than ten percent of the GNP in any country.

The worst thing that can happen, I think, is that we get government intervention. It's not going to be fair for a while—not everybody's going to have online access. But we can really slow this thing down if we start to demand universal access and guaranteed universal access. You obviously don't want to have discrimination. But being online is going to be a huge advantage.

Those who are online will get access to huge amounts of information, to distance learning, to faraway places. They will get a view of the world that anybody who is not online just won't be able to get.

Two-thirds of the planet (or pretty close to that number) dies without making or receiving a phone call. Isn't that cool? In some ways, I think it is. In others it isn't, because you're fundamentally cut off. So it's not going to happen that each of us will have an IP address connected online as universal access. What we've got to do is go hard, go like crazy, and drive this technology through the private sector as aggressively as possible, with as little government intervention as possible. I think the government will have to get involved in some areas and sort some things out.

One of the big issues is security. I always laugh when people say, "Do you send email on that topic?" I say, "Well, yeah. Have you ever sent a letter? Are *you* worried about security? You take this envelope, paper thin, stick your content in, and seal it with a little spit. Then you give it to the government for three days, who may or may not put it in the right little tin box with a tin door, no lock, on a public street, available to anybody with a car. And it sits there till you decide to get it. And you're talking to me about security?"

Electronic security is actually far more valuable. I was on a trip through Omaha, Cincinnati, Fort Lauderdale, Bentonville, Arkansas, and about three other places in four days and my wife got a phone call from Visa and they said, "We think your card's been stolen." Somebody had lunch here, bought something there, a room there, hotel, car there. And she replies, "Oh, that's my husband. Thanks for calling." Click. But see, electronic allows much better audit trails, much better exception reporting, that sort of thing. So I think actually electronic commerce, electronic mail, and all these kinds of things, give us audit trails, give us access. Makes it a lot less anonymous.

And certainly the tools and the pieces are all there. We don't yet have it sorted out that it's illegal to read somebody's email in the same way it may be a felony to go into somebody's mailbox and steal their mail. So all the laws have to get sorted out, all the encryption. You're not allowed to encrypt anything in France, and you're not allowed to shoot a bazooka down the Champs Elysée. Those two things are illegal.

Now it seems to me one is kind of destructive and the other is actually an enabler. But, you know, we have to sort through all of these issues and get used to being online. And you're going to hear a lot about CyberCash and digital cash, and whether we really want digital cash. One of the reasons why you want cash is there's no audit trail. You don't know where that bill's been and it's laundered. It's completely laundered as soon as it changes hands because there's no audit trail. So we're trying to figure out how to do Cyber-Cash, and it has no audit trail.

Why do you not want an audit? Because you did something wrong with that money before. Maybe you bought something you shouldn't have with it. So there are privacy issues that still need to be sorted through with online commerce. But they will get sorted out and people will get comfortable with it and we will move forward in a fairly aggressive fashion. Eventually, one hopes, everybody gets access to this. We started with email. That was the first killer app, then we went to publishing with HTML. Email got about 100,000 users on the Internet. Then HTML and publishing got millions and tens of millions of people actually out there surfing. I guess chatrooms helped a little, too.

All of a sudden now, with Java, we're moving to hundreds of millions of users on the Internet. Then at some point, with videoconferencing, point-to-point, you can move to getting at the limit: every man, woman, and child will be on the Net in some way, shape, or form, and it really will move the world forward.

A capitalist has a fairly Darwinian view of how things work, and I think this is going to change a lot of business models. It's going to turn a lot of the franchises upside down in the computer industry, in the technology industry. For instance, when was the last time any of you saw a bank teller? Do they exist? I can't remember the last time I was in a bank. I don't need to go to a bank anymore. That kind of change is what matters in a bank. Now they're doing telephone calls over the Internet. This is all going to change very, very quickly.

We're trying to implement all of this new Network technology inside Sun—we're trying to get off our mainframe, we're trying to implement Java and get everybody retrained. Bill Joy was at our staff meeting recently and somebody said, "We've got to move faster." Then Bill Joy said, "You got to make it happen, you got to *make* it happen." And finally I said, "Bill, the stuff's not ready and we can't move too quickly." He looked at me and he laughed and said, "Scott, Sun is in absolutely no danger of moving too quickly."

I think that's an absolutely accurate and fair criticism. I don't believe there's an organization, institution, enterprise, whatever, on this planet that has more than 50 people around more than a couple of days that has the ability to move as fast as the Network's going to move. We are all hopelessly, hopelessly behind adopting the technology and moving as quickly as we need to at the rate at which this stuff is going to go.

It reminds me of the bear in the woods story. All the computer hikers are hiking in the woods and this 60-foot bear starts chasing them down the path. I stop because I'm putting on my running shoes and the DEC hiker says, "Hey, you can't outrun the bear in those things." And I say, "I've just got to outrun you." That's what this is all about. You can't move as fast as the technology, you can't hope to move that fast. But what you can do is try to move faster than everybody else.

The by-product of all of that is what the market economy, what capitalism, drives.

The empirical evidence is so ragingly obvious. I hadn't been there when I was in college so I really couldn't argue with my professors, but I've now been to Moscow and I've been to New York, I've now been to East Berlin and to West Berlin, I've now been to Beijing and to Hong Kong. I don't care what any theory book says, market economies blow the doors off of planned economies, controlled economies, theoretically perfect economies. What this is all about is Darwin: it's winners and losers, and you can't have winners without losers.

What's scary right now is the whole sentiment about losers, bankruptcies, corporate layoffs, and all of the rest—in this environment you can't have losers. The day there are no more losers is the day you eliminate winners. When everything's a tie, you fundamentally have a planned and managed economy. The biggest impact statement that I want to share with everyone here is this: we cannot let the Internet and intranets become a managed planned ecosystem or economy or market.

The day we don't have losers is the day we don't have winners; without winners you don't get the improvement in the standard of living, the improvement in the quality of life, the improvements in the technology and innovation that will allow us to take it to more and more and more and more people. Just not to everybody at the same time.

It scares me to death that with the current perspectives, and with the feeling that government ought to be at least 40 or 50 percent of GNP, we're really going to start applying those kinds of theories to something that has worked so well, to being totally, absolutely out of control. In spite of the fact that everybody is talking about how it doesn't work, there are people stepping up to the bar and providing the online service which has much more access, much more predictability, and more reliability. And I hope the solution comes from the private sector.

This will also create some very new entities. I think it's pretty interesting to look at the Fortune 500 companies of 30 to 40 years ago and see how many of them are still there, and go look at the Fortune 500 or even the Fortune 200 of today and see how many are new, how many weren't there as few as 20 to 30 years ago. One of the really powerful things that is happening today is that ideas are much more powerful. We're moving power into the hands of the author, not the publisher. And I'll talk a little bit about that in the context of Java.

One of the other opportunities is NetDay, which was the brainchild of another Harvard student at Sun, John Gage. Out in California we got thousands of schools all wired up. We got all kinds of organizations motivated and targeted it on one day—I don't know how many schools we wired up, how many tens of millions of dollars of equipment was donated, and how many volunteer hours were spent. But we understand that getting the Net into the universities and the K-12 environment will really change the learning experience.

We're actually helping them organize a NetDay here in Massachusetts in October [1996]. It's actually getting rolled off fairly aggressively in a whole bunch of states here in the United States. And in fact, many countries around the world are now starting to take this model of a totally online organized event.

There were no meetings. It was just orchestrated online and organized through home pages. People registered and organized online and it became a virtual community. It was probably one of the biggest statewide efforts that has ever happened in the state of California and done without any government intervention, through private organizations, nonprofit organizations, that sort of thing. Pretty exciting idea. The Network really enables that.

So this is the old model. You do some research, create a product, go out and make lots of noise, beat some drums, start supplying and get some volume, and create some market share. This old style starts off with Windows 1.0, then 1.1 and

Windows 2.0 and Windows 3.0. Then Windows 3.1 works, right? Profits, yeah! Well, there's a new model. Are your ears ringing, Billy? And that is, you launch it. You give it away for free. You get everybody to use it, you get really famous, get an incredible brand going, then you take your company public with no revenues, a little loss, and you name it something like Yahoo! Right? That's what's going on right now. We still haven't gotten to that last little square up there called profits, but never mind.

So how does this thing work? We're still stuck in this world of, which environment do we write to? If we're going to go online, if this is really going to matter, if we're going to add content, if we're going to add value, if we're going to create applications, if we're going to do distance learning, if we're going to have email clients, if we're going to bring all of these benefits, electronic commerce and home banking, home shopping, distance health care and all of those other things to the masses, we can't know what client environment is going to be in every home, in every hospital, in every office.

In fact, every time you create content, you'll have to port it to each one of the many, many different dialects. And in fact, that's a huge, huge problem. One of the biggest problems we have with communication among nations and with people in the land is that we don't all speak the same language. And imagine how cool it would be if we all were fluent in one common language. That won't happen in the written and spoken language because governments mandate the language. It is mandated that the courts and the road signs and all the rest of it will be in French in France. Is there any other reason why we'd have French around? (I only say that because I learned French a little bit in school and it was painful and I didn't like it.) Quebec is the other answer to that.

There is no government mandating that we speak a written and spoken language of computers. Well, that's not entirely true. We do it *de facto* by buying a proprietary language with government taxpayer dollars, which has always been a big beef for me. Why do they tax me to go buy a propri-

etary language and operating environment and then deploy it in schools and government offices and that sort of thing. And then as they invent new letters in the alphabet like *N* and *T*, upgrade to that. I've never really understood why we use taxpayer dollars to do that but there's actually a better answer.

That is, to start off with a whole new language, one that's available to anyone. Anybody can write in this language. You will not get sued if you write an application in Java. You will not get sued if you create a Java-based computer. You will have the ability to innovate above, below, around the Java interfaces. It's a great architecture and what's nice about it is that you can run it on anything. If you write it once, it will run on your Macs, your Windows, your PC, your Unix machines, and your Java clients. And you can do it safely. You can download content and applications.

Most computers are veritable petri dishes out there on the Internet. You know, you download something from the network and then you have a computer science project growing on your computer before you know it. And it keeps growing and growing and it's pretty ugly. What Java allows you to do is set up, if you will, (can I say this?) on the Internet, a prophylactic layer. (The censors are really bad these days.) Then you can actually do safe computing on your computer. I know, the MBONE [Multicast Backbone] just shut down. But this is a very, very powerful environment.

What it really addresses, though, is a suite of issues. One is, you write your application once and you put it on a server and it's available to the world. You can put it on the Internet or you can put it inside a firewall and make it available to your intranet, or you can give people access to it if they pay you money. I talked about the security issues and the save features. I won't get into all the technical details. You can also lower your costs per seat by not giving everybody a CD and a floppy. Why should you have to?

Can you imagine distance learning with 50 Pentium Pros whirring away, running NT in the classroom? Just doing computer-based training and having that many computers, 50 Pentium Pros in your room? The white noise would be deafening. You'd have to give a PA system to the professor; put headphones on the students for all the white noise. The whole concept of the Java clients is they get all of that into the server.

Think about the telephone model. The way we're going to really take this to the masses, and get the Internet to the masses, is not to give my parents a mainframe.

Think about a Pentium Pro NT PC and what it takes to manage one of those things. First of all, try keeping it up all day. There are some PC users here. Right, they're saying. Then think about the difference between the telephone, which is the model we want to get to. When you pick up the telephone, if you don't have a dial tone by the time it gets to your ear, you're angry. Think about the difference when you turn on your PC and it boots. Yes! I'm going to have a good day today, right? Or if it crashes and you actually recover your files? You know you're lucky then. That's when you go to the track.

It's a different model we're trying to get at. If I wanted to install a telephone in your office, do I install the switch there, too? And say, "Now here's the switch, now load some software in there, program it a little bit, configure it, and oh, by the way, when you're done, back it up?" AT&T will shoot you if you get within 30 yards of their switch. For good reason. It's CNN news when they can't make a phone call.

What we're trying to do is provide datatone from a server room to a Java client, which is nothing more than a microprocessor that runs the application. When you need it, you download the application.

Now you're all thinking, oh, yeah, I'm going to download Microsoft Office as an applet. Applet just doesn't describe Office does it? Appton. You'd have to reshave while it was downloading. No, this new architecture actually allows you to re-engineer your applications into what I call subset ware. Now you all use word processing, right?

Have you ever seen the manual for Word? Do you need all of those features? The reason they do it is "superset wares" because they can't afford to have 40 different versions of word processing tested and stocked at Egghead.

What I want is the Java word processor. It's got five functions: backspace, delete, cut and paste, and print. That's all I need. I don't even want spell-checker because if it doesn't have a couple of typos, people know I didn't write it. And you can download those kinds of applets very quickly or you can have a little disk cache to download all the applets you need at the beginning of the day. Then you go, you run, and you exist. It's going to be a very, very different model of computing.

And this is the one that is easy enough to use. You turn it on and you click, you're immediately up in a browser. You download your applications, they come in and just start running. Even I could load an application if all I had to do was click. This is the model that will drive you.

This conference is useless if we can't get everybody on the Internet. But giving everybody a mainframe—you know, PCs are like fingerprints, no two PCs on this planet that are configured the same. That's true. Even if you put the same software and boot them up, they're going to come up different. It just happens. And then you have so many bells and whistles and ways to configure this environment. To try and expect that the mere mortals on this planet will be able to deal with that kind of an environment. Most PC operators today are better system administrators than most VAX-VMS system administrators were ten years ago. Think about that. It's true.

Think about how much you know. As PC users, how much do you know about computers that you don't really wish you knew about? X of bat dot something or other. I've seen some of these things in the trade magazines, I've never seen some of this stuff before. This is really the problem we're trying to solve. I think this actually turns on a red light to get somebody to push a button. So what we're trying to solve is the situation where you don't know which ones of these environments to port to. Porting has to go the way of the punchcard.

There's been a very interesting announcement recently, and that is that every major operating systems vendor has agreed to embed the Java virtual machine into their operating environment. This has never happened before. Never before have the Macintosh world, the Novell world, the IBM world (including the mainframes), the Windows world, the Unix world, and the Java clients' world (these network computers, these reference profile network computers that everybody's signed up on), all agreed to be able to run the same application without changing, without re-engineering, without reprogramming across all environments. This has never before happened.

I'm hoping Windows can some day get to a unit buy-in that makes it a standard. Because this supersets that. Literally, I don't know of any technology that is going to go from 0 to 100 million seats as fast as this technology because it's embedded in this environment, in all of these environments, that are made available. This is, I believe, going to basically make this conference worthwhile because it's instantly going to create an opportunity where everybody can get on the Internet and get access to the content and applications and that sort of thing that will make the societal impact and issues actually relevant, because we'll actually be dealing with a large group of people.

So the zero administration client will be whatever you want it to be. It will be embedded in your hub router, switch, printer, copier, set-top box, game machine, television. It will be in your car, it will be on your desktop, it will be in your hotel room, it will be in your classroom, it will be at your office. It will be everywhere and you won't care. And you'll have a home page, you'll log into that home page with security, and you'll get access to the files and applications that you need. It will have every kind of device you can imagine connected to it and it will be a very exciting different world.

For your desktop computer, instead of having a CD, you'll buy yourself more D-RAM. Instead

of putting an Intel chip in there, you might actually put a fast, low cost chip in there. Take the disk drive out and give yourself three more ultra-spark chips. People think about these network computers as being slow, they're going to be way faster. You'll have incredible amounts of horsepower at your fingertips. But it won't be there driving some big OS. It will be there driving your applications. I'll get faster Network ports. And all the money you save running this environment, you can do to get more applications, more Network access, and put the user administration back where it belongs, in the hands of a computer scientist.

> *The cable modem is going to happen, ATM is happening. ISDN, I have it in my home. I'd never see my son if I didn't have ISDN.*

So this is the model. This is what we're driving. And we really think it has a lot of implications and you can think about how this would change the education environment. Where you check into your dorm room and there's a Java client just as part of the furniture. You don't need a desk, you need a Java client. It's probably cheaper than some of those big old desks we have in the dorm rooms. You register online, you turn your papers in online. You check into your home page and see that your professor has hot-linked into your home page the next week's assignment and references to the books or papers you need to read.

It can all be done, regardless of what kind of client environment you have. It can really re-engineer the whole learning process. I talked about the reference profile. You have every computer maker basically charging as hard as they can to create these Java clients and it is going to be a much lower cost and exciting way. We're at the very early stages. Think about the PC or workstation business in 1980. That's where we are today. For those who underestimate this, are betting against bandwidth, the cable modem is going to happen, ATM [asynchronous transfer mode] is happening. ISDN [integrated services digital network], I have it in my home. I can't imagine not having ISDN. I'd never see my son if I didn't have ISDN. I don't know, maybe it wrecks my quality of life. I don't know, but that's where we're headed.

So this is what we're doing and this is how we're driving it. It's going to change and create the impacts that we're all looking for, the very positive impacts. There's a lot more I can talk about but I want to let you all get on with the rest of the conference. Good luck, thanks for listening.

About the Speaker

Sun Microsystems—a company which **Scott McNealy** helped to found in 1982—is the quintessential Silicon Valley success story, with revenues last year of more than seven billion dollars. For more than a decade, NcNealy has been advancing Sun's networked vision and slogan, "The Network is the Computer."

Since taking the reins as CEO at Sun in 1984, he has steered the company to constant growth and profitability. In 1995, Sun was named one of the world's 100 best-managed companies (by Industry Week) and McNealy himself as one of the nation's top 25 managers (by Business Week). The Technical Business Research Group have recently rated Sun the #1 technology company, praising its market, technology, product, manufacturing, and management strategies.

Most recently, Sun has been garnering the headlines as part of the Internet craze, with the phenomenal success of its Java programming language. Time magazine recently said: "Java is the hottest thing in cyberspace."

Personally, Scott McNealy is married, and he and his wife Susan have a one-year old son named Maverick. He is an avid hockey fan and still plays in his local league.

HARVARD NEWS

CONFERENCE ON THE INTERNET AND SOCIETY

May 29-31, 1996   Cambridge, MA

Intel's McGeady Says Web Will Launch a "Digital Reformation"

By Shawn Zeller

Despite being introduced as "an early hacker," Steven McGeady, a developer of software technology that enables personal computers to transmit, receive, and display digital information, laid out his vision for the future of the Internet and society with a keen awareness of world history and without reference to the corporation for which he is a Vice President and General Manager: Intel.

Framing his speech around the metaphor of the Protestant Reformation, McGeady called for a "Digital Reformation," in which the future of the Internet would focus on making the Net a more personal space for community-building. He warned of excessive commercialism and stressed that the Net should be about human interaction on a peer level, separate from the hierarchical relations defined by client/server.

An audience tired of what they perceived to be self-aggrandizing advertisement from earlier keynote speakers expressed their approval with loud applause and laughter.

Indeed, while many of McGeady's listeners expected the "nuts and bolts" of Intel's technology innovations, what followed was a detailed vision for the role of the Internet in society, encompassing both a warning and a hope for the future.

McGeady noted that the pronouncements one sees every day proclaiming the "Internet revolution" are contributing to a lot of unwarranted hysteria about the future. With a cinematic projection of a 1950s advertisement featuring a woman spraying her furniture with a hose, McGeady warned that pronouncements about cyberthis and cyberthat fall into the same realm of "bunk" as the misguided notion from 40 years ago of futuristic waterproof furniture.

Noting the Internet's 25-year history and mocking the recent hysteria, McGeady joked, "With this technology we're talking about an overnight success that took 25 years."

Rather than making claims about the future to enhance commercial marketing ploys, McGeady said that he preferred to "look as carefully as I can at the past for a vision of the future."

Turning to the metaphor of the Protestant Reformation, McGeady argued that what is needed for the Internet is a "Digital Reformation."

"The Gutenberg printing press was a necessary but insufficient mechanism to make the information revolution really take off," McGeady said. "It was Martin Luther who translated the Bible from Latin to German and created the incentive people needed to learn to read. He encouraged individuals to make their own interpretations, separate from those of their own parish priests and, therefore, Rome."

McGeady sees the Internet as a modern day printing press: merely an enabling technology. The Net alone will not transform society without the type of literacy promotion that Luther provided for his generation.

McGeady framed his plan for spreading Net literacy under the subheadings of "Freedom," "Risks," and "Responsibility."

Under "Freedom," he stressed that he meant more than simply freedom of speech, but freedom that allows both individual creativity and communication between individuals.

Noting the marketing bonanza which is hounding the "Information Superhighway," McGeady argued that the Net must be more than a marketing device; it should be a vehicle for human interaction.

And McGeady warned that the Internet is still a mechanism dominated by the upper classes and the highly educated. "I am optimistic about the future," he said. "I'd like to see Joe Sixpack out there making Web pages."

Regarding risks, McGeady took a different tack than that of the federal government. Mocking the naïvete of the Communications Decency Act, but hesitating to join Microsoft's Bill Gates and Sun Microsystem's Scott McNealy in their libertarianism, McGeady called for government intervention, not in restricting the Net, but in making it more widely available.

Saying he foresees the next great status revolution, McGeady warned of the danger for society of allowing a class of the "digitally clueless" to develop. Just as the Industrial Revolution displaced agriculturists, he argued, the increasing importance of the Internet could displace a new generation of people not taught to adapt. Only with education could this displacement be avoided.

"The Internet is only useful if we can band together and cooperate," McGeady said. "In cooperation of individuals comes a great deal of strength."

Finally, McGeady stressed that those shaping the Internet have a responsibility to mold the Net into a community-building device. Presently, he said, the Net is often considered a place of alienation and isolation.

"Being on the Internet is like being in a mall that has been neutron-bombed," he quipped. "There are no people. It's an eerie feeling."

In explanation, McGeady said there is little place for human contact on the Net. When one looks at a Web site, there is no sense that others might also being looking at the same thing, except for the slowness of the server. He further lamented that home pages are set up as immutable edifices that others cannot add to or comment on. The popularity of chat groups, he explained, is a manifestation of the natural human need for community-building.

Although he said he sees the Communications Decency Act as "lunacy," McGeady argued that government at its best is a community-builder.

"I'm not sure if the federal government is the appropriate vehicle, but we do need to create a means and a mechanism to build communities, otherwise the Net will remain a trinket and a novelty device," McGeady said. "We are not a monoculture anymore. The Net needs to turn into a neighborhood, allowing cultural groups and interest groups to gather."

Creating this neighborhood, McGeady said, is "an absolute moral obligation for all of us."

Keynote Address
May 30, 1996

Steven McGeady
Intel Corporation

The Digital Reformation: Total Freedom, Risk, and Responsibility

It's an honor and a privilege to be invited to speak at this august institution. I want to really thank the conference organizers. I'm from Portland, Oregon and this weather makes me feel right at home. I have to admit to being a little worried about speaking here when I first got the invitation. It is a very august institution and the other speakers are illustrious, at the very least. And I became even more worried during the last couple days because I didn't come here to actually *sell* you anything, which seems to put me at odds with some of my colleagues.

So I'll have to work from that point of view. I'm going to talk about the topic of the conference, the Internet and society, and see where we get. I'm worried about some of the pronouncements I've heard over the last few days here. Worried that our imaginations here are limited to pronouncements of the sort: "In the future, we will do electronic banking at virtual ATMs, or with virtual tellers." Or that, "In the future, my car will have an IP address," or "In the future, I'll be able to get all of the old *I Love Lucy* reruns that I want over the Internet," or "In the future, everyone will be a Java programmer."

I think this is bunk. I'm worried that our imagination about the way that the Net changes our lives, our work, and our society is limited to taking current institutions and sort of dialing them forward: the more, better school of vision for the future. We've taken these things and we're just putting the word "electronic" or "cyber" in front

of them and pretending that that's what the future amounts to.

This habit reminds me of predictions of the future we have seen in the past, some 40 or 50 years ago. I remember one in particular: "In the future, housework will be easy, because all your furniture will be waterproof" (Figure 1). This actually appeared in *Popular Science* magazine or something like that. Now we don't have domed cities and we don't have personal hovercraft and, for the most part, our furniture isn't waterproof. Furthermore, back at that time, no one was thinking about stagflation, two-income households, and a 50 percent divorce rate. Those were visions of some future than the much stranger one in which we now live.

Because everything in the home is waterproof, the housewife of 2000 can do her daily cleaning with a hose.

Figure 1

I try to be pretty careful about predicting the future. I like to try to follow Yogi Berra's advice that "There's one thing I won't predict, and that's the future." You might consider this a handicap in my job, as the director of a research lab, but the way I get around it is to look as carefully as I can at the past.

I didn't go to Harvard. I went to this strange little place out on the West Coast called Reeve College, which is best known as the place that Steve Jobs dropped out of. Like the speakers who attended Harvard, they also made me study the *Iliad* and the *Odyssey*. The difference is that I stayed awake. In fact, I even took the following course, Humanities 210, and they made me read

Max Weber's *The Protestant Ethic and the Spirit of Capitalism.*

While writing this speech, thinking about an apt metaphor for the change the Internet will bring, I started rereading the book. It's a polemic, really, the thesis of which is to expound the link between the Protestant Reformation and the Industrial Revolution; in particular, the rise of entrepreneurial capitalism. If that hasn't put you to sleep, just wait.

Upon reading Weber's book, I changed the title of my talk from the time I sent the abstract to make it a little bit clearer. People bandy about the word "revolution" and think they're being brave. Revolutions change political systems, governments: they're disruptive. But the Reformation, at least in Western society, changed *everything.* That is the mode we're in. I'm not going to try to tell you exactly how things are going to change, but I picked three words that I hear often on the subject of the Internet, or rather two words that I hear a lot and one I wish I heard more. I've chosen *freedom, risk,* and *responsibility* as a way to frame my comments.

Figure 2 shows a plate from the *Book of Kells,* one of the most beautiful of the surviving illuminated manuscripts from Western antiquity. Western Europe, until the late 1400s, had extremely limited access to information. The ability to publish anything was essentially limited to governments and the Church, which was almost indistinguishable from a government at the time. The ability to own books was limited to the most wealthy merchants, the Church, and kings and princes, partly because of the sheer expense of creating them. The *Book of Kells* was the work of probably almost a lifetime, probably by my distant Irish ancestors in dark abbeys in Ireland.

There's an anecdote I read in William Manchester's *A World Lit Only by Fire,* about the Baron of Castellane. He bequeathed to his only daughter a copy of the *Corpus Juris,* the premiere legal book of the time (early 14th century) with the mandate that she marry a lawyer in order to receive the book. Imagine a piece of information so valuable

Figure 2

that you'd marry an attorney just to get it. This just puts things in context for where Gutenberg picked up.

The Gutenberg Press has by now become such a completely hackneyed metaphor for the Internet that I'm not going to spend much time on it. Gutenberg, you know, took us from a time of hundreds of books to one of thousands of books. Most of what we know about Gutenberg, we know from just bankruptcy records. Gutenberg was not a stunning success as a businessman, but he is not entirely to blame. The technology to print comparatively inexpensive copies of manuscripts was necessary but insufficient to really make information accessible in Western society. It took something far more radical.

It is worth commenting on the reason it didn't take off: less than five percent of the people in Western Europe were literate. Gutenberg invented a technology for which there was a very small number of buyers. It took Martin Luther to do something completely heretical—he translated the Bible from Latin to the vernacular German and convinced people to learn to read and interpret it for themselves.

I'm not making a religious point, I'm making a social one. He promoted the radical decentralization of the canon of the time, and the religious dogma of the time. He encouraged individuals to make their own interpretations at a time when the model of the Roman Catholic Church was to encourage people to seek interpretation from the institution, from their parish priest. That was the only interpretation that was supposed to be trusted. Luther turned this on its head and said, "Go find your own deeper moral code. Go find your own interpretation that is distinct from that of the government" (the Vatican, essentially).

This was an incredibly radical idea and, in fact, Weber's thesis in *The Protestant Ethic and the Spirit of Capitalism* is that one of the Protestant reformed Reformation sects, the Calvinists, and in particular, their dogma of predestination, led to moral obligation for the first time, away from agrarian experience and toward a calling, a profession or a craft—and the encouragement toward the accumulation and investment of capital rather than a consumption of capital. Because of that encouragement, based on the tension between the desire to be successful in a worldly life and the injunction against sin and conspicuous wealth, this led to the first widespread institution of entrepreneurial capitalism.

The period of the beginning of the Reformation proceeded from the late 1460s to 1520—about 50 years between the invention of the press; i.e., the invention of an enabling information technology and the event that caused the radical decentralization of the political and social power in Western Europe, the Reformation. From that point on, it was just a series of steps that led to the Industrial Revolution.

This year is the 50th anniversary of the first digital electronic computer, the ENIAC, at the University of Pennsylvania. It's the 25th anniversary of the microprocessor. The Internet is over 25 years old, depending on where you place the beginning, and it's the 20th anniversary, more or less, of the personal computer. This is something I haven't heard so far this week. The technology we're discussing has become an "overnight success" in 25 to 50 years. It's been around for a while, and I think that having had the 25 to 50 years to gestate, we are in for some changes on the order of magnitude of the Reformation. I'm going to examine each of those three words—

freedom, risk, and responsibility—and hope that they give us an idea of what may change.

Freedom

Freedom is a word that gets bandied about quite a lot on the Internet, and in the context of new digital media. People talk about freedom, in the context of the Internet, when what they mean is the freedom to watch any TV channel you like. This is not my idea of a fundamental human right—the freedom merely to consume information. I am talking about a more traditional definition of freedom of speech and the arts, but more importantly, the freedom to create speech and the freedom to communicate speech: in particular, what we can call personal authoring or personal publication. Both of those words, authoring and publication, are mired in a little bit of "oldthink," implying overt acts of volitional publication, like the printing of a book. I have in mind a more expansive notion, but these phrases will have to do for the moment.

I pulled the Web page in Figure 3 off the Net a while ago. It's not the most attractive home page that I've run across, but it's interesting because it was "authored" by a nine-year-old. I'm sure there have been a lot of people talking about children getting on the Internet, but one of the things I think we discount, especially when we start talking about the Internet as a place simply to receive information, is the intense creativity inherent in many people, most people, and especially in children—at least before we often grind it out of them.

We had a great talk last night with Dr. Rudenstine about the educational process as a mutual creation of sharing of ideas. I think that the thing that we need to emphasize about the Internet is not that it's a giant digital library or a vast encyclopedia—two metaphors I've heard people use—but that it is a mechanism for person-to-person communication; a mechanism for personal authoring.

We mistakenly went down a very strange road a few years ago. Al Gore coined the term "Information Superhighway," and for George Gilder, it

Figure 3

was the "Telecosm," for Nicholas Negroponte it was "Being Digital."

These digital pundits were all predicting interactive television—a mechanism that existed solely for delivering vast amounts of advertising and entertainment to your home and possessing only the ability to send back enough information to pay for it. This misguided prediction of the future set us back a number of years. The telephone companies and the cable companies spent years— and tens of millions of dollars—saber-rattling over who was going to own the pipes that carried this digital tidal wave into your home. They all failed to realize that the Information Reformation is about *personal* information, not about the same old stuff turned into bits and delivered to your doorstep in a slightly new way. It's about creating things on one's own.

Allen Ginsberg had an operative quote here:

> Whoever controls the language, the images, controls the race.

As a society, we are at a juncture where we have to ensure that the Internet becomes something more than a new vehicle for all the old advertising, the old journalism, and the old politics in place today. It must become a mechanism for personal expression in an analogous way to the rise of personal expression after the Reformation. Like Luther's Reformation, this one is about shift-

ing who controls the dogma, and who controls the canon and the images that define our culture.

Risk

Free speech, such as I just talked about, is a precarious enterprise. Free speech is fine as long as it's your speech, and when it's somebody else's speech that you don't like, you get kind of worried about it and you end up with things like the Communications Decency Act. Many of the risks of the Internet overall have been covered here, so I'm going to concentrate on just one of them.

I'm concerned that a lot of people in this country and around the world are going to end up more like this guy: Nicholas Negroponte. He, I think, coined the phrase "the digital homeless." I'm less concerned about the digital homeless than I am about what I call "the digital clueless." The digital clueless are those who will become nearly unemployable because they don't understand the new technology. Soon the only jobs for those people will probably be in the U.S. Congress.

The Reformation was not entirely about decentralization. The Industrial Revolution replaced an agrarian society that was, by and large, self-sufficient. One produced enough to meet one's consumption. Occasionally you'd gather a bunch of people together and raise a barn or something like that, but by and large, it was a distributed, largely self-managing economic and social structure. The rise of industry required the construction of hierarchical management systems to ensure communication within the organization, within the factories. Now in digital communication, however, I think we're beginning to see a shift back toward decentralized management and work models.

This is not always by choice. People are working more independently of central institutions but, in many cases, they're doing so because they have been involuntarily downsized. The unemployment rolls are swelling with the ranks of middle managers from the central part of that hierarchy essentially with very few of the tools to do so.

Personal computers help and the Internet helps but, by and large, we don't yet have the right technology for effective distributive cooperative work—a form our industry of knowledge work will be taking as it moves onto the Internet.

In small instances, we have seen quite effective cooperative work on the Internet. The Internet itself is an example of cooperative work, in many cases. But we don't have the technology yet for peer-to-peer communication. Technologically, we're stuck in this mode of client/server. Our networks still model a hierarchical organization, and we need to pay a lot of attention to understanding the technology that enables distributive cooperative work and, on the social side, to understanding what it means when we decentralize our fundamental organization. I've addressed work here, but we need to understand the process of decentralizing government and other institutions on which we have come to rely. Disruptive as this will be, I believe it is inevitable.

It is important to note that the PC and the Internet—now, and increasingly, as we get new technologies for distributive work—become truly useful only if we can find other people and band together and cooperate. The creative ability for an individual in this distributed, cooperative environment, while greatly expanded over previous institutional structures, is still limited by limited technology for distributed communication and that technology's poor ease of use. We must build new technology that allows for interpersonal cooperation on the Internet. In the cooperation of individuals, we get great strength.

Responsibility

I don't know how T.S. Eliot knew about the Internet, but he wrote this sentence which Ambassador Dougan paraphrased yesterday. He identified one of its main problems:

> Where is the wisdom that we've lost in knowledge? Where is the knowledge that we've lost in information?

I think that we need to remember that the thing that turns information into knowledge in most cases is context. The context is what distinguishes something from a random piece of data from a fact that fits into a larger whole, and a piece of information that makes a point makes a difference.

Context is provided by society, but being on the Internet today is a lot like wandering around a shopping mall that's been neutron-bombed. There are beautiful store windows and all this beautiful merchandise enclosed behind glass: you can wander around in this place, but there are no other people there. It's a very spooky, very lonely feeling to be in this place where you see lots of rich information but have no idea whether there's a crowd of people around it (other than maybe the server's really slow), or whether it's completely vacant. There is no context provided by the Internet.

Is it any wonder that people are so interested in chat grounds? They at least provide a little bit of social context. Unfortunately, it's not a lasting social context; it doesn't have any permanence. We have very, very few mechanisms on the Internet to provide a kind of lasting social context. Much of the talk in fact of government regulation of the Net is aimed at providing some kind of social context for the extraordinarily wide range of information available there. As I was pulling this presentation together, I've been thinking about the motivation for that regulation, the need for context, and about what I can call "small g" government.

It occurred to me that at its best, government is community. At its worst, government is tyranny. At the moment, in light of things like the CDA, maybe we're in a middle ground of government being just lunacy. But at its best, the government or our community provide the social mores, the context in which we can interpret the information that's around us in the communication. I think the network does need some control, but I am deeply uncertain as to whether that control can come from any of our existing national governments.

We need to create the means and the mechanisms to build community on the network. In absence of it, I think we're doomed to see the Internet continue as a technological trinket and not as a fundamental social force. But in building these communities, we have to realize the Net is not a monoculture anymore. Perhaps it was a monoculture back in the '70s and early '80s, when guys like me with propeller beanies were the only people online. But, at this point, we need to take some instances of our community, and turn parts of the Net into neighborhoods: turn places on the Net into the analog of our neighborhood streets or our corner café, or whatever helps define our particular culture.

It's not the end of some of the problems that people ascribe to the Net, such as alienation and a sense of separation from society when we're working, especially as we are forced to work in these distributive environments. So let's work on the neighborhood aspect of the network.

Summary

I want to summarize my points briefly. The freedom we're talking about on the Internet is not the freedom to be the recipient of mass-produced information. It's the freedom to create that information, the freedom to communicate it, and the freedom to interact with other people on the Network, not just other information. The means and the mechanisms to do this are through placing and giving individuals creative abilities. And many people will say, "Well, you know, Joe Six-pack isn't going to sit down and create something on the Internet."

I fundamentally and vehemently disagree with that conjecture. It is perhaps true that very few people write novels, but lots of people make phone calls. It's perhaps true that very few people paint, but lots of people decorate their homes. It's perhaps true that very few people design clothing, but lots of people choose to wear fashion in a way that's self-expressive. We need to think about casual creations—the acts that we do to live our everyday lives—as acts of personal authoring, as ways of being creative and expressive on the Internet.

This is the reason I was unhappy with the word "authoring" earlier. It connotes a formalism that I'm not trying to express here. We need to create the mechanisms to allow people to casually—as they use digital technology in their everyday lives—create information which persists and represents who they are in a digital world.

We run a great deal of risk. The institutions we have are going to be decentralized. They're going to be destabilized by the Network. You have heard and will continue to hear much talk this week about what the Net does to national borders, what the Net does to things like taxation, what the Net does to intellectual property. (Incidentally, intellectual property is a notion, however dear we may hold it, that didn't really exist for all intents and purposes before the Reformation.) There's a lot of radical decentralization of the social and government structures that is going to take place.

We need to think about casual creations—the acts that we do to live our everyday lives—as acts of personal authoring, as ways of being creative and expressive on the Internet.

Specifically, I think we're going to see ever more decentralization of work, and we need to mitigate the harmful effects of this by ensuring that we have the tools to allow us to work in a distributive manner; tools and applications that allow us to take the incredible power of the personal computers we have and use them to greater effect. It is ironic that the PC industry sold about 60 million personal computers last year and those computers largely sit on desks, unused. The total amount of computer power memory and disk space available on those computers vastly exceeds all of the mainframe computers, or servers, for that matter, ever sold or that most likely ever will be sold—and by several orders of magnitude.

We need to be able to effectively use those tools now in place (or rapidly being put in place) in a cooperative way to give individuals greater power to work together. That establishment of community is what will really knit the elements of this vision together. We have an absolute moral obligation to bring our community to the network. If we don't do that, the Net will continue to be nothing but a technological marvel, and we'll continue to hold conferences on it until its hype bubble bursts and we go on to the next big thing.

I said that I wasn't going to try to predict the future; that it's a dangerous enterprise, but what I meant was said best by Alan Kay:

> The best way to predict the future is to invent it.

Some of us are in the business of inventing technology that will make this vision of the future possible. All of us are responsible for inventing the culture and the community that will create the network of the future, and all of us are responsible for carrying forward this digital reformation and ensuring that it turns out the way that we want.

About the Speaker

STEVEN MCGEADY is Vice President of Internet Strategy for the Internet Communications Group of Intel Corporation. Mr. McGeady's work focuses on technology innovations for end-to-end internetworking solutions. He has led the company in the development of advanced software technology and applications that enable personal computers to transmit, receive, display, and manipulate new types of digital information such as graphics, audio, and interactive video over high-performance full-service digital networks. Mr. McGeady chairs one of Intel's Research Council committees, which oversees Intel-sponsored university research efforts, and currently serves on the International Review Board for the Institute of Systems Science in Singapore.

HARVARD NEWS

CONFERENCE ON THE INTERNET AND SOCIETY

May 29-31, 1996   Cambridge, MA

Pesatori: Digital Will Use AltaVista to Get into New Businesses

By Lori Valigra

It was a seemingly incongruous setting. Enrico Pesatori, Vice President of Digital Equipment Corp., took center stage at Sanders Theater yesterday, the same place Microsoft Corp. founder Bill Gates stood just the day before while extolling his company's leadership in the Internet.

Next to Microsoft, Digital may seem an unlikely player in the glittery world of cyberspace. The company has been known most recently for a massive restructuring that shucked off businesses and thousands of employees.

But Pesatori painted a picture of a new Digital, one that has made a name for itself with the AltaVista Internet search engine. Since AltaVista hit the Net last December, it has become one of the most-used Web sites and is more popular even than Yahoo!

"AltaVista is accessed more than 12 million times a day, far exceeding our expectations," Pesatori said.

AltaVista is the outgrowth of an internal project at Digital's Palo Alto research laboratory, which in six months built the indexer to provide full text searches of the entire World Wide Web.

Pesatori said Digital will leverage the AltaVista brand name and technology to get into new businesses, adding that other companies will build businesses around AltaVista. Digital plans to help them sort through what Pesatori calls the "chaos theory" that is the hallmark of the Internet.

"If you have heard all the speeches at this conference, you already know that the number of visions roughly equals the number of speakers," Pesatori said. "But there is no reason that there should be a single vision of the Internet."

Digital built the AltaVista Web site using the expertise for which it is best known. For the past 30 years or so the Maynard, Mass., company made its name by selling high-performance computer hardware.

Though that computational horsepower might not be as sexy as the AltaVista search engine, it is the power that makes AltaVista able, within a second, to leaf through more than one million pages of information in 1,100 Web sites.

Keynote Address

May 30, 1996

Enrico Pesatori

Digital Equipment Corporation

The Convergence of the Internet and the Enterprise

I'm delighted to be part of this very important program. It is really easy to get excited about a phenomenon like the Internet. But it is critical that we step back every so often to reflect on the power of the technology we have before us and what it means for us as a society, as businesses, and as consumers. We have learned over the years that technology alone does not solve problems or open new opportunities. It is the application of that technology to new, innovative, and thoughtful business solutions that allow us to create economic and social value. So I want to thank Harvard University for putting this program together and for inviting Digital to be part of it. It is appropriate that this event is taking place here in Cambridge. While my friends on the west coast might disagree, many of the most innovative companies in the Internet business are right here in the Boston area: companies like BBN, Open Market Inc., and of course, Digital.

To begin my remarks today, I would like to show you a brief video:

> The Internet will be the biggest thing to hit business since the Industrial Revolution. The Internet will be nothing more than a chat line for physicists and video game addicts. Some day, your web address will be more important than your phone number. One day on the Internet, a modern day Attila the Hun will loot and pillage all in his path. One day on the Internet, the Colonel's secret formula will whiz past the secret formula for Pepsi. There are many visions of what the Internet will become. The truth is, no one really knows what's going to happen. But as the computer company with the most Internet experience, we've learned to engineer systems that anticipate this vast

uncertainty so that you and your company can approach it as one huge opportunity. Digital. Whatever it takes.

I use this video not to make a marketing point but to underscore the fact that there is no single vision of the future of network computing. If you have heard all the speeches at this conference, you already know that the number of visions roughly equals the number of speakers. In fact, there is no reason that there should be a single vision of the Internet. This is such a dynamic environment that we can expect a vast number of Internet users and applications to coexist, including publishing, collaboration, commerce, education, entertainment, and many more.

I was in a meeting recently, and someone raised a frequently asked question, "What is the business model for the Internet?" I found the answer quite interesting: chaos theory. The Internet is where it is today not because it was carefully planned and managed. Quite the contrary. It grew, unrestricted by boundaries or regulations or preconceived notions of what it should look like. It was nurtured by hundreds, then thousands of people, each with his own vision of what was possible. As a result, use of the Internet, specifically the World Wide Web, exploded. It may be too much to expect that we can entirely tame the Internet. And perhaps we should not even try to do it. After all, the chaos sparks an incredible burst of creativity that continues to drive the growth and utility of Internet work. But we are finding new ways to harness its power. A year ago, customers were asking us to help them understand this Internet phenomenon. Six months ago, they were coming to us for help in setting up a web site. Today, they want to know how to use the Internet technologies to solve their business problems.

Let me give you an example. One Internet growth area is online banking. And one of its leaders is a Digital customer, Wells Fargo Bank. Wells Fargo is providing its customers with a wide variety of financial and investment information over the Internet. Customers can use the Internet to submit loan applications and balance their accounts. And the bank plans to use emerging technologies to enable video communications, fund transfers, and credit card transactions.

This is not a business experiment. Wells Fargo is using the Internet to redefine banking.

What I want to focus on today is one of the most compelling trends in the explosive growth of the Internet: the convergence of the Internet and the enterprise. It is a trend that has significant implications for all companies in all industries, and in all parts of the world. It is creating new business models and new measures for success. First, I want to discuss our vision of the Internet, how this new computer paradigm is changing the rules of competition. Second, I want to talk about a few of the Internet technologies that are helping businesses achieve real results. Third, I want to give you some examples of companies that are using the Internet to create virtual organizations and to reach new markets. Finally, I want to discuss how Digital Equipment enables emerging Internet applications.

At Digital, we believe that the Internet will become the work environment of choice, an environment that allows companies to access old information within the enterprise and around the world, seamlessly, to meet the needs of an increasingly flexible and mobile workforce; to create virtual corporations with partners and suppliers; and to create new distribution channels direct to customers. To compete in this new world, companies are rethinking the models that have guided them in the past: the notion that large is more powerful; that you have to be big to compete globally; that the best route to success is the traditional way. Of course, this does not mean that the large businesses are reinventing themselves as small businesses. It does mean, however, that large companies are thinking more like small businesses, becoming more responsive, more agile, and more innovative. It also means that small companies can obtain the global reach they need to challenge larger, more entrenched competitors.

Consider the success of another Digital customer, a small book retailer in Palo Alto, California, called the Future Fantasy Bookstore. The store primarily served a local clientele to their extensive catalogue of science fiction titles. But once the bookstore started taking orders on the Internet, it became a global business. International orders now represent 40 percent of the store's business.

The ability of the Internet to meet the needs of individuals or companies will depend on a technology that is powerful, reliable, secure, and easy to use. The industry in general is making significant progress on all these fronts. We see continued advances in security, search engines, and collaboration tools, improvement in bandwidth, and the introduction of powerful web servers to meet the expanding needs of millions of users.

To illustrate my point, I would like to tell you a story about two Digital researchers. During the past four years, our researchers have been developing a high performance query engine to serve Digital Research Labs. Eighteen months ago, when the Internet was first capturing the attention of the world, one of our researchers asked what would happen if we took this lab research and applied it to the Internet. What contribution could Digital make to millions of Internet users? In April of 1995, Louis Bonnier and others from our Palo Alto Research Laboratory began a six-month crash program to develop a web crawler and indexer to provide full text searches of the entire World Wide Web. The technology they developed became the Digital AltaVista search engine, which we introduced last December [1995]. Many of you may have used it already. It gives fast, easy access to more than 30 million pages and 3 million newsgroup articles on the World Wide Web. AltaVista has quickly become the most comprehensive and effective search engine available in the Internet, anywhere. The index is 30 gigabytes in size and growing, with an average query-answer in under one second. The growth is incredible. Currently, AltaVista is accessed more than 12 million times a day, far exceeding our expectations. And it is winning awards around the world.

AltaVista's success in helping Internet users find the information they need from hundreds of thousands of sources on the Internet convinced us that the same technology could help companies and individuals manage their own information. Many companies, for example, find that one of the biggest challenges is determining what information actually exists on their networks. For Digital, for instance, we now have AltaVista running on our intranets. And it has already helped us to better understand what information exists on our networks. The first day of the pilot, the AltaVista Spider found over one million pages of information and 1,100 web sites, twice the number of web sites we thought existed. Customer demand for this kind of information led us to announce the extension of AltaVista to the enterprise, to work groups, and to the desktop. Innovative companies like Xerox are already using the AltaVista version of this new product to increase productivity and reduce the time to market.

But AltaVista is not just a search engine. It is enabling a significant change in the way businesses interact with information. It used to be that individual employees had access to individual databases; but everything was separated and partitioned. Now AltaVista empowers people to access information across the enterprise and across platforms. Today, it provides access to web pages. Very soon, it will provide access to all the legacy data, thereby allowing companies to turn that information into knowledge and competitive advantage.

But providing access to information is just the first step. The next step is linking people, organizations, and information in a whole new way: the virtual private network. In today's environment, companies want to do business anywhere, any time, using an interconnected work force and interconnected networks of partners and suppliers deployed around the globe. The approach most companies rely on today, private networks using leased lines and dedicated connections, meets their needs for security and reliability, but it requires a very costly infrastructure. It is not only expensive to manage; it is costly to change, whether you are adding a new supplier or changing a connection to a remote location. But the Internet offers a much better alternative. By using the low cost infrastructure of the Internet, companies are creating secure virtual organizations through the use of virtual private networks.

Rather than hard-wiring their business with leased lines, they are using the Internet to softwire their organizations, linking remote locations and users together and increasing their flexibility to respond to a rapidly changing business environment.

At the heart of the virtual organization is the intranet, the private networks that use Internet technology to connect people with information throughout the enterprise. You can hardly pick up a trade publication or an analyst's report today without reading something about intranet. It is one of the hottest information technology topics of '96, and for a very good reason. intranets promise to eliminate many of the barriers that prevent companies from taking full advantage of their information assets and the knowledge of their people. With Internet technology and technical standards like TCP/IP, web servers, and browsers, you can build a universal network that bridges multiplatform computing environments, whether the information resides on a mainframe or a Unix server or a Windows NT platform.

Customer service representatives, for example, gain access to a much broader array of information to answer questions, respond to requests, and make sure that customers' problems are solved quickly. Instead of searching through individual databases to find the information they need, they can point and click their way across the entire enterprise. The source of the information is transparent to the user. Many companies are also using the intranet to communicate more effectively with their employees. In fact, a survey of the Business Research Group found that the three leading intranet applications are human resources, financials, and order entry.

This is proof that the Internet revolution is real. We have moved beyond the flash and hype of the early battles, and are now on the quiet revolution that is changing everyone's life. You know that the revolution has arrived at your doorstep when even the most mundane activities—employee directories, policy and procedure manuals, and software ordering—happen routinely on the Web. It is easy to see why DataQuest predicts that every Fortune 1000 corporation will have an intranet installed by the end of this year [1996]. Now, no one company can deliver all of the systems, software, and services companies need to take full advantage of the intranets. So Digital is forming alliances, like the one we have with Microsoft and MCI, to deliver end-to-end intranet solutions.

The true value of the intranet is realized when a company links up with its partners, suppliers, and customers over the Internet to create a virtual organization. This allows companies to share information and collaborate across a wide network of trading partners.

DataQuest predicts that every Fortune 1000 corporation will have an intranet installed by the end of this year.

Let me give you some examples of what I'm talking about. At Digital, we have created web sites that allow our partners to download new software and to find information about all the new products and services. These sites also include tips on how to close business and provide access to online technical support. By providing these services on the intranet, our partners can access the information they need, when and where they need it. The intranet is our customer-partner connection.

Other companies are using the intranet to reduce their costs. One of our customers, a midwestern manufacturing company, wants to get out of the business of providing office supplies directly to its employees. So it is setting up a web site managed by its office supply vendor. Authorized individuals in the company will use the Web to order office supplies, which will be shipped directly to them. The company therefore will be able to shift the ordering and accounting workload to the vendor and eliminate its own office supply inventory, while also making it easier for its employees to order the supplies they need.

Business use of the intranet has expanded dramatically over the last year. And the same thing is about to happen with Internet commerce. The issues around secure transactions are now being solved through authentication and encryption technologies. As a result, the use of the intranet for buying and selling products and services and information is beginning to explode. Input, a market research group, estimates that commerce over the World Wide Web is growing at an annual rate of over 370 percent, to a projected $165 billion of revenue in the year 2000.

Digital is one of the companies that is already engaging in Internet commerce. Last year alone, we sold more than $200 million in products over the Internet in the United States. But there is more to the Internet commerce than just transactions.

A good example of innovative use of the Internet is the Canadian realtors who are using the Network to market real estate. I'm sure many of you have had the experience with multiple listing services. You have sat in a realtor's office, reading through page after page of black and white photos and small type, that tell you very little about the home available on the market. By accessing the Canadian multiple listing service on the World Wide Web, prospective buyers can search for properties that match their requirements, and get full information and images before they actually visit the site they are interested in.

This example illustrates a key phenomenon of the Internet: *disintermediation.* That is, the Internet frequently eliminates the need for a middle man between the actual seeker of the information and the information itself. In this new paradigm, end users directly access the specific information they need. This does not mean that the Internet is going to wipe out real estate brokers. But it is going to free them to spend more of their time on high value activities, such as developing new services and building stronger relationships with their customers.

Finally, let me tell you about a company that is breaking new ground and building a global business on the Internet. The company is called CD

Now, and it sells compact disks directly to customers all over the world, using the Internet. By arrangement with several distributors, CD Now maintains an index catalogue of 165,000 titles. Visitors to its web page can view a picture of the CD cover, read the reviews, and see a list of the album tracks. Once the customer has set up an account, he can use a credit card to order a CD which is delivered within 48 hours. CD Now has some distinctive advantages over its more traditional competitors. It has no store. There is no inventory. It has virtually no overhead. The product is stored and shipped by distributors. And since every transaction is paid by a credit card, the company has no accounts receivable. This gives CD Now a significant cost advantage. Even when you factor in the cost of shipping the CDs from the United States, the company can undersell distributors in countries like the U.K. and France, where distribution costs are much higher.

One of the nice things about the Internet is that you do not have to know how it works in order to use it. However, since I am from Digital, I am going to tell you how it works. I want to make the point that the technology behind AltaVista has benefits that extend well beyond this one product. AltaVista is a very clever software and contains a huge database. But the only way to provide that one-second response time the users demand is the combination of Digital's high performance 64-bit alpha architecture and high performance networking.

The power and scalability of 64-bit computing is important to the Internet for several reasons:

Sheer computational speed. This provides the ability to exploit high bandwidth communications.

Virtually unlimited memory addressability. This gives instant access to massive databases that are loaded in virtual memory.

Affordability. Mainframe performance at the price traditionally associated with that of workstations and servers.

This kind of performance is going to be essential in delivering new data-intensive Internet applica-

tions such as multimedia, interactive video, 3-D animation, searching, and indexing.

Not every Internet application will require 64-bit computing. For instance, to support the web site for the introduction of Windows 95 last year, Microsoft used five of Digital's high end Intel-based Priori servers running Windows NT. In the first 24 hours, more than 1.8 million hits were received by these machines, representing about 200,000 customers. It would have required 2,500 people answering the telephone to provide this level of service. And the Internet provides immediate response, compared to the 40-minute phone queue for those who did call for information over the telephone.

One of the keys to Internet performance is the technology that switches traffic from one branch of the Internet to another. Digital is one of the industry leaders in delivering high performance switches and other network products that form the backbone of the Internet. In fact, the web page you see on your computer probably came through one of our switches. A growing list of Internet service providers, like BBN Planet, as well as the three largest network access providers, rely on Digital switches.

Since the Internet market is still immature, customers are looking for a wide range of services and support. Customers come to us with four basic questions:

1. What can the Internet do for my business?

2. How do I connect to the Internet?

3. How do I do business over the Internet?

4. Who can manage and operate my server?

So we offer services ranging from business planning and Internet pilots to training, collaboration services, and server management. And we are providing more and more of our services directly over the Internet.

Whether you are drawn by the technology or by the business opportunities, the Internet is an exciting place to be. By the year 2000, we expect the Internet to connect over 300 million people worldwide and to become the communication infrastructure globally, nationally, and locally. We fully expect the Internet to become as pervasive as the telephone is today, and just as revolutionary in redefining the way we work, the way we do business, and the way we view the world around us.

My message to you is very simple: To grow your business, to prepare for the competitive realities to come, you should start thinking today about how the Internet can become an integral part of your business strategy. You can be sure that your competitors are.

Thank you very much.

About the Speaker

ENRICO PESATORI is currently (as of October 22, 1996) President and CEO at Tandem Computers Inc.

While at Digital he served as Vice President and General Manager of the Computer Systems Division, which represented two-thirds of the revenue for the company. It included two worldwide business units.

Prior to Digital, Mr. Pesatori served for two years as President and CEO, Zenith Data Systems (ZDS), a leading worldwide supplier of notebook and desktop personal computers, owned by Goupe Byull of France. Mr. Pesatori also served 21 years with the Italian computer electronics firm, Ing. C. Olivetti & C., S.p.A., where his positions included President and CEO of Olivetti North America.

Mr. Pesatori earned his master's degree in electronic engineering from Polytechnic University in Turin, Italy.

CHAIR: SCOTT BRADNER
Technical Consultant
Office of Information Technology
Harvard Univerity;
Co-Director
IP Next Generation Area
Internet Engineering Task Force

Technology

THE NEXT GENERATION INTERNET

MODERATOR: David Clark
PANELISTS: Vinton Cerf
Ron Skelton
Mario Vecchi

THE WIRELESS INTERNET

MODERATOR: David Goodman
PANELISTS: Vernon Fotheringham
Tom Freeburg
Tomasz Imielinski
Kendra VanderMeulen

POST-WWW

MODERATOR: John C. Klensin
PANELISTS: Cecil Bannister
John Markoff

GLOBAL AND LONG TERM IMPACT OF ATM

MODERATOR: John M. McQuillan
PANELISTS: Peter Newman
John Swenson

SECURITY AND ENCRYPTION ON THE NET

MODERATOR: Ronald L. Rivest
PANELISTS: Butler Lampson
Michael Rabin
Jeff Schiller
Clint Smith

HARVARD NEWS

CONFERENCE ON THE INTERNET AND SOCIETY

May 29-31, 1996   Cambridge, MA

Driving Faster on the Information Highway

By Andrea Early

Mario Vecchi wants to drive a Maserati on the information highway—but the road is cluttered with traffic, it isn't large enough, and the speed limit is too slow. But as Vecchi, Vice President of Networking at Time Warner, and officials from MCI and the Electric Power Research Institute told a full house audience yesterday, he and others in the communications business are building a highway that will impress even the fastest drivers.

The panel of experts, moderated by Dave Clark, Senior Research Scientist in the Laboratory for Computer Science at the Massachusetts Institute of Technology, discussed plans for increasing the bandwidth of the Internet so it will handle larger capacities of information faster and in real time.

For his part, Vecchi announced plans by Time Warner for LineRunner, an asymmetrical but high-speed, two-way cable modem that is currently being deployed in three major metropolitan cities with the goal of upgrading some 10 million computers by 1998. "I wanted to create a network that was not a bottleneck," said Vecchi. "There is hardly any machine out there that will keep up with the speed of what we'll provide."

Vinton Cerf, Senior Vice President, Data Architecture, at MCI Telecommunications Corp., is more interested in how efficiently the highways will connect than in how quickly he can navigate them.

But the same revamping of the Internet that Vecchi is after will also help Cerf provide the real-time connections that are in heavy demand from his company right now. "I think it's safe to say we are in the middle of a gold rush," said Cerf, who has seen the number of networks on the Internet double each year since 1988. "We're about to go into a wave where businesses will want to be interconnected. If we are to provide real-time quality of service, we have to increase the bandwidth. This is really a WYGIWYG service, 'What You Get Is What You Get.'"

Other issues of quality service that still need to be refined are those of cost and security. None of the panelists could say exactly how the multibillion dollar costs for this exciting new superhighway will be passed on, but all agreed that they will be passed on to Internet users.

Ron Skelton, of the Electric Power Research Institute, suggested that the monthly meter and bill methods used by utilities might prove a good model for the Internet. Vecchi alluded to an as-yet-undefined flat fee billing scenario that will "not likely be based on connection time."

"We'll encourage people to log in and never log off, or at least to stay on for a very long time," he said.

Security, the age-old problem of the Internet, remains an issue for the future. According to Vecchi, "It's a mess right now, and anything we can get from the next IP generation will be a real boost."

Skelton, too, expressed concerns about security issues and offered that authentication and encrypted payloads might help.

As for the long term implications of this new and improved technology, Cerf offered some amusing thoughts. He believes that once interactive games go over the Internet, people will have a compelling need to hear and see their real-time conquests in action.

"Teleconferencing will be a funny side effect of this," he said.

Cerf also suggested that someday in the not-so-distant future, Internet-smart appliances—such as those that could receive a message from the electric company to slow down during a major power surge—might really have a place in society.

Clark, the panel moderator and former chief protocol architect for the Internet, offered his thoughts on the new directions of the Internet. "I have a good feeling," he said. "There is a short-term sense that consumer Internet ventures are viable. A lot of people have decided they can make money and the technology has to play catch-up. Right now the Internet is like a toy, but what happens when the device that's on your desk gets smart? It could be very exciting."

But before Vecchi can drive his Maserati, and before Cerf can build his bridges and see his Internet-smart appliances, all panelists agreed that a global backbone will be essential for moving the Internet to the next stage. And that will require larger providers such as Time Warner and MCI to work together with other competitors, and with local providers.

Technology

May 28, 1996

The Next Generation Internet

MODERATOR: David Clark
PANELISTS: Vinton Cerf
                  Ron Skelton
                  Mario Vecchi

CLARK: Because this is the first session in a technology track, one might ask what role a technology discussion can play here, given the focus of this conference. Because in some sense, aren't we done? Isn't the technology there? Aren't the questions for tomorrow "what is it good for" and "how are we going to use it"?

Ten or fifteen years ago, we were building technology to prove that it could be done. Now we're building technology to try to meet well-articulated needs, something like "remedial" technology. And that raises two questions for the panel:

• What are those needs?

• How well are we doing?

I once described trying to write standards in this community as being chased by the four elephants of the apocalypse because the faster you innovate, the faster somebody who thinks he can make a billion dollars tramples you from behind. And the only thing between him and that billion dollars is some silly little problem you haven't solved yet.

So today we're struggling with a variety of problems. We're worried about security. We're worried about the support of new services such as real-time audio and video. We're concerned with quality of service, since somebody who has more money can buy better service. And that raises the question of whether we need a mechanism in the Internet to deal with more sophisticated pricing.

I think that's why we're having this session. We have speakers from several different communities. I want to introduce them in the order you'll hear them.

RON SKELTON is from the Electric Power Research Institute [EPRI]. You might wonder what they have to do with the Internet. The answer is: Stop and think who has wires to more houses in the United States than anybody else. It's just that you didn't think about their wires. They are very concerned with the question of what data network can mean. Ron Skelton is a manager of strategic projects at EPRI in computer science and telecommunications. He's worked in that industry as well as on communication projects in the military.

MARIO VECCHI is from Time Warner and represents the cable industry—they own wires too, right? You're going to get data over them real soon now. Mario has been with the cable industry in some form for several years. Prior to that, he was at Bellcore, so he's done time in both of those communities.

VINTON CERF deserves a great deal of recognition for all of his contributions to the Internet. He is one of the two authors of the original paper that defined the core architecture of the Internet. So in some sense, he goes back beyond the very beginning. Aside from continued involvement in the Internet itself, he's gone off and done time twice at MCI; the first time to invent MCI Mail and the second to define their data network architecture. He's also primarily responsible for the creation of the Internet Society.

So we have significant speakers representing three industries here. Ron Skelton will speak first.

SKELTON: It's a pleasure to share some thoughts about the future direction of the Internet. Though I'm offering my personal perspective, it will be close to that of the electric utility industry in general.

Our industry actually created standards which achieve the ubiquitous coverage and the "plug-and-play" goals that we're still striving for on the Internet. One of my favorite stories about the era in which these standards were set was when

Thomas Edison, who favored DC, was competing with Westinghouse, who favored AC. Edison tried to portray AC as more lethal than DC, so he invented the electric chair. As you know, he didn't succeed. Westinghouse's AC succeeded, but Edison can claim to have invented the first "killer" application!

In celebrating the success of the Internet, let's consider the many factors the success is based on. We must appreciate the role of the U.S. government for the initial and continued funding of data communications science and honor the leaders of that science, like Vint Cerf (here today) and Bob Kahn (at CNRI [Corporation for National Research Initiatives]), who pioneered the TCP/IP protocols. Others who no longer share the spotlight include Doug Engelbart, who virtually invented the mouse and the graphical user interface.

I believe Doug's current work in nonlinear methods of information navigation will become increasingly important in dealing with the information firehose. Let us also credit the many IEEE committees that gave us 10BASE-T, the 802 series of subnets standards; the ISO [International Organization for Standardization] standards that gave us modems; and Xerox, who gave us the Ethernet addressing mechanism. Without these standards we would not have the universal connectivity of the Internet we enjoy today.

Before discussing the technology, I will establish a business context. After all, technology is a means to achieving some business or social objective, a fact that we tend to forget at our peril. This is a simple model of one aspect of the utility industry which might soon benefit from the Internet. It's the deceptively simple matter of reading a utility meter and obtaining payment for the energy consumed. Bear in mind, roughly 100 million meters are typically read once a month.

The example in Figure 1 does not involve high security operational data, so it's likely that an improved Internet could be readily applicable. Now assume that a data network is used as a basis for electronic meter reading, payment, collection, and settlements, and that we gain eight days in

preparation of the bill and 30 days in collection of the bill. That still leaves us two days to read meters and five days to actually process payment. That shouldn't be too difficult in this era.

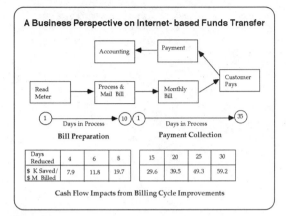

A Business Perspective on Internet- based Funds Transfer

Days Reduced	4	6	8		15	20	25	30
$ K Saved/ $ M Billed	7.9	11.8	19.7		29.6	39.5	49.3	59.2

Cash Flow Impacts from Billing Cycle Improvements

Figure 1

If we calculate the value of the float at six percent interest, we recoup nearly $80,000 per $1 million of monthly billing. Now our industry is a $200 billion annual revenue industry. So in theory, the savings would be $1.33 billion. We could imagine going even further into near real-time pricing and financial transactions. If instead of billing monthly, we bill daily, the present value of the cash flow increases by $454 million. Not too shabby.

We know from the history of electronic data interchange that those kinds of savings take much more than simple connectivity. Nevertheless, there is a huge incentive for our industry to help fix the problems of using public networks and to make the necessary investments in the metering and data processing technologies. In my experience it's unusual to have such a clear business case for making an investment in information technology.

Our industry today is only a moderate user of the Internet. For obvious reasons, we've taken a very conservative position where the nation's power supply is at stake. It underpins almost everything in our economy. We've opted for the more formal international ISO and IEEE standards. And traditionally, most of our communications are carried out over facilities we own and operate. Now this is beginning to change as the market for power is becoming competitive.

For instance, we are now required by the federal regulators to make information about the grid available to independent generators of electricity. To do this within the time frame the government allotted, the use of the public Internet was made almost mandatory. Quite a shock for our industry. The challenge is to provide secure access to utility information.

To do so, we've chosen to use the World Wide Web and the Internet, and we are using public key encryption with an international standard of X509 as the key repository (see Figure 2). I think this general diagram is a model that will apply to many commercial situations in the future. This configuration is now considered a secure Internet commercial-strength application. Over time, we may voluntarily place even more critical operational data on public networks as they become more secure and economical.

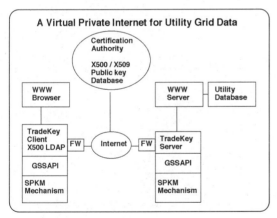

A Virtual Private Internet for Utility Grid Data

Figure 2

Let's look at some specific Internet protocol technology design issues. We joined in the debate over the next generation of IP because of our critical requirements for managing a very intelligent power system in the future. For the Internet to support our commercial environment, we require near instantaneous monitoring and control of many hundreds of thousands of intelligent devices with security, service, quality guarantees, and

multicasting. You can almost imagine every insulator on every transmission line with an embedded sensor and microprocessor in it and communicating with it.

The following list highlights the features of the new version of IP (version 6) that are of most value to our industry and to many other commercial users of the Internet.

- Integral security. Authentication and encrypted payloads.

- Autoconfiguration. Neighbor discovery.

- Advanced routing. QoS, flows, and transit lists.

- Transition and coexistence. Tunneling, automatic identification/translation.

- Expanded address space. 128 bits each for origin and destination; multiple address allocations, NSAP, Geog, Multi.

- Simple header processing. 64 bits, 6 fields, extension headers for options.

Although we did not get all we wanted in the formation of IP V6, Alison Manken and Scott Bradner must be congratulated on shepherding consensus, which required an enormous accommodation of individual and collective points of view. I'll talk briefly about security, IP V6, autoconfiguration, and routing and network performance below.

Security. We think security is far and away the most important aspect of V6. We think it will be a big inducement for service providers, in particular, to shift to V6. For instance, it allows you to construct a steel tunnel between two remote firewalls of an organization. And having the complex algorithms for security built into the network as a network service will simplify the development of applications. In any event, routing protocols should be secured.

IP V6. IP V6 provides authentication support for sender verification and nonrepudiation and is required as an option in all V6 implementations. The algorithm choice is flexible and the current minimum is the keyed MD5 protocol, designed by Ronald Rivest.[*]

Autoconfiguration. This is the "plug-and-play" requirement. It means that a device must automatically configure itself to participate in the network. IP V6 is purported to fix this problem, but I'm not entirely sure that it does. In any case, it requires a unique interface token, usually the 802 address. How the market will behave with regard to the inherent, recommended provider-based addressing mechanism and the amount of actual renumbering that would have to take place remains to be seen.

It's curious to me that we haven't yet really made much more use of the global positioning system [GPS], for example, as part of an addressing mechanism. As a yachtsman, I would like to see a bit more of that featured in IP.

Routing and network performance. The processing load on routers is both an immediate and a long term issue. Though it will ultimately be a problem or a cost for all of us, we see this initially as more of a problem for network service providers. Now the problem should be eased by this simpler header format and extension design of V6. How we will fix the explosion of the routing tables in practice, again, remains to be seen.

The nature of the communications traffic is changing. Message sizes are increasing while acceptable response time and latencies are decreasing. We expect this trend to continue. To my mind, there are still many unresolved performance and service quality problems and issues. How the Internet will evolve to provide the varying degree of service quality needed by a mix of first, stream, and bulk traffic and how these service levels will be charged for is anybody's guess.

Now we have to think about the transition. The Internet Engineering Task Force [IETF] has decided to support transition from V4 to V6 to use a dual strategy. The downside of this difficult

decision is managing two sets of addresses. It's claimed that the dynamic address, configuration, and automatic neighbor discovery mechanism should make this almost invisible to the network managers.

The future, experience has told us, is that superior technology is no guarantee. Even with the recommended solutions of IP V6, the issues of controlling the routing table, enabling service guarantees, provider selection issues, the relationship to ATM [asynchronous transfer mode], the provisions of mobility all seem far from settled. Incidentally, the IETF is also looking at a new version of TCP (see Figure 3), which compounds our concerns about stable environments.

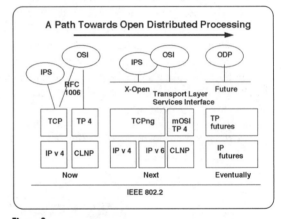

Figure 3

I want to make one point here: we're not sure that the right formula for the future is the so-called wine-glass architecture, where the concept is one single transport protocol. We think the better way, in the future, is to have flexibility at the lower layers as well as at the upper layers, where the transport layer of service is the interface between them. Something along the lines that we saw in Larry Desward's presentation.

In summary, the long term question is whether the public Internet will deteriorate or improve. I think it was Winston Churchill who said,

One should never watch either sausages or laws in the making.

[*] Ronald Rivest moderated the session entitled "Security and Encryption on the Net" also in the Technology section of this book.

Had there been data communications protocols around at the time, no doubt he would have added those to the list.

CLARK: Thank you. Mario, you're on.

VECCHI: The following list goes back more than two years and was the basic outline of what we planned to build at Time Warner. (Mind you, two years is almost prehistory in public awareness of the Internet.)

Connectionless access. LAN-like service, no dial-up, permanently connected, automatic "bandwidth-on-demand."

High speed. 8-25 Mb/s downstream, 1-3 Mb/s upstream, shared bandwidth.

Standard datacom. Mainstream Internet technology (TCP/UDP/IP), leverage new multimedia extensions (IPng).

Client/server infrastructure. Enables Time Warner Cable environment to evolve to new services.

"Connectionless access" means that we were going to provide an environment similar to what your local area network provided to your office, in your home, both in terms of speed and also the connectionless nature of the service.

Next is high speed over cable networks, comparable to Ethernet speeds.

The third bullet is one that is very relevant to this conference. I made it clear from the very beginning that there was only one communications protocol that we support, and that was TCP/IP and all the related families of applications around it. This decision was made over two years ago and we've been working steadily in that direction.

Finally, what we're building is a general end-to-end solution. It's actually a client/server infrastructure to support our business.

Figure 4 is a quick view of our Excalibur model in detail. I want to point out that the model we have is, loosely speaking, a regional federation of broadband IP networks interconnected on a national and global scale. We like to think of the Internet as one of those interconnection networks

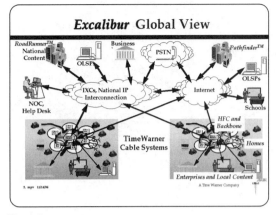

Figure 4

as well as general IP carriers as sort of parallel environments over which connectivity is offered.

This is a bit of a loose definition, after all. What is the difference between the Internet and an IP carrier? It's something we could debate for a long time, but we have to dwell on this issue if we are to deploy a commercial rollout, because all these things do have owners, and money changes hands across each of the arrows that are indicated in the figure. So it is not just an academic exercise of putting things where we can, and being casual about it.

Figure 5 amplifies one of the regional clusters Time Warner Cable owns. Each one is a fairly large metropolitan area. A primary head end subtends approximately 300,000 homes. We have a backbone network based on fiber with ATM over SONet [synchronous optical network], in most cases, down to distribution hubs, where we then serve about 20,000 homes. Then we have the cable industry hybrid fiber coax [HFC] architecture over the fiber and the coax that reaches your home. This is the real seat of broadband access to the residence.

Figure 6 shows the Excalibur reference architecture in a little more detail. You can see the different components, going across the hybrid fiber coax networks, starting from your home PC. A cable modem interfaces with 10BASE-T Ethernet to your computer, and then goes over the fiber coax network into a device of the distribution

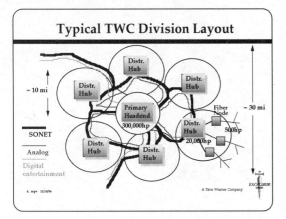

Figure 5

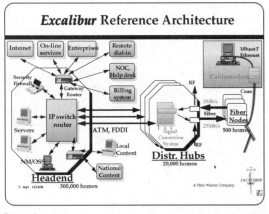

Figure 6

hub we call a "signal conversion system," or SCS. The SCS essentially terminates the physical and link level protocols that went over the HFC network, and injects IP packets into the backbone network. Typically, it's ATM over SONet, but it could be FDDI [fiber distributed data interface] in those regions where we don't yet have a SONet deployment.

At the head end is the main switching and routing as well as all the server capabilities, which provides connectivity to other parts of the world. This includes the delivery of content as well as connections to the public Internet, connections to enterprises, and so forth. I could elaborate on this, but I hope you have a sense of what we are building at Time Warner. It is essentially a metropolitan area, a broadband IP network with as

many of the distributed computing capabilities as we can manage to put together to actually deliver services and run a business. This is much more than just providing connectivity.

The following list summarizes the basic features of the cable modem, because you may wonder what this cable modem technology is leading to.

- Asymmetrical, but high speed both ways. 64QZM, 25 Mb/s in 6 MHz down; QPSK, 1-3 Mb/s in 1-2 MHz up.

- Ethernet 10baseT to PC. Multiple PCs in the home/small business; filter network traffic on MAC address.

- Vendor-specific MAC protocol, future standard. Time Warner is part of the industry effort to define the interoperable cable modem.

- Link-level encryption required over HFC.

We've been working very actively for the last couple of years with a number of vendors and these things have begun to come to light just in the last year. These are the basic characteristics of the cable modem. The cable modem will be an asymmetric device. In other words, there will be more bandwidth coming down then there will be going up. On the other hand, the reverse bandwidth will also have to be high. Time Warner Cable will not deploy any of these solutions that you may have heard of with little or no bandwidth in the reverse, based on telephone connections. We don't believe that makes sense from either a technical or fiscal standpoint. So all our reverse bandwidth will be between 1 and 2 T1's. And it will be certainly in the 10 to 25 megabits per second in the downstream, depending on the cable modem technology. But the ultimate limitation here is the 10BASE-T interface into your home PC.

One of my goals when we started pushing this idea within Time Warner was creating an environment where the network was not the bottleneck, where I would push the bottleneck right into the PC sitting on your desk. And in fact, we have succeeded in doing that. The trial we have been conducting for the past year, running with cable modems in the multimegabyte per second range, clearly indicates that the real bottleneck for higher-speed access to data, essentially, is the PC.

Even Pentium machines running at very high speed cannot keep up with the downstream bandwidth. By the time you consider all the overhead of the interface card, the NDIS [Network Device Interface Specification] disc driver, the video display, and so forth, there is hardly any machine today that can keep up with the speed of the 10BASE-T delivery. This will change, of course, in the future, as you hear from Apple and Intel and many other computer manufacturers. Computer speed will grow, and, one hopes, this will be a healthy race where the network will push the computer and the computer will push the network and we'll just keep going.

Now that I have given you a quick summary of what LineRunner is, let me give you a wish list in the spirit of this session—based on what we have learned and what we would like to help us better deploy the services that I've described.

First on the wish list is lots of IP addresses. (I guess that's on everybody's wish list.) Give you an idea of what Time Warner Cable's situation is and why our company has been upgrading the cable plans at a more aggressive pace than most other cable companies—Time Warner Cable has about 11 million homes. But now, in 1996, we have more than 4 million homes that have been upgraded to the two-way HFC architecture, and our plans indicate that by the end of 1998, the number will be in excess of 10 million.

We're using public class C blocks that I got a year and a half ago after a discussion with my friend here, Dave [Clark], about how to resolve this issue. We are going to run out of those literally in the next three to six months. We will be running the *lrun.com* domain and will subdomain it by each one of these regions.

In addition to the users, there are many network elements we need to address. In addition to which, because of the nature of the routing and the architecture, as with any network, there are subnetting limitations and inefficiencies. So we can't use every single one of those IP addresses

that we have available. And last, we are using dynamic host configuration protocol. But DHCP [Dynamic Host Configuration Protocol] will help us only marginally because the model for LineRunner is a connectionless access model. So we're actually going to encourage everybody to log in and never log out.

There will be no connection charges based on time or data usage, so we do expect users to log in and stay logged on, if not forever, for a very long time. Those IP addresses are not going to come back as quickly as in a model based on telephone service, where there are connection charges. So DHCP is there not so much for efficiency of IP usage but for managing our network and our assignment of subscribers. It has a lot of other beneficial factors in our architecture. We need a lot of IP addresses. And IP next generation should provide them for us.

The other issue is, who is going to carry all that traffic? This is a question that has to do with the fact that even though the Internet includes, in general, any network or any subnetwork that interconnects, that we all subscribe to the same Internet-related standards. But unfortunately, when you start running a business, each one of these things actually has an owner. An owner who expects to be paid for every wire you connect to.

And one of the characteristics of LineRunner is that it is completely open, not only technologically but also from a business perspective. People who want to connect to us should be able to connect any way they want, in any manner that is most appropriate, and in any manner that makes the best business sense to them.

In some cases, we have already run into difficulties providing more than one "IP pipe" into our environment. It's very difficult to manage routing tables and so on to actually satisfy a vendor or a partner's desire that their service be accessed to the facilities they own rather than some other facilities. So here is a generic wish: we would like to have the equivalent of "10-222" or "10-288," or whatever functionality, to actually enable you to selectively route which path the IP traffic goes on. Will IP next generation provide this? Perhaps. So just put a question mark on this one.

Security. Security has to do, of course, with protecting our servers and our content. As Time Warner, we have a good deal of content we want to make available. But it also has a lot to do with how I manage my business. Security is a handle I use to define who has access to whom, who to restrict from a particular class of service, and so on. We want flexibility in the security policies. Right now, the technology is developing; there are many firewalls out there, IP filtering rules you can set at the routers, and so on. It is a mess. Anybody who knows security knows about that.

Anything we can get from IP next generation that will help us improve both the management and flexibility in the way that we manage our network will be greatly welcomed.

Multicasting. Multicasting is a key function. I point out just a few reasons of many. For content distribution, as I said, we are a federation of regional IP networks. We need to deliver content to all of these places. The equivalent function of multicasting or broadcasting over IP networks is very important. It facilitates and makes a lot more sense, economically. In addition, there are many applications. But now we want to deliver to the end user, and not just for delivery and storage for further retrieval of content that would greatly benefit from multicasting.

Our requirements and our LineRunner architecture specifically requests that all of the devices—all of the cable modem requirements—that run over our HFC network support multicasting. We need to ensure that the physical and the MAC layers of a lot of the networks that are built will naturally support the multicasting function. This could become a problem even if IP supports it. So that's an important issue that we need to watch.

What do we do about quality of service? (In our service, this is like a red herring.) LineRunner is definitely a best effort service. When somebody asks, "What are you delivering?" (in other words, what is your speed, what is your bandwidth), my

answer is very simple, "Try it, you'll like it." Again, I borrowed this from Dave Clark. And there is a lot you can do when you have a broadband network and you use a little bit of common sense in your engineering.

I should point out that LineRunner is not intended to be an entertainment video, on-demand service, or a telephone service. It is really intended to be a multimedia computing application. Nonetheless, as more audio and video streams become part of those applications, some quality of service will be required. My strong inclination is that soft guarantees will be the way to go here, but this is an open issue for now.

As far as defining the architecture for Line-Runner: we're not making any commitment now in terms of the support of this quality of service. Will IP succeed in supporting real-time traffic in a really cost-effective way? We will wait and see. Is ATM the solution to this problem? Is MPEG transport the way to go? A lot of open questions remain. My strong inclination is to hold back and wait for IP to deliver soft guarantees of quality of service.

It's not really the domain of the network level or the IPng work, but obviously we're looking at applications and more applications. And the talk that preceded this from Apple [Larry Tesler] is really a good indication of where a lot of these battles will be fought. We are certainly looking at the evolution and extensions of HTML and VRML. Java, of course, is attractive. We have collaborations with Sun Microsystems for building content and taking advantage of Java.

What we expect is the combination of better computing platforms, high speed, and a truly enabling environment where the computer platform will facilitate the creation of applications.

So let me finish with what the future points to. I just want to emphasize that this is not an academic exercise. In 1996, we will be deploying several major systems. We have already publicly announced three major metropolitan area deployments, and quite frankly, I am not having an easy life nowadays at the hectic pace we're keeping to launch this service. I look forward to talking to you in the future.

CERF: What we've noticed over the last thirty years with respect to networking is that when we started, the only important thing was just getting bits to go from one computer to another. Then we discovered that it was important to get information to go from the place where it was to where somebody wanted it. We're in the middle of the information wave, where people are using things like the World Wide Web, Gopher, WAIS [Wide Area Information Service], and so on, to reach out to get information and bring it back.

The point here is that we're about to go into a wave where business processes are going to be connected to each other through the Internet. We have operating, running systems communicating with each other on an inter-organizational basis and intra-organizational basis. And in a sense, some of what you hear about Java leads you down the path of thinking about active processes communicating with each other. So that's the next big wave demanding capacity.

It's fair to say we're in the middle of a gold rush and Figure 7 is just one example of what a gold rush looks like. The number of networks in the Internet has been doubling every year since 1988. The rate has not diminished since that time, nor do we expect it to diminish until the end of the year 2000.

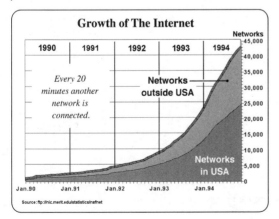

Figure 7

Another example of a gold rush is shown in Figure 8, which shows the number of host computers (in thousands) in the Internet over the last six years. At the end of 1995, there were slightly fewer than 10 million computers in the Internet, according to Mark Lottor and others.

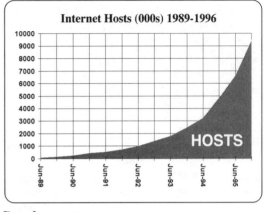

Figure 8

Some interesting facts: There are 134 countries connected by the Internet system today. Fortunately, the number of countries isn't doubling every year. The number of users in the Internet is an unknown figure. Estimates vary widely: 23 million in July 1995 by one study; 19 million by another; 35 million estimated in June 1996. None seems to be too far out of kilter. If you ask how many people can get to the Internet using email, the numbers get even bigger. In particular, the number of countries that can be reached that way (about 186) is larger than those that are directly connected to the Internet.

The chart in Figure 9 gives a log-scale projection of the number of hosts on the Internet in different regions of the world. The point is that the number of machines on the networks in various parts of the world is doubling every year in every part of the world where the Internet habit has taken hold. So we can assume this growth is going to continue.

The chart in Figure 10 shows the fraction of the NSFnet [National Science Foundation network] backbone taken up by Gopher traffic and by World Wide Web traffic during the period from

November 1992 to November 1994. The point here is twofold. First, although it looks like Gopher flattened out at four percent of the backbone, the *actual* traffic in the backbone more than doubled every year.

So something which looks like it's only taking up a constant percentage of bandwidth is generating or consuming an exponential amount of actual traffic. Moreover, the World Wide Web was growing more than exponentially, in terms of absolute data rate. Today it's estimated that the World Wide Web traffic takes up about 50 percent of the Internet.

I want to point out something that the data in these figures and other comments today suggest. Just when you think you've got the best thing since sliced bread, somebody comes along with a toaster and toasts you. The World Wide Web is not the end of this story. As Java and other programming languages become common on interpreting platforms scattered around the network, I think you'll see an even more rapid growth of software moving back and forth on the network, and not simply HTML pages.

One of my favorite charts (Figure 11) plots the growth of human population through the end of the year 2000, and charts the number of users in the Internet. By the end of the year 2000, every human being on the face of the earth will be an Internet user. Now even if that doesn't happen—and there are a lot of reasons why it won't—this is the number of hosts in the Internet. If that projection holds, it would amount to about 200 million machines on the Internet by the year 2000.

I believe that is an achievable and likely outcome. But it may not be for the reasons you think. Last year about 65 million PCs went into the marketplace. This year, maybe more than 50 million will go in. Even if the number is stable, you can generate enough computers in the marketplace—all of them equipped with either the Apple Mac OS or with Microsoft Windows, or what have you (all of them Internet-enabled)—and you could project that a significant fraction of all the computers sold may very well wind up on the Internet.

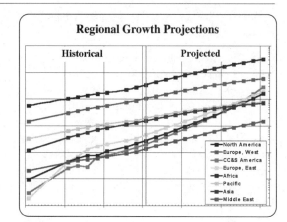

Figure 9

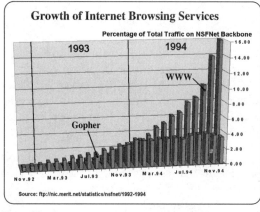

Figure 10

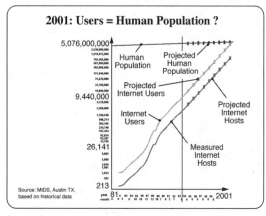

Figure 11

Even if you forget that for a moment, something else is going on that's terribly important. It has to do with appliances, it has to do with control, it has to do with putting computer controls into appliances like toasters, microwave ovens, and washing machines.

As a consequence, we may find that this projection is actually low, and that although it might reflect the number of conventional computers, like this laptop on the Internet, it won't necessarily take into account all the hundreds of millions of devices that might very well end up in the system as well. All of which, by the way, is tremendous motivation for having a larger address space than the current IPv4.

The set of applications running in the Internet today has become almost classical. One that has not shown up too quickly is interactive multiuser games on the Net, except on college campuses, where they sometimes consume so much bandwidth that you have to ask students not to play them during the school day. I understand that several of the video game manufacturers, Sega and Nintendo, will be producing Internet-capable interactive game devices this year, probably by Christmas-time [1996].

So my guess is we will see a significant increase in demand for Internet service as a consequence of people playing games, which will drive something else. If you think about people playing interactive games, wanting very fast response time, shooting at each other, you're going to want to hear those people go "Aaah" when you shoot them out of the air. So there will be a need for audio communication among the players. And it would be nice if you could actually see them when they bite the dust.

My prediction is that when these things finally hit, they'll come with these little $100 cameras and you'll get multimedia videoconferencing out of these games as a funny side effect. Last year everybody and his dog started some kind of an electronic commerce experiment and I think that's what these all are. Some were very successful. CyberCash looks like it's doing well on the stock market. Now a lot of these do well on the stock market. It's not as clear how well they do when you start looking at profit and loss. But the fact of the matter is, there's a great desire to use the Internet for electronic commerce. And there is tremendous pressure for doing so. But there are real problems with cryptography and its widespread availability. That's a challenge for IP Version 6: to have a common high quality crypto capability everywhere in the world, without leading to arrests for violation of arms regulations.

Multimedia keeps coming up again and again and, from my perspective, from the point of view of a telephone company, we are under tremendous pressure to deliver real-time services that the Internet wasn't designed to do.

There are two contrary trends going on at once. One is that the Internet is being used to support conventional telecommunications services like telephony, video, radio, and multicasting. It doesn't work terribly well everywhere on the Net, because the Net doesn't have enough capacity to handle it in all the places people try. And so this is really a WYGIWYG service: What you *get* is what you get. And sometimes it's worth what you pay for it.

The other inverse phenomenon is that conventional transmission media—television and radio, direct broadcast satellite, and cable—are also being used to carry Internet services. That's important, too, because the Internet is influencing two different directions. One, it's supporting conventional services, and two, it's influencing the existing conventional ones to carry Internet traffic.

We have to have real-time quality of service support on the Net. To really do a good job, we have to increase the bandwidth on the Net dramatically.

So the kind of feature that my company and many in the Internet community require is an ability to produce assured performance levels. At MCI we're moving in several directions. One is to experiment with RSVP [Resource/Reservation Protocol]. The other is to start projecting some of the requirements into ATM networks. Another major issue is that the more mobile these computer devices become, the more necessary it is for people to get convenient access to Internet no matter where they are, anywhere in the world.

International roaming, to borrow a term from the cellular phone system, is absolutely a requirement and it is not yet well resolved. Plainly we will have to solve the same problems the cellular telephone community has had to solve to allow people to easily connect to the Internet wherever they are. I have hopes that you could go into a hotel and simply plug your PC into a cable modem and, through the magic of dynamic host configuration and so on, plus some roaming capability, you can establish that you're *bona fide* and get into operation.

I'm going to predict that there will be Internet lightbulbs in 2005. When you screw the thing in, it will use the power wires in the house to communicate with the light switch.

Another big problem shows up not so much in the cable case, but in the direct-broadcast satellite case because, typically, those are one-way channels. If anyone here has ever dealt with communication with submarines, you'd know something about the problem of radio silence, emission control, and one-way channels. Using Internet with a one-way channel is tough, considering the way TCP works. It would be expecting acknowledgment from things that can't respond.

As a result, multicasting may be the most immediate and obvious way of using some of these high bandwidth one-way channels, and they're terribly attractive. The 24- to 27-megabit per second data rates you can get out of a 6 megahertz television channel is extremely attractive for delivering all kinds of content, if you could assure the quality of the delivery at, say, 10^{-10} bit error rate. You'd still have to figure out how to recover from failures. Nonetheless, I see those one-way channels

as an important new element for distribution of content over the Internet.

More than enough has been said about the need for security, privacy, and authenticity. The big problem here is not just the technical definitions of the specs, it's getting the administrative framework in place; getting organizations in place that can accept the liability of handing out certificates and maintaining keys; and determining who can authoritatively say that a given key was allocated to a given person so when you try to authenticate a contract, you can verify with whom you are dealing. Finally, this vast increase in address space is absolutely necessary.

So let me just toss a few thoughts about the distant future into the picture. First, we will start wearing computers in our shoes and antennas in our hats, giving a whole new meaning to "talking through your hat" and "booting up." We've heard lots about Java and other kinds of languages, knowledge robots, or "knowbots," and intelligent things. I'm seriously expecting to see all kinds of appliances become part of the Internet environment. I don't know what the toaster has to say to the refrigerator, but I can tell you that the power companies would have some real interest in being able to say things to the water heater like, "Hold off on heating up that next gallon of water until I get past this peak."

Finally, just to give you a solid projection that you can test, I'm going to predict that there will be Internet lightbulbs in 2005. There will be an IP chip in the base and when you screw the thing in, it will use the power wires in the house to communicate with the light switch. The light switch won't interrupt the current, it will just tell the light bulb to go on or off, or dim or bright. So you can test me in 2005, when I hope I've retired to some island in the South Pacific.

What we have had to do as a result of demand—just to give you a sense for what's happening in the real world—we started with a 45-megabyte network. We upgraded it in April to 155 megabytes on most of the backbone channels. We already know we're going to have to upgrade to OC-12 by the end of the year or sooner, just to keep up with the demand for communications on our part of the Internet. Moreover, we absolutely must have a globally managed backbone—or more than one—in order to make the Internet reliable on a global scale. Today you can't just tie 100,000 networks together and expect to get any kind of well-defined service.

Here's what happened to us. We have customers in about 70 countries with 160 circuits connecting them to our backbone network in the United States. And they look at this and say, "That's the dumbest way in the world to use expensive, transoceanic capacity," and I completely agree. What we need to do is to reorganize all of that capacity so that it's part of the network. And just like the undersea cable business, I believe that competitors are going to have to cooperate to build that global network and to provide the kind of service that's required.

Questions & Answers

Q: *What are the addresses for your material?*

VECCHI: Oh, it's *ftp://ftp.excalibur-group.com/*.

CERF: See "Cerf's up" at *http://www.mci.com/*.

Q: *How do you see the local telephone companies and the cable companies playing out in terms of the vigor of their deployment and their posture over the next few years?*

VECCHI: Let me just quickly address that. I don't want to represent the whole cable industry, but the phone companies are by no means sitting back and playing dead. In fact, the fact that we are so aggressively operating our HFC and spending literally multi-billion dollars of investment is because we are getting ready for the phone companies to be a viable broadband competitor of the local axis networks. So that's what we would expect would happen.

CERF: I'm very egalitarian about all of this. You know, I have a T-shirt that says IP on everything and I want to make sure that we can run the Internet protocol on HDSL, ADSL, one-way satellite, cable systems, anything that we can possibly use: I don't believe in the apocalyptic view that any one technology or any one organization will dominate everyone else. I actually believe that Internet will find niches and convenient uses in all the various media, whether it's wireless or otherwise. So I actually encourage the telephone companies to make use of any of the technologies that make economic sense, including ISDN, where they can be of benefit to a customer.

CLARK: I might add something to that as an additional comment. I was recently involved in a study that came out from the National Research Council in which we went out and asked a variety of industry sectors what they were going to do over the next five to seven years, and in the context of that study, we detected a real difference in tone between the cable industries and the telephone. You might say that it's a gift from God to be given only one path to walk down, because then the only decision is how fast you walk. The cable companies have a legacy of coax, which means that the only obvious technology option for evolving their system is hybrid fiber coax.

If you're in a telephone company, you almost have an excess of options. You can try to deploy ISDN or you can go with one of the DSL technologies, but then you have to choose between HDSL, ADSL, VDSL, or BDSL, or you could do fiber to the curb, or you could deploy a hybrid coax technology. And the uncertainty, of course, of rolling the dice and blowing $100 billion on the wrong answer has induced a certain amount of conservatism in the telephone company. Whereas, of course, the entrepreneurial spirit of the cable companies says, "Let's roll it out." So right now, I've noticed a difference in tone. On the other hand, telephone companies have deeper pockets so eventually they'll buy the cable companies or at least they'll try again, right?

Q: *Does MCI expect to get telephony running over the Internet too?*

CERF: Two answers to that. First of all, we can do it just like everybody else does, you know, by clearing a 100 megabit per second channel and putting 28 kilobytes across it and it works great.

The fact of the matter is that there is a lot of stuff that has to go on underneath to handle any significant quantity of Internet telephony. And I don't expect to be able to do that until probably some time in 1997. We of course can't stop people from doing it, so they'll do it anyway. It's a self-limiting effect because if the service is really crappy, if things congest, then it won't work very well and people will stop doing that.

I'd like to be able to support it better than I can today and I have ATM running underneath our OC3 network in anticipation of putting up special channels to handle this sort of reliable service or better quality of service. But I don't think we have the capacity and the routers to handle any significant fraction. The last calculation is that we could handle maybe five percent of our total voice load on the rest of the voice network that MCI runs on the current capacity available to the Internet.

Q: *There are some applications for which the best effort service of the Internet are not adequate; what's going to happen to deal with those sort of guaranteed services?*

CLARK: I'm going to give a partial answer myself because that's part of the stuff that I've been involved in. I'll let some people here comment on whether they think I'm crazy.

Over the last three or four years, there's been a project that's moved from the research stage to the standards area to try to define some new service models for real-time applications. The specific models are called "guaranteed service and controlled load," as well as a protocol named RSVP [Resource Reservation Protocol] to set up a "call," although those are words that cause people to throw me down and wash my mouth out with soap. The major router vendors are experimenting with these enhancements in their Beta code today and they're going to ship it into corporate Intranets within this year.

The thing that's needed in order to roll it out in the public Net, other than the natural cycle of getting technology out, is a model of how we're going to charge for it.

CERF: Let me make two observations. First of all, I'm finding that the use of level two networks like Frame Relay and ATM underneath of IP is giving me some flexibility in routing some traffic by preferred channels to remove some potential for congestion. It's not a perfect mechanism, but it's the beginning for support and for better qualities of service. Of course I have to say, when you reserve capacity or do anything else like that, somehow you have to get compensated because it uses up more resources.

Q: *What kind of pricing models do we expect to come into the Internet and what will the impact of those be?*

CERF: My expectation is that there will be multiple classes of traffic and they'll have different kinds of price points. The best efforts traffic will probably continue to have a flat rate kind of price. But when you start asking for special quality of service, especially if that's transoceanic service, you have to expect that there will be different price points associated with it. It may not be priced per packet or anything like that, but it might be that if it's a flat rate service, it will be a higher level flat rate than the conventional best efforts. I don't know how we will work it all out, but plainly you can't provide service unless you can pay for all the costs of doing it.

SKELTON: From our view, the flat rate is the preferred model. In the cable industry we're really providing service to the consumer rather than selling a certain amount of bandwidth. But as Vint is saying, it's very hard to maintain that model if applications develop to the point where users actually reserve amounts of bandwidth that are not available to other users. So we will have to work through that; there will be some charges associated with either time or usage as we evolve to the future. But we don't envision that happening as we roll out these services in the first year or two.

Q: *Are the "big bad" telco's or other big companies going to gobble up all the little guys?*

CERF: The answer is, it depends. First of all, customer service turns out to be absolutely vital in today's Internet. That's not easy to supply—a lot of the local access providers are really good at it because they're nearby and they make a business, not simply out of selling Internet service, but selling advice, configuration assistance, application development, and the like. I think they do a good job of that and it's a wonderful sales channel for the backbone services that we offer.

So, in one sense, I see those as partners. There are plainly competitors; my competitors are mostly backbone type suppliers. It comes down to how much fiber you have in the ground, how fast the routers are, and how many partners you have overseas that can nail up capacity on the transoceanic cables. That's not a game for the local access provider so I don't think they're hurt by that.

Skelton: I do want to make a comment: our vision is that we will be deploying these services region by region, and our emphasis is in having strong partnerships with the local company and a very open environment. We don't envision that the Internet access provider will disappear. It will probably evolve to be a different kind of a business, but certainly will not disappear. We are relying very strongly on all the existing activity in the local communities to make it attractive for our customers to sign up for the service.

About the Speakers

Dr. David Clark is a Senior Research Scientist in charge of the Advanced Network Architecture group at MIT. His research interests include networks, network protocols, operating systems, distributed systems, and computer and communications security. After receiving his Ph.D., Dr. Clark worked on the early stages of the ARPA-net and on the development of token ring local area network technology. Since the mid '70s, Dr. Clark has been involved in the development of the Internet. His current research area is protocols and architectures for very large high speed networks, computers, and communications security.

Dr. Vinton G. Cerf is Senior Vice President for Data Architecture at MCI Telecommunications, where he is responsible for the design of MCI's data services including its Internet service offerings. Dr. Cerf also served as Vice President of the MCI Data and Information Services Company where he developed MCI Mail. Formerly, Dr. Cerf was Assistant Professor at Stanford University in the Computer Science and Electrical Engineering departments. While at Stanford he led the development of the TCP/IP protocols and, with Robert Kahn, designed the basic architecture of the Internet. He is married, has two sons, and has an abiding interest in fine foods, wine, and mind-rotting science fiction.

Ron Skelton is Program Manager of Advanced Information Technology within the Strategic Development Group at the Electric Power Research Institute. He is responsible for the assessment of emerging information technologies and assisting electric utility member companies with business case development, strategic planning, and systems integration of information technology. Ron represents the utility industry on the Executive Committee of the Cross Industry Working Team [XIWT] which aims to advance the development of the National Information Infrastructure [NII] and recently conducted a study of the NII impacts on Business Opportunities for utilities. He is currently investigating aspects of information security, wireless technologies, and data visualization related to power system operations.

Dr. Mario P. Vecchi is currently Senior Vice President and Chief Technology Officer of the Excalibur Group, a new Time Warner venture dedicated to the product and business development of LineRunner services (broadband data services: Internet, online, etc.) based on cable modem technologies. Dr. Vecchi has defined the functional and architectural model to develop products for the delivery of high-speed data services to home personal computers over the broadband hybrid fiber/coax network using multimega bit-per-second cable modems. Dr. Vecchi has held numerous other positions, including Vice President, Network Engineering at Time Warner Cable.

HARVARD NEWS

CONFERENCE ON THE INTERNET AND SOCIETY

May 29-31, 1996   Cambridge, MA

Amid a Blossoming of Cellular Phones, Panelists Predict Wireless Will Be Internet's Future

By Alessandra Bianchi

The Internet in your pocket? *Wired* magazine delivered to you wirelessly? As Eric Clapton might say, Internet Unplugged? Promises like these were delivered in yesterday morning's panel "The Wireless Internet," in Sanders Theater, which directly followed the bomb scare, after Bill Gates's keynote. Curiously, a clue to just how these wireless scenarios will come to pass was provided by the synchronous and rapid-fire unflipping of cellular phones that followed the bomb scare in the Computer Center. Future wireless technology, specifically devices that connect to the Internet without the necessity of being plugged into a wall, will rely on the very same technology that brought us cellular phones. Cellular carriers have spent roughly $18 billion to date, buying up chunks of the airwaves—or spectrum—in an effort to make wireless Internet devices as ubiquitous as telephones.

Though most people in the audience might agree with Gates' prediction that widespread use of wireless Internet devices is two years away, several of this session's panelists begged to differ. "We're delivering wireless broadband media today," asserted Advanced Radio Telecom CEO Vernon Fotheringham, referring to the amount of spectrum (a broad amount) these types of services require. As evidence of the demand, he added that his com-

pany has "customers in more cities to serve than we have employees to serve them."

Kendra VanderMeulen, VP and General Manager of AT&T's Wireless Services Wireless Data Division, supported Fotheringham's assertion with a visual aid. She held up before the audience her Wireless Internet Device, scarcely bigger than a calculator, and proceeded to tell the group how she relies on it wherever she is. "It's a phone, it's a modem, and it can also run small applications like notifiying me of important email, checking stocks, or telling me when a flight I'm scheduled on is going to be delayed. What wireless is all about is delivering spontaneously and on-demand high-value information to people where there are, when they need it," she said.

There are drawbacks, though, to all of this wireless hype. As moderator David Goodman of Rutgers University rightly pointed out, bandwidth is neither free, nor infinite, and therefore the trick to making wireless technologies widespread is to make the best use of limited resources. VanderMeulen put it another way: "We're all going to remain bandwidth-challenged and learn to like it."

Tom Freeburg, a VP of Motorola, struck a more optimistic note. He pointed out that the $18-billion investment on the part of the cellular carriers translated into approximately $6 per person in the U.S. "That's a small price to pay for bandwidth availability," he noted. Another way to look at it, he offered, was to consider that equipping a neighborhood with wireless capabilities cost about the same as installing streetlights in the area. Adopting a chicken-and-egg logic, Freeburg speculated that the reason why wireless isn't as widespread as other forms of communicating today is the fact that "we haven't developed the will, because developers haven't developed applications yet. Revolution happens," he says, "when developers for applications recognize breakthroughs."

In mentioning application developers, Freeburg could have indirectly been referring to one of his fellow panelists—Tomasz Imielinski, Professor of Computer Science at Rutgers University. Imielinski, who spoke perfect English with a heavy Germanic accent, has been developing wireless Internet applications for the past several years. One of the constraints to the widespread proliferation of such devices, notes Imielinski, is their mammoth battery appetites. "None of us thought we'd be worrying about extending battery lifetimes to this extent, but since their capacity is only expected to increase slightly—by seven percent—over the next ten years, we must focus on ways of saving energy," he stated. He added that keeping wireless Internet devices turned on in order to wait for email will drain it of all of its energy within one to two hours.

Following the panelists' presentations, the audience raised several pertinent questions regarding cost, pricing models, fraud, and consumer confusion from an ever-increasing array of communications devices. Most of the panelists ably and authoritatively answered these questions, but at one point Freeburg of Motorola revealed a welcome sense of humility. "Sitting here right now, how can we predict what's going to happen in the future?" he asked. "It would be like having our grandfathers be able to predict the effects brought by the invention of the automobile—the national highway system, and the development of the railroads, for example—well before they happened. We have to leave a little up to imagination," he cautioned.

Technology
May 29, 1996

The Wireless Internet

MODERATOR: David Goodman

PANELISTS: Vernon Fotheringham
Tom Freeburg
Tomasz Imielinski
Kendra VanderMeulen

Editor's Note: Because of a bomb scare immediately prior, this session was not taped. The following text is a transcription of the Session Notes by moderator David Goodman.

DAVID GOODMAN, director of the Wireless Information Network Laboratory [WINLAB], which examines wireless technology in conjunction with many university and industry players, introduces the questions at issue:

• How can we use wireless?

• When can we do it?

• Why should we?

VANDERMEULEN makes these preliminary remarks:

• Infinite bandwidth is a myth. We will all be bandwidth-challenged and still enjoy technology.

• Wireless internet is available today in over 50 cities.

• The protocol for Cellular Dual Packet Data [CDPD] is the means; this is a forward-error-correction-enabled, secure version of TCP/IP for wireless connections. This runs at 19.2 Kbps currently, which is a slow link, but people can still do a lot of work with this link.

• People are urgently in need of some information and are on the run; a wireless connection seems to be the best solution to meet these needs.

• Over 70 to 80 percent of what goes on on the Internet is really an intranet application involving high-value information being spread among a finite number of users.

• Applications include delivery of high-value information to people where they are, when they need it: e.g., email, customer status information, price schedules.

VanderMeulen demonstrates a new cellular phone that serves as a interpreter/browser that uses CDPD to update files on servers, download information on stocks or flights, all of which involves less than a megabyte of data.

• The business goal of wireless technology is to find high-value information so as to make people satisfied with their immediate needs for information, not their high-bandwidth information with superfluous data.

FOTHERINGHAM makes the following observations:

• Wireless has many meanings and serves many solutions.

• The key of wireless technology is its mobility, speed to installation, and ubiquity for wireless cable, yet it is consolidated in one band.

• Many cities and areas are served.

• Bill Gates [who spoke immediately prior to the panel] assumed that wired media will deliver the bandwidth. This is not true, since the last mile will need a quick solution; many wired systems already in place are over 10 years old and will need to be revised, with a solution that does not involve rebuilding the entire building. DS1 or DS3 installation for these buildings can involve at least three to four months, or more often, longer.

We can expect a tremendous wellspring of capabilities soon.

FREEBURG notes that:

• Bandwidth is not infinitely available.

• Wireless is fairly limited, yet per-person bandwidth costs are fairly cheap; each person could afford a substantial channel at a cost less than that for installing common street lighting. The driving force here must be the these types of solutions.

- Wireless is analogous to the VisiCalc scenario, when applications only really became available after engineers made assumptions that people will invest in creating computers with sufficient memory.

- The cable modem will offer realistic broadband solutions.

IMIELINSKI notes his interest in three main issues on wireless computing:

1. Mobility

- No longer will there be a fixed address associated with a user; and therefore standard TCP/IP addressing cannot be relied upon any longer.

- There needs to be a new proposal for mobile protocols.

- GPS [global positioning system] can be used to assign and identify addresses for computers, servers, local services, and even personal home pages. The computer itself becomes a pointing device with the ability to identify objects, their properties or characteristics, directions, etc.

2. Varying Bandwidth

- Some areas will have more bandwidth, others will have less.

- High and low bandwidth solutions will be offered in parallel.

- High bit rates with small range devices will develop to fulfill niche applications.

3. Energy Equals Battery Life Time

- None in CS previously thought about the duration of batteries since the doubling of processors capabilities were the focus concern, but now, power is the constraint.

- Using a LAN to wait for your email alone consumes enough energy to exhaust a small battery—even before you begin reading any email!

Questions & Answers

Q: *Setting aside the mobile capabilities of wireless, can it serve as the last link to the home?*

FOTHERINGHAM: Sure, since the bandwidth on a per channel basis allows microwave links to be applied immediately to a particular footprint without intense regulation.

Q: *What is holding up the infrastructure construction for PCS?*

VANDERMEULEN: Some is actually being built, but expenditure on the order of double what was paid for the spectrum in auction must be made to reach satisfactory deployment. In Washington, D.C., there is now a successful operation. Thousands of cell sites still must be created. The magnitude of this task is challenging, but the problem of local authorities derailing the process of setting sites is the ultimate delay. A second delay is the clearing of private microwave users who have previous claims to the microwave bandwidths now allocated to the same range.

Q: *Do line-of-sight obstructions play a problem in the 38 GHz band?*

FOTHERINGHAM: Yes, line of sight is required now, but the technology and costs will address this in the future.

FREEBURG: These bandwidths can be used even though people initially believed they could not be used at all; similarly, the line-of-sight problem will be solved with alternative technology.

Q: *What about satellites for the Internet?*

GOODMAN: The real issue that we have not solved includes the problems of ubiquitous coverage, especially reaching indoors into large buildings;

terrestrial substations may be needed for solutions in buildings.

FOTHERINGHAM: The problem with satellites is that they fall apart quickly in the cost-model of bandwidth; they have the potential for success, but if too many people want to use and adopt the technology, the benefits will decline; significant attenuation from the atmosphere, moisture, and buildings has forced narrow footprint applications, which in turn require more satellites. Soon, instead of tens of miles, thousands of miles may be in the future footprints.

Q: *The American Superhighway was apparently heavily criticized by Australian journalists along the following line of attack: why is cellular and wireless so expensive in the U.S., and won't this hurt America's competitive position with respect to other countries like Australia?*

VANDERMEULEN: A lot can be done for not a ton of money here; the competitive dynamics will evolve and allow multiple carriers; people will be forced to be more efficient in their use of the bandwidth; we will not be second rate!

Q: *How will the pricing models evolve or "shake out" in the wireless arena: on a per packet, per minute, or per month basis?*

FREEBURG: Wireless cellphone services in the U.S. are the cheapest anywhere. *[He backed off a bit, however, in response to an audience member's assertion that, because Australians must purchase their phones, and the caller pays, users end up paying less for similar services when examined over five-year periods.]* Different packages for pricing phones and services can create packages that are as hard to compare as apples to apples.

VANDERMEULEN: Cellular sells at about 3 each kilobyte. Attractive rates develop to meet applications; for example, with credit transactions, the value rendered is significant, even if sold in large buckets of consolidated bandwidth.

IMIELINSKI: Examining the charging algorithm (per month, per packet, per time) can be calculated by the software on your computer or cell phone, which can then determine the optimal consump-

tion patterns based on the pricing preferences of the users and delays.

Q: *Is it true that fraud is a heightened concern?*

VANDERMEULEN: Digital technology enables more complex and facile encryption techniques, and this can robustly avoid fraud; as more digital technology is embraced, however—while outside fraud will decline—the relative frequency of more types of fraud by inside people will become more likely.

Q: *What about the consumer confusion about rates and services—won't this get worse?*

FOTHERINGHAM: This situation is actually better; more choices gives the consumer more power. For example, the long distance phone rates have dived; Canadians on the U.S./Canadian border who recognized pricing differences have been upset by prices on their side of the border, which were much higher; the construction of unmetered local services was based on a goal (which has been successful) of allowing universal access voice services. This is now being misused to serve growing number of computer users on modems connected to Internet. Thus the existing system consumes numerous public resources that were previously properly allocated on a universal basis, but should not be doled out this way now. Cable modems and wireless solutions will force a general public policy examination of waste in the telephone system.

GOODMAN: Industry people are uncomfortable about service guarantees in the wireless communications industry; some even suggested [yesterday in the "Next-Generation Internet" Session] What You Get Is What You Get. How are wireless Internet providers going to face the quality-of-service issue?

FREEBURG: ATM addresses quality of service squarely; WYGIWYG is only fine if you get great services. Once one steps off this continent, quality declines precipitously. As the cost of long distance has gone down, there have been predictions of long-distance fees disappearing entirely, creating one global calling area.

Freeburg points out that allegedly 15 times more undersea fibers exist than what is projected to be necessary. He foresees cheaper bandwidth and capacity through all media—wireless or not. Remember, it took 15 years from the creation of cellular until the business took off. Thus prediction is impossible in this industry.

FOTHERINGHAM: The wireless broadband aim is to deliver low-cost services: a bit is a bit, so that everyone will eventually charge by the bit. Future modulation techniques will also be outdated and replaced, since they only use about three percent of the theoretical capacity of fiber.

VANDERMEULEN: The quality of the wireless network needs to match that of the existing wired network. The cost of such a universally available, predictable performance will be picocells. This will enable creative alternate solutions on a small scale, which will spread to homes and lead to vast improvements in quality and capabilities to induce people to rely on this type of information transfer.

IMIELINSKI: Wireless permits freedom of connection at almost any point: TV remote controls and cordless phones have demonstrated that the users prefer devices that enable mobility. This is a big advantage that people are willing to achieve by trading off quality. This is not a goal, but a reality.

About the Speakers

DAVID GOODMAN is Director of WINLAB, the Wireless Information Network Laboratory at Rutgers University. WINLAB is a National Science Foundation Industry/University Research Center specializing in mobile communications and mobile computing. Before joining Rutgers in 1988 as Professor of Electrical and Computer Engineering, he was a Department Head at AT&T Bell Laboratories. His research spans several areas related to wireless communications, including multiple access protocols and network control. Presently, he is Chairman of the National Research Council Committee On the Evolution of Untethered Communications.

VERNON L. FOTHERINGHAM is a founder of Advanced Radio Telecom Corporation. Mr. Fotheringham has extensive experience with the successful formation and operation of new enterprises within the telecommunications industry. Prior to his association with Advanced Radio Telecom, Fotheringham was the President and CEO of NORCOM Networks Corporation, a nationwide provider of mobile satellite services. Mr. Fotheringham also serves on the board of directors of Digital Satellite Broadcasting Corporation, Washington, D.C., where he was founding chairman, and as a Director of American Wireless Corporation.

TOM FREEBURG currently heads the Radio Research Organization in the Messaging, Information, and Media Sector. He has spent most of his 31-year career at Motorola working on Wireless Data in one form or another. His 33 patents cover many of the basics for cellular-like data transmission (Ardis and CDPD), as well as techniques for achieving RF data transmission rates at 15+Mbps, a new technique for achieving reliable radio coverage at microwave frequencies, and a way to take advantage of directional antennas in portable equipment. Most recently, he has championed development of technologies aimed at wireless ATM communications and spearheaded formation of the Motorola Corporate Steering Committee on ATM and Wireless ATM.

TOMASZ IMIELINSKI is currently Professor and Chairman of the Department of Computer Science at Rutgers University. He formulated one of the first approaches to provide intentional answers to database queries, and co-edited a book on this subject, *Nonstandard Answers and Nonstandard Queries*, published recently by Oxford University Press. His current interests include database mining and mobile wireless computing. Dr. Imielinski is a co-editor of the book *Mobile Computing* (Kluwer, 1996) describing the current state of research in this area. He is also a member of the steering committee for the ACM/IEEE Mobicomm Conference and an associate editor for *ACM/Baltzer Nomad Journal of Wireless and Mobile Communications and Computing.*

KENDRA VANDERMEULEN currently serves as Vice President and General Manager of AT&T's Wireless Services, Wireless Data Division. She is a twenty-year telecommunications veteran and has full operating responsibility for AT&T's growing wireless data business. Prior to joining the Wireless Data Division, VanderMeulen was with Cincinnati Bell Information Systems, where she served as chief operating officer and President of the Communications Systems Group. Earlier Ms. VanderMeulen also held a variety of business and technical management positions at AT&T in the fields of software development, voice processing, and signaling systems.

The Game's the Thing (and It's Not Only Boy Toys)

By Alec Solomita

Silicon Valley is in what time zone? If your answer is Pacific, you're up on your geography but not necessarily your Net savvy.

According to John Markoff, New Media correspondent for the *New York Times* and a member of the "Post-WWW" panel, Silicon Valley sets its watch to "Internet Time," a zone in which "everything is accelerated and everything is upside-down."

To a large extent, says Markoff, the "hyper" activity in the Valley is what is driving new Net technology and speeding up the already rapid transformation of the World Wide Web. "I see the Web," he explains, "as an ecology which is mutating rapidly. Any prophecy about the future forms of the Web based on what's going on today is very tentative because it's an ecology out of which new protocols are bubbling continually."

That explains "accelerated." But what's "upside-down" about the Internet Time Zone?

"Until seven or eight years ago," says Markoff, "technology was driven by companies making supercomputers, and then the technology 'trickled down.' Over the last decade, this phenomenon has been turned on its head: the leading edge of computing is now consumer driven. You see this everywhere in Silicon Valley.

"These days, when a large company breaks a conceptual barrier, the first place the new technology is deployed is in personal computers. It's the bottom of the market that's targeted first, then the technology 'trickles up.'" And, according to Markoff, one of the areas most clearly consumer driven and most dramatically "leading edge" is that of multiplayer games.

"I was recently in Los Angeles at the E3 Conference, which is a sort of intersection of Hollywood, software, and the video industry," says Markoff. And there, it became clear that one aspect of the World Wide Web, which is often characterized as a potentially profitable arena for companies, is already a huge money-maker—and that's multiplayer games. Like the shoot 'em-up games in the arcade, the web versions engage the player in simulated combat, but unlike in the arcade, the multiplayer games, as their name suggests, allow you to battle in apparent synchronicity with other players on the Internet.

This new "interactive space" activity is quietly gobbling up customers as voraciously as PacMan (remember him?). "The 'boy toy' industry," reports Markoff, "is currently taking in more revenue than the movie industry." And multiplayer games are the hottest thing in "boy toys."

Markoff cites two recent games, Warcraft Two and Command and Control: "When they were released, about 800,000 each were sold at $60 per [unit]. You do the math." (The calculator puts it at $48 million.)

Markoff speculates that the new multiplayer games may help to bridge the famous WWW gender gap. While simple "twitch games" are used overwhelmingly by "teenage" males of all ages, there are a number of "text-based adventure games being developed which could prove far more compelling for women," says Markoff.

The MUDD (Multi-user Dungeons and Dragons) phenomenon has already proven that these interactive text fantasies are capable of drawing in users of both genders. And single-player fantasy games such as Myst are popular with women. "Communication" environments which can be shared with others, and adventures which can be extended in interaction with others, are multiplying quickly on the Internet and signal, at least in part, the configuration of the Web to come.

Technology
May 31, 1996

Post-WWW

MODERATOR: John C. Klensin
PANELISTS: Cecil Bannister
            John Markoff

KLENSIN: We have two speakers today and enough controversy; I hope to produce a lot of questions and discussion. Our first speaker is **JOHN MARKOFF** who is New Media correspondent with the *New York Times* and watches technology in the Internet, in particular, for the *Times*. John can always be counted on for controversy, and I gather he's going to reward us with more today. The second speaker will be **CECIL BANNISTER**. Cecil is Senior Advisor with the Wireless Technology group, Advanced Wireless Services of Northern Telcom (NorTel). He's been with NorTel for about 15 years. His background is in electrical engineering.

MARKOFF: You know, the idea of a New Media correspondent at the *New York Times* has to be something of an oxymoron. And in fact I'm not the New Media correspondent—I'm not even the Internet reporter at the *Times*. I covered it for the *New York Times* until 1992 when I moved out to Silicon Valley; Peter Lewis now writes about the Net. Actually, I've been trying to run away from the Net for the last four years but I haven't succeeded. There doesn't seem to be anything that you can report about anymore that doesn't have something to do with the Net.

I thought I was going to be the one person who wasn't building post–World Wide Web applications, but I have been an observer of the emergence of the Internet and the Web over a couple of decades. I have no clue what's going to come next, but I do think that as a veteran observer of Silicon Valley I've been able to watch this remarkable industrial process that's given rise to the Net and the Web over the last two decades. I want to try to give you something of an unortho-

dox context from a reporter's perspective, and I offer some suggestions as to what's going to come next.

I see IP [Internet Protocol] as this remarkable petri dish out of which all kinds of protocols emerge and just keep bubbling up. A remarkable juxtaposition of two events happened in May [1996] that really gets at the heart of the context, or the platform, on which the Web and the Net will move forward. Two events that I reported on—at the time I missed the lead for them, actually. It always galls you as a reporter to have that happen, but I can tell you. At least now I have a small audience. These two events happened within a week of each other. First Silicon Graphics [SGI], which now owns Cray Research, lost a contract to a Japanese supercomputer maker, NEC Corporation, which sold a machine to the National Center for Atmospheric Research. The National Science Foundation purchased this machine, and SGI and Cray raised a stink, suggesting that the Japanese were selling MIPS [a measure of CPU processing power] below cost, which they were dumping in this market.

Not a week later, I was in Los Angeles and there were a bunch of executives from SGI with the Nintendo Corporation. To do what? Well, they were selling cheap MIPS to the United States. And if you think about this juxtaposition, this is the introduction of the N64, which has been designed by Silicon Graphics. It's a remarkable computing machine. Essentially, the top of SGI's product line in 1992, that cost upwards of $20,000, is now being put in a little box and sold for $250. Probably by the time it gets to this country, $200. That's four years from the top to the bottom.

So you have these two events. I like to think of it as this inversion going on right now in the computer industry, which is going to define everything that comes hereafter. The way I see it, from now on, the cheapest computers will also be the fastest. And that's a remarkable change.

So what's at work here? Well, a couple of days ago Bill Gates invoked Moore's law: the industrial process by which the number of transitions on a given piece of silicon doubles every two years. Bill seems to see it through a very Popperian view. You know, it's just an upward straight line over time. And I think what it means to Bill is that, over time, we're going to be able to have bigger and faster versions of Windows and little more. But what if he's wrong? What if Moore's law is actually a dialectical or a more Hegelian process? I'd like to argue that case.

Moore's law means that by the turn of the century we're going to have billion byte memory, which is a startling concept. And that four or five years after that, the cost of billion byte memory will be $3.12, because all chips fall to that price over a given period of time. I also might mention to this audience that there's Andy Grove's corollary to Moore's law. (Gordon Moore was one of the founders of Intel.) Grove's corollary is that chip density doubles every 18 months and bandwidth doubles twice a century, which I think is very profound.

So if Gates is wrong and we're not just embarking on bigger and faster versions of Windows, what is next? What does it mean that this industrial process that was set in motion by Moore's law allows each generation of computing to consume the former? If that's true—if you go from mainframe to minicomputer to personal computer—or if you're in Silicon Valley and you go from digital watch to pocket calculator to video game to personal computer to PDA [personal digital assistant] to more or less, the network computer, what's next?

So my argument, which I think is in direct opposition to Gates's, is, why should this process stop with the personal computer? Why should the personal computer be the end of history in terms of this technological evaluation? But if you go up to Redmond [Microsoft headquarters] right now, what you'll find—and this is really quite remarkable—is that one to two thousand people are engaged in software development with, I would submit, no possible revenue that will derive from their work.

Because what Gates is up to is that he's basically trying to cut off the air supply, as a friend of mine mentioned, from his competitors. So he finds revenue out there in this space. He finds revenue on the balance sheets of his opponents and he is basically throwing programmers at writing code that will essentially be sucked down into the operating system, and the operating system will get bigger and bigger. At the Worldwide Developers Conference Microsoft had a couple of months ago, they gave a brief glimpse of the web browser as part of the basic desktop of the next version of Windows which will be released later this year [1996].[*]

The one thing I came away with was that we've reached the state I think of as the pre-computer-icon era of user interface design. What I mean is this: the operating system and the user interface are getting more and more baroque. Microsoft products are already baroque, and if you add an order of magnitude of complexity to what users are going to have to deal with, you get this very, very strange situation. So Bill Gates has essentially decided that the enemy is Netscape and he is going to deny them a market. And that's because he has this pauperian view of Moore's law.

I think that Gates and Microsoft have missed the picture and that the more interesting action, if you follow this argument [that each generation consumes the next] is going to be in this space of things. I actually think the network computer people have missed the picture too: if you look at Larry Ellison and Scott McNealy, their notion of a network computer is a personal computer minus. It's as if everybody has this notion of something that you sit at, something that sits on a desktop.

But I think that the next growth space will shift to the platforms—things that run Java or Inferno, or whatever applet language emerges—these will have IP addresses, they will not be computers, and they will be connected to some wireless fabric that will also emerge.

---

[*] This is to be included in Windows 97, which has not yet been released at the time of publication.

So this is what makes Silicon Valley an interesting place for a reporter. Each one of these industries has tended to eat the last one over time. My sense is that the personal computer era is really just the prehistory of the Internet and that we're even before the Model T period: only when these next generation platforms emerge with the characteristics listed above, will things get very interesting.

I would submit to you that the personal computer industry right now is actually more monopolized than the mainframe era was at its peak, where you had seven different architectures. Here we supposedly have this remarkably innovative industry where, in fact, we have one and a half architectures. We have Apple, on its way spiraling to who knows where, and we have Windows. Not a very competitive space.

But I don't think that the future is really about the war between Netscape and Microsoft: it is about this other space that is emerging. Each one of these circles of computing over time reaches a broader portion of the population. And as these things trickle down, the war will be fought beyond the personal computer space. Not that personal computing will go away, it will just become a boring and sort of dull industry (if you heard the speeches earlier this week—with the exception of Steve McGeady's—maybe you can already see that. I was just amazed at all the advertising that went on).

It seems to me that technical innovation doesn't trickle down the way it did once upon a time from supercomputing to the generations that followed, but now it is actually surging up. You see that everywhere when you start to look at the world that way. The notion of the information technology industry is now being driven by companies that make things that go under Christmas trees. And that's a profound difference from where we were five or six years ago.

A classic case in point. Last month, IBM broke a barrier. They broke this barrier of magnetic storage media that can now store more than a billion bytes of information per square inch. Where do they deploy it first in the marketplace? Not at the high end. They put it on their two and a half

inch disks that go into portable computers. I mean, if you look around the industry, you see this happening everywhere. The only people who have the capital to move to this next layer are the companies that are building the things that go under Christmas trees.

Another thing I wanted to mention is this context in the notion of price point. We're at this wonderful juncture where we have a class of machines that sell for $3,000 and they have a 100 MIPS processing power more or less, maybe going to 200 MIPS. And then we have this other class of machines that sell for $200 and they have more than 100 MIPS. I think that there's a disconnect here and it's a very unstable situation. This other class of machines are the Sega, Nintendo, Sony, 3DO video game players. This is just pure processing power, it's just pure MIPS.

Some smart graduate student is going to figure out how to tie all those Nintendo computers together and build a very, very fast machine. Or there will be other killer apps that will emerge for that kind of processing power at that price point that will move the industry and move the innovation in that direction. A company called MicroUnity in Silicon Valley is a wild gamble. And this year, their first machines will ship that will go into set-top cable boxes. The processor in the MicroUnity box is going to start out between one and ten giga apps and this thing is going to sell for $300 to $500.

This price performance disconnect means that this is an incredibly unstable time, and that means things are at a very interesting point. What are the implications for this price/performance disconnect, and how does it affect the Web or whatever comes after the Web? In a way, I'm more interested in the hardware trends than the software trends.

I was just at the Society of Information Display Conference in San Diego this month and it's pretty clear that the flat panel guys are really on the Moore's law curve. I mean, there were inexpensive 15-inch flat panels there. There were 22-inch flat panels. That technology is finally going to get on the same price/performance curve. I mean, if you've seen the Xerox displays, we can finally start talking about a world in which paper is a last resort. The Xerox displays are $10,000 now, they're able to resolve two point type. They're easier to look at than paper and CRTs [cathode ray tubes]. And that is just one more aspect of the Moore's law process.

The other thing is you bundle in wireless technology. I think in the Bay Area, within the next four or five years, we're going to have five or half a dozen competitive wireless digital providers. And that will emerge as a platform for all of these new devices that have IP addresses.

So it's going to be a remarkably interesting platform for this IP petri dish to continue to bubble along in. It's not a world in which I think I would feel very comfortable being Bill Gates. Thanks very much.

BANNISTER: Today I will be sharing some ideas with you on where the Web may be heading. We'll focus on voice communication services for obvious reasons. But first, to apprehend the future of the Web, we need to comprehend the present.

In today's Internet, the Web paradigm is primarily seen as an effective database access, enabled by a browser-server technology. The information being accessed is mainly text and graphics, although it is moving fast to include animations, sound, and voice. But in essence, the Web still represents an individual accessing stored information from a database in a server. There are emerging applications today on the Internet that allow two individuals to communicate with real-time voice and some video. The nature of these communications exploit the Internet and are, in essence, independent of the Web.

Let's focus for a minute on the list of uses all of which fall well within today's Internet or Web paradigm. They involve advertising, marketing, online publishing, and a number of uses you probably already know.

What is interesting about popular web sessions is that nearly all of them have the potential for real-time voice connectivity. For instance, if I'm accessing a Yellow Pages web site, I see a phone number and I then have to go to a phone and dial that party. That call is independent of my session with the web page. What we're proposing is a mechanism whereby a voice connection can be made in association to that data connection with a call button. When I select the call button in that page, the system phones the business that is advertising, then phones me and makes a connection—all in one step.

This functionality represents a shift of paradigm of what the Internet is today, which is database access, to more real-time interactivity. At NorTel, we've been researching and implementing a number of prototypes that deal with this notion of bringing the voice networks to serve the Internet. I will illustrate this using two examples: Yellow Pages and the 1-800 ACD application, which I'll describe below.

In the Yellow Pages, as I explained, there may be a call button in each page for each ad. When the consumer selects the page and presses "call button" in that page, the connection will be made to the business associated with that specific page or ad.

In the ACD 1-800 example, it's a bit different. If you go to, say, the NorTel home page, you may then navigate to the Wireless Network's page. From Wireless Network, you navigate to Wireless Products. From Wireless Products, you may go into a CDPD [cellular digital packet data] page. At that point, you may want some more information.

As a result, the agent and the customer share a visual space together with a voice connection. At that point, the agent can actually navigate for the customer and present new information, even in areas that normally would not be available for anybody coming into that server (price lists or customer specific information, for example).

An interesting aspect of this concept is that since the call is originated by the system to the customer, it's a virtual 1-800 service, which now has the added value of being associated with the content of the customer screen. The call to the customer is paid by the service provider. In today's

1-800 service, incoming calls to an agent are often put on hold, and the business providing the 1-800 service has to pay for those calls. In contrast, if I press a call button on a page and the agent is busy, the server can report back that I'm on the fifth position of the queue. No additional phone calls are made until that agent becomes free. So this system benefits everybody.

If this call closure service in association with web pages is indeed a useful thing, then many server-based applications will incorporate it. Entertainment services on the Web are one example—you can assume, in fact, that just about every server in the Internet will start incorporating this voice capability of originating calls to the network using call closure.

During the time service providers engineer their servers to allow for proper traffic flow, robustness, and so forth, this solution would be an expensive proposition. Another model is for businesses like Inter-Exchange Carriers, for example, to sell this call closure service on the Internet. In other words, any server on the Internet can request call closure service from this IEC in real time.

This model can be compared to a Computer Telephony Interface model, where you have a computer, a switch, and an interface between them that allows a computer application to control the telephone functions in a switch. Similarly, on the Internet you have a large number of servers replacing the CT computer, and a switching entity at the IEC serving all these Internet applications. Offering call closure service is advantageous for IEC, since they are in a very good position to offer least cost routing for the calls. And that means that application providers on the Internet don't have to implement and invest in the switching capability associated with their servers, they just contract the service through the Internet.

I believe that the concept of applications contracting specialized services on the Internet will become more and more common. This concept is a shift in the Internet paradigm, This call closure service, for example, with an open standard

interface available to any Internet web application, offers a substantial paradigm shift for the Net, and allows numerous web applications to enter a new functional dimension.

What will happen, then, with voice over the Internet? As Internet networks evolve by increasing capabilities such as capacity, latency, and robustness, it's likely that the boundaries and capabilities of the existing voice network and the Internet will become blurred. Voice traffic may be routed over either network, where central offices may connect to other central offices through the Internet, and as the terminals and workstations on the Internet with voice capabilities increase in numbers, the central offices will bridge the calls over the two networks.

The Internet of tomorrow will be a new and improved ATM-based network, where virtual networks and virtual businesses will be common, driven mainly by Intranet business requirement. As Intranets also become ATM-based, many services, such as voice and data, will be supported by the same network. Telephone services will be supported on both data and voice terminals. We'll have integrated wireless and voice data services along with a communications controller to orchestrate many of the voice communication needs, particularly to support mobile uses.

The value offered by the future, new and improved Internet/Intranet will manifest itself through services that synergistically integrate functionality provided by the different entities. For example, controlling environmental factors such as the light and room temperature through a wireless terminal. Like Intranets, the residential networks will be interconnecting many of the intelligent and controllable entities in the home, allowing appliance manufacturers to diagnose problems remotely, and owners to monitor performance of key systems such as alarms and environmental controls. Voice and data devices will be able to provide services associated with several virtual networks. Users will be able to make and receive business calls on their home phone. From their home computer, they will be able to simultaneously log into different virtual data networks.

Imagine, with so much distributed computer power available in the Net, it may get to be an out-for-rent resource...why not? Central offices on the Net may become front-ends for wireline phones to customers without ATM-based home networks. Wireless user-base stations will be controlled by a mobility service providing mobile users with seamless service, regardless of Intranet, residential, or Internet location.

In summary, the Internet will be an environment where multiple service and virtual networks will coexist and integrate in a synergistic fashion. Well, I wish we were there today: I would be making this presentation, instead, from the comfort of my office. Thanks very much.

Questions & Answers

Q: *How do you see Sun's notion of Java?*

MARKOFF: Though I agree with Scott McNealy that Java will be everywhere, including on Bill Gates's Windows system, so far I think Sun has been pretty weak in having much vision with respect to their clients. It's hard for me to see what Scott's vision is. I think the truth of the matter is that Java snuck up on Scott and wasn't part of his original vision: it just exploded and he is frantically trying to hold onto the Java reality.

BANNISTER: Recently NorTel and Sun announced the use of Java for hand-held devices, specifically for Orbiter. Orbiter is a NorTel wireless device with a touch screen. The intent is to have a Java engine in silicon and be able to download the Java applets for applications. It allows the wireless service provider to provide wireless communications—specific services—at the same time allowing third parties to download their own Java applications. So I see Sun, at least from a Nortel perspective, in an interesting position to support future devices with IP addresses all the way down to the portable device.

Q: *Do you see Netscape's vision as being any different?*

MARKOFF: I think probably the sad reality is that Netscape's vision is very close to Microsoft's

vision. They just see Netscape in Microsoft's place.

Q: *As Microsoft takes over larger and larger percents of the market, do you see them using that to stifle innovation of the various types that you're seeing, and if not, what prevents it?*

MARKOFF: I think it's difficult to assess that right now. I don't think Microsoft is the same as IBM, which simply practiced account control. The net effect was that innovation was stifled. Microsoft is pushing ahead in a lot of these spaces, but all within the same restricted vision, which is that you have a mainframe on your desktop and it runs Windows. And I think that's one single vision. Given that the market is monopolized, I think that the net effect may be to stifle innovation.

> *The sad reality is that Netscape's vision is very close to Microsoft's vision. They just see Netscape in Microsoft's place.*

Q: *As we move towards things which require increased bandwidth and as the bandwidth goes up, how do those costs manifest themselves to users on the network and who pays the costs? We're in a situation now in which for small amounts of little dialog, the user cost is essentially zero. Presumably that can't continue as the bandwidth requirements rise.*

BANNISTER: It's not an easy question. How this will change in the next five years would certainly be a wild guess. One thing is for certain: we have to assume that whoever is providing the service has to make some revenue out of it. So as you mentioned, increased bandwidth on the Internet may reflect increased fees for access and maybe pay for the amount of information being transferred. That has to change though. Somebody has to pay for that. But I don't have the answer, honestly.

Q: *Given the power of chips in 2010, what's the computer software going to be post-Netscape during the same period?*

MARKOFF: Well, Alan Wong, who was an optical researcher at Bell Labs, argues that the Internet will be the first petaflop computer. I think that's what Java gets at. I'm not a technologist but this notion of a distributive computational fabric with these little small programs flitting around doing different tasks is a very compelling vision. My only refuge is in science fiction—I think you have to look to a book like *True Names** to understand the real potential of this kind of process. *True Names* was one of the first books that looked at the kind of virtual community that might arise out of the conjunction of infinite bandwidth and infinite processing power. And it's still, I think, a remarkably prescient view even though it was written at the time that the first bulletin board societies were emerging.

You will essentially be able to synthesize reality. You will be able to build these synthetic realities with all of the MIPS and the bandwidth that you have. And I have no idea what kind of strange societies are going to emerge from that.

Q: *Do you see that new operating systems will be required to take advantage of this, and if so, who's built them?*

MARKOFF: Well, I think Sun. I announced this thing called Kona and Inferno is running around out of Bell Labs. There are lots of plays. The Newton OS Digital House has an interesting chip called Strong Arm. I think that if the Java vision is actually pulled off, it won't matter what the operating system is because there will be this layer of abstraction that interesting things happen on top of.

Q: *Do you see new protocols needed in network architecture to make that happen?*

MARKOFF: I think that they're emerging constantly. I was just at E3 and all of the buzz at this digital entertainment conference in Southern California was about multi-player Internet games. What these companies like Total Entertainment Network and Impact are doing is building their own protocols to guarantee. You know, the issue is

latency in the Internet—how you make these twitchy games work, to make it at least look real even if it isn't real.

So protocols were built to do that. I think there's a whole series of protocols that will emerge over time to handle different specific needs in that space.

KLENSIN: If I can add to that, there's a tremendous amount of activity and innovation out there. Most of it is short-sighted: focused on a particular application or two and not very good. And whether that kind of stuff will take over the marketplace because it's there, or whether other better things will come along to secede it is one of those interesting open questions.

Q: *What are the technical impediments to real-time use of the network today, especially for voice? Are there efforts to find audio compression and transport standards for interoperability?*

BANNISTER: Certainly there are some deficiencies in today's Net. Latency is one of those, as is lost packets. That has to change. Now, are there any efforts to define audio compression? Yes. A lot of it is being driven from a wireless, which has a limited bandwidth. What is interesting is that, looking at applications for voice on the Internet today, many offer the same compression or the same bandwidth as used on wireless applications. So they're adopting a technology that is coming from wireless.

KLENSIN: A part of the answer is that we just do not have the bandwidth. We can build the bandwidth if the money is there. But the voice telephone networks are not where that money's going to come from. The total amount of Internet capacity in this country across all suppliers is a tiny fraction of the bandwidth we've got devoted to the voice network. And if you want to do voice on the Internet, even at high compression ratios, some of that stuff has to shift over and the economics have to be there to support it.

---

* Vinge, Vernor, *True Names*, Baen Books, 1987.

MARKOFF: Just another small little anecdote. If you go to the office of HotWired, which is this wonderful postmodernist newsroom run by a bunch of twenty-somethings, you walk in and there's a sea of terminals and there's incredibly loud music playing. And then you realize that everybody's got their own headphones on listening to their own music. And so I don't think it's a very big step. We're already there at least from a fashion point of view.

Q: *Does anyone in the audience have a post-WWW vision?*

___: I don't really care about the Web; I use it but I really care about my family. So the Web has to move to where it's more like a refrigerator, like a kind of utilitarian entity. That's a very bland, abstract statement, but right now [the Web] is a very cumbersome environment manipulated by people who are trying to make a lot of money, trying to convince us that we need to be a part of it. My vision is that the mass of people will force it to be easy and very inexpensive.

Q: *Do you see the next generation as being an automatically restocking refrigerator?*

___: Sort of. My question is really about bandwidth: what is the actual technology and where is the demand for it coming from?

BANNISTER: The demand for bandwidth will come from businesses. The corporations are the ones that would be driving and adopting this technology, they are the ones demanding the network bandwidth, and they are the ones who have the resources to pay for it. Obviously, the rest of the world will benefit from that too.

MARKOFF: I think that the good news is that the demand is clearly there to build these fiber networks. The bad news is the demand is probably going to be driven by entertainment. If you think of America today as a population of couch potatoes—I mean, what are sitcoms and dramas but one-way immersive fantasies—and then you go down to something like E3 and you see these multi-player interactive immersive fantasies, you know we're going to come out the other end of this World Wide Web period with the nation sitting at personal computers playing with these fantasy games.

This is the interactive television reality coming to fruition. It's just happening in the web space instead of in interactive TV. So there'll be plenty of bandwidth; I'm just not sure that we will like the result of the cultural level, which will probably settle somewhere around Fox TV.

Q: *Will the wireless technologies ultimately drive out the wired system in this country as they're doing in Asia?*

MARKOFF: I think the situation in Asia and some developing countries is that they lack a wireline infrastructure. That's why the adoption of wireless is so huge and the ratio is not the same as here in the States. Certainly the wireless is doing well here in the States but it's for different reasons.

BANNISTER: I think the issue here is more from a services perspective. As I mentioned earlier, you can go and retrieve the information from a database in the Web. However, if you want to talk to somebody, you have to go to a different network and request a service which is disassociated with your data connection. I think the value of this interaction is how those services will be exploiting and synergistically exploiting the capabilities of the voice and the data for services. So it's not so much who carries what, but how those services exploit the capability of having both.

Q: *What is the short term future of free phone calls? Who's the best positioned to take advantage of that market? Netscape, Porterdec, Vocaltech, or someone else?*

MARKOFF: I think it has to be the people who can set standards, so it has to be a Microsoft or a Netscape.

KLENSIN: Or a phone company.

BANNISTER: When we say "free call," truly there are no free phone calls today. Even in the Internet. You are paying an access fee today.

The question of how cheap it will be is a different issue. As far as who is the best positioned to offer cheap voice, I think it's a matter of how those services are provided and in what context.

Q: *What are your thoughts about the future of the rest of the Internet, the non-WWW? Does it have a future?*

MARKOFF: Obviously electronic mail has a huge future.

Q: *If the Internet gets to have enough bandwidth, do you envision it totally replacing the telephone network?*

KLENSIN: No.

Q: *What will the relationship be between the Internet and the phone network in the future?*

KLENSIN: At a given level of bandwidth, the Internet technology looks like it's much better at transmitting things other than audio. It's really good for video, especially stop motion video. There's a hypothesis floating around that Internet-based videoconferencing may drive Internet-based audioconferencing back to the telephone because the telephone's a really good technology for doing that. But again, it's a question of economics, it's a question of bandwidth, it's a question of usage. Patterns in business environments where they're paying for a lot of bandwidth may turn out to be a lot different from patterns in home environments.

About the Speakers

DR. JOHN C. KLENSIN is Senior Data Architect in MCI's Data Services Architecture Department. His activities there include product design and evaluation for MCI's Internet offerings, especially for Internet applications. Outside MCI, he has had significant responsibility for the present generation of Internet applications standards. He was one of the principal designers of the framework for extensions to the Internet's mail transport protocol and later served as chair of the working group that developed the standard in that area. He also made contributions to the design of the MIME standard for multimedia and structured electronic mail.

Born in Chile, CECIL BANNISTER joined the Department of Geophysics, University of Chile, as head of the Seismological Service after graduating from Electrical Engineering. During his 14 years with Bell Northern Research/NorTel, Cecil managed a number of projects from product development to exploratory work on advanced wireless and Internet/Intranet services. He holds a number of patents on wireless services and technology. Currently, as Senior Manager at Omnipoint Technologies, he develops exploratory wireless service concepts to exploit the unique features of the IS-661 radio access technology.

JOHN MARKOFF is based in San Francisco as West Coast Correspondent for the *New York Times* where he covers Silicon Valley, computers, and information technologies. Before coming to the *Times* in 1988 he covered Silicon Valley for the *San Francisco Examiner* beginning in 1985. He has also been a reporter at Infoworld and in 1984 he was West Coast Technical Editor for *Byte Magazine*. He is the co-author with Katie Hafner of *Cyberpunk: Outlaws and Hackers on the Computer Frontier* (1991) and with Lenny Siegel of *The High Cost of High Tech* (1985). In January 1996, Hyperion published *Takedown: The Pursuit and Capture of America's Most Wanted Computer Outlaw*, which he co-authored with Tsutomu Shimomura.

Acronyms Abound at H C on the I & S

By William J. Cromie

I know that ATM does not mean "automatic teller machine," at least to most (but not all) those attending the Harvard Internet conference. I know it means "asynchronous transfer mode," and that knowledge would at least allow me to carry one of those neat tote bags they give you when you register.

The next step in my education, I thought, would be to find out what an asynchronous transfer mode does and what one might do for me. So I went to the "Global and Long-Term Impact of ATM" session on Thursday morning.

John McQuillan, president of McQuillan Consulting, started things off. He's a nice, distinguished-looking fellow, who got both his undergraduate and Ph.D. degrees from Harvard. In fact, he told us, the University was one of the first sites of the ARPA network, the government parent of the Internet. As far back as 1970, Harvard had connected a mainframe called PDP to the ARPAnet.

He said that "we are already measuring the age of the Internet in dog years."

Then McQuillan did something that really impressed me. He asked the audience if there was anyone in the room who didn't know what ATM means. There was no way I was going to raise my hand. Fortunately, a few did, but not very high.

He said, and these are my words, not his, that it is a really fast switch that can send data, voice, and video over a single cable simultaneously. "How do they do that?" I wondered.

The key to such technological wizardry is in mind-numbing switching speeds. Text, voice, and video are broken up into electronic packets 53 bytes long: ATM switches between packets so fast that two or more people can receive different messages simultaneously.

At this point, I felt that I was really going to learn something. I settled back in my chair, pen and notebook at the ready.

McQuillan introduced John Swenson, from Lucent Technologies, born of one of the greatest corporate spinoffs in history. Lucent, that is, not John.

Swenson pretty much convinced me that, in the future, ATMs will provide invaluable support for the Internet by managing all the traffic it carries. He mentioned that the Net was growing so exponentially that faster, better routing of messages is a must.

About this point, I began to miss words. Then sentences, then entire slides, then the whole drift of Swenson's talk. I was in astupid transfer mode.

I thought about leaving, but I was sitting in the middle of one of those really wide rows. I had my brief case, my tote bag, my umbrella, and my top coat to move. Even if I made it, I'd reach my office just in time for a staff meeting.

I decided to stay and do something productive—count acronyms. I made it to 22, then got bored.

At the end of Swenson's talk, I, like him, was convinced that the Internet could not traffic into the future without ATMs. He described switches that could handle millions of information packets every second. Or was that billions. Doesn't matter, it will soon be hundreds of billions, maybe even trillions. They would surely form the backbone of all global and regional business, government, and academic networks, and maybe LANs, too.

At this point, McQuillan introduced Peter Newman as the man who designed the first ATM that failed. Newman is a witty Brit from the other Cambridge who works for Ipsilon Networks, Inc. McQuillan noted that almost everyone who has anything to do with ATMs belongs to, or subscribes to the views of, an organization called the ATM Forum. He (jokingly) described the Forum as the Church of ATM and Newman as part of the rabble outside.

Newman promptly demolished my impression that ATMs will make possible The Grand Unified Network that would be everything to everybody, everywhere. It will not, he emphatically stated, provide the hoped-for seamless ubiquity.

I was crushed. I tried to follow his acronym-rich arguments but I couldn't.

What I did get out of it was that ATM hardware is very useful, but not the controlling software.

Newman says that IP (Internet Protocol) software plus ATM hardware is the way to the future. He also maintains that ATMs are unsuited for WAN-LAN integration.

By the way, his company makes some nice IP software that it will sell you.

I'm sorry if my summary doesn't do justice to Newman's heresy.

I left the meeting not knowing how the world is going to achieve the virtual ubiquity it seems to want.

One thing is clear, however. No matter how we tie ourselves together electronically, acronyms, like web sites, will multiply exponentially. Newman pointed out that the ATM Forum's "bible" contains 42 pages of them, some 500 in all.

And he displayed a neat colored slide that tracks numbers of acronyms per millions of dollars in computer industry revenue. It shows a steep decline from billion of dollars to $700,000 per acronym, and the rate of fall shows no sign of decreasing.

That's something to think about during your next staff meeting.

Technology
May 30, 1996

Global and Long Term Impact of ATM

MODERATOR:　John M. McQuillan
PANELISTS:　Peter Newman
　　　　　　　John Swenson

McQUILLAN: Good morning, everybody. It's nice to be back. I have fond memories of going to the computer lab night and day to write software. And in 1970, I built the hardware and the software to connect Harvard's PDP-1 to the ARPA-net with some help from a few friends. I built it, but then Ben Barker debugged it, so I think Ben probably deserves more of the credit than I do.

Then I went on to build the routing algorithm for the ARPAnet which I called SPF [Shortest Path First], which was later improved and extended to the OSPF [Open Shortest Path First], and is some of the work that is now behind the routing algorithms in the Internet. Success has many fathers; failure is an orphan. I've also had a terminal in my home and in my office since 1971, and I've been getting email with an @ sign since 1972. So none of this seems very new to me. There's no "overnight" about this at all. It's been around a really long time, and for me, it's been quite a remarkable experience to work in this field continuously my whole career.

I sometimes feel as I imagine an astronomer might have felt if he had gone to school with Galileo and was still a practicing astronomer today, working with arrays of telescopes and radio telescopes and space telescopes. It's almost like having lived for hundreds and hundreds of years. We're now measuring the Internet in dog years, and I think it's going to be remarkable for another good 20 or 30 years.

More recently, I've been focusing on ATM (Asynchronous Transfer Mode), and the next generation of network technologies. So let me explain briefly how I think ATM represents one of the next key steps for the Internet.

The Internet has almost all of the ingredients to become a really enormous success, and I don't think it is, though it's certainly much bigger than it was 26 years ago. We have an enormous potential market with 180 million personal computers. We have heavy publicity, even hysteria. The Internet is now a fad. We have remarkable ease of use with the Web, and we have really high value on the Net; certainly higher than it was a couple of years ago, and it gets higher every time anyone adds a web site (there are 300 added every day). We can keep low costs because computers are cheap: 28 kilobyte modems now cost $150 and the software is bundled into your operating system.

So we have everything we need on the Internet: ease of use, low cost, wide availability, high visibility—everything except good performance. Specifically what the Internet doesn't have is the following:

• Good throughput

• Good delay

• Good reliability

• Good security

And this is where ATM comes in, or where it's going to try to come in. In the U.S. high tech industry we know how to do this. We know how to observe a large, well-identified, well-established, rapidly growing market that has new entrants all the time, and how to introduce into that market a continuous stream of innovations that make things cheaper, better, faster.

This is where Silicon Valley shines. You've heard from the CEOs of Microsoft and Sun. You've heard from the Chief Technology Officer of Apple and a high-ranking executive at Intel. They're all targeting this. So are Oracle, Cisco, Bay, and Netscape. The best and the brightest in the high tech business are all focusing on the

Internet and pouring billions of dollars of R&D into this. Tens of thousands of very highly motivated and very talented people are working on making the Internet cheaper, better, and faster.

The story of ATM is that it is one of the key underlying transport and switching technologies to make the Internet faster. That's my new view of it. It may be many other things—ATM is such a big issue that it's a lot of things to a lot of people—but I think that the Internet has become the killer application for ATM.

Let me just do a sanity check here. Is there anyone here who really doesn't know what ATM is? Okay, I was afraid of that. This usually takes days, but I'm going to do it in two minutes.

ATM stands for "asynchronous transfer mode." It's a cell switching technology. A cell is a fixed length unit of information, 53 bytes long. The rest of the world works with variable length datagrams. The Internet and the Ethernet work with datagrams, or packets, which are all basically the same thing. ATM is a revolution: it suggests that you can chop things up into these cells instead. This has several advantages: you can switch them in hardware instead of a mixture of hardware and software. You get very low latencies because the cells are short. And you get very low variability of the latency because you can control multiple queues in hardware, and run just the stuff you want to send through the switch at the time you send it through.

We can now build multigigabyte ATM switches for under $10,000. It's remarkable! People are now building multigigabyte ATM switches on a single chip. They haven't been built into products yet but we know how to build terabit ATM switches. We know how to build them for the local environment, and for the wide area. We know how to send voice and video data over ATM switches. And there's interest in ATM in the public carrier environment as well as the enterprise environment. You can use it with copper, fiber, wireless, and satellite, so it's a very ambitious attempt to rethink the underlying infrastructure.

Now this is not the same as the effort to make ATM into the next generation of Internet. In fact there's some intellectual rivalry between the ATM community and the Internet community. This morning we're going to hear from one of the experts in the ATM field. Then we'll hear from, I would say, a heretic: someone who is also an expert in ATMs, has worked in the field for many years, but is also an expert on the Internet and has a different suggestion to make.

Our first speaker is **JOHN SWENSON**, from Lucent Technologies [*http://www.lucent.com/*], recently the largest initial public offering in history. John joined Bell Labs in 1976. He used to work in human performance of computer systems and he's been working on ATM standards since 1988. He's been involved in all the different standards activities and is currently on the board of directors of the ATM Forum. He chaired the committee that was central in the development of the adaptation layers that are the fundamental building blocks of ATM. At Lucent, he's involved in network systems, product architecture, and is responsible for ATM standardization.

SWENSON: I'm going to be talking today about ATM's role in supporting Internet traffic as well as aspects of where ATM will be deployed. My perspective is that of a person who's providing equipment to the public network provider. While Lucent does provide equipment use on premises, that is not the area of the company I represent, although I do have some understanding of the direction and the thinking in that area, which I will touch on briefly. Suffice it to say that, in our view, ATM will be a fundamental part of the evolving public network. We believe it will also hold a fundamental place in enterprise networking.

I'm going to touch on a number of topics this morning. I want to look at some of the environmental factors that affect the deployment of technologies, such as ATM, which is aimed at providing support for integrated services—not just Internet, but telephony services, video services, and whatever other communication services are needed to be transported in the public or enterprise network. I'm also going to touch on some of the technology issues and some of both the consumer and business needs that are driving the deployment of this equipment and services.

John alluded to the controversy in the industry as to the future of ATM—that is, whether there are other technologies that could be profitably deployed in its stead—and there are a number of reasons as to why this is. One issue is the standardization process. People feel that the standardization process may have created a certain amount of confusion. There may be some truth to that, at least from the public network perspective. But we don't believe that is the fundamental cause of a slow down in the deployment of this particular technology.

You're probably quite aware that there's been a huge increase in the use of all communication services. Some technologies that some of you may actually loathe, such as voice mail and answering machines and what have you, have been very beneficial to your local service provider and your long distance service provider because they've increased call completion. So there's been a huge increase in the number of minutes on the public network as a result of those things. Also things such as facsimile have increased the traffic markedly.

When was the last time, in the course of business, you received a business letter as opposed to email or a fax? During the last couple of weeks we saw that people were actually emailing from Mt. Everest. My brother, in rural Maine, now has email. It's something that some of us have grown up with, and that many more people are embracing each day.

Then there's another source of some of the most interesting traffic: the Web. Also creating huge increases in service usage are MBONE [Multicast Backbone] and medical imaging. Things that were once just a glimmer in people's eyes are becoming a reality today, increasing demands on public transport. Together, these have done some very interesting things already to the communications industry. There has been a marked increase in the sale of local telephone switches to meet this emerging demand.

What has happened? A few years ago, video dialtone and interactive TV were just around the corner. All the local operating companies were actively pursuing very aggressive deployments of new access technology for switching. Since the cable companies have good bandwidth capabilities for the delivery of information, all the local exchange carriers were actively beginning to deploy high bandwidth distribution facilities and switching facilities.

Well, Congress upset the tea kettle a bit, perhaps just temporarily, when they basically said we're going to deregulate the industry. And that suddenly prompted some new decisions that had to be made by the planners in the public network provider companies. Whereas before they had developed a business case and calculated that they could make money providing video services to the home, suddenly they had alternatives they hadn't realized they had just a few weeks earlier. In particular, they were allowed to get into long distance services and some other services as well.

When one computes the business case, one finds that the risk for getting into long distance services is, at least on the surface, a lot lower; hence, the business case looks an awful lot better to get into those types of services. That and the FCC [Federal Communications Commission] beginning to auction off Personal Communications Service [PCS] and cellular spectrum seems to have changed those investment directions. (One of the aspects of the PCS spectrum auctions is that you can spend a lot of money to obtain the rights to bandwidth, which is two-spectrum, but having done so, you then have an obligation to develop the equipment to provide the service behind it. And that isn't going to come cheap.)

Then, finally, you have the Web going wild. Providing Internet services and other services to Internet providers as backbone, or becoming Internet providers themselves, became an attractive business. So everybody had to go back, redo the business cases, and now we find ourselves with some new priorities.

Another force that's driving some of these changes in the rate at which technology is being deployed is consolidation of the telecom provider. You've seen some mergers in recent weeks—big mergers—of Southwestern Bell Communications acquiring PacTel, and NYNEX and Bell Atlantic merging. This has a number of implications. Because of the competitive nature of these changes, there is very, very strong pressure for those companies to streamline their operations drastically to be competitive with their brethren in the LEC [local exchange carrier] environment and the interexchange carriers [IEC] getting into that market.

Further, one of the big problems that is often experienced, at least in the datacom world, is that when companies merge, they must have some kind of common architectural vision so they can move their operations and their infrastructure toward a common goal. We'd argue that ATM serves that particular vision.

In terms of technologies, I think these concepts and Moore's law* are quite familiar to most of you. There are a lot of debates as to complexity of technology *A* versus technology *B*, and I would argue that these amazing advances in the underlying technologies will probably wipe out any real differences between those basic technologies. I don't think they're the kind of thing that will really make a big difference in the future.

On the other side, this is extremely beneficial to those of us in the business of providing public communications services because it will create end points that have the ability to demand increasing amounts of bandwidth.

Again, from the perspective of a provider of public communications services and underlying equipment, the Internet and its amazing growth is just wonderful. The growth is near exponential. The important thing is that it's now becoming a fundamental way people are beginning to do business in this country and worldwide. And

we only hope that Metcalfe's law† holds true over the longer term.

One of the areas of a great deal of debate in the last year has been where the role of ATM ends. I don't think you'd find a lot of people who would argue too strongly that it has a major role in the support of the public network. There is a lot of debate, however, as to whether or not ATM will actually make it to the desktop, which I, personally, would like to see. However, I think that people who advocate other technologies have good reasons for their arguments to the contrary.

Today, Ethernet underlies most of your services within the campus and it does quite an adequate job. One hundred megabyte Ethernet will do an even better job. And if you're the person responsible for maintaining your company's or your building's communications services, and you know that your people are happy—their applications work just fine on an Ethernet—you'd hesitate to come in and try to propose something entirely different. There's such a risk-averse, perhaps pragmatic view, that augurs against the introduction of new technology.

However, there are some implications to extending that further into the enterprise network. One will be, for the foreseeable future, encumbered by the realities of the public network plan. Lower bandwidth facilities, in particular, will always be a reality. Consequently, ATM may have some strong advantages in integrating services. Techniques that don't use such a small cell-switching approach may not provide adequate quality of service.

There will always be competing technologies and, especially in my position in the industry, this is just a wonderful thing. Competition by industry for providing more bandwidth to the desktop will bring the price down and create greater and greater deployment of that technology. As

---

* Moore's Law: The logic density of silicon integrated circuits follows the curve *bits per square inch* $= 2^{(t-1962)}$ where t is time in years; that is, the amount of information storable on a given amount of silicon has roughly doubled every year since the technology was invented.

† Metcalfe's Law: The value of a network is proportional to the square of the number of users connected to it. For more information about Metcalfe's law see *http://www.discovery.org/metcalf.html*.

they've always been in the past, people will be bandwidth hungry. Applications will be bandwidth hungry and there will be more information flowing to the public network.

My guess is that over time, owing to the competing technologies, we will see a hybrid approach: that is, the large enterprise hub switch, the backbone switch, will likely have ATM capabilities, certainly, as it goes into the public network, and there may well be some ATM networking within the campus. I do believe, however, that many of the Ethernet approaches will prevail in their particular places, and we will end up with a mixed solution over the long term. Which, in my view, isn't a bad thing at all.

I think that the people who try to declare one technology dead should be a little bit careful. We've seen many examples where people have made such proclamations and have been proven quite wrong. Today ISDN [Integrated Services Digital Network] is selling very briskly. I know what our sales are like. I would hazard a guess that our major competition in North America, NorTel, is doing very well selling ISDN switches these days.

And it's all attributable, for the most part, to the growth in the Internet services, fax machines, and what have you—things with longer holding times than the typical phone call. Also asymmetrical digital subscriber lines [ADSL], high-speed access over twisted pairs to the premises, was dead some time ago. It's now coming back in force.

Taken together, some of these technology changes have already provided some pretty good advances. Within Lucent, we are already deploying 5 gigabyte ATM switches on a chip. All the fundamental ATM functions are being captured on one chip. In our lab, we have a working 160 gigabyte ATM prototype, and this technology is quite manufacturable.

Moving on to some of the drivers. From the consumer perspective, what they are looking for is a full service network. The service provider, in order to differentiate themselves from their competition, would like to provide such a full service

network. You probably see that in the ads the various service providers are airing these days. They'll provide for all of your communications needs: telephony, broadcast video, enhanced pay per view, interactive TV (perhaps in the future), and basic Internet access and transaction services.

There are a number of drivers, some of which I touched on earlier. In the near term, the service providers need to have a rapid return on their investment. Their stockholders won't allow them to take any huge risks. This is why you see some of the changes in the investment directions of the operating companies. And part of that, of course, is that the appropriate service mix—whether or not they should be providing just telephony and Internet access, or they should be providing telephony and video distribution, or what have you—it's quite uncertain, which compounds to the risk.

There is, however, increasing competition from the cable companies. They are beginning, in certain areas, to provide telephony services. And as I said, they do have some advantages in terms of the bandwidth they can deliver. So at least the local companies, and certainly some of the long distance companies in conjunction with the cable companies, are constrained to make a decision sooner rather than later. And clearly there is already a demand for information services.

One of the things that's happening as these networks evolve is the expansion of the areas being served. Various companies are invading each other's historical territories. To be competitive, these service providers must:

- Increase the operational efficiency.

- Provide a wide range of services to gain market share.

- Provide new, enhanced services, including interactive multimedia.

In the far future, we see things such as virtual neighborhoods, full interactive entertainment, electronic commerce, and what have you. The fact that all these services need to be integrated into some efficient method of delivery, again, argues for deployment of ATM technology.

From a business perspective, the main drivers here are LAN to LAN connectivity and Internet access. In fact, the Internet is being used commercially by a large number of companies today. There is greater and greater work group collaboration over electronic media. (My organization is split over four states and yet we have to communicate on a daily, hourly basis to get our work together, and we can't afford to be flying all over the place to do so.) And finally, from a competitive standpoint, there's a need to upgrade the network infrastructure to provide more efficient, robust ways of providing private line services for various enterprises.

There is a similar set of drivers for the business from the service provider perspective. The data services are an area which they have to quickly move to capitalize on in supporting enterprise networks. Again, cost control is fundamental to their competitive health. There is also a greater emphasis on some issues that relate to interconnection of carriers as well as some legal issues in that area. To avoid becoming the dreaded dip pipe, they have to evolve to higher value services—like multimedia and some vertical applications—which provide more of the content (or at least that's the view).

One of the things that's driving the need and demand for communication services is the growth in interenterprise networking between different companies. And again, the notion of broad-based electronic commerce is fundamental in the long term, as is virtualized distribution: doing away with the middle man and using the network to basically provide direct contact with the customer.

Other factors are driving the demand to deploy ATM in the wide area network. One of the major factors today is the deployment of personal communication services [PCS] and cellular networks. As I'm sure you're quite aware, the growth of these types of networks is astronomical. And as one moves toward PCS, with it smaller, microcell topology, one finds the need for an underlying infrastructure to interconnect these various radio sites. That is a major cost to the PCS or cellular provider.

One of the ways they hope to contain those costs is to use ATM technologies to multiplex traffic from the radio to the switch. And this has worked. It's actually active in standard today. There are systems being deployed today that use this type of technology.

Another aspect of ATM technology is improving the performance of the service provided to the end user. In today's network, it's a compressed voice approach. And the newer Code Division Multiplex Access [CDMA] and other approaches are highly compressed voice, which, when one feeds it into a LAN-linked network, introduces some delays. If, as the call moves, one goes mobile and moves toward the called party, one has to do successive transcoding; that is, going from digital to analog or from one coding format to post-call modulation, 64 kilowatt approach, used within the LAN-linked network. This introduces additional delays and distortions. By using ATM—if ATM is ubiquitous—one can get the call to the destination without a lot of transcoding.

There has been a lot of work on the backbone of the Internet and also frame relay traffic—a burgeoning source of traffic today. ATM switch providers perhaps got a black eye in terms of the first generation, particularly in the way it handled IP traffic from a traffic manager's standpoint: a lot of congestion, a lot of dropped packets. Our company and my competitors are doing a lot to address those issues, including introducing beeper buffers, ingress traffic-shaping, random early discard, per VC queuing, and a lot of approaches that will help mitigate the problem.

There are some additional capabilities of closed-loop traffic control that have come out of the ATM Forum that are just now being introduced, and we'll see how well they work. But again, the goal is to provide a good infrastructure for transport of the Internet to directly address some of these problems meeting the real capacity demands.

One of the areas under debate is the IETF [Internet Engineering Task Force]. The ATM Forum has a number of different approaches to routing Internet traffic, and I think these things are still open. Some good ideas come out of the raging debates going on, and Peter will touch on those. His company has some interesting ideas. Voice is one of the things that ultimately must come onto the ATM network to realize the goal of being an integrated services network. It's still a preponderant source of traffic in today's network.

There are some demonstrable operational efficiencies from moving voice onto a common network infrastructure. Investments in existing circuit switches make realizing those gains an issue. But there are operational efficiencies. Despite what people might think in terms of protocol overheads to ATMs, as the amount of bandwidth being carried increases, ATM becomes more efficient than circuit switching.

Another area we're looking into are some better quality, high fidelity, ATM-aware codex. Today's voice networks basically only give you part of your aural spectrum, clipping the high end of the conversation, reducing the fidelity. Being able to provide for and make use of some of ATM's capabilities in terms of variable byte-rate services, layer-coding, increased bandwidth utilization, and what have you, has some interesting prospects.

There are also a lot of areas we'll see capitalized on in voice-trunking between PBXs [Private Branch Exchange] and in support of local service resale. This is being driven by the new competitive environment we find ourselves in.

We see an evolution over time from a circuit environment to an ATM-overlay environment. We begin to interwork the narrowband and broadband services, and the operations become integrated. Then finally, there's a fully integrated ATM network providing for all the services in an ST environment.

Some quick conclusions:

- We firmly believe that ATM's future is very promising, particularly in the wide area network.

- There will be continued competition to wire the desktop, which is good for all of us.

- We think there is a strong role for ATM to play in the enterprise. One of the reasons is that, in many areas, ATM has a big lead on some of the alternative approaches being proposed.

- Finally, if one moved all the services people talk about onto the Internet, we don't believe that current routers would be able to serve them. We think an ATM approach will be fundamentally necessary.

McQuillan: I mentioned that John is on the Board of Directors of the ATM Forum, a worldwide consortium of about 750 organizations that is responsible for establishing the implementation agreements. All the major chip vendors, local area and wide area network vendors, carriers, most of the leading software companies and even cable companies, are in this forum. So it represents the unified view of how to do ATM, except for a few rebels.

And now it's a great pleasure to introduce one of the leaders of this rabble, **Peter Newman**. Peter is a senior member of the technical staff at Ipsilon Networks [http://www.ipsilon.com/], a company that introduced an idea called IP [Internet Protocol] switching, which was voted the Best of Show at Interop. At my conference a couple of weeks ago on ATM, it was really the hit of the show as well. Previously, Peter was the ATM systems architect at Adaptive, which, as he says, were the designers of the first ATM switch to fail commercially. Peter also survived the traffic management group at the ATM Forum, and I don't think they'll ever want to talk to him again.

In his previous life, he was a research fellow at the computer laboratory at the University of Cambridge—that's the other Cambridge, where he received his Ph.D. for research in ATM switch design.

Newman: If at first you don't succeed, give up and try IP.

ATM: myth, marketing, or virtual reality? In the beginning was the requirements document, and the market requirements document was without form. And void and darkness was upon the face of the engineering team. And there was evening and there was morning, the first day. And the darkness was not good. So two celestial standards bodies were brought forth to shed light upon our darkness. One to rule the packet switching and one to rule absolutely everything it could get its hands on, including the packet switching. And there was evening and there was morning, a second day.

Now this is a long story so let me cut to the chase. By the fourth day, it was clear even to marketing that there was a problem with the schedule. Shipping on the sixth day was unlikely in the extreme, big bang or no, even should engineering sacrifice its day of rest. So there was a reality gap. And to bridge this reality gap was conceived the greatest marketing machine the networking industry had ever seen: the ATM marketing machine.

The great ATM marketing machine is a virtual machine. You feed it reality and out comes virtual reality. Virtual reality is cool, way cool. It's almost indistinguishable from actual reality. Virtual reality is what reality will look like after the next spin of the die, after the next rev of the spec, after we deliver the next generation. Let me demonstrate the great ATM marketing machine in action. Feed in local area networks, and out come virtual LANs. (Not that anyone has yet found a use for virtual LANs.) It's an attempt to offer some of the features of routing in a bridged network. Virtual LANs are the poor man's routing.

Try another one: feed in Ethernet and out comes LAN emulation. Almost as fast as switched 100 Mbps Ethernet—as long as you don't try giving it any multicast traffic—though I wouldn't try to squeeze the driver into boot ROM [read-only memory]. Now there is a theory that states that if you take the virtual reality output from the great ATM marketing machine, delay it just a tad and then feed it back into the reality input, you achieve the legendary perpetual marketing machine. As long as the cash flow is maintained, the output is sustained…though it does get a little thin on reality after a while.

There is another theory that states that this has already occurred and that nobody noticed, because how else can one account for the emergence of the recent cells in frames proposal? But here we must leave the big picture so as to offer at least one or two little facts to substantiate our marketing story.

There are two sorts of ATM networks:

The ATM cross-connect network. It offers a leased line with bandwidth control. This is very useful. It allows us to provision permanent virtual paths. It allows the phone company to offer fine-grained but fixed bandwidth. It's used for bandwidth provisioning. It's here now, it exists, it is very useful but rather dull.

The ATM multiservice network. This is the brave new networking world for the '90s that you mostly hear about. This is the voice, data, video, image, TV, and absolutely everything network: the grand unified network. Everything to everyone everywhere. This is the ATM network that I shall address.

What are the advantages of ATM? I went back to the papers that I and others were writing about three, four, or five years ago. These are the advantages we were preaching back then: ATM offers high-bandwidth links, scalable bandwidth links, high capacity switches, scalable capacity switches, low latency. Low cost hardware is available for the local area because of the research investment that the wide area carriers have poured into this technology. It offers quality of service guarantees for multimedia traffic and, I shudder to say it, but we were preaching seamless local area and wide area integration.

So let us review those advantages:

- High-bandwidth links

- Scalable bandwidth links

- High capacity switches

- Scalable capacity switches

Very true. ATM offers 25 Mbps links, 155 Mbps links, 622 Mbps links, 2.4 Gbps links. But then Ethernet offers 10 Mbps links, 100 Mbps links and, soon to come, 1 Gbps links. It seems that Ethernet can also scale. Scalable link bandwidth is a direct result of switching. High capacity and low latency results from switching in hardware. And you can switch Ethernet, too.

Service classes. Now we're getting into the concept of offering guaranteed quality of service. There are only two services. There is capitalist switching and there is socialist switching. This is a concept we all learned at about the age of two. There's a big bowl of candy and we share it, or Mother gives a piece to you and a piece to me, etc. Socialist switching: there is a big pool of bandwidth and we share it. Capitalist switching: there is a big pool of bandwidth, and the phone company gives some to you and some to me, and you don't have to share your bandwidth with anyone, even if you're not using it. Both classes of service are potentially available in both the Internet and in ATM.

Fixed bandwidth service. This has already been solved for ATM mostly because ATM came out of the phone companies and this is the concept of switching that the phone company has developed. "Guaranteed service," which is what it's called in the Internet, is still an item of research.

Shared bandwidth. Socialist switching and the Internet developed with Unix and became popular through the People's Republic of Berkeley, Version 4.2, in part because it was hip, but mostly because it was distributed free with the operating system. Therefore, shared bandwidth is more the concept that underpins the Internet. You get two types: you get shared bandwidth with congestion control and without congestion control. So in the Internet that's TCP [Transmission Control Protocol] or UDP [User Datagram Protocol]. These services have been available for a long time. In ATM, shared bandwidth without congestion control is called ABR [Available Bit Rate]. This is still a subject of research even if the ATM Forum has finished the traffic management specification for ABR. In ATM, shared bandwidth without congestion control is called UBR [Unspecified Bit

Rate]. Combinations of the above may be possible, but any service beyond these is the subject of current research.

Quality of service. Guaranteeing a quality of service to a particular user. It has two components: making a promise and keeping a promise. Making the promise happens at call establishment time. You ask for a certain quality from the network, or you ask for a certain amount of resource from the network: for example, bandwidth. The network thinks about it and then says yes or no.

When it says yes, it's making a promise. This is hard. It requires signaling. It's called Q.2931 in ATM, it's called RSVP [Resource Reservation Protocol] in the Internet. Q.2931 is finished, RSVP isn't. It requires admission control—thinking about whether you can actually satisfy this request for the entire duration of the call. For some services, that's finished; for some, it's not. It requires quality of service-based routing. This is still a subject of research even if the ATM Forum has finished the PNNI [Private Network-Node Interface] specification. We still have to try it and see if it works. And it requires certain political decisions or economic decisions, like who is permitted to request the resources and how do they pay. That is very hard.

Keeping the promise, surprisingly, is not so difficult. Once the promise has been made, keeping it is the job of the hardware. Keeping the promise occurs when data actually hits the network. Making the promise occurs when a request hits the network. So keeping the promise is usually done in the switch in hardware with policing, queuing, and scheduling. The next generation of switches will all include variations on that theme. So quality-of-service support in the data path is available now in ATM hardware. Quality-of-service support in the control path requires some further work.

Ah, seamless local area and wide area network integration! We should have known better. This is a utopian ideal, totally unsuited for the real world. The goal of seamless integration forces heavyweight solutions from the wide area into the local area. We have baroque 1970s ISDN sig-naling on the workstation. We have an unneces-sarily complex physical layer. SONet-Lite [Syn-chronous Optical Network] is still too heavy. We didn't need that. We have very complex ABR traffic management in the workstation itself to handle connections that span the known universe.

It's totally unnecessary. Yes, we need compatibil-ity. Yes, we need the same cell size; changing cell sizes would be very inconvenient. Yes, we need easy interoperability. But seamless? Absolutely not. Keep the phone company out of my local area network. Remember 15 years ago how the phone company tried to convince us to use the digital PBX as a local area network? Ethernet won for a very good reason.

Finally on this theme, the politics of compromise is impossible, and it often yields a poor solution when we have to seek a technical compromise between the requirements of the wide area and the local area. Very difficult. Easy, however, to stand up here and say that.

So to summarize the advantages of ATM:

- High bandwidth links? Yes, in the hardware.

- Scalable bandwidth links? Yes, in the hardware.

- High capacity switches? Yes, in the hardware.

- Scalable capacity switches? Yes, in the hard-ware.

- Low latency? Yes, in the hardware. I think you're getting the idea here.

- Quality of service? We've still got some work to do on making the promise, but keeping the promise, yes, we've done that. It's in the hard-ware.

- And seamless local area, wide area integration—we should have known better.

So the advantages of ATM are here and they're in the hardware. But a network requires both a data path and a control path. In ATM, the data path is in the hardware, the control path is in soft-ware. So now let's turn our attention to the speci-fications for the control software that have recently been coming out of the ATM Forum.

I feel there is a certain amount of complexity in the solutions that have been delivered by the ATM Forum for the control path: not the physi-cal layer, not the hardware, the control path. My first example, my first measure of complexity is acronyms-per-unit revenue. (I have the official ATM Forum glossary, April 1996, 44 pages, 500 acronyms.) Alright, not all of them are ATM but more than half are.

So I tried to track when the acronyms came in, and there we have a curve: acronyms per million dollars revenue. It's falling, it's falling fast; but we're still at a scary 0.7 acronyms per million dol-lars revenue. Now you may not think that 0.7 acronyms per million dollars of revenue is particu-larly scary; but just think—to get to a billion dol-lars in ATM/LAN-switch revenue we will need at least another several hundred acronyms. And it's the IS departments that will to have to under-stand this complexity if these switches are in the campus network.

The next measure of complexity: new software. In the network, to implement the ATM Forum's solution for IP over ATM is going to require an estimate of 200,000 lines of new software. That represents 60 percent of the stack. In the host we estimate it's going to require about 60,000 lines of new software. That's 75 percent. Networking software is hard to get right and it takes a while.

Another measure: new networking standards. If the ATM Forum continues to meet for another six months, I think we're going to have more of a protocol heap than a protocol stack. Now, my favorite, reproduced verbatim from a vendor's advertisement: the 14 steps required to build a LAN-emulation connection. It takes three steps to do it with IP and Ethernet. It takes 14 steps with LAN emulation. No further questions.

Moving on. Back in the early '80s, there was a movement to develop a new set of vendor inde-pendent networking-protocol standards. A Brave New Networking World. It was called OSI, Open Systems Interconnection. It wasn't tremen-dously successful. I think we're frighteningly close to making history repeat itself with the ATM Forum. The goal seems to be becoming the same. A Brave New World, a Brave New Set of vendor independent networking protocol standards.

There are three approaches to standards development. There is ready, aim, fire. There is ready, fire, aim. And there is fire, rape, and pillage.

Ready, aim, fire. You implement, you evaluate, you standardize. This has given us such classics as Ethernet, TCP/IP, and the network file system [NFS]. The problem with this approach is that you have to give away the first implementation. In order to get it accepted, in order to get it standardized, you've got to give the stuff away. This frightens people.

Ready, fire, aim. This is the guided missile approach. Fire the thing and then see if we can steer it towards a target. The dynamic here is that when I go to the standards committee, I want my stuff in the standard. But failing that, I want my competitor's stuff kept out of the standard. So this results in a standard either with multiple options so that it isn't particularly standard, because we both got in, or it results in a standard that has never yet been implemented because my stuff and his stuff is the only stuff that's been tried. So whatever we end up with has nothing that has actually been tried before. (Perhaps I exaggerate a little.)

Oh, the third approach:

Fire, rape, and pillage. To be politically correct, I think we call it merger and acquisition these days. This is standardization by purchasing the entire market. It typically helps to at least own 80 percent before you start down this track.

So a funny thing happened on the way to the Forum: the Internet. We've all heard about the exponential growth and so on. Eighty percent of corporate desktops are going to have browsers by the end of the year. The number of web sites doubles every 23 weeks. More than 30 million people have access to the Internet today. We've all heard it. Another funny thing happened on the way to the Forum: fast Ethernet. No longer is the lucrative desktop market available to ATM technology.

So where does ATM fit now? The ATM control methodology (the basic philosophy for control in ATM), and the basic philosophy for control in the Internet and in the local area networks that form your campus network, are completely different. It's the socialist versus capitalist theme again. Two completely different views as to how you control a network.

We have shared bandwidth on the one, guaranteed on the other. Packet switching on the one, circuit switching on the other. Connectionless versus connection-oriented, datagrams versus signaling. We have the Internet or the phone system. We have monthly fee-type stuff or usage distance fee. They are very different. The philosophies are very different and they were developed by people who were thinking along completely different lines.

There are three approaches to standards development. There is ready, aim, fire. There is ready, fire, aim. And there is fire, rape, and pillage.

It is not surprising, therefore, that it is very difficult to convert between them. Witness the MPOA [Multiple Protocol Over ATM] standard that is being developed by the ATM Forum. This stuff is complicated. But all the benefits of ATM are due to the hardware. So a thought strikes us. Can I use the ATM hardware but with the Internet control software? I gain the benefits of ATM from the hardware, but I keep the control philosophy that's already established in my campus LAN and in the Internet. Basically, I take IP and just speed it up by applying hardware. Of course, the answer is yes, otherwise I wouldn't have set up the question. We call it "IP switching."

You take the ATM hardware, you delete any software you might find hanging around, and you install IP (Internet) software. I mean verbatim. IP itself. And all you need is a little bit of protocol in between them to glue the two together. And the surprising thing is, it works! So now you've got a choice. Every ATM switch looks like this. It's a lump of hardware connected to a control processor. In our case, it's 16 ports at 155 Mbps connected to a high-end Pentium processor. Sometimes the controller is inside the box; sometimes it's external. We've left the option of external so you can mix and match your controller and your ATM hardware.

So either you get to install the ATM Forum software, and it is bona fide regular ATM, or you get to install the IP software (which, incidentally, you can get from us, including that little bit of glue that glues it together). And you've got what we call an IP switch. But what is an IP switch? It's a router that goes fast because it uses switching technology. You have the benefits of ATM, you have the control philosophy of the Internet.

Drawing to a conclusion, it's now safe to invest in ATM. Most of the benefits of ATM are in hardware—the hardware's here. You can use the Internet protocol suite for control now. It's easily compatible with the existing installed base. It's mature and it's a well-tested protocol suite. There's a lot of it out there. And later on, you can choose to move to the ATM Forum stack, if you like, when it's finished. After all, it's just a software change.

The fabric of the Internet is constructed from routers. What we have here, what we've constructed, the IP switch, is a router that offers an order of magnitude more performance: ten times the speed of traditional routers by integrating switching technology. And friends, I know this is true. I got it myself, directly from the great ATM marketing machine.

Finally, the benediction. God bless your ATM switch, every cell that sails through her, every sale that sells her, and may they all make a packet.

Questions & Answers

Q: *Do you really think that ATM will be used for carrying voice and video, or will it just be used to carry* *more data, like any other wire? Do you think it will really happen?*

SWENSON: Yes, I do. And the main reasons are twofold. One, there is a growing need to consolidate disparate networks under one fundamental network infrastructure. It's just a competitive requirement. The second is, in order for our customers to grow their businesses, they have to find new revenue sources. I think, ultimately, they will begin to offer both distributed and interactive video services over those networks. And I think that will ultimately drive them to ATM technology.

Q: *What makes it possible for us to do ATM now that's different than it was five years ago?*

SWENSON: First of all, the fundamental agreements in terms of the ATM and adaptation layer weren't really solid five years ago. They were solidified about four years ago. In fact, there were systems that anticipated ATM techniques that have been available for 15 or more years; so a lot of experience with the underlying techniques has been gained over those years. From a technological perspective, I think that has been the case for some time. I'm referring to the Datakit switch, to some of the Stratacom equipment. Those fundamental techniques have been available and are viable.

McQUILLAN: Peter [Newman] was building things that had cells in Cambridge back in the '80s, too, so it's been around a long time.

NEWMAN: Actually in Cambridge, they were variable length packets. There was some work on looking at the jitter you got if you decided to use fixed length cells. And from that point, fixed length cells certainly offered you lower jitter, and they happened to agree with the fast Cambridge ring which was around there at the same time.

To comment on that question, I do think that we shot ourselves in the foot somewhat when we adopted some of the phone company's carrier methods in the local area. I think we could have done a much better job if we had avoided the heavyweight signaling, if we'd stuck to our guns and kept to a lightweight signaling method in the local area. And if we'd made switches with plentiful virtual channels and plentiful buffers, there would be far less chance for my own company to do what it's doing. I think that ATM would have been good enough to offer datagram service.

SWENSON: For what it's worth, I'll agree with you. I think the whole history of the Internet is to put something out and see how well it works and improve it. And if the early ATM switches had been pretty good, they would have been improved. Instead, we were waiting for the software. But the Internet being the impatient place it is, a lot of people have given up on it. Not everybody, by any means. There are a lot of Internet service providers that are running ATM and, in fact, probably something like half the Internet's backbone traffic is flowing over ATM switches right now.

NEWMAN: But is that ATM just bandwidth provision, just for raw data?

SWENSON: It's just big pipe ATM.

NEWMAN: In which case that's dull ATM.

SWENSON: It's dull ATM and it doesn't take the time to wait for all of the ATM Forum standardization efforts. But I don't take issue with that.

McQUILLAN: It is cost-effective deployment of the technology. That's an important point that people must understand and it is financially, economically motivated. But I agree that it is dull.

NEWMAN: I disagree with you.

McQUILLAN: Okay, the Internet's dull. But just to drive this point one step further, the providers of much of the Internet backbone right now are not the traditional telephone companies to a great extent. Not the RBOCs [Regional Bell Operating Company]. A lot of the ISPs are little companies like PSI, UUNET, and Netcom. And a lot of the backbone providers include MCI and Sprint, who are of course providers of telephony, but not on that same network.

So the debate between these two speakers comes down to the vision of whether we'll soon see voice on the ATM switches or whether we'll

soon see voice and telephony on the Internet, or whether neither one of those things is going to happen and we'll just see telephony as an independent network. Does anybody want to comment on that?

SWENSON: I know that a lot of companies are actively working toward providing voice services on the trunk side of their switches, and they're doing that for basic efficiency reasons: to contain costs. (Basically, the tariff they have to apply to their long distance carrier or their local exchange carrier.) It's just a mechanism to efficiently carry compressed voice in ways that can get around some of the historical inefficiencies of the digital hierarchy that has grown up in the phone system. Ways to do it more cheaply.

On the trunk side of equipment, that's something that's already beginning to happen, and the carriers are beginning to see some of the advantages of that as well.

NEWMAN: In the converse, the integration of voice and data has been under active consideration for the last 15 years. There have been small start-ups with neat technologies that have died little deaths or sometimes long, lingering deaths over the last 10 or 15 years. So I'm not going to pin any of my stock on hopes of the integration, the market drive for the integration of voice and data, in the campus network.

McQUILLAN: I was trying to distinguish between the lines, to sort the axis from the workstation to the switch, versus from the switch between either PBXs in an enterprise or from between a PBX and a virtual private network. That's where there is some efficiency to be gained today.

Q: *The ATM and Internet debate is over. The current Internet backbone's already ATM. Vint Cerf ["The Next Generation Internet"] pointed out MCI's running OC-3 and is going to OC-12. Any major ISP will need to carry this speed, and speeds only work sensibly using ATM switching. So once an Internet service provider is using ATM, they'll be able to offer total quality speech with only a very small fraction of the data bandwidth they're carrying. The company that can do this, that can connect PBXs to it, will put all the* *telephone companies into bankruptcy. Are you worried about that?*

SWENSON: I'm a little bit worried. I'm still a stockholder of a lot of the RBOC and interexchange stocks. But my current company is in the somewhat beneficial situation of being an arms merchant, happy to sell equipment.

NEWMAN: We, on the other hand, are in the drugs kind of role model. We give the stuff away and hope to hook people.

MCQUILLAN: To summarize, what we heard from this presentation is that the Internet is getting relief in the form of ATM. That ATM will be used to reach higher performance levels and higher quality of service levels.

The significant question still is, who will the providers of this ATM technology be? Will they use the conventional wisdom as developed by the ATM Forum, some new unconventional ideas as developed by Ipsilon, or some combination? The main point is, we think we can deal with a lot of the performance limitations of the Internet; we're just not completely sure how we're going to do it. Thanks to our speakers and participants.

About the Speakers

DR. JOHN MCQUILLAN, President of McQuillan Consulting, is one of the world's foremost authorities on advanced networks, both as an original contributor and as a consultant to industry. He spent the first decade of his career at BBN with pioneering work on the ARPAnet, the first packet switching network. Since 1982, McQuillan Consulting has advised many of the major communi-

cations and computing organizations as well as leading end-users and investors. Dr. McQuillan's current focus is ATM and the broadband Internet. He has authored over 100 monthly columns in *Business Communications Review*, developing a reputation for accurately predicting and clearly explaining each major new development in communications technologies.

PETER NEWMAN is a senior member of technical staff at Ipsilon Networks Inc., Sunnyvale, California, the IP Switch company. Previously he was an ATM systems architect at Adaptive, manufacturers of the first ATM switch to fail commercially. He is also a survivor of the Traffic Management Group of the ATM Forum. In a previous life he was a research fellow at the Computer Laboratory of the University of Cambridge where in 1989 he received a Ph.D. for research in ATM switch design. He began working on fast packet switching in 1981 for the Telecommunications and Computer Systems Research Laboratories of the G.E.C. (UK). He can be found on the Web at *http://www.ipsilon.com/staff/pn/.*

JOHN S. SWENSON is the manager of strategic applications in the Network Systems Broadband Multimedia Division of Lucent Technologies in Warren, New Jersey. He joined Bell Labs in 1976 and has worked on a wide range of projects in human performance technology and data communications. In addition to his ATM and data networking product architecture responsibilities he is responsible for standards development and representation for ATM products. Mr. Swenson chaired the ATM and AAL working groups in T1S1.5 and is on the Board of Directors of the ATM Forum.

Government Called Chief Obstacle to Encryption

By Anna Aleksandrowicz

Computer hackers break into an Internet server that provides service to 50 regular customers. The hackers insert a "sniffer" file, so that each time the customers access the server, the file tracks them back and documents their personal information, including which Internet sites they visit.

The server company, said Jeff Schiller, instead of alerting its customers to this break-in, hides the information and lies to the customers, who are left surprised and violated when the server is taken offline.

Schiller's horror story was one of the examples of the need for electronic security and encryption on the Internet, which he and fellow panelists discussed yesterday in Science Center B. According to Michael Rabin, Professor of Computer Science at Harvard University, the fundamental issues in the area of computers and the Internet are security and privacy.

Data security, he said, was very much a public concern—and very much like the debate over the safety of nuclear power. "The public is very apprehensive and is not willing to blindly believe all is in order."

"Information is not physically secure," said Butler Lampson, a Microsoft architect. "People from all over the world can try to attack you, and it is difficult to track them down. It happens too fast." While the actual losses from such attacks today are small, according to Lampson, the potential danger is large and growing.

The basic technology for security already exists. Using encryption for secrecy, digital signatures for integrity, and directory services for connecting names with keys are all options that are currently available. But most users don't understand security issues, Lampson said, and they try to get away with using as few security measures as possible. Unlike encryption, most security systems are expensive and time-consuming, Lampson said, and most people are not willing to spend the time and effort to buy and use them.

The panelists agreed that the main obstacle to international Internet encryption was the Federal government, which wants to establish tight encryption regulation.

"We call government regulation of encryption the 'Bosnia of technology,'" said Clint Smith, an attorney with the Washington, D.C. law firm of Steptoe and Johnson.

Smith pointed out the main reasons why any government would want to regulate encryption were control of intelligence for national security and access to criminal activity for law enforcement. Governments would also be interested, Smith said, in controlling less threatening areas of encryption, including access control, authentication, financial transactions, and weak encryptions, but these are issues over which the government was less willing to fight.

Which leaves corporate and private users of the Internet exposed to electronic attack, unless they are willing to incorporate other, often more costly and difficult to use measures. The government solution to this impasse: the key escrow initiative.

Key escrow would ensure that all financial and other sensitive personal or corporate information that is gathered on the Internet would be deposited in escrow with a designated company, or government agency.

The problem with this solution, according to Schiller, the security area Director for the Internet encryption steering group and Network Manager at the Massachusetts Institute of Technology, is the government's demand to keep a copy of your personal encryption key, for "safety" reasons and easier law enforcement.

"You'd like law enforcement to be easier and convenient?" Schiller asked. "Why not use torture? Governments and states where police have an easy job are called police states." Instead, he recommends government drop the key escrow initiative and leave the work up to businesses.

"Businesses will want key recovery for documents. The industry will create key recovery systems which can then be obtained with a subpoena," he said.

Smith felt that key escrow could be workable if both government and industry were more willing to compromise.

Governments, he said, must let businesses hold on to their own information keys rather than insist they deposit them with a trust company.

And businesses must realize key escrow is the solution to getting government approval of Internet encryption.

Technology
May 30, 1996

Security and Encryption on the Net

MODERATOR: Ronald L. Rivest
PANELISTS: Butler Lampson
                  Michael Rabin
                  Jeff Schiller
                  Clint Smith

RIVEST: Welcome to the "Security and Encryption" session. I'm Ron Rivest, and I'll be moderating our panel of four very distinguished experts in this exciting and important area.

Our first panelist is Professor **MICHAEL RABIN**, who holds a joint appointment at the Hebrew University, and has a Ph.D. from Princeton. He's been a visiting professor at many universities: Yale, Berkeley, MIT, University of Paris, CalTech, and so on. He has won many, many awards and prizes, including the A.M. Turing Award in Computer Science and the Israeli Prize for Exact Scientists. He is a member of the Israeli Academy of Sciences and Humanities, the U.S. National Academy of Sciences, the American Academy of Arts and Sciences, and has been awarded many, many other honors.

His researches include parallel computation, randomized algorithms, and, of special interest to this session, computer security. He has made numerous contributions—practical contributions—to the area of cryptography. He worked with Doug Tygar on the implementation of ITOS, a computer security system based around the Unix system and extensions of that. So I'm pleased to welcome Michael Rabin.

RABIN: I would like to discuss some of the fundamental issues that are facing us both in the areas of computer security and privacy. I am guessing that the audience here is very mixed, so I'm going to concentrate on the various policy and fundamental issues. I think everybody realizes that they are presently at the watershed junction with respect to computers and Internet security.

In fact, several of the speakers, for example, Larry Tesler, Scott McNealy, and especially Bill Gates, have highlighted in their presentations the importance of Internet security. There is really a heightened awareness and, we hope, a willingness to go forth with these issues.

As background, we also note that the public is very apprehensive. As long as computing and data processing were limited to a select group of bankers and people in charge of data processing—even though it impacted every one of us because our private data was in various databases—the problem was not as pressing and as clear as it is now. Everyone now can see all that information shuttling over the network, including personal data. And the public is not willing to just blindly trust that everything is in order.

Many people are convinced they definitely do not want to entrust their social security number or their credit card numbers and other personal information to the network, even though doing business over the network in that manner is, of course, a considerable convenience. I'm going to touch a little bit later on the question of whether this apprehension is justified or is it just paranoiac. But in general terms, our situation now in the computer industry is somewhat similar and has some of the same characteristics as the issues of security that we are facing in the nuclear power industry.

Obviously, nuclear power is an avenue for cheap electricity, yet there are problems with nuclear waste. But the public is most preoccupied with the question of nuclear safety. You can make a dramatic comparison between what's happening here in the United States and what is happening in France. In the United States, maybe less than 20 percent of the total electric power is generated by nuclear stations. In France, it's 75 percent. Here there is enormous resistance to the installation of any new nuclear power station. In fact, there is an essential standstill in that area.

In France, except from small, politically motivated segments in society like the Greens, you do not have resistance to that technology. Here, for example, people had to change the name "nuclear magnetic resonance," or NMR, which is used in medicine, to MRI to expunge the offensive and threatening "nuclear." In France, there was much greater openness and a much better dialogue between the nuclear power industry and the government on the one hand, and the population at large. And people have a feeling, rightly or wrongly, that they understand what's going on and they have, again, rightly or wrongly—I think rightly—a sense of safety.

I think we ought to be extremely careful in our industry not to create the same kind of apprehension and eventual resistance with respect to, let us say, the Internet and computer security in general, that we find with respect to nuclear energy. There are potentially very serious problems with computer and network security. I think the only person of the three I mentioned who fully acknowledged it was Bill Gates. He said that these problems are solvable, and I'm with him on that. He said within five years, and he may be somewhat overly optimistic. But he also said that, in the coming five years, we are going to have problems, breakdowns, and various (these are my words) potential calamities.

But the fact that something has to be done is undeniable. Even now there are periodic break-ins, which are probably under-reported. From time to time we read about some hacker, some kid either in Brooklyn or in the Argentine who got into some database, some computer system, and did something mischievous. I think that these occurrences are minor in comparison to what might happen in the future—I want to remind you of the Internet breakdown a few years ago, where roughly 3,000 sites went down as the consequence of the actions of one person.

What are the sources of the problems that face us? In that respect, the problem of computer and Internet security is really quite different from problems in many other areas—the chemical industry, for instance—and various other hazards

that face us. First, we have an explosion in the number of users and their degree of interaction with the system. From a situation where computing and data processing were in the domain of experts and we, the public at large, were just very important but passive users, now there are many, many more people involved.

Obviously, this multiplies the dangers by orders of magnitude. So it is clear that we need some way, for example, of authenticating people who have access. Even with the wonderful technology that, say, Ron Rivest is responsible for, the issue of authenticating millions of people is by no means a trivial matter.

Another point is that the Internet is only as secure as the operating systems and the computers which are the servers that feed it, the computers that are being used by the people who access the Net, and the links and switches that carry the traffic. So one can have a very good scheme, a supposedly very safe language. But if I get an applet on my computer and my operating system does not have the appropriate protections, then actually I am exposed.

Another issue which is not sufficiently dealt with is the danger from malicious insiders. Take the people, for example, who write the code. There isn't very good control on who is writing code and certainly not very good control, in many cases, of what they put into it. We have a danger of time bombs, Trojan horses, spurious back channels, and (when it comes to managing the systems) abuse of superuser privileges by managers.

How do we deal with these issues? The solution by and large lies in computer technology itself. The same power that makes a subverted program or a computer so dangerous, the very same power and the same technology can and should be harnessed to create the proper protections. Let me mention just one area. How do we guard against insiders? How do we guard against the theft of our keys? One solution that was proposed in the ITOS Project was the notion of a secure committee. With all the other technology and encryption, we also rely on safety in numbers. Authority is not vested in one person, but rather in a group of people or a group of agents who have to cooperate and who are, one would hope, independent of each other.

Doing our RSA* signatures in a distributive way is itself a challenge. But it can be done. So the problems are very sophisticated and the solutions are very costly. But the requisite science is here, and all we really need is the will and the commitment to solve those problems. If we ignore the problems, it will definitely be at our peril.

Now I want to say a word or two about privacy. There is no doubt that this new technology, the collection and dissemination of personal information, poses an enormous danger to our privacy. It's a danger of misuse and intrusion. And that is not just the Internet. Let's not forget the Intranet, the mode whereby within organizations such as hospitals, this technology will be used for much enhanced and easy and convenient access to data. But with that also comes an enormous exposure.

The legal protections right now are very, very weak, and I could spend 20 minutes listing what is not protected by what amounts to a patchwork of laws right now. So here is the concept which may serve as a key to the solution. The new legal framework would declare personal data we surrender when we go to a doctor, when we are students at a university, in any kind of interaction between us and a commercial or governmental agency, data held in personal trust. So this is an overall concept of data as a trust. With this comes an implied obligation that this data is held by whoever holds it and whoever has it, only for the purposes for which it was surrendered by the person to whom it relates. So, for example, I am being treated at the hospital and I want to get well but I don't want to be exposed to denial of insurance at some later date. And if the relationship between me as a patient and the hospital is well defined by a general and clear law, that will be our protection.

I'll end by making a comparison with pollution. We have a tension in industry and in commerce between efficient, low-cost manufacturing, and environmental pollution. Here we are in danger of some sort of informational pollution, and I think we ought to take the same care to protect ourselves and to have continued success of our industry in that area as well. Thanks.

RIVEST: Thank you, Professor Rabin. The next speaker is **BUTLER LAMPSON**, who is an architect at Microsoft Corporation, as well as an Adjunct Professor of Computer Science and Electrical Engineering at MIT. He's worked in many areas, including computer architecture, local area networks, operating systems, programming languages, computer security, and WYSIWYG editors. He's one of the co-designers of the Alto Personal Computer Distributed System and several programming languages.

He got his Ph.D. from Berkeley and is a member of the National Academy of Engineering, a fellow of ACM (which granted him the Turing Award), and he has also received a number of awards for his work on the Alto.

LAMPSON: I'd like to discuss some of the same issues that Michael dealt with but from a slightly different point of view. To begin with, a brief introduction on the subject of Internet security. First, there is no physical security. There's no reason to believe that the actual channels over which data travels are physically secure. Second, and more important, because of the connectivity of the Internet, people from all over the world can try to attack you. In this respect, Internet security problems are qualitatively different from the problems we've addressed in the past. In general, it's very difficult to track down the source of an attack, and things can happen very fast because computers can do things very rapidly.

On the other hand, what we've observed until now is that the losses from failed security on the Network have been small. Certainly one can imagine scenarios under which major losses would be incurred as a result of bad security on the Net. But nothing like that has happened yet.

---

* A public key encryption scheme patented by Rivest, Shamir, Adelman.

Newspapers like to write scare stories about how terrible things are and how the Internet worm brought down thousands of computers. Then people multiply thousands by other large numbers and conclude that hundreds of millions of dollars were lost because of the worm. But as far as I can tell, there's absolutely no basis for believing any of that. It was only a small ripple that didn't really make much difference.

Unfortunately, there's no reliable record of losses owing to inadequate security. If it's a computer-related security problem, companies prefer to cover it up because it's embarrassing. And that makes it very hard to understand what is really going on.

As Michael said, the basic technology definitely exists to make the Information Highway safe:

- There is *encryption* to maintain secrecy in spite of the fact that you don't have physical security.

- There are *digital signatures* to maintain the integrity of information in spite of the fact that you can't lock it up and you can't rely on older techniques such as nonerasable paper.

- Finally, there are *directory services* to connect meaningful names for people in organizations with the numeric keys that are used by the encryption and signature technology.

This is all well understood and has in fact been well understood for more than a decade. Not only have we had this technology for a long time, but from the size and the growth of the Internet, its trajectory has also been very clear. Why is so little of this technology deployed? Well, there are various theories. My own private theory actually is that it's all an elaborate plot by the NSA [National Security Agency] to delay the deployment of encryption because the NSA's goal is to make sure that the Libyans can't go down to Radio Shack and buy secure communication. And the easiest way to ensure that is to make sure that nobody can go down to Radio Shack and buy secure communication. But aside from that, I think that there are also issues of ignorance and irresponsibility.

For a number of years, I worked for Digital Equipment. For much of that time I worked on security, and it all came to nothing in the end. The reason for that, basically, was that people didn't want to buy it. Users fundamentally don't care about security. They don't see much value in it. It gets in the way. You have to pay money for it. Worse, it makes your life inconvenient. Furthermore, bad things very seldom happen in the world of computers, at least bad things that could have been prevented by better security.

This is exactly the same situation you see with respect to security in the everyday world. Having locks on your doors, keeping things locked up, running an information classification program in your business—all that is expensive and it's a pain in the neck, so people do as little of it as they think they need to. It's exactly the same in the computer world. The difference is that people's houses get broken into fairly routinely, at least in many parts of the country. So there's some clear motivation to put locks on your door in spite of the fact that it's a pain in the neck; whereas your computer gets broken into very seldom so there isn't much motivation.

Second, very few people understand information security. The technical details are complicated, there are lots of different ways to do things, there's not a lot of experience by which you can judge what's adequate and what's flakey, and there's an enormous amount of misinformation circulating. As a result, organizations don't want to pay for security; therefore, vendors don't provide it or they provide something that's so clunky that nobody wants to use it.

To take a somewhat extreme example, the government for many years has had an elaborate system for certifying secure computing, and military organizations are supposed to buy these certified secure computers. If you look at what actually happens, hardly anyone buys this stuff. Instead they get a waiver because the stuff that you can buy costs a lot more than uncertified computers, it's three or four years out of date, and it doesn't do the job. So if you actually want to get your work done, you get a waiver instead of following the rules. Exactly the same thing is true, and I think will continue to be, in the civilian sector.

This all arises from a distinction that people who study this problem like to make between vulnerabilities and threats. A *vulnerability* is a bad thing that could happen that your system technically can't defend itself against. A *threat* is a vulnerability combined with someone who might actually exploit the vulnerability to do harm. You can do a technical analysis of your system to try to understand its vulnerabilities, and if you're sufficiently clever, you can do a pretty good job of finding them. Understanding the threats is much more difficult. Certainly every vulnerability is potentially a threat, but every system has lots of vulnerabilities, and it's expensive to correct them.

Only a threat can cause harm, and the only way to determine whether you have a threat is to understand who the potential adversaries are. For instance:

- Who is out there that could exploit your vulnerabilities?

- How much damage could that do?

- How much benefit could that damage do the adversary?

- How likely is that scenario to play out in practice?

These are not the kind of questions that can be answered by a technical study, because obviously it has to do with the social world, with judgments that a lot of potential adversaries out there are going to be making.

You can sit back and try to imagine what an adversary's capabilities and intentions are. But you can never really convince yourself that you've done the analysis correctly. What happens in practice is that you have to rely on experience. To take a concrete example, should you put bars on the first floor windows in your house? Well, if you live in Manhattan, you probably do. If you live in a suburb of Boise, you probably don't even lock your front door. Who is behaving irrationally? The vulnerabilities are exactly the same in both cases, but the threat is very different. If

you live in Manhattan and you have not had your house or apartment broken into, chances are, your neighbor down the block has. So you recognize there's a real threat. If you live in Boise, you recognize there isn't a real threat because these things don't happen. So neither party is behaving irrationally. Both people are doing exactly the right thing; both have the benefit of past experience on which to base judgments about what the threat actually is. Unfortunately, in the world of computer security, we don't have an enormous amount of experience, and the experience that we do have says that the threats so far are not very significant.

Another important thing to bear in mind is that a lot of the work that's been done on information security has been done by or for the government. And the government, especially the military, faces a different set of threats than you or I do.

Since this is a technology track, I ought to say a few words about the technical aspects of this. Supposing you decide that the threats are real and you actually want to try to do something about it, what sort of technology is available? As I said, all of this stuff is very well understood from a technical point of view, and you can even buy some of it. Because the newspapers like to run articles about security, a lot more of it will be stuff you can buy in the fairly near future. But it won't be free and, more important, you will incur costs in the form of inconvenience and administrative hassles as well as dollars to do these things.

Safety at home comes first. Firewalls are a good technique. If you have a bunch of computers inside an organization, it's very attractive to surround them by some sort of barriers to control communication between the inside world and the outside, which is filled with millions of Argentine hackers. Virus control is also important. You want to make sure you don't import anything into your system software that can do damage.

You want to be able to identify people in organizations so that when someone walks up to your web server and says "I'd like to access this page," you have some basis for deciding whether to grant the access. The technology for that will be based on encryption. To make it reasonably secure you will need "smart card" devices that can store your keys securely, and directory services that can connect meaningful names of people and organizations with the keys. For integrity of transactions, you need digital signatures on documents and, even more important, you need audit trails on transactions so that if something has gone wrong, you can come along after the fact, find out what actually happened, and have some chance of tracking down the wrongdoer.

For privacy and secrecy, there's "tunneling" technology, based on encryption, for constructing secure channels between two end points through the insecure worldwide Internet. And there's also encryption technology that can keep messages and data private.

So, to recap, all this stuff exists. The technical basis for it has all been pretty firmly in place for about a decade, and a fair amount of it you can buy. On the other hand, it's relatively inconvenient to buy it, it's overpriced by the standards of software in general, and it's typically not very well hooked up with other parts of the computing environment. So it's a real pain in the neck to use these things today.

What can actually be done to improve security over the next few years?

Demand it.   From the customer's viewpoint, certainly the most important thing is to demand security from the vendors. Fundamentally, the reason you can't buy security is that customers *don't* buy it, and companies won't invest a lot of development and marketing effort in things that customers don't buy. It's not because we don't have the technology that you can't buy good security, it's because people haven't been demanding it.

Some of these protective measures are pretty simple, pretty cheap, and pretty unintrusive, and they should be routine. Signed code (as

opposed to the current scheme for detecting viruses by looking for telltale patterns of evil-looking code), firewalls, "smart cards" for protecting keys, and audit trails: these are really basic things that ought to be part of any system.

Record losses.   A second issue that I think is quite important is to have a repository of data on actual losses that occur. Without that, it's very difficult to do rational planning. Customers need a reliable way to know what the real threats are, and currently it's extraordinarily difficult to do that. About the only source of information is the newspapers, and that doesn't give you a very rational, well-organized, unbiased account of the costs and dangers.

Assess losses.   Third, try to assess the threats realistically. Stories have been published claiming $150 to $300 billion a year of losses from computer hackers. As far as I know, that number was made up, and it was probably made up by multiplying two other numbers together that were both made up. There's not the slightest basis for it that I'm aware of.

To conclude, I would like to give you a few references. Ron mentioned one of them at the beginning of the session, the National Academy's report on cryptography. The other is a 1991 National Academy study on computer security in general called *Computers at Risk.*[*] Things have not changed that much in the last five years, so this is still an excellent, relatively nontechnical summary of what the issues are and also of the available technology.

RIVEST: Our third speaker in this session is **CLINT SMITH**, a colleague of Stewart Baker's at Steptoe and Johnson, a Washington, D.C. based law firm specializing in encryption policy, particularly in export and international issues.

SMITH: I'm from Washington, so naturally I will talk about government regulation of encryption, and I'll focus on the international dimension of government regulation. In Washington, we call

---

[*] System Security Study Committee, National Research Council, *Computers at Risk: Safe Computing in the Information Age*, National Academy Press, 1991.

encryption the "Bosnia of technology policy," and I think for good reason, as people learn once they get involved in it.

With the market for encryption, we see three factors emerging.

Technology migration.   While 20 years ago encryption was the domain of governments, it's migrating to the private sector. While encryption was the domain of the United States, now it has migrated to Japan, to Israel, to South Africa. And as a result, the U.S. is no longer the sole source of good encryption.

Emerging global demand. With the astounding growth of computer networks, with more individual users using the networks, with more companies putting valuable information into electronic form, you are seeing demand emerge for information security—and encryption is the technology to provide that security.

Product proliferation. They may not all be good products, but the Software Publishers Association has identified more than 1,000 information security/confidentiality products out there. And more than 450 are made outside of the United States, and that's telling.

Now the question is, if demand for encryption is growing, why isn't it in use everywhere? Encryption is not in Windows 95, it's not in my *cc:Mail*. I would suggest that one reason for this—and I may disagree with Butler Lampson of Microsoft on this—is government regulation.

Let's step back and ask why the government is regulating encryption. The traditional reason has been for intelligence. Governments are interested in any information that affects their national security. They cast a wide net. What are they trying to find? A typical piece of intelligence would be the landlord of a terrorist saying: "My tenant got a bus ticket for city X." That's what governments are looking for; to find it they cast a very wide net. If all this information collected by the government were encrypted, government intelligence functions would be crippled.

An emerging government interest is law enforcement. This is much more narrow than the intelligence function; it's evidence of criminal activity. Governments are interested in communications and phone calls, but they're most interested in stored data. And the FBI is increasingly coming up against encrypted stored data. When they have a search warrant, they go in, and they see computer files. Up to three percent of the computer files they seize now are encrypted. It's not a lot but the law enforcement agencies don't have the ability to decrypt the files—and the Los Angeles Police Department doesn't know what to do with encrypted files.

What encryption is not a threat to government? Encryption used for network passwords, access control, authentication. You hear talk about digital signatures, which are no threat to government because they don't encrypt the substance of a communication or document. Encryption for financial transactions? By and large, this is not a threat to government. Because they have good relations with the bank, governments can get that information otherwise. Weak encryption? It may not be a threat to sophisticated intelligence agencies, like the National Security Agency, but it *is* a threat to the Los Angeles Police Department or Spain or Egypt. They can't deal with that.

So, given these interests, what are governments doing? Let me run quickly through some of the approaches that you see.

Laissez faire. Scandinavia thinks: "Oh, our citizens have strong encryption, that's good, it protects their privacy." It's not that way all over the world.

Industrial policy. Japan is spending 30 billion yen this year on encryption and digital commerce pilot projects and R&D. They see a market there. They're going to be regulating it, but they're also investing heavily in the technology.

Export controls. The United States uses export controls to regulate encryption technology, and that's a reflection of the U.S. interest in intelligence gathering outside our borders. If you keep encryption out of the rest of the world, you can conduct your foreign intelligence more easily.

Import and use controls. This is obviously the most restrictive. In France, you can't import or use an encryption product for confidentiality purposes without registering it with the Prime Minister's office. In Israel, you have to register and get the Defense Ministry's approval but they're much more lenient. In Singapore, you are more likely to get a knock on your hotel room door and have someone tell you, "You're using a telecommunications device that is not authorized to interconnect with our PSDN [Public Switched Data Network]." (It's a little more loosey-goosey.) In Russia, Boris Yeltsin has issued two decrees regulating the use of encryption. I suspect that if you want to go in and register as an encryption user with the Russian Defense Ministry, you'll probably pay a nice fat registration fee. China also has import and use restrictions. We have several clients who have dutifully gone in and asked for permission to use encryption devices—and they're waiting and waiting and waiting.

What's the problem here? You see a lot of variation in international policies. International policies are inconsistent. You can't build one product for various markets. Policies are uncoordinated. Well, who is this bad for? It's bad for the user—it's bad for Chevron which wants to have Kazakhstan and Peru and its Bay Area headquarters hooked up to one secure network. It's bad for vendors—it's bad for EDS who might like to sell GM a secure global communication system, but to do this they have to comply with 30 or 40 different laws.

And in the long run it's bad for governments because you're beginning to see migration of technology to the areas of the lowest regulation. There's a South African product, an Internet browser, that advertises itself as having the quality of encryption that's in Netscape Navigator for the U.S. market but which Netscape cannot export. Well, if encryption migrates to the regulatory equivalent of the Cayman Islands, governments won't be happy with that situation.

You have to ask yourself, is it good for anybody? I'm happy to say it's good for lawyers! We get paid by the hour, and it takes time to sort through all the regulations and find a good loophole to sneak through.

But, seriously, there's a need for an international consensus on encryption policy that balances government interests and user interests. What are the essential requirements? I see them as three:

1. Strong and trusted encryption for users.

2. Global interoperability, if electronic commerce is really going to take off and reach its potential.

3. Government access.

And this is where I may disagree with others in the audience, but I think any solution must provide a reasonable degree of government access to private information.

What's on the table now that solves this? Commercial key escrow is a fluid concept that's constantly changing, but it's basically the idea of ensuring access to encrypted information by storing the key required for decryption either with a trusted third party or within your own company. Commercial key escrow will allow the company to have data retrieval if information is lost and the government to have access to encrypted information when authorized to do so by national law.

What is going on in the international sphere? Are there international efforts to form consensus behind the concept of commercial key escrow? Well, the United States government likes key escrow and is pushing it in the international sphere. In December 1995 they organized a meeting in Paris at the OECD [Organization for Economic Cooperation and Development]. Basically, the U.S. got together with the OECD governments and told them widespread availability of strong encryption is bad news for us. The other governments agreed. This had a strong sobering effect on U.S. industry, which had long been fighting to relax U.S. export controls. And U.S. industry is beginning to realize that if you relax export controls in the U.S., you're going to face controls, import controls, use controls, in other countries. The impact of the OECD meetings was this: They made U.S. high tech companies realize that defeating export controls may not be the answer some people once thought it was.

What is the goal of the OECD negotiations? I'm speaking for myself here, and I have just a vague sense of what the governments want. But, I think, in the next year you'll see an OECD guidelines document—a recommendation that's not binding, but encouraging governments to remove restrictions on the export/import of use of encryption products that support a key escrow feature.

What are the obstacles to making this system work? First, Japan has a tradition of privacy. They are very leery about key escrow solutions. They don't like the idea of government access to their information or communications.

Second, OECD is a small party. There are other encryption players out there—China, Russia, South Africa, Israel—which are not part of the OECD discussions.

Third sticking point, government to government cooperation. If you're going to have a key escrow scheme, you will need an unprecedented amount of cooperation between governments. For instance, if the U.S. government suspects there's somebody in Barcelona sending email messages about drugs, they will have to go to the Spanish authorities and cooperate in terms of exchanging private keys. This need for cooperation worries the government as it worries users.

Finally, market reaction really is the key. Will there be a market for key escrow products? Governments sure hope so. I want to close my talk by suggesting what governments will be doing in the years ahead to encourage key escrow solutions.

France may mandate commercial key escrow. There's a bill right now in the French Assembly which says encryption products which have an encryption key escrowed with a French escrow agent can be freely imported or used. All other encryption products with the capability for confidentiality must be approved by the Prime Minis-

ter. Don't expect quick approvals unless the French can break your code. (Well, that's a little draconian, I don't think you'll see this approach in Britain or the U.S. or Australia. But those governments, too, will be encouraging a move to key escrow.)

The first strategy is *differential controls*. The U.S. government will say you can export 40-bit encryption that's unescrowed, but if you have an escrow feature you can export 80-bit encryption, you can even export 128-bit triple DES [Data Encryption Standard] encryption as long as the key is escrowed.

The second strategy is *bundling*. You see this in a white paper that the White House issued May 17 [1996] that is still in draft form, but which will be made final in the coming months. Bundle key escrow with other important aspects of digital commerce, with digital signatures, with time stamp functions, and put it all together in a single package offered by a single entity, so you don't even know the key escrow is there.

The third strategy is *government benefits*. An awful lot of Americans interact with the government. Knowing this, the White House has proposed adoption of a mandatory standard for all federal computers that would include key escrow, digital signatures, and other features. So, if you want to do business with the government, you're going to have to buy a similar system that meets that standard. And that system will have key escrow.

Finally, there is *government procurement*. There are two million computers out there that are DoD [Department of Defense] sensitive but unclassified and DoD contractor computers. That's a pretty good-sized market. They'll be buying key escrow and so will all the civilian government agencies. Vendors may very will build to that government spec, then offer the same model to the private sector—and that model will have key escrow. I think government procurement will be a big driver.

Where are we heading? Where will we end up? I think governments will favor key escrow, but are ready to accept that there are some products and applications for which key escrow is not a solution. Web browsers? You don't need to keep those keys in escrow. Cable modems? You don't need to escrow. Cellular telephones? I think the governments will have to give up on them.

I also think industry will see a need for key escrow, and it will be in the data recovery area. You're going to see businesses warming to the idea of having some data recovery escrow function as part of their network. So I predict that you will see a middle ground emerge: there will be use of key escrow, it won't be as broad as the governments might like, but there will be a market for it.

RIVEST: Next is **JEFF SCHILLER**, a founding member of the Steering Group of the New England Academic Research Network, NEARNET, which provided Internet access to a lot of the institutions in New England.

SCHILLER: Thank you, Ron. It's interesting to be involved in a voluntary standards organization such as the Internet Engineering Task Force. If anybody wants to have a leadership role in that, a good way of practicing is to herd cats.

Why all the fuss? We hear all this noise about cryptography, and cryptography is relatively new on the scene. We didn't talk about cryptography when we talked about telephone networks. We don't talk about cryptography in other applications. Yet suddenly, the Internet comes along and everybody's talking cryptography. Part of the reason for that is that the Internet is not owned by anyone. There is no accountability on the Internet. If you send information across the Internet, that information may well be handled by ten different service providers.

But the real killer is, and this has really happened, I know of a service provider [ISP] that had a computer in their infrastructure broken into and converted into a sniffer. So all the data from about 50 different customers who crossed that service provider was being intercepted by hostile parties. And they were looking explicitly for names and passwords. That Internet service provider did not tell his customers this had happened. They were worried that they would look bad. In fact, when

some of the customers noticed that service machine went down and they asked why, the ISP said, "Oh, it had a head crash."

So they actually just plain lied. Why? Because they're not required to say what's happening. So the bottom line is, if you have confidential information or you have information where integrity needs to be protected, you have to do it yourself because these guys aren't going to do it for you. And to be honest with you, if your confidential information is intercepted, it's very hard to figure out where the leak was because a passive intercept leaves no trail.

I might add, by the way, today on the Internet we hear a lot about passive attacks; namely, somebody listening into the wires and getting all the passwords. Within a year or so, we'll see active attacks, where somebody grabs a running session. I've already seen the technology that can do this. I understand it's already being done, although it is not very widespread yet. It will become more widespread. Again, cryptography provides the solution there.

And I have to agree with Clint. If it wasn't for the government role, I think we'd see a lot more cryptography. And in fact, look at the Clipper Three paper Clint referred to, I forget its exact title but it's something like "Providing Commerce Security and Privacy and Public Safety." All right, that's public safety. That's called "the government gets to watch everything." You read all these key escrow things and they talk about balance. We have to balance the requirements of law enforcement with the requirements of privacy. I claim that that argument is lost the minute you say, "Let's have the discussion." As soon as you say we must find a balance, we must take into account the requirements of law enforcement, the game's over.

We don't design houses that way, right? If we designed the front door of your house with the requirements of law enforcement, there would be a master key for everybody's house at the police station. I mean, after all, kicking the door down is inconvenient. If we consider balance, what I like to think of is the balance in public safety and window blind design. Can you imagine window blinds that are designed to be transparent when looked at with the proper goggles? That's what you would get if you had to consider balance and law enforcement requirements every time you considered a technology.

Today you have privacy of your thoughts. I can't read your thoughts or innermost feelings unless you display them on your face somehow. We don't consider writing laws that say government can't read your thoughts. But imagine if the technology came along that allowed that to happen. Of course it would be abused. Law enforcement would use it, the Mafia would use it, everybody would use it. And after a while, we'd say this is really bad, we have to regulate this.

If there were any way to regulate the dissemination of the technology for reading thoughts, it would be done. But invariably there would be a rule passed that when a court order is issued, the police can read your mind, maybe prevent you from committing a crime. Wouldn't that be convenient? *Stop crime before it happens.* (I can see the slogans now.) But then along comes somebody who invents a skull cap. When you put it on, they can't read your mind anymore. You'd hear law enforcement saying, "But we have to have a back door. We're only trying to preserve the capabilities we already have."

You see all the same arguments today. So when the law enforcement people say to me, "Don't you understand, Jeff, that by advocating against key escrow, by saying that people should have the privacy to protect their information, we can't get to it," what they're saying is that they'd like law enforcement to be made easy, because there are other ways of getting information from people. You can bug my house if you're really that interested. It costs money, but you can do it. So you want it to be convenient. I can give you an even better way of getting evidence, much more convenient: torture. Torture people. Remember government and states where police have an easy job, we call those police states. Not many people want to live in them.

The other thing I'd say is the bad guys already have it. If the bad guys want to encrypt information, they can already do it. At the MIT Distribution Site for PGP [Pretty Good Privacy], we hand out between 500 and 1,000 copies of that program every day. Now I can't tell you how many of them are really being used because it's not the easiest program in the world to use, but it's out there.

Furthermore, you say, "Well, that's easy. Government outlaws PGP." You say, begin PGP message, go to jail. But I've already seen a program called *stealth* that takes the output of PGP and turns it into something that's indistinguishable from random noise and another program [for hiding information in a JPEG image] called *JSteg* that takes that random noise and mixes it in the low order bytes of a JPEG image. And with the advent of cameras on every single computer you can find these days, it would be really easy. We have a camera in my office pointing at our iguana. So we can PGP encrypt a message and hide it in the lower order bits of the JPEG images coming out of the Iguana Cam!

So, in fact, you could not prevent the bad guys from using this. What does this mean? The effect of key escrow has been to delay legitimate users from getting technology. That's where export control laws are used as a club. By the way, whenever you deal with the NSA on these sorts of issues, most of the communication is oral or through telephone calls. Very little of it is written down on letterhead that you could ever produce later. And that makes it very hard to categorize what's going on. I mean, somebody told me (and this is a secondhand story I can't actually validate) that if they advocated a strong cryptography in a certain domestic product, they would lose an export license on an unrelated product they sold overseas. Because there's no rule that says you have to get an export license.

There is uncertainty in export licensing, uncertainty about producing a crypto product and putting it up for an FTP on the Internet or making it available on the World Wide Web. Why is the Netscape version that everybody downloads in the United States the export version? Because of that uncertainty. You can't get a straight answer to the question: Can I do this? Will I or won't I get prosecuted for export control violations if somebody figures out a way to download it? So we take risks when we do that.

What does this all mean? To summarize in some sense, Internet security is not a one-way problem. Butler said this. We know how to do this, this technology's been around for years. It's a will problem. We don't have the will to deploy it and of course the U.S. government throws up blockages. Probably one of the other really bad effects of this is that NIST [National Institute for Standards and Technology] is losing credibility. They say we should standardize in this technology and somebody asks, "Where's the back door?"

At a meeting last week someone said, "We really want to have cryptographic programming interfaces." And I asked, "Why do you guys care so much about cryptographic programming interfaces?" And they said, "Well, we want to make sure that Fortezza card* could be used with an application and we want the crypto APIs [application program interface] to make sure they can support the Fortezza card." So again, you wonder what's the point of this fighting? And it's causing some very good people to lose credibility, I might add.

I'll give you briefly what I think my recommendations would be if I were advising the U.S. government. Drop the key escrow initiative. It's a mistake.

I did an interesting analysis on the Clipper Three† document, the document Clint referred to. Chop up the document into its words and see how often certain words occur. Providing "public key infrastructure" occurs a few times, providing "privacy" occurs maybe once or twice. But every

page mentions "key escrow" and "law enforcement access," and it's a 24-page document.

So it's really a key escrow document. Everybody sees through this. This time they're saying, if you give us key escrow, we'll give you something in return. Maybe. But yet, if you drop the initiative (as Clint said, and I think Butler said as well), business will want key recovery. Business requires it. In my job, if I receive an encrypted document and I've left the company or I'm just otherwise not available, there's a real business need to be able to get to that. If something bad happens to me, all the business records I have shouldn't go with me.

So industry will create key recovery facilities. And those keys, by the way, will be subpoenaed. You can subpoena them because—by the way, the only defense against a subpoena is to not have the data. If you have the data, it can be subpoenaed, it can be obtained with a search warrant. All the due legal processes are there. Now what that means is the government will not get private communications of individuals, which may be what they really want, but there will be no business reason for individuals to key escrow themselves unless they habitually forget passwords.

The government will not get telephone calls. MIT is not recording my phone calls. So if I encrypt my phone calls, they have no need to ever get the keys back. And I think what the government has to recognize—the people in the government (and I think they actually do, we're just playing out this dance), is that ultimately technology giveth and it taketh away. It changes the landscape. Just as it provided the facility for enabling electronic surveillance of all the international telephone calls, it will provide new capability for individuals to protect those telephone calls.

And stored communications of businesses will be obtainable. That may not be what you really

---

* The Fortezza card is a U.S. Government-developed PCMCIA card, intended to provide digital signatures and confidentiality, which uses the Clipper Chip (complete with government key escrow) for its encryption engine.

† Clipper Chip is the unofficial name for the U.S. Government (May 17, 1996) attempt at key escrow, by claiming that key escrow should be built into a public key infrastructure.

want but it will be there. In the end, I believe that's the most workable solution. Thank you.

Questions & Answers

Q: *What is the legal right of employees to keep encrypted files on their office computers, especially if they don't inform their employers? These files could, in fact, be confidential company files which are being slowly assembled for removal offsite at some future time.*

SMITH: Employers are very interested in this issue and more and more of them are coming up with policies. First, you must inform your employees that the computer is only for work. And that gives the company access to everything. Second, companies are developing encryption policies as to what encryption you can use—and by the way, that encryption is going to come from the network manager, not the PGP you downloaded from MIT. It's a very important issue and many large and small companies are looking at how to manage it. But the bottom line is that an employee at work has no privacy rights, and has no rights to encrypt information unless she has the permission of her employer.

Q: *(For Professor Rabin) How can we implement your vision of privacy protection when big money is being made by firms who are in the business of selling personal information collected from anything from a grocery store to a hotel to web sites?*

RABIN: Well, I think that's really a key issue here and we have to make a choice. On the one hand, we are getting certain utility from the fact that people, say, monitor our purchases. If I buy a few books on a certain topic and then all of a sudden I get a letter (as has happened to me) asking whether I'm interested in this or that magazine or this or that book, I may benefit from this. But I think there are some benefits which industry and commerce better forgo before there is an adverse reaction. The wealth of information is now so extensive that they can get to customers and they can very easily develop the marketing base. And I think this has to be done not surreptitiously but in the open and not the way it's being done now.

Mainly, what everybody is worried about is personal information. When you go to the hospital, there are no very strong, clear rules that prevent the hospital and certainly people in that hospital from releasing information concerning your health, disease, medical history, and so on. One indication of the public's apprehension is the case of the two Marines who refused to give their DNA into a DNA bank for subsequent identification. They were court-martialed. I think that they were exonerated. But the worry is a very, very real worry and I think that we better, as I said, address it and react to it.

The bottom line is that an employee at work has no privacy rights, and has no rights to encrypt information unless she has the permission of her employer.

Q: *What off-the-shelf products exist for online authentication of an individual? How will one be able to authenticate the source of information on the Internet? For example, if one finds a web page with government regulations in it that purports to be an official page of a government agency, will there be a failsafe method of verifying that the page is really the product of the government?*

LAMPSON: Well, the technology for this is straightforward. You use digital signatures. The tricky part is getting the encryption key that's used to make the digital signature hooked up in a reliable way with the identity of the government agency, the individual sending the email message, or whatever it is. The jargon for this is "public key infrastructure."

You can do this in an informal way by making one-on-one arrangements. For example, the government agency could publish an ad in the *New York Times* that says, "Here's our public key." It would be a string of 200 characters, you could type it into your computer, and subsequently you'd be able to authenticate information from that agency's web sites. If you want to do it in a more systematic way, then you have to set up a directory of services and webs of trust and all kinds of other complicated things which people have been struggling to do for quite a number of years without much success because of the NSA plot.

RABIN: The technology is there, as we've said, on the whole field of security. But I think the technology is extremely complicated and very difficult to understand. Consider the directories that Butler outlined for key authentications and for establishing a relationship between the key and the agency which supposedly is the owner or the user of that key. For the average user, as he or she is now sitting at their personal computer, to really understand and be convinced that this is so, the whole technology also needs a certain user-friendliness component which I think we are very far from establishing.

SCHILLER: I'll give you an example of where this has actually gone today. The Computer Emergency Response Team [CERT] run at Carnegie-Mellon University has a PGP public key that you can download from their FTP site. You have to recognize that there's a risk that you're not really talking to their FTP site, but assuming you actually get their key, they are now sending out all of their vulnerability alerts digitally signed with PGP. That is an example of where that technology is being used. Obviously it requires you to have and understand PGP.

Within the context of the IETF [Internet Engineering Task Force] and the World Wide Web Consortium [W3C], a lot of the web browser and server manufacturers are actually working together on security technologies and this is certainly one of the places where discussions are happening. So I think we're going to see user interface improvements coming up in the next couple of years, if not sooner.

SMITH: I think some of the larger companies are holding back because of liability concerns. Whether you're maintaining a directory of public keys or whether you're issuing certificates, there's a wide amount of liability you could be exposing yourself to. So you have smaller companies like

VeriSign into the market already. But bigger ones like AT&T and Motorola are standing on the sidelines thinking it out.

Q: *Should the government have a role in this directory service? Should the U.S. Post Office or some other government agency be playing a role? Is this a place where you want the government to help us out?*

SCHILLER: Not if it means that you have to escrow your private keys with them. The Post Office was in fact looking into providing a public key infrastructure, probably still is. I think this is the place where the government really could help. But again, every initiative these days is sort of colored with, "Of course, we have to keep a copy of your private key." And my personal view on this is, sorry, that's not a price I'm prepared to pay.

Q: *Is it possible to build effective distributed trust systems that don't require a central issuing authority?*

LAMPSON: Well, it's definitely possible to do that technically. It makes life more complicated for the users. How that tradeoff is going to play itself out is unclear at the moment.

SCHILLER: I think settling that tradeoff is going to be one of the more important issues that are going to have to get settled because it is a clear tradeoff. You can make it under the control of the end user, in which case you have to hope that the end user is clued in (which in general they are not). One solution to this problem is to have a very limited certificate hierarchy where everybody must be authenticated through a single hierarchy.

But what has happened is amazing. People are reptiles at some level. You try to set that up and the people at the top of the hierarchy, those in charge, say, "This is great. I'm a monopoly." And guess how people in a monopoly position behave? They behave like monopolies.

RABIN: May I add a comment about distributed security? I think the added overhead could be made transparent to the user. Networks and computers and processors are so fast that this is not going to cause a delay. I think that this distributed concept is important because you may not be sure about one of the sites that you are talking to, be it the Bank of America or the U.S. Treasury Department. But if there is some distributed security structure to authenticate users, you can assume that unless four or five or six sites were subverted, then the assurance which I got from a subset, from a quorum of those sites, is really sufficient. And I think that is also going to alleviate congestion problems arising from having completely centralized solutions.

SCHILLER: We've got all kinds of wonderful technology. I think the market will sort these issues out over the next few years, and people will vote with their keystrokes and their dollars.

Q: *We have the technology, but how do we verify that the implementations of that technology really are secure?*

SCHILLER: Not to plug PGP, because believe me I get no money from it. If you can get a product in source code form, then obviously, as an individual, you have the ability to read it and convince yourself it's good. However, more to the point, many other people are doing so and chances are, if there was a significant flaw, it would be uncovered and you'd get to read about it. There's a real risk when you don't have the opportunity for independent evaluation of security technology and must wind up trusting the reputation of the company involved. And a large company with a large pocketbook would probably be more trustworthy than some guys in their garage.

Of course you do have to worry about that warranty, which basically says the only thing we warrant is that you have some plastic in these floppy disks.

RABIN: Somebody had to consult me about a certain project and concept. There was a start-up company in the domain of computerized cash, digital cash. We were talking about this and that about the technical issues, encryptions and so on, and I said, "Who is going to implement it?" The answer was, "Well, we will get some people. We are calling up universities, graduate students and so on." Essentially people from the street in some sense. And that is a very big problem.

I do not think that examining the source code is sufficient protection because, after all, everybody's trying to write correct code. I'm not even talking about security, and still there are crashes and there are bugs. I don't think that there is a single large program in the world that doesn't have about five or six bugs in it, even now. And think about what somebody may put in maliciously. So the question of the insiders, of the people to whom we entrust our money, our health, our privacy, has to be sorted out in a very thorough way.

About the Speakers

RONALD L. RIVEST is the Webster Professor of Electrical Engineering and Computer Science at MIT, an Associate Director of MIT's Laboratory for Computer Science, and a leader of that lab's Cryptography and Information Security research group. He is a Fellow of the Association for Computing Machinery and of the American Academy of Arts and Sciences, and is also a member of the National Academy of Engineering. Professor Rivest is an inventor of the RSA public-key cryptosystem, and a founder and director of RSA Data Security. He has served as Director of the International Association for Cryptologic Research, the organizing body for the Eurocrypt and Crypto conferences.

BUTLER LAMPSON is an Architect at Microsoft Corporation and an Adjunct Professor of Computer Science and Electrical Engineering at MIT. He has worked on computer architecture, local area networks, raster printers, page description languages, operating systems, remote procedure call, programming languages and their semantics, programming in the large, fault-tolerant computing, transaction processing, computer security, and WYSIWYG editors. He was one of the designers of the SDS 940 time-sharing system, the Alto personal distributed computing system, the Xerox 9700 laser printer, two-phase commit protocols, the Autonet LAN, and several programming languages.

MICHAEL RABIN is T.J. Watson Sr. Professor of C.S. at Harvard University, and Albert Einstein Professor of Mathematics at the Hebrew University of Jerusalem. He is the recipient of numerous scientific awards and prizes, and is an elected or foreign member of several scientific and philosophical academies. His research interests include complexity of computations, efficient algorithms, randomized algorithms, parallel and distributed computations, and computer security. He is also interested in bringing traditional mathematical tools to bear on computer science problems of foundational as well as of practical significance.

JEFFREY I. SCHILLER has managed the MIT Campus Computer Network since its inception in 1984. Prior to his work in the Network Group he maintained MIT's Multics timesharing system during the timeframe of the ARPAnet TCP/IP conversion. Mr. Schiller is the Internet Engineering Steering Group's [IESG] Area Director for Security, where he is responsible for overseeing security related Working Groups of the Internet Engineering Task Force [IETF]. He is also a member of the Privacy and Security Research Group [PSRG] of the Internet Research Task Force. His recent efforts have involved work on the Internet Privacy Enhanced Mail standards (and implementation) as well as releasing a U.S. legal freeware version of the popular PGP encryption program.

CLINT SMITH is an assistant technology counsel in the Law and Public Policy Department at MCI Communications Corporation, where he is responsible for legal issues relating to MCI's Internet and electronic commerce services. He has been actively involved in the roll-out of MCI's line of encryption-based Internet security products and the development of MCI's policy positions on government regulation of encryption. Prior to joining MCI, Clint was an associate in the technology and international practice groups at the law firm of Steptoe & Johnson LLP. He received his J.D. and an M.A. in political science from the University of California at Berkeley.

CHAIR: SIDNEY VERBA
Carl H. Pforzheimer University Professor
Director of the Harvard University Library
Harvard University

CO-CHAIR: DALE P. FLECKER
Associate Director for Planning and Systems
Harvard Library

Library & Publishing

OPENING THE GATE

MODERATOR:	Edward D. Horowitz
PANELISTS:	Willy Chiu
	Shikhar Ghosh
	Christine Maxwell
	Martin Nisenholtz

THE PUBLIC LIBRARY ONLINE

MODERATOR:	Arthur Curley
PANELISTS:	Deirdre Hanley
	J. Andrew Magpantay
	Betty J. Turock

HARVARD NEWS
CONFERENCE ON THE INTERNET AND SOCIETY
May 29-31, 1996   Cambridge, MA

Panelists Predict Content of Internet Will Broaden, Deepen, and Remain Free

By Phyllis Albert-Mitzman

A lot of people complain that the Internet offers far too much information, but it's not enough, according to Willy Chiu of IBM's Worldwide Digital Library group. Digital libraries now offer only one percent of the content of printed text libraries, he said, and more content is being produced every day.

So the real problem is for the library and the librarian. The library "maintains the collective memory of society," Chiu said, and librarians establish order in the chaos and information overload of the Net.

"We need someone to place information in context, to provide order and structure and documentation to help patrons search and find related information." Chiu added, "There is absolutely no quality control on the Net. Anyone can put anything on the Internet, and they will!"

He said the Net is an opportunity for content owners, for technology providers, and for society to distribute its collective memory. "But just getting all the content up won't allow us to maximize its power. Only digital librarians will allow this."

Chiu was one of four panelists in the session "Opening the Gate: Increasing Content on the Internet." All emphasized the importance of building new relationships to realize some of the Internet's potential. This is true for business, for libraries, for indexing companies, and even for newspapers.

Christine Maxwell, president of the McKinley Group, a search engine and indexing company that produces the Internet Directory and the Magellan Online Directory, said the most challenging issues are the Internet's implications for content and intellectual property owners. They will probably no longer realize the chief benefit from publishing, she said, and will focus instead on what people do with information. She spoke of rethinking "how to distribute the content free but sell the services, relationships, and ancillary products."

She perceived the added value coming from evaluating and rating existing resources and helping people sift through the vast amount of digital information. "Browsing has now hit the masses, but in the next ten years searching will hit the masses," Maxwell said.

She urged people not to fear letting go of the way intellectual property has been traditionally viewed, but to "build bridges and bring publishing integrity and standards to help the Internet grow into the new interspace of the future."

Shikhar Ghosh, head of Open Market, at two years old one of the older Internet technology businesses, observed that, "Although everyone believes the Internet is an important paradigm shift, few have any understanding of quite how this will be felt." He described how the new medium is reshaping business boundaries and alliances and how entrepreneurs will need to build new, innovative partnerships to be successful.

"Every information company will have an identity crisis," he remarks, "but relationships will be essential. We will need to pay attention to the complete value chain and offer several services to customers, not just one."

Edward Horowitz of Viacom Interactive Media, who moderated the panel, foresaw a problem of separating development of consumer applications for the Internet from their own Intranet business environment. In the first, he said, the emphasis must be on openness, adding value, and easy ways to find and access information. In the second, the emphasis is on ensuring the security and privacy of content information and business transactions.

For Martin Nisenholtz of the *New York Times* Electronic Media Company, the question was how to achieve scale in the new electronic business markets.

To do this, even for a well-established content provider like the *New York Times*, he stressed the importance of finding a new identity, of providing added value, of helping advertisers and agencies to a new vision of interactive marketing, as well as developing new ways to measure those marketing strategies.

"In a sea of content," he noted, "industry needs to work harder to make services easier to use, the cost of access needs to fall, and the selection of content must expand. But," he cautioned, "the process can't be forced. Above all, we will need patience."

Library & Publishing

May 28, 1996

Opening the Gate
Increasing Content of the Internet

MODERATOR: Edward D. Horowitz
PANELISTS: Willy Chiu
Shikhar Ghosh
Christine Maxwell
Martin Nisenholtz

HOROWITZ: My name is Edward Horowitz. I am responsible for the overall management of Viacom Broadcasting's five network affiliates and 14 major market radio stations, and I also oversee Game Development. It's really a pleasure to be here. It's not often I get a chance to join such a distinguished group of colleagues and spend the time discussing and debating the questions and answers to which we all devote a lot of time, but don't get a chance to have high-level discussions about.

With me are **WILLY CHIU**, Director of the IBM Digital Library, Santa Teresa Laboratory; **CHRISTINE MAXWELL**, Publisher and Senior Vice President of the McKinley Group; **MARTIN NISENHOLTZ**, President of the *New York Times* Electronic Media Company; and **SHIKHAR GHOSH**, Chairman of Open Market, Inc.

Our topic today, "Opening the Gate: Increasing Content of the Internet," presents nearly as many opportunities as the Internet itself. I feel safe in assuming that everyone here would agree that the Internet has not yet approximated even a fraction of what it can and should be. It has, however, captured the interests and attentions of millions of users and billions of investment dollars around the world. Getting the Internet to the next stage—making it more than just a promotional and marketing vehicle, transforming it into a revenue-generating enterprise—is what we are here to discuss.

As content providers, we at Viacom view the possibilities with a healthy mix of enthusiasm and skepticism. Some of the issues that we, as content providers, are wrestling with, and which I hope that we can tackle together on this panel, include:

- How do you separate the development of consumer applications for the Internet from the business development of the Intranet?

- What are the opportunities in both environments?

- What are the applications that the Internet, with its enormous capacities for accessing and storing information, offers businesses?

- What consumer applications can be developed?

- What are the easy ways to find them and to navigate them?

- What is the value that you can add and charge for them?

- How do you ensure privacy and security for the consumers for information that is important within the business?

- How do you develop transactional web sites?

- How do you protect and secure copyrights and branded content? (This is perhaps most important from a content provider's point of view.)

Let me start by introducing Willy Chiu. Willy is currently responsible for IBM's worldwide digital library and he is the Director of the digital library mission within the IBM Corporation. He is also the Director of IBM's Multimedia Software Technologies Group. He joined IBM at the T.J. Watson Research Center in 1974, and has since received numerous outstanding innovation awards within the computer software industry. He recently chaired the Asian Business Forum Conference in Digital Libraries in Singapore.

CHIU: I'm very pleased to be here today. As the Director of Digital Library Technology at a technology company, I'm often asked about the technical barriers to placing content on the Internet.

What generally transpires is a discussion on the five elements essential to the successful development of any digital library:

1. Content capture

2. Content storage

3. Distribution

4. Search and access features

5. Rights management or ownership protection

Despite the enormous growth in digital content generation, the majority of the global information resources remain outside of the digital domain, subject to inefficient manual access.

Information not yet in digital form exists in tens of thousands of libraries, museums, and archives around the world. It has been estimated that nearly one percent of all stored information is in digital format. The remainder—99 percent of all information in every conceivable form—still needs to be captured and digitized if we are to store, distribute, preserve, and protect it for global usage. It helps to have some idea of the electronic storage equivalents for information when looking at the task that faces us.

One page of text equals roughly three kilobytes. One page of graphics is 20 kilobytes. One black and white page of a scanned manuscript equals 50 kilobytes. After compression, a one-page color image is five megabytes. And an X-ray is roughly double that. One minute of CD quality audio is about ten megabytes. And finally, one minute of impact II compressed video is 30 megabytes.

One of the biggest challenges is merely converting physical material into digital information. High resolution digital, scanning, and color calibration technology must be used to capture and reproduce images with near perfect color and quality. Equally important is the ability to convert fragile materials without damaging them during the capturing process. Time and cost represent major inhibitors for converting material. Each scan can cost between 25 cents and five dollars, depending on the resolution that you desire.

However, as digitizing technology advances, the cost of capturing will continue to drop. With current trends in digitizing equipment, it will take decades to digitize even ten percent of the unstructured content that exists today. But fortunately, the majority of new texts and graphics-based content today is created digitally. And over the next decade, digital creations will become the norm for the graphic, video, and motion picture content, thus reducing the growth of material that remains to be digitized. Once physical media has been scanned or transformed into digital format, it must be enriched and stored to be effectively organized for searching.

It is estimated that there exists over 50 exabytes of data in the civilized world. Incidentally, one exabyte is equal to one million terabytes. By 1995, the worldwide shipment of that storage was 100 catabytes, which is 0.1 exabyte. Worldwide, CD-ROM and tape storage shipped was estimated at anywhere between two and four exabytes. Think about that. There is 25 times the amount of data in the world than all raw storage ever manufactured.

As I mentioned earlier, converting text, image, audio, and video content into digital form required a tremendous amount of storage capacity. But we live in an era when IBM's Zurich lab scientists won the Nobel Prize for picking atoms. The scientists designated a single atom as one byte, thereby making it potentially possible to fit the contents of the entire Library of Congress, all 115 million objects, onto a single diskette the size of a quarter. In this environment, storage is increasingly becoming less of an issue. While the cost of storage is an inhibitor, the cost has been dropping by 40 percent growth rate per year.

To any Internet user, the tools used to search for and access information are essentially the system. It doesn't really matter how many bytes of information one has access to unless one can carefully choose the right byte of information that is needed. The particular search method—whether it's technically most efficient or offers the use of the highest information quotient—depends upon the kinds of data, the size of the data, and the user's objectives. Obviously, it is important to include tools for text and image analysis as well as content search of digitized video and audio.

The Internet makes rights management a key concern for content owners and hosts as they make intellectual property available outside their organization. Copyright owners must be assured that reasonable techniques are used to prevent excessive, unauthorized redistribution, misuse of assets, and royalties lost to piracy. On the Internet, where it is desirable that published information be widely distributed, users must not be able to get more or less than they pay for and their privacy must be maintained (particularly with respect to individual transactions).

> *If a library's core mission is to serve as a storehouse of information and knowledge, then there is no question that the Internet can be viewed as the world's library.*

Thus, a primary objective of the Internet must be to provide a comprehensive family of electronic intellectual property management tools to address the issues of control: that is, access and usage, monitoring property, and authenticating data. Digitized content such as images, audio, and video is large in size relative to the Internet's existing network capabilities, and this presents a very real challenge to our ability to successfully distribute information. Moreover, real-time delivery of audio and video is dependent on bandwidth that can assure this paced and continuous delivery.

If a library's core mission is to serve as a storehouse of information and knowledge, to maintain, in essence, the collective memory of a society, then there is no question that the Internet, and especially the World Wide Web, can be viewed as the world's library. And yes, what I have just discussed are the main technical challenges or key infrastructural issues to placing content on the Internet. But what I think is ultimately more interesting are the sociological challenges we face in placing this content, this memory, on the Internet.

Throughout history, in times of war, society is chaotic. People are doing what they can to make sense of the environment, and rarely is there any sense of structural order. Then, when the war is over and the dust settles, when the custodial forces take over or are restored to power, the communal structure returns and a sense of order reigns. Ironically, this paradigm mirrors the current situation with the Internet and society. While not exactly a war zone, the Web is a chaotic environment, with people trying to make sense of information where no one organization is in power and everyone is attempting to take their advantages where they can. We are suffering from information overload and an inability to structure all the information available on the Internet.

When Mosaic was introduced in 1993, there were only 50 known web servers; now there are more than 100,000. With this phenomenal growth we can be sure of one thing: the Internet is a force so powerful it may soon take on a life of its own. Anyone who has been on the Internet knows it offers both benefits and hazards and absolutely no quality control. Unlike traditional forms of publishing, which involve layers of project management and legal clearances, anyone can put anything on the Internet, and we know that we do.

What we need on the Internet, more than key infrastructural elements, is an establishment of order, a system to weed through and navigate the environment. A custodial force, if you will. Remember when you were a child and you went into a library for the first time alone. You walked into a large physical structure and most likely the first thing you did was seek out someone who could provide you with guidance, who could place all this information in a context for you to understand and be able to master. You looked for the librarian. She or he represented order and structure, a knowledgeable force familiar with all that was held in the imposing building.

In a physical library, the librarian carefully selects the books, the materials the library will purchase. The librarian is familiar with all the material, and catalogues it according to appropriate sections within the library. The librarian generates documentation to ensure that patrons can easily search for and find not only what they're looking for but also any related information they deem of interest. Librarians consciously place bestsellers in a prominent location of the library because they know what their patrons want to read. They are careful evaluators of both content and audience.

If content is to flourish on the Internet, I believe the most daunting challenge that must be faced is filling the role of digital librarian. While online directories offer search mechanisms and technology companies provide the tools and mechanisms necessary to ensure the quality of the content and maintenance of the infrastructure, we are randomly increasing content on the Internet without custodial intervention.

Now I'm not suggesting that we need to enforce restrictive policing. (I was recently visiting a nation where I was asked repeatedly if IBM Digital Library solutions could closely monitor citizens' Internet usage and completely restrict access when necessary. I gave a technological answer, of course.) Obviously, I'm not in favor of the *1984* scenario with regard to the Internet. Quite the contrary. I believe that the natural forces of society will eventually provide self-filtering and self-monitoring.

Currently the Internet is like a small town where its citizens are tolerant of its insufficiencies. But as the Internet starts to grow out of control we will start demanding certain limitations, filters, and monitoring techniques if we are to participate, if we are to deposit content into the world's memory bank. We will demand some force to help qualify select content. Even if we can't control what content is assessed by whom, over time we will empower digital librarians to help us create barriers and to filter and index information; to weed out unsuitable material and set up racks of bestsellers, based on our own tastes and security requirements.

In summary, it's clear there is immense opportunity on the Internet—opportunity for content owners, opportunity for technology companies, and above all, opportunity for society to preserve and examine its collective memory. But in order for us to take full advantage of this opportunity, we must face a variety of obstacles, the basic one being how do we get all this stuff onto the Internet and safely distributed. We will overcome the technical barriers, I have no doubt.

We are already developing exciting digital library technologies that integrate information capture, storage, management, search and retrieval, rights management, and distribution technologies. These innovations are already allowing businesses and institutions, such as the Vatican library, to securely distribute vast amounts of information over networks to users around the world.

However, simply getting all the content of the world on the Internet and overcoming the technical challenges to distributing it safely still won't allow us to maximize the power of the Internet. To do that, we will need digital librarians. Only digital librarians can bring order to such an immense collective memory bank.

HOROWITZ: Thank you, Willy. I think a digital librarian might be a useful control tool for certain countries. I think one is Singapore, the other is China, which is looking to create a gateway, and take on the gatekeeping role. And Germany is in there as well, which actually is a bit surprising.

Talking about search engines, our next speaker, Christine Maxwell, is one of the founders of the McKinley Group, the publisher and creator of the Online Internet Directory. In her present position as Senior Vice President and Publisher of the McKinley Group, Christine has a special charge to develop new publishing and a special focus to acquire, republish, and locate intellectual properties in a new way on the Internet. She also is spearheading McKinley's push into the European market. She's the inventor of the greenlight concept in Magellan for marketing safe sites on the Internet. She's one of only two women named on the Web's 100 most influential people in c|net's special article entitled "Movers and

Shakers." Something really interesting deep in her past, she taught elementary school in Oxford, England.

MAXWELL: Ladies and gentlemen, I'm very happy to be here today. I find the heading of this session fascinating, "Opening the Gate: Increasing the Content of the Internet." I'm sure there are many of us right now who'd be quite happy to close that gate. There's so much already there, how can we possibly take anymore. Interestingly enough, the reason I founded the McKinley Group (with my twin sister and our husbands) was because we felt that the Internet was such an important arena, we wanted to create a publishing Internet company and have it as a separate entity.

My sister loves mountains. We thought, well, we've got a mountain of information to climb and Mt. McKinley is the highest mountain in America. And that's how we decided on the name of our company. Actually I first created the Internet Yellow Pages, which at the moment is a pebble on the beach compared to what the Magellan Online Directory has become. A few years ago I realized that what was out there at that time was just books written by computer people for computer people, and there was no attempt whatsoever to organize the information.

I could never understand why I was supposed to look up *medicine* on Gopher. (I still haven't figured that one out.) So that's how I got the idea to create a Yellow Pages where ordinary people could find car under "C" and horse under "H." So that was the beginning of the Internet Yellow Pages. The Magellan Online Directory has come a very long way since then. The challenge for us today, and particularly for our company, is to help people to locate quality information quickly and easily.

The Net itself poses very interesting challenges for owners, creators, sellers, and users of intellectual property. I think what we really are facing today is an enormous need for change in the way copyright works and how people expect to get return for their work. This has come about because the Internet essentially allows for costless copying of content. Esther Dyson has noted very dramatically in many articles that this really does change the economics of content. So what we really need is a different definition of intellectual property.

And why? Because the shelf life of information is so much shorter today. The intrinsic value of content in aggregate will remain high, but most individual items will have a short commercial half-life on the Net. So companies should therefore not try to own all the intellectual property. It is much more important, I think, to focus not on what you own but on what you do with the information. This really does imply a new definition in publishing.

I think that the likely "best defense" for individuals and content providers today is actually to exploit the situation and to distribute intellectual property for free in order to sell services and relationships. The provider's task becomes figuring out what to charge for and what to give away, as well as how to set up relationships or develop ancillary products and services that cover the costs of developing content.

At the moment, the existing models in terms of search engines and directory services are those of supported advertising. The McKinley search engine, Magellan, is also a directory. And what we have done very differently from the beginning is try and add value to the content we find on the Internet. We spend a great deal of time evaluating and rating resources. And that is a very first effort at sifting through the content.

So where will the value in intellectual property be found in the future? People, I think, are going to be increasingly rewarded for their personal effort with processes and services rather than for simply owning the assets. It's a kind of intellectual property which today is called "context." Information itself can't be so easily replicated over the Internet; it depends on the activity or presence of a person or persons, locally or remotely, who are dealing with content in real time.

In a moment, I'll to show you a few different resources on the Internet that I think are very interesting beginnings of what's going to happen on the Internet in the future.

The basic difference is that the first kind of intellectual property is really an embodiment of the automation of the effort. The second kind of value is for the effort of the service or the process itself. And because it's scarce and not so easily replicable, it's the second kind of value that I think is likely to command the highest rewards in the commercial world of the future. Let me just give you a few examples.

The home page of the Magellan Directory [*http://www.mckinley.com/*] is one of five directory services that is up on the Netscape search page today. What I have done is look for some very specific pages that demonstrate some very real changes. I'm going to tap into one called "Beyond." We're going to look at a very interesting site that I like a lot called Beyond the French Riviera [*http://www.beyond.fr/*], which focuses on the south of France.

What's particularly interesting about this is the process created by the individual who's been working on this site. The site has been up just for over a year, and it's a process that shows some tremendous attention to detail as well as a process that perhaps is a kind of intellectual property.

Over time, people are going to have to focus on how can they get mileage out of the information they put on the Net. As wonderful as it is having lots of hits, the biggest trouble today is that the many special jewels on the Internet are not actually able to keep going because they just don't have the money or the advertising to support them.

So this individual has figured out a process of going into all the villages in the south of France and has coordinated that information and organized it, putting it up on the site. And it is a fabulous resource for anyone traveling around this area, both from the point of view of a tourist as well as a business person.

Another site that provides very interesting access to information and a way of processing it differently is Maximov [*http://www.maximov.com/*].

This is a directory service that focuses on who in fact is governing the former Russia. What they have done is made a connection with the Interfax News Service and, by going into the news, they have attached actual telephone numbers and contact names to the corresponding articles in the news service. What that means is that, for once, when you get a story, you can actually find the phone number of the person in the story and can immediately make a complaint. And the Russians are loving it.

What's really interesting about that is there are 5,000 phone numbers in Maximov's directory. And I do know that's going to be online soon. What you find is that many people have tremendous fears about putting their crown jewels up on the Internet; they fear that they're going to lose control of the information, they won't be able to make money out of it, and so on. Yet the fact of the matter is that much of the efforts by others to actually put full content on the Net is in fact increasing the sales of hard copies, not detracting from it.

I want to read something I came across very recently which talks about the Net of the 21st century. Bruce Shaft wrote a very interesting paper called "Information Analysis in the Net: The Interspace of the 21st Century." And he said:

> The Net of the 21st century will have a very different character than at present which will see the beginnings of enabling ordinary people to solve their information problems. The past ten years have seen browsing hit the masses so that document fetching is now standard. In the next ten years, we'll see search hit the masses so the distributed repositories will become standard. This trend is already well underway with a federal R&D program and digital libraries. But to be ready for the world of 2005, the plan for major R&D and analysis environments must be implemented so that it will become possible for information correlations to become standard in the years beyond. The Interspace is a vision of what the Internet will become, where the users cross-correlate the information in multiple ways from multiple sources.

I think the transition from the Internet to Interspace is happening, where the Internet is going to evolve into the basic model of user interaction and that model will change. Physical machines and files of bytes will have disappeared transparently, to be replaced by information objects and classification of collections. I do believe that we are really in the Golden Age of indexing. It is amazing when you go into some of the major bookstores in Berkeley, for example. I actually asked where their books were on indexing, and the response was, "Can you think of another word?" It took me an hour and a half to find one book on indexing that was buried in Computer Science.

I think that when one thinks about the role of universities in the future, the library itself won't be just an archival repository of information, although indeed it is that as well. But I think we're going to be looking to a future where individuals will be a large part of actually interacting with that information and helping to create new indexes because there will be a consistent need to create indexes on the fly. So we hope that as we go forward, Magellan will help to provide the value-added content in a much more focused way through vertical market product, answering needs with the help of specific communities around the world.

We shouldn't be scared of letting go of how we have looked at intellectual property for the last 50 to 100 years. As a publisher, I think we need to let go of "I've-got-to-own-this-stuff" and try very hard to work on building the bridges and bringing in the publishing integrity that has been the hallmark of publishing in the past. Because at the moment, a lot of that is lacking. The trust element is a very, very important one.

I believe that a very important part of McKinley's mission is to grow publishing standards on the Internet to define the new Interspace of the future.

Horowitz: Thank you, Christine. We've gone from the custodian to the sorting, searching, changing paradigm for intellectual property. So now let's go on to transacting business. Here to discuss that is Shikhar Ghosh, Chairman and cofounder of Open Market, Inc. Open Market, Inc. is poised to redefine the electronic age by providing the first complete solution for conducting business on the Internet.

In the last year, Open Market has been selected as one of the hottest companies by *Upside* magazine, one of the 25 coolest companies by *Fortune* magazine, and in the high tech city of Cambridge, Massachusetts, one of the best new businesses of the year. *Business Week* selected Shikhar Ghosh as one of the top entrepreneurs of 1995.

In his past, he was a consultant with the Boston Consulting Group; he graduated with an MBA in 1980 from the Harvard School of Business.

Ghosh: I think that before we redefine business on the Net, it's worth making an attempt to define business on the Net. And that is essentially what I'll do. I'll try to give you a picture of who we are in the context of what some of our customers are doing and how they see the Net starting to change business.

I have a quick story to tell before starting. A few weeks ago, I was listing to an NPR [National Public Radio] story about a conference that was held at the end of the last century, where eminent scientists and philosophers got together to discuss what the world would look like at the end of this century, some time around now. And one of the predictions they made was that a primary mode of transportation between cities would be flight. At that time, that was a radical thing to think about, that people would fly from city to city. And in order to justify this or to lend some credence to their prediction, they actually designed what a system of transportation might look like. So the first idea of it being flight was something we could all accept. What they did then was to design a system where they basically strung wires between cities, where balloons and horses dragged these balloons across, and where people were strung up.

I think we're sort of at the same stage on the Internet. I'm going to define what I *think* the balloons and the wires are going to look like, but fundamentally we don't know. It's a radical change, and we're all speculating.

Just a quick overview so that you can judge how much you want to set store on what I think. Open Market is three years old, one of the older companies on the Internet. We make systems, transaction system servers, stuff like that. We have worked with a number of companies that are really on the cutting edge of doing business on the Internet. So it's *Times*, it's Davis, Hard Core, Bank One, Visa, people like that, and a number of service providers that are trying to get one degree above the fray. People like MCI, UUNET, and so on.

Looking for a definition of business on the Internet, the best one that came to mind was the classical definition of theology: faith and search of understanding. I think that most of our customers and their businesses are really at this stage. They have some belief that the Internet is going to be big for business, but not much of an understanding of how this is going to affect the core businesses of these companies.

I'll start with a quick perspective on what the Net is. To us, it is a change in paradigm. One of the things that happens when paradigms shift is that there are many more losers than there are winners. I think that if you look at the history of warfare, if you look through the history of other major paradigm shifts, you find that it takes a long, long time before the real impact of that change is felt. For example, in warfare, gunpowder had been around a long time before it was used effectively on the battlefield.

In Japan, it was used for about 30 years in traditional warfare with virtually no impact. And that was because the orthodoxy of battle was that the knights who were the highest in status would come up in front. And before a battle, the two armies would line up and their best soldiers would come up and do drills, ostensibly to frighten the other side. Then they'd start the battle. But the people with muskets would be at the back. So used at close range, these were pretty much ineffective. This went on for 30 years until, in a famous battle, one of the sides lined up and had all their best knights come up and the other side shot them. I think you will see a lot of that.

I think two big things are going to happen in business:

The distribution chain will collapse. I was at MasterCard two or three months ago and they were asking us what we thought would be the transaction volume. We said, "Well, we think books and computers will be sold on the Net but planes and cars wouldn't be." And the person sitting opposite me said, "I just bought my car on the Net."

If you think through that example, one U.S. dealer's transaction costs are a couple of dollars, but he can sell a car for a $5 profit. It changes the business of every car dealer in the U.S. It's the same car delivered to a dealership next to you. It completely changes the economics of that business. And you go off to industry after industry, and the same thing happens.

Business boundaries will get reshaped. Bank One is a customer of ours. Time Warner is a customer of ours. Banks are not very good at content. So if you look at the Bank One sites, in my opinion, they are kind of boring. You look at the Time Warner site and it's wonderful because that's their business. So we asked Bank One to get together with Time Warner and said, why don't you license some content from them because that's their core business.

Now imagine the meeting between these two companies. The first item in a business meeting is who should pay whom. Time Warner is a company that depends upon advertising. Bank One has 10 million customers that they are bringing to Time Warner's content. So maybe Time Warner should be paying Bank One for giving them the customer base. Or maybe it should be the other way around. And so you start to rethink these businesses and then you take one more step. Time Warner happens to own *Money* magazine, which, on its page, happens to have the ability to do banking transactions.

All of a sudden, they are competing with Bank One for the same customer. And you start to look through these mind games: who's the wholesaler and who's the retailer in this business? Who owns the customer relationship?

The other big change I see is that people talk a lot about transactions—we sell our systems on the basis of transactions—and yet it really isn't about transactions, it's about relationships. What you're trying to do at this stage of the development of the Web is preserve relationships with your distribution, with your customers. In a way, access is very, very easy where everybody is theoretically on the same global web. And I think that finding ways to strengthen relationships through information is really the area that will be the battlefield.

The way you secure relationships is through brand identity. Brand, in most hard goods products, has the disadvantage of specifying what you're going to get. In my example of buying a car, if I want a Nissan Maxima with a particular option package, I know exactly what I'm going to get. I don't care who I get it from. So it starts to level a lot of the distribution strategies and ways that large companies extract value and put resources into creating this aura of brand. It starts to level those things in ways that are quite frightening to a lot of companies, and rightfully so.

The final point I want to make on the overall perspective is that when you're picking systems, pick those that have technical integrity, that do what the Net can do well. There are a number of companies that have started to do this. But what happens a lot on the Web is that people say, "Who are the big companies that have done information systems?" And they go back to traditional companies like the chemical industry, for instance, to make the process work. In doing that, you get systems that look suspiciously like systems in the chemical industry. So you need to think about what an open network does well; think about what you can do on one of these open networks that you cannot do in any other kind of information system.

There are three or four things that fall in that category. The first is that everybody's on the same network, so you have to keep things open. You have to make sure that the servers you use, the browsers you use, the kinds of features you put

into your system, are accessible to anybody you want to get to. Increasingly, we see companies go out on the Web, and then they put the most recent tag on their HTML or something that's only available, say, through Netscape or only available through Microsoft. And that immediately restricts the market. It looks great in a controlled environment, but the Web is about openness and it's about transactions that go all the way across.

Second, the Web really changes the way you do business. It changes the way in which one can operate, let's say, an information company. All of a sudden, what you have is the ability to offer multiple business models in the same platform. So the Pathfinder side could be worked with the Time Warner side by offering the following:

- Soft goods

- Subscriptions

- Private currencies

- Pay-per-page

- Premium services

- Affinity groups

And if you look through publishing, each of these business models represents a different sector; in the physical world it's quite hard and very expensive to offer all these things to support all of these business models. And when you start to do that, the boundaries start to blur. Where does Time Warner end and where does the bank stop? Where does Time Warner end and where does the retailer start? Take subscriptions. Where does Time Warner end and where does America Online start? All these distinctions start to go away. And then you've got to go back in and rethink, what is my business, what is my identity?

So to sum up, this is what I think is going to happen with business on the Net:

- First, every information company is going to have an identity crisis: who they are, what's the value, who's their friend, who's their enemy, and so on. And that's going to be quite hard to do going forward because all around distribution chains are collapsing and boundaries are getting fuzzier.

- Second, the people who don't go out and get relationships are, over time, going to find it more and more difficult to get them back. The banks and the consumer side, with Intuit and Microsoft sort of interposing themselves between them and their customers, have already started to see some of this happen. In that case, banks did not pay enough attention to the complete value chain as they went through it. And I think that's likely to happen in industry after industry, particularly in information-based services.

(Sprint has a rule; they call it "the rule of 3.5." If they can sell three and a half things to you, then you stay on as a customer. Whereas if they only sell you long distance, the next great deal you get where someone gives you 100 bucks to switch long distance services, you will do that.)

- Finally, a lot of the emphasis today, and for the last year in conferences, has been on technology—what's going to happen with Java, what's going to happen with security, and so on. I think we're at the stage right now where all the big changes in technology have already occurred. The things that are going to make the world change have already occurred. They will all be refined and every month we'll get some new version of something. But the big things have happened.

The changes that remain, the changes we've got to think about, and the changes that are still completely in their infancy are those of business model. Companies need to think through, what is my identity, what's my business, how do I start to make this happen, in a world in which it's very hard to economically justify changes based on traditional ways of accounting.

HOROWITZ: Thanks, Shikhar. Clearly changing the transaction paradigm, shooting the incumbents, redefining the concepts of brands, understanding the concept of an open network, and how lines

of business change, are very intriguing and astute questions. Our last speaker is Martin Nisenholtz.

Martin is President of the New York Electronic Media business unit. He joined them in 1995, and is responsible for the development and delivery of electronic products centered on a brand you know of, the *New York Times*. And he comes to this position from the other brand, Ameritech Corporation, where he was responsible for the development of video programming opportunities in the interactive environment as well as trying to marry advertising to this interactive world.

NISENHOLTZ: Thanks, Ed. It's very nice to be here today. I'll describe, from the perspective of the *New York Times*, some of the things that must happen for content to flourish on the Internet. This is really a wonderful topic, one I spend a considerable amount of time thinking about and working on. But naturally, it sort of begs the question, flourish for whom? For years, the *Times* has had a business selling our content to business markets through services like Lexis-Nexis and we've expanded this business year after year.

So online access to the *New York Times* has been available through these upper-end services for a decade or more. There's nothing new about that. What makes the question about flourishing content more interesting is when it's asked in the context of markets that are much more price sensitive than the traditional, commercial markets were, and where our information services group operates. So clearly, the Internet and the proprietary online environments like America Online create these market opportunities, as the others have suggested.

For example, our "@Times" service on AOL garnered over a million hours of use in the month of April. That's a lot of time. Our World Wide Web site, *http://www.nytimes.com*, has attracted over 300,000 registered users since its launch four months ago. And there are a dozen or more major advertisers now paying to reach these people. But by almost any standard, I think it's safe to say that these are small businesses. So the obvious question—and perhaps the purpose of this meeting in part—becomes, how do you achieve scale in these new markets? How do we, the *New York Times*, create meaningful businesses online, and what must happen for our content to flourish among this new group of users?

So in an effort to answer these questions and perhaps motivate some discussion, I've developed five areas that I believe must be significantly enhanced as a basis on which to build our business. The fact that these areas are still nascent puts us in a kind of prehistorical phase. I think Mr. Ghosh sort of suggested that in a balloon metaphor, but that's really true. This is a time that we are not yet capable of seeing sustainable year over year revenue growth, which is very scary for a lot of companies who are making investments in this area.

First, let me put the responsibility for our success on ourselves. There's a lot of talk about how all of this stuff has to happen for this nirvana to be reached, as though businesses exist on the outside. And that's not the case. The fact is that we're responsible for making our business a success. We also believe that the notion of building a scale business by simply porting the content of the newspaper online is bankrupt. We have never believed this, do not view the Internet as a replacement for the printed page, and will not pursue this definition of content.

Two weeks ago, someone at a party asked me where my children's grandchildren (I get these questions all the time) would be reading a newspaper. Now after explaining that I would be dead by then (unless some paradigm shift in medicine takes place pretty soon), I say I have no idea what's going to happen in 60 years.

But it goes two ways in the newspaper business these days, although I'm strongly on one side. I speculate that unless a radical flip in the economics of newsprint versus electronics takes place— that is, unless for whatever reasons the cost of providing a printed product in the middle of the next century turns into the functional equivalent of the illuminated manuscript—the print on paper is, *for what it does,* superior in almost every way to almost any imagined electronic equivalent. Again, for what it does.

My point is that the Internet and the other electronic forms perform fundamentally different tasks than does a newspaper or a magazine. It is an oddity of technological history that today the bandwidth and device attributes of the electronic world happen to intersect with the output of our Atex systems in a way that allows us to port this content online and add a little bit of value to it. But just as technology has made this possible, so will it render this notion mute over the next five years.

So again, we will look back on this period as sort of the horseless carriage phase of interactive media. The point is that it is incumbent upon us to find a position, apart from the newspaper, in the consumer's life. I think an "identity crisis" is a good way to put the struggle for that position.

Now at the *New York Times* newspaper, I think it is safe to say that our duty is to cover the world, and I think we do that pretty well. Our Sunday magazine, which has been reinvigorated over the last two years, is now created for the pleasure of taking some time out on a Sunday afternoon. But on the electronic side, we believe we're in the business of creating a context for service. Context is very important to us.

This means that you will see our web site deliver consistently higher levels of practical content that will help our users through their busy lives. We'll create some of that ourselves, but we'll also partner to find the information and applications that will make the *New York Times* on the Web undeniably useful to our customers. And again, as someone else said, there is a struggle, there is a basic definitional issue about how you partner in this world today. We will be very flexible as we go down the road with these partners; we'll create some content ourselves, but we will partner much of it.

I think this is a very distinct editorial mission. It's differentiated from the newspaper and it's one for which we believe, through our research, is based on considerable consumer demand. For those of you who have used our web site, and there may be a few of you in the room, you may have seen that we've already begun to execute this strategy.

Our archival travel and entertainment reviews, our cybertimes navigator, which highlights the best of the Web, our late sports, our financial updates—these are examples of a departure point. But we will soon offer a much more highly personalized view of the editorial, richer access to our archive, and a much expanded and personalized online business section. By the fall, we hope to have a prototype for Version 2, which will really raise the bar on value.

Another notion of ours is this whole idea that you come out with one of these things and you feel like this is the last word, when in fact, this is only the beginning. The notion of versioning, which is so common in software, is really still new to electronic publishing. So again, we're taking the responsibility to make our site irresistible.

For content to flourish, our first rule is that we must *make* it flourish for our customers. Second, for content to flourish, we think it's very important to create interactive marketing—state of the art. The fact is that advertisers and their agencies must begin to discover how to create and measure interactive media. Without this development, there can be no large consumer online publishing business, at least not one with an editorial sensibility distinct from the marketing message.

Yes, advertisers are content providers too. We've already seen marketing sites like *http://ups.com/* begin to offer value to their consumers. Today these are marketing examples that exist largely apart from sites like ours. They promote their URLs through traditional media, television, and print, and spend very little, if any, media money online. Agency media departments still don't have the analytical framework to evaluate the online buy; they act more or less intuitively. Agency creatives, at least at the larger agencies, don't yet have the skills to create for this forum.

This situation impoverishes content providers, who are caught between the traditional dynamics of consumer media spending and nonexistent advertising dollars. The obvious danger is that without a dynamic relationship between advertisers and publishers we run the risk of turning the World Wide Web into an extension of the 800 telephone business—a huge business, to be sure, but certainly not an intellectually interesting publishing platform for the consumer.

The third thing we need for our content to flourish is a bigger user base. At conferences like this it's sometimes easy to forget that fewer than ten percent of U.S. households subscribe to an online service.

So I divide this marketing challenge into five areas.

1. Just as we have the responsibility to lead on the editorial and interactive marketing sides, *we must do a better job marketing our service.* And that's critically important. It's hard, even at the *New York Times*, to get your message across in this sea of content.

2. The industry must work harder to *make these services more accessible and easier to use.* Internet access should be as simple to get and use as the telephone, and it just isn't. Anyone who has downloaded yet the latest version of the Netscape browser for the 59th time, knows that for the average user, it's still not easy.

3. *Cost of access must fall.* A content business can't flourish when vast numbers of people are locked out simply because they can't afford the equipment and services. And we've heard about a number of solutions there.

4. For content to flourish, *the selection of content on the Net must expand.* It's no secret that entertainment basically drives the media business today. Entertainment is the primary product of television and radio, video games, and CD-ROMs. Some would argue that until the Internet becomes a platform for entertainment, it will remain marginalized among consumers. After all, television flew into most American homes because people wanted to see Uncle Miltie, which created the critical mass for the evening news. HBO started the cable revolution, which led to CNN and C-SPAN.

Now this isn't to say that we can't create a profitable business on a pre-entertainment Internet, but we probably won't reach the kind of scale we're capable of without the markets that entertainment helps build. The Net-based interactive entertainment business is still in its infancy, and many will argue (and it would be interesting to hear from Ed on this point) that it won't truly exist until a video on-demand capability is possible.

I happen to disagree. Nascent companies, like Willisville in Los Angeles or the Ridler in New York, have begun to pioneer new forms of entertainment product on the Net, even in a narrowband world. Certainly broader bandwidth is desirable in this context, it will create new opportunities, but we're already beginning to see the seeds of these new forms appearing in the current environment, and we look forward to their success.

5. Last, but not least, for content to flourish—for *our* content to flourish, *we're going to need some time.* I said at the outset that there were five points to be made and this is probably the most important one. If you look back on the content of services that were developed in the early '80s, you'll find many of the same issues and problems that still confront content providers online today.

The point is, again, as others have said, we're witnessing a pretty profound shift from analog to digital media. Massive infrastructure changes, content sensibility distinct from analog media, the knowledge of how to market these new products, and finally, understanding the consumer perspective of why these new products exist and why they add value—all of these things take time, even in the most optimistic scenarios.

Impatience is natural. Where money is invested, returns are expected. But the process cannot be forced. It often takes many years before a true state of the art appears for a new medium. This was true in film even though film is much closer to the traditional dramatic arts than is the Internet to almost any other means of providing information or entertainment. So I think we need patience in order to

make content flourish. It will happen, but it will take time.

Now the message is that the *New York Times* is committed to being a full participant in this process. As I said, we will diligently raise the level of value in the products we create, we will work with advertisers and their agencies to develop a legitimate and measurable interactive marketing industry. We will build our online brands among consumers wherever they wish to reach us, and support hardware and software products that make this process easier and more accessible for consumers. We will encourage our friends in the Internet business to create along with us. Perhaps most important, we will scale our activities and investments to the appropriate level of consumer demand and be patient as we participate in the birth of this new media form.

These are the five things we will do to create a flourishing content business online. We look forward to hearing what others will do so we can work together to make this happen.

Questions & Answers

Q: *What do you project, in dollars, the value of the Internet market on your company will be in the year 2000 and in the year 2005? And if you are owned by a larger company, what do you think those total revenues will be as a percentage of overall revenue for the parent company?*

NISENHOLTZ: I'd rather be asked what my grandchildren will be reading 60 years from now. I mean, obviously it's impossible to answer that question because we are in this prehistory. Going five years out is difficult. Going ten years out really is impossible. But I'll go out on a limb, just for the fun of it. Just as a *guess*, I would say that in the year 2000, revenues from online in total, not just the Internet but online in total, will be somewhere in the $40 to $50 million range. Ten years out, I don't know—in my view it makes a lot of these IPO [Initial Public Offering] values kind of ludicrous. But that's about what we think it will be, and as a percentage, it will be very small. You know, the *New York Times* company is a $2.5 billion company. So you do the math.

MAXWELL: Okay, the McKinley Group is a private company and we are in a rather interesting position because directories are indeed the gate through which virtually everyone goes when they start their daily or hourly or minute by minute journey on the Internet. So today, we are receiving millions of impressions a day. Exohits. Hundreds of millions I hope by then.

GHOSH: We just went public last week, so I think I can't even answer the question. But just to give you a sense of what the market expects, you know, we're a company that's two years old. We did $2.5 million in the first quarter in revenues and our market cap is $1.2 billion. So, you know, every investor who's come into that value expects—because it's obviously risky—to get a substantial return on their investment. You can do the math. But the only point I want to make on that is that there is a belief in the market that, you know, in the time frames that are mentioned, this market is going to be a big part of the economy.

I think Forrester did a study a little while ago of asking CEOs of companies how much of their business they thought would be done electronically in the same time frame, by the year 2000. The number was 30 or 32 percent. So it's a big chunk of what's going to happen.

CHIU: IBM is a technology company and I hate to say anything that will affect our stocks, so take this as off the record. We believe that this area is a very tremendous opportunity for us. We are technology enablers. We do not own content and we believe that the content owners will get the bulk of the opportunities. If you look at the overall projection of the Internet marketplace as an electronic commerce marketplace, transaction-based revenue is obviously where a lot of the opportunity lies. IBM certainly is investing very heavily in this area.

We believe that this is the new way of doing business for many of the companies; finance, banking, any kind of transactions that you're conducting

today. There will be many more of those to come and many of the speakers have talked about that already. And I would only say that, as a percentage of revenue (I hope I don't get a call from my chairman) I think it will be a significant percentage of IBM's revenue by the year 2000. In the 20 to 30 percent range.

Q: *What sites do each of you visit on a regular basis for content, for purchasing goods, and for services?*

CHIU: Library of Congress [*http://lcweb.loc.gov/*].

Q: *How about for services and do you buy anything?*

GHOSH: I like two. I like Pathfinder [*http://www.pathfinder.com/*]. Once you get used to how to use it, you can actually find a lot of stuff with it. And I like Amazon [*http://amazon.com/*].

MAXWELL: Oh, I will start with the Magellan [*http://www.mckinley.com/*]. But actually Magellan's content is inside Pathfinder. Purchasing goods. I also consistently enjoy looking at CyberCash to see how that wallet transaction system is progressing. So that's fun.

NISENHOLTZ: I have not become a brand loyal web user. I surf. I mean I skim and do five or ten sites at a time. There isn't anything that I go to every day, other than email of course.

HOROWITZ: Well, I think that we've had an extraordinary one hour and fifteen minutes. I want to thank you for your questions, your participation. And I'd like to, at this point, also thank our panelists for being quite revealing.

About the Speakers

EDWARD D. HOROWITZ is Senior Vice President, Technology, Viacom, Inc., and Chairman and Chief Executive Officer of Viacom Interactive Media. He also serves on Viacom's seven-member Executive Committee. As the company's senior technology officer, Mr. Horowitz works closely with each of Viacom's operating segments, worldwide, in assessing the global impact of technology-dependent issues on their current and future core businesses. In addition, he determines Viacom's international satellite distribution strategy. Mr. Horowitz is on the Board of Directors for Star-Sight and Ariel. He also is on the Advisory Board of Corbis, the Cable Labs Technical Steering Committee, and is a member of the Executive Committee of the Montreux Television Symposium.

DR. WILLY W. CHIU is currently the Director of IBM Digital Library, in San Jose, California. In this position, he is responsible for the worldwide strategy, planning, product development, and market development of the IBM Digital Library solution. He is also responsible for IBM's Multimedia Software Architecture in the IBM Open Blueprint as well as 3D Virtual Reality Technologies. Recently he chaired the Asian Business Forum on Digital Libraries in Singapore. He is also a member of BAMTA, a Silicon Valley Joint Venture.

SHIKHAR GHOSH is Chairman and cofounder of Open Market, Inc. Open Market, Inc. is poised to redefine the electronic age by providing the first complete solution for conducting business on the Internet. Open Market has received praise from companies such as *Upside* magazine and *Fortune* magazine; it was selected as one of the "Best Businesses of the Year" in Cambridge, Massachusetts; and Mr. Ghosh was selected as one of the "Top Entrepreneurs of 1995" by *Business Week* magazine. Prior to founding Open Market, Ghosh was the CEO of Appex Corporation from 1988 to 1994. *Business Week* magazine selected Appex as the fast growing entrepreneurial company in the US in 1990.

A 25-year veteran of the publishing and research industries, **CHRISTINE MAXWELL** is busy focusing her extensive research, publishing, and Internet expertise on creating a new Internet publishing vehicle for the publication of high value content. Ms. Maxwell cofounded the McKinley Group's Magellan Online Directory and also co-authored the original "New Riders Official Internet Yellow Pages" in 1994. She has since brought out the third edition of this work under the revised title of "McKinley Internet Yellow Pages."

MARTIN A. NISENHOLTZ joined the *New York Times* as President of its electronic media company in June 1995. He is responsible for development and delivery of electronic products centered on the content of the newspaper. Prior to joining the *Times*, Mr. Nisenholtz was Director of Content Strategy for Ameritech Corporation, where he was responsible for guiding development of new video programming opportunities and interactive information and advertising services. From 1983 to 1994, he worked at Ogilvy & Mather Worldwide. In 1983, he founded the Interactive Marketing Group (IMG), where, upon his departure, he was a Senior Vice President and a member of the operating committee. He is married, has two children, and lives in Armonk, NY.

HARVARD NEWS
CONFERENCE ON THE INTERNET AND SOCIETY
May 29-31, 1996   Cambridge, MA

The Public Library: On-Ramp to the Information Superhighway

By Marvin Hightower

The public library has long served as "the people's university" in America, the one place where citizens from all walks of life could explore virtually any topic.

Is the Internet making the public library obsolete? Hardly, according to panelists at yesterday's Science Center session on "The Public Library Online."

The Internet offers "an extraordinary opportunity" for public libraries to expand on their "core" mission of reaching out, said panel moderator Arthur Curley, Director of the Boston Public Library.

Convinced that "getting the nation connected [to the Internet] is essential to the public interest," American Library Association President Betty Turock argued passionately for national policies that will maintain the same "free and open access to information in the 21st century that we have today."

During the past five years, she said, "telecommunications corporations have spent more than $40 million to influence legislation." As a result, "technical and financial interests have [thus far] dominated decisions about the Information Superhighway, overshadowing what it can do for the people. In a democracy, the electronic frontier must enhance the public interest as well [as the private]."

Turock maintained that the public library is the most practical "on-ramp" to the Information Super-

highway. But before cruising off, the nation must first negotiate a road potholed with issues like intellectual freedom versus censorship, copyright restrictions, and the economics of access in a world of increasingly privatized online services.

If such questions are not carefully resolved, "the evolving infrastructure threatens to exacerbate the chasm that already exists between the information rich and the information poor," she warned. "We must continue championing the public interest to ensure equity on the Information Superhighway for people of all ages and all circumstances."

Statistics from Andrew Magpantay, Director of the ALA's Office for Information Technology Policy, bolstered many of Turock's points on the centrality of public libraries to the common good.

Public libraries have traditionally served as cost-effective means of providing community access to expensive reference materials, Magpantay said, and these facilities serve a similar function in the electronic Information Age, with its swiftly changing hardware, software, and services.

A recent national survey showed, for example, that while about 39 percent of American households have a personal computer, only about half of those have a modem. "That's less than 21 percent of the population in the U.S. who have even the capability of getting access to the Internet from their homes at this point," Magpantay said.

By contrast, the National Commission on Library and Information Sciences recently found that about 44.6 percent of public libraries are now connected to the Net—up from about 23 percent in 1994. By 1997, the figure may reach 60 percent or more.

The "bad news," Magpantay said, is that less than 23.6 percent of Internet-ready libraries have graphic access to the World Wide Web, and areas with populations of 25,000 or less are "less likely to be connected than those in large urban areas such as Boston."

At the same time, 1996 figures from the National Center for Education Statistics indicate that roughly 52 percent of public library facilities lie outside metropolitan areas and that public libraries as a whole have at some point served about 66 percent of adults and 75 percent of children nationwide.

"About 40 percent of public libraries have budgets of under $50,000," Magpantay said. Only about 9 percent have budgets exceeding $1 million. "Within those budgets, libraries are performing a wealth of services."

For all these reasons, he argued, the 16,000 facilities of the nation's 9,000-odd public library systems will remain important as places where people can get personal guidance in navigating the Net.

Deirdre Hanley, Director of the Reading (Massachusetts) Public Library, spoke from daily practitioner's perspective. "In Reading, it has made sense from the beginning to our community that we be the gateway to the Internet. We positioned ourselves as a technology center, [and] we've become viewed as a very critical service to the town."

Hanley urged everyone to keep a level head in today's technological wonderland. "We must be very careful to not make a bigger deal of the Internet than it actually is. It's a source of information and a means of communication, and we should really view it in this context to make it work for us.

"Sometimes it's appropriate to use the Internet to answer a reference question. And sometimes it's easier to just look in the *World Book*."

Library & Publishing
May 28, 1996

The Public Library Online

MODERATOR: Arthur Curley
PANELISTS: Deirdre Hanley
Andrew Magpantay
Betty Turock

CURLEY: I am the Director of the Boston Public Library and this is the portion of the program that takes seriously the title, "The Internet and Society." This is not one of the sessions about the Internet and money. Public libraries are, of course, social entities and, in that respect, librarians take quite seriously the challenges of the electronic revolution and their historic role of representing the needs and interests of all of the citizenry, and not just some of it. Before I introduce the panel, I want to congratulate them for showing up. If, as some project, the Internet will render the library obsolete, they probably ought to be back home job hunting. But I think their being here suggests that they subscribe to a different perspective, and it is that the Internet represents an extraordinary opportunity to the public library. Reaching out has long been at the core of the missions of public libraries in this country and, frankly, around the world. And the technological revolution has had quite the opposite effect of rendering the libraries' mission obsolete. It has given it the means of reaching out.

In Boston, we've been able to link every one of the 114 public schools in the city to our library's central computer, to give every student in the city access not just to our own databases, our own collection and bibliographic databases, but, through our computer, a gateway into the Internet. And this is a wonderful thing.

We also know from our own statistics that while electronic inquiries to the library quadruple about every month, since we've been on the Internet (about four years now), use of the library's print resources have gone up between five and fifteen percent each year. So, far from in any way replacing print literature, the knowledge explosion is occurring at such a geometric progression that we need virtually every format available to us just to run fast enough to stay in place.

One of our speakers yesterday [Scott McNealy] suggested that the dynamic needs of the Internet and its development are such that government should be kept to an absolute minimum in its involvement therewith. This, I hope, is an issue our panelists will address. Public libraries are certainly entities of government. We're dependent on government not just for our funding but to exercise its regulatory authority in a way that benefits the public interest, and not just the economic interests of those who are the producers rather than the users of information. The same speaker also called for a form of social Darwinism. He also mentioned, however, that two-thirds of the world's population, by his calculation, has never either placed or received a telephone call. Well, public libraries are very much committed to the notion that no segments of our population should be left behind. And I know our panelists will address this matter.

BETTY TUROCK is the Director of the Graduate Library Science program at Rutgers University and President of the American Library Association. During her service, Dr. Turock has made issues surrounding the Internet the centerpiece of her presidential activity.

ANDREW MAGPANTAY is the founding Director of the American Library Association's Office for Information Technology Policy in Washington. Andrew brings a very thorough perspective and background to the program.

Then we have the true specialist, an actual practicing librarian. **DEIRDRE HANLEY** is the Director of the Reading Public Library, one of the finer and more pioneering libraries in the Greater Boston area. Deirdre also is the president of a major regional council that plans for cooperation among public libraries, particularly in areas of automation.

TUROCK: Good morning. A momentous telecommunications revolution is sweeping our country... so momentous that for the first time since 1934, the Telecommunications Act has been rewritten. Nothing happening today will offer more challenge and more opportunity for the people of our nation than the emerging national information infrastructure, better known to the American people not as the Internet but as the Information Superhighway. I believe so strongly that getting the nation connected is essential to the public interest, I have made public policy on the Information Superhighway the focus of my year as President of the 58,000 member American Library Association, the oldest and largest library association in the world.

The Information Superhighway is a major focus at the highest levels of government as well. Political leaders from both sides of the aisle agree that all Americans must be connected. But we need more than words to guarantee the same free and open access to information in the 21st century that we have today. In the past five years, telecommunications corporations have spent more than $40 million to influence legislation. It's no surprise then that until now, technical and financial interests have dominated decisions about the Information Superhighway, overshadowing what it can do for the people and how it can address society's needs.

My opinion on the electronic expressway travels in the opposite direction from the opinion expressed yesterday by Scott McNealy. While I applaud the opportunity for financial gain the superhighway presents for entrepreneurs, I believe that in our democracy, the electronic frontier must not only enhance business but must also enhance the public interest, and the government has an indisputable and appropriate role in making that happen.

The American people are being barraged with promises and proposals for this swiftly evolving infrastructure. Amid the rhetoric, questions arise about who's going to reap the benefits. Major national public policy on four issues will ultimately decide whether access remains free and open. They are:

1. Universal service

2. Intellectual freedom

3. Intellectual property rights

4. Equity

Universal Service

The signing of the Telecommunications Act of 1996 was historic.[*] It provides the opportunity for unlimited economic gain in the private sector. But for the first time, libraries are slated for special telecommunications discounts and given the designation "universal service providers," a designation that brings with it an ongoing infusion of funds for technological transformation.

Intellectual Freedom

At the same time, the Communications Decency Act [CDA], a provision of the Telecommunications Act, threatens intellectual freedom by making it a crime to transmit or distribute "indecent" material. Under the CDA, material that is perfectly legal for youth to view in books, films, or other media, is made illegal to view electronically. In February [1996], ALA became the lead plaintiff in a Constitutional challenge to the CDA. That case was assigned to the Fifth District Court in Philadelphia, and I have been told that will have an opinion from the judges at the end of this week or the beginning of next week. We expect that the case is on a fast track and will be heard in the Supreme Court in the fall.[†]

Intellectual Property Rights

The third major public interest issue is the protection of intellectual property rights. Contrary to

---

[*] Vorys, Sater, Seymour, and Pease. See *http://www.vssp.com/fcc2.html*

[†] The CDA was shot down by a three-judge court in June, 1996. However, on December 6, 1996, the Supreme Court agreed to hear the government's appeal for the legal challenge to the CDA. See *http://www.cdt.org/*.

some opinions I heard in the previous session of this conference, original copyright legislation not only fosters the development of creativity in the arts and sciences, but also encourages the dissemination of that creativity broadly to the public. The National Information Protection Act, now before the Congress, tips the delicate balance in current law toward those who make financial gains; that is, authors and publishers. Any change in policy must continue to protect the public's right to reproduce copyrighted materials in limited quantities for educational purposes.

I have skimmed over the first three major issues, because Andrew Magpantay will bring you information in greater depth on each of them. He will also give you an up to the minute report on where we are in the Capitol on each of the issues.

Equity

The fourth major issue is equity on the Information Superhighway, a stake for the people in equitable, just, affordable access. Today we who are here know that more and more of the information we need is in computers, but we are among the information rich. Most people in the United States do not realize the importance of electronic access to their future. The powerful technology of the Information Superhighway can help us find a job, research a medical condition, participate in government, connect a student or a scholar to information they need around the nation and around the world.

But what if we don't have a computer or know how to use one? What if we can't afford one or we can't pay the online charges to get access? The evolving infrastructure threatens to deepen the chasm that already exists between the information rich and the information poor, even as it revolutionizes how we live, learn, work, and connect to one another. In an earlier session, I was ecstatic to hear Bill Gates put the issue of the information "haves" and "have nots" on the list of important problems we have to face, even though he did not propose any solutions.

According to a recent *New York Times* article, two-thirds of all computers are sold to households with incomes of over $40,000. But only one in three households reaches that level. Statistics also show that only one in ten Americans has access to the vast network of databases that are already part of the infrastructure. High cost and rapid change in technology could make many more of us information poor. Were I not part of a faculty, I doubt I would have a Pentium chip, with all the bells and whistles, sitting in my office. If computing came from my home budget, that setup plus the laptop I usually take with me everywhere would probably be beyond the dollar figure I could invest.

> *In a country troubled by balancing its budget, it is cost-effective to concentrate on the library for public access rather than to think about connecting every home.*

Public libraries have historically served as the nation's great equalizers, providing people with the information they need, regardless of their ability to pay. They can also make technological costs more reasonable. In a country troubled by balancing its budget, it is cost-effective to concentrate on the library for public access rather than to think about connecting every home. That, *Barron's Business and Financial Weekly* estimates, would take over $250 billion. And librarians are in the libraries to help the public find the right information from the sea of information available over the Highway, and to teach the people how to use the technology.

But high costs and rapid changes in technology have also made it difficult for public libraries to keep up, just at the time technologically sophisticated libraries are needed in every community. The Career and Work Force Development Act, which includes the Library Services and Construction Act (even as we meet the Act is undergoing a metamorphosis), will send most public library grant funds—up to $250 million authorized—to state libraries for new technology and service innovation. But clearly, state and local government as well as the federal government will have to make commitments, if the development of the electronic infrastructure is to include libraries. For that to happen, the people must know the benefits they will get when libraries are on-ramps to the Information Superhighway.

As the centerpiece of my year as President, ALA sponsored the summit, "A Nation Connected," held at the Annenberg Center in Rancho Mirage, California, to bring greater attention to the problems and promises of the Information Superhighway. Harvard Law Professor Charles Ogletree, moderator of the widely acclaimed PBS series, "Ethics in America," facilitated the discussions. A nationally renowned panel of 20 experts accepted my invitation to participate. Among them were Arno Penzias, Nobel Prize winner; Richard Rodriguez, Pulitzer Prize winning author and journalist; Gwendolyn Baker, President and CEO of the United States Committee for UNICEF; Esther Dyson, Chair of the Electronic Frontier Foundation; and Deborah Kaplan, Vice President of the World Institute on Disabilities.

Panelists described communication in this century as dominated by a medium with a limited number of speakers, transmitting programming and information to essentially passive audiences. Now, they observed, the public square of the past is being replaced with electronic communication which allows millions of people to take part in discourse on a national and global level. Craig Howe, Director of the Center for the History of the American Indian, worried about the effect of this superhighway on existing communities and their ability to get the kind of information they need. His concern sparked discussion about our lack of understanding of the average person and of diverse people's information needs, and the politics of information that determines who gets what, who creates and controls the infrastructure, and what it contains.

Most panelists were enthusiastic about the promise of the electronic future to facilitate communication and exchange information across national economic, ethnic, and social boundaries, to create communities united by similar interests, where none had existed before. But they recognized the evolving structure's ability to separate, exclude, and depersonalize, even to the extent that it affects a loss of cultural identity.

Panelists applauded the superhighway's ability to improve participation in government and the way we are governed. They viewed the availability of more information than ever before as empowering, informative, and educational. But they warned that increased privatization could turn the electronic frontier into a virtual shopping mall.

While describing the superhighway as providing easy access, quick response, informality, accessibility, and independence, they recognized it as chaotic and disorganized, a pathway where it was difficult to sort quality information from the glut available, and to trust the authority of what was found.

They saw the superhighway as offering the opportunity to do the following:

- Develop skills and abilities in a world where, by the year 2000, it's predicted that 60 percent of the jobs available will require knowledge of information technology.

- Improve access in communications for disabled persons.

- Create and enter new markets and optimize business processes.

But in applauding the beneficial long-term effects of the highway, they did not ignore the adverse effects in the short term on our work life, which they believed could be substantial. Some even doubted results would ever be beneficial, citing the nature of information technology, its severe impact on low-skilled workers, and increased international competition as reasons for their pessimistic outlook.

Panelist Andrew Cohill from Blacksburg, Virginia's Electronic Village, sounded a bit like Scott McNealy. He wanted us to put all of our fear of the future aside, calling the Information Superhighway the greatest egalitarian tool the world has ever known. He celebrated superhighway anarchy when he said, "No one is in charge any more," and dismissed the information poor by saying, "They've always been with us, and they always will." Itibari Zulu countered Cohill's generalizing from his experience in other locales, by explaining that a confluence of factors hardly made Blacksburg a model for the American community. Blacksburg has a small, homogenous, college educated, upper middle class population, and influential venture partners in Virginia Polytechnic Institute and Bell Atlantic.

Zulu agreed with panelist Major Owens, United States Representative from New York City and the only librarian in Congress, that government must intervene if the underserved are not to experience acute information disenfranchisement. Owens denoted the government's role in shaping the infrastructure as providing at least a part of the financing to connect all communities. He recalled the GI Bill and the Morrill Act as steps to the fiscal foundation the federal government must establish to ensure equity on the Information Superhighway.

Richard Rodriguez argued for a continuation of tradition in the role played by librarians. He supported the thesis of Jim Billington, the Librarian of Congress, about the transformational role the public library has played in this society in the past and will play in the future. They agreed that for democracy to be dynamic in a multicultural society, it must be based on knowledge freely available to the people. The two spoke of our knowledge-based democracy as threatened by the flood of information generated by new technologies, saying, "We talk about the Information Age, not the Knowledge Age. We cannot let a flood of unsorted, unverified information replace knowledge." Words, sounds, and images factored into zeros and ones in the digitized process are, for them, dehumanized unless they are rehumanized at the end of the terminal by librarians, whom they referred to as knowledge navigators.

Panelists strongly defended the role of the public library as a location and wanted it preserved. (Let me assure you that these panelists were not picked because we knew they had an affinity for libraries.) Besides offering access to the digital world, they offered the continuation of public libraries as stimulators of dynamic debate and intellectual exchange among Americans, who will be more easily engaged electronically in community decision making.

Twenty-six library leaders from all parts of our nation, nominated by their peers, listened to the day-long Socratic dialogue to distill what it might offer to help them prepare the nation's libraries for the 21st century. They focused on the library and how its presence on the Information Superhighway could serve the public interest. Toni Bearman, the only librarian on the National Information Infrastructure Advisory Council, set up by the President and Vice President, added two new roles for librarians to the traditional ones of organizers and dispensers of information. The first role is as a partnership builder, taking the lead in gathering public and private groups as participants in the design of local on-ramps to the Information Superhighway. The second role is as a publisher and producer of multimedia information packages, moving the basis for the development of public library services and collections from the comprehensive basis of "just in case someone might need them" to collections and services "built just for you." In the latter, electronic sources built locally and globally are combined by selecting text from one source, data from another, still images, moving images, and voice from yet another, to customize individual resources to meet the individual information seeker's specific needs and demands. Even now at Rutgers, as we teach graduate librarians both at the Master's and Ph.D. levels about the professional life of the future, they are exposed to a course in structuring, organizing, accessing, and producing multimedia.

For Michael Koenig, Dean of the Graduate School of Library and Information Science at Rosary College, and Luis Herrera, Director of the Pasadena Public Library, the most critical role for libraries and librarians is as the vehicle and the voice for equity, acting as advocates to develop Information Superhighway policy and making the public aware of why we're leading the charge to ensure equitable, just, and affordable access.

The message from the Summit was clear: We can't quit now. We must continue championing the public interest to ensure equity on the Information Superhighway for people of all ages and all circumstances. The Summit will serve as the jumping-off point for discussion by American Library Association members and guests at the President's program during the national conference in 1996 in New York City. Join Richard Rodriguez, Jim Billington, Gwendolyn Baker, Charles Ogletree, and me, to contribute your thoughts about what libraries and librarians must do to serve the public interest in this age of electronic information.

Over the past two years, I have logged more than 267,000 frequent flyer miles to meet with legislators, policy makers, and the media in our national capital and across the country. It's obvious I'm very serious about delivering the message that Americans cannot wait for equity on the Information Superhighway, so you'll understand the compelling need I have to engage you in informing the public about what's at stake. Promote having a public discussion at your library on the promises and problems of the Information Superhighway. Write an op-ed piece. Send a letter to the editor. Visit or write state and local officials as well as Congressional representatives, to urge their support for libraries as the people's on-ramps.

The superhighway of information is not about the future, it's about now. We cannot allow ourselves to be diverted from the great opportunity we have to demonstrate how we can use electronic technology to redefine community in a new and empowering way. ALA is hoping for your support to ensure equity on the Information Superhighway for all Americans. But more important, our children and grandchildren are hoping that all of us will work to ensure a free and open Information Society for the 21st century. Thank you.

CURLEY: Thank you, Betty. We're indeed fortunate to have you as our president and superb advocate. I feel sorry for the editorial board of the *Boston Globe*. She's meeting with them tomorrow. They will go home exhausted but inspired.

I want to underline just one point you made with an anecdotal reference. Even if we were able to put a PC in every home and apartment in the country, consider this statistic. We do annual user surveys at the Boston Public Library. And one statistic that jumps out from every study is that 65 percent of the people who use the library seek the help of a reference librarian nearly every time they visit the library. We're talking about not just access to information, but we're talking about an enormous body of people to whom access is only the first step. Help is needed in migrating into this technological world.

I'm now delighted to call on Andrew Magpantay, who is known as the technology wizard of the American Library Association.

MAGPANTAY: Both Betty and Arthur have set forth very well the role that libraries (and librarians) play in society. And as you can see, particularly from Betty's presentation, librarians are very passionate about the role that libraries and librarians can play in helping bring the Information Superhighway to the public. What I'd like to do is build on what Betty has said, and provide you with a current scan of the environment about where public libraries are today in terms of their connectivity, who they're serving, and also some of the policy issues that public libraries, and probably all libraries in general, are facing as we begin to connect them up to the Internet.

I'd like to begin with a simple proposition about the role of libraries in society. Libraries collectively invest in and provide access to valuable, specialized, high-end information services and resources for their local communities. Even before we'd entered into this new Information Age, this high tech age, that's traditionally what libraries have done. They've invested in things like specialized dictionaries, encyclopedias, atlases, indexes, and other special high-priced information tools. They've done that so that communities, whether it be an academic or a neighborhood community, can have access to these things. It was economically more efficient to do that than, say, to have every individual household, or every individual student or faculty member purchase these resources themselves.

Now, I believe we're seeing the same parallel thing today with digital information resources. It doesn't make sense for everybody here to have a T1 line coming into their home, at least not yet. A report from Grunwald and Associates, who did a survey along with another organization called "Find SVP," found that something like 39 percent of households have a PC, and only half of those actually have a modem in them. That's less than 21 percent of the households in the U.S. who have even the capability of getting access to the Internet from their homes at this point. Estimates of the number of actual Internet users are (and for this statistic I refer to John Quarterman in Texas, who has done some work in this area) somewhere upward of about 40 million people worldwide. Contrast that with a United States population of somewhere around, I think, 250 to 255 million, 122 million adults.

It doesn't take an advanced degree to see that not everybody is on the Information Superhighway just yet. And again, I think that is where the role of libraries will come in, and will continue to come in, as resources both for access to these advanced telecommunication/information resources, and places where people can go to get guidance and instruction as to how to navigate this Information Superhighway.

To give you a little background about public libraries, there are nearly 9,000 public library systems in the United States today. These 9,000 public library systems represent almost 16,000 individual public library facilities. (I'm making a distinction here between the administrative unit, such as the Boston Public Library which Arthur heads, and the number of, say, main and branch libraries that may be included within that system.) According to the National Center for Education Statistics, about 52 percent of those library facilities are located outside of metropolitan areas. Libraries again play a very major role in bringing information out to rural areas.

We know that public libraries serve about 66 percent of U.S. adults. Almost two-thirds of adults have been to a public library. In the same vein, about three-quarters of U.S. children come through public libraries at some point. So you see, these public libraries do play a major role within the communities, serving both adults and also acting as places for children and kids in the K–12 grades, to come and do their homework and pursue other educational endeavors.

And yet, libraries do this on an incredibly small budget. The National Center for Education Statistics 1995 report on public libraries reveals that about 40 percent of public libraries have budgets of under $50,000. If you take that threshold up to $100,000 you find that a little over half of the public library systems have budgets under $100,000. Surprisingly enough, less than 10 percent have budgets over $1 million. And within those budgets, libraries are providing a wealth of services—not only print, but as you will see, more and more of them are beginning to provide access to the Internet.

A survey recently completed by the National Commission on Library and Information Sciences in Washington, D.C., just this year, found that currently 28 percent of public libraries offer public access to the Internet. That's up from about 12.7 percent in 1994. They further found that an additional 22 percent of the overall sampling said that they had plans to offer public access to the Internet by 1997, meaning that it looks like about 50 percent of public libraries could be offering public access to the Internet by 1997.

Furthermore, libraries that are serving population areas with less than 25,000 people are actually less likely to be connected than those in large urban areas, such as Boston. Bill Gates brought up this morning, the notion of the "haves" and "have nots." And as he said, there are various demographic characteristics. People in rural areas are much less likely to be connected than those in urban areas. Low income people are much less likely to be connected than people who have household incomes of, say, above $50,000. This is a societal problem that must be addressed.

Let me mention some other statistics about libraries and how they're offering access to the Internet. About 48 percent offer access offer through their electronic card catalogue. About 38 percent offer access through a local area network they have in their library. And another 14 percent (the remainder) use some other means to get hooked up to the Internet. The typical speeds you'll see, in terms of connectivity rates in the library: about 73 percent, the majority of them, have about a partial T1 line running at about 56 kilobits per second. A small percentage of them, 18 percent, have a T1 line, and 9 percent are using some other bandwidth.

Libraries are very cooperative creatures. And you will see that a number of them actually have come together to form what we call consortia to share resources. This is especially true in terms of automation resources. A lot of libraries will come together, including the North Boston Library Exchange, to try to facilitate purchasing bandwidth, purchasing training and support resources that can be shared among consortia members. And I've just listed a few. As you can see, they are in all parts of the country, and both in rural as well as in urban areas.

To wrap things up, I just want to talk about some of the American Library Association projects and some of the policy issues we are facing right now, that concern us. One project the ALA is involved in right now is helping the public to understand what this new Information Superhighway about. It's called ICONnect, and it's run by a division in the ALA, the American Association for School Libraries [AASL]. This program instructs students as well as teachers on how to use the Internet and be responsible netizens.

We're also involved with a number of corporate partners in other projects to help explore how we can better bring the Information Superhighway to underserved areas. One of these projects is a three-year partnership with MCI Corporation. MCI Library Link provides grants to assist libraries in training and other aspects of getting connected to the Information Superhighway. Grants have been made to public libraries in Albuquerque, New Mexico; Austin, Texas; Richmond,

Virginia; Sacramento, California; Memphis, Tennessee; and about 12 other public libraries to date.

Another major project we are running is with Microsoft. It's called "Libraries Online!" This is a $3 million pilot project that's running this year, to look at ways to develop innovative approaches for extending information technologies to underserved areas. There are nine library systems involved in this project. They include the Baltimore County Public Library; Brooklyn Public Library; the Public Library of Charlotte in Mecklenberg County in Charlotte, North Carolina; the Mississippi Library Commission; Pend Oreille County Public Library in Pend Oreille, in eastern Washington; the Los Angeles Public Library in Los Angeles, California; South Dakota State Library; the Seattle Public Library; and the Tucson-Pima Public Library in Tucson-Pima, Arizona. These libraries represent a mix of inner-city and rural areas. These are all exciting projects, as we find and learn more about ways that we can extend the on-ramps to the Information Superhighway to underserved communities.

The area I usually work in when I'm in Washington involves public policy. And there are a number of policy areas Betty has alluded to that affect the development of this Information Superhighway. Yes, there's a technology component to it. Yes, we need to be able to bring high bandwidth interactive capabilities out to the libraries, not just text capabilities. We need training, we need equipment. But we also need to address these other legislative and public policy issues before us, which determine what the rules of the road will be for the Information Superhighway.

The following list illustrates the policy issues affecting public libraries at this time:

- Universal service (see *http://www.ala.org/alaorg/ oitp/univserv.html*)

- Cyber-censorship—Communications Decency Act (see *http://www.cdt.org/ciec/*)

- Copyright (see *http://guess.worldweb/net/DFC/*)

- Government information

One of them is universal service. Betty mentioned the 1996 Telecommunications Act that was signed into law in February. Two provisions in that law directly affect libraries. One of them is universal service. In that universal service provision, it has been mandated that public libraries and school libraries receive discounts from telecommunications rates so that they can proceed to hook up and begin to deliver these services to their communities. This goes back to the notion of libraries as instruments of universal service, as institutions that provide their local communities access and availability to sophisticated information and telecommunications technologies. We have a web site up on this issue, if any of you are interested in finding out more about what we're doing there [*http://www.ala.org/*].

Having been passed into law, universal service rule making has now fallen to the FCC [Federal Communications Commission]. The FCC is dealing with this along with about 79 other rule making proceedings that resulted from passage of the 1996 Act. A Joint Board, composed of three FCC commissioners, four public utility commissioners from various states, and a consumer advocate who is on the Joint Board, will be making recommendations to the full FCC commission on rules to implement discounted rates for schools and libraries. This Joint Board recommendation is expected this November, with a final FCC ruling in May of 1997.

The other provision of the Telecommunications Act that affects libraries is the cyber-censorship issue, more commonly known perhaps as the Communications Decency Act. As Betty said, ALA is a lead plaintiff in a suit challenging the constitutionality of some of the provisions of this Act. To find more information about this suit visit the web site at:

http://www.ala.org/alanow/cda/lawsuit.html

The reason ALA and others have challenged the Telecom Act is because some of the language in this Act is much too broad in scope. The primary problem is with language that essentially criminalizes anybody (and this includes public libraries) that provides access to material considered "inde-

cent" in nature. And it's really a problem with that language of what is "indecent." What do I consider indecent? What do you consider indecent? How do we define indecent stuff? Particularly when you think of the role of the public library as a place where people can come in, that is a resource for people to use and explore and find whatever knowledge or information they seek. Given the language of this Act—given particularly the use of the word "indecent"—it did not, does not, provide guidance to the average citizen as to what kinds of materials might be prohibited, and we felt that the potential chilling effect of such a law could be really threatening to free speech, to the rights of all citizens to get onto the Internet and search for material that was constitutionally protected.

This issue is being pursued in the courts. And as Betty said, we expect, once the decision comes down within the next few days or by next week, that it will be kicked up to the Supreme Court, and we are likely to see more on this issue in the fall.

Another issue—one that was discussed this morning—deals with copyright. One of the issues the ALA is very much concerned with is copyright. The American Library Association has always maintained that creators of intellectual property certainly are entitled to have their original works protected under copyright. We must continue to preserve this balance between protecting the rights of creators of original work and the rights of users, which includes the rights of people who use libraries. And that is the doctrine commonly referred to as "fair use" of material, whether it be for scholarly research, for scholarly debate, or for researching a report for a sixth grade assignment. There has always been this balance within the intellectual property regime that says, yes, we'll grant to authors limited monopolies on their work, but at the same time we recognize that, as the Constitution says, "for true progress in the sciences and useful arts" to continue, you need to be able to have that information flow for legitimate purposes, and you need to allow people to make use of that information—again, for legitimate purposes—so that we can build on what we have learned, so that we can share ideas, so that we can share our learning.

Currently there is pending legislation on this in the Congress; in the House, it's HR2441, and in the Senate, it's S1284. These issues are being discussed and debated in Washington right now... and also internationally, I might add.

We sometimes forget that the Internet is really a global network, and that laws, whether they be Decency Act laws or copyright laws, when you apply them to this medium, apply beyond the national borders of the U.S. Your public library today now can take you anywhere, literally anywhere in the world, to find information. And these international harmonization issues constitute an underlying theme that runs through a lot of what we're talking about today, in terms of policies that will enable public libraries and enable our citizens to make the best use of this medium to meet their needs.

The final issue I want to talk a bit about is government information. Our president, Betty Turock, was in Washington not too long ago, testifying before Congress on this, because there is a proposal now, put forth by the Government Printing Office, to accelerate the electronic dissemination of federal government information. Again, this is something that the American Library Association has always supported, and has particularly advocated that there be sufficient resources behind any such effort. However, we feel there are some serious questions to be raised as to whether or not government agencies are sufficiently equipped right now to begin to disseminate information electronically. Nobody really knows how many agencies are prepared. The example I use is the U.S. Congress. At this time, about three-quarters of the Senate—and I think it's a little less than half the House—even make active use of their email or have web pages of some sort. When you're looking at that sort of indicator for how far the government itself may be automated, the question is whether or not two years is a realistic timetable to expect all agencies to disseminate government information *solely* electronically.

The second issue that comes up when you talk about government information and its dissemination is whether or not the distribution channels are ready. As I noted earlier, if we're lucky, by 1997, perhaps 50 percent of public libraries will be offering public access to the Internet. Will they have the kind of access they truly need? Will that be the high bandwidth, interactive types of access they need? What about the remaining 50 percent? If electronic media is the only way you can get access to a certain government document or a government speech, or some other critical piece of government information, are we saying we're going disenfranchise the rest of the population whose libraries still may not offer public Internet access? This is clearly not desirable. This is another issue that we are grappling with in Washington that has implications for the public, and institutions like the one that Arthur and Deirdre head up.

So these are the policy issues.

CURLEY: Thank you, Andrew. Andrew and the office he represents have brought enormous credibility to the efforts of the American Library Association in Washington. When ALA was founded more than a century ago, its mission statement was very simple: to encourage a love of reading. You can see that today there is a complex framework of regulation law that influences the ability of people to have unfettered access to information.

Now, from my colleagues on the national scene, I want to turn to a valued colleague on the local scene. Deirdre Hanley has been not only a pioneer in her own library but has been a strong champion of information services in the very kinds of consortial development to which Andrew referred.

HANLEY: Thank you, Arthur. Thank you to Andrew also, for referring to me as a practitioner and a specialist. I must tell you that I'm the library Director, I'm not a reference librarian. I really can't find my way out of a paper bag on the Internet. But my staff is actually quite adept, and that's what really matters.

I'm very honored to have the opportunity to talk about what we've done in my public library in Reading, Massachusetts, which is just 12 miles from here, 12 miles from the hub of the universe, as we very laughingly refer to ourselves. I'm sort of curious, if you wouldn't mind telling me, how many of you are librarians? Given the cost of this conference, I'd be very interested to know.

___: I'm from what used to be the Welfare Department. And also, I write for the area's black newspaper. And I paid my own way.

___: I'm a computer consultant who was asked by a public radio commentator in Minnesota if I would come and give her feedback, especially on public policy.

___: I work for the Centers for Disease Control and Prevention, the CDC, in Atlanta. One reason I'm here is an interest in libraries as a place for the public to get access to health information, particularly information about disease prevention and health promotion. It seems to me, that's a natural partnership.

HANLEY: Great. I think we all agree with that.

___: I work for the United States Information Agency, which of course has all of the same kinds of concerns as perhaps the public libraries, but in this case, abroad. So the "haves" and "have nots" is a question we deal with, and information dissemination issues.

HANLEY: Thank you. I hope that what I have to say about what goes on in my public library, which I think is pretty typical of how people use the public library and how they use the Internet in it, can be helpful to all of you, librarians and otherwise. (I have to tell you, I'm rather overwhelmed to be here talking about this, at such a prestigious conference.)

At the Reading Public Library, we don't feel that we're doing anything particularly exciting or risky. The Internet is a means of communication. It's a source of information that our customers want and need, so we provide it to them. It's really that simple. And I use the word "customer" very deliberately. Public libraries produce library services. That's our product. And it had better be a good product, or we will be out of business, just like any of the other businesses that are so well represented here at this conference.

I'm going to talk briefly about the impact of the Internet on the organization of the public library, on how it's helped us to do our job, on the finances of the public library, and what we've learned, based on how we have implemented it in Reading. I have about six points I want to make.

The Internet's Impact on Public Libraries

First of all, as Arthur said, the Internet is really an incredible opportunity for public libraries. We are, I think, the perfect institution to provide Internet access to the public. We have been called "the people's university." We encourage and enable lifelong learning, and our professional expertise is organizing and providing information to customers.

In Reading, it has made sense from the very beginning to our community that we be the gateway to the Internet. We positioned ourselves as the technology center in the town. We demonstrated that we knew about this technology stuff when other people didn't. And as technology has become more important and the Internet has become more mainstream, we've become viewed as a very critical service to the town. The result has been more credibility for us. It has translated directly into more money and increased political support.

To provide some context, Reading has always supported the library pretty well financially and has used it quite vigorously. Our annual circulation per capita is about fourteen. The state average is about seven. We answer about 40,000 reference questions a year. So you can see it's quite a busy place. And we take great pride in being out in front, on the bleeding edge, as they say. But despite this widespread community support, our budget was regularly cut during the bad times of the early '80s, and the town manager was never shy to tell me that while he was required by law to provide police, fire, and public education, he was not required to have a public library. I'm happy to say that he does not say this anymore. He now knows that the public library is the place where people come, where they expect to find the Internet that they can't afford to have in their homes. This is something that he knows that he needs to do if he wants to continue being town manager.

It was interesting to me yesterday to hear the session on "Press and the New Media" and to listen to Scott McNealy. There's a lot of talk about expanding the customer base for the Internet, identifying who is the audience. I would submit to you that the public library has the customer base. Everybody can have a library card. We know who the audience is. They come into our library every day, and they use the Internet in an incredible variety of ways. Sometimes they don't even know why they're using it, but they want to use it. They use it to find jobs. The latest thing is to go to web sites that companies have put up, to look at. That's the best way to find information about a company when you're job hunting. It's just incredible, the variety of ways that people use it.

Technology in Context

The second point that I would like to make is that I think that we must be very careful not to make a bigger deal of the Internet than it actually is. It's a source of information and it's a means of communication, and we should really view it in this context to make it work for us. The public library has to integrate the Internet into existing services and policies. Sometimes it's appropriate to use the Internet to answer a reference question, and sometimes it's easier to just look in the *World Book,* my own personal favorite reference book.

Sometimes it's better to use email to communicate with someone, and sometimes you should just make a phone call or walk out of your office into the next room and actually talk to somebody.

Public library staff need the proper training to have the comfort level with the Internet to know the difference.

When a customer calls the reference desk, as one recently did, wanting to know the price of a bond today that she had bought some time ago, I want my reference librarian to be ready, willing, and able to search Lycos, find the right web site, enter the purchase price of the bond and today's date, and initiate the computation. That was the perfect example. We could never have answered that reference question if we didn't have access— well, I shouldn't say "never," but it would have taken forever, and it took about five minutes, because this librarian was trained as a librarian. She was trained on the Internet. She was comfortable with it. She knew exactly what she had to do, and she did it. And she filled that need. The public library customer does not need to know how to search Lycos, and so forth. The library customer has a need, and just needs to articulate that need; then it's the librarian's job and expertise to figure out the best way to fill that need.

Quality in Context

Number three. There's a lot of talk about the reliability of information on the Internet, the quality control. And while I think this is certainly a valid concern, I think it's very disingenuous to say that it's a new concern, specific to the Internet. I think every medium has its flaws. I know that I read a lot of newspapers, and every day there seem to be a couple of paragraphs devoted to correcting errors in previous editions. So I think, again, we shouldn't make a bigger deal out of this kind of problem than it actually is. We teach classes to the public regularly, and one of the things that's an integral part of the class is reminding people to evaluate the information that they get. I think we've been doing that throughout our professional career, whether it be in a book or a video or on the Internet. And I think we are ideally suited to help our customers be smart shoppers and educated consumers.

Censorship

The pornography thing. This is my favorite Internet "red herring." Do we really think pornography or indecency is the sole property of the Internet? I don't think so. I happen to know because my customers have told me, in no uncertain terms, that I have plenty of pornography in my library, in all different formats, whether it be books or videos or CDs. In fact, videos are a bigger problem for us right now. There's something about a picture that's worth more than a thousand words to parents of teenagers, when they find out that their kids have watched *The Unbearable Lightness of Being* or *Henry and June* or some of these movies. And I think of what Andrew said, what is indecent? My idea of "indecent" is certainly not the same definition of "indecent" as some of these people who have been yelling at me in my office.

Don't get me wrong. This issue does make me very nervous, because I think the emphasis on pornography or indecency on the Internet is just going to highlight all the rest of the indecency that's available in the public libraries. I think it's a really slippery slope, once we start saying what's pornographic and what isn't. And I think that it's another example of why we can't treat the Internet any differently than any other resource. Once we start filtering Internet sites, what are we going to filter next?

Somebody gave the example at one conference that one library was filtering out anything that had the word "breast" in it—which is fine for kids. On the other hand, for the woman who's trying to do research on breast cancer, this is kind of a big problem. She's not going to find the information she needs.

Promise versus Threat

The most exciting aspect of the Internet to me is that it really tears down the walls of the library. It really *does* create a virtual library. And I do not feel threatened at all by the Internet. I view it as this incredible opportunity. I view it as a way for us to provide more service to our customers, greater access to resources. It's really just a breathtaking improvement in service. And for us to not embrace it fully is to not fulfill our responsibility as professionals.

We have a web home page [*http://www.netcasters.com/rpl/library.html*], and we're using it to answer reference questions. People can submit reference questions. They can ask to renew books. They can join the Friends, send money. (We accept Mastercard and Visa.) They can reserve museum passes. We have a homework bulletin board, where kids or parents can check on what the latest assignments are. I think we just have to look at it, as I say, as another means of communication for people.

There are a few problems, as Andrew has talked about. Generally, we have the Internet available through our consortium, which does not provide graphical access. We've had to go out on our own in order to provide that, because that is what people want. But fortunately, in Massachusetts, the state library agency has a plan, and we hope the legislature is going to fund it. That will provide full graphical access, sort of the underpinning for all members of the library consortia. So that will be a big improvement for everybody.

The Paradox of Progress

I think there's a paradox, which is that librarians are afraid of change. I think that often librarians become librarians because they want to avoid change. Of course, they also become librarians because they want to help people and they want to create order. But we really have built our reputations as, I think, preservers of the past. And I think our society is extremely focused on change right now. It's in love with change for its own sake. And I think that we have to be really determined to shed this sort of "retro" image and just embrace the possibility of facilitating this change as much as we can. We're information professionals. We organize it, we synthesize it, we evaluate it. I don't know what skills are really more critical in this Information Age.

Finally, I would just like to say that I think there's plenty of money to go around, plenty of money to be made from the Internet. And I would hope that a small portion of it could just be sort of siphoned off to support public libraries having the right kind of access to the Internet so that we can provide that people, and our society, continue to progress. Thank you.

CURLEY: Thank you, Deirdre, for a very meaningful perspective on the role of the Internet in libraries. What you do that is so special is treat the Internet as though it is not some bandwagon passing through town, but something that needs to be put at the core of what libraries are all about.

Questions & Answers

Q: *Can the ALA advocate for additional federal funding if, when the U.S. government requires, for example, Social Security information to be disseminated online instead of in local offices?*

HANLEY: It would seem to me that the ALA can advocate for additional federal funding for the Internet, no matter what. Wouldn't you say, Betty?

TUROCK: Yes, I would certainly say so. In fact, the legislative policy and information policy agenda of the American Library Association is set pretty much by our members. But I think your question is, if the library is a disseminator of information or a receiver and transmitter of information for the Social Security system, should we then be reimbursed in some way, as that transmitter? And indeed, that is one of the things which could be approached.

Q: *If everyone had ready online access to everything in the Library of Congress, would there still remain a need for local public libraries?*

MAGPANTAY: I'll go first. The answer is yes. One is the roles of the librarian is as a knowledge navigator that people can go to, not only to ask an expert about information, but also to get access to those facilities that are out there. Yesterday I heard one panelist quote that only about one percent of the available information worldwide is actually in digital format.[*] You have to argue about how soon everything will be converted to digital format.

Even if it were, you would still need places where people could go to talk to people, like the experienced people Deirdre has at her library, to guide them through getting access to more advanced types of telecommunication systems and information systems. This is going to be a constantly evolving environment.

You could argue that the library fulfills other roles in society as well, as community centers and other things.

TUROCK: It's interesting to me to see that in the summit [conference] we had in Rancho Mirage, where people were experts from all walks of life except librarianship, not one of them suggested the library as a place that would disappear in the Information Age. It's always in the librarians' literature that I see that debate going on. The rest of the country seems to have a romance with the public library, which we really need to translate into an active advocacy for the library. The arguments or concerns about the library seem to be more within our profession than outside of it.

The idea that everything will ever be digital is not cost effective, in business terms. It is not cost effective today, and it probably won't be tomorrow, to download a 415-page book. Publishers are making money because, in fact, books are a good format in which to store information. So electronic information has a different purpose, a different perspective.

Q: *What coordination exists between the Internet and libraries in the United States and schools?*

CURLEY: The truth is that there is no single national pattern, although there are hopes along these lines.

I mentioned earlier that in Boston we've been able to link every single public school in the city to the central computer in our library, which gives students and teachers access through the schools—not just to our own bibliographic databases but through our gateway into the Internet.

However, the sad news is that this wasn't accomplished with public money. Boston Public

---

[*] Willy Chiu, in the session "Opening the Gate: Increasing Content of the Internet" also in this track.

Library is a big and visible institution and we were able to get a major grant from Raytheon, as well as matching funds from NYNEX. With this grant, we were able to wire all of the schools.

I've used the Boston example not so much to brag about what we're doing in Boston, but to demonstrate that it had to be done with special private funds, and that this cannot be the pattern we rely upon elsewhere. In the legislation we're attempting to put through in Massachusetts, there are specific provisions for trying in every community to bring all of the schools online, into connection with the public library. And it certainly is central to what we've been trying to do nationally.

HANLEY: Massachusetts has the distinction of being 51st in the nation in the funding of school libraries. In Reading, for example, we have started a pilot project with one of our middle schools to make it sort of a branch of the public library. One of the big benefits that will produce is that they will be part of our consortium and will have access through the Internet to the databases the consortium can provide to all of the members, because they can buy in quite a large volume. So I think the Internet should improve a lot of school libraries, at least in Massachusetts, if we can manage to organize ourselves properly.

About the Speakers

ARTHUR CURLEY is the Director of the Boston Public Library. He was formerly Deputy Director of the Research Libraries of the New York Public Library and Deputy Director of the Detroit Public Library. He has directed libraries in Massachusetts, Illinois, New Jersey, and Ohio; served on the staffs of the Boston Public Library and the Widener Library at Harvard; and has taught management in the graduate library schools at Rutgers and the University of Michigan. Mr. Curley is the founding editor of the quarterly journal *Collection Building: Studies in the Development and Effec-*

tive Use of Library Resources, and the author of numerous books and articles.

DEIRDRE HANLEY has been the Director of the Reading Public Library in Massachusetts since 1991. She was previously Director in Swampscott and Amesbury, MA, and Assistant Director in Winchester, MA. After graduating from the Simmons College Graduate School for Library and Information Science in 1979, Deirdre dabbled in various types of libraries, including special and academic, before discovering that her true vocation was public libraries. Her first public library job was in 1981 as Beverly Farms Branch Librarian in Beverly, MA.

J. ANDREW MAGPANTAY is Director of the American Library Association's Office for Information Technology Policy in Washington, D.C., which was established in June, 1994. This office provides policy development and analysis for the ALA's legislative and public policy agenda in the areas of technology and telecommunications. Mr. Magpantay has held positions as special assistant for innovative projects and planning at the University of California, as computer systems manager at Earl Gregg Swemm Library at the College of William and Mary, and as visiting librarian at the William R. Perkins Library at Duke University.

BETTY J. TUROCK, librarian, library educator, and library advocate, is immediate past president of the American Library Association (ALA), the oldest and largest library association in the world. Currently, she is a professor in the School of Communication, Information and Library Studies at Rutgers University. Ms. Turock has held management posts across the U.S. in public, school, and academic libraries. She has also served as senior advisor in the U.S. Department of Education, office of Educational Research and Improvement Library Programs. A frequent lecturer and consultant to libraries, Turock is the author of more than 60 publications and is the founding editor of *The Bottom Line: A Financial Magazine for Libraries*.

CHAIR: SIDNEY VERBA
Carl H. Pforzheimer University Professor
Director of the Harvard University Library
Harvard University

Education

THE INTERNET IN THE CLASSROOM

MODERATOR: Linda Roberts

PANELISTS: Paul Reese
Margaret Riel
Colleen Wheeler

THE MARKET FOR EDUCATIONAL APPLICATIONS OF THE INTERNET

MODERATOR: Martha S. Wiske

PANELISTS: Geoffrey Fletcher
Denis Newman
Roger Rogalin

HARVARD NEWS
CONFERENCE ON THE INTERNET AND SOCIETY
May 29-31, 1996   Cambridge, MA

Net in the Classroom: Teachers Provide Access, Despite Sense That They're Tilting at Windmills

By Eileen K. McCluskey

Seventh-graders in the Olympia, Washington, public schools are using the Web to research and present data about the health of local waterways. Elementary school students at the Ralph Bunche School in New York's inner city are publishing their own newspaper, both in print and online.

At the same time as kids across America demonstrate their keen interest in applying themselves to Net-based learning on every imaginable subject, teachers are shelling out their own dollars to buy tables to replace desks, so as to fit the computers—also purchased out of pocket—in the classroom. Educators also find themselves wiring their schools for the Internet, and maintaining the technology, on top of full time teaching responsibilities.

Initiatives to bring the Net into public schools are out there, but as the teachers at yesterday's "Internet in the Classroom" panel discussion pointed out, there is much to be done before this technology is in the hands of the nation's future, its children. The panel focused on the technological picture in the public school system's grades K-12.

Despite a sense of tilting at windmills as expressed by the panel's educators, they're taking the initiative to open the Net to their students. Paul Reese, Computer and Technology Coordinator at the Ralph Bunche Middle School (online at *http://ralphbunche.rbs.edu:70/*), glowed with pride as he spoke of "attempts to involve the students…in articulating, in their own words, what they're doing."

Sometimes the learning, Reese said, doesn't start with the large ideas. "Our school has a local area network, and every student has his or her own email account."

Reese noted that the students tend first to email their pals in the same class, then move on to reaching out into the wider web world.

There are more than 3,000 schools on the Web, according to Reese, and the networking possibilities, both kid-to-kid and teacher-to-teacher, was an idea that sparked the speakers.

Colleen Wheeler, a music teacher from Wheaton College, said "The most important thing is that you can grab people and people can grab you." Another benefit of the Internet, she noted, "is the global perspective" students can gain. "Students from all over the world are writing each other."

Wheeler also said, of her own use of the technology, that "Falling into the Internet meant finding colleagues. It's an apprenticeship sort of culture—you mentor me with the understanding that I'll mentor others."

Wheeler spoke of her students' email relationships with composers who, through the Net, helped them to shape their musical pieces: "It was amazing how close these students felt to [them]." She said her role shifted when she used the Net as an educational tool. "I was no longer a judge; I was a collaborator," she said.

On the subject of whether the nation's educational administrators are willing to finance the Net's migration into public schools, Linda Roberts,

Director of the Office of Educational Technology in the U.S. Department of Education, said 50 percent of all public schools had some kind of Internet access, but only 9 percent had any meaningful classroom access. "I think we will see, by this October, probably close to 65 to 70 percent of schools [hooked up to the Net], with classroom access up to close to 25 percent. This is really quite significant," she said.

Yet when addressing a number of audience-generated questions about whether resources, especially those of a financial nature, are being committed to bringing Internet technology to our public school students, Roberts admitted that "the financing is complex."

The "single most popular approach," she noted, "is to pass a bond referendum." This remark was greeted by groans and laughter from the attendees.

Roberts said the "problem is it's a blip," a short term influx of dollars with no long term commitment. "We now see demands for per pupil allocation," she continued, but did not present a picture of how such demands may be met.

Reese noted that "keeping the school wired is one of the biggest headaches," and "maintaining the [Net's] environment can and should be a full time job."

She said, "almost all the money we have comes from grants," and, to general murmurs of audience sympathy, noted that they try to "survive between grants. Over ten years, we've spent about $500,000 on the infrastructure."

Roberts estimated it will cost "$50 billion to bring schools up to snuff," including infrastructure, hardware, and teacher training, with $10 billion annually for upkeep.

"How do we help make it happen all around the country?" Roberts asked. "This is one of the real public policy challenges."

Education

May 30, 1996

The Internet in the Classroom

MODERATOR: Linda Roberts
PANELISTS: Paul Reese
Margaret Riel
Colleen Wheeler

ROBERTS: My colleagues and I are very pleased to be here because we truly believe that the Internet and advanced telecommunications are critical for all of our educational institutions and for learning in society. If we have any lessons to be drawn from both schools' and higher education's experience with new technology, it's that if we don't think about learning, if we don't think about what our education goals are first and foremost, we miss some very, very important opportunities.

With that in mind, I think President Neil L. Rudenstine's address gave us a framework for thinking about this session and thinking about what we want the future to be, in terms of the use of the Internet and other interactive technology. But as the moderator, I'd like to set the stage for the remarks to come.

Our goal in this session is to give you a sense of the use of interactive and networking technologies in our schools, in settings that are too often criticized for a lack of innovation and for the inability to change. Schools around the country have literally been under siege in terms of trying to respond to the changing needs in our communities, the changing demographics of our populations, and trying to do a better job but oftentimes being reviled for a lack of progress. In fact the truth is that in many schools—particularly in the

sites that we are going to talk about today—some truly remarkable things are being done.

Let me give you some figures that I think are really quite extraordinary. When I came to the Department of Education in 1993, the first question I asked in terms of how do we set policy and programs for technology was, "What do we know? What's the status of schools' access to technology?" And while we had a clear sense of the number of computers in our schools, we had very little sense of whether or not networking technology was available and used.

So in 1994, the National Center for Education Statistics surveyed K–12 schools across the country and, surprisingly, we learned that 35 percent of all public schools in the United States had some access to the Internet. I say "surprisingly" because nobody expected the penetration rate to be that high. That was the good news. The bad news was that only about three percent of classrooms in these schools really had access that would make these resources useful for teaching and learning. Furthermore, as you can see in Figure 1, access to the Internet is not equal.[*]

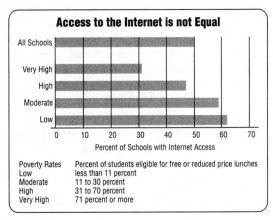

Figure 1

In 1995, we went out again. We decided it was very important to continue tracking this data and what we learned was that the number of schools with access had grown to 50 percent. And while

---

[*] Source of the figure data: U.S. Department of Education, National Center for Education Statistics, Advanced Telecommunications in the U.S. Public Elementary and Secondary Schools, 1995 (U.S. Government Printing Office, February 1996).

I'm not usually someone to predict what will happen next, based on my visits around the country and on state and local level investments in infrastructure, I predict that when we conduct the survey in October, 1996, school and classroom access will have increased again.*

The really important question is, Does it matter? Are we using these capabilities to advance learning? To change the way in which students think about the world? Are students in fact improving their skills, their most fundamental skills of reading, writing, research, and problem solving? 80 percent of the public believes that computers and new technologies are basics and should be integrated into the curriculum. The public is ahead of the curve of some of our educators and their thinking.

Let me begin this session by describing what's going on with students in the Olympia, Washington, public schools. There are students in elementary and secondary schools gathering data online, searching interactive libraries, talking to experts, and creating their own electronic publication and World Wide Web sites. The educational goals of this district and, in fact, the educational goals of the students are being reinforced by the use of technology. In addition, these students have become mentors to their teachers and to their parents. This is a district that has solved its professional development problem largely by tapping into the knowledge and the expertise that seems to come much more rapidly to the young than to the experienced. So it's a very, very exciting place and it's a very exciting model.

That's the good news. The bad news is this is that this school is an "island of excellence." Districts 30 miles or 3,000 miles away are largely unaffected by the kinds of things that have happened in Olympia. And this is one of the real public policy challenges that we face as a nation. We see lots of innovation, lots of exciting ideas, and the real challenge is, how do we help make it happen all around the country? How do we move beyond the isolated examples?

I believe this conference can play an important role. We need to make clear where technology makes a difference in student learning, how it can support teaching and learning, and how it can support professional development of teachers. We also need to understand what directions are most promising, what cautions must be considered, and what we need to do next.

So let me turn the session over now to **PAUL REESE**, someone I have known for almost a decade. I visited his classroom at the Ralph Bunche Elementary School and was truly astounded by the work that he was doing. You need to know where Paul's school is situated. You look out of his classrooms windows and you look right down into the public housing project that surrounds the school. If we want to think about how the technology enables us to literally go beyond the reaches of our community, I think this is one of the most important things that Paul has been able to do with his students.

REESE: Thank you, Linda. Yesterday morning I had no scheduled classes, but typical of the day, there were kids in and out of my room, and last minute changes to some reports that they were doing on Mexico. Perhaps a little exasperated, I finally said to two or three fifth grade girls, "Will you please be quiet? I've got to finish the notes on this presentation at Harvard." And one of the girls says, "What's Harvard?" (I'm not sure whether I should tell the rest of this) and the girl sitting next to her replies, "Oh, I think it's something like Yale. I'm going to go to Yale and study law!"

Let me begin with some of the notes I was trying to prepare during those interruptions. I'm a school teacher. For 15 years, I taught fourth grade at the Ralph Bunche Elementary School in central Harlem. I was a good classroom teacher. I learned fairly successful classroom skills so that I could manage my students. That made my principal very happy because it meant that they were

---

* By the time this publication is printed, the Department of Education will have released the findings of this survey. See *http://www.ed.gov/Technology/*.

orderly in the halls and there were not too many eruptions into his office. They also did fairly well on standardized tests. That made my principal even happier.

I almost quit teaching 15 years ago. I was professionally dead. I was isolated. I had been in that classroom with my students, whom I loved dearly, although was admittedly sometimes happy to say goodbye to in June. But there was no more energy. I hadn't had a challenge to learn or change my techniques during most of those 15 years.

Since then, through a number of wonderful opportunities, I began using technology. A lot of it I learned myself. I locked myself in a closet, learned how to use the computer, and it's changed my professional life. I feel very strongly that the technology offers a great potential for communication—the possibility to give teachers, as well as students, the opportunity to design and control their own learning environment—and, perhaps, even to revolutionize our schools. (Although I may have some caveats on that as I go on.)

The Internet is getting lots of press these days and, certainly, the people at this conference don't have to be told about that. A number of very slick commercials by computer companies and telecommunications giants are appearing on public television and on the commercial television networks as advertisements, painting rosy pictures of a Brave New World where children are using the computers to talk with world leaders and great scientists and assumedly preparing themselves to assume those roles as they step into the world.

I hope I can give you a picture of what goes on at the Ralph Bunche School. There are lots of wonderful things there. But I think we need to be careful about assuming that those pictures prepared by the computer companies and the telecommunications companies give an accurate picture of what goes on in schools. Sometimes the learning, especially at the level of student I work with—third, fourth, fifth, and sixth graders—isn't the large ideas, isn't going out on the network and getting information from somewhere across the world. Sometimes the communication takes place right within the walls of our school.

Like the school Linda just referred to, our school has a local area network, where all the children have their own portfolios and access to the tools, word processor, and database. We start our fifth graders using some spreadsheet applications, some computer programming. Every student in the part of the school where I work has an individual email account. Our school had the very first K–12 goal ever, over four years ago on the Internet, where we published our school newspaper, which I'll talk about in a minute. We had probably the third K–12 web server ever set up in cyberspace.

The story about it is one that's fun to me because it wasn't my decision to set it up. A student of mine, Hammadu Diori—a marvelous young boy whose social skills are sometimes not up to his computer skills—met somebody at a conference who showed him how to run CU-SeeMe, and he pestered me to get it running on one of my computers. He then met somebody in Norway one Saturday morning who mentioned that he had a home page, and showed him that it was running on his Apple SE. That day, before he left, Hammadu had started the Ralph Bunche home page [*http://ralphbunche.rbs.edu:70/*]. (He was 13 at the time.)

Now the other two K–12 servers were started by universities for their schools. So at one level, Hammadu probably has the distinction of having started the first K–12 server by a K–12 student. (I think: the Internet world is very competitive, and if I posted that, we might get challenged on it.)

We have a long tradition of using the computers for tools, and the publication of our newspaper started long before I even had heard the word Internet. But it was a very natural extension for us to publish the work that was being done by our students first on our school Gopher, and now our web server, in addition to publishing it in hard copy.

We have tried very hard to make sure that our newspaper publication challenges the students to find their own voice. This can be frustrating because sometimes as adults, we know that there are perhaps better and more sophisticated ways of doing things. But encouraging students to explore has always been central to the way we've used the Internet. So one of the objections I have to many of the slick commercials I talked about before is that they have adult perspectives on what's important to children and superimpose them and try to say that "this is education."

I could give lots of examples of students using the Internet to get information. Yesterday, just before I caught the plane here, a fourth grade class was looking up information about animals and found out that the horn of the rhinoceros is made with keratin, something like the hair on their head.

Another story illustrates how important it is that students begin to own this electronic space. Fernando, one of the many students in our after school program (that often runs until six o'clock and is staffed by volunteers), has a bit of bravado, and is occasionally a bit of a bully. When I saw him headed to the door in tears, apparently ready to leave the building, I intercepted him to try to find out what the matter was. It appears he'd left his computer with friends for a few minutes, telling them to watch it while he went to the bathroom. When he'd returned, they had opened his email and read some of his correspondence with other classmates.

He was deeply hurt and touched and confused and angry with his friends about it. Of course it was a wonderful opportunity to talk about the value of correspondence and the fact that writing, just like our baseball cards and everything of importance, belongs to people. And the boys who had looked at his mail listened carefully, apologized for it, and we emphasized the importance of respecting other people's property. It also says something about how we begin to develop the sense that students value their own writing and value their own ideas and value their own communications.

Very often the successes at Ralph Bunche School are very small ones and I think that's symbolic of them. They often don't require Internet access, although that access to the wider world is always there when they need it. Ninety-five percent of the mail in the fourth grade is exchanged between students and their classmates, often with students sitting at the same computer right next to each other. Very short. But I often compare it to how young children use the telephone. We have to learn how to talk about age appropriate subjects with our grandparents, parents, and other members of our community.

ROBERTS: I urge you all to get on the Web and not only visit the Ralph Bunche School, but the more than 3,000 school web pages that are up and running and doing wonderful things.[*]

Let me just tell you an interesting story. When I was at the Ralph Bunche school last September, I brought along Peter Max, the noted artist. We were doing a "back-to-school" visit. And Peter, who uses technology in so much of his work now, was just astounded at what these students were doing. He was convinced that these kids were really different, "wired from birth."

That morning when I got on the Internet to send a message to another school that was linked to the Ralph Bunche School, the student who was at my side watching me said, "You know, you've got a mistake in your message." And I said, "Is that important?" She said, "You're not just writing to yourself, you're writing to the world." When we work to get kids to think about their writing, having a "public voice" clearly makes a difference to them. In this new public arena, the students understand what's important.

So with that, let me turn to **COLLEEN WHEELER**. Colleen is a former classroom teacher with a new baby of her own, who may be the youngest citizen in the United States with her own World Wide Web page.

WHEELER: Good morning. I'm going to quickly launch my web page [*http://www.wheatonma.edu/*

---

[*] See Web66 International Registry of School Web Sites (Stephen E. Collins, University of Minnesota, *http://web66.coled.umn.edu/*).

Temp/Harvard/agenda.html] and then introduce myself. I've been a music educator for, well, a little more than ten years and I'm going to focus my remarks on what went on in my classroom in a junior-senior high school in a suburb close to Boston. I've spent a couple of years developing web sites for educators in the state of Massachusetts, and I'm now at Wheaton College developing educational resources and their intranet. But, again, I will focus my remarks today on teaching and learning with technology and the Internet in the K–12 realm.

I stumbled upon the Internet for many of the reasons that Paul mentioned early in his remarks. I was really feeling a bit burned out and even a little bit bored. I loved my students and I loved my classroom and I loved my colleagues, but it wasn't quite enough.

In 1987, I met a musician who recommended MIDI [Musical Instrument Digital Interface] technology to me. It was brand new technology. It allowed me to connect a computer to a synthesizer and, later on, to many other devices (including a Nintendo Power Glove, which I'll tell you a little bit about). Using these devices revolutionized the way I thought about both teaching and learning.

Traditionally, we teach music upside down. We start with visual systems and "train" our students to turn them into sound. Students interpret other people's work. We train them to be performers, and, often, performers only. Creativity is something that is left for the future. (You know, maybe some day, as an octogenarian, you will be good enough to compose—you'll have what it takes when you've spent many hours by candlelight writing tiny notes.)

Well, this isn't correct, but it is what goes on in many of our music classrooms. And it was certainly what I was doing. Computer technology helped me turn things around: students could work first from a sonic environment. They could compose for one another, they could ask "what if" questions, they could perform a musical idea on a synthesizer and then see its notation.

Students that walked into my classroom not knowing how to read traditional music were not necessarily at a disadvantage. We invented our own symbol systems. We experimented with MIDI's editable, electronic "piano roll," where notes were indicated in an approachable way, much the way chant was.

And then, there was the Internet...

I'll give you one illustration of how the Internet became very important to us; it made crucial primary source material available anywhere. A colleague and I were teaching a hands-on art/music course. We were exploring the Middle Ages, and the students were asked to create an illuminated manuscript, which was to be representative of their lives, and which was to include the beautiful gem-like colors we *thought* we had shown them.

One student, John, came in the next day with a black and white and gray rendition. And we said, "John, what happened to the beautiful colors?" And he said, "It was the Dark Ages. They didn't have any color."

Well, something went wrong somewhere: he definitely had "dark" in his mind and nothing we had done had corrected that impression. So we went back and looked at the books in our library and, sure enough, the reproductions were nothing to write home about. They were yellow and very old. Nothing to get excited about.

So, we jumped on the Internet and headed over to the Vatican Music Library where we found a 15th century music manuscript, which I have here for you to see [*http://lcweb.loc.gov/exhibits/vatican/music09.jpg*]. This did the trick! The students saw the intense blues and beautiful greens first-hand and it made an impression. And now when John thinks of the Middle Ages or the Dark Ages, I hope that he thinks about these vibrant colors too. I hope he thinks about stained glass windows and light.

The Internet also offers a unique opportunity for relationships with people. A lot of people think of the Internet as a big information bank, where you can zip around and grab data. Well, that's true. But the most important thing you can grab is people and people can grab you. You can grab subject matter experts. You can talk to composers who are very willing to help you with your work. Soon, we were emailing student compositions back and forth to professional composers and to student composers all around the world.

Eventually we realized that our email/pen pal relationship had become a drafting process. John Lamar, a composer from the Berklee College of Music, might write back to an aspiring student composer, Cynthia, and say, "This looks like a really interesting piece. But why did you orchestrate it this way? Why did you chose this timbre, as opposed to that timbre?" And zip, the email goes back to Cynthia and she thinks about it. She might make some changes and she might send the changes back to John. This sort of thoughtful give and take went on every day and I was amazed at how close my students felt to people outside the classroom.

The surprising thing for me was that my role changed dramatically. I was not a judge anymore, I was a collaborator, I was a resource. My students were writing for other people and I had experiences and insights that they found genuinely useful. And, as mentioned earlier, there's probably no greater motivator for student writing than to know that another human being knows you only through your written word or creative work. It's very important to students that they craft their work just perfectly before they send it out. They begin to understand that a piece of music or art doesn't just happen: it's a process that takes time and thought, an evolution of ideas.

Eventually some of the "virtual" composers were so close to my students that they came to our school and spent time working with them. One man, John Lamar (whom I mentioned), brought a Nintendo Power Glove along. This Power Glove was one of the most amazing things I'd ever seen in my life. John put his glove on several students who had no interest, they thought, in sound and expressive gesture. And as they moved their hand through space, a synthesizer was tracking the position of their hand and the movement of their fingers, and translating that into sound.

You could tell by the expression on their faces that these kids were immersed suddenly, and totally, in a sonic realm. There was no notation in the way. They were inside a sound world and they were conducting. (I didn't tell them that's what they were doing, but that's certainly what they were doing.) It was amazing! And it would have been impossible to experience any other way.

John and I are hoping that we can take the Nintendo Power Glove idea and develop some real-time, interactive composition over the Network. Technically, it's a little tough right now but sound technology is catching up quickly. I know David Reider at BBN has been working on the World Band Project, which is doing similar sorts of things. The Internet can make all kinds of collaboration a reality.

It can also connect disciplines. Another composer and artist came out from the Massachusetts College of Art. When Neil Leonard arrived, he had "chaos theory" under his arm, ready to go. We had a math class come down to check this chaos theory out, and we created artwork and music based on mathematical formulas. Suddenly math formulas took on a life of their own, and kids were asking questions about sound and structure that probably wouldn't have occurred to them in math class or band rehearsal.

The Internet encourages cultural exchange. There's a man in the United Kingdom who is a clarinet player; for years he has been collecting folk music from all over the world and categorizing it. He organizes it according to key signature or time signature, genre, and country of origin. Since folk music is one of the greatest sources there is for composers, we blasted over to the United Kingdom, and we were able to look at and listen to some of this folk music online. [See *http://celtic.stanford.edu/pub/tunes/RRTunebook/*].

An example is the "Sweets of May" [*http://celtic.stanford.edu/pub/tunes/RRTunebook/RRtunes/02/00000252.gif*]. One of the students' projects was: find a folk song, learn how to play it, memorize it, make it part of yourself, and then incorporate it into a larger piece, into a broader musical idea. Either use it as a theme and variation source or perhaps take it and orchestrate it. And the kids were able to do this fairly easily, and enjoyed it tremendously, using MIDI technology and the Internet.

The Internet connects people and cultures through students' creative work. There is a student newspaper in South Africa called *Grab* [*http://www.ru.ac.za/departments/journ/grab.html*] that illustrates this. Certainly Paul's work at Ralph Bunche school is another example of how students from all over the world are publishing. And at the Buckman School in Oregon [*http://buckman.pps.k12.or.us/buckman.html*], second graders are writing and publishing haikus to a global audience. It's very easy, with a click of a mouse, to be in almost any culture now, enjoying creative work. And this certainly enhances what we're able to do in a classroom.

For me, falling into the Internet meant finding colleagues who were asking the same questions I was asking, people that were able to give me some feedback, some support, some resources, and a very large community. Certainly in those days, the Internet's culture was based upon teaching and learning through apprenticeship. Online colleagues said, "I'm here to help you" with the understanding that you would then return the favor by mentoring others.

And that's a final lesson that the Internet can help us teach—a habit of contribution—a culture of giving; not just taking. What we try to model for our students today is that 50 percent, at least, of what you do should contribute to the growth and resources we call the Internet.

ROBERTS: At this point, let me turn the panel over to **MARGARET RIEL**. When I was at the Congressional Office of Technology Assessment, Margaret was one of the experts that we consistently turned to as a voice of reason and objectivity and, most important, as someone who was pioneering use of the Internet and evaluating what actually made a difference in the classroom.

She has continued her work in this field and has put together a superb paper on "The Future of Networking" for the Department of Education. These papers and others are online.

RIEL: Thank you, Linda. That means a lot to me. Many people, including Bill Gates in his talk yesterday, describe the Internet as "a goldmine of information." But the truth is that even our poorest schools are rich in disconnected information. There are critics who claim that the Internet itself or the prospect of wiring our school children to the Internet is the "snake oil of the '90s." Silicon snake oil[*] leads to a future that doesn't compute.[†]

> *We try to model for our students…that 50 percent of what you do should contribute to the growth and resources we call the Internet.*

While these critics play an important role in alerting us to the possibility of negative aspects of the Internet, they often miss the most important point. The real power of the Internet for schools is not the delivery of information. I have a cartoon drawing showing what some people think of when they think of wiring kids to the Internet. But the Internet is not about isolation, it is fundamentally about communication. As we heard from Steven McGeady this morning, the Internet can link people in contexts in which we use information. It connects information to people and it provides a way to share the value that communities place on information. These communities can be both local and global at the same time.

---

[*] The book *Silicon Snake Oil*, by Clifford Stoll, discusses fears of what is wrong with having students work with technology [*http://www.obs-europs.de/obs/english/books/nn/bdsto105.htm*].

[†] Steve Talbott is another place to find a negative image of the future of schools with technology. Read his book: *The Future Does Not Compute* (O'Reilly & Associates, 1995), or look at his online newsletter on the Web called Netfuture [*http://www.ora.com/people/staff/stevet/netfuture/index.html*].

Education is also primarily about communication. Schools are places where we try to pass on what we know, what we value, do, and think, to the next generation. Today I will focus on the way the Internet extends this mission of schools. Neil L. Rudenstine did a great job yesterday of describing how the Internet is extending student learning at the university level. I will try to do the same for primary and secondary education. I'm going to describe the changes and challenges of Net learning in terms of the following:

- Who teaches? Who is involved in the educational process?

- What is taught? How is the classroom curriculum designed?

- Where does teaching take place? What are the places and spaces of learning?

Who Teaches?

In the time of slate boards and chalk, the teacher, and what the teacher knew, was the primary source of information for classroom students. As textbooks became widely available, they augmented the teacher's knowledge. Curriculum packages, lab materials, posters, filmstrips, radio, television, phones, videotapes, and finally computer programming mediated a form of indirect interaction between adults and students in classrooms. While many forms of technology—radio and television, for example—did not have the predicted revolutionary impact on the classroom,[*] they did serve as mediators, bringing more human resources into the classrooms as resources. With each new form of telecommunications—communication over distances—more people have turned their attention to education. In the classrooms of today, it is now possible for people around the globe to play important roles in classroom education. They do not have to leave work to be a part of the classroom life.

Some of these interactions involve the development of a long term relationship between "telementors" and students, while others are short "Ask an Expert" exchanges. Judi Harris's Electronic Emissary Project, for example, matches a specific expert to work electronically with a classroom of students for one year. The Education Development Center [EDC] has launched efforts to match female high school students of physics with practicing female physicists. The goal of this project is to provide talented students access to role models who can help them chart their own path in what is frequently a male-dominated context for learning. "Writers in Residence" is a partnership created by Trevor Owen in Canada in which professional writers work with classes to provide comments and guidance on student writing. Colleen's description of composers working with music students provides another example of this form of telementoring.

There have been ongoing "Ask an expert" opportunities on the Internet: "AskEric" librarians, "Ask a mathematician," "Ask a geologist," "Volcanist Online," and "Science Question and Answers," are some examples of this type of short term exchange.[†]

Teachers and students in distant locations are also providing a source of expertise to enrich classroom learning. Sharing their local expertise on community issues and current events, historical periods or events, geographic formations or patterns, and a range of science topics related to their physical environment, is a way to help extend student understanding in new directions. Networks help facilitate the formation of groups to teach and learn from one another. Examples of cross-classroom collaboration can be found in the Learning Circles and in project conferences on networks such as I*EARN. Teaching is a very powerful way to learn; therefore placing students in the role of teaching other students is one of the best ways for them to understand a topic or issue.

---

[*] See Larry Cuban's book, *Teachers and Machines: Classroom Use of Technology Since the 1920s,* for descriptions of how technology that was to revolutionize classrooms ended up in classroom closets. (New York: Teachers College Press, 1986.)

[†] Students can send "Ask an expert" questions to *http://www.askanexpert.com/p/ask.html.* Teachers will find "AskEric" a place where they can have any question answered.

Finally there have been a number of contests aimed at increasing student collaborations with people who would not have otherwise been a part of classroom instruction. ThinkQuest and Cyberfair are two excellent examples of how a contest can motivate school community ties. These contests reward collaboration rather than individual excellence. Cyberfair encourages partnerships between students and their local community organizations and worldwide contacts to create new spaces on the Internet to "Share and Unite." ThinkQuest turns students around the country into teachers with the Web as their podium, blackboard, and microphone. The quest is for students to teach other students through the development of a web site. In these cases and others, the contest organizers are using the contest as a way to reach and teach students in new ways.

My experience has been largely with students working across distances with one another, and I can tell you that this type of contact changes the way students think about themselves and their peers. I am reminded of a native American student who said he was no longer afraid to leave the reservation for college. His confidence came from his work with students around the world through telecommunications. He understood how he was both similar and different from his peers from different places and he was eager to explore new relationships.

I am struck by a different change that I think is equally important. In Judi Harris's research on the Electronic Emissary project, she finds dramatic changes to the subject matter experts who work with classroom students. Working with students changes the way adults think about themselves and their careers.

I think I can illustrate this change by a short story about what happened to a set of fellow prisoners who were invited to share their expertise with a theme-based Learning Circle. This Learning Circle—a group of ten classrooms—was working together on the theme "Society's Problems." Bill Burrall, a very creative teacher in West Virginia, saw how he could use the anonymous nature of networking to provide more direct contact between classes of students and inmates.[*] The prisoners were given the opportunity to reflect on what they did, why they did it, and what they could have done in response to questions sent by classes of students. The advice they gave to students was impressive. Here are a few excerpts:

From Smeagol (pseudonym):

At age 15 I thought I knew everything.

At age 16 I knew that I knew everything.

At age 17 you could not tell me anything, because it was a waste of my time to listen to anything anyone was telling me when I already knew everything.

At ages 18, 19, and 20 no one older than me could tell me anything—they simply did not know what they were talking about. But with all of my belief and knowledge of knowing everything during those years there was one thing that I could not know at that age or be told and that was WISDOM. Wisdom that only comes with age and experience. Wisdom has to be learned with time, of what to do and how to handle different situations that you may find yourself in. So in any situation where you think you know everything and can handle it, take the time to ask yourself one question: "At this time in my life do I have the wisdom to do what is right for me and everyone concerned?" If you cannot respond with a yes, then back off, get out of the situation and get advice from an older person that you trust and who takes you seriously and does not treat you like a kid. Remember even when you know everything and know that you know everything you still need Wisdom!

From Thorin (who spent hours each day with a dictionary to write his responses to the students):

I really care about you all and what happens to you and your future. The streets don't really care about you, drugs don't care about you and most of all, gangs don't really care about you. You must care about yourselves first! Think #1. Remember this: no one but you, and you alone are responsible for your own education, future, way out of the inner city, and a much better life. You have the power within you.

---

[*] The text of prisoners' exchanges with students over three years can be found online at *http://168.216.210.13/mjhs/pproject/pproject.htm*

I would like to say to you all, thank you for being part of my life. You may not know or understand how much you have changed Thorin for the better. I really didn't think Thorin could care about anyone until this special opportunity came along. You all have given me a new dream, and that's to take all that has happened in my life and give it to you, and other young people that is on the same road I was on, and that's the road of death, drugs, gangs, and most of all, a life of hurt and pain.

Some joined this project, no doubt, to have something positive to show a parole board, but those who worked with these prisoners reported real changes in their attitudes and behavior. In fact they were the same changes that Judi Harris reported for the subject matter experts she worked with. They were changed by their interactions with students.

There is an African bit of wisdom that is often quoted and recently appeared in part in a book title by Hillary Clinton: "It takes a whole village to raise a child." But from the work that I have seen on the Internet, I would like you to consider the other side of the equation. Interaction with children can make a village whole. Teaching children is a very rewarding and life-changing activity. Anyone who is a parent or teacher knows this. Getting more people in the village involved in education may be one small step toward making our village whole.

The Challenges for Increased Human Resources

Not everyone who wants to work with children has good intentions. Open any big city newspaper and you will read examples of how adults, even parents and teachers, abuse children. It takes careful planning to make schools a secure and safe environment for learning. As the participation of more people in the classroom becomes possible, there is an increased need for screening them and protecting students. In the same vein, not everyone is who they say they are on the Net, and not everyone is motivated by good intentions. How can we make the vast resources of the adult world available to students without risk to their safety and innocence? We have faced this challenge in creating schools, and we will need to tackle it on

the Net. It takes careful planning. We need to find reasonable procedures to protect young learners and to help students develop new strategies to protect themselves in this changing world. Just as we have worked out rules and procedures for how children should interact with strangers on city streets, we will need to teach our children how to interact with strangers in the world of the Net.

The second challenge of increasing human resources in the classroom is more difficult. It's the issue of balancing subject matter expertise and teaching partnerships. Just because somebody knows a lot and cares a lot about a certain subject doesn't make that person a good teacher. Helping students learn is more complex than giving them information. Subject matter experts often need to be prepared for their work with students. Anyone who has established programs like the ones I have mentioned knows that it takes much more work than finding some experts, making them available to the classroom for magic to happen in the classroom. It takes careful preparation and planning because experts have to realize that mutual discovery, rather than telling, promotes intellectual curiosity. If we find ways to address these challenges, then the involvement of more people in the classroom instruction is an exciting prospect for improving the education we provide our children.

What Do We Teach?

We want to share with the next generation what we know, think, do, and value. But how do we decide to do this? Who is the "we"? What is it that we should be teaching in schools? The "scope and sequence" of current curriculum are attempts to distill information from different groups and find that information that is commonly held as true by most groups. This information is then arranged in a way that makes it easy for students to learn (memorize). Yet this distillation of what we know takes away the sense of discovery and controversy that surrounds the construction of knowledge. The Internet opens up ways of offering students access to information in the context of the communities that value specific information. The Internet can provide a place for students to explore the multiple perspectives of communities that are often missing or barely cited in state-approved textbooks.[*]

But schooling is not only about learning information, it is also about developing the skills students will need to take their places in society. Cognitive science tells us that the more different task situations resemble one another, the higher the likelihood of the transfer of skills learned in the first task to the second. While this may appear too obvious to be important, we find that if we examine educational tasks in school they are often so different from the context of use in the world that there is little or no transfer of learning. If we looked at each of the three basic skills—reading, writing, and arithmetic—and compared how these skills are taught in school with how they are used by adults, we would find vast differences.

Consider writing. If you go into a classroom and watch a writing lesson, you might see kids with a set of sentences they are supposed to organize into a paragraph, with a topic idea, three supporting details, and a summary sentence. They might then be instructed to write their own topic sentence, supporting details, and summary sentence. Is that writing? Is that what you think of when you think of writing? No, writing is fundamentally an act of communication. It has to do with conveying ideas to specific audiences. Can you imagine a child asking "who is my audience?" when asked to write something? Yet most writers want to know this basic information before they begin writing.

Curriculum in Context

With Internet links, we can provide kids with worldwide audiences that can help them find their voices through writing, in just the way Paul [Reese] described is happening at the Ralph Bunche school. When kids become involved in writing their ideas to *share* them with distant peers and in *evaluating* other students' work for publication, they develop the type of writing skills they will need as adults. The best way to get students to understand the need for grammatical conventions is to have them try to make sense of the writing of students from distant places who fail to use them.

Computer technology makes it possible to create more precise simulations of the context of skill use in the work place. One of the best ways to get students to learn is to have them teach others. In the classroom setting, it is sometimes difficult to supervise and evaluate peer instruction. However, the slow-motion, recorded teaching conversations that happen online provide a perfect medium for students to teach and learn from one another and for teachers to supervise this process.[†]

What we do or should teach in school is a politically charged issue. There are many people who want to help shape the answer to this question, and increasingly more groups are becoming involved as I mentioned earlier. If we don't let the students play any role in these decisions, the outcome may not be what we hoped for. Consider this quotation:

> Education is what survives when what has been learned has been forgotten.

It may surprise you to learn that B. F. Skinner is the author of these words. I think it's important that we remember that much of academic content learned in school will be forgotten. When adults were asked about what they remember learning in school, they most often told stories about significant interpersonal relationships and what they learned about themselves and others as a result of these exchanges.[‡] I think the fact they mentioned these issues rather than the algebra,

---

[*] To see a great collection of different communities and organizations involved in teaching history and social science, see *http://execpc.com/~dboals/boals.html*. For a good collection of resources that deal with diversity, see *http://execpc.com/~dboals/diversit.html*.

[†] For some examples of project ideas, see Oz projects at *http://owl.qut.edu.au/oz-teachernet/projects/oz-projects.html*, I*EARN projects at *http://www.peg.apc.org/~iearn/*, or the Global Schoolhouse Network at *http://www.gsn.org/*.

[‡] The adult reflections on education come from Alan Peshkin's book, *The Color of Strangers, the Color of Friends: The Play of Ethnicity in School and Community*, Chicago: Chicago University Press (1994).

grammar, and spelling they also acquired underscores the social dimensions of learning.

Challenges for Curriculum Design

Who makes the curriculum decisions and what flexibility is there for change? Will textbooks be replaced with materials that are more current and projects that evolve from current affairs? Will communities take a more active role in producing classroom materials? Will teachers have more freedom to find materials from a range of sources? Will students have more flexibility in selecting and pursuing topics? If the answer to some of these questions is yes, it will lead to fundamental changes in the current education structure.

Teachers who are learners and students who take a more active role in learning require more human resources. Teacher training is the right term to use if you are talking about packaged curriculum that is delivered in a standardized way. The Internet can provide new models of professional development for teachers, by allowing for partnerships with other adults who care about what we teach in schools. Isolated teachers and packaged curriculum work well together, but if we are talking about a different way of learning, a connected kind of learning, teachers as well as kids need to be connected. Teachers need the same partnerships as their students. If producing lifelong learners is our goal, we need to start in the classrooms and specifically with teachers.

The other point I want to make has to do with project integration with skill development. We've spent years designing scope and sequence to make sure that learning builds on past knowledge and skills in an organized and orderly fashion. And yet we know that kids learn so much better when we embed things in rich context, in project-based learning. So how can we combine the best of project-based learning with the scope and sequence of packaged curriculum to make sure that students have a comprehensive education? It's not impossible but it will take some rethinking of the curriculum.

Many people get frightened and want to go back to basics. I think we have to move *forward* to basics. We have to think of new ways to see that kids get the necessary skills; but at the same time, they get new skills, and, through more personal involvement, their learning survives the test of time. Equity, reciprocity, sustainability—these are all critical issues in designing these networking projects for classrooms.

How can we make sure that these kinds of partnerships last? What can we do to make them part of the curriculum in a real way? Equity has been talked about a number of different times in this conference. It's a big issue and I don't think it's one we can afford to ignore.

Where Learning Takes Place

That brings us to places of learning. What are the new places of learning that exist in a Net world? We can create a sense of place for students that is more real than virtual. We can use all our technology in an integrated way to take kids around the world. By combining television, networking, and classroom activities, kids can actually join researchers, get on the plane and go off to Antarctica, do their own research, watch the scientists do research there, compare notes, see how their findings compare with the research carried out in this distant laboratory. Using technology, they can even operate the tools remotely in exactly the same way that scientists do.

We can create communities of learners. We know how to do it. It's been done in many pockets on the Internet. It's what Steven McGeady was talking about this morning. Creating these communities and getting kids involved in them will really change the way we educate our children. We can also make classrooms places that other people can visit. We used technology to "virtually" visit two classrooms today. Linda encouraged you to visit others. How many times have you helped a child practice and practice a presentation and then, when you ask how it went, he or she just says, "fine"? If your school has networked computers, the technology to allow you to take a short break to tune into that classroom and watch your child give that report is very inexpensive. In many cases the window into the classroom is already there; all we need is to open it.

So what are the challenges we face in creating these new spaces for learning?

- We need to assure student safety in Net explorations.

- We need ways of making the classroom on the Net an inviting educational environment.

- We need to help students evaluate and value knowledge in terms of its ties to communities.

Evaluating information and applying it so it becomes useful knowledge will be far more important than memorizing facts. And yet, in many of our schools, kids are still memorizing disconnected information.

We want to create ties to society as we maintain clear educational objectives. I'll just say that the ties, the partnerships between schools and businesses, are very important. But we also want to make sure that we don't end up in a situation where the kids are workers again. We want to make sure that what they're doing has very strong educational content.

I'd like to close with a message I received as I was preparing this talk. It's a closer look into one person, but she is representative of many others.

Six years ago Marilyn Kennedy was troubled about teaching. It had become repetitive and she was losing the motivation that had attracted her to teaching. She went to a computer conference hoping to find that piece of magic that would energize her students. She was intrigued by the prospect of working with other teachers and providing her students with global contacts. But there were no computers, and no budget for computers, in her school. She made the decision to buy a computer and a modem, and started a process of complete transformation. The magic was that she was learning and, with other teachers as partners, she was not alone in this process. She learned from others and she taught what she was learning to her students, to students in other class-

rooms, and to other teachers. Each year, she would describe how excited her students were becoming about learning and how her whole orientation to teaching was changing. And while I watched her transformation, I knew she was changing others. This is the message she sent me on May 23rd, as I prepared this talk:

> Hi Margaret,
>
> ...
>
> I want to share with you the news of our test scores, as I know you will be interested. As you know, I'm only able to dabble in technology as long as my students do well on those state and national test scores. Well, I got the results. I was the only 4th grade teacher to have 19 of my 20 students pass the state writing tests, including ESL students! My students' Iowa Test of Basic Skills (ITBS) average scores were in the 80s and 90s, while the other students in the school were in the 50s.
>
> Remember Josh? He began 4th grade reading at 2.1 grade level. He now reads at 5th grade level. I'm convinced my students' achievements resulted from their collaboration through telecommunication and multimedia. The work they do in our classroom motivates them to read, write, imagine, and create. They have become inspired because they know what they are doing has value. They are connected with the real world. They're not just filling out another workbook page. Instead they are doing real work. Their achievement using technology gives them confidence in themselves. My students know they are winners.

Marilyn Kennedy, like Paul Reese, has become an explorer, a learner who has led her students in an adventure to new places, with new teachers, and new technology.

Questions & Answers

ROBERTS: Let me begin our discussion by focusing on the questions that deal with the issues of financing.

Q: *Did Netday in California, the voluntary effort to wire California schools and connect them to the Internet, produce results? What is the role of the private* *sector; how do we get them engaged? How do we get parents engaged?*

ROBERTS: Netday yielded 20,000 volunteers in California on March 9th, who laid six million feet of cable in 5,000 schools. An average of five classrooms connected in each of the participating school sites. California's Netday will be replicated by some two dozen states during the four Saturdays in October.

Why does this effort matter? I believe it brought resources into the schools and it worked best in the locations where there was a real partnership between the high-tech industry and education. And it worked best where people had already thought about what they wanted to use the technology for.

Q: (for Paul Reese) *How did you get Netday started, and who funded your project?*

REESE: We've been running Netday at the Ralph Bunche School for the last ten years. I'm one of the few teachers in the New York City school system who keeps a masonry bit in the closet. I've wired the school four times, beginning with a Harvest Network (for those of you who have a little history of the technology). And it has continued to be one of the biggest headaches and challenges to keep the infrastructure going. Working with Denis Newman (then at Bankstreet, now at BBN), we've done some very innovative work in understanding and designing the infrastructure and creating an environment that is relatively seamless and very comfortable for kids.

Maintaining that environment can and should be a full time job. I have a network, all with Internet access and all with access to local file servers, of just under 100 Macintoshes. I teach full time and I keep those running. I have a paraprofessional who helps with some things, but it's not enough. I would imagine those of you in industry could tell us something about the ratio of technicians in your firms and organizations to keep the technology running smoothly. It [system administration] is one of the major problems.

We tried to put a price tag on this, and over the ten years, almost all the money for our project has come from grants. We've lived and we've survived between them. My annual predictable hardware budget is about $2,000 or $2,500 from the state. But we've estimated that, over those ten years, we've spent about a half million dollars on the infrastructure in various grant programs. Some of that's what I call "funny money." We have a T3, one of the fastest lines, in the school right now because we're doing some experimental work. If we had the money, we probably wouldn't need quite that much bandwidth.

RIEL: How you get started is what I think underlies the issue of cost. In many cases, if you can get a teacher connected with other teachers in other places, through one of the support groups, the community-building groups are on the Internet, like Global Schoolhouse. If you get teachers involved with other teachers, they get this kind of information and ask questions of other professionals. Starting as a group, a partnership with other teachers, is one of the fastest ways of getting teachers to understand what this change is about.

REESE: On the other hand, I really think we need to challenge ourselves and think. When universities realized that the Internet was important to them, they built the infrastructure and hired the people and committed the resources to support that so that the professors and the teachers and students were not running wires. And I don't mean to diminish the tasks of running wires and keeping the infrastructure going. Very few schools have designated positions so it is usually a teacher who takes the responsibility. I don't mean to diminish that. But if we are going to scale, we really need to understand what it means to find and train and develop a climate that sets those resources aside.

ROBERTS: Let's talk a bit about financing strategies that have been used. The most popular approach is to pass a bond referendum. But the problem there is it tends to produce a blip of investment that is not sustained over the long term.

Some states are taking a long term strategy by passing a per pupil allocation every year in the budget. States like Texas and Florida have been very successful in continuing to sustain legislative interest. A report prepared by McKinsey and Co. estimates that technology funding is about three to five percent of the total educational budget. And while the good news is it's only an additional three to five percent, the bad news is that in many districts budgets are shrinking!

Q: *What are the models we know already work that need to be expanded to engage teachers and support them in the effective use of technology for teaching and learning?*

WHEELER: I will tell you a quick story about the problems that we have with teacher assessment. And unless we have administrators that understand what it is that we're doing in the classroom, we take awful professional risks. I asked my supervisor to visit my classroom one day. I was very excited about this; I had kids working in collaborative groups and interesting things were happening. When my supervisor arrived, he didn't see me lecturing at the front of the class, he didn't see worksheets, and there was quite a bit of noise. So he kindly tapped me on the hand and he said, "I'll come back when you're teaching."

Now I had my work cut out for me. How do I explain to him that yes, I am teaching? That's probably the biggest hurdle we face regarding assessment. Certainly in schools, teachers are very concerned about their assessment but we tend to focus only on teachers; we don't always bring the administrators along with us. Certainly this has implications for colleges of education as well.

RIEL: Well, I'll tell you a little story too and it's about this teacher, Marilyn Kennedy, that I read the quote from. In talking to her, when I asked her permission to read you her letter, she said, "You know, the other fourth grade teachers in the school all have their desks in a row and they stand in the front and teach." And she had to buy her own tables because she said she couldn't teach without tables. So she bought the tables in her classroom at a hundred dollars a table. She also bought all her technology.

The principal has told her on various occasions, "You're rocking the boat. All the parents want their kids in your fourth grade classroom. Would

you stop using technology because you're causing too much trouble in my school?" And seriously, he said this to her. And she said, "I can't teach without it." And so she ended up teaching all the different fourth graders that came into her classroom. And she said, "You know, I can't teach this way either. I don't see the kids long enough to make an effect. You know, I really need to have my contained classroom."

But those are the pressures a good teacher has, like the teachers here and like hundreds of teachers that I deal with. They're in this kind of sea change situation; there are those who don't want to change who they work side by side with, and it's going to take some real dialogue to get teachers to see that isolation is not the best way of doing things.

REESE: There are a lot of issues. One of the very serious ones is the problem of time. We often have to, particularly when we have project-based learning, rethink the way school time is divided up into very arbitrary segments. The one thing that has been very encouraging at my school is that as we've developed this core of teachers and students who are really excited about the technology, we find them spending time outside of the classroom. So our computer center, which includes both computers in the classrooms and in the lab, often doesn't empty out until 5:30, 6:00 in the evening.

And I kind of laugh at 3:00. There's always the chaos around dismissal. But one of the biggest problems we have is to get the kids to get up and out at 3:00.

ROBERTS: Let me just mention a couple of things. Yesterday, at the White House Ceremony on Blue Ribbon Schools, the President announced a joint effort by the administration, the National School Boards Association, the AFT, the National Education Association, the National Association of Secondary School Principals, the Association of Colleges of Teacher Education, and other organizations. These groups plan to recruit the teacher technology leaders across the nation to help their colleagues get online and use computer-based resources in their classrooms. I believe this effort can work because it uses the people who know, who have done it in their own classrooms.

It is also an opportunity to overcome institutional barriers and create a new mindset about teachers. Technology can be our greatest asset because, for the first time, we have a way to link Paul Reese with Marilyn Kennedy that is easy, that can sustain them both over time. And I think we have to think about how we reach out to others.

When I was a teacher, my biggest challenge was that I could innovate as much as I wanted in my own classroom, but the next year, it could all be undone! And so we not only want to talk about communities of learners, but we want to talk about communities of professionals. And we are the only professional institution that I can think of that is so terribly isolated in what we do.

REESE: Something we have not discussed is that there are a number of initiatives at the national level that may profoundly affect K–12's and other institutions' ability to participate fully in Internet access. The implementation of the recent Snowe-Rockefeller Amendment to the Telecommunications Reform Bill in Washington, that is now being sorted out in the FCC, has very important implications for schools. At state levels, the regulatory agencies that affect the tariffing of networking access can have a profound affect on schools. And schools don't have a tradition of getting their voices together to realize that they have a major interest in those things.

To the extent that community, industry, higher education has a better experience in that I hope they will continue to be advocates for the schools at that level.

ROBERTS: I concur with Paul and underscore that the Department of Education is in the thick of the FCC Public Utility Commission negotiations. Secretary of Education Richard Riley testified before the FCC joint board, urging the board not to let technology become the fault line between the haves and the have nots. He argued that we have to find a way to make access affordable for every school and library across the country.

If the FCC Board makes the "right" decision, the legacy of the Snowe-Rockefeller provisions will last into the next decade and beyond. The provisions can subsidize school connections fairly and generate billions of dollars in benefits for our schools and our children. We think it's critical.

At the end of our session, I would urge all of you to get onto the Internet and tap into the many online educational discussions and explore the resources that are available. Visit the Department of Education's web site [*http://www.ed.gov/*] as well as other federal agency sites. They are literally information goldmines.

About the Speakers

LINDA G. ROBERTS is Director of the Office of Educational Technology and Special Adviser to the Secretary of the U.S. Department of Education. Dr. Roberts coordinates the Department's technology activities and plays a key role in developing the Clinton Administration's Educational Technology Initiative. Her leadership efforts include creating affordable access to the Information Superhighway for schools and libraries, and mobilizing state, local and private, and non-profit efforts to wire our schools, upgrade the base of hardware in classrooms, train teachers, and create effective products and services that transform teaching and learning.

PAUL REESE is the computer educator at The Ralph Bunche Computer mini-school in Community School District Five in New York City, and also the District Computer and Technology Coordinator. The mini-school, founded six years ago by a group of seven teachers, is committed to school restructuring, and is currently a partner with Columbia University Teachers College on a New York State and NYNEX-funded project to investigate the issues of student access to high-bandwidth applications including video conferencing and video-on-demand. Mr. Reese is a founding member and Chair of the Consortium for School Networking. *Electronic Learning* magazine named him 1990 "Teacher of the Year."

MARGARET RIEL has developed and researched models of "network learning," specifically cross-classroom collaboration designs. She designed the Learning Circle model initially for AT&T and currently for the International Education and Resource Network (I★EARN). She has written research reports and articles on network learning and designed curriculum books for online projects. In her recent publications she describes how schools, teachers, and learners are forming partnerships within, across, and between schools and other communities to form new contexts for learning in the Networld of the communication age. For links to web publications see the URL *http://www.iearn.org/iearn/circles/riel.html.*

COLLEEN F. WHEELER is a musician, educator, and web developer. At Wheaton College, she develops technology education resources and tools for teaching and learning. Ms. Wheeler has won numerous awards for outstanding teaching and curriculum development as well as commissions for compositions. She has been integrating MIDI technology, computers, and the Internet into her performance ensembles and classrooms since 1987. She and her husband, Ken, are the proud new parents of a delightful baby daughter, Meghan.

Educational Publishers See Opportunities on Net

By Phyllis Albert-Mitzman

Publishers producing educational materials—what used to be called textbooks—say if they do not take advantage of the Internet and the possibilities opened up by electronic media, they will be left behind, trying to distribute out-of-date products in a very competitive field.

Roger Rogalin, School Division Publisher at McGraw-Hill, told a panel on educational applications of the Internet that most publishers had a tepid reaction initially to the medium and to the possibilities of electronic publishing.

But he said market forces rapidly forced them to re-evaluate that judgment and they now see lucrative new opportunities for distributing ancillary materials via the Internet, as well as for developing web-linked activities using important national databases and resources, such as the Library of Congress's Civil War archives.

Teachers will also be able to download worksheets and a much richer set of information for students to use than could have been developed by individual publishers, he said. He did not say whether publishers would cut their prices to make up for the increased reproduction costs schools will face.

Geoffrey Fletcher, former Agency Associate Commissioner for Technology, of the Texas Department of Education, said the state will be investing heavily over the next ten years in hardware, software, connections, teacher training, and distributed instructional materials that could be available from home computers as well as from those in schools. He added, "The need in technology is to have it just in time, not just in case."

Denis Newman of BBN emphasized that organizations and groups must collaborate to develop content and tools to make the most of the Net. He spoke of "the convergence necessary to bring the Internet into the curriculum and to draw on the Net as well as on individual school resources."

The panelists said education will take place beyond the classroom and will not stop with the end of formal schooling. And parents will participate in this process along with teachers and students.

Quoting from Tom Peters' *In Search of Excellence,* Fletcher said people will need to be "flexible, devoted to perpetual learning, disrespectful of the status quo, and a little crazy." He added, "In technology, we will need to be unreasonable, crazy risk-takers."

Education

May 30, 1996

The Market for Educational Applications of the Internet

MODERATOR: Martha Stone Wiske
PANELISTS: Geoffrey Fletcher
Dennis Newman
Roger Rogalin

WISKE: Good morning. It's nice to be here. This is the second of only two sessions specifically focused on education at this conference, a fact that might seem somewhat surprising since the conference was organized by a university. It struck me, until today, that this conference on the Internet and Society has focused a great deal more on the Internet and technology than on people and society. I think the shift in the balance of attention is really noticeable today, starting with the keynote this morning [Neil L. Rudenstine] and certainly continuing with the session on education that previously took place in this room ["The Internet in the Classroom"].

Finally, we began to think much more carefully about issues of teaching and learning and about the fact that education is always essentially a human endeavor, more than a technological one. I hope that in this session we will continue to shift this balance toward the people side of the context.

My own interest in the questions addressed by this conference centers on action research in schools to support teaching for understanding. I am, therefore, interested in the potential of new technologies to contribute to this agenda, and in

the processes of change involving learners, teachers, and school systems.

It seems to me that the Internet has the potential to make very big changes in the lives of end users in terms of the products available to them, their own role in producing, selecting, tailoring, and using educational resources, and potentially in the process of accessing and distributing resources.

My colleagues today are experts in various institutions that play a part in the educational marketplace. They'll be focusing on several questions:

- What is the market for educational applications of the Internet?

- Who are the sellers and buyers?

- What are the products in this marketplace?

- What are the economic realities and the social structures that define this market?

- How can the participants in this marketplace collaborate with one another to produce appropriate technologies?

One of the questions embedded in the last question is, what is the meaning of "appropriate"? What defines quality educational products? What makes them educationally powerful and workable? Who participates in answering those questions? A second part of this question is, how are the roles of these producers and consumers shifting, and who makes decisions about what to produce and purchase? How are the participants in the marketplace learning to play their new roles?

Finally, we will talk about the implications of the Internet for changing the educational marketplace. How does that alter the kinds of products that are marketable and the economic dynamics of participants? How does it influence the equity of access to educational resources across individuals and institutions from different geographic regions, different socio-economic strata, different cultural-linguistic backgrounds?

Each of our speakers represents one of the institutional players. **ROGER ROGALIN** of McGraw-Hill will go first. Roger is a Senior Vice President of McGraw-Hill, in charge of the school division of publishing. He's responsible for overseeing the development of instructional materials and their distribution. He's going to explain to you how, in the age of the Internet, the nature of products at McGraw-Hill is shifting, the process by which they are distributed to users, and how the relationships between consumers and producers is also changing.

ROGALIN: Good morning. It's a pleasure to be here; I'm in very good company this morning. I'm the commercial guy, the one who's "next to the money," in theory. I work for a for-profit company. I've only worked with this for-profit company for about a year. Prior to that, I headed up the school division of the Association of American Publishers. AAP is a nonprofit company in the business of making the publishing environment better for for-profit companies, if that makes sense.

At AAP, I represented the entire industry to the media, to the state departments of education, to the U.S. government, and to the interests of school publishing—formerly called textbook publishing. The reason we don't really use that term anymore is fairly obvious, and it's one of the reasons I'm here.

Several years ago, the Internet, which has been around for years and only recently gained its current critical mass, garnered some attention via some of the writing and preparation of the Telecommunications Act. It also got some attention because the technology hit a certain point for people who determined that perhaps there was money to be made. But at that point, regardless of the attention it was getting elsewhere, publishers looked at the Internet with fear and trepidation. These publishers were members of AAP. At the time, several CEOs came to me and said, "Well, what are you going to do about the Internet?" The publishing companies didn't want to be buggy whip manufacturers in the age of the automobile. The Internet was important, providing a different kind of open architecture and access to learning that a book couldn't. So after their initial concern, publishers embraced the Internet.

My presentation this morning is in three parts. In part one, I will talk about the market environment. How are educational materials purchased and looked upon around the country? The second part is about obstacles: how commercial publishers view the Internet's obstacles; how they view it as an obstacle itself; and what the obstacles are to making money on the Internet. The third part will be about opportunities, so at least I can end on an upbeat note.

The Market Environment

The United States is divided into mega markets, if you will, for textbook publishing. In the "Open Territory" states, decisions are made at the district level, either school by school, town by town, or citywide. But the buying decisions in these states are made at the district or local level. The "Adoption" states have a two-part selection process. Instructional materials go through a screening process at the state level. If they pass at the state level, they can be purchased by the local school districts, either with state funds or local funds or in combination.

Geographically, there is an interest in state control south of the Mason-Dixon line. North of the Mason-Dixon line, buying decisions are more provincial—purchasing goes district by district. There's a long history to this. In fact, there was a whole war fought over the issue of state control.

But this geographical and purchasing distinction makes a big difference in the way publishers publish. The state of Texas, with seven percent of the student population of this country, is buying biology books in one year, but the state of New York buys them district by district in random fashion. A New York district might wait ten years before purchasing new books. The fact that Texas is buying them all in one focused effort in one year gets publishers' attention. The Texas curriculum, against which the textbook submissions of the different publishers is measured, has an enormous influence on what kinds of textbooks publishers publish.

Another consideration is that, should the Texas State Board go off the ranch and ask for something really weird that you can't sell anywhere else in the country, publishers might have second thoughts about that. They may not participate in the Texas submission but focus on the other 93 percent of the student population. If the Texas curriculum is more or less all right with the rest of the country, it's worth pursuing and you'll see that every publisher has a new copyright that year—new books are produced and lots of money is spent. So there's an interactivity between what the states do, particularly in the south and in California, and what publishers do with instructional material.

These adopting states have definitions of instructional materials. These definitions used to refer to textbooks as "paper between two hard covers," but these definitions have been changing. Texas's definition now says a textbook can be "a system of instructional materials which conveys the information to the pupil or otherwise contributes to the learning process." That's pretty broad. It could mean a book, it could mean a CD-ROM, it could mean something on the Internet.

Who pays for these instructional materials? When you're in a commercial enterprise, you have to follow the money. Seven percent of the money for instructional materials comes from the federal government, approximately 50 percent from the state government, and 43 percent from local government. Now this is obviously all connected to public school education, so those dollars are tax dollars. Clearly in those southern states, the influence is a little higher on the state level; it's more than 50 percent. The federal government has very little influence on curriculum despite the Improving America's Schools Act. That fact is fairly unique to this country, by the way.

So that's the marketplace we're dealing with: heavily localized, paid for with tax dollars, and a very emotional issue because these are taxpayers' children you're talking about. When I worked for AAP, the Association represented freedom of expression, the First Amendment, except in the school division. This is because material must be age-appropriate, and freedom of expression for a six-year-old may not be appropriate.

Obstacles

Let's talk about the obstacles to publishing educational materials on the Internet.

Hardware and wiring. In the preceding session ["The Internet in the Classroom"] Linda Roberts talked about the $50 billion it would take to really develop the infrastructure. If you're going to publish something for profit, you do want a ready market. You want availability.

The fearful publishers say, "Well, I don't know how many times I came out with programmed instruction for Plato and that didn't go anywhere and I lost $10 million and my job. Apple IIe, Texas Instruments, Radio Shack, and everybody went wild in the early '80s. That was the way to go. So I put $50 million in investment into that. Lost my shirt and my job. And now they're telling me about CD-ROM and multimedia and this Internet. Do I want to lose my shirt and my job again? Or is this an opportunity? If I don't do it, will I lose my shirt and job?" That kind of fear is an obstacle.

That ready market doesn't yet exist because the hardware and wiring is not there. You'll hear publishers say over and over again, "I'd be happy to do it, but the market's not big enough, it's not there yet."

Access. The pipe into the schools is the needed access, and Linda Roberts gave a very encouraging statistic in her talk about the number of schools. Then she said the average classrooms wired in those schools was four or five classrooms within the school. That was very encouraging to Linda, but it's not big enough for me yet. I'm not looking to invest $50 million for four classrooms per school.

Teacher training. You saw some wonderful teachers in the last session who had no difficulty with technology. They trained themselves. They developed an interest and they did it. If you travel around to all the schools in the country, not just the ones that are doing something great in technology, you get a picture that's a little less optimistic. The saying goes that once the teacher closes the classroom door, he or she does what they want to do. And maybe what some of them want to do is something other than technology. Keep in mind that I'm giving you the obstacles here. Don't ascribe this necessarily to the way I feel about the realities of the market.

The conservative shift movement. A very, very important part of all the difficulty in educational materials being online, and something that I'm struggling with right now, is the conservative movement. Let's think about the November '94 elections. Here's my theory (call it "Rogalin's Theory of the Political Pendulum"): Government at that point was Democratic in the House, Democratic in the Senate, and Democratic in the Executive branch. People were unhappy with government. And so you have this big wave in the November '94 elections toward a group of people leaning more to the right.

The results of the '94 election enabled and empowered people who had been disinterested or disenfranchised to say, "Well, I'm going to run for my local school board, I'm going to run for a seat in the California Assembly. I'm going to get out there." The voters came out and showed up. It's the disenfranchised who turn out to vote. The people who are comfortable don't necessarily come out and vote—that's why we get these pendulum swings. So the pendulum had swung to the right, maybe the far right. Maybe it's coming back. It depends on where you are in that cycle.

These swings of the pendulum affect what is published for the public school market. In a minute I'll show you which content is affected. (Some of you already know which content is most affected.) But the movement also affects pedagogy and instruction. I'm hearing more and more from the radical religious right about the real problem—of course they don't want evolution in there and they don't want some of the social content—but what they're really con-

cerned about is why we don't have directive instruction. Why don't we just teach kids? What's this about inquiry and exploration? What's this "feel good" education?

When I was a kid in the 1950s and walked eight miles to school in my bare feet, I was taught. Somebody taught me the "right" answer. Can't you imagine that as an important issue to the right? That there is a "right" answer? Only one answer? So imagine how these people feel when you come in and say, "It's great, my kids are surfing the Net, surfing the Web, and they're talking to kids in Ghana." This isn't what these conservative parents—and arguably, any parents—want to have happening in the short amount of time that children are in school.

What they want to see happening is phonics instruction, spelling, direct spelling exercises, computation without a calculator (because you may be stranded in a desert someday without a calculator and you've got to know how to compute). Memorization of multiplication tables, memorization of grammar facts. It's coming back, folks, it's coming back strong, and Geoff [Fletcher] will support that it's happening, I think, in Texas. But it's not just Texas, that bastion of conservatism.

So we always think of the radical right as having an interest in content, but they also have an interest in pedagogical approach. And the advantages of the Internet and some of the advantages of technology may not be in concert with those interests.

Copyright protection on the Internet. Of course this was the big thing that commercial publishers were worried about: copyright protection is all a publisher has. How many of you have ever visited a publishing house, a book publishing house? I don't mean a newspaper. Or worked in one? How did you like those big presses you saw in there? What? You didn't see any? That's right. Because publishers don't own presses, all they own is copyrights. Intellectual property is what publishers own. That's their whole asset.

So when something threatens that, when people say we want an open architecture and everything on the Internet will be free and it's improper to have anything that you might charge for, that worries publishers. Now the Telecommunications Act and Bruce Lehman, the Commissioner of Patents and Trademarks and Copyrights, protect copyright and intellectual property rights on the Internet. This is very controversial. A lot of people don't agree that the Internet should be so constrained. But publishers do agree that copyright should be respected on the Internet.

And who decides what's on the Net? The state or the local school district? That's another major concern for publishers about what gets published on the Net.

Opportunities

Now we see the opportunities.

Product costs. People think publishers are making a whole lot of money. If Mr. Gates were to look at the AAP data from 1982 to 1992, he'd run away from this business as it exists.

What you see is a tremendous decline in operating profits for publishing houses. That's not to say they're not profitable. The ones that are not are out of business. Today there exist—and this was predicted 15 years ago by publishing sages—there exist five large publishers of instructional materials in this country. Only five. Fifteen years ago there were about 32. The number has declined through mergers, acquisitions, and bankruptcy.

We're down to five large publishers, and I'm pleased to say that McGraw-Hill is the largest. Then there are a lot of little publishers. In fact, there are more small publishers today than ever existed in all of U.S. history. So there are big publishers, little publishers, and nothing in between. And that is part of the economics of the problem.

So what do publishers provide?

Development cost. I'm going to skip this for now. Just take my word that the cost of developing four-color textbooks is massive.

FWO. "Free with order." The textbook industry is an aging industry—when you have five providers, they all do the same market research, which results in a similarity in appearance and content. This is especially true when you're all targeting, let's say, a Texas adoption. I contend that they're all different if people look closely enough. But if you're part of a commodity, price becomes an issue and therefore, you have to give more value, more materials for free. Since the unit manufacturing cost on the Internet is virtually nil, it can help provide lower cost FWO.

What are publishers' big advantages in publishing materials on the Internet? This overhead is our home page.

The Internet provides access to an enormous amount of information, but publishers provide the all-important context.

Production costs. The biggest advantage is lower production costs. Our home page [http://www.mcgraw-hill.com/] displays all the resources and activities available through McGraw-Hill. We have web-linked activities like Grade Five, Civil War. You can get into the American Civil War home page and you can get into the Library of Congress. The Internet allows our users to view and interact with great resources that could never be attained before in an 800-page textbook. So what publishers are creating are online activities in which they link students to the Library of Congress or the American Civil War home page and ask questions of the students as they go. And these are very, very valuable activities that can be provided at little cost to the publisher. Or a teacher can download worksheets from the Internet should he or she want to work on paper activities with the students.

Instructional expertise. There's a rich set of information as we heard this morning, but the important part is the context. Steven McGeady talked about these things: "information, knowledge, and wisdom."

I'm going to leave you with the idea that the Internet provides access to an enormous amount of information, but that publishers—whether they're commercial publishers or universities or schools—provide the all-important context. Publishers turn that information into knowledge, essentially, by organizing it within a context. And I contend that it's the teacher interacting with this knowledge and with this information who provides the wisdom. We need to train teachers, we need to get them involved, and these resources will become more valuable and available. Thank you.

WISKE: Our next speaker is **GEOFF FLETCHER**, who has already been introduced by Roger as coming from one of those states that's in the area below the Mason-Dixon line. Geoff is the Associate Commissioner for Technology in the State Department of Education in Texas, where for some time he has been responsible for the divisions that oversee curriculum assessment, textbooks, and technology.

Texas is a very large state and has been quite forward-thinking in its definition of what educational materials to include, and it has been on the forefront in including electronic materials on that list. The purchasing process in Texas has also been unusual in the way educational materials are funded. So he will tell us about both of those things. At the end of the day, literally, he changes jobs and becomes a telecommuter, he tells us. He will be starting a new division for *T.H.E. Journal* that will focus on professional development. So perhaps we'll get some insight from the new perspective as well.

FLETCHER: Thank you. Good morning. I've been involved in education for about 25 years now. I've taught seventh grade through twelfth grade,

I've taught at the university level, I've been a coordinator of gifted programs, of future studies programs (my doctorate is in future studies), and technology programs. And I think, for the last 11 years, I've reached the pinnacle of success. I've been a bureaucrat in state government. (That was a joke!)

I've learned a lot over these 25 years. I've learned, for example, that Will Rogers never met an eighth grader. I want to talk today about three major issues that are related to our topic, the market for educational applications of the Internet:

1. How do we define the education market?

Roger has given you a definition from the textbook publishers' perspective and I think it's a very important one, but I don't think it's quite broad enough, as I hope you'll see.

2. How do we address equity in education?

This is extremely important to me in this day and age of technology. I'm not quite sure how to fix it, but how do we at least keep the gap from growing? How can we not bring the top down and at the same time, bring the less enfranchised, poor folks, up?

3. How do we use professional development and training to make technology in education work?

Let's first look at the definition of the education marketplace. The typical complaint you will hear from providers to education is that the marketplace is fragmented, it is small, and in some cases, it's actually shrinking as fewer and fewer state dollars, in proportion, go to school districts and schools. The problem is getting worse with certain trends, such as site-based decision making. In Texas we have 1,048 school districts. *One thousand and forty-eight school districts.* That includes over 6,300 campuses. And we have a state law requiring—this is ironic—bottom-up reform. We have a state law mandating site-based decision making, which is an interesting twist.

And Roger already mentioned the significant impact of the extreme right upon the education establishment. It is not something to sneeze at. It is a very, very important force that is occurring in education in general. I call this market I've described "the two-by-four-by-six-by-nine-by-twelve concept view of education." That is, the two covers of the textbooks, the four walls of the classroom, the six periods of the day, the nine months of the school year, and then the traditional twelve years we have in education. Nice little algorithm to help us remember things.

However, I think there's a vastly different definition of the education marketplace we need to begin to heed. That is, the education marketplace is any place where education takes place. It's not rocket science. The education marketplace includes the home, it includes the community, the church, the library; it includes everywhere learning can take place, including (I see somebody with a Newton here) outside. That's the education marketplace to me.

If 38 percent of all homes have computers, as I read recently, and 10 percent of the homes can connect to the Internet (and that number is growing significantly, as we all know), the market all of a sudden—if you think not just about the two by four by six, etc. classroom, but you think as well about the home and everywhere learning can take place—the market gets significantly bigger. This technical connection between the home and the school, if you have such a connection, can help get parents further involved.

The research is pretty clear that the more parents are involved in a child's education, the better the child has an opportunity to learn and succeed in school. So not only would the market be expanded, but education would also be improved with this new definition of the marketplace.

How many of you have tried to help your child or other children with algebra homework? (And I'm a product of the new math.) If you had access to the Internet, wouldn't it be nice to just click on a little QuickTime movie of a teacher explaining the same concept you cannot explain to your kid? So that's an example of how the market connecting the home and the school can work. There are a lot of opportunities, I think, if we just think a little bit differently.

Clearly one problem is that those are two very separate and distinct marketing channels. One channel goes directly to the school, one channel goes to Egghead Software and places like that. The Internet can help to bridge those two channels. In addition, Roger (and other people in the textbook industry who are thinking wisely about this topic) will begin to say, what if we provide, in some cases, a CD-ROM in the back of our textbooks for teachers?

What if we said, for an extra ten cents or perhaps even for free (it's not too much, it's one of those ancillary materials), what if we give those little CD-ROMs to the parents and let them have some of the same materials the teachers have? To me, that's another attempt to close the gap between the home and the school that could be beneficial. So I think the market can grow, and the technology we have out there can really help that market to grow.

The second issue, and obviously closely related, is equity: 62 percent of the homes in this country do not have computers and 90 percent of the homes are not connected to the Internet. And in schools, the upper middle class suburban schools are more likely to have computers and connections to the Internet than most other schools nationwide. These students and teachers are more likely to use the computer as a tool than the other schools.

And what the research shows—continues to show, unfortunately—is that those rich schools have the technology to browse the Web. They are using *tools*, whereas in the poorer schools, the concentration of their technology is in computer labs, where students are doing *drill and practice*. So the computers are acting on the students, as opposed to the students using the technology as a tool.

That equity issue is something that urgently needs to be addressed. We not only have the issue of the quality and quantity of the technology in the hands of the richer kids, but we also have the use of the technology that is not nearly as powerful with the poor kids. We hear these threats, promises, whatever, of these $500 to $600 machines coming out over the next year that will have the tools installed, that will have connections—in some cases, maybe not even wired connections—to the Internet. Still, even that is not sufficient, I think, to address the equity gap.

Despite what Scott McNealy of Sun said the other day, I truly believe there is a role for government in addressing this problem. Let me give you an example of how one state can address the equity issue in some ways. In Texas, there was a telecommunications deregulation bill this last session. In exchange for being deregulated, Southwestern Bell and others had to put some money into a pot. (By the way, those folks were the primary authors who proposed that bill, as opposed to the legislature.)

And that pot of money is now the Telecommunications Infrastructure Fund: it is $150 million a year for ten years. Some of that money is tied up in court, but the legislature will fix that problem. So the promise is, $1.5 billion dollars over ten years that goes primarily to schools to wire schools, to wire to the doorstep, to also buy hardware, software, and training, and to connect schools. That $150 million a year helps to expand the marketplace a little bit.

Another fund the legislature has created is the Technology Allotment: $30 per student goes to the schools every year. Not one year, but every year. That $30 per student totals over $100 million a year. Actually it's $106 million to go toward purchasing hardware, software, and training for schools in technology.

A third area, as Roger [Rogalin] talked about, is textbooks. In Texas, we spend somewhere around $175 million a year, which will rapidly move to $200 million a year, on textbooks, instructional materials. Roger didn't read the whole definition of a textbook to you, but you can drive an electronic truck through there. And they even specified that it includes online services. So if you have content that can be delivered online, if you have CD-ROMs or any kind of media that will meet a broadly defined textbook definition in Texas, you can play in that $175 to $200 million a year market.

Now let's put all these numbers together. $150 million a year, $100 million a year, $175 to $200 million a year. Pretty soon you're talking money. And that is *one* state. Granted it's a big state, but it's in one state and it's focused on technology in the schools.

Here's another example of how to achieve equity and getting the technology in the schools to work together: Texas, California, and Florida got together and each put in $400,000 (that's 1.2 million bucks), and said we have a problem in our states. We have a growing population of limited English-proficient kids in our middle school who are not doing well, who are dropping out of school. We need to fix or at least alleviate that problem. So we went out with an RFP [request for proposals] to the world and said, "We want you to design a multimedia program that addresses this population."

The winner of the bid was Addison Wesley, in conjunction with Davidson Software. Together, they produced a product called Vital Links, which is now sold on the market. Florida, California, and Texas pay a lower price because we helped to take the risk out of that, and we get some of the royalties until our initial investment is made up. So that's another example of state governments working together with the private sector to create a product to absorb some of the risk—to create a product that will work for schools.

The fourth area I want to touch upon is professional development. It was pointed out in the last session that we need professional development both for teachers and for administrators. So we don't have the horror stories of a principal coming into a classroom and saying, "Oh, I'll come back when you're teaching," because kids are working off in small groups [see Colleen Wheeler's presentation in "The Internet in the Classroom" session].

Boxes and wires and content are getting into the schools. You've heard me describe some of those efforts to make that happen. By one survey, there's overall about a ten-to-one computer to student ratio across the country. (I think it's closer to twelve-to-one in actual fact.)

Linda Roberts mentioned the bully pulpit that the President is using to drum up support for things like Netday, to promote the mentoring of other teachers. That's out there. However, few people seem to be addressing the human element in general. Few people are spending time helping teachers learn to use the technology and, more important, few are helping teachers *integrate* technology throughout the schools. Less than ten percent of the technology allotment in Texas has been used for training over the past four years. *Less than ten percent.* And not surprisingly, we're seeing little impact on student achievement, as measured by statewide tests.

Now you've heard some stories from the last session ["The Internet in the Classroom"] that there are all kinds of wonderful things happening with kids. We just don't measure them very effectively at the state level. But that's what the public looks at. As a result, we're seeing many classrooms with hardware and software, using exactly the same approach to content instruction as before the technology was there. Thus, we have minimal gain in student learning, as measured by state tests. Teachers feel frustrated and guilty and are bearing the weight of school boards, the public, and the students' unrealized expectations.

So we need professional development for educators and parents in how to use the technology and, more important, how to integrate this technology throughout the teaching and learning process. We need professional development that is just in time, not just in case. We need it whenever and wherever teachers want it and we need it through all media. Again, the Internet is a very logical place to help make this happen (as well as some of the other technologies). So not only do I see this as an important need in education, I think it is a potentially huge market.

In summary, let me say this: I think the educators and those selling and creating this new education marketplace need to have a different approach and a different attitude. And this attitude, I think, is illustrated by three quotations. (I'm a former English teacher so I have to use this stuff.) The first quote is from George Bernard Shaw:

> The reasonable man adapts himself to the world. The unreasonable one persists in trying to adapt the world to himself. And all progress depends on the unreasonable man.

The second is from Tom Peters, author of *In Search of Excellence*. Tom Peters was addressing the graduates of the Naval Academy. Note the audience. He cited some key characteristics of a naval officer in today's world:

> A naval officer must be flexible, devoted to perpetual learning, disrespectful of the status quo, and a little crazy.

And finally, the last quotation is from Winston Churchill, who saw Americans as risktakers and experimenters. He said,

> The American people will, in the end, do the right thing. After they have exhausted all other possibilities.

In order to make and grow this most important marketplace and to help it succeed, we need to be unreasonable, crazy risktakers. Sounds like a lot of fun.

WISKE: Our final speaker today is **DENIS NEWMAN**. We've heard from a producer side and a consumer side. Denis is perhaps from the linker side. He's the Director of Marketing of Internet Products at BBN, which, as you may know, was the institution that had a large role in the development of the Internet. Denis said he's been using the Internet since 1978. Doesn't look that old, does he? He is one of the originals. So we are interested to hear from him about how the participants in this new marketplace can collaborate.

NEWMAN: Thank you, [Martha] Stone. There are a number of Internet technologies that show promise in the school marketplace. There are, in fact, solutions to scaling up school participation in the Internet to the point that it becomes a viable commerical market. But I want to cast back to what now seems like a kind of prehistory; that is, before the Web.

We started some research back in 1991, funded by the National Science Foundation, to look at how to scale up access to the network, which was beginning to look very interesting on a small scale. We came up with this notion that what was needed in school technology was a convergence between the local area networks within the schools and the wide area networks which schools usually accessed with a modem.

Over the last few years that convergence has actually been taking place. And I want to take this occasion to look at what has been happening, what problems remain, and to examine some of the technologies that will need to be in place for the convergence to continue as we look forward to the year 2000.

Some of what I present here can be found in a paper written in 1992, based on that research. The paper was written with Paul Reese, who presented in the earlier session. Although it was never actually published, it was distributed widely in Xerox form and has now found its way onto the Web, published by an elementary school in New York City. You can see it at:

http://ralphbunche.rbs.edu/WWW/PROF/infra_ paper_92/Infrastructures.html

Now if we look back, 1992 was when Al Gore challenged industry to wire up all the classrooms by the year 2000. So we are about halfway there in terms of time, but we are nowhere near wiring up half the classrooms. Now remember, Gore's challenge was not just to bring the wire to the school, which is what the telecommunication companies are doing: it's actually getting it *into the classroom*. It is only when the wire gets into the classrooms that the teachers and students can use Internet resources in the curriculum. This is why the convergence of local area and wide area networks is essential.

The problem we were dealing with back in 1992 was that there were a lot of schools that were getting on the network, using what was called telecommunications; that is, the familiar modem and phone line. It was all very exciting, kids getting linked with other kids, teachers communicating with other classrooms, and all these telecomputing projects. But the question was, "That's great, but how are we going to scale this up?" Because if you are to get all the classrooms involved, there

has to be something going on in a school beyond a single modem, which obviously can be used by only a few people in the school—usually one or two teachers in the school who are interested and have the modem. Since many schools *did* have local area networks, it seemed at the time that if we could somehow tie the local area networks to the telecommunications networks, there would be a solution to distributing network access to many more teachers and students in the school.

We knew that the Internet technology existed— BBN actually has been working on Internet technology for 25 years. However, at that point, it was almost nonexistent in the schools. Internet was not seen as a way to connect local area networks. What you had was a computer with a modem connected as a dial-up terminal to a host computer. What teachers saw on their screen was a text-based interface to a host computer, often located at a local university or host for a state network (in those days, a state network consisted of a host computer to which teachers connected as terminals). The host computer, of course, was connected to the Internet, and the teachers could *telnet* or *ftp* from the host to other Internet sites. The Web, at that point, was unknown, and the idea of the kind of Internet connection that would support a web browser was far into the future. [It was in 1993 that NCSA's Mosaic program popularized the Web.]

To understand how schools could connect their LANs (not just isolated modem-equipped computers) to the Internet, we began a search for schools that had done it. We got some survey data from the California Technology Project and re-analyzed it to identify specific schools that had both a wide area connection (in other words, they declared they had a modem) and schools that had local area network. As you can see in Figure 1, we identified 43 schools we could call up, and we actually got on the phone and asked how they were connecting their telecommunications network—their wide area network with their local area network.

We discovered that none of the schools we contacted had any connection at all between the

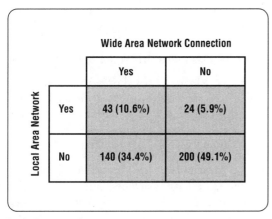

Figure 1

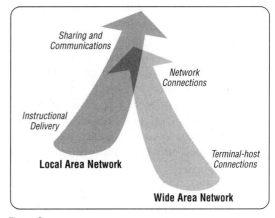

Figure 2

local area network and the wide area network. Usually the modem wasn't even on a machine that was in the computer lab. And there were two reasons for that. One is, as I said, the wide area connections were all terminal-host connections. They were connected to an Internet computer but they weren't themselves on the Internet. And none of the local area networks were running Internet protocol either.

More important, the purposes of the two kinds of networks were quite distinct. While the purpose of the telecommunications network was project-based learning, communication, and sharing of data and information, the purpose of the LAN was to distribute courseware to workstations in the school. So we came up with a theory of a convergence that was going to have to happen. We thought that as wide area networks stopped using terminal-host connections and started using real network connections, and the local area networks started being used more for communication and sharing data, they would come together (see Figure 2). And to some extent, that is what happened.

What we see in 1996 is absolutely that where they're connected, the local area network and the wide area network in schools are extensions of each other. They have converged, from a technical point of view. The Internet in the schools is pretty much an absolute standard even for dial-up.

So the technical convergence we thought necessary has happened. It's moving rapidly even in states that had widely implemented a terminal-host kind of network. Even administrative networks that are being put in are increasingly using the same Internet protocol that is being used for instruction. For the schools, we are seeing that this is increasing the access, as we had predicted. The broader access is letting students become producers of information, get experience in the information economy. So arguably, the technology is helping them be better prepared for the kind of roles they will take in the future of the Information Age.

Now it appears that a different kind of convergence is needed to fuel the continued expansion of Internet. The convergence on the network technology side is well along, at least in principle. That is, with the emergence of the Web and web browsers, everybody agrees that the appropriate kind of wide area connection is the kind of Internet connection that allows you to use a web browser. That is true whether that connection is for a single computer with a modem or a whole local area network. But the necessary convergence is only beginning to happen with respect to the purposes of the technology. What we understand now is that the convergence of purposes has to bring the "top-down" content from outside the school together with the "bottom-up" purposes from inside the school.

This view is somewhat different from the one we had several years ago, when it appeared that the goal of supporting the project-based and communication-based curriculum would drive the adoption of the Internet standards. It now appears that the delivery of the more structured curriculum from the large commercial publishers will help to drive the wide spread adoption of Internet connections, as well as changes in the school-based technologies that will help schools take full advantage of the connections.

Consider textbook publishers as a powerful force outside the school. Traditionally, they have been involved with delivering content. Content is beginning to become available on the Web. We're starting to see it right now at McGraw-Hill, among others. All the publishers have web sites, and they are beginning to address the issues of how you sell this content into the schools and how you put the curriculum onto the Internet. But they can't deliver their content until the schools open up their networks to them. So we can look at a new kind of convergence that will have to happen; the publishers adjusting their model of the structured curriculum to take advantage of how the Internet works, and the schools adopting the kind of technology and opening up their connections so the publishers can use them to distribute licensed material.

From the school side of this convergence, there is still a long way to go. The use of the Internet in schools has inherited the pedagogy of the project-based learning and is still dominated very much by the pioneering kind of teacher. As a result, it is generally not very well integrated into curriculum. The web sites are usually a construction of individual teachers, who are really excited about this.

On the technical side, within the school, there are still infrastructure limitations that interfere with publishers bringing in web content:

- The instructional management systems that are running on the local area networks are generally incapable of actually managing connections to the outside. For example, the schools are concerned that students are protected from inappropriate content as well as how we focus attention on the content that is useful for the curriculum so that you can get kids actually working on things that are meaningful.

- The LANs are still based on a kind of model of five to ten years ago—not a model in which teachers exert control over how the curriculum is presented, what resources are made available, and so on.

- The personal computers are still designed as, of course, personal machines, and the operating assumptions in the local area network are incapable of dealing with what you actually need in a school, which is machines that are network-centric.

Now the other limitation on the school side is, of course, the dollars. We've heard a lot about this. Netdays are not going to be enough. It will take billions of dollars to wire all the classrooms. And then once you actually put the wire in there's the ongoing costs of Internet service and staff development, and other costs that Netdays aren't going to cover.

The basic problem for the school Internet marketplace remains reaching into the school to the computers to which large numbers of students have access.

I'd like to talk a bit now about the direction we think things are headed in the final years of the century. I think the convergence will continue to bring the Internet into the curriculum. This will require continued improvement of the school technology, as well as a synthesis of the traditional structured curriculum with the project-based approach that takes advantage of the power of the Internet for communication, interaction, and research using primary source materials. (Roger used an example of that, where a curriculum unit now ties into the Internet so that the curriculum draws not only on the wide area network resources, but also on information that's in the school, say in the textbook or other kinds of resources, and that the schoolwork begins to combine both the tutorial kinds of things—teaching kids to do the basic skills—with the more constructive kind of activities for which the Internet connections are best suited.)

I believe we will continue to see a lot of competition among publishers for this market as it develops and that there will be continuing attempts to infuse the curriculum materials with the Internet connections. We will also see the combination of instructional and administrative networking using the whole district Internet or network infrastructure. That is, the two are now actually using the same infrastructure, so we ought to see pairings of companies sell content with companies that offer the basic administrative infrastructure.

This raises one important role of government. These new technologies that address the very specific characteristics of schools are not something that Bill Gates or Scott McNealy or [Jim] Clark are actually going to develop, because the market is very small. So, similar to the project Geoff mentioned in Texas, Florida has been working on a project to develop some of the underlying capabilities schools will need to combine their administrative and instructional networks. Now Florida and Texas are way ahead in implementing Internet. They need capabilities in their school district sites for access control, authentication, licensing their materials, setting up systems so kids can go to any computer and get access and be authenticated from that location; and where the server now serves as a local cache for outside information to reduce the requirement for and cost of a lot of bandwidth into the school.

I want to show you the design of a system, initially developed by the state of Florida, to create the kind of infrastructure that would support commercial web-based content, and integrate it with the emerging teacher-initiated, project-based school work that until now has been driving the early introduction of the Internet. This is just a quick picture of what the environment would look like to a student in one of these schools using this system, the "Network Access Manager." (I'm not going to show you the system by which teachers administer the system,

which is being built as a Java application, but rather the environment that gets created). If you were here last session for the presentation by Paul Reese, this system is actually modeled on how his school uses its networked computers.

First the student has to identify himself before any kind of local network or Internet access is granted (Figure 3).[*] A file server that opens up when the student logs in, and from there he or she can get into personal work places that are carried through from year to year. He or she can get into the newspaper area where all the group files are, the connections to get their mail, and that sort of thing. This student has access to all this by virtue of being a member of a group that's been defined in the management system. And if the student clicks on this little piece of Netscape in the Level 2 *Tools* folder, he or she actually comes up with a *Bookmark file* that then leads him out into various places on the Internet to which students have been given access (Figure 4).

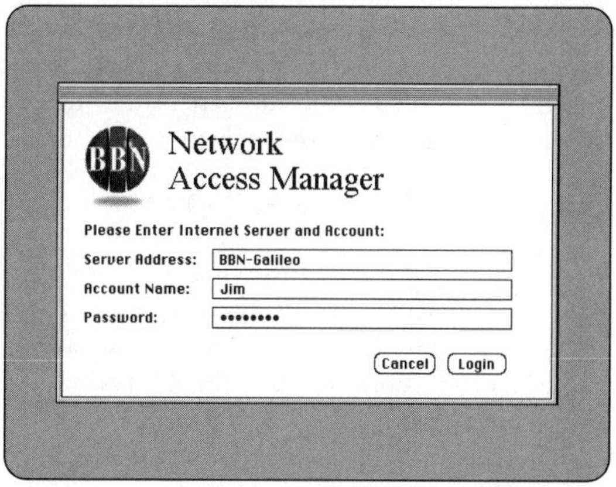

Figure 3

For example, PBS is part of the curriculum so the student can click on the PBS link and get to PBS. But if the student tries to edit the location line and go to somewhere else like Nintendo, he gets a message that he can't get to it and that will be an important capability.

This bookmark screen in Figure 4 is a bit dull, but we imagine that publishers will add interest

---

[*] Note that Figures 3 and 4 are only a partial representation of the screen shots described.

Figure 4

to these pages with graphics and instructions and deliver them as part of curriculum material. In the Network Access Manager, these web pages can be assigned to groups of students and, in the assignment of that file to a group, each individual, by virtue of being part of the group, is given access to the appropriate resources (coded as URLs in the file). And these resources can be local, as you see. Some of them are on the file server itself, which is actually part of the Internet server or on the web site, which is part of the school's Internet server or outside the school entirely.

In summary, the Internet working model for connecting school networks to the Internet is firmly established. Publishers are poised to take advantage of connections to the school. Technology that will let schools take full advantage of Internet connections will also soon be in place. But it will be costly to wire up the schools to a point that the volume will be great enough to make it a profitable market. So where will the dollars come from? And what else needs to change?

The cost issue can be addressed in several ways.

1. One push may be from changes in the publishing industry. Given the increasing cost of production of paper, schools will be looking for more efficient delivery of textbook content, so the increasing costs of producing textbooks with the decreasing cost of telecommunica-

tions make the possibility for the growth of that marketplace.

2. There is another important role of government. The huge Chapter One program in the federal government is actually designed for creating equity. Yet it currently is very difficult to use those funds for these kinds of projects because, with the way the Internet has been used in schools, there has been no clear connection to the curriculum such that you can clearly assess its effectiveness. As traditional publishers enter the market this can change, and that money, which has actually funded a huge amount of the technology in schools so far, could be used for this purpose.

3. As I said, administrative systems and instructional systems need to be combined and this will produce a cost savings.

On the technology side, there must be a shift in paradigm to a more network-centric approach to the school computing systems. The traditional file server has to encompass the functions of the Internet server and become a local cache for the external licensed content that is integrated into the school curriculum. The network management systems must encompass both the local and the remote resources.

Finally, there is the critical issue of the convergence of the purposes for which technology is being brought into schools. Bootstrapping is in order now. The major publishers won't play until there's a market, and the infrastructure won't be built out until the Internet can address the standard curriculum. In the short run, the current "bottom-up" forces that are driving Internet connections in schools—that is, the attempt to open schools up to a more constructivist curriculum based on the mostly free external resources so that students are better prepared for the Information Age—will continue to be an important political force in providing funds for connections. Ultimately, the economics of providing standard curriculum on a large scale will have to come into play for penetration into the schools to become universal.

But I think the most important thing is for the two sides of this convergence to realize the value of the other. That is, the pioneers in the schools who have been creating the capabilities will have to accept that content can be more efficiently distributed commercially, and that a lot of the services and information that is now free will be part of licensed offerings. On the other hand, the textbook publishers are going to have to live with the fact that the inherently distributive model is going to change the whole nature of what the content is, such that the customer will inevitably be participating a lot more than they are now. Thank you.

Questions & Answers

Q: *How will publishers make a living in this era?*

ROGALIN: That's an important question to me obviously. There are two ways to think about a technology can help you on your balance sheet. On the positive side of the ledger, you can think of how you can deliver instruction or content in a way that you can charge for it, so you develop a revenue stream from using technology. Denis [Newman] assured me or reassured me that there is a mechanism for that.

On the negative side of the ledger, where you're not charging for products, you can save money in different parts of your business and thereby increase your operating profit. And certainly the Internet provides opportunities for that: it really has to do with the technology. One thing I didn't mention that I think is very, very important, that we often forget, is that the technologies used are appropriate to the instructional goals.

One question I'm always asked is if I see books going away or some indication of that. I don't because there is an appropriate use for ink on paper, there's an appropriate use for standalone personal computers, and there's an appropriate use for online or Internet or World Wide Web.

Q: *Part of the shift in paradigm has to do with the ability of information interactivity to flow in two directions instead of in one, and with more members of this mar-*

ketplace connecting with one another. *Geoff raised the question of how the Internet itself may address one piece of the equity problem by facilitating support for teachers, administrators, and others. Can you say a bit more about how the Internet will be a medium for supporting the development of school teachers, parents, administrators, and the rest of us?*

FLETCHER: Well one of the things we clearly hear teachers say time and time again is that they are isolated. They are usually stuck in a classroom, they don't have time. As a former English teacher, I know I had about 150 students at the high school level. Somebody used the term "wall-to-wall time"—you get up in the morning and you're grading papers and you're preparing four different classes and you do the same thing in the evening. So part of what the Internet can do is break down some of that isolation between and among teachers, and allow teachers to communicate with each other.

Q: *How can these institutional participants—content providers, infrastructure providers, and schools—develop relationships that allow our expertise and resources to flow more freely?*

NEWMAN: I think what we have to avoid as much as possible is creating school-specific technology. Although I outlined one, it's actually designed as a very thin layer on top. The advantage the home market has is that it can participate in a much, much broader technology infrastructure. Schools need to use standard stuff as much as possible. So I think in terms of partnerships we have to make sure that we don't put ourselves in a special situation.

WISKE: I'd like to just conclude our session with the following question that brings the content of this conversation to the individual level (we've talked a lot at the institutional level).

Q: *I'm interested in the problem of professional development and training of teachers. Since grassroots efforts can be quite powerful, how can I, one person, who has a great store of knowledge and access to technology, make an impact on my local community?*

WISKE: This person probably has good answers for that question already, but I invite all of us to embrace the question in hopes that the conversation we've started today will be mediated via the Internet and other more direct contacts. So that, as individuals, we are able to participate in meeting some of the challenges that we discussed today and in taking advantage of the opportunities. Thank you.

About the Speakers

MARTHA STONE WISKE is a lecturer at the Harvard Graduate School of Education and Co-Director of the Educational Technology Center there. She teaches about issues of new technology in education, including the evolution of distance education with computer-mediated communication and the process of integrating technological innovations into schools. Her recent research focuses on teaching for understanding (with and without new technologies) and on systemic approaches to school improvement.

DR. GEOFFREY H. FLETCHER is Executive Director of T.H.E. Institute, a company dedicated to providing high quality products and services for professional development concerning technology and education. T.H.E. Institute is a division of *T.H.E. Journal*. Prior to starting T.H.E. Institute, Dr. Fletcher held numerous positions during his 11 years with the Texas Education Agency. His most recent position with the agency was Assistant Commissioner with responsibility for curriculum, assessment, textbooks, technology, and professional development. Dr. Fletcher has a B.A. in English from Miami University, an M.A.T. in

English from Miami University, and an Ed.D. in Futures Studies and Curriculum from the University of Cincinnati.

DENIS NEWMAN is Director of Marketing for Internet Products at BBN and Product Manager for software tools used in administering Internet resources in the school environment. Previously at BBN, Dr. Newman directed research and development on communication networks for schools, including the National School Network Testbed which is investigating the functionality and implementation costs of large-scale networks of K–12 schools. He has written for a variety of journals including *Cognitive Science*, *Discourse Processes*, and *Journal of Educational Computing Research*, and is the co-author, with Michael Cole and Peg Griffin, of *The Construction Zone: Working for Cognitive Change in School* (Cambridge University Press, 1989).

ROGER R. ROGALIN joined Macmillan/McGraw-Hill School division in July, 1995 as Senior Vice President, Publisher. Mr. Rogalin is responsible for all editorial departments, production and design, and software and multimedia development. Mr. Rogalin comes to Macmillan/McGraw-Hill School division from his position as Vice President, Director of the School Division of the Association of American Publishers, where he was involved in major legislation and rule-writing. Prior to that, he was at D.C. Heath as Senior Vice President, Director of School Publishing. During this time he directed product development for elementary and secondary programs, and oversaw all school publications.

CHAIR: MARCELLO PAGANO
Professor of Statistical Computing
Harvard School of Public Health

Health Care

AIDS AND THE INTERNET

MODERATOR: Richard Marlink

PANELISTS: Geoff Eisen
Lauren Ferguson
Michael Immel
Kiyoshi Kuromiya
James Marks
Nancy Marks

TRANSFORMING MEDICINE

MODERATOR: Marcello Pagano

PANELISTS: Mark Boguski
Douglas A. Perednia

HARVARD NEWS

CONFERENCE ON THE INTERNET AND SOCIETY

May 29-31, 1996   Cambridge, MA

Helping People Live with AIDS via the Internet

By William J. Cromie

"I'm going to rain on the Internet parade," Geoff Eisen said yesterday as he opened a conference discussion session on AIDS and the Internet.

Worldwide, few people who have the disease are computer literate, educated, or financially well-off enough to get much out of it, said the International Data Manager for the Harvard AIDS Institute. Only about seven percent of people in this country have access to the Internet, and most of them are not at high risk for the disease.

Twenty-five percent of the world's people are illiterate, and that includes one in five Americans. Outside of English-speaking nations, the Net suffers from what he calls "linguistic imperialism." Then there are the problems of free speech restriction, and reliable electronic and communications systems.

The five other panelists, however, discussed various "umbrellas" that do keep "rain" off both AIDS patients and those who attempt to help them via the Internet. Richard Marlink, Executive Director of the Harvard AIDS Institute [HAI] moderated the sparsely attended session.

Lauren Ferguson, a project manager at HAI, pointed out that most AIDS patients get their information from physicians and other health care workers, rather than directly from the Internet. She maintained that it is up to the technically fortunate to communicate the latest knowledge quickly to caregivers all over the globe.

Ferguson insisted that this knowledge must be presented so it is comprehensible, not just as medical text.

"We have to develop innovative ways to communicate that include audio and video information," she said. "Besides the latest medical treatments, we must provide information about prevention and survival. We want to tell people how they can live with AIDS instead of just die from it."

Fellow panelist Kiyoshi Kuromiya told the audience that he is doing both, and he talked about how he and other AIDS activists use the Internet. The founder and director of a Philadelphia-based organization called Critical Path, he provides the latest information on trials of new drugs, and on use of approved and unapproved treatments via printed, phone, and web page form.

"We on the 'bleeding edge' of science cannot wait months, even years, for research results to be analyzed and published," Kuromiya said. Critical Path updates its web site (which gets as many as 6,000 hits a week) daily, or "hourly, when needed." The site also hosts other web pages. He provides free software and dial-up service in Philadelphia.

Kuromiya expressed concern that government efforts to keep sexually explicit material off the Internet would hamper efforts at AIDS education. "To convey life-saving information to young people at risk of the disease, you have to get sexually explicit," he said.

The majority of the ten million users of the Internet in the U.S. are young males, the same descriptors of the main group that dies of AIDS, noted James Marks, who runs a New York AIDS action group called The Body.

Like Kuromiya, he wants to inform people of drugs that may be used for treating conditions for which they have not been approved. He used the example of thalidomide, which once caused horrific birth defects, and is now being tested for treating tuberculosis and several AIDS-related illnesses, such as wasting.

"Pharmaceutical companies are limited by law in what they can say about those and other drugs under testing or not yet approved," Marks pointed out. "We need to figure out how to wisely mesh our new technology with these old regulations."

Mike Immel of the AIDS Action Committee praised the rich sharing of information among researchers made possible by the Internet. But he noted it should be adapted for those who need help with their treatment. He is establishing a system that lists the trials of new drugs and evaluates the results to date. "Patients don't want to read medical information they can't understand; they want to know if a drug 'sucks' or looks promising," he noted.

In closing the session, Ferguson acknowledged the limits of the Internet in helping to break the AIDS pandemic, but she insisted that it has its place.

"The Internet can't be used by everyone, or for everything," she said. "But it is a part of a global information, education, and research system that can save lives. It's up to us to be more creative in finding new and better ways to use it for that."

Health Care

May 29, 1996

AIDS and the Internet
Networks of Knowledge and Infection

MODERATOR: Richard Marlink
PANELISTS: Geoff Eisen
Lauren Ferguson
Michael Immel
Kiyoshi Kuromiya
James Marks
Nancy Marks

A note from the Chair, Marcello Pagano:

This session is a bit different from the others, because once we advertised it, there wasn't much interest in this topic among the other conference attendees. Rather than cancel the session, however, we thought it was important to keep it on. Rick Marlink suggested we open it to the public and that is what we've done.

MARLINK: AIDS [Acquired Immune Deficiency Syndrome] is often a disease of isolation. And as the illness progresses, people with HIV [Human Immunodeficiency Virus] may find it harder to track the latest treatment strategies, to visit their physicians, and to maintain the sense of community we all need. While these difficulties may be fairly common, they are not inevitable. Recent studies have found that installing network computers in the homes of people with HIV can lessen their sense of isolation. The Internet can also be used for access to the latest treatment information, perhaps as a policy tool, which the AIDS epidemic and AIDS activism have honed as perhaps no other patient group or disease-related effort has done. It could also be used to speed research, clinically, or in the basic sciences of epidemiology. And last, it could be used to bring some of the same legal issues to the forefront,

concerning AIDS prevention messages, safe sex messages, and confidentiality.

With that, I'd like to ask the panelists to speak briefly about how they came to be involved with AIDS and the Internet, and to comment on the role of the Internet in fighting AIDS.

GEOFF EISEN, the International Data Manager at the Harvard AIDS Institute laboratories, is an anthropologist involved with managing our international HIV research projects in Africa and in the United States.

EISEN: I think I was invited to participate because Rick is aware that I am a bit negative about the Internet. (I don't know to what extent my feelings are shared by the panel. We'll see.)

There are a few questions I think are important. The basic one is, can the Internet improve AIDS research and the provision of treatment and support? I can break that down into five parts:

1. Dissemination of AIDS prevention and treatment information.

2. Support for persons with AIDS and care givers.

3. Organization of information about AIDS and HIV.

4. Communication among AIDS researchers and among public health professionals.

5. Facilitating the research process.

Now I intend to rain a little on the Internet parade. Before touting the Internet as an AIDS information resource, let's not forget that the computer literate are a very small minority. I find it difficult to be sanguine about a system that serves the better educated and more affluent, inasmuch as these people already have access to what society has to offer.

A few statistics might help. According to an April CNN news report, only seven percent of the American public has access to the Internet. Among minorities, this percentage is substantially lower. There is also a concern that access to the Internet by minorities is not likely to improve. I refer you to a *New York Times* report on May 24, 1994, that talked about electronic redlining, where plans for building the Information Super-highway seem to exclude poorer neighborhoods and minority communities.

Literacy is also a problem. It is estimated that 25 percent of the world's population is illiterate, according to a survey commissioned by the Department of Education. The DoE also reports that nearly half of American adults have limited reading and writing skills. One in five Americans is functionally illiterate.

There is also the matter of linguistic imperialism. Most communication on the Internet is in English. As a native speaker of English, I don't object to this. But if I could only read Spanish, I might feel differently. I grant that English is the *de facto* language of international business, science, and technology, but I wonder how useful and accessible English-language AIDS information is internationally, beyond the health care researchers and service providers who do, in fact, read English.

Then there are the minimum requirements for access to the Internet. You have to:

- Live in a country or a region that has a reliable electrical and communications infrastructure.

- Have a government that is not too suspicious of unrestricted communication.

- Read English to make use of most of what's available.

- Be wealthy enough to afford a computer and online charges, or fortunate enough to have free access to a computer with a free Internet connection.

- Have at least intermediate computer skills and an understanding of the Internet; for example, how to navigate it, how to find information, and transfer files.

I'm willing to bet that, at the moment these criteria are met by, or are within the reach of, most health care professionals in the Western industrial-ized world, but not by too many people beyond that group. I would ask, what proportion of the

people at greatest risk for HIV infection actually meet these criteria?

There is also one inescapable limitation: there are only 24 hours in the day. This means that there is a saturation point for information use. If you have, say, 100 TV channels right now, and some-one provides you with a way of getting 1,000 TV channels, have they given you anything you can really use? I don't think so. Providing people with access to vast amounts of information and data is fine. But when will they ever have the time to absorb more than they already do?

As a source of information for the general public, I think the Internet does provide some good material, bearing in mind that again we're talking about better educated and more affluent Ameri-cans. Some of the interesting, useful, and reliable web sites are represented on the panel: The Body, the AIDS Action Committee, and Critical Path, I think, are fine. But there are also a num-ber of web sites and sites on the Internet you may have run into that are unconventional, to say the very least, *vis-à-vis* AIDS and HIV.

As a source of information for persons with AIDS, I have to ask what proportion are being reached in this way. In browsing through the AIDS-related newsgroups, I'm troubled by some of the postings. I think it's fine to be a "proactive medical consumer," but some of the comments I see posted in these newsgroups make me think there are a lot of people out there who are man-aging their own treatment. I wonder if their phy-sicians are aware of what they're doing. They seem to be conducting their own experiments. And although this may be fueled by desperation, I don't think it does much to help the doctor-patient compact. I also wonder why these people could not get the information they needed from their physicians. Why did they have to turn to the Internet? For instance, toxicities of drugs taken in combination is a commonly requested bit of information.

I also have a few things to say about virtual sup-port groups. The comparison of virtual support groups to real support groups is a false parallel if we're talking about social interaction. Virtual groups are real, it's just that they're different. My question is, are they sufficient substitutes for real face-to-face interaction? When you consider that the virtual support group is operating using a very narrow conduit, the written word, you lose information from other channels. You lose the visual and auditory cues, facial expressions, body language, and so forth. And I don't think there is a smiley that's as good as a hug.

But there are some advantages to virtual support groups. One is that, owing to the stigma that still surrounds HIV infection and AIDS, it allows people to participate in support groups without revealing their identities, and I think that's an advantage. It may also be that virtual support groups are all the support you can get in particular communities that don't have "real" support groups.

There might be another useful role for the Internet in terms of research. There's an old bromide in engineering that you learn more from your mistakes than you do from your successes. In biomedical research today, publication is usually limited to reports and studies that achieve statistical significance. We continue to worship the .05 level. There are, I'm sure, reams of material, unpublished studies in filing cabinets, that never see the light of day because they failed to reach statistical significance or because there was some design flaw. What that does is prevent us from learning from other people's mistakes. We talk about the waste of reinventing the wheel; we should also consider the waste that goes into reinventing the square wheel. I think the Internet would be an interesting way of publishing a sort of reverse journal, a journal of studies that did *not* achieve significance and that *may* have flaws, so we can learn from (and not repeat) the mistakes made by our colleagues.

In terms of data management, I don't have much use for the Internet. In the process of research design and data gathering, at some point in the planning process, somebody decides what kind of data is going to be needed to answer the questions you want to answer and how to best go about gathering that data. Data-gathering instruments are designed; typically they are paper forms that are administered by field researchers. For lab-based projects, data is entered into a lab book. These data are then entered into a database on a computer, cleaned and exported to a statistics or graphics program. The data is then analyzed, reported, and so forth. In all of these steps, I don't see much of a role for the Internet. It's nice to be able to transfer files, but the Internet is not something that is solving a problem we didn't have solutions for before.

My basic feeling is that the Internet is no panacea. The Internet's contribution to the improvement of AIDS research and the provision of treatment and support, I think, will be marginal because it's tangential to the obstacles we face. It's just another means of communication, which is not something we didn't already have. I grant you it can cut down the time it takes to find and retrieve bits of information, and it may be a more cost-effective way of finding and retrieving this information, but it can also bury you in information. For researchers, I see the Internet as a great convenience but no great help. Finally, what bothers me the most is that it reaches such a small proportion of the general public and the people who have AIDS.

MARLINK: Thanks, Geoff. Next is **LAUREN FERGUSON**. Lauren is a student at the Harvard School of Public Health, as well as the WebMadam for the Harvard AIDS Institute [*http://www.hsph.harvard.edu/ Organizations/hai/home_pg.html*].

FERGUSON: I come to this discussion with a very different perspective. The World Wide Web has unwittingly become a centralized point for information and services for people living with HIV/AIDS, their care providers, and researchers. The Web demonstrates the efficacy of empowering individuals to help themselves by making their own informed decisions about health care and psychological well-being. The interactive capabilities of the Web provide a bridge over the information gaps that many agencies cannot process or fulfill.

When Rick and I first talked about developing a web presence for the Institute, the very first question was how to take this innovative communication medium and create a unique information intervention. How can the Institute accurately, effectively, and quickly communicate that information to the basic scientist, the clinician, the social science researcher, and the policy maker?

As a student, I also wanted to take advantage of the Web's ability to actively and interactively transform information consumers into information providers. So the question becomes, what are the information needs of people living with HIV and how easily can they access the information that's available?

Before coming to Harvard, I had a great opportunity to work at the AIDS Library of Philadelphia, the only library of its kind in the country, and to work with Kiyoshi [Kuromiya] on Critical Path. Much of my focus is looking not just at the barriers but at the opportunities to take this new medium effectively, as public health officials, and use it.

We must confront the issues of access to information. We must remove barriers, such as language barriers, illiteracy, and deafness, that impede empowerment. In an information-rich society, having access to information means having access to services. So I ask, how are we going to give people who need access to this information greater access to it, and, with that, greater access to services?

It's recognized that in communities of color, people are becoming infected at a rate five times greater than our white counterparts. But is that simply due to services, or to lack of information? The question that arises when you look at the Internet and surveys by people living with HIV is, what is their greatest need? Their greatest need is access to treatment information.

Looking at the World Wide Web, can we say that treatment information is culturally and linguistically appropriate? Are we still putting information out there that is directed at the researcher? Or are we giving people with HIV who do have access to the Internet information

which empowers and fosters the management of HIV disease?

The next steps to assess the Web's role in this process are to ask what do we know and what don't we know. We know the Web is a tool that is only available to people who have expendable income. But as public health professionals, we must start investigating answers to these questions:

- Who is actually using it?

- Where are they getting their information?

- How are they using what they find?

- What role do they play in the HIV community?

- Are they case managers? Primary care providers? People living with HIV?

> *We must confront the issues of access to information. We must remove barriers, such as language barriers, illiteracy, and deafness, that impede empowerment.*

Last semester I was enrolled in a class where three of the things that I specifically examined included how the need for information about HIV services parallels the expansion of the epidemic; the recognition of the knowledge of HIV and AIDS and the ability to act on that knowledge since the beginning of the epidemic; and the recognition that the typical public health message is simply not going to work. We must incorporate the perspectives of people who are living with HIV.

What *are* their perspectives? How do they deem the information to be valuable? Here we have all this valuable information on the Internet, but what purpose is it serving? I think that what often happens is, as professionals and as researchers and as public health policy makers, we need to remember that if information is not community-based, if the community is not oriented toward the community, you're not going to be able to pass that information on to empower a community to change its surroundings.

The World Wide Web offers us that opportunity. It offers us an opportunity to go into the community and ask, "What information do you need?" and to ask, "What is the best way to present it?" Because the Web is such a dynamic medium, all of the capabilities can be effectively used to carry a clear message that HIV is a preventable disease and that if you are living with HIV, you can become part of a society that's living with HIV, rather than a person who's dying from HIV.

I think what happens, when we look at the Internet as simply a database for information management, is that we disconnect the information from the person who's living with HIV. The Internet *does* offer us an opportunity to keep that connection between the information and the person, and a chance to give them a culturally and linguistically appropriate message that achieves a level of understanding that is not dictated by those of us who use this secret public health language. Thanks.

MARLINK: Next we'll hear from **MICHAEL IMMEL**, the manager of HIV information at AIDS Action Committee. Mike runs an HIV treatment, education, and information program at AIDS Action Committee.

IMMEL: We recently won one of the National Library of Medicine grants to "Internetize" our library offerings and the work we do at the AIDS Action Committee [*http://www.aac.org/*]. It was basically a grant to buy a lot of hardware, $25,000 worth of plastic, plugs, and that stuff. So at this point we're basically discovering how to use the Internet. One of our first approaches in the grant was to look at integrating the electronic information with our print information family of products, and see where that takes us. So we're going through the paces and seeing what's useful and what's not.

We just got the web site up, and the major portion of work on our agency's web site is the HIV treatment information. While a lot of the products we have are in print and they're useful in print, the information is also quite useful on the Internet.

Since 1989, we've had this treatment resource library at AIDS Action. What we've done is catalogue and index the community-based treatment information, which I would characterize as different from the professional literature of public health and medicine. This is the literature that sprung up in the '80s, in response to the epidemic. Then there are a half-dozen or more journals that are widely read by people with AIDS and their community-based service providers. I think the term "community-based" helps you to understand and locate where we are in this world of information.

The literature has become more sophisticated over the last decade, but, compared to the professional literature, it is readable by someone with a mere Master's degree. So it's somewhat more accessible.

In our library, we publish this one-page newsletter on a monthly, bimonthly, or quarterly basis, depending on our volunteer capacity, that tells about the new articles in the library. And it's all about treatment information. This is now on the Net. The way our library has always worked is that people phone in and ask for some information on particular articles or on a collection of topics, typically core topics that people with HIV want to know about: disease conditions, or drugs, and such. So that's on the Net. We just got our first request from Halifax, Nova Scotia, a fairly distant site. There is probably not a lot of community-based treatment information for that person up there. So we're quite pleased to be able to do that. We see that as something quite hopeful.

I think one of the most unique information products our core group of volunteer librarians have created is a subject index to community-based literature, across about seven journals [*http://www.aac.org/hivtreat/index/subj.htm*]. Most AIDS service organizations around the country have all these journals in their libraries or in different offices around their sites, but when you want to find that article on PCP [*Pneumocystis carinii* pneumonia] in children, it's not an easy trick. But now we have indexed all those articles for the last seven years, and this should be up on the Web in a week. And it's updated every month.

We now have 100 print subscribers around the country. We don't know what effect this is going to have on us, in terms of growth and demand, but this is really the core of our collection. It's going to be a very useful tool for people who want to access information that's readable, and be a boon to a lot of service organizations around the country.

We also list as many clinical trials in the region as we can—in the New England region and in Massachusetts, in particular. While there are trial directories of all sorts out there, none of them are comprehensive. You have to work a few different angles to get the information you want. We're doing one just for the Massachusetts area, and the only distinction is that we provide a comment or a review, a critical voice that says, "This trial is good," or "This trial sucks." And the voice comes from a person with AIDS [PWA] who is considering participating. The motivation for trial participation is that the PWA wants the new therapy. This is not something that the AIDS research industry has realized yet. It has a great deal to do with trial design and compliance and people staying in the trials. And as trials become more and more competitive for patronage, we're hoping that this document actually gives some feedback to the research community, including the pharmaceuticals, as well as a very helpful, readable guide to clinical trials.

This is mainly what we do. We're discovering where to put our information. We're trying to identify the unique characteristics of the Internet and how it's going to be useful to our 1,500 PWA clients as well as the public. We haven't found that yet. We've found that we spend a lot of time funneling through the muck, but we have these beautiful and productive moments on occasion, where information converges and provides real assistance to someone struggling with the treatment.

A case in point is people with HIV *do* have some treatment opportunities, which have been recently expanding at a terrific pace. But in later stage AIDS, or in early stage AIDS, when you're off the graph—where most of the action is, with respect to research or clinical practice—doctors don't know what's going on. Research doesn't know what's going on. And patients are, on occasion, trying things in collaboration with doctors and researchers to try to push the envelope. Some of the sites on the Internet are useful in identifying discussions around those issues. One does have to wade through and see what's of value, but there is a kind of productive field to garden for on-the-edge treatment information that people need to know, to advance their options.

MARLINK: Thank you, Mike. Now I'd like to introduce **KIYOSHI KUROMIYA**. Kiyoshi is director and founder of *Critical Path AIDS Project*.

KUROMIYA: By way of introduction, I should say I'm wearing three hats today. First, I'm an Internet consumer. Second, I'm an Internet content producer. Third, I'm an Internet service provider.

First, as a person with full-blown AIDS for a number of years, I use the Internet daily to get the vital information on which I make my treatment decisions. This is important to me because I am a survivalist, living on the cutting edge (some would say the bleeding edge) of current AIDS research. I need to know the unpublished and yet-to-be analyzed data on the experimental drugs of which I'm a consumer today. This information may make the difference between life and death for me.

Second, I am also a content producer. Since 1989, I have edited and published an AIDS treatment newsletter called *Critical Path AIDS Project*. It's a 96-page periodical with a circulation of 10,000. I've also operated the nation's only 24-hour peer-operated AIDS treatment telephone hotline, an early excursion into cyberspace, and since 1992, an AIDS treatment BBS [bulletin board system]. Now we operate Critical Path AIDS Project, the hypertext edition, on the World Wide Web, at *http://www.critpath.org/*. Currently, we get up to 60,000 hits per week from 1,300 unique domains in 65 countries.

Third, for over a year, I have been an Internet service provider in the Philadelphia area. Critical Path, a small grassroots organization with one full-time employee, one part-time employee, and an annual budget of under $100,000, provides free software and free dial-up access to the Internet in the Philadelphia region for persons with AIDS and the staffs of over 80 AIDS service organizations in the area. We host 20 web pages besides our own, for regional and national and, soon, international organizations. Our system also hosts a dozen electronic mailing lists.

Our cutting edge approach to information gathering and problem solving was inspired by the polymath, the late R. Buckminster Fuller, with whom I collaborated on a number of books including *Critical Path*, in 1981; *Grunch of Giants,* in 1982; and posthumously, *Cosmography*, in 1992. Fuller constantly graphed the exponential increase in data rates and travel speeds for humans. Its relevance is becoming more and more apparent by the very people who scoffed when Fuller tried to convince them that humans would travel at speeds approaching the speed of light by the mid-'80s. Fuller died in 1983, while working on *Cosmography*, and unfortunately did not live to see the fulfillment of some of his prophetic explorations into carbon, the Fullerenes, and the communications of the World Wide Web.

Fuller described the exponential increase in the speed at which a message can travel around the world. He felt we were about to realize the post-Newtonian world, in which the normal or baseline was the speed of light, what we have come to think of as instantaneous. This exponential increase in speed of travel and communications is about to turn a corner, the proverbial paradigm shift.

When I was in Cambridge a year ago, David Clark told the Internet Economics Workshop at MIT, "Instant is within a second or so. The U.S. is 100 milliseconds wide, and Australia is 300 milliseconds away. It is a nice, flattening effect that everything is this close." Over four years ago, I wrote a cover story in the Critical Path newsletter about AIDS information at the speed of light.

Why is the Internet so important to me as a consumer with AIDS? By the time AIDS research and treatment information is published in a book, it is historic; some would say ancient. Even with the new bending of rules by such peer review journals as the *New England Journal of Medicine*, by the time a journal publishes AIDS research findings, the data is six months to a year or two old. For years, most activists have obtained their treatment information from grassroots newsletters like *Treatment Issues*, *AIDS Treatment News*, *Project Inform Perspectives*, and *Critical Path AIDS Project*. A newsletter can publish information within two to eight weeks. Randy Shilts, who wrote the best seller *The Band Played On*, described these newsletters as the prime and most important source for current and late-breaking treatment information for persons with AIDS.

This year, we have seen the future of AIDS information on the Internet. Critical Path's web page updates its late-breaking news daily, and hourly. We FTP information to our online publication from laptops in hotels while attending medical meetings, or at the conclusion of conference calls. Through patient advocacy, we have demanded and secured abstracts on disk and CD-ROM, including late-breakers at the beginning of AIDS medical and research conferences.

We are the same activists, fighting for our lives, who gained seats on the scientific core committees of the major federal clinical trials networks. And now we at Critical Path post on the World Wide Web the full text protocols of clinical trials of the major federal clinical trials networks. We are the same patient advocates who marched on the NIH [National Institutes of Health] in 1990, amid multicolored clouds of smoke bombs, and who stormed the FDA [Food and Drug Administration] in 1988, with bullhorns and ladders.

A few years ago, it took ten years to get a drug approved by the FDA. On March 14 of this year [1996], I sat on the FDA Antiviral Drug Advisory Panel that, through the accelerated approval process long fought for by activists, approved the Merck protease inhibitor Indenavir in a mere 42 days. As is true in other arenas, we're still spending far too much time putting out the wildfires of bigotry and misinformation, when we should be fighting for new drugs and life-saving treatments.

Critical Path was the only litigant continually invoked by Judge Dalzell in the current preliminary injunction hearings on the Communications Decency Act, which ostensibly would keep sexually explicit information from teenagers on the Internet. We know, however, that the new ill-defined law, which makes no exceptions for libraries and institutions of higher learning, will also block important speech, and in this case, life-saving speech. Critical Path has continued to provide sexually explicit safer sex information anonymously to teenagers, and in fact, is contracted to do so by the same federal government that regulates this medium, a medium that, in five days of testimony, has been shown to resist every attempt to censor, regulate, and monitor expression. To do so (as was evident from the testimony) is impossible, except at the consumer's workstation. And it will get more difficult as the sophistication of the technology improves.

How does one avoid or label indecent or patently offensive materials on one's host system, when Critical Path will soon be providing, among other things, prevention and treatment information in ten or more Asian languages, and when the text in the newsgroups we provide each day amounts to the equivalent of the full text of three entire sets of Encyclopedia Britannica?

The *Critical Path AIDS Project* has conceived and designed a blueprint for what AIDS activists, lacking a better metaphor, said, "What we need is a Manhattan Project for AIDS."

MARLINK: Thank you, Kiyoshi. Next we'll have **JAMES MARKS**, president of The Body [an AIDS action organization], based in New York [*http://www.thebody.com/*].

J. MARKS: I come to the world of AIDS information as a lawyer by training. For years, I was a civil rights lawyer and consultant on new media, and I saw the potential of putting the two together in the area of AIDS. It might be helpful to touch on some demographic information about usage of the Internet. Various studies put

American usage at ten million by the beginning of next year. We may have already hit that number. And the demographic skews highly male, skews young. We know also that AIDS is the leading killer of young males. There are some statistics from industry sources that we've seen at The Body, which we're debating how much credence to give to, which say that AIDS is the most highly represented chronic medical condition online.

So while there are other examples of disease topics being treated successfully—OncoLink, run by the University of Pennsylvania, is one of the better-known examples, which gets over a million hits a month, and has very, very extensive cancer information used by patients and physicians alike—resources like that for AIDS are being developed by people like Kiyoshi and by us. We think that AIDS has a special role to play in the world of the Internet and health because of the demographic factors I mentioned, and also for some of the reasons Kiyoshi [Kuromiya] mentioned, in terms of how AIDS lobbyists have led the way for accelerated approval processes at the FDA, for different government treatment of a disease population, for knowledgeable patients seeking to reform reimbursement structures.

Let's take an example—is there anyone here from the pharmaceutical industry or from the HMO [health maintenance organization] industry? No? Take the example of protease inhibitors, approved in March [1996] by the FDA. They're expensive, as much as several thousand dollars per year, per patient. And not all formularies of HMOs reimburse for patients to receive them, and certainly not all states, through their Medicaid programs, reimburse for this.

The Internet can be an absolutely fascinating place to inform a patient population that these drugs exist. They've passed safety and efficacy trials at the FDA. They're approved. And many doctors would recommend including them in the treatment regime. If you go to your HMO doctor, however, he or she may be discouraged from prescribing them at this time, based on the HMO's reimbursement policy. This gets at the crux of a larger trend in health care, that people with AIDS are facing on the frontlines: greater patient information, greater patient involvement in health care decisions, and how information that can be available—at least to those educated patients online—can factor in a treatment decision. A patient can effectively become his or her own best advocate by going in to the doctor informed.

Rick asked me to address several regulatory issues involving health care online. There are two sets of important regulations that one might bear in mind. (A word of caution: Don't rely on this as a legal opinion.)

Full descriptions of risky sexual behavior can be chilled, because to describe the behavior could be deemed indecent under the Communications Decency Act, and the Act bears a jail term and a fine. But others at the conference have referred to that as a red herring. And I would hope that in this context, because of the tenor of the government's briefs in that case, that law will be overturned as unconstitutional.*

Another key area of regulation that could be far more inhibiting, in terms of the funding to support the provision of AIDS information online, is FDA regulation. Given that major supporters of online medical information are often pharmaceutical companies, and pharmaceutical companies are regulated by the FDA, and are loath to jeopardize their good relationships with the FDA because they're constantly placing new drugs in the pipeline for approval, FDA regulation of direct-to-consumer advertising affects what drug companies may say online. And this plays out as follows.

Most major drug companies today have their own web sites. But at those web sites, they do not describe in great detail the research that they're conducting. They may describe their overall philosophy. They may have a questionnaire you can fill out if you're a patient for an approved medication they already have on the market. But when a drug is approved in the United States, it's approved for indicated uses. And if the drug has not yet been approved, or if the drug is being prescribed by doctors for non-indicated uses, the FDA severely curtails what a drug company may say about that. The reason is to avoid confusing the consumer, and also perhaps because the drug has not been tested to verify its efficacy for those particular nonindicated uses.

What online services can do is describe nonindicated uses. And in fact, many of the newsletters on AIDS do just that. Classic example: thalidomide. (I'll cut to the chase here.) Thalidomide is the notorious drug that gave rise in the 1950s to efficacy and safety testing by the FDA before a drug could be prescribed. Many doctors are now prescribing it for "wasting" among AIDS patients. There may be very useful applications of this drug, but the FDA would not permit the manufacturers of the drug to talk about it.

So one of the challenges online is how to provide a robust array of information in a way that can be funded by those sources that have the funds available without violating regulatory requirements from a prior era. We have an old regulatory regime and an exciting new medium that makes a lot more information available to those consuming the care. But we have to figure out how to use it most wisely.

MARLINK: Thank you, Jamie. Our final panelist is **NANCY MARKS**, Public Policy Manager at AIDS Action Committee.

N. MARKS: I'm here to talk about how AIDS Action Committee [Boston, MA] uses the Internet as a tool for public policy advocacy. My specific work at AIDS Action is to develop ways to make public policy accessible to a range of people—from AIDS service providers who don't have the time to keep up with the many policy issues to people living with HIV who may not

---

* The Communications Decency Act (CDA) was shot down by a three-judge court in June, 1996. However, on December 6, 1996, the Supreme Court agreed to hear the government's appeal for the legal challenge to the CDA. The case is expected to be heard in March, 1997. See *http://www.cdt.org* for more details.

have daily access to this type of information. My education and outreach work also includes anyone in the community who wants to gain a greater understanding of how our political system intersects with the issues of HIV.

In Massachusetts alone, there are over 100 bills filed each year that address issues that affect people with HIV. Over two-thirds of these bills, if passed, would negatively impact the lives of those living with HIV/AIDS. Some of the most important work of our Public Policy Department is to make sure that these bills don't make it through the legislature, while at the same time proposing and advocating for proactive legislation which would help people affected by HIV/AIDS.

I coordinate a program called Mass Action, a 1000-person legislative response network which makes AIDS policy information available to people throughout Massachusetts. Until recently, it was run only as a phone network. When there's a specific issue on the state or federal level which can be influenced by a concerted grassroots response, we issue a "legislative alert." People on the phone tree get a message asking them to call or write their senator or representative. Legislators are then asked, for example, to "Vote yes on this bill," or "Increase AIDS funding," depending on what the key issue is. It can be quite an undertaking. But it actually works. We've gotten a lot of feedback that our calls often make a significant difference.

When the Internet became more popular, AIDS Action began to consider how we might utilize its capabilities to our advantage. To be honest, I approached the use of technology with great reluctance. As an organizer, I have always understood that people are moved to action based on several factors—the most important being a personal connection to an issue or a problem. It was unclear then, and remains unclear still, whether or not using the Internet for organizing and advocacy purposes engages people in all the ways necessary to inspire sustained activism. But as I considered these more lofty questions, I also couldn't deny what I was seeing—how quick and easy it was to reach people throughout the state through the Internet. All of a sudden our "rapid response" legislative alert system really had a chance of being rapid. So we expanded Mass Action to add a new component called CyberAction.

CyberAction allows us to send out legislative alerts over the Internet once our members send us their email addresses. A complement to our phone network, we are able to reach our online membership in under an hour. When members receive an alert, they can now receive more background information on an issue than we are able to provide when we activate our phone tree. We have had a great response to this new program, which we advertised through an ad campaign called "The Mouse that Roared."

CyberAction has clearly been a success in the community. We have received feedback that our members like getting updates on AIDS public policy issues, and find the Internet an easy way to receive them. It has also been relatively easy to build our membership. In one month's time, 150 people signed up; it took four years to build our phone network to 700.

My job is really that of a community organizer, and it is through this lens that I approach my work. What this means in real terms is that while the "ends" is ultimately important—i.e., making sure that bad laws don't get through the legislature, it is equally important to me that people fully participate in the debate and dialogue which surrounds an issue. I know many people use the Internet for these exchanges. However, for dialogue to be most successful, I believe there needs to be face-to-face interaction between people.

The Internet gives us speed, great amounts of information and broad access. Even for me—I can't deny that it is exciting to reach so many people by pushing a button. What it doesn't give us, however, is the human touch. I may be from an old school of organizing, but I believe that the only way people will ultimately become invested in a movement is if they put their bodies on the line (metaphorically speaking). I fear that reliance on advanced technology which is, in fact, only truly accessible to a few, will both limit the kind of work we take on and will cause us to fall short of our goals.

Many questions have been raised for me through my use of the Internet. What do we gain as a movement when we use the Internet as an organizing and advocacy tool? It's clear we gain numbers. I can come up here and say we got 150 people online in one month. And now I can reach people who might never have become active in AIDS public policy had it not been for access to it through the Internet. On the other hand, I'm not sure if people will commit to sustained activism by getting a legislative alert from AIDS Action once a month on the Internet.

I'm not yet sure that access to information through CyberAction will encourage a person to become a more socially conscious individual. For many, this may be too far-reaching a goal for a program whose objectives are to influence a concrete legislative agenda. However, while this may be the goal of my work in the capacity of Manager of Public Policy, it does not satisfy my vision as someone committed to making this a more equitable and just society.

Questions & Answers

Q: *If AIDS hit today instead of 15 years ago, how would the history of the disease be different? And what difference would the Internet technology make to that?*

J. MARKS: I have a quick thought in response to that. Getting the prevention message out. Fifteen years ago, our mass medium was television. And the television networks had policies of not carrying public service announcements with condom messages. That wasn't necessarily FCC [Federal Communications Commission] regulation, but it was network policy not to talk about condoms. The Internet isn't restricted, as of yet, in terms of being able to get a prevention message out quickly. So that would be one mass media response that exists today that didn't exist 15 years ago.

KUROMIYA: Much of the information on AIDS is anecdotal. We get it in the corridors at medical meetings. We get it before it hits the newspapers. And the word would have gotten out very quickly when the first few cases were spotted in Los Angeles and New York. We would have known that there were hundreds more that just hadn't made the newspapers yet. We would have gotten the very earliest prevention information out in our communities. I know the connectivity of various individuals in these cities is very great on the Internet.

For example, if we're working on a project to get information out, we can set up on Critical Path a mailing list or discussion group overnight, as we did for new ones last week: one for ACT-UP [AIDS Coalition To Unleash Power] Network, the active chapters around the country; one for a writing group within the CPCRA [Community Programs for Clinical Research on AIDS]. The community constituency group will be communicating with local groups. We also have a group of activists who are going to be meeting in Vancouver at the International AIDS Conference, and we set up work groups overnight on that. With the Internet, word would have gotten out very quickly in our communities.

EISEN: I'll grant you that if the epidemic hit today rather than 15 years ago, things would be somewhat different. But I keep thinking of the people who aren't paying attention. Well, the mass media delivers messages about AIDS through network news and so forth. But how many Americans really listen? There have been surveys that are somewhat amusing, I guess, where people are asked who's President, where is the city of Boston located. Despite the mass media, some people can't locate themselves on the map. They're not aware of who their political leaders are. I think that the Internet is fine, and it does serve a purpose. I'm concerned that the proportion that it actually reaches is rather small and rather select. This is the zero point now for some underdeveloped nations, but what use is the Internet to these people? For those who have access, I think it's great, but access is limited.

Q: *Sometimes I get very frustrated. I've worked with community-based organizations like AIDS Action, and I come from a world of high technology. I think that* *there's the technology there to prolong life now, and even possibly a cure. The problem is really one of coordination and a different approach towards looking at information. I don't know if clinical trials look at a broad enough picture, in terms of the way they analyze data. Does anyone share my frustration with the tools available? The Internet is very much a facilitator for data warehousing, for data mining—there are much better tools than there used to be a couple years ago. And I urge the community-based organizations to become more technically sophisticated. (I think that this idea of tracking clinical trials is a good first step.) Kiyoshi, maybe you have an opinion about this.*

KUROMIYA: I serve on a panel called the AIDS Research Evaluation Working Group, that just finished a report on March 14 [1996], for the Office of AIDS Research, that looked into all the aspects of AIDS research. One of the outcomes of this was, by 1999, to integrate the clinical trials networks into at least a network that would serve a vast number of people and integrate all the data so the data could be shared, so there would be less duplication of effort, so it would be more cost effective.

Q: *What are the impediments to that happening? Do the pharmaceutical companies not want to share their data?*

KUROMIYA: Well, many of these systems were set up in a crisis situation. We're now looking back to see if we can evaluate this. I'm on the national advisory board of HIV Cost Services Utilization Survey, which is a project of Rand Corporation and AHCPR [Agency for Health Care Policy and Research], another federal agency, looking into HIV care. And for the first time we're going to look at the costs of all people accessing HIV care. It will be a 3,300-person database. The baseline survey began in January. We should start seeing results next year. It will continue into '98. But we're looking into all these systems that were set up in a crisis emergency situation. And we're evaluating them to make them more cost effective and better.

Q: *Do you think that the community-based organizations like AIDS Action have a data-gathering function as part of this effort?*

KUROMIYA: I think that we're going to depend on these community-based organizations to provide the important information because they're community-based. They're the experts in their own areas.

IMMEL: I'm in contact with research people. Some of them are volunteers at our library. I hear a rich kind of exchange among researchers on the Internet, and an ability to talk more rapidly together worldwide about issues. What I understand you saying is some kind of advocacy around information sharing and database work around treatment information.

MARLINK: I think clinical trials (although I'm not an expert on them) seem to be very narrow in focus, in terms of the variables that they look at. A database would have the computational ability to look at a much larger array of variables and say which factors relate to longevity, etc.

IMMEL: The way we see our treatment work in AIDS Action Committee and a community-based setting is, in large part, to make information available that's out there right now.

MARLINK: I'm not suggesting community-based organizations would do the analysis, necessarily. But they would have the role of gathering the data. Because there are data warehousing tools available and because the Internet facilitates the ability to build a data warehouse, community-based organizations would have a function as part of a larger national research plan.

KUROMIYA: One area where this is happening is in the OAR, the Office of AIDS Research report that I mentioned. A whole new area is being investigated, and that is alternative and complementary therapies, therapies in wide use in the community. Also off-label uses of approved medications. This is an area that at the last minute, within two months of the report being issued, was incorporated as an area of interest and an area of concern for research. So for the first time, we're going to be looking at treatments in wide use in the community, for which we have no data collected in the past.

Q: *I'm a computer scientist. How soon do you see having the patients' data channeled into an epidemiological model? And where do you think that someone like me with technical skills would be most useful at the moment?*

___: I've often felt that it would be quite convenient to be able to talk to my physician over the Internet. And I have, on occasion, forwarded information. It might even be cheaper than a consult price. So I look forward to that some day, and to some more sharing along those routes.

KUROMIYA: At Critical Path we have an electronic mailing list of HIV clinicians and researchers for the Philadelphia area. We also are hosting dissemination of RFPs [request for applications] and RFAs [request for proposals] through the city AIDS office and through the Philadelphia AIDS Consortium to AIDS services organizations. This would be for monthly data reports, etc. Thus far the city has purchased 31 computers for small grassroots agencies that don't have access to that. We're providing the link to the Internet.

FERGUSON: I'm grateful that we have this opportunity to have this type of discussion. But I think that we really seem to lose sight of a few things. The Internet should not be seen as the only tool. It's seen as one of a number of intervention methods that are available. It's seen in the scope of prevention and education, it's seen in the scope of public policy activism, it's seen in the scope of treatment information, it's used as a tool for communication among researchers. It's seen as not necessarily the answer to everything. It should first be used to reach the members of communities that are already accessing this information, with the goal of mobilizing them toward the common goal of ending the epidemic. The second task is to effectively bring in other communities that don't have access.

The Internet is going to lose that interaction if we don't keep in mind the need to maintain the human connection, regardless of the medium. It should be understood that you will lose certain things only available through that face-to-face personal contact. But yet and still, there are a lot of alternatives that we haven't looked into when we look at the Internet. The possibilities to bridge the human gap in an impersonal communication form are only limited by our imagination.

You need to take something else into consideration when you're talking about data management and putting personal information on the Internet. You need to guarantee confidentiality, you need to protect the interests and freedoms of all types of information that you're looking at when you're dealing with divulging people's HIV status.

One of the issues that Nancy [Marks] really brought to focus is the ability to take those connections that you've been able to establish via the Internet, and foster those communications using all of these other alternatives which already exist. The World Wide Web and the other components which define the Internet have only given us an opportunity to be creative, to develop new initiatives in dealing with HIV and AIDS. It shouldn't be looked at as an only alternative, or the last step.

About the Speakers

DR. RICHARD MARLINK, the Executive Director of the Harvard AIDS Institute [HAI], is also the Senior Research Director and Lecturer in the Department of Cancer Biology at the Harvard School of Public Health [HSPH]. Dr. Marlink's initial research involved collaborative trials of new anticancer agents; later he turned to trials of antivirals used to treat HIV infection. As part of the team that identified HIV-2, the second AIDS virus, he became involved in laboratory research at the Harvard School of Public Health, focusing on epidemiological and clinical studies in West Africa. Dr. Marlink has also directed a Harvard AIDS Institute program that provides laboratory training and support to AIDS investigations around the world.

GEOFFREY EISEN received his Ph.D. in anthropology from Tulane University. A specialist in ethnopsychiatry and medical anthropology, he was formerly a research associate at the University of

Hawaii's Social Science Research Institute, and is currently a data manager/analyst at the Harvard AIDS Institute and in the department of Cancer Biology at the Harvard School of Public Health.

LAUREN M. FERGUSON began her work in the AIDS World more than ten years ago, when, in 1985, she cared for terminally ill babies at the pediatric ward at Robert Wood Johnson Medical Center. After studying and working in Uganda, Ms. Ferguson returned to the United States and embarked on an information career at the AIDS Library of Philadelphia. From there she was employed by the City of Philadelphia Health Department to coordinate the HIV Prevention Community Planning Group. She is presently employed by the Harvard AIDS Institute as their WebMadam and as a Graduate Research Fellow for a Metropolitan Life Grant which is looking at the Challenge of HIV/AIDS in Communities of Color. She can be reached via email at HSPH at *lferguso@hsph.harvard.edu*, or via the Web at *http://world.std.com/~lauren/*.

MICHAEL IMMEL is HIV positive and has been involved in AIDS treatment advocacy, information, and education in the Boston area. In 1988 he was one of the founding volunteers of the community-based HIV treatment library (The Resource Library) at the AIDS Action Committee [*http://www.aac.org/*]. He was a member of the HIV treatment issues committee of ACT-UP Boston, and served as their representative to one of the first community advisory boards to the AIDS Clinical Trial Groups in 1989. At AIDS Action Committee, Mr. Immel manages the HIV Treatment Information and Education Program.

KIYOSHI KUROMIYA, a person living with AIDS, has been editor and publisher of an AIDS treatment newsletter, *Critical Path AIDS Project*, since 1989. He operates a number of cutting edge electronic services in Philadelphia, including a 24-hour AIDS treatment hotline (215-545-2212) and a comprehensive World Wide Web page on AIDS [*http://www.critpath.org/*]. An author and former collaborator on several books with the late R. Buckminster Fuller, Kuromiya is a founding member of ACT-UP Philadelphia and has been prominently active in civil rights, gay liberation, antiwar, and human rights movements for 35 years.

JAMES D. MARKS is the President of The Body, a leading web site dedicated to providing comprehensive information and building online community related to HIV/AIDS. Since its founding in 1995, The Body has come to carry materials provided by agreement with over thirty of America's top organizations and publishers working with HIV/AIDS. The Body can be found at *http://www.thebody.com/*. Prior to The Body, Mr. Marks served as a consultant on emerging media to various organizations, and as a cooperating attorney to the ACLU [American Civil Liberties Union], for which he brought a number of leading cases in gay and lesbian civil rights. He is a graduate of Yale College and Columbia Law School.

NANCY MARKS is currently Manager of Public Policy at AIDS Action Committee, where she has worked for the past five years. Her job includes coordinating Mass Action, a state-wide grassroots advocacy network of 1000 members, and developing community-based advocacy groups such as Women of Action, a group for HIV+ women, and community advocates interested in working on AIDS-related policy issues. In addition, she organizes public policy trainings and events, including the AIDS Public Policy Institute and AIDS Action's annual AIDS lobby day. Nancy cut her teeth as an organizer in her previous job as Director of Organizing for Local 509, SEIU [Service Employees International Union].

HARVARD NEWS

CONFERENCE ON THE INTERNET AND SOCIETY

May 29-31, 1996   Cambridge, MA

Web Changing Health Practice, Panelists Say

By Patricia Guthrie

When he hit page 135 of *Jurassic Park*, Mark Boguski wondered: just where did author Michael Crichton come up with his amber-preserved DNA dinosaur sequence? Surely it couldn't add up to a prehistoric creature, so what *did* it create?

To find out, the biotechie scientist jumped on the Internet and dumped the lengthy code to match it with DNA sequences already dissected and listed in the virtual world.

His discovery? The code was an exact match of a segment of bacterial DNA, used in every genetics lab across the country as a cloning vector. Crichton's dino DNA was in actuality a kind of Piltdown Skull, the infamous find once thought to be the missing link of man, later discovered to be an elaborate hoax consisting of a human cranium attached to an orangutan jaw.

"I was rather disappointed with Crichton," Boguski revealed during his presentation at Thursday's "Transforming Medicine" seminar. "I expected more of a Harvard Medical School graduate. It took me just 20 seconds on the Internet to undo his code."

Boguski, a Senior Scientist at the National Center for Biotechnology Information that is building the Human Genome Project, turned his quirky quest into an academic paper, "A Molecular Biologist Visits Jurassic Park." His cyberspace research also led to a reply from Crichton and a thanks in *A Lost World*, Crichton's DNA adventure-packed sequel.

Boguski challenged the audience to unravel Crichton's next fictional sequence, explaining how to do it with GenBank [*http://www.nchi.nlm.nih.gov/*]. GenBank contains all publicly available information on gene research and sequences, and is updated daily from its base at the National Institutes of Health near Washington, D.C.

High school students routinely call up the servers, called Entrez and BLAST (Basic Local Alignment Search Tool), as do researchers around the world who are at work unraveling the codes of diseases.

Internet technology is adding tremendous speed to the detection and eventual treatment of diseases by providing a way to instantly match DNA sequencing in organisms once thought to have no relation to one another, Boguski said.

One such example of the process, called *homology*, was the research of the disorder ataxia-telangiectasia, a childhood immune deficiency often followed by lymphoid tumors and cancer. About 2.5 million people in the United States are carriers of this gene that stumped scientists for decades.

"It took 18 years for the scientist to unravel its DNA sequence, but only 5 minutes to find its similarities to other genes" once it entered cyberspace, Boguski said.

While technology has always advanced health research and care, from the breakthrough invention of the microscope to minuscule laser surgery tools, perhaps no technological advance will prove as terrific and troubling as the Human Genome Project, Boguski said.

At a cost of $3 billion over 15 years, the Human Genome Project will reveal the genetic blueprint of humans by the year 2003, two years ahead of schedule. It will consist of three gigabits of information, three billion base pairs of DNA, and between 50,000 and 100,000 genes.

"It will be as profound as getting the first alien communication on earth," he said. "We will know the entire blueprint of humankind."

Linking far-flung patients to high tech research and urban doctors is the most cost-effective and useful application of the Internet, explained Douglas Perednia during the session's second presentation, "Making Sense of Telemedicine."

Currently, there are 120 sites in the United States using phone lines and computer images to transmit medical information ranging from chest X-rays to skin disorders. Perednia, Assistant Professor of Dermatology and Medical Informatics at Oregon Health Sciences University, explained how telemedicine helps doctors in his field assist patients by reviewing skin disorders on the screen from patients living in rural places where specialists seldom live.

A map he flashed on the screen marking where licensed dermatologists live confirmed that few live in isolated rural areas. "You will note dermatologists all live in nice places," Perednia said, flashing his penlight on the East Coast and California. "None live in the pits of Nevada and Oregon."

But consulting with far-flung patients in rural areas by doctors hundreds of miles away cannot be done without the expensive electronic equipment of telemedicine, the paradox posed to Perednia by an audience member.

He replied the Internet and telemedicine is the "most appropriate use of technology" if it saves money normally spent on traveling long distances to medical care and it saves health insurance companies (and in some cases the federal government), the reimbursements of those trips.

For example, federal health programs, such as the Veterans Administration and the Indian Health Service that serves American Indians in remote regions, should consider the costs of telemedical diagnosis versus reimbursing its patients and doctors for travel.

The critical cost of telemedicine, according to Perednia, is this: "Is the cost of seeing someone in person higher than the cost of transmitting the information over electronic wires?"

The cost of long-distance medical diagnosis will continue to come down, he predicted, as technology invents cheaper and more efficient tools. One such example is the color camera needed to photograph dermatology patients so the images can be transmitted to a referring doctor miles away. That camera has come down in price from $9,000 to $3,000, Perednia said.

"You don't have to prevent a whole lot of travel and lost work (of patients) to pay for that $3,000 camera," he concluded.

The Internet is also providing a world of consultation for doctors across the globe when they send queries about baffling cases to colleagues with a mere touch of the send key, noted seminar moderator Marcello Pagano, Professor at the Harvard School of Public Health.

He cited a recent letter on the Net from a doctor in northern India who needed help diagnosing a patient. Soon doctors from London and California responded, ending the long gone days of doctors toiling away by themselves in white lab coats, trying to save their patients.

Health Care

May 30, 1996

Transforming Medicine

MODERATOR: Marcello Pagano
PANELISTS: Mark Boguski
   Douglas A. Perednia

PAGANO: Today we want to look at how the Internet is going to affect medicine and health care. Technology has a long history of impacting medicine, of course, ranging from the microscope and the stethoscope to tremendous developments of the artificial heart and magnetic resonance imaging, etc. We will be looking at two aspects of medicine: one is basic research and how that's impacted by the Internet, and the other is care.

For the first speaker, we're very fortunate to have **MARK BOGUSKI**, from the NIH [National Institutes of Health]. Mark first got an M.D. in pathology, and then got a Ph.D. in molecular biology. He's presently at the National Center for Biotechnology Information, a division of the National Library of Medicine, where he's a senior scientist. His main research interest has to do with gene mapping associated with the human genome. Mark will now address us with his talk, entitled "Hunting for Genes in Computer Data Bases."[*]

BOGUSKI: These are the items I want to discuss:

1. A progress report on the Human Genome Project.

2. A bit of the flavor of biology on a computer.

3. How DNA databases and analysis tools will completely transform the scientific foundation of medicine in the next century.

Hunting for Genes in Computer Data Bases

I'd like to begin with a report on the Genome Project. Rapid DNA sequencing technology was invented in 1975. However, it took us 20 years to get the complete genetic blueprint of a completely free-living organism, the bacterium *Hemophilus influenzae*. It has 1.8 million base pairs in its genome, about 1,700 genes. That research was finished last summer.

Going up the tree of evolutionary complexity here, the complete genome of the budding yeast *Saccharomyces cerevisiae* was just reported in April. It's about an order of magnitude larger in size. The important thing here is that these yeast cells more closely resemble human cells than bacteria. They have nuclei and look a lot more like the cells in our body. So this was a landmark as well.

The next organism, once again in ascending evolutionary complexity, is a nematode worm, *C. elegans*. Now, this worm is only a millimeter long and has exactly 1,000 cells in its body. Yet it has a primitive nervous system, a reproductive system, and all the complexities involved in a multicellular organism. This is another landmark.

The human genome won't be done until about the year 2003. It's 3 billion base pairs of DNA, 50,000-100,000 genes. I've heard Francis Collins use this analogy before: if sequencing *H. flu* is like Alan Shepard going up and doing that suborbital flight, *S. sereveciae* was like John Glenn circling the globe, and this is the Apollo project. This is getting to the moon.

Figure 1 shows the genome sequencing milestones discussed above.

These numbers don't impress most people in astronomy or computer science or weather forecasting. When the genome is done, it's only going to be three billion bytes, three gigabytes of information. But, that's not the point. The point is, biology is complexity. And how all three gigabytes of data specify what you and I turn out to be, from a fertilized egg to an adult, is really an indication of the complexity of the process.

---

[*] Boguski, M.S., "Hunting for Genes in Computer Data Bases," *New England Journal of Medicine,* 333, 645–647 (1995)

Genome Sequencing Milestones

ORGANISM	GENOME SIZE (base pairs)	NUMBER OF GENES	COMPLETION DATE
H. influenzae bacterium	1.8×10^6	1,734	July 1995
S. cerevisiae budding yeast	12.5×10^6	6,330	April 1996
C. elegans nematode worm	100×10^6	~13,100	1998
H. sapiens you and I	$3,000 \times 10^6$	50,000-100,000	2001-2005

Figure 1

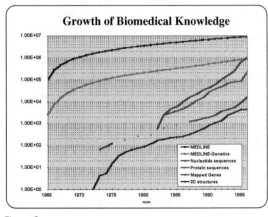

Figure 2

Let's take a look at genome information historically, as a subset of biomedical information in general (Figure 2). I'm using MEDLINE, a computerized database of all biomedical literature, which the National Library of Medicine has maintained and operated for a long, long time. It was computerized in the early 1960s and has increased significantly. MEDLINE currently contains about eight million abstracts or records, and is growing at the rate of about 400,000 articles a year, abstracted from about 3,500 biomedical journal titles. This is just a subset of MEDLINE having to do with genetics. That's 800,000 articles, and it is increasing at a greater rate than MEDLINE as a whole. As I said, rapid DNA sequencing technology was invented in 1975, but it really took off once the practice was reduced to a commercial kit. It has now been reduced to a robot, and this data is doubling every 12 months.

Right now, in the database called GenBank, there are 700,000 DNA sequences from 18,000 different biological organisms. This represents only about a half of gigabyte of raw data, so there's about a one-fifth human genome equivalent in GenBank today. These are mapped genes, protein structures, just different indications of how fast the information is growing.

Now, it's really the NCBI's [National Center for Biotechnology Information] job, where I work, to take this data and make it available. We were called the "Claude Pepper" Bill in Congress, and we date from the last Reagan Administration—

the last Reagan budget, that is. This is our [the NCBI's] mandate:

- To create automated systems for knowledge about molecular biology, biochemistry, and genetics.

- To perform research in new methods for analyzing and interpreting molecular biology data.

- To enable biotechnology researchers and medical care personnel to use the systems and methods developed.

To fulfill this mandate, we build and provide data to GenBank, Entrez, BLAST, and many other Internet-accessible databases and software tools I'll describe shortly. We're also a center for basic research and training in computational biology.

We're right outside Washington, D.C. on the NIH campus, in the National Library of Medicine complex. Buildings don't really matter any more, do they? It's the age of the Internet and World Wide Web. I'd like to point out to you, though, that there is a dark side to the Web. It's like the Wild West—all of those millions and millions of web sites out there exist, yet very few of them have any real content. We're one of the content providers. And even on those web sites that do have content, it's rare to find editorial oversight, quality assurance, or peer review in any of them. Once again, we take our job as a responsible content provider quite seriously, making sure the data you see is of high quality and data that has been reviewed.

Buildings may not matter any more but institutions still do. And the National Library of Medicine has existed as an institution since before the Civil War. It's been around for more than 160 years, and it was one of the first institutions to really embrace computers in communicating biomedical research information to the community.

GenBank is where all publicly available DNA sequence data ends up. And even the name "Bank" implies what the value of this data really is. Since the beginning, about 15 years ago, GenBank has been an international collaboration between the National Center of Biotechnology Information, the DNA Database of Japan, and the European Bioinformetics Institute. There's an international collaboration that exchanges data daily. So anything you find in GenBank you can also find at European and Japanese sites, synchronized on a nightly basis.

How does data get into GenBank? Traditionally, it was abstracted from journal articles. And the National Library of Medicine still does that, to maintain absolutely comprehensive coverage. However, authors submit data directly to us as well. There's a tradition in biomedical publishing that, if you're doing research with taxpayer dollars and you produce a DNA sequence (even if you haven't done it with taxpayer dollars), and if you hope to publish it in the open literature, you must, as a condition of publication, submit that data to GenBank. There's peer pressure. There's history. There's tradition about doing this. And that's been a boon for the biomedical research community. So any published article with a DNA sequence has a corresponding entry in GenBank. This entry can be retrieved with a unique identifier called an accession number, which we issue to the authors.

Those are three of the ways data gets into GenBank. Increasingly now, with the Genome Project ramping up to its rapid sequencing phase, we basically have our information systems talking to information systems at the production level, where the centers at which the data is produced

(and there are only about a dozen worldwide) push a button on their laboratory information management system, it comes into GenBank, and it's distributed to the public.

Now, how does it go out? Anyone can anonymous FTP this stuff—the whole database or updates any night. There's email distribution too. We're phasing out CD-ROMs for obvious reasons, but the CD-ROM subscription at GenBank did have its heyday. At one point, it was the second most popular title in the Government Printing Office. (The most popular title was OSHA [Occupational Safety and Health Administration] regulations on CD-ROM, which shows that there are more lawyers than scientists, I suppose.)

In any case, the most popular and powerful way to use our data these days is using two network servers available on the World Wide Web: the Entrez and the BLAST network servers, which I'll describe in a minute. I should add that access is absolutely free. Your tax dollars have already paid for this, and our job is to make it as easy as possible for you to go in there and access these sequences. High school students use it to work on their term papers. We process about 30,000 intellectual queries a day on this data, and we were connected to by 100,000 different Internet sites last year.

So what is biotechnology information? I know most of you in the audience aren't scientists but it's not that hard to understand. DNA is just a sequence of letters, a chemical code. This DNA code codes for proteins, and proteins have structures, and these structures have functions. They make us what we are. The powerful thing about this kind of information, though, is that the databases and retrieval tools not only allow us to look up things but to make discoveries by computing on the data. The whole game here is, when you get a new DNA sequence from isolating a disease gene, you compare it against all the genes that everyone has isolated to date and see if they're similar enough to allow you to infer a common or similar function.

To give you an example, about a year ago, a gene for a disease called ataxia telangiectasia [AT] was cloned. Now, AT is a rare disease, although the carrier state is fairly common. And even those people who aren't affected by the disease but who carry one of the defective genes have a predisposition to develop certain kinds of cancer and immunodeficiency syndrome. So it's an important disease from a basic research point of view.

Yosi Shilo, a physician-researcher at the Sackler School of Medicine, in Tel Aviv, set out 18 years ago to clone the AT gene. It took him 18 years from the time he decided to do it until he actually got a DNA sequence. What did he do with that DNA sequence when he got it? He sent it over the Internet to search GenBank and MEDLINE, and within five minutes he got back a putative function for that gene, just by searching the database.

So here we have a tremendous compression phenomenon. Once again, this gives you an idea of the power of being able to compute the data. Eighteen years of effort were compressed into five minutes, in terms of figuring out the function of that gene. And this happens, as I said, 30,000 times a day at our site. Not every day does it make the headlines, but it happens all the time. It's a routine technique for molecular biology.

Another example is colon cancer. The gene for that was described two or three years ago. The first thing that was done with that DNA sequence, was to search GenBank. It turns out that that sequence was, beyond a reasonable doubt, similar to corresponding sequences in yeast and E. coli. Since these sequences had already been characterized as proteins that repair damaged DNA, this immediately led to fundamental insights into the pathophysiology of colon cancer. By realizing the similarity to sequences in other organisms, it was clear that a DNA repair defect was underlying the disease (Figure 3).

The whole theory that makes this all work is the theory of molecular evolution. It's the expectation that if we clone a disease gene in humans, and there are similar genes in these other organisms, we can infer the function of the human disease gene by comparison with genes in other organisms; that is, as long as this relationship here,

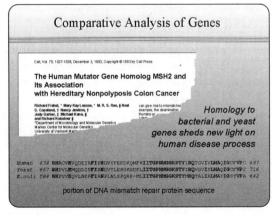

Figure 3

this alignment, this string-matching, is statistically significant, it could not have occurred by chance. So when these search programs that we use return a P value and the P value is sufficiently low, we can infer that the human and protein have the same function, and that underlies the disease phenotype.

Now I want to share with you the results of a database search I did a few years ago. When I was reading the book *Jurassic Park*, I came across a DNA sequence on page 135 which was presumed to be dinosaur DNA. Dr. Wu, the fictional head of the fictional biotechnology company, said that this amount of DNA probably contains instructions to make a single protein— say, a hormone or an enzyme. Well, this couldn't really be dinosaur DNA, right? My scientific curiosity got the best of me. I read a few pages on, but my curiosity kept drawing me back to this page. So I went down in my basement, typed the whole darn thing into my home computer, sent it over the Internet, and did a search. The search revealed sort of a Piltdown hoax.

For those of you who remember your history of science, Piltdown was a story where someone fraudulently buried a human cranium with an orangutan's jaw, only to have it rediscovered and concluded to be the missing link in human evolution. It was revealed to be all a hoax, but it took 40 years to uncover. It required the development of scanning electron microscopy, chemical dating procedures, and so on. In fact, after uncovering the hoax, it took another 20 or 30 years to find out who did it. It was reported in the journal *Nature* last week that the culprit was a disgruntled employee who had been refused a raise at the British Museum.

At any rate, this is what I found in my Piltdown hoax. When I compared Crichton's dinosaur DNA against GenBank, I found that with a *P* value of zero, it was perfectly identical to a bacterial sequence called PBR322, which is a cloning vector in common use in every molecular biology lab in the world. I was really kind of disappointed, because Michael Crichton, after all, is a graduate of Harvard Medical School, in addition to being the producer of "ER," author of *The Andromeda Strain,* and a lot of other things. I expected a little more of him, in terms of a phony sequence. He could have done a bit better job of disguising it, because it only took me about 20 seconds by doing a search over the Internet to find out what it really was.

In any case, I was quite proud of this. When you do a nice piece of work, you want to publish it. So I actually wrote this up. It was rejected from some of the best journals, including *Science* and *Nature* and *Cell.* (I mention *Cell,* in particular, because their editorial offices are just a few blocks away. *Cell* sent me the most amusing rejection letter. They said that they thought this was a hilarious story. They were afraid if they published it, however, it would increase their circulation, and they were already having trouble keeping up with the demand. So they turned me down.)

Because I had wasted enough of your taxpayer dollars by working on this research project, I put it on the shelf for a year. But when the paperback came out, I just had to give it one more try: it was published in a journal called *Biotechniques* under the title, "Molecular Biologist Visits Jurassic Park."[*]

Now, when you're a young graduate student and you publish your first paper, you send reprints to your mom to prove to her that all that hard work

and toil and expense was worth it. When you're a junior faculty member, you send them to your senior colleagues, hoping to impress them with your work. Well, I sent a copy of my reprint to Dr. Michael Crichton, because I was really curious about where he got this DNA. And he sent me this letter back, saying:

> Dear Dr. Boguski, Many thanks for your entertaining article. I'm sorry I was not clever enough to insert a more interesting sequence. Frankly, it never crossed my mind that anyone would have the interest to investigate it.

And I must say, he really underestimated the power of scientific curiosity.

But he didn't learn his lesson—here is the sequel to *Jurassic Park*. If you look on page 105, there's another DNA sequence. I will leave it as an exercise to the audience to figure out what the secret message in this sequence is. If you type it in and paste it into a window on our web site, it will search GenBank for you and tell you. So that's your incentive to do it.

Going from the ridiculous back to the sublime, Figure 2 is a scary growth chart, showing the database doubling in size every 12 months. How on earth will we ever be able to keep up with it? NCBI started out five or six years ago to try and at least link this data. This was before the World Wide Web, before HTML, and all of that. We tried to link all this information, which previously existed in separate databases, taking advantage of the laws of molecular biology to link it in an intelligent way. After all, genes encode proteins, and proteins have sequences, and DNA is composed of genes, and genes have applications. All this is described in the biomedical literature.

We set out to create a system called "Entrez," where we simply made explicit links among all these data sources. And we did better than that. We were able to add more value, once again demonstrating the power of using computational molecular biology data to create new knowledge. One is able to compare all the DNA sequences, as I did with that dinosaur DNA sequence,

---

[*] Boguski, M.S., "A Molecular Biologist Visits Jurassic Park," *Biotechniques* 12 (5): 668–9 (1992).

against all the other data, and precompute and store all the results, so that a biologist coming in here can click on it and get the top 30 or 40 most closely related sequences in the database, without having to do the search anew every time. Same thing on protein sequences. These are examples not of explicit links, like DNA codes for proteins (they're described in publications), but implicit or emergent or computed links that you can create from the data itself, by analyzing the data. The early Entrez system is show in Figure 4.

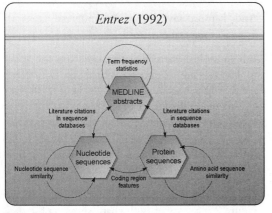

Figure 4

Now, there's an analogue of this for the literature, which I'll describe briefly because it's most relevant to some of the web search engines that exist today. John, who works in our group, invented something called "term-frequency statistics,"—if you take two articles from MEDLINE (which consist of a title, an abstract, and medical subject headings) and ask a statistical question such as how closely related are these articles to each other, you can develop a statistical measure of that by looking at the frequency of use of meaningful terms. Here is an example:

Genetic analysis of cancer in families
Genetic predisposition to cancer

Both articles have the words "genetic" and "cancer" in their titles, so presumably they're related to each other. And you can do this throughout the text.

Now, to make this work, we first had to go through and throw away the words that added no meaning—prepositions, conjunctions, and things like that. The local jargon for this is "stop words" because, when we get to them, we stop and throw them away because they don't help us. (It may interest you to know that two of the stop words we found were the terms "novel" and "important," because scientists always describe their work that way.) Therefore, they're of absolutely no importance for specific information retrieval.

Once again, before Mosaic, Netscape, and other sorts of web browsers, we had our own Internet client for this, which we still support, called Med Entrez. There's also a web Entrez. All the functionality here migrates to the Web, although the generic solutions to information retrieval on the Web do not take full power of the implicit knowledge we have of molecular biology. So our own client, in many ways, is more powerful than the generic solutions possible with HTML on the Web. Perhaps Java will change that. I don't know.

Our Entrez client is just like web browsers. It runs on every platform—the Macintosh, Windows 95, VMS, any platform out there—because it's built on a portable software base. Because of that, it's very easy for us to add in new modules as they become available. So originally Entrez was just DNA sequences, protein sequences, and the literature. We've recently added in protein 3D structures and something called "complete genomes," which I'll describe in a minute.

Although MEDLINE now contains only the abstract of an article, we're working closely with a number of scientific, technical, and medical publishers to link up MEDLINE records to their online publications. A lot of scientific publishers are experimenting with, if not committed to, full text online in some way. What we're trying to do at the Library of Medicine is to provide a card catalogue of the Internet for access to the full text of their articles. So when you come into Entrez and find an abstract in MEDLINE, and if it corresponds to a full text online publication from the *Journal of Biological Chemistry*, for instance, another button will appear in the Entrez interface, which you can click on and go to the full text of the article. These links are bidirectional, so if you're reading an article in the *Journal of Biological Chemistry* and you come down to a GenBank accession number, you click on that accession number, come right into GenBank, and see the DNA sequence.

Moreover, if you look at the bibliography or reference section of an article, each reference is hotlinked to the MEDLINE server. So not only do you get the abstract of the article cited, through this Entrez neighboring technology you get the top 30 or 40 most closely related articles in MEDLINE, whether or not they were cited by that publication. It's a very powerful way to explore and expand into the information space.

Figure 5 shows the way Entrez looks today: DNA sequences, protein sequences, structures, complete genomes, and MEDLINE. We're considering adding more links all the time. Links between nucleotide sequences, MEDLINE, and structures are increasingly being made to full-text online journals. It's our mandate and commitment to take the information in the public domain and make it all easy for anyone to use.

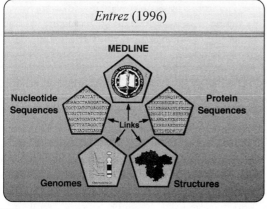

Figure 5

I'd like to end with the implications of all this for medicine in the 21st century. As I said, all this data is going to change the scientific foundation of medicine in the next century. Right now, it's of most interest to biomedical researchers, but, increasingly, medical practitioners, genetic counselors, and physicians will be tapping into this in

the future to do their jobs. The availability of the complete human genome research creates all sorts of problems, from an ethical, legal, social, economic standpoint, and so on. For those of us who have been working on the technical and scientific aspects of it, we haven't thought too much about that, because we've been trying to get the data out. But in looking around for an appropriate description for the way I feel about this, I was drawn to a poem that was written 300 years ago by Alexander Pope. This is from his *Second Epistle on Man*. Pope writes:

> Know then thyself, presume not God to scan,
> The proper study of mankind is man.
> Placed on this isthmus of a middle state,
> Of being darkly wise, and rudely great:
> With too much knowledge for the sceptic side,
> With too much weakness for the stoic's pride,
> He hangs between; in doubt to act, or rest;
> In doubt to deem himself a god, or beast;
> In doubt his mind or body to prefer;
> Born but to die, and reasoning but to err;
> Alike in ignorance, his reason such,
> Whether he thinks too little, or too much:
> Chaos of Thought and Passion, all confused;
> Still by himself abused or disabused;
> Created half to rise, and half to fall;
> Great lord of all things, yet a prey to all;
> Sole judge of truth, in endless error hurl'd:
> The glory, jest, and riddle of the world!

Postscript

Since my presentation at the conference, an important new development in human genome research has occurred. A gene map containing 20 percent of all human genes has been constructed by an international consortium and co-published as a peer-reviewed journal article in *Science Online*:

http://www.sciencemag.org/science/scripts/display/274/5287/540.html

The web site:

http://www.ncbi.nlm.nih.gov/SCIENCE96/

can be utilized by the general public and physicians, as well as by cutting edge researchers. This gene map is being used to accelerate the isolation of genes underlying human disease.

PAGANO: In the next part of this session, we will discuss how all this technology actually gets used in the clinic.

When I was growing up, I recognized that there were only a few canonical stories that Hollywood used over and over and over again to make movies. And one of them that keeps repeating is the high tension, isolated incidence: A group is isolated, and there's a medical emergency. It could be a woman delivering a baby or something. The physician can't get there, communication is always through a telephone or radio, and there's always this tremendous tension. And always, the baby gets delivered well.

A few months ago it struck me—I was on the Net on a Saturday morning—that life indeed does mimic art. I'm on the Net and see this letter from somebody in northern India, an isolated World Health Organization officer in northern India, who needed help in diagnosing and helping a patient. So he sent out this message on the Net. Here I was, sitting in Boston, when somebody in London responded. Then later, somebody in California responded. And I was thinking, gosh, this is the Internet mimicking Hollywood. So I figured, it's here to stay.

And to convince us we have the talk entitled "Making Sense of Telemedicine." We are very fortunate to have **DOUGLAS PEREDNIA**. Douglas is the Director of Advanced Telemedicine at the Oregon Health Sciences University.

PEREDNIA: To show you how the Internet brings people together, Dr. Boguski and I actually went to medical school together. We haven't seen or heard of each other for 12 years, and now the Internet has brought us together.

Making Sense of Telemedicine

Telemedicine is something that is intuitively pretty obvious. But when you try to get your head around it, it grows and grows and becomes very difficult to understand. I want to explain briefly what telemedicine is, where it comes from, and why it works or why it doesn't work, and then discuss how that relates to health, the Internet, that sort of thing.

What is telemedicine, anyway? The essential ingredients are these:

You have to have data. If you don't have data, there is nothing to transmit. If there's nothing to transmit, why are you bothering? If there's no distance, it's unclear why you would want to transmit the data. If we're in the same room, why should I use the Internet—or any other means—to call you, tell you about something?

You need expertise. If you don't know any more than I know about the problem we're trying to deal with, transmitting the data to you does absolutely no good at all.

You need a way to electronically transfer the data over the distance to the expert. You could use mail. (You could use Pony Express, whatever.) But the "tele" in telemedicine means medicine at a distance. And electronic transfer is the most efficient way of accomplishing that.

So a reasonable definition is that telemedicine is the electronic transmission of information for use in medical care. It includes the delivery of anything you can deliver over an electronic link.

The reason telemedicine is useful or interesting can be exemplified by imagining a distribution of dermatologists within the continental United States in 1991–92. What you'll find is that dermatologists are all located in nice places to live: here in Boston, San Francisco, Los Angeles, Portland, Seattle, that kind of thing; whereas, in the whole area of Nevada, or the whole area of Oregon, there's not a single dermatologist. This is a very long way, actually. It would be very useful to be able to transmit data over a distance, to come up with some kind of clinical aid. Dermatology is actually a pretty good example, because most physicians don't know much about dermatology or skin diseases. The average primary care provider, or in fact, the average provider of any type, has had a total of 30 hours of dermatology training by the time they finish their formal training. That includes courses, rotations, and everything. So odds are, if you go to somebody in an area like this, they are not going to have had a lot of background in whatever kind of skin problem you have.

The first concept to understand about telemedicine is that all medical problems lie in a spectrum of diagnostic and/or management difficulty. If we graph this out, there is a distribution. An axis on such a graph would show the number of cases and the relative difficulty of diagnosis or treatment. When we talk about difficulty of diagnosis or treatment, essentially what we mean is the amount of information or analytical skill required for the correct diagnosis or effective treatment.

For example, if you go to a doctor who has no idea what's going on with you, what does he do next? Well, the answer is, the doctor orders an expensive or invasive test. And the reason to do that is to get more information of the type you can't get without that test, to try to figure out what's going on.

This spectrum is a very real spectrum. We actually call these simple or easy problems "doorway diagnoses." That means you walk into the room, you look at the patient, and you say, "How long have you had hepatitis?" or "How long have you had that melanoma sitting on your face?" or whatever. On the other hand, on the other side of the spectrum, are what I have taken to calling "autopsy diagnoses," which means, regardless of the expense or invasiveness of the test that's taken—until it's so invasive that you're examining little bits—we won't have any idea what was going on. And almost everything falls somewhere in between.

If you don't believe a range like this exists, there's an outstanding paper that was published in 1991 in the *Journal of the American Medical Association* called "Melanoma: It Can't Be Melanoma." It's about a subset of melanoma that defies clinical recognition. What happened here was, at Columbia Presbyterian Hospital, they examined 178 cases of malignant melanoma. Then they looked at what the physician thought it was. In 13 cases, melanoma was very, very far from what they thought it was. And when they approached the

physician about this, the response was, "Melanoma? No way! That didn't look like a melanoma. It didn't act like a melanoma." And the reason is that melanomas pretty much overlap with something else that you can have, as do all other diseases.

We typically recognize melanomas, a potentially fatal form of skin cancer, by clinical clues. A melanoma is bigger than usual moles or things like that, and it tends to be irregular in shape. It tends to be multicolored. It tends to be asymmetrical; one side is not like the other. And if all those characteristics are present, you have a doorway diagnosis. You can walk in and say, "You know, that sure looks like melanoma. How long have you had it?"

On the other hand, if it's round and not irregularly margined, and it's all one color, then it starts to look like a lot of other things, like basal-cell skin cancers, like seborrhea keratoses. And soon you get something you can't believe is a melanoma. In these cases, it isn't until a biopsy is done that the diagnosis can actually be made. The kind of information you're getting now is on a cellular level rather than just a clinical level.

The second topic is that all telecommunications modalities represent tradeoffs between the cost and amount and type of information relayed per unit time. Imagine a graph that shows the relative resource cost of transmission of information, and the amount of information relayed per unit time. Telephone or radio relays relatively little information per unit time, but it's very inexpensive: really cheap. On this graph, in fact, smoke signals would be on the bottom, and telegraph would be somewhere in between.

If you then start adding video or images, it starts increasing the amount of information relayed per unit time, but it also comes with a cost. A picture is worth a thousand words. On the other hand, a picture is also worth many thousands of bits. So you may recognize that picture you're transmitting immediately, but it may take many minutes to get to you because of the amount of time required.

Now, that still might be a lot more efficient than having someone sit there on the telephone describing it. That's typically what happens in something like dermatology, where people say, "It's a rash. It's a red rash. It's sort of a fuzzy red rash, actually. It's a fuzzy red rash all over." By the time you finish the description, 15, 20, 30 minutes have passed. And you might as well have sent a picture—it would have been a lot faster and a lot cheaper.

When you start adding video, the cost starts rising fairly dramatically because video transmits about 30 frames per second, or 15 frames per second if you're accepting lower resolution rates. And then when you get to virtual reality, it becomes relatively expensive to transmit, because you're transmitting information not only about what the front of something looks like, but also what the back looks like, what the side looks like, and perhaps in some cases, what it feels like. So there is a relationship between the amount of information transmitted per unit time and the resource cost.

Here I bring in the Internet. One thing the Internet does, or has the potential to do as the bandwidth devoted to the Internet increases, is lower the cost of this cure. So it may become less and less expensive to achieve any one of these particular pieces of information, or to communicate this stuff.

One thing you should be asking yourselves is, where does in-person consultation fit on this spectrum? That's actually a key question. I worked out this whole scenario with Jim Grigsby, at the University of Colorado, in Denver. We were scratching our heads, trying to figure it out. It turns out, in terms of information relayed per unit time, it lies over here somewhere, because not only can you talk to someone but you can examine them, palpate them, listen to them, and everything else.

But where does it fall in terms of resource cost? This is really the key to telemedicine, because the answer to that question is, it depends. If we're in the same room, as we are now, the resource cost of getting all of this information about you is about zero, because all we have to do is expend

the calories to walk over to one another. On the other hand, if you're on the dark side of the moon, the resource cost is literally pretty astronomical, because you have to mount a multimillion dollar space mission to see someone in person, on the dark side of the moon.

So where telemedicine really fits in here is that, when the resource cost of seeing someone in person is higher than the cost of transmitting the amount of information you need there is a potential for achieving efficiency and lowering the cost of seeing somebody by use of telecommunications. That can be represented on another graph, which combines both of these concepts: the data transmission capabilities of various telecommunications modalities allow one to diagnose or manage some specific fraction of medical problems.

Let's say that of all the melanomas in the world, there is a significant fraction that, if you just described it to me over the telephone, it would be easy to make the diagnosis. That happens all the time. In fact, the average primary care provider spends about 25 percent of the time on the telephone. And if it weren't possible to do this, nobody would waste that much time talking. The exact fraction depends on what it is you're trying to do, what kinds of conditions you're talking about. But all the evidence I've been able to dig up from the medical literature and studies we've done in our own lab is that roughly 70 to 75 percent of all medical problems are amenable to being taken care of quickly and efficiently over a medium such as the telephone.

Any time you add more information to that, you increase the fraction of cases you can handle. All of these cases, for example, with still images and two-way audio, could be handled that way as well. But there's an additional fraction of cases that require pictures for some reason—either X-rays or skin images transmitted, or whatever—that allow you to take advantage of the medium to give you the additional information to make the diagnosis.

Now, if you just want to take care of this 75 percent or of cases using, say, virtual reality, it essentially is the equivalent of sending a man to do a boy's job. You've expended a lot of extra resources and a lot of extra capability, but it doesn't add much. The key is figuring out what it is you want to add, how much you need to add, to fulfill the purpose clinically or medically, and then add that much and no more. Then there's also some fraction here that requires in-person assessment or complex invasive testing, because there's just not enough information transmitted by any of these modalities. So that basically sums up telemedicine.

> *Roughly 70 to 75 percent of all medical problems are amenable to being taken care of quickly and efficiently over a medium such as the telephone.*

It's also important to understand that telemedicine is not one thing, any more than medicine is one thing. For example, telemedicine is made up of teleradiology, teledermatology, telemental health, tele-this and tele-that, just as medicine is made up of radiology, dermatology, and mental health. And one modality—say, two-way interactive video—is not necessarily sufficient for some things, whereas it's overkill for other things. And so, when figuring out what it is you want to accomplish in the way of clinical care, it behooves one to try to determine how the technological requirements match the clinical requirements, and vice versa.

Where telemedicine fits is sort of depicted by this model. If you can imagine a Swiss cheese layer cake as all of medical care, conventional services occupy a very large portion; in fact, the vast majority of what we do right now. And there's a dermatology component, and a CME [continuing medical education] component, and a neurology component to that. But there are holes in this cheese, because there are certain things we cannot do in dermatology right now. One thing we can't do is to treat somebody on the dark side of the moon with in-person, conventional care consultation. For that matter, we can't treat some-

body on the eastern half of Oregon, because it's so expensive to get out there, it's not worth it.

Another example I like to use is one given to me by Kathy Britton, who runs the mental health telemedicine program in eastern Oregon. There they frequently have to have precommitment hearings or similar sorts of exams, medical-legal type exams. To do that from eastern Oregon now, they have to put the person in the back of a caged police car and drive them to Portland to be seen by a psychiatrist and a judge. As Kathy likes to point out, if they didn't need to be institutionalized when they left, they need to by the time they arrive, especially if it's winter, because it takes hours and hours and hours. And probably, the policeman who brought them needs to be institutionalized, too.

Telemedicine basically adds another layer to this range of services that we can provide. But there are a lot of things you can't do in telemedicine. You can't, for example, palpate someone right now. You may be able to in the future, but you can't now. So there are holes here as well. But the holes are complementary; some things you can't do in one place, you can do in the other. And this is really becoming the totality of medical care services that we can provide. And the Internet is just another means of providing them. To my mind, it's not much more and not much less, except that in some circumstances it may be more convenient.

This is not a new idea. In *Radio News,* from 1924, they talked about the radio doctor. This idea has come and gone, and just recently, in the mid-1990s, it's really started to take off. The number of interactive television programs in North America has skyrocketed recently. An example is a program that existed between Harvard and Boston's Logan Airport. There was a clinic out at Logan Airport with a full television link. It was actually fairly expensive to maintain, but it fulfilled a pretty good service, until it was deemed not worth the cost for the number of patients being seen. And so telemedicine actually has gone through a number of cycles—where interest has burgeoned, people have installed telemedicine systems, then they've gone away.

What's going to be different this time around is that that cost—the cost of carrying this out and the number of applications you have for a given investment—has really come down. As of February 1996, there were over 120 telemedicine programs in the United States. The reason this is happening now is that the conversion from analog-to-digital storage and transmission has lowered the cost, and made it more efficient for many more purposes.

And actually, the provision of health care services has changed as well. For example, in Oregon, where there is a lot of managed care, it turns out that, to cover Medicaid in Oregon, many managed care providers are obligated to provide more or less the same level of services to all the patients in the state. It won't be economical to do that without the use of telecommunications.

Here is a quick look at some applications:

- Teleradiology
- Teledermatology
- Psychiatry
- Mental health
- Cardiology
- Home health care

Radiology is one of the very first applications for this. And the reason is obvious: because radiology is all images. So if you can transmit images, you're no better or worse off than if you are seeing this image in person.

Dermatology is a slightly different case than radiology, because of the need to handle color: How much color do you need? How much can you compress and get away with it? What types of color do you need, that sort of thing. And also, the resolution issue has not been well worked out. People have been fiddling with teleradiology for many, many years. Teledermatology is pretty far behind, but it's catching up quickly.

Let me give you some examples of the work we're doing in my lab, back in Oregon. We're trying different kinds of compression to determine

when the informativeness of the image falls off. Radiologist Dr. Harold Kundel points out that every image has three characteristics: fidelity, informativeness, and aesthetics.

Fidelity. Fidelity says, how close is that image to reality? And a good example of that is, if you look at a deer crossing sign and it's a nice sharp yellow deer crossing sign, that image has high fidelity.

Informativeness. If you look at a deer crossing sign that's a little bit blue and just a little bit out of focus, you think, "That's a terrible image of a deer crossing sign, but it's a deer crossing sign. I can tell that in two seconds." Those images are equally informative. They tell you what you need to know about the presence of wildlife on the road, even though one has terrible fidelity and the other has excellent fidelity.

Aesthetics. You wouldn't think aesthetics are important, except that many very otherwise intelligent people routinely buy cars based on looks rather than performance. And if you have images that are thoroughly informative but people don't like to look at them, your system is doomed for failure, no matter what. So all of those characteristics are important in their own way.

Another example is trying to figure out what you need to transmit and how you need to transmit it. Cardiology, for example, uses many different modalities. You use EKGs [electrocardiograms], which can easily be faxed. Then again, you use auscultation, which requires the transmission of sound. You just put an electronic stethoscope on the patient's chest, it digitizes the sounds and then sends them over. Cardiology also uses images in the form of things like catheterizations and echocardiograms. So you have one modality here where, depending upon what you're trying to achieve and what equipment is located on the transmitting end, the requirements may be very different.

My last example is home care. Japan makes extensive use of its fairly broadband transmission system that exists throughout the country. This is in a nursing home environment, where the patient can interact with a television screen. There are some less expensive models for the same kind of interaction going on in the United States, where what you're after is not so much making a diagnosis on the patient, but deciding when the patient should be seen in person. Just the act of not having to send someone to see if the person needs to be seen can save a lot of money.

This principle applies to almost everything. A guy named Ogilvy, who is in advertising in New York, once observed that people don't want cars, they want transportation. In the same spirit, people don't want telemedicine, they want to feel better.

One of the problems in telemedicine is, as soon as the funding is taken away from any telemedicine programs, they fold. And you think, if they were so valuable, why did they fold? It turns out it wasn't the telemedicine people really wanted; patients wanted to feel better physically. Doctors wanted to feel better financially and emotionally. And payers wanted to pay less. They wanted to feel better, mostly financially. And every telemedicine program that has failed, has failed in one of those three areas. By the same token, people don't want the Internet; they want what the Internet provides. And if the Internet is not providing content, as Dr. Boguski pointed out earlier, I suspect people won't be on the Internet very long, either.

Again, telemedicine is only a tool. It is applying computer technology to find the right wrench to pound in the correct screw, as typically happens. And in that spirit, the caption of one of my favorite cartoons is, "If we can't cure you, at least we'll awe you with modern medical technology." And this happens more times than I care to admit.

In terms of the implications of telemedicine in practice, how it affects your life and your providers' lives, providers see some potentially profound changes this is likely to produce. One is that interstate and possibly international commerce and health care delivery is not only likely to explode, it is actually exploding right now. The example I like to give is that medicine used to be a cottage

industry. You had a cottage, and as a provider, you would either go to someone's cottage or they would come to your cottage to deliver care.

Around the late 1950s, when third-party payment started to become popular, we developed factories. Of course we don't call them factories, we call them hospitals. We call them managed care organizations. But basically, you've got your raw materials in, which are patients and chemicals and catheters, and you have your finished goods out, which are patients (hopefully, although not necessarily) who are better off than when they went in.

The factory model served us pretty well until the late 1980s, early 1990s, when people began to move a lot of production and a lot of the intellectual addition of content to items overseas, or to other regions, for various reasons. So cars aren't necessarily made in America any more. They're made all over the world and assembled here. By the same token, you don't have to get your health care from providers in the state where you live. You can get your health care from out of state. If it turns out the doctor you want to talk to is the cheapest or the best or the most efficient or the friendliest, whatever your requirements are, that may be in another state.

And that's already happening in south Florida. There's a company called Harris Corporation, a large electronics firm, actually, a multi-industry conglomerate that set up a medical imaging center in partnership with UCLA. Harris Corporation has 23,000 employees in south Florida. All of a sudden, they started sending all of their employees to this medical imaging center, and the images are either sent via post or transmitted electronically to UCLA, where they're read.

Harvard is actually a member of a similar consortium called TeleQuest, a consortium of Harvard, UC/San Francisco, the University of Pennsylvania, at least one organization in North Carolina, and I know I'm missing one. But like it or not, this interstate commerce in health care is growing quite rapidly.

Second, as far as patients and referring providers are concerned, telemedicine gives you more choice. So that's really nice. But it may affect referral patterns, which have almost always been geographic until now.

And it may affect the number of specialists needed. It depends on whether the increased access to specialists brings people out of the woodwork who never before would have consulted a specialist. From the research we've done on our National Library of Medicine contract in eastern Oregon, to learn everything we can about teledermatology, that seems to be the case. One other observation is a possible decrease in the number of specialists. There is actually a theory now that by the year 2000, every X-ray in the United States and probably the world will be read by five radiologists in Kansas.

Another possible and potentially important change is that, as physicians, you may add telemedicine rounds to your other hospital and clinical obligations. There is the potential for a more efficient use of time when reviewing clearcut cases. This happens a lot in radiology, where you can hold up an X-ray and say, "Normal chest." You know, "Normal chest: That's $75."

In dermatology, for example, when you see a patient, you have to examine that patient, talk to the patient, educate the patient, that sort of thing. Nowadays, you may be able to look at an image and say, "I know exactly what that is. That's seborrheic dermatitis. Here, I'll send the seborrheic dermatitis reply." And all of a sudden you've gone from what's typically been a 15- or 20-minute visit to a 3-second visit, depending upon how fast you operate.

There may also be a potential for less efficient use of time and more interruptions, if you don't limit interruptions to routine tasks. So if I'm seeing patients in my clinic, and all of a sudden I'm called out to do a telemedicine consultation, instead of being there until 9:00 at night, I'm there till 10:00, and my life is a lot worse.

The effect on practitioner time, right now is totally unknown. We're facing a number of unknowns: effect on practitioner, income, effect on cost to patients—are all unknown at this point. A lot of it depends on how appropriately the technology is used. And effect on satisfaction is essentially unknown, although all the evidence so far suggests that people really like this, just as people really like the Internet.

There are some potential barriers, as far as liability. Interestingly enough, this is probably not that significant a barrier since now physicians handle patients over the phone anyway, so you're typically adding more information this way. So if you keep your perspective and don't try to do more than you have information to handle, odds are that your liability won't change. And based on the current policy of Northwest Physicians Mutual, theoretically, people are provided, although the first suit has yet to be filed. I suspect, as soon as they finish with the OSHA requirements, that will happen.

Reimbursement is a very interesting issue. The Health Care Financing Administration, the people who run Medicare, do not currently reimburse telemedicine. And the reason is, it's hard to know how much to reimburse unless you know what a given service is worth. It's hard to know what it's worth unless you have a lot of good data to go by. You don't want to do a telemedicine consultation and then duplicate your efforts by doing another kind of consultation, an in-person consultation.

Licensure, malpractice, and privacy are all issues that must be addressed. A final reminder is that this is a means to an end, not an end in itself. And if this whole thing doesn't make people feel better, it's not worth much.

I want to point out a few sources of telemedicine information:

The Telemedicine Information Exchange. The URL is *http://tie.telemed.org/*. This is run by the Telemedicine Research Center, an organization with which I'm affiliated. It is currently the most comprehensive database of telemedicine information available anywhere.

"Telemedicine Technology and Clinical Applications". This is an article I published in 1995.[*]

The Association of Telemedicine Service Providers [ATSP]. The URL for the newly established (as of January, 1997) organization is http://www.atsp.org/. This should be of use and interest to anyone trying to create or grow a telemedicine program.

Questions & Answers

Q: *Medscape recently announced that it will make MEDLINE available at no cost over its web site, with advertisements, of course. Will either the abstracts and/or the collected full-text articles be available at no cost directly through the NIH MEDLINE?*

BOGUSKI: I can't answer that question directly, but let me give you a few basic facts about MEDLINE. MEDLINE has always operated on a cost-recovery basis only. We don't make a profit on it. MEDLINE is available through the Entrez system, which is free now, but it's only a subset. It's a large subset of MEDLINE. It's 1.5 million out of the eight million records. But it's that subset most relevant to molecular biology, genetics, and biotechnology research. The third thing I wanted to point out is, it's been possible for a long, long time to license MEDLINE for redistribution, for repackaging or whatever. And plenty of companies have licensed MEDLINE, put their own retrieval system interface on it, and so on. I'm not sure how the licensing agreement applies to web distribution. In fact, I don't know about Medscape, so I can't comment directly on what they're advertising.

Q: *Given the "managed care" reality with fee-for-service a foregone institution, will IP become the cost-driven result of health care reform?*

PEREDNIA: Actually, I think what IP has a chance to do is, to some extent, to unify the babble of communication that's currently taking place over direct phone lines and other telecommunications lines. Virtually no telemedicine equipment that's currently used or available follows much of a standard. There are some putative standards, h.320 for example. But most people have their own proprietary standard. I think the biggest thing needed for the Internet is to follow at least some sort of standard so that we're all talking the same language.

Managed care is likely to be a very heavy user of telemedicine services, because of the efficiencies that I was talking about. The VA Hospital, for example, pays for most travel for all of its patients, as does the Indian Health Service. And so if you can avoid travel cost, then it makes telemedicine a much more effective proposition.

Q: *How does the Human Genome Project affect society?*

BOGUSKI: I think it's time for all of us to start thinking about how the Human Genome Project is going to impact society. As I said at the end, it's going to impact economics, almost every dimension of human activity, I think. In a sense, it's going to be as profound as getting the first alien communication to earth. I mean, we're going to know every single detail of the blueprint which makes us human. It's a question for philosophers and economists and social scientists, and I can't answer any more specifically than that.

Q: *What are the ethical issues of the Internet and health care?*

PEREDNIA: Well, the ethical issues have to do with actually problems of anonymity, I think. Right now, if you go to a doctor who is in your state, odds are, you're going to be able to look at his wall or her wall, and see that they have a license, and see that they've been trained somewhere, and they have a reputation within the community. Part of the problem is, over the Internet in particular, there is not a very high signal-to-noise ratio in many aspects of things that are done. And that's probably not going to be any different for health care. Is the person that you're communicating with truly a qualified provider? If they're not a qualified provider, well, who the heck are they?

---

[*] Perednia, D., and A. Allen, "Telemedicine Technology and Clinical Applications," *JAMA*, 1995; 273(6): 483-488.

And should you be doing what they say you're supposed to be doing?

That's also a problem that's come up already in clinical studies, even in clinical studies that are supposed to have placebo controls. Patients that chat amongst one another over the Internet can unfortunately mess up the clinical study which really should take place unaltered, if it were to advance the knowledge of clinical care.

So it really has to do with two problems. One is anonymity, and the second is not being able to use some of the really useful tools that we've had to work with in the past.

Q: *How are people paying for telemedicine services today? How will they pay in the future? And how does (or will) the cost/price compare with that of conventional medical services?*

PEREDNIA: There are a number of different ways in which people are paying for medical care, for telemedicine currently. The first is, in teleradiology. Teleradiology is reimbursed by virtually everybody. And the reason is that you can't demonstrate any difference between images interpreted remotely and images that are interpreted in person, as it were, right where the image is generated. The other thing is that, from the Health Care Financing Administration's point of view, it's not face-to-face interactions. And the face-to-face requirement is what is required for reimbursement in clinical care to date. So teleradiology is already being reimbursed by just about everybody.

Other aspects of telemedicine are being reimbursed for a variety of sources. There are a lot of demonstration programs going on, that are funded by the Office of Rural Health Policy, the Health Care Financing Administration, the National Library of Medicine, Rural Utilities Service. Those are your tax dollars that are paying for them.

And then, in situations where institutions or organizations are paying, especially for travel, Medicaid frequently pays for travel of patients, as does the VA and the military. The travel money is basically being used to offset the cost of equipment and services provided.

It will probably also evolve that people will pay out of pocket, because many of the travel costs that people save are their own travel costs—the cost of being missing from work, and the cost of actually depreciating your car by driving it hundreds of miles to see a specialist.

Q: *Three very similar questions: What other infotech incentives will become available to patients, consumers, and health professionals; Comment on the problems and opportunities of telemedical physician and patient education; and What is the impact on patient's knowledge of their disease due to the Internet, and how does that impact the doctor-patient relationship?*

PEREDNIA: One aspect of telemedicine that I didn't talk much about, because I was emphasizing the applied clinical parts, is patient education. Patient education is what a lot of providers spend a lot of time doing right now. And if they don't, they should. Having ready access to large pools of information, help groups, and that sort of thing, is potentially very valuable and can only help, actually, if the information is accurate.

That's another major problem with the Internet as it now stands. When you log onto a home page, it could have been put up by somebody whose intention, God forbid, is to mess up everyone with that disease or that problem.

The opportunities are pretty considerable, and so are the problems potentially caused. For one thing, virtually no provider in the United States or the world today has been trained in an era in which they are expected or trained to provide health care remotely. So there are issues of establishing rapport and trust, how you provide advice, what types of information you need, and that type of thing. And then, when to say, "I don't know." And so all of those are problems that pretty much need to be worked out.

The opportunities are also enormous. For one thing, it would be very nice to live where you want to live, and still be able to practice medicine. One big problem in rural areas right now is that people get very lonely. They don't have the support of their colleagues, and they often don't have the patient base needed to support them. So no one goes out there. And that's why there are no dermatologists in eastern Oregon. There are probably not enough patients to support them. On the other hand, if you're seeing people in person and also seeing patients over a much broader area, you may be able to support yourself. And the quality of overall care will rise in the entire region.

Q: *Putting aside your individual interests for a moment, what do you think are the greatest issues for potential patients concerned about the prospective health of their families and themselves, when the single best health care measure they can take is to buckle their seatbelt?*

PEREDNIA: This is a problem. You can't make a silk purse out of a sow's ear. And if people don't want to help themselves, for whatever reasons, then it doesn't matter what we do, or it doesn't matter whether you're seen in person; it doesn't matter whether you're seen remotely. All providers can do is provide advice and prescriptions, and sometimes surgery. But if you don't take care of your wound, your wound will get infected. If you don't take your medicine, it won't do any good.

BOGUSKI: I'd like to address that issue obliquely, too, by underscoring something that Doug said and that I stressed also. It's *caveat emptor* when you go out to the Web and look for information. For patients in particular, there is as much misinformation out there as information. And it's our job as physicians to be conveyors not of information but of wisdom. I think it's possible for a patient to come to your office and say, "Well, my son was just diagnosed with embryonal rhabdomia sarcoma," and you haven't seen a case since medical school 30 years ago. They're going to be better informed about that tumor than you are. And that's not the point. It's not the knowledge; it's the wisdom of a physician/patient contact. And you also have to educate your patients that not all sources of information are of equal quality. It's the content issue, once again.

Q: *How can we get other disciplines to make their data public?*

BOGUSKI: Outside of science, I suppose you mean. Well, it's all economics, right? GenBank is free because taxpayers all over the world have supported basic research, and it's their right to enjoy the fruits of that research. And it's basically who pays, and what their motivations are for producing the information in the first place. I think GenBank in particular has earned many times its initial cost, in the amount of good that it's created, in terms of advancing not only research in the public domain but also in the private sector as well. Ten to fifteen percent of our use is by U.S. pharmaceutical companies, for instance. And basic research, not only that leads to DNA sequences but that the NIH supports in general, I think, is the life blood of our biotechnology and medical care in this country. So I encourage that. I don't know how to get people who are holding onto data to release it, though.

Q: *One benefit of having telemedicine is to small hospitals in rural areas, where there is shortage of experts and specialists. Nevertheless, these hospitals are likely to treat poor people and don't have much money. The hospitals themselves are likely not able to afford telemedicine setup and facilities. So the question is, will telemedicine still be the solution for the shortage of specialists in these rural, poor hospitals?*

PEREDNIA: Great question. The answer is yes. And the reason the answer is yes is because you have to remember, it's the most appropriate use of technology. Telemedicine is a pretty large thing, and there is an awful lot you can do with more efficient use of the telephone. There's also a lot you can do with more efficient use of still imaging. The mandate we have from the National Library of Medicine is to try to figure out the most efficient, lowest cost way to do teledermatology in particular, and then measure the impact that that had on the community.

The most expensive part of our system is a $9,000 camera, which is $9,000 because we haven't quite finished the research to determine if we can use a $599 camera. So the entire cost for our system will probably end up being around

$3,000. You don't have to prevent a lot of travel to pay for $3,000. Remember, we're using standard, ordinary phone lines.

The assumption that rural hospitals and rural people may not be able to benefit because the cost advantages aren't there, just isn't true. Rural hospitals will continue to be a major beneficiary, I think.

Q: *Do you need really high bandwidth to accomplish good things?*

PEREDNIA: The answer is no. The more bandwidth you have and the cheaper it is, the more things you can do. But it's just sort of like icing on the cake, icing on the Swiss cheese layer cake, as it were.

About the Speakers

MARCELLO PAGANO is Professor of Statistical Computing at the Harvard School of Public Health, where he has worked since 1978. His research interests have been closely associated with computers, and now he is also very much interested in the use of the Internet as an educational tool, in its very broadest sense.

DR. MARK BOGUSKI is a Senior Investigator at the U.S. National Center for Biotechnology Information (NCBI), a division of the National Library of Medicine. NCBI is the organization that builds and distributes GenBank, which is the largest and most comprehensive public DNA and protein sequence database in the world. Dr. Boguski is an expert in computational molecular biology and has written and lectured extensively on bioinformatics. Several years ago he and Dr. Carolyn Tolstoshev created dbEST, a new division of GenBank for cDNA sequence data. More recently he has worked with Dr. Greg Schuler to create the UniGene set of human genes which is being actively used to create a gene map of the human genome and to study gene expression on a genome scale.

DR. DOUGLAS A. PEREDNIA is a clinical and research physician with considerable experience in both the diagnosis and treatment of skin conditions and the applications of computer imaging in medicine. He is currently the Director of the Advanced Telemedicine Research Group at Oregon Health Sciences University, and a founding Director of the Telemedicine Research Center (TRC), an Oregon-based non-profit public service research corporation dedicated to supporting multisite collaborative research in telemedicine. Dr. Perednia, a medical internist and Assistant Professor of Dermatology, has authored many works on telemedicine, and has become one of the most referenced authors on this subject in the medical literature.

CHAIR: BILL KOVACH
Curator of the Nieman Foundation
Harvard University

CO-CHAIR: MARK S. BONCHEK
Director, Political Participation Project
Massachusetts Institute of Technology

Press & Politics

UNIVERSAL ACCESS

MODERATOR: Nolan Bowie
PANELISTS: Prudence Adler
Richard Civille
Jock Gill

LIFE AND POLITICS ON THE NET

MODERATOR: Charles Firestone
PANELISTS: Doug Bailey
Peter Kollock
John Mallery
William Mitchell

PRESS AND THE NEW MEDIA

MODERATOR: Norm Pearlstine
PANELISTS: Denise Caruso
Janice Kaplan
John Markoff
Brock Meeks

HARVARD NEWS

CONFERENCE ON THE INTERNET AND SOCIETY

May 29-31, 1996   Cambridge, MA

Fairness Is Fundamental in Thinking About Net Access

By Marvin Hightower

"The fundamental issue involving universal access [to the Internet] is fundamental fairness, whether or not in the long term we will have a society based on inclusiveness or one based on privilege."

With that declaration, communications attorney Nolan Bowie staked out the territory for the "Universal Access" panel he moderated as part of the Conference on the Internet and Society.

As the Temple University Associate Professor pointed out up front, the title phrase is hardly as self-explanatory as it seems. "It means different things to different people—often far less than service to 100 percent of the universe."

So why is universal Net access an issue at all? In part, because as the nation's earlier experience with telephones demonstrates, "the more people you hook up to the network, the more valuable the network becomes—not only for the provider of the network, but for the individual private user, too," said Richard Civille, Executive Director of the Center for Civic Networking. "Ensuring universal access and universal service is simply sound economic policy, if nothing else, and I think it's a lot more."

Civille chose an electrical metaphor to distinguish "universal access" from "universal service," terms that often morph back and forth in casual usage.

"You can craft policies which may assure that you get the plug on the wall [i.e., access] but nothing beyond the plug [service]. If our policies focus too much on the access question, we may provide hook-ups in a lot of schools, a lot of libraries, and a lot of health clinics," without factoring in the resources required to teach people how to use the new tools productively. If that happens, the network just won't multiply in value as it should, he said.

With the addition of a simple prepositional phrase, Prudence Adler, Assistant Executive Director of External Relations for the Association of Research Libraries, turned the panel topic into a question: universal access to what?

And thereby hangs the complex tale of copyrights, which Adler believes will stir up "probably the most contentious of all debates in terms of how we access information in the future. Intellectual property issues may well be the defining element of how the network thrives or fails."

As more and more copyrighted material goes online, a huge question looms ever larger: "How do you impose a very tightly controlled, legally enforceable system of access to information on the culture of the Internet, which is encouraging the free flow of information?" And to further complicate the problem, the Internet just won't sit still: it keeps evolving.

Similar challenges surround universal service and universal access, generating endless assessments and reassessments of needs and rights. "The laws need to be flexible and provide room to accommodate some level of change," she said. "It's not going to be a one-stop shop."

Adler proposed that copyright provisions on the "fair use" of protected materials (as in bookstore browsing, copying an encyclopedia entry for educational use, or singing pop tunes in your car, royalty-free) be "extended appropriately" to the digital domain.

"How the intellectual property issues are resolved will determine the value of the universal service provisions [of telecommunications laws and policies]. If we in the library/education communities and the public arena cannot get at information at an affordable rate or in a meaningful manner, what have we gained?"

Jock Gill might reply, "Another story to tell." Gill, who is the President of Penfield Gill, Inc., waxed lyrical over the Net as "the most powerful storytelling mechanism that has emerged in the last 50 years. Maybe the reason it's so important is that the stories we tell ourselves and each other determine who we are. If that's the case, then we must have universal access in order that all of us may be storytellers."

Gill displayed several charts delineating major differences between information media old and new. In what is perhaps his favorite polarity, the "target" nature of older media-like books (in which the author aims one-way communications at multiple readers) squares off against the "partner" nature of interactive electronics (in which everyone constantly switches between reading and writing).

Like maps, good stories provide us with useful information and suggest courses of action, Gill said. "Storytelling is critical because how we tell our stories—the ones we tell inside our heads in traffic jams, the ones we tell each other at dinner parties and lectures, at the movies, over our newspaper—determines what we know, how we know it, and, in fact, the dreams we dream."

Press & Politics
May 30, 1996

Universal Access

MODERATOR: Nolan Bowie
PANELISTS: Prudence Adler
                  Richard Civille
                  Jock Gill

BOWIE: It's a pleasure and a privilege to participate in this conference, and particularly on this panel on the subject of universal access, which I personally believe is the most important of the issues being discussed at this conference. I say this primarily because the issue of universal access and how we decide what it is, who ought to get it, how much, under what circumstances, what costs, and who ought to pay for it, ultimately will decide in the long term what kind of society we choose to become.

I'd like to introduce our panelists, a very distinguished and interesting group, as you will hear.

PRUDENCE ADLER is the Assistant Executive Director of External Relations of the Association of Research Libraries, where she focuses on information policy issues, intellectual property rights, telecommunications issues, and issues relating to access to government information. When I first met Prue in the 1980s, she was the Assistant Director of the Congressional Office of Technology Assessment program on communications and information technology.

Next is **RICHARD CIVILLE**, the Executive Director of the Massachusetts-based Center for Civic Networking. He is co-founder of CAP access, a community network in the national capital area, serving over 12,000 individuals, and author of a chapter in a book published just last year, where he writes about the poor and access to the Internet.

Then we have **JOCK GILL**, President of Penfield Gill, Inc., an organization located here. He is the former Director of Special Projects in the White House Office of Media Affairs, where he ran the electronic public access during the 1992 Clinton/Gore campaign.

I think you're going to hear some interesting viewpoints from them all, in terms of what universal access really is. One might infer that the term "universal access" implies 100 percent of the universe. We'll see, in fact, that it means different things to different people, often far less than service to 100 percent of the universe.

I'd like to mention some of the comments I heard earlier at this conference by Scott McNealy, who said he thought: the worst thing that could happen would be government guaranteeing universal access; that what we needed in this society was losers in order to enable the winners to win a higher quality of life; and that this structure ought to be based on something called "fierce Darwinism." This connotes a sort of electronic feudalism, much like the medieval societies in Europe, with the "haves" and "have nots." The fundamental issue involving universal access is fundamental fairness—whether or not in the long term we'll have a society based on inclusiveness or one based on privilege.

I'd like to begin with Richard.

CIVILLE: Looking at census data over several years, where the Department of Education polled the population about their use of personal computers and how they used electronic mail and such, we see between 1989 and 1993, for example, the level of literacy of high school graduates—that is, their access to personal computers and the fact that they were using electronic mail or some form of online service—increased quite dramatically. It suggested to us that there is a kind of a "driver's education" level of skill that can be acquired, where a lot of people with basic literacy can learn how to use online services quite effectively. The problem is, those who are below the levels of marginal literacy are going to get left much further behind, much more rapidly, without support.

Bowie: Now let's hear Prue's definition, both of universal access, and what might constitute essential information, particularly in regard to public information and copyrighted information.

Adler: Thank you, Nolan. When I first discussed this presentation with Bill [Kovach, track co-chair], we agreed it would be useful to discuss universal access from the perspective of access to what. In that spirit, I will focus on universal access issues in the context of two current debates: debates concerning copyright and intellectual property issues and the NII [National Information Infrastructure], in particular, the relationship between these important discussions and universal service and related provisions in the Telecommunications Act of 1996—namely, the Communications Decency Act. The basic premise common to these debates is that universal access is more than a connection. It is meaningful and affordable access to information and needed resources.

First, it is important to try to capture the challenge facing all of us in these discussions and why it is important. The following statement by Pye does just that.[*]

> Communications is the web of human society. The structure of a communication system with its more or less well-defined channels is in a sense the skeleton of the social body which envelops it. The content of communications is of course the very substance of human intercourse. The flow of communications determines the direction and the pace of dynamic social development.

This statement captures the challenge and what we stand to lose if in the debates regarding universal service, access, and copyright, we don't get it right. How do we ensure the "flow of communications?"

To appreciate the challenges before us, some context for how these topics are interrelated and a review of the recent debates regarding copyright and universal service will be helpful. Let me state the obvious: promoting universal access broadly and through many channels should be a national priority.

We are living through a time when the network is undergoing extraordinary changes in its size, scope, the types of users, and thus uses. Each new user makes the network more robust, a richer resource, and may spark the development of new services and applications. Thus, attracting new communities and users to the network is closely linked to promoting universal access.

Recently, the focus of the debate has been on content and what flows over the network. It is now widely recognized that to be successful, the NII and the GII [Global Information Infrastructure] must be more than an entertainment, economic, or functional force in our lives. It must assist us in how we communicate, how we educate, and how we participate in the democratic process. Thus, the second focus is on access and universal service issues. Access to information, both public and proprietary, is essential to all of these activities: education, participation in the democratic process, and communications.

Many of you heard the session yesterday on intellectual property issues ["Intellectual Property Online"] and the NII. The NII will undergo a dramatic change as more and more copyrighted information is available, and rules and procedures are put in place to manage those proprietary resources. Part of the difficulty in designing new mechanisms to deal with intellectual property issues is the clash of cultures, if you will. How do you impose a tightly controlled, legally enforceable system of access to information on the culture of the Internet, which encourages the flow and exchange of information? And how do you impose such a system on a entity such as the Internet, which is more like a growing organism, given it's ability to grow, reshape itself, and change? Laws should be flexible and provide room to accommodate some level of change. It is difficult to find that room for the Internet and copyright issues because the change is so rapid and because we really aren't sure where we will end up. That is the same challenge for defining universal service: how to define an ongoing

---

[*] Pye, Lucien (ed.), *Communications and Political Development*, Princeton University Press, 1963, p. 4.

process for assessing and reassessing the needs of educational institutions and libraries as technologies and our institutions change.

A friend in Minnesota notes that whenever he hears the "C" word [copyright], he feels a migraine coming on. Truth be known, he is on to something. Grappling with copyright and universal service issues in the network environment will lead to many migraines for all of us before we find workable solutions. The issue of copyright will also be the most contentious of all debates regarding access to all types of information in the future. Intellectual property issues may well be the defining element in how the network thrives or fails. And importantly, how these issues are resolved will determine the value of the universal service provisions. If we in the library and education communities and the public cannot get at needed information in a meaningful manner or afford the information, what have we gained? What will we have universal access to?

Given the importance of copyright issues regarding how the NII may or may not evolve, some context for the current discussions would be useful. The genius of the copyright law is that it balances the rights of authors, publishers, and copyright owners with society's need for the exchange of ideas. Balance is achieved through many provisions but most importantly, fair use.

In a nutshell, fair use and other provisions of the act are, in fact, much of what we take for granted. It is being able to go to a bookstore and browse before you decide to purchase or not. In the network environment, this is also called browsing. It is a student going to the library and copying an article in an encyclopedia for a class project. In this setting and others, this is fair use. It is also your right to buy a book and to pass it along to a friend. And, it is your right to listen to music, sing along in your car as loudly as you'd like, and not declare it a public performance. How much of this can be directly translated to the Internet remains to be seen, but all of these opportunities or rights should be appropriately extended to meet the unique medium of the digital environment.

Why the heightened interest in intellectual property issues? Stimulating the growth and development of the NII is a continuing priority for the Clinton Administration, and there are bills (HR 2441 and S. 1284, the NII Copyright Protection Act of 1995) in the House and Senate seeking to update the Copyright Act.

If implemented, the provisions in the bills would dismantle the current balance between the rights of copyright owners and those of libraries and users of proprietary information. It is critically important to continue to maintain the balance between the rights of users of proprietary works and the rights of the owners of those works in the print and digital environments. The full potential of the NII for the education and research communities and the public will not be realized if the current balance in place in the print environment is not appropriately extended to the electronic environment. Indeed, it would be a very hollow definition of universal access if these bills are passed as introduced.

It is important to note that provisions in the bills have implications well beyond copyright and intellectual property issues. In particular, the proposed revisions raise a host of issues relating to privacy, confidentiality, and the potential liability of libraries and educational institutions in the delivery of information in the networked environment. Of most interest to the library and education communities are those concerning fair use, first sale, third-party liability for transmissions on a network of resources, and the impact of these proposals on distance education.

Of utmost concern and, again, a notion that is cropping up in other legislative forums, is the conclusion that those who use the NII to transmit information should be legally responsible for all transmissions on their network (users of Harvard's Widener Memorial Library, for example). Libraries and educational institutions would be responsible, thus liable, as providers of online services. This kind of proposal mirrors the recent congressional discussions concerning third-party liability by providers of material considered to be indecent.

Finally, there is also a subtle and less tangible but important link between the online service provider liability discussions, freedom of expression, and universal access. Institutions, including schools and libraries, will be more cautious in the provision of information if there is concern regarding third-party liability. Over time, this would have a dampening effect on the role of libraries and educational institutions in the provision of information and on the ability of users to access information resources. This could also include the severely needed software tools and training.

In comparing the Copyright Act and the telecommunications and universal debate, it is interesting to note that the Copyright Act has been modified many times over the years, yet the Communications Act of 1934 was not changed until this year. And whereas the proposed changes to the Copyright Act have been characterized as "modest," they are as sweeping as those included in the Telecommunications Act of 1996. It is also interesting to note that, increasingly, changes to the Copyright Act are driven by international trade concerns rather than sound domestic copyright and intellectual policies. Telecommunications providers called for radical changes to the communications infrastructure in order to compete effectively on both the national and international arenas.

There are two parts of the telecommunications legislation of interest to the universal access discussions; one of which Richard has discussed, the opportunity. Although not the focus of the Telecommunications Act, it does speak to universal service as a goal—namely, ensuring that the basic tool of electronic information is available to everyone. Congress, much to its wisdom, left most of the details of defining universal service to a Joint Federal/State Board. The work of the Board will be based on six principles, one of which requires that K–12 schools, libraries, and rural health care providers have access to advanced telecommunications services at lower rates than those for comparable services provided to other parties. This discount should be sufficient to ensure affordable access to and use of such services. This is the first step in defining the functionality that is needed for core services. It is to define an ongoing process of assessment for our institutions.

This is a unique and historic opportunity. This is the first time that schools and libraries are included under universal service policies. And schools and libraries are not merely beneficiaries of these services. They will help create markets, support training and education, be points of access, and more.

The challenge is, of course, the Communications Decency Act, or CDA.[*] Title V of the Telecommunications Act includes provisions that make it illegal to knowingly transmit or display "indecent" or "patently offensive" material over the network, where minors might view it. In the case of universities, it could be illegal for enrolled students under 18 to view health information, considered "indecent," via the campus network. On a similar note, educational institutions could under certain circumstances be liable if a student was able to access a web site that contained indecent materials.

Several lawsuits challenging the act have been filed with the ultimate goal of reaching the Supreme Court. Even if these onerous provisions are overturned by the Supreme Court, it's clear that there will be more proposals on the national, state, and local levels to try to grapple with these important issues. All educational institutions, indeed all providers, need to be prepared to implement policies to set the rules of the road for students, faculty, and the public. Our institutions also need to educate our users concerning their rights and responsibilities in this new environment. Again, the current debates will define what universal access means in the years ahead.

---

[*] The Communications Decency Act (CDA) was shot down by a three-judge court in June, 1996. However, on December 6, 1996, the Supreme Court agreed to hear the government's appeal for the legal challenge to the CDA. The case is expected to be heard in March, 1997. See *http://www.cdt.org* for more details.

Again, in considering the link between the copyright and telecommunications debates, there is a not-so-subtle shift in responsibilities. Provisions in both the CDA and in the proposed copyright bills would hold online service providers liable for the acts of their users. Universities and libraries have invested in a technological infrastructure to promote access to information and resources, not to monitor use or label information resources. We have built a digital "commons" in support of a robust definition of universal access.

As mentioned earlier, the NII will be the means by which we will communicate, educate, and participate in the democratic process. Thus it is critically important that we actively participate in how it evolves to meet the needs of the public and commercial interests, and more important, to ensure the flow of communications. Ensuring the flow of communications is the defining element of universal access. Thank you.

BOWIE: Jock Gill, will you tell us your version of universal access and how we learn about our own definitions through the stories we are told—how it either expands or limits what we think about it.

GILL: Thank you very much. I need to answer Nolan's question, but I'd also like to comment on Scott McNealy's very amusing presentation. Cowboy capitalism and market fundamentalism are interesting phenomena, but they're only one story. I'd like to get on with perhaps telling some other stories. I like Prue's question, "Access to what?". But I'd like to also suggest: Is it important? Why should we have it? I mean, maybe it's irrelevant. Maybe only 10 percent of the people are going to use it and the other 90 percent are going to ignore it. So it's a moot point and we can all go home. But I think that you'll see I believe [universal access] is incredibly important. How we handle this is going to determine the markets that emerge.

Part of the access/service question is that it is not only about the market. I'd like to question whether, in fact, the Web-Net is about markets, and whether it's really even about information. Maybe it's more about stories. And maybe "access to what" is the access to the most powerful storytelling mechanism that has emerged in the last 50 years. Maybe the reason it's so important is that the stories we tell ourselves and each other determine who we are. If that's the case, then we must have universal access in order that all of us may be storytellers.

Now on this map (please see my web site for the slides—look under "What's new" at the URL *http://www.penfield.gill.com/gill/*), for which I am indebted to Dr. Michael C. Geoghegan from Dupont, you'll see that information is on the bottom left, where there's a lot of it but it's relatively low value. Knowledge is more important. It's in the middle. It's sort of the "how" that we get from the "what." But understanding is really much more interesting and more important. And wisdom is—well, there's much less of it, and it's of much higher value.

President Neil L. Rudenstine's talk last night was absolutely splendid and extraordinarily important. However, I did afterwards ask him, "Where does knowledge come from? And what is the role of knowledge creation?" As we move forward into the new economy, where we're not going to be competing with our backs or with natural resources or with access to capital or manufacturing technologies, we're going to be competing on our ability to create understanding and wisdom. I believe that the Web/Net is fundamental for this process. And I believe it's therefore fundamental that we have universal access to this new tool for creating understanding and wisdom from knowledge, information, and data.

Now, a little history is in order, in part to rebut—or to question—Scott McNealy's and Bill Gates's comments. The 1920s were, I believe, historically the last period of rip-roaring cowboy capitalism, which led to some rather interesting events in the 1930s, sometimes known as the Great Crash or the Great Depression. Not exactly shining, glorious moments.

However, it also led to the Communications Act of 1934. And one of the interesting questions is if, in 1930, between 30 and 40 percent of the people had dial tone, did we need the Communications Act to promote the concept of universal service or access, or not? We had the Rural Electrification Act in 1936, because the Great White Way ended at the town limits. The companies, the private sector, were more interested in building power trusts that generated capital profits but did not deliver electricity to Americans. In fact, Lyndon Johnson rose to political power, in some sense, by his ability to bring electricity to west Texas farmers.

Clearly there was a market failure in the delivery of wired services. The Rural Electrification Act was expanded to cover telephony in 1949, by President Truman. An interesting question is, why was this necessary? I do not have the answer. The NII, the National Information Infrastructure, had field hearings in 1993 and 1994, which were published by the IETF [Internet Engineering Task Force] in 1994, about the need for universal access. They had meetings scattered around the country. That's great research. If you do a search on "universal access" in AltaVista, you'll find references to the field hearings, and you can read the report. There is a substantial body of research and evidence that this is, in fact, a very important issue, not only for health care, for politics, for education, for the sense of community and culture, but also for the creation of social as well as market capital.

We then had the Communications Act of 1996, which was the first revision of the 1934 Acts. And we now have, peculiarly, the FCC [Federal Communication Commission] hearings, dealing with universal access. I'm not clear why it's in the FCC. But history shows that this is not a pure market phenomenon. One might speculate, at least within the realm of education (and since we're at Harvard, that would be an appropriate speculation), that there is a terrible mismatch between markets and education. The market has a tendency to look in 90-day time frames. The market in general will not invest in R&D that doesn't show a positive return in six to seven years, because of the projected value of the dollar that far out. Education at Harvard is a 16-year

experience. You have 12 years before you get to Harvard; you have four years at Harvard. And somehow, a 90-day time frame maps very poorly to a 16-year time frame. Therefore, I would suggest that we need a rich and diverse set of metaphors, of which the market is but one.

The book changed both how we told stories and the context in which the stories were told. And I love President Rudenstine's discussions of what Germans thought about reading, and the great impact of the library program on Harvard in the late 19th century. Clearly, the book made certain that nothing would ever be the same again.

I would suggest, as we have heard in the entire conference, that the computer is changing how we tell stories, and again, the context in which we live. Nothing will ever be the same again: the landscape in which we live is very dynamic.

But what is a good story? A good story is relevant. So when is it relevant? When it provides a useful description and it maps to observed situations. I would argue, in fact, that stories are maps. A good story provides useful explanations. It helps us to understand the process of our lives, our businesses, our education, even our health. It provides useful suggestions for action. And one hopes it will improve or maximize our evolutionary success, or the prospects for evolutionary success. So storytelling is critical, because the way we tell our stories—the ones we tell inside our heads in traffic jams, the ones we tell each other at dinner parties, at lectures, at the movies, when we read a newspaper, and so on—determines what we know, how we know it, and in fact, the dreams we dream, as well as the stories we tell. It's a self-referential, circular, nonlinear process. The one influences and changes the other.

One of the things we have not yet talked about at this conference is the difference between old media and new media.[*] We have not described the new media as a storytelling mechanism. I find it extraordinarily useful to do so. But part of understanding the importance of new media is to

---

[*] This subject is discussed in the session entitled "Press and the New Media".

understand the difference between the old and the new. My web site contains several slides on "a difference" matrix. Let me just review them with you briefly.

We're moving from an age of objectivity, sort of a Newtonian physics approach, a Cartesian ideal, to a more constructive reality. We're moving from an industrial paradigm to perhaps a more biological paradigm. We've heard a good deal of talk about ecologies.

We're going from a situation where information is strictly controlled, with concerns about copyright and intellectual property rights, to an area where I would suggest information is largely out of control. (Some of you may have read a book by that title, published by the fellow Kelly at *Wired* magazine.[*])

We're going from a system of communications, a storytelling mechanism, where we rely on very few intelligences—simply linear text, pretty much black and white—to something much more complex. Howard Gardner, a very famous professor here at Harvard, suggests in fact that human beings have many intelligences. There are many ways of being smart and knowledgeable. The new media allows us to use music, multiple links, sound, graphics, and call on many more forms of our human intelligences, and therefore it is far more satisfying to use than the more limited old legacy media.

Information is much more static in the legacy media. It comes to you in dead, flattened trees (which is really not very useful). Or it can be very dynamic on a screen. There will be interesting changes in what a document is. A product has been demonstrated called FutureTense, which uses Java. Scott McNealy would be very happy. It allows you to have areas on the screen that change dynamically every time you call it up, which calls into question the definition of a document. In fact, the definition of a document will be the set of programming commands that create the document, because the actual presentation will be different every time. And what that does for information rights and policies, I don't know. But it's clearly very different.

Community. Because we can all participate, the new media is an inclusive community. The old media—I don't think very many of us own newspapers or TV stations, movie studios, radio stations, so forth and so on. We're leaving an exclusive era, I think—all to the better.

The legacy media has a very high barrier to entry. Computers are cheap. I've been on the Internet in Washington with a computer we saved from a dumpster. I put in a $100 disk drive, a $100 modem, and I was broadcasting on the Internet.

> *Computers are cheap. I've been on the Internet in Washington with a computer we saved from a dumpster. I put in a $100 disk drive, a $100 modem, and I was broadcasting on the Internet.*

Communications flow is one-to-many on the legacy media. And more accurately, in new media, it's many one-to-many, which looks like many-to-many. But we don't really have this "and both" operator yet.

The organization in the old media is top-down. In the new, organization is more bottom-up. But in fact, it's "and both." There are components of top-down vision, and there are components of bottom-up innovation and application.

It's linear versus hypertext. It enables dialogue. This is critical. You can tell stories in a one-way fashion. But you can't engage in the storytelling process unless you can all talk to one another. Critical difference.

---

[*] Kelly, Kevin, *Out of Control*, Addison-Wesley Publishing Co., 1994.

If I could use just two words to differentiate the old media from the new media, I'd use the words "targets" and "partners." For the last hundred years, those of us who do not own media outlets have been treated as targets. We have become passive. In the new media era, we can become partners. We can become (as Prue [Adler] helped me see today) participants, and it's a very active process.

So you can see, given these differences, that the storytelling capabilities of the new media are radically different from the storytelling capabilities of the old media. Because of this, they will enable entirely new sorts of stories to be told. And because the stories we tell determine who we are, we will see ourselves in remarkable new fashions.

Let me quickly give you a couple of examples. The United States used to be the largest market producing over 50 percent of the world gross product, and the reserve currency was clearly the U.S. dollar. (I thank Lester Thurow at MIT for these facts.) Europe or China will be the largest market. The U.S. now produces, I believe, less than 25 percent of the world gross product. And the reserve currency of the future is probably not the U.S. dollar. Who's telling us that story?

Another story. This is more chilling. Television tells us that there are lots and lots of crimes, and the TV shows (stories) best solve these criminal problems with guns. The FBI wants to tell us that all Americans have a "realistic" chance of being murdered. But the statistics in 1992 show that only one percent of violent crimes required hospitalization, and less than one half of the armed robbers showed a gun, and those armed robbers who showed a gun harmed fewer people. Very interesting why television tells us the solution to the crime problem is through guns. I suggest it may be a logical consequence of treating people as targets for 100 years. We are so numb, you've got to poke us hard. If we were actually being engaged in dialogue, would we need to have crime and violence and blood and guts on television? What will the new stories be? And who will tell the new American story? And if we do not tell it, who will tell it?

In the end, I would suggest it's the trust we build with the stories we tell that really matters; and that the best stories increase the ideas we have access to, maximize the diversity of the ideas that we have to work with, reveal new solutions for problems, and improve our chances for evolving…but not necessarily in a market context. Some of it is market-driven, some of it is government-driven, some of it is entertainment-driven. It's a much richer model than pure, simple market fundamentalism and cowboy capitalism.

Bowie: Thank you. Perhaps no one will tell the stories. I point to the fact that the Telecommunications Act passed in February [1996] with very little public awareness, apart from those who were following it very closely as a business story, as opposed to a story that had a great impact on the way society will be governed in the future. Prue mentioned the Telcom Act and the provisions regarding the Joint Board that is considering what universal service will be. Richard actually participated in comments. Will you comment on key points you made?

Civille: We submitted to the Joint Board of the Federal Communication Commission what we thought the framework for universal service ought to be. We suggested several points to the Board:

- Consider a policy framework that would combine market incentives and individual tax credits, such as the earned income tax credit, to increase computer ownership among low income households and small, low income businesses.

- Provide electronic mail services for low income children and job seekers.

- Promote the development of public access to network services that address community needs and life.

- Fund network literacy programs through adult education programs, such as JPTA [Job Training Partnership Act], through public libraries and schools.

Around this is a framework that the government should improve federal data collection on the individual use of networked information. If we're going to come back and revisit these definitions every couple of years, we have got to have good baseline data on how the National Information Infrastructure is affecting individuals. And that can be only be done through the Census Bureau, through the current population survey (and those surveys cost about half a million dollars a pop to do). They're done piecemeal, once in a while, and we think they should be done on a very regular basis.

Questions & Answers

Q: *Must the United States expand global access?*

GILL: I think this is a question of scale. I think we need to chuck out the old ideas of how we do this. It's been pointed out that we increase the value of the Net by increasing participation. Therefore, if I own a net, it would be in my self-interest to ask how I could increase its value. For example, if (as was suggested to me by a Nieman reporter this morning) telephony came with a web browser built in, and if Internet access were charged at a flat fee rather than per-minute, per-unit of distance, we could say, "We'll increase the value of the network that way. We'll increase the size of the storytelling group or the market group. And it is by having a larger market and a more valuable net that I make my money." So to that extent, we should clearly ensure that the rest of the world is involved.

There are also arguments for social stability. And it's in the United States' best interest to have worldwide social stability.

Q: *The harder questions are, how do we achieve universal access, and how do we pay for it?*

ADLER: There are a number of ways to achieve universal access. First, it will entail partnering with a variety of communities and providers. Second, with regard to federal activities in support of universal access, the FCC adopted the interconnection rule, allowing the states to open markets for local telephone service to competition.

The FCC's interconnection rule calls for states to utilize the total element long run incremental cost [TELRIC] when deciding the charges new entrants will pay to local telephone companies (if there is not agreement among parties). TELRIC is the discounted rate that should be adopted for schools and libraries, thus moving toward implementation of universal service goals. It is important to note that with this cost-based approach, deeper discounts could be available to rural, high cost, and low income communities or applications. It's through partnering, and it has to be through many diverse channels, not only through libraries and schools. We need a great deal of participation for this.

Q: *If universal access is good economic policy, why not leave it to private companies rather than the government?*

ADLER: There is another factor I would add. One of the more important roles government provides is equity. Government provides the assurance that in a whole host of arenas, including telecommunications, there is equity for all participants.

Q: *How is democracy affected by universal access?*

GILL: When I was at the White House, my mission, as I saw it, was to increase the participation in democracy, because after all, our form of government is based on self-governance. We, all of us, are the government. When I was with the government, I'd go out and say, "We are the government," and there would be a huge groan or a chuckle: "What do you mean?". It was an oxymoron. "You're from the government. You can't be one of us." But in fact, that's a very sad state of affairs.

The government *does* have an important role. I think the role of the people is to establish the constraints which they believe will optimize the system, and then to ask the government to enforce those. A level playing field is a desirable environment, so that the winners and losers at least start in the same place and we don't tilt it toward one group or another, based on whether you happen to be born in northern New Hampshire, southern Texas, or the Four Corners area of this country. It's also true, as the Vice President says, that competition has just these two really horrible enemies: one is bad regulation, the other is unfair advantage. So I think one role of the government is to keep a level playing field and to make sure that regulations are sensible and realistic.

Q: *How is the information underclass different from an ordinary economic underclass?*

GILL: I think an extraordinarily undesirable business environment is an unstable social configuration. And if we have a social system that is badly bifurcated, where the gap is accelerating to a point where the laws of decreasing returns are driving the "have nots" further down, and the laws of increasing returns are driving the "haves" further up, this is exactly what we will create. It's bad for education. It's bad for health care. It's bad for democracy.

ADLER: I would add to the definition of an information underclass. It's not just access to information, but it's what you heard from many of us earlier, with regard to literacy: the needed information skills, training, and access to tools. Those tools and access to them must evolve and keep pace.

Q: *Why should everyone have a computer and Internet access in their home? Why isn't library access enough?*

GILL: No one is suggesting that we provide hardware to people, although I think this will become "the textbook of the future" within our lifetimes. Information doubles every four or five years, and textbooks tend to last 10 to 15 years in most public schools. It's pretty inappropriate and expensive to be educating people with stuff that's two or three generations out of date. So we are, in fact, going to have to learn how to issue electronic textbooks.

As to the home, some people elect to have five telephones and some elect to have none. Some choose to read the newspaper at the library, some

read it at home. And I expect that we will preserve these distinctions.

ADLER: It is a notable goal to have universal access in each home. But in recognition that that may not be possible in the near term, the question becomes how to build on the infrastructure we already have in place, through these other social institutions, and use those as the mechanisms to provide universal access to needed resources.

GILL: I think that the single most effective thing we can do for universal access is to get every school in this country wired, so that every K–12 child has a 12-year experience with these modalities, these storytelling tools, and can make up his or her own mind whether they are valuable to that child; where they are appropriate; what works better on a paper book or on a screen; what works better with a paintbrush rather than electronic media. It's only by having the ability to make informed choices that we will truly have some sense of equity and of responsibility.

Q: *Will the new media create societies that are more similar to oral societies?*

GILL: Mark Bonchek [Press and Politics Co-chair] threw that out prior to our meeting. It's interesting. I think there will be more elements like that. There's a book about Australia called *The Song-lines*[*] about how the Aborigines use songs to navigate across great expanses of "unmarked" Australia. And I think we will find a similar richness in storytelling. We have been deprived of participating in storytelling for 100 years, because we weren't part of the process, and we were treated as targets.

Think of your own personal relationships. In the ones that have worked, you've probably treated the other person as a partner, as a participant. In the ones that have failed, you've probably treated that person more as an object or a target. How do you like to be treated?

With the new media we can all start engaging in dialogue, talking to one another, listening. No

---

[*] Chatwin, Bruce, *The Songlines*, Penguin Books, 1987.

one has said this yet at this conference. The fact of the matter is, half of new media is *listening*. It's not advertising. It's not selling. It's not storytelling. It's listening.

Q: *Aren't the costs of what is being proposed prohibitive? The public sector has other pressing priorities.*

GILL: Many of these priorities, particularly education and health care, can be enhanced by appropriate use of an information infrastructure. One example is that the U.S. Postal Service is being supplemented by use of email, which is much more efficient.

ADLER: I would add that if the Internet continues to grow to the degree that we believe it will, and the knowledge economy evolves the way we all believe it will, the Internet and providing universal access will be the predominant mode of communication. It will be the predominant mode for education and participation in the democracy. So by default, it *is* the priority, in terms of making sure people have access and use this resource.

BOWIE: I'd just like to leave you with the Chinese proverb to think about, in terms of universal access:

> If your vision is for one year, plant rice. If your vision is for ten years, plant trees. But if your vision is for one hundred years, educate children.

About the Speakers

A widely respected communications attorney, **NOLAN A. BOWIE** is an Associate Professor at Temple University, School of Communications and Theater, Department of Broadcasting, Telecommunications, and Mass Media. Mr. Bowie has also served as an Assistant Special Prosecutor with the Watergate Special Prosecution Force and as an Assistant Attorney General in the Civil Rights Bureau of the New York Sate Department of Law. His primary policy concerns are with promoting public interest regarding issues of equality and access to information for those whose voices are generally underrepresented in policymaking regarding broadcasting and telecommunications.

PRUDENCE S. ADLER is the Assistant Executive Director of the Association for Research Libraries. Her responsibilities include federal relations with a focus on information policies, intellectual property rights, telecommunications, issues relating to access to government information, and project management for the ARL GIS Literacy Project. Prior to joining ARL in 1989, Ms. Adler was Assistant Project Director, Communications and Information Technologies Program, Congressional Office of Technology Assessment, where she worked on studies about government information, networking and supercomputer issues, and information technologies and education.

RICHARD CIVILLE is the Washington Director of the Center for Civic Networking, which promotes the public interest in communication policies and creates community networks. He started a distance learning project which used telecommunications to link school children around the world to do joint work on an ecological issue, and also co-founded Econet. He is a board member of CapAccess and serves as the Director of Information Services at the Center for Budget Policy Priorities. Civille is a leader at bringing together people from different grassroots telecommunications initiatives to learn from each other and organize politically. He consistently stresses the importance of access for everyone, especially disenfranchised and low-income groups.

JOCK GILL is President and Founder of Penfield Gill, Incorporated, a consulting firm specializing in New Media communications, marketing, and strategic planning. The firm also provides investment banking services for Internet-based enterprises in the areas of communications, education, and health. From 1993 to 1995, Mr. Gill was Director of Special Projects in the Office of Media Affairs at the White House, where he was a key member of the communications innovations team which developed the first White House web site, "Welcome to the White House." Previously, he was a consultant to the 1992 Clinton/Gore presidential campaign, and a senior Product Manager at Lotus Development Corporation.

HARVARD NEWS

CONFERENCE ON THE INTERNET AND SOCIETY

May 29-31, 1996   Cambridge, MA

Virtually Real: Life, Politics, and the Net

By Katrina Roberts

"Think of the Internet as a large scale piped water system," William Mitchell, Dean of the MIT School of Architecture MIT, was saying.

Historically, a central water supply such as a village well was a place where people collected to gossip and share information. "Once you've put in piped water, there are certainly advantages, but you destroy a fundamental thing keeping people together," Mitchell added.

"The glue of the physical community is really face-to-face interaction. Online communities pose a threat to places that traditionally bring a necessary density of people together in a public way."

Mitchell suggested that architects face the challenge of recognizing the intimate connections between the structures of electronic and physical worlds: "It's essentially a design issue: understanding the properties, potentials, and affordabilities of physical presence. Where are you bringing someone back to in virtual space? What are the essential physical points, without which we lose our essential human core?"

Mitchell, whose book *City of Bits* has been simultaneously distributed in hard copy and on the Web, was one of four panelists in the session "Life and Politics on the Net." Participants addressed questions about how online communities might impact geographical communities, and the social and political implications of virtual communities and Internet use.

"If we assume that [Bill] Gates' predictions this morning are right, if virtual space substitutes for physical space so that real estate becomes unnecessary, what kind of communities will we have?" asked Mitchell.

"There's more than a grain of truth in the old maxim, 'all politics is local,' but what does local mean anymore? Of course, we'll still have to park ourselves somewhere; we'll still have possessions, material belongings. And face-to-face interactions in a physical world are crucial to us; there's always the physical dimension."

Successful virtual communities have some of the same attributes as physical ones, but there are some differences. In a virtual world, the bomb threat that necessitate the move of this real-world session from the Science Center to Emerson Hall wouldn't have had the same effect.

"The key challenges we're going to face are not technological," said Peter Kollock, professor of sociology at UCLA. "We're here today for social reasons. It's not just a question of designing a better dialogue box and 'there: society's better.' There is no algorithm for a community, but there are social heuristics." Kollock noted that many of the flashiest exciting 3-D communities lack ongoing and supportive interaction; they are, he said, "lonely museums."

Charles Firestone, the Director of the Aspen Institute who moderated the panel asked, "Is it politics 'as usual' on the Web? And, will web sites change voters, or are campaign sites really preaching to the already converted?"

Fellow Washingtonian Doug Bailey, publisher of *PoliticsUSA OnLine*, a major bipartisan web site, replied, "Online politics is in its infancy." He suggested that online voting is inevitable, "but the Internet won't have an enormous impact on the '96 election, although the technology is going to be used as a new campaign vehicle. It's powerful from an organizational and informational standpoint, because it will provide an opportunity to gather input from people, though it's not yet terribly effective as a two-way communication system."

About Presidential campaign sites, Bailey said, "The Dole campaign site is pretty good." He clarified: "That's the web site, not necessarily the campaign."

Bailey said that *PoliticsUSA*, a "one-stop shop" informational site, will merge next week with the *Washington Post*'s and ABC's *ElectionLine*: "To make a business of it, we need the backing that a TV network can provide. The keys are building a community, understanding, and learning to trust what people want, then bringing them back with ever-changing content." Despite Bailey's enthusiasm, he did voice wariness.

"What concerns me about the trend toward online politics is that as we increase our knowledge and capacity to communicate around the world, we're cutting off our neighbors in a physical sense." In addition, Bailey cited maintaining secret ballots as a pressing challenge for developers, as well as addressing the situation created by divisions based on discrepancies in income, education, age, race, and availability of technology.

"In the year 2000, online voter registration will happen," Bailey said, "but the division between the 'haves and have nots' will grow dramatically."

He noted that, although the Web will make political figures more accountable, "Who is to say what's true on the Internet? Whose judgments and descriptions do you trust?"

John Mallery, Technical Director of the Intelligent Information Infrastructure Project and research scientist at MIT's Artificial Intelligence Lab, suggested that as society starts to have "deliberative systems in the public sphere online," they will create a problem for those with limited access.

Issues arose about individualism and isolation. "Isolated on the Net, compared to what?" asked Kollock. As we sit in our underwear typing email to millions around the world and surfing the Web, are we any more isolated than we are anyway, sitting in our suburban homes, he asked.

But Mallery plugged the interactive online communities that MUDs [multi-user dungeons] provides. Mallery, who was one of the architects of the White House web page, and instrumental in the developing the 1994 open meeting for Vice President Gore, sees the Networld "as a major city. You get a high rate of channeled interaction," he said. "You can interact productively with many people in a narrow slice," something you couldn't do in the physical world.

"What's missing in virtual space," says Mitchell, is "persistence of identity and sites. In physical architectural sites, site-specific kinds of discourse emerge. Here in this hall we speak in a language unlike the one we'd hear in the Square."

Mitchell suggested that our behavior and discourse change when we physically enter architectural structures such as churches, but, he continued, "in web sites, there aren't such traditions and expectations. It's easy to wear masks, but it's tough to build trust—a key component in creating a working physical community."

Firestone prompted a discussion about the veracity of information received over the Web. From the audience, Jock Gill suggested that "the great political contribution of the Net will be new storytelling capabilities, to explain our world to us in meaningful ways that ring true. Right now, we're telling each other bad stories in a 1950 framework."

Press & Politics
May 29, 1996

Life and Politics on the Net

MODERATOR: Charles Firestone
PANELISTS: Doug Bailey
                  Peter Kollock
                  John Mallery*
                  William Mitchell

Editor's Note: Because of a bomb scare immediately prior, this session was not taped. The following text is a transcription of the Session Notes, by online moderator Chris Kelly.

FIRESTONE: Will there be politics as usual on the web, or some significantly different approach?

BAILEY: Politics on the Web is in its infancy. The Web won't have much of an impact in 1996, but it will later on. The Web is very powerful from an organizing and information-providing standpoint. Providing information and the opportunity for input is a valuable political tool. About 150 to 200 campaigns are up on the Web right now, generally using it as an electronic brochure, which is not terribly effective. Two-way communication sessions over the Web will get results, however. This will involve people, give them the opportunity to participate, and must be updated frequently.

Politics USA is a bipartisan info site, one stop shop. It will merge with ElectionLine for the brand name of ABC/*Washington Post*—called Politics Now. (The big question was not technology but the name of the site.) Trying to make a business out of it was a wonderful learning experience. On the Web you need to change content regularly, give people a chance for involvement,

and respect their desires in providing them with what they want to see.

FIRESTONE: Will political web sites change votes, or are they preaching to the converted?

BAILEY: It will have an impact in the year 2000, maybe 2004. There will be online voter registration, online voting (once the problem of electronic signatures is worked out), online town meetings. The Web is great organizing tool. The majority of Americans will be online, but there will still be big "have/have not" problems.

FIRESTONE: What is the best way to work town meetings, and many-to-many communications?

MALLERY: This works in the area of mass listening and defocusing the broadcast model. The big question is how to use digital communication networks differently. You can get information from many different people, but it must be structured in some way. The organizational process was tested in doing a mass meeting on National Performance Review (*http://www.npr.gov/*). The big problem is that bottlenecks will inevitably develop. For example, the White House communications office and their classification of letters is helpful in seeing questions that arise:

- How will we aggregate responses while still allowing for adequate expression?

- What are the limitations of survey research and closed surveys?

- What are the questions to ask?

What's needed is a wide-area collaboration, where the process is decomposed with respect to content and number of people, and it must be asynchronous. There must be some structure imposed, and annotations that make sense; structure that focuses the comments to arrive at something cogent.

Among the possibilities is an online presidential debate. This is possible because position papers are already online; nonpartisan moderators and basic organizational structures are available. One

---

* Please see an outline of John Mallery's talk at *http://www.ai.mit.edu/projects/iiip/talks/1996/malleryd/index.html.*

would expect this to reduce appeals to emotion, and encourage the reasoned provision of information, developing both better communication and a better democratic process. However, the big communication "haves vs. have nots" problem remains.

FIRESTONE: How are we to judge the success of an online community?

KOLLOCK: Look at online communities in their own right, not just in comparison to actual communities. Study both successes and failures. The key challenges are social interaction and architecture. There is no algorithm for community. The most successful online community is arguably the ugliest, in terms of user interface: Worlds Away, on CompuServe, has silly avatars, only three bodies to choose from per gender, but it has a number of necessary traits for success:

- Consistency of identity
- Eternal economy
- Private property
- Risk (moderate is good)
- Documents/history
- Easy space to understand
- Casual social interaction required by need to walk everywhere.

FIRESTONE: What is the effect on geographical communities?

MITCHELL: All politics are local, but the question is, what does "local" mean? If there is free bandwidth and reasonable access, to what extent can virtual space substitute for real space? The fundamental difference between an electronic community and a physical community is in the meaning of physical threat.

FIRESTONE: But what about viruses? Is there a loss of core values with the network?

MALLERY: The Net is really like a big city. You can interact with more people, but on narrow issues.

FIRESTONE: What is your expectation of online voting?

BAILEY: It's inevitable, but like working at home, it offers the capacity to shut people out. Is there a loss of security? Does the capacity to connect with the world lead to a neglect of one's local community?

JOCK GILL:[*] It's new media as a storytelling vehicle. The problem is that the same old stories are being told. A great political mechanism of the new media allows the creation of new stories.

BAILEY: That's an apt description of the shortcoming of the current Net, and a problem of present politics. But it has the potential to break the limitations of time and space. But there are major downsides to new possibilities—Congressional nightly town meetings may just amplify the current problems of risk-averse politicians.

FIRESTONE: Isn't authentication also a difficult issue?

MALLERY: The Net is response to society. There is uneasiness in current political discussion on the Net because of underlying economic issues.

FIRESTONE: Will there be more political accountability?

BAILEY: Absolutely. But the downside is the lack of "truth" on the Net. For example, *http://www.dole96.org/* is not the real campaign web site, *http://www.dole96.com/* is. Voting records and the more or less accurate presentation of voting records will be available on the Web from many different sites.

MITCHELL: These issues connect with the persistence of identity of both people and sites. It is easy to put things up, but hard to build trust because sites come and go.

Audience Questions

- Can the current model of web governance survive?

---

[*] See the session "Universal Access" in which Jock Gill is a panelist.

- What constitutes the physical threat on the Internet?

- Comment on the social isolation and the factor of time. How much time to we have to participate in virtual life?

- How does the Net address Robert Putnam's *Bowling Alone?*[*]

- What is the role of the Web in moral/character development?

- Will electronic voting undermine the ideal of one-person/one-vote, or the secret ballot?

- Will there be more of a move to direct representation?

- How will the "have/have not" issue affect developed and developing countries?

- What are the leadership roles and power structures in virtual communities?

- How will the possibility of both isolation and interaction posed by the Web affect individualism?

MALLERY: A distinction must be made between the Net and the Web. The technology is neutral. We need organization and the formalization of rules to accomplish tasks on the Net. Increasing options on geographical location can disburse the Net and the technology, and thereby politics, back into rural areas.

MITCHELL: There is developing competition between physical space and virtual space. We must ask where value is added by physical presence. With purchasing books, for example, if you know what you want, then can just send out your agent to negotiate the best price over the Web. But if what you're seeking isn't a commodity, you may need to talk to the rare bookstore owner. The question is, what is the optimal mix of the physical and virtual? What we are designing virtual communities to do?

KOLLOCK: Isolation is real in real life. Voting in electronic communities has been tried in MUDs [multi-user dungeons] and MOOs [multi-user object-oriented dungeons], and has failed. It ends up in a (usually) benign dictatorship, with a "helper class." It is also important to note that the Net contradicts the *Bowling Alone* thesis. There *is* more social involvement as a result of the Net; it's merely virtual.

BAILEY: In politics, the change of the reintroduction of time into the process is real. Sound bites will never go away, but more is available now. Online voting will inevitably happen, but we must pay attention to the "have/have not" division to avoid severe political problems. Education is a major part of the answer.

About the Speakers

CHARLES M. FIRESTONE has been the Director of the Aspen Institute's Communications and Society Program since December 1989. The Program is a neutral forum for public policy conferences and seminars relating to the societal impact of the communications and information sectors, particularly as they relate to democratic institutions and values. As director of the Program, Firestone is responsible for all of its operations. He is also Program Director of the Institute for Information Studies, a joint project of The Aspen Institute and Northern Telecom. Firestone is the editor or co-author of three books: *Television and Elections*; *Television, Radio, News, and Minorities*; and *Toward an Information Bill of Rights and Responsibilities*.

Together with the *National Journal, Washington Post*, and ABC, **DOUGLAS L. BAILEY** is the founder of PoliticsNow, a comprehensive online service for the political community of professionals and activists on the World Wide Web. Mr. Bailey is also the founder and chairman of the American Political Network, the publisher of *The Hotline, American Health Line, GREENWIRE*, and *The Abortion*

---

[*] Putnam, Robert, "Bowling Alone: America's Declining Social Capital," *Journal of Democracy*, vol. 6, no. 1 (1995), pp. 65-78. This article may also be found online at *http://muse.jhu.edu/journals/journal_of_democracy/v006/putnam.html*.

Report, as well as the founder and president of Bailey, Deardourff & Associates, Inc.—political and media consultants to clients including former President Ford, as well as numerous governors and senators.

PETER KOLLOCK is Associate Professor of Sociology at the University of California, Los Angeles. His research focuses on cooperation and the role of trust and commitment in groups. He studies a wide range of situations in which group members gain by cooperating but where a temptation to behave selfishly exists, examining the factors that encourage or discourage the emergence of cooperation and community. His recent work has concentrated on studies of computer-mediated communities, and he has several projects in progress examining social interaction and organization in online groups.

JOHN C. MALLERY is technical director of the Intelligent Information Infrastructure Project at the Artificial Intelligence Laboratory at MIT. His research interests center around new ways to model international interactions and new ways to incorporate political communication. His current research explores intelligent information access, wide-area collaboration, knowledge-based organizations, and global knowledge webs.

WILLIAM J. MITCHELL is Professor of Architecture and Media Arts and Sciences and Dean of the School of Architecture and Planning at the Massachusetts Institute of Technology. He teaches courses and conducts research in design theory, computer applications in architecture and urban design, and imaging and image synthesis. He consults extensively in the field of computer-aided design and was the co-founder of a California software company. Mitchell, the author of *City of Bits: Space, Place, and the Infobahn*, as well as numerous other books and articles, is the Chair of the Editorial Board of The MIT Press.

Emerging Journalism Forms on Internet Are Blurring Traditional News and Advertising Lines, Panelists Say

In the new Internetted world, awash in raw information, why does anyone need journalists?

For openers, said Denise Caruso, "You don't trust everything you read on the Net. Journalism brings with it standards and some sense of credibility. "There's a big difference between raw information and people who check out the facts," said Caruso, the Director of Digital Commerce for the *New York Times* and a panelist yesterday on "Press and the New Media" at the Conference on the Internet and Society.

Janice Kaplan of News Corp. agreed. "The good news about the Web is everyone has a voice. The bad news about the Web is that everyone has a voice. Unfiltered voices is not necessarily what we have time for."

She noted, however, that people seem to want to read first-hand accounts and some Internet pages now offer that.

Brock Meeks, chief Washington correspondent for *Wired* magazine, said he uses The Well, a San Francisco electronic bulletin board, for raw accounts. He said he enjoyed the fact that eyewitnesses to events were encouraged to give their views before the traditional journalists got to the scene.

"There's a place for someone on the ground in Nicaragua, someone working with a relief agency," to report on an earthquake.

"People aren't stupid," he said. "People playing journalist on the Net and spouting off unconfirmed facts will be branded as such."

He said AT&T's Lead Story page (*http://www.leadstory.com/*) was a good idea in making details about breaking news readily available. But Meeks said the page was subject to commercial interference, citing what he said were the largely negative stories the site carried about the proposed merger of Bell Atlantic and NYNEX.

John Markoff, who writes about new media for the Times, warned of a "nightmare scenario" for journalism where "we can all rush to wherever the news is." Citing the coverage of O.J. Simpson's freeway drive, he said it may be real-time reporting but "whatever it is, it's not journalism."

Panelists were generally critical of the web sites that they said simply repackaged the stories that other publications have created. In particular, the PoliticsUSA site (*http://politicsusa.com/*) was heavily criticized, with the panelists arguing that they were "shoveling" material online without trying to organize it in meaningful ways.

Caruso suggested one valuable role for online journalism comes from its ability to provide links to related information. She said traditional media should consider providing links to more alternative views of issues, such as those offered in *Mother Jones* magazine (*http://www.motherjones.com/*). The panel was equally concerned with how the Net is bringing a convergence of news and advertising, blurring what were once sharp differences between the two.

Caruso noted that the Web has no rules about who is or who is not a media organization, so there was nothing to stop Toyota, for example, from developing advertising content and posting it as "news" on a web site. "I'm not sure there's anything you can do about it," she said.

Meeks noted that Miller Brewing Co. sponsored a home page (*http://www.mgdtaproom.com/*) called Taproom that had news content from "alternative" publications and did so without pressing advertising of its beers. He also noted that "Advertisers right now are pretty stupid...throwing their money at sites they think are hot."

The process may produce a lot of hits, but not much in the way of sales, and the advertisers "are getting hip to the fact that they're getting rolled." Markoff said he found it "spooky" that when he conducts an Infoseek Net search it returns with advertising content closely related to the news stories.

Caruso agreed that she was "really freaked out" by that sort of matching, but "it's almost unavoidable given this media and what it's designed to do." The panel moderator, Norman Pearlstine of Time Inc., said the bottom line on web advertising was the bleakness of the bottom line. He said the Web looks to publishers like "the biggest black hole there is" because no one makes money on it.

Press & Politics
May 28, 1996

Press and the New Media

MODERATOR: Norm Pearlstine
PANELISTS: Denise Caruso
                   Janice Kaplan
                   John Markoff
                   Brock Meeks

PEARLSTINE: I'm going to briefly introduce my colleagues so we can get right to our subject. **JOHN MARKOFF** is the national correspondent for the *New York Times* who focuses on Silicon Valley. **BROCK MEEKS** is the chief Washington correspondent for *Wired* and HotWired. **JANICE KAPLAN** is Editor-in-Chief of the iGuide, News Corps' online service. And **DENISE CARUSO** writes the "Digital Commerce" column for the *New York Times*, and more importantly to me, for better or worse, she has taught me most of what I know about new media.

We've been asked to talk today about press and the new media. And if you turn to your books, while it will suggest that the moderator is Michael Kinsley, he seemed to have the wisdom to go to Seattle, get his face on the cover of *Newsweek*, and try an Internet product. Those of us who are still in traditional print are left to try to figure this out. Filling in for Michael, one of the questions we've been asked to talk about is the impact of digital media—this coming together of information, communication, and entertainment—and the way that, from one perspective, it looks like the very large media companies have tried to get a piece of this action. The flip side of that is that, at the same time (as some of you may have heard from Dr. Tesler), one of the true components of the Internet itself is that it changes the business models completely, raising the possibilities, at least in theory, for a more democratizing environment than many people have felt we've

had in traditional media over the last few years. So we're going to talk about some of these different strands through the perspectives of the panelists, who come from very different places.

Before we talk about where the media is and what is happening particularly on the Net, I think it is worth asking who the audience is, what kind of opportunities are there, and what the technology allows for. Are we far enough along to make judgments about what the business is? Or are we still at a point where we have some interesting technology but are still trying to figure out who the customer is?

MARKOFF: You know, I was picked as the poster boy of Nicholas Negroponte's book, *Being Digital*, as someone who could be part of this new generation of journalists (which I think, from our conversation at lunch, Brock [Meeks] fully intends to do), where you could go off on your own and become a cottage industry unto yourself, take advantage of this microtransaction technology that's supposed to emerge shortly, and become an instant millionaire.

Well, I haven't left the *New York Times* yet for a couple of reasons. One is that I have no desire to be an entrepreneur. I've seen what the lives of entrepreneurs are like in Silicon Valley. But the more important issue for me is that I have no idea who the audience is. And that's a problem that I don't think the Net has dealt with yet. As a reporter for the *New York Times*, I'm very comfortable with who my audience is, and I feel like I have a relationship with that audience. I think that's much less clear on the Net. For all the sorts of new technologies, I don't see a notion of audience, at least in the traditional sense. There's lots of interactivity, but I haven't seen an identifiable audience emerge.

PEARLSTINE: Brock, could you talk a little bit about your experiences?

MEEKS: One of the things that's interesting is, I don't care who the hell my audience is. I've been out there writing for the Net for 12 years, and only in the past three years, I suppose, formally with my CyberWire Dispatch publication. I didn't do it with any kind of financial gain in mind, and I still don't. Nobody pays me to do it, and I don't charge anybody for it. I am still waiting for the day when you can just click on the F1 key, or click a button, and three cents will be debited. I think I'll rake in a hefty piece of change when that happens. But until then, my straight gig at *Wired* has to subsidize that.

The difference is I've never been concerned about the audience. As it turns out, my audience is not very different than the best guess we have about the demographics on the Net: overwhelmingly white Anglo-Saxon Protestant males with a fairly hefty income. But I'm also getting something that I think the traditional media, especially newspapers, are drooling after. And that is the 13 to 18 crowd. My best guess, from feedback I've had from various lists and so forth, is that I have about 30,000 13 to 18-year olds that are reading my stuff. This comes from kids who send me messages. So I know that's one demographic I have that newspapers would just love to have. How that happens, I don't know. I just write like I think—coming from that Net community, I publish and write as somebody who's been in it, let the chips fall where they may, and it seems to happen. So I'm not really concerned about that.

PEARLSTINE: Brock, your experience suggests that there is room for journalism on the Net, as at least those of us who have been engaged in print or in broadcast look at it. Janice, is that your experience with News Corp., trying to develop the I-way?

KAPLAN: Absolutely. I think the audience issue is an important one because the attitude many of us now have about this new media is, if you build it right, they will come. I came from *TV Guide*, where 13 million people would buy the magazine every week. And News Corp. would not be putting the effort and the finances into its web site right now if it believed that the people who are on the Web are the only ones who are *going* to be there. They expect it to become far more of a mass media.

What some of the larger companies are trying to do as we enter into this world is to bring the peo-

ple onto the Web who haven't been there before. Certainly, some other companies are aiming at women, planning many sites that will appeal to women, and hoping to bring in a totally new audience. If we were only worrying about who's there right now and what the demographic is, that wouldn't make a whole lot of sense. A lot of us feel that we're on the verge of something. And if we do it right, we'll get a whole new crowd.

The Internet has brought new meaning to the words "black hole" when it comes to a business investment.

PEARLSTINE: I think one of the issues some of us are struggling with is the great deal of commentary about media concentration. Many of you may have seen *The Nation*'s cover story of last week, with its first-ever gatefold, describing the tentacles of four very large media companies (one of which I happen to work for), suggesting that this has led to a homogenization of content, and raising very serious questions about the future of the Net—whether indeed these behemoths will gobble up content the way they seem to have done in other areas. As someone inside the behemoth, I think often of my colleague Don Logan, the CEO of Time, Inc., who says that so far as he's concerned, the Internet has brought new meaning to the words "black hole" when it comes to a business investment.

For a number of us, we still seem to be struggling not only to figure out what the business is but who the competition is. There was a tendency, for example, in the *Nation* piece, to focus very much on the content players who are either in print or in broadcast or in film. Yet your most recent cover in *Wired*, Denise, laid out very clearly the ambitions of Microsoft to be a media player. You listen to people like Ray Smith at Bell Atlantic dismissing cable and saying, "We're going to be the content providers." I just wonder if you could try to make some sense of this. Are we at a stage where the dinosaurs are trying to band together to get bigger, even as a whole new group of players comes in to take over? Or is there something about size and about marriage of distribution and content that really is worrisome to you?

CARUSO: I think there are a couple of ways to look at that. One of them has to do with whether or not the Web continues as a viable publishing medium. If nobody's on the Web consuming, it doesn't matter who owns what. But what I see is Microsoft is modeling itself after big media companies, doing this aggregation thing, where it's sort of a cable channel model. I haven't checked AltaVista lately, but the last time I looked, there were 21 million pages on the Web. I don't know how many thousand actual home pages were actual sites. Let's just say a lot: kind of overwhelming. So companies like Time Warner, Microsoft, and Viacom will become aggregators and create the cable model, where you have a basic service, you have premium service. As a consumer I have a familiar brand name, people that I allegedly trust, to give me the information they think I would be most interested in. The problem I see in terms of media consolidation is that, *de facto,* alternative voices drop off the end, because if what you're trying to do is make a site manageable, you can't put too much stuff in it.

Earlier, you asked who the audience was for the Web. Well, we don't know who they are because interactive media actually splits the market into subject areas—those are audience segments. So we're like a newspaper. For example, you could think of the *New York Times* as an aggregator of content. They edit, and the editors decide what everybody is supposed to see on a daily basis. When it comes to electronic stuff, you search by subject. So you ask to have delivered to you what you're interested in. And that changes the whole model for everyone. It's very tricky.

PEARLSTINE: With that as background, why don't we home in on a couple of specific subjects that I think are relevant to this discussion. One is the whole role of advertising on the Net. Most of the models that I've seen so far suggest that it's a fairly important component. Yet the advertisers

themselves, I think, are raising serious questions about whether database marketing is really what the Net is designed to do, and whether the marriage of content and advertising that has been so much a model in print and in television really will apply. Perhaps we could also talk a little bit about any privacy concerns you might have. John, would you like to pick up on that?

MARKOFF: The clearest example of the marriage that I've seen on the Net is InfoSeek, where, if you do a query, your ad frequently matches very nicely to your query. It always gives you this sort of spooky feeling, this Brave New World. But once you get over that, it's not such a bad thing, I think.

So much of this is prehistory. It's so difficult to gauge the Web as it is today, because it's not going to be that way tomorrow; it's going to be something fundamentally different. I'm very optimistic about advertising, based on what I've seen. And in particular, it seems like there are real revenue streams that are emerging. I think c|net in their seven-figure revenue stream is talking about $3.5 million of revenue this year, and I imagine a fair amount of that comes from advertising. So taken out of this period I think of as prehistory and moved to a much broader audience, I don't know why advertising wouldn't subsidize much of what's going on now.

CARUSO: Actually, I'm really creeped out by the fact that you get advertising to match editorial when you do searches. But I also believe that is almost unavoidable in this world, because of what the Web is designed to do. You brought up c|net, which is actually very interesting. They have a team on staff that tries to educate advertisers about good interactive advertising.

I have a pretty strong belief that I don't want anybody to gather demographics on me without my foreknowledge. And I could go into a whole explanation about my reasons for that, but I won't. I will say, however, that one of the really interesting things about the Web is this: if you do have my permission, then you can do a lot more than just wait until I do a search on Yahoo! to deliver the ad to me. I can enter into a relationship with an advertiser and provide them with a really qualified lead. And that is really good for advertisers.

The thing I haven't figured out yet, that I think is sort of queer and funky, is that in order to make money as an editor you need to drive people away from your editorial and into an ad. In any other medium, it's serendipity. You're watching TV, the commercial comes on. You're reading the magazine, the ad is always down there somewhere, waiting to catch your eye. You actually have to leave the editorial, and that's a desirable thing. So what happens is kind of interesting. Do ads become editorial?

How many people fly United Airlines? Have you ever seen that Bunting's Window thing that they show, that guy who's the kind of groovy thirty-something guy in the work shirt? Those are "advertorials." That is not editorial, those are paid for. Do they ever tell you that? No. So that's part of the model I see emerging on the Web, that actually the Web is very good for. But it's strange for writers and journalists to think about what that does to our credibility and our world.

KAPLAN: It seems to me that the one model least likely to work is all of the advertisers coming up with their own web sites. I love it when I read a magazine or a newspaper and everybody has their web site address now—as if you've just seen the ad for Jeep and you're going to run to their web site and buy one.

But I agree with John that we're in a prehistory stage here, and that the advertisers' expectations may not end up being the direction this takes in a couple of years. One hope for Denise is that rather than users having to leave the editorial, perhaps the Web will start following more of a magazine model, where indeed the ad on the page becomes satisfactory to an advertiser.

The other possibility is that as we start doing more video, as we start doing more rolling in real-time audio and real-time video, maybe we'll follow more of a television model, where for better or for worse, you will indeed be sitting there, watching your computer as something rolls by and the ad comes up.

MARKOFF: But that won't be the Web. That will be broadband digital delivery of television.

KAPLAN: It's being tried on the Web.

MARKOFF: I think it will be another creature entirely. It will be something new. It won't be television, either.

MEEKS: Advertisers right now are pretty stupid. It's a new world for them. A friend of mine likes to say there's a lot of dumb money out there. And advertisers are throwing their money at web sites they think are hot. Now, what is a hot web site? Well, nobody really knows. People have all these wild guesses as far as hit count goes. And anybody that tries to tell you, "Advertise on my site because it gets 250,000 hits per week," doesn't mean—I probably shouldn't swear—doesn't mean B.S. People are lying to you about hit counts. It could be that one person going to a page could equal five hit counts, or whatever. There's really no good way of judging how many people are seeing your site by hit counts. So advertisers are getting hipper all the time to the fact that they've been rolled on this whole thing, and they're paying $10,000, $30,000 for a site, and somebody's going, "What the hell are we actually paying for?" They're demanding a better type of accounting mechanism.

I wrote a column about year ago where I laid out a nightmare scenario: some big media person, Murdoch or somebody like that, who's very aggressive and has what seems to be an endless checkbook, goes out and commissions the best study he can to find out the top 50 web sites around. (The most popular ones are getting the most hits.) And he pays a lot of money for a very quantitative study. Now he has the top 50 web sites on a little list. He opens his checkbook, he goes out, and he buys the top 50 web sites. Then he goes to advertisers and says, "Look, I have the top 50 web sites in the entire Web. I can give you this many hits, so and so, on a rotating basis." Then he's able to sell advertising on a volume basis, undercut everybody else's advertising costs, and then all of a sudden we move closer and closer to what we're getting in traditional media, with the media concentration, with the top 50 web sites owned by Mr. X.

PEARLSTINE: Wrong mogul, Brock.

CARUSO: That's MSN's model. That's Microsoft's model exactly. It's happening already.

MEEKS: Let me assure you that at the moment it's just a nightmare. It's not happening.

PEARLSTINE: One thing implicit in all of this, though, is that media on the Net will continue the one-to-many model that has been prevalent since Gutenberg. Given the technology itself, is that a logical conclusion? Or do you think that more exotic forms of bulletin boards with true interactivity among special interest groups becomes a more prevalent model?

MEEKS: I think it's prevalent now. There are all sorts of Usenet lists and so forth, that spring up over the most arcane topics, where there is a small niche of people that use that list very regularly—they argue amongst themselves, and topics rise and flow. John can probably do this better. We were talking about this earlier, about having to define the Net and how it changes.

There are two different types of components. There is the web side of things, where you basically can go in, choose the information, and it comes back at you. But even now, some of those web sites, like HotWired, have the thread section where you can go in and interact, just like you are interacting with a newsgroup. The other side of the Net, which is more the email model, is where you can go out and participate in these distributed newsgroups or email lists, where you send a message and everybody that subscribes to that list can read it and then respond, and everybody else can read that as well. So I see that as very interactive right now.

KAPLAN: I think one of the surprises has, in fact, been just how powerful bulletin boards and chat rooms have been. Those of us in the business of creating content believe that what we do is what attracts everybody. I believe at America Online they've said that—and don't quote me on the number—but roughly 75 percent of their use is

in three areas: email, bulletin boards and chat, and Internet access. And one would think of America Online as a place people come to exclusively for content. But quite to the contrary.

MARKOFF: But clearly, the Web is this ecology right now, and new protocols are showing up. And the protocols increasingly are moving toward push, which moves back toward this traditional journalistic model of where an editor shapes the news for you, with an interactive component. Point Cast is probably the most recent and best example of somebody trying to get beyond the library pull model of the Web. And they've done a fairly invasive job of it. But the idea of pushing a predefined or slightly interactive content to you, I think, is increasingly going to be the model.

Actually there are a number of other people trying to do the same thing as Point Cast. What they've done is, sitting on top of the Web, they've taken a slice out of the desktop of your personal computer and inserted the newspaper into the screen saver. And they've taken advantage of tossing ads at regular intervals into that. And that's what's paying the freight in some part. It's a channel model on top of the Web, so that newspapers like the *Los Angeles Times* and *Boston Globe* are doing regional things for their own market. But it allows all kinds of personalization—using the screen as a canvas to paint it more like a traditional newspaper than the Web, which, as it first started, was more like a library.

PEARLSTINE: The traditional newspaper that you get to personalize. You get to pick which kind of news you want to hear and which sports teams you want to know about.

MEEKS: I think if there's a trend, that's it: filters and agents over the next ten years will make it possible for me to not have to go out to the Web at all, unless I really want to browse for something that's not a specific part of a personal profile that I fill out. That's actually what I'm looking forward to, because I find the Web incredibly annoying. And I have ISDN.

MARKOFF: At the same time, look at that in light of the monopoly question you started with. I saw the number just recently (somebody correct me if I'm wrong), that there has been a ten percent decline in the last three years in evening news viewership. If that number is true, that seems to be free fall, like a collapse. Coincidentally, over that same three-year period, you could probably say that the Web has picked up about ten percent.

PEARLSTINE: I think that the Pew Foundation Report actually had the number dropping even more. And the question was whether it was as a result of information on the Net, or because there was no local news crime report as good as *NYPD Blue*.

MARKOFF: Will this be optimistic?

PEARLSTINE: If you can get Jenny Jones at 11 o'clock, why watch news?

MARKOFF: But no. Maybe people are leaving television entirely.

CARUSO: Actually, there was a study done on that. I forget the name of the research company. They did a study on pay-per-view, and found the only reason anybody wanted pay-per-view is because they were spending more time on their computers. They actually quantified this. More time on their computers, and they didn't want to pay $30 a month for HBO if they were only watching one movie a week. So I think that is a direction that things are moving in. And that was actually quantified a couple years ago.

MARKOFF: The other example I have is, there's this new wave of multiplayer games coming on the Net that are the big rage right now. And the folks at (I believe it was) TEN, which is the Total Entertainment Network, one of the two big protocol people, said that their beta testing has shown that they can see when *Seinfeld* starts every night, because the game players fall off. And then when *Seinfeld* is over they all come back.

PEARLSTINE: Brock, from your Washington perspective, is the privacy issue one that's likely to bring the legislators into the game? Or is it just an issue we tend to talk about at conferences like this one?

MEEKS: Yes, it's going to bring the legislators in. The nose of the camel is in the tent already. We let them in through things like the Communications Decency Act, which was part of the Telecommunications Reform bill, which is really a rat bastard bill and should never have been passed. (That's my editorial comment for the day.)

MARKOFF: Preaching to the choir.

MEEKS: "Preaching to the choir," John said. I'll take it. Just throw dollar bills. But what happens is the Congress just can't keep their fingers off of things that generate or have a potential to generate commerce. Furthermore, the folks on the commerce end, while they buck and spit about all the regulation, in a lot of cases they demand it, because they want to make sure that the rules of the road are there, that have to be followed, they need level playing fields, and blah blah, woof woof.

Right now what's going to happen, just in the first week of June, is that the Federal Trade Commission is holding a two-day series of hearings, looking at whether or not there should be regulations about marketing on the Internet. Who should be able to be marketed to? What rules should guide that marketing data? One of the big issues that's being pressed right now in Washington is, what about kids and taking information from kids?

There's an organization—Center for Media Education—that wrote a fairly scary document about these companies that were having children fill out all sorts of information—name, rank, and serial number, shoe size, and all this kind of stuff. And they would send them a little T-shirt. And then, all that information was being sent to a federal prison, where hardened criminals—rapists, child abusers, and so forth—were sitting down with this information on these little kiddies at their hands, and typing it in and creating the databases. And the group painted a fairly draconian picture of what could happen if this information got outside. The FCC stood up and took notice. And right now we're facing some very real possibility that there will now be an extra layer of regulation put on the Net.

Questions & Answers

Q: *Certain commercial web sites, such as Toyota, have undertaken strategies to publish content, lifestyle, and other articles that have nothing to do with automobiles in an effort to attract a certain demographic that parallels its target buyer market. How do you see this trend developing? And does it pose any conflicts or ethical issues for "legitimate" publishers?*

CARUSO: Geez, I don't know. So far, I don't think there are any regulatory bodies in this country that say who is and who is not a media organization, for better or worse. And when it comes to stuff like that, if it's information that's not lying, and if it's not about "Toyota is Number One" and it's just them saying so, I don't know that I'm crazy about the idea. But I don't know what you can do about it. I think it feeds into that advertorial thing I was talking about earlier, with "Bunting's Window." It's very easy to do this stuff on the Web.

PEARLSTINE: Well, there also is a model in the custom publishing that already exists in print, where some very large companies have pushed a model very similar to this for their customers.

MARKOFF: One model I like so far, that I think does it well and keeps the distinction between church and state, is AT&T's Lead Story [*http://www.lead-story.com/*]. What they do is, they take one subject and give you pointers to things that they've found on the Web. And you know when you leave their site, and you know when you're there.

MEEKS: I love the site, by the way, because it's very well done and so forth. But one of the things that I saw very early on, was when there was one of the big mergers that happened—I guess it was between Bell Atlantic and NYNEX—the stories that AT&T chose to highlight were, of course, very negative stories on that merger. You know, direct competition.

PEARLSTINE: It's a public service!

MEEKS: I happen to agree with that, but that's a really bad deal, again thanks to the 1996 Telecommunications Reform Act. However, it was very odd to pop into that at AT&T. The Lead Story site is very slickly done—I mean, it really is a good model. However, to see AT&T pointing you to articles saying, "Hey, this is a bad deal," and "Oh, this portends ominous things," makes you think, hmm, does AT&T maybe have an agenda here?

KAPLAN: The other thing to be said about that, from what I hear, AT&T is trying very hard right now to get out of the content business. Any number of big corporations that said, "Well, this is an easy way to advertise; we just do content. What's content? It's no problem to do," are discovering that really, there is a reason that journalists get paid, however meagerly, because it is more difficult than some of them understood. So maybe they will be leaving and others will be following.

MEEKS: I hope somebody takes over their site. It's very well done. Let's go back to talking about whether these web sites that are sponsored by corporations are any good. I don't know if it's still around or not, but Miller Beer, Miller Genuine Draft sponsored a site called Taproom [*http://www.mgdtaproom.com/*], which I thought was great. In fact, they went out and they hired a journalist from all the alternative weeklies in major cities, and they had them running lifestyle stories and stuff. The times I was there, you never found any reference to Miller Beer, Miller Genuine Draft, or beer at all. They were talking about what was happening that was hot in those specific cities, and I thought it was a very well done site.

But the point I'm bringing up here is what happens when there is a commodity, a product that is looked down upon—let's say cigarettes. Let's say Joe Camel goes onto the Web and wants to produce some sites that are very hip, and draws kids in, and of course it has Joe Camel all over the place, when R.J. Reynolds, the tobacco company, is getting hammered everywhere else, but now they can go onto the Net.

A few weeks ago you saw the tobacco company take out this big advertisement saying, "Look, we'll agree to legislation that does this, this, and this. We'll pull advertisements from sporting events. We promise not to advertise here. We'll pull cigarettes from vending machines." And they promised to do all this stuff, as long as they weren't regulated as a drug by the FDA. One of the things that was glaring to me in that whole list of things that they agreed to, it was as if the Japanese were signing the surrender document on the *Missouri*. I mean, it was incredible. They were surrendering this whole thing. The one place they did not mention that they would stay out of—the Internet.

Q: *In 1992, the number of journalists who were online was effectively zero. The new media were not a major factor in the 1992 election cycle. In 1996, this has changed. How much will new media change the process in the 1996 election cycle? Why or why not?*

MEEKS: In the '96 election cycle, I don't think it's going to change very much at all. This my primary gig at *Wired* and HotWired, covering the '96 election. And from the other web sites that I've seen—by the *Washington Post* and so forth—they're just repackaging the same old horse race-style journalism and putting it on electronic format. All of a sudden that's supposed to be hip. I don't think that that's what the Net community wants to see. And something that we're trying to do on Netizen, just the exact opposite. Now, what kind of effect is that's having? Zero.

PEARLSTINE: We have a couple people in the audience who may want to add something to that. Bob Merry, Editor of CQ [*Congressional Quarterly*], I see, is here, and Mike Riley from the All Politics web site of *Time* and CNN. What have your experiences been?

MERRY: Mike and I can talk together, since we're working together on a web site that is *Time/CNN*. Essentially, what we're trying to do is go beyond what Brock is talking about, not just give the web people the same thing we're giving them, but go beyond that.

MEEKS: Are you using links? Can you talk about some of the specifics?

MERRY: Well, in terms of Congressional elections, for example, we've got something that we call "Rate Your Rep" [*http://voter96.cqalert.com/cq_rate.htm*], where we give the user about ten questions, and it's designed to determine how they would vote on certain issues. And then we tell them, well, this is how your Congressman voted. So we give them an opportunity to determine whether they're in sync with their Congressman.

CARUSO: The central thing that is different about the Web are the links, the hyperlinks. And I think it would be a brave move and certainly a welcome move if some big media company sites started linking to alternative press, to alternative points of view. Give them a space. I'm not just interested in the questions that are posed by the $100,000-a-year journalists who get paid to not ask hard questions, basically, but instead the people who are serving a completely different part of the population.

Q: *Denise, will you elaborate on your suggestion that Brock's nightmare is the Microsoft model? How do you think that Microsoft will try to corner the market on available popular web sites?*

CARUSO: Actually, they're trying to go out and create those web sites in a variety of ways. MSN, the Microsoft network, right now is still a proprietary network like America Online. Some time this year, probably later this summer, they're going to blow the walls off it and turn it into a web site. In order to do that, since there is no business model for the Web and nobody really knows how to make money on it, they're financing a number of content companies, ranging from news all the way to entertainment. Michael Kinsley's publication [Slate] is one of them. And they are financing them in a variety of ways—with royalties, or owning the whole thing, and every sort of configuration in between—and configuring those into what they call the cable model. They are going to be aggregators. And then they will split up those sites into basic service, premium service, and probably some kind of pay-per-view service. Nobody knows if it's going to work. But they're the first company I've seen that is moving aggressively to create a demographic, to create popular web sites by dint of the fact that they basically own the PC desktop. That's where the nightmare part of the scenario comes in— you're basically on MSN when you install Windows, if you want to be.

MARKOFF: The other part of the Microsoft scenario is that they have 840 programmers at last count, working on their browser, for an indeterminate return. They're bravely trying to suck the Web down into the OS [operating system] so they can put it on the OS model. But I think that Bill is faced with herding cats here. The Net is going to be a huge energy sink for Microsoft.

Q: *There have been some predictions that the Internet was never designed for the current level of use, and it will collapse, technically or organizationally. If the Net crashes, what might replace it?*

MARKOFF: There's been a lot of reporting on the imminent demise of the Net. But so far, what's happening is local congestion, and the backbone seems to be scaling up with the traffic demands. There have been brown-outs, but that's one of the wonderful things about this technology. It was designed to survive nuclear war. It tends to be resilient. And so I think IP [Internet Protocol] will scale fine until the next generation, and there will be a series of technologies that will arise.

Q: *Does all media go national on the Web? Does the Internet bring the end of geographically defined markets, the end of the dominant metropolitan or regional news organization?*

KAPLAN: Actually, quite the opposite. (Denise disagrees, but I get to speak first!) The national model is what we're all starting from. But there is a great awareness that local news and local stories are what sells everywhere. Certainly, we are pursuing some localized content, and there are many others who are doing the same. One of the easiest reasons to go onto the Net is for a simple service, or to find out where something is. There are sites that will do that for you, and there are becoming more and more of them.

One of the greatest successes we're having right now is in offering localized listings from the *TV Guide* on our site. So I do think that localization is going to be a model that many are pursuing right now.

MARKOFF: Denise, isn't Microsoft building regional news organizations?

CARUSO: Yes, absolutely. Everything becomes international when it's on the Net. Local, obviously, will be very important to people who live in a geographic area. But for people who are trying to publish and have a national or international reach, they have it *de facto,* the minute they put up a server.

Q: *Will the new media inevitably be in English? And will U.S. values predominate? How will you accommodate the new Asian markets?*

KAPLAN: I think it's going to be a matter of partnerships. And I think it's going to have to be localized content. Because News Corp. is a very international organization, the question has arisen many times. We don't really feel that we can ship out most of our content, so there are local services that are currently being built all over Asia and elsewhere. I think that some American content, just like some American movies, translate. Some of what is on the Internet will translate, but much of it is going to end up being nationalized.

PEARLSTINE: We had an interesting example of our own, where we recently reached an agreement between Pathfinder, which is our own Internet project, and Hong Kong Telecom. And in that deal, they were particularly interested in *Entertainment Weekly* and *People* magazine, and specifically requested that *Asiaweek* not be included on it. I'm not quite sure what that says, but it does suggest that customers operate in ways you can't always imagine.

CARUSO: I don't know if it's the largest. I don't have the numbers. But one of the largest exports out of the U.S. is media. We've already been accused the world over of cultural imperialism,[*]

---

[*] See the panel "Cultural Imperialism on the Net" for an in-depth discussion about this topic.

probably for good reason. But there are buyers and sellers. I'm not really sure what to do about it in terms of the Net, because the truth is that technology does not create any new problems or situations; it magnifies things that already exist.

So if we want the Internet to be multicultural, then the people who are in cultures that are not the dominant U.S. one, which is what most of the Internet is now, are really going to have to work on that. I don't know what the solution is. I know some people are working on software that does automatic translation, which would be kind of cool. But I'm not holding my breath for that. I think there are going to be a lot of legal issues around this, as well.

Q: *Perhaps the decline of TV viewership, as well as newspaper readership, is due to inferior, inaccurate information. I have canceled my subscription to many news magazines and newspapers because the topics I consider to be important are not covered. Do you think new publications will emerge that we haven't thought of yet, that will be attractive to people?*

CARUSO: Yes, I think that's certainly one thing that will happen. But I would caution the questioner to keep in mind that I wouldn't believe half of what I read, if not three-quarters or 90 percent of what I read on the Net. The good thing about journalism, when practiced well, is that you have some small assurance at least, that whoever's done the reporting has done some work and has checked with a couple sources. I do not call *Eyewitness Reports* journalism. There's a big difference between raw information and people who go check out facts.

That said, I think that absolutely, there's an enormous opportunity for new journalism on the Net. I am thrilled about the possibility of alternative voices and points of view finding their way—news straight from Nicaragua and El Salvador, rather than what we get filtered through western media here. So I think that there are caveats to that, but as a general rule, that's true.

KAPLAN: I would agree. I think the good news about the World Wide Web is that everybody has a voice and the bad news about the Web is that everybody has a voice. Most of us would not

be happy reading *Time* magazine if they printed every one of the letters to the editor they received. And that has frankly been one of the problems on the Web—endless unfiltered voices don't always hold our interest. There is a role for good journalists on the Web who can make sense of some of those voices.

MARKOFF: The nightmare scenario is the end of journalism, like the OJ car chase. That's not journalism. And I think, to a certain extent, it threatens to displace journalism.

KAPLAN: To some extent, we do like to hear those voices. When something happens, the local news reporters for your local television station rush out, and they talk to the neighbors. "What did you see? What was he really like?" And there certainly is a role for that on the Web. But again, they need to be in a context, and a context that some other form can hold together.

MEEKS: You know, people aren't stupid either. If somebody is out there trying to play journalist on the Net, and he's just spouting up all sorts of unconfirmed facts and so forth, people are going to label him as an idiot, and nobody's going to read him any more. People will be able to pick and choose, and you'll say, "Okay, this guy is good, but Mr. X over here never knows what he's saying."

Q: *Do you worry about the death of print journalism or its dumbing down to web site length, attention span, graphic, sound bite?*

MARKOFF: Actually, yes. That's the down side of more bandwidth. We were in this wonderful period, sort of a renaissance for print, largely created because there wasn't adequate bandwidth. And we're about to reach this world where there will be video messaging and teleconferencing. I think we might find that print was like this—electronic mail and similar things were this wonderful little period that we'll look back again on fondly. So I think it's a real issue.

Q: *Editors and journalists are supposed to be gatekeepers, and have traditionally played that role. With AT&T, Toyota, and everybody else rushing into the* *content business, is there still a role for gatekeepers? Is the role of the journalist as we've known it, eroding?*

CARUSO: Yes, I think, just because of the sheer mass of media that's out there. What would be really interesting to me about the John Markoff channel would not necessarily be what he would write, but that he would be out there finding things to link me to. That has a very strong editorial voice. It would be a lot less egregious than five or six white guys sitting in New York, deciding what you're going to read every day. At least it's *one* white guy, and you know who he is, you know what his biases are, and you choose to participate in that world with him. I think there's a really strong role for a different kind of editor that really takes advantage of what the Web has to offer, which is this hyperlink thing. I keep hammering on this. But that is what makes the Web different from other media.

PEARLSTINE: One thing to keep in mind is that in the last 15 to 20 years, at least in print, the growth has been in niche publishing, not in broad publishing. When people tend to think of the Web as an alternative to mass consumer publications, it fails to recognize the hundreds of new publications a year that are started, that really address, if you will, the same kind of narrow niche that there is potential to address on the Net.

MARKOFF: Is the national edition of the *Times* an exception to that rule, in your mind?

PEARLSTINE: That's clearly a niche publication. It's 400,000 circulation outside the New York metropolitan area, which is small. First of all, people who read are a niche in our culture today! But people who read the national edition of the *New York Times* are reading a niche publication.

Q: *Yahoo! has created a highway on which it can post billboards. What do you think the other highways will be?*

KAPLAN: Yahoo! is actually getting into the content business, or trying to. It's begun with *Yahoo! Internet Life*, it's trying kids' programming. I think they're realizing that with 20 million pages and 200,000 web sites and those growing every day

by quite dramatic amounts, putting the Web in any sort of order is starting to get to be a difficult task. Nor do people necessarily want to go into a Yahoo!, or an AltaVista, looking for something specific, and end up being given 20,000 different sites to go to. So ironically, the openness is starting to devolve into something where we do need those editors. Not necessarily gatekeepers, but someone who you trust, who you can go to for content. That's what Yahoo! seems to be trying to become.

CARUSO: But I think it's going to disappear, too. I think that all the search engines are going to just disappear. They're going to get built right into all the applications. I think about the trend someone mentioned earlier, about AT&T and Toyota and all those people getting tired of having content on their sites. That technology, the search technology, will become as much a commodity as word processing is now.

Q: *(For Brock Meeks) Isn't it good for the advertisers that there are only a few media owners? It's too hard to deal with many, many publishers for the likes of Proctor & Gamble and Unilever. They want their size to entitle them to bulk discounts.*

MEEKS: Sure, it's good for advertisers. But I'm not sure it's good for the content. I hate to keep picking on Murdoch, but he's an easy target. So you get Murdoch, and you've got the top 50 web sites, and he's done this specifically so he can generate this ad revenue model. And all of a sudden, some of his advertisers are saying, "Well, you know, there's this one Net site that you've got way down there, number 49 or number 50, that's run by Brock Meeks. And he keeps writing this really liberal, off-the-wall stuff. We don't like it." So maybe advertising gets moved off my site. Maybe I get dropped from that site. If everything is generated towards that advertising, I can see advertisers having a very real effect on the content. If you don't think that Murdoch is concerned about ideology and so forth, you have to look no further than his justification for creating the all-news channel as a competition to CNN. He thought CNN was getting too liberal, so he wants to create an all-news channel specifically to have a conservative voice.

About the Speakers

NORMAN PEARLSTINE became Editor-in-Chief of Time Warner Inc. on January 1, 1995. He is the fifth Editor-in-Chief in the company's history, and the first to be chosen from outside the company. Pearlstine worked for Dow Jones & Company from 1968 to 1992, except for a two-year period when he was an Executive Editor at *Forbes* magazine. He joined the *Wall Street Journal* as a staff reporter in its Dallas bureau in 1968, and subsequently worked as a reporter in Detroit and Los Angeles before being named the Journal's Tokyo bureau chief. From 1983 to 1991 he was the managing editor of the *Wall Street Journal*, during which time the paper expanded its coverage and won four Pulitzer Prizes. He left Dow Jones in 1992 to start his own multimedia investment company, Friday Holdings LP.

A longtime analyst and observer of the industries of digital technology and interactive media, **DENISE CARUSO** writes the "Digital Commerce" column for the *New York Times*. She is also Executive Producer of Spotlight, an executive conference for the interactive media industry, and a contributing editor for "The Site," produced by Ziff-Davis Television. In 1994, Caruso launched Technology & Media Group, an information services company, for Norman Pearlstine's Friday Holdings. Before Technology & Media, Caruso was founding editor of *Digital Media*, then acclaimed as the seminal newsletter in the emerging new media industry, published by industry. She lives and works in San Francisco.

JANICE KAPLAN has an extensive background in television, magazines, and new media. She was a writer and producer at ABC-TV's *Good Morning America*, senior producer of the syndicated show *A Current Affair*, and producer of many other shows for cable and network television. A former columnist for magazines including *Vogue* and *Seventeen*, she was most recently Deputy Editor of *TV Guide*, and Editor-in-Chief of the web-based magazine iGUIDE. Kaplan is the author of six books and a regular correspondent on the E! Entertainment channel. She has appeared on numerous television shows including *Today*, *CBS This Morning*, and *Entertainment Tonight* discussing media and entertainment

JOHN MARKOFF is based in San Francisco as West Coast Correspondent for the *New York Times* where he covers Silicon Valley, computers, and information technologies. Before coming to the *Times* in 1988 he covered Silicon Valley for the *San Francisco Examiner* beginning in 1985. He has also been a reporter at Infoworld and in 1984 he was West Coast Technical Editor for *Byte Magazine*. He is the co-author with Katie Hafner of *Cyberpunk: Outlaws and Hackers on the Computer Frontier* (1991) and with Lenny Siegel of the *The High Cost of High Tech* (1985). In January Hyperion published *Takedown: The Pursuit and Capture of America's Most Wanted Computer Outlaw*, which he co-authored with Tsutomu Shimomura.

BROCK MEEKS is currently Chief Washington Correspondent for MSNBC. Previously he was Chief Washington Correspondent for *Wired* and Hot-Wired, where he helped develop the company's first political web site, Netizen. Brock also wrote the weekly "Muckraker" column for HotWired. His net-based CyberWire Dispatch is an award winning publication that has set the tone for hard-nosed reporting in cyberspace. Dispatch is "journalism with an attitude." It reaches 800,000 readers. Brock has won several journalism awards for everything from investigative reporting to his coverage of the war in Afghanistan while a foreign correspondent for the *San Francisco Chronicle*.

CHAIR: LEWIS BRANSCOMB
Professor in Public Policy and Corporate
Management
John F. Kennedy School of Government

CO-CHAIR: BRIAN KAHIN
Director, Information Infrastructure Project
Science, Technology, and Public Policy Program
John F. Kennedy School of Government

Public Policy

THE GOVERNMENT'S ROLE IN THE DEVELOPMENT OF THE INTERNET

MODERATOR:	Anthony Oettinger
PANELISTS:	Michael Fricklas
	James Kamihachi
	Sharon Nelson

THE PARADIGM OF INTEROPERABILITY

MODERATOR:	Brian Kahin
PANELISTS:	Fred Baker
	Marvin Sirbu

INSTITUTIONAL STRUCTURE FOR THE INTERNET

MODERATOR:	Jeffrey F. Rayport
PANELISTS:	Paul Callahan
	Mike O'Dell
	Tony Rutkowski

THE PLACE OF THE INTERNET IN NATIONAL AND GLOBAL INFORMATION INFRASTRUCTURE

MODERATOR:	Lewis Branscomb
PANELISTS:	George Conrades
	Joseph Duffey
	Howard Frank
	Richard Zeckhauser

State Regulators Test Internet Options

By David Eddy Spicer

The state of Washington is worried about The Big One, and it's not because the San Andreas stretches all the way up the West Coast.

According to Sharon Nelson, Chair of the Washington Utilities and Transportation Commission, this Big One is due to a fault line right through the middle of the Internet, and it has to do with the price of access. Decisions about how to price Internet access portend an upheaval that will change forever the landscape of the communications industry throughout the country, and the first tremors are coming from the Northwest.

Everyone knows major shifts in pricing are going to happen, "but no one knows how or when," says Anthony Oettinger, moderator of the panel "The Government's Role in the Development of the Internet" in which Nelson also took part.

Oettinger, Professor of Information Resources Policy in Harvard's Division of Applied Sciences, calls pricing the "central question" whose answer will either lead the Internet onward to what some believe to be its manifest destiny as the "network of networks" or leave early promises forever unfulfilled.

The question comes down to who's going to pick up the tab for maintaining and fostering Internet access in an era of rapidly diminishing government subsidies and expanding commercialization. In the state of Washington, home to industry heavy-weights Microsoft, Intel, and Hewlett-Packard, the debate about pricing is intense.

Interconnection requires cooperation among competitors. Local telephone companies, like US West and GTE, worry they will be stuck with the bill at the end of the multimedia meal, after years of receiving a steady diet carefully prescribed by federal and state regulations. Those providing conduits to and content for the Internet, ranging from Microsoft to local Internet service providers, call traditional pricing, based on distance and time, out of sync with emerging technologies.

With the accelerating convergence of computer technologies and communications networks, a culture clash has emerged between new and existing telecommunications industries.

"In the Internet, new interconnecting systems generally are viewed as adding value to the system overall," says Nelson. "By contrast, many traditional telcos are more concerned about maintaining their existing market share than they are about generating new lines of business from a growing local exchange market."

Nelson, and her counterparts in other states, are the seismologists who should be most keenly attuned to the subterranean forces now at work in the field of telecommunications.

Federal regulation of the telecommunications industry, most recently codified in the Telecommunications Act of 1996, gives great latitude to the states for overseeing affairs within their borders. Nonetheless, Nelson admits that only a handful of states—Washington among them—has emerged as visionary in handling the dismantling of traditional regulatory structures and creating new forms that fit the rapid changes now underway.

As a regulator attending this conference of Internet enthusiasts, Nelson told the panel audience that she worried she would be "about as popular as a skunk at a garden party." She found, however, the image of a raccoon to be more apt. "People look at me sideways, wondering where I'm going to poke my nose next." Throughout the many conference panels that have touched on the roles of governments *vis-à-vis* the Internet, the predominant theme has been one of government's benign neglect.

Oettinger was reminded of the rabbi's reply to Tevye in *Fiddler on the Roof* when Tevye asked if there were a prayer for the czar. "Of course, my son, there is a prayer for everyone," Oettinger recounts the rabbi's reply, "May the Lord bless and keep the czar...far away from us!"

The czar of telecommunications—at least in Washington state—appears to be an instrumental and essential arbiter of change. Conference attendees skeptical of regulators should take heart in Nelson's readiness to apply Internet experience to the regulatory model she is now shaping. "The Internet community, with its experience of cooperatively managing a system of systems, has a lot to contribute to this debate," says Nelson.

Nelson and the economists on her staff have taken a particularly keen look at prices based on capacity, as measured by bandwidth versus per-minute charges.

"To complete a toll call, a long distance company must pay a local telephone company for access based on the number of minutes of that call," she explains. Most local telcos want to extend that model to "anything that looks, acts, feels, or smells like a telephone."

Given such a scenario, she says, "Internet service providers would spend all their time writing and cashing checks to each other" for such things as email messages and access to web pages. To settle the matter in Washington, Nelson's office has ordered local providers US West and GTE to come up with interconnection pricing based on capacity, not minutes of use.

Playing the provocateur, Oettinger questioned why the government should intervene at all. Why not let the market shake itself out, perhaps bankrupting those phone companies too entrenched in traditional approaches, thus making way for new, more flexible, and innovative carriers?

Nelson replied that her goal was to create a situation in which the network remained robust, in which "all carriers have incentives to invest," so that a "reliable, innovative, and flexible network of networks" can flourish.

The shock waves now felt in the area of pricing promise to have far reaching effect on the Internet's potential for interconnection and interoperability. "It's more than just issues of content and censorship, it also involves who is in control," warns Nelson.

Can the creative, independent, and occasionally cooperative chaos that we know as the Internet survive? Nelson is worried. "If we don't get this one right, if we botch it, it's back to oligopoly."

Public Policy
May 30, 1996

The Government's Role in the Development of the Internet

MODERATOR: Anthony Oettinger
PANELISTS: Michael Fricklas
    James Kamihachi
    Sharon Nelson

OETTINGER: This panel is on the government's role in the development of the Internet. What might that mean? Those of you who saw "Fiddler on the Roof" may remember a line where Tevya asks the rabbi if there is a prayer for the czar. And the rabbi says, "Of course, my son. There is a prayer for everything." "What is the prayer for the czar?" "May the Lord bless and keep the czar...far away from us." That's one extreme view of the role of government in anything. The other is epitomized by the Congressman who once mused to me and to my associate John McGates, who helped plan this session, when we were talking. He said, "Everybody is after me, everyone wants the government out of their hair. Except that they would like me to give them a fair advantage." That's the other view of the government, as the agent for giving a fair advantage.

Our speakers this morning occupy several points on this spectrum. Indeed, several aspects of this inhabit their individual heads, we've discovered. So they are conflicted within themselves as to who should play what role. Let me introduce them, and then we'll open the floor for discussion among the panel and for questions.

The first speaker will be **MICHAEL FRICKLAS**, Senior Vice President and Deputy General Counsel at Viacom. In case there is anyone here who has never heard of MTV or Nickelodeon or Nick at Night, I remind you that Viacom is not in the health care business, but in the entertainment business.

JAMES KAMIHACHI is Deputy Comptroller for Economics and Policy Analysis in the U.S. Department of the Treasury in the Office of the Controller of the Currency [OCC]. He worries about banks and worries about money, an area again where there is a certain amount of ambivalence about what the government should or should not do. Again, in case some of you are unaware of this, the Controller of the Currency is a branch of the federal government.

I remind you that this is a federal republic, and that we have 50 states, not only with legislatures and governors and things like that, but also with organizations with names like PUCs and PSCs and so on. And in the case of the state of Washington (not to be confused with Washington, D.C.), it is still called a Utilities and Transportation Commission, reflecting back to its roots. I also remind you that the Communications Act of 1934 had a strange provision in it that retains considerable power in the hands of the states. As for the Communications Act of 1996, among the many things it did not do was to remove that power; indeed, it reinforced it. So that when one speaks of government in the United States, one needs to keep in mind not only the federal government in Washington, D.C., but also the governments of many states, among them the state of Washington. We are privileged to have with us as our third speaker today **SHARON NELSON**, the Chair of the Washington Utilities and Transportation Commission.

I now turn it over to Michael Fricklas.

FRICKLAS: Thanks, Tony. Viacom has a unique perspective, or I should say perspectives, on regulation on the Internet. Sometimes I like to point out that the first two letters of Viacom really refer to "varied interests." We are such a large and varied company that we have a hard time deciding what our own point of view is.

As a cable programmer and a cable system operator, we've been in the business of delivering content down wires for a very long time. As Tony pointed out, our content ranges from cable channels like MTV, Nickelodeon, and Showtime to movies and TV shows produced by Paramount Pictures and Spelling Entertainment, to interactive games produced by companies like Virgin Interactive and Viacom New Media. Our content is seen by literally billions of people around the world.

Several years ago, we made a big bet that a little company like ours (we have a market capitalization of only a little north of $30 billion) would never be big enough to be a dominant player in the distribution of information. So we decided the right thing to do was to sell most of our distribution and compete on the strength of our creative ability and content. It's in our interest and we would love to see a competitive, efficient Internet develop that would provide every content creator with the ability to reach every viewer who wants to watch. It would also enable the creative community to reach its customers with existing products and entirely new experiences, flavored by the promising new medium of the Net. We believe that free enterprise and competition are the best ways to achieve the promise, a position surely colored by our experience with the "on again, off again" nature of regulation in the cable business, our historical core.

However, as with any free enterprise system, we believe that government has a role to play by assuring the efficiency of the markets and information, in particular, by protecting intellectual property rights and ensuring that all of us have access to the means of distribution and that our children know how to use it. On the other hand, we have a strong desire to see the government avoid slowing things down with complex regulatory schemes or politically expedient regulations such as those that now apply to indecency.

At Viacom, we believe strongly that it is content that will drive Internet development. Sure, a few of us techies surf the Net just to see what great applets have been created. But at the end of the day, unless consumers can find reliable or highly entertaining sources of information, the Net is going to become a great wasteland of promotions, sales, and clutter. If we are to get the private sector to upload to the Net, the valuable, up-to-date, often customized information and creative materials that we believe add real value, it is essential that the creators and rights holders have a means of being compensated for their work. In other words, we want to be assured that their copyrights will be enforced. Indeed, even the advertiser-supported information now prevalent on the Net will not meet its promise if a thief can freely copy the content and sell the promotional space to advertisers.

Today, the copyright industries of the United States (publishing, software, movies, music, television, and the like) control over $100 billion in annual sales and are growing at a rate faster than any other sector of the economy. As a major producer of copyrights, we hope the Internet will, over the long run, provide us with an economically efficient way to reach our customers and provide us with the opportunity to unleash our creative strengths in what is in many ways a unique medium of expression. In the absence of such a regime, the Net offers the potential of limitless perfect digital copies of material being freely distributed, sucking revenue from the creators and harming the creation of new ideas.

The factory of a copyright infringer in the digital domain is no more than the ubiquitous personal computer. For example, at one of our subsidiaries, Simon and Schuster—the world's largest English language publisher—we are creating a digital archive that will eventually contain every image and all text for which Simon and Schuster holds the rights. Currently, that would be over ten terabytes of text, images, video, and sound, all indexed in a meaningful way and tied back to their relevant rights.

At present, very little of that content is being made available on the Internet, because we are far from convinced that it is safe to do so, from a copyright standpoint. Ignoring copyright protection or supporting those who seek to circumvent it will create a virtual wall around the Internet and will ensure it never attains its full creative promise. We believe that the Internet only will grow as fast as people figure out how to make money on it. By that I mean it will develop only as far as content on the Net is protected in a meaningful way by the copyright laws.

I have a few examples that illustrate the problem. The first is the Star Shop Enterprise Internet site, devoted to selling *Star Trek* books that infringe on our *Star Trek* properties. As you can see, the owner of this site has quite a business enterprise going in selling infringing material.

The second is a web site devoted to *Mission Impossible*. This example was taken in March 1996, more than two months before the picture that is now in the theaters was released. And it shows that more than 10,500 people hit the site since it was launched in September of 1995. It's not clear how many of those downloaded the script to the movie, which is clearly available on the site.

The third example is our publishing unit's worst nightmare. Available now in Japan, it's a copy machine that actually turns the pages of books. So imagine putting one of the textbooks that one of you has worked so hard to put together, and changing the copy mechanism to a scanner. Basically anything can be put on the Net easily and cheaply.

For these reasons, we have our eyes fixed on Washington, where Congress is now considering issues of crucial importance to Internet development. In our view, the NII [National Information Infrastructure] legislation holds the promise of enabling rights holders to manage their own intellectual property and protect their own interests. We're not asking the government to take on this role for us, except perhaps in the case of head-on massive theft of intellectual property. But to us it seems obvious that as enforcers of our own rights, we need Congress to supply the fundamental copyright management technology tools to protect our content. We also need meaningful remedies against those who would defeat that technology or otherwise steal our property.

In the context of the pending NII legislation, that means we need to do the following:

- Outlaw devices that circumvent copyright management technology now under development.

- Outlaw attempts to alter or delete the copyright-identifying information we need for intellectual property management.

- Reaffirm that transmission is, in fact, copying.

- Ensure that the online service providers and Internet service providers are held to a standard of responsible copyright conduct.

Two of those issues, I think, bear a bit of elaboration. The third item, that transmission is copying, turns out to be a pretty controversial issue in the Internet area. It really shouldn't be too hard, with respect to those who would make the kinds of copies I referred to earlier.

On the other hand, it seems to be harder for us to win the hearts and minds of Negations that there should, in fact, be a charge for reading books by Internet from your local library. The reason for our position is one of degree. The need for one copy of a book for each reader and the inconvenience of a library and its associated time constraints means that we'll sell a reasonable number of books to interested people. The virtual library, in which one library would scare up and digitize one copy and make it available around the world instantly to everyone, holds out the promise that copies of our materials would be freely available to everybody in the world, on the basis of selling a single copy—not the kind of incentive that encourages creation of a meaningful work.

Second, we believe commercial online service providers should have substantial responsibility for copyright education and enforcement on the new medium they control, albeit with some recognition of the special characteristics of that medium. For the government to enact legislation to exonerate these parties from responsibility that bookstores, newsstands, music, and software retailers now have for the materials they carry, is to breed a climate of lawlessness and piracy that will end up stealing the promise of the Internet future before it can be fully realized.

OETTINGER: Thank you. Jim Kamihachi.

KAMIHACHI: I'm from the federal government, and of course I'm here to help you. Before proceeding, I have the standard disclaimer that the views I express are my own and not those of the OCC or the Treasury Department.

My charge is to talk about the government's role in the development of the Internet. And while some at this conference have said, "Well, it's a pretty simple thing: there isn't a role," actually I think it's really a very complex subject. What I want to focus on is the part of this subject I know best from my work at the OCC, which is the promise of Internet technologies for commercial banking.

Today, the volume of Internet commerce is only about $200 million a year, and that's a tiny fraction of consumer retail transactions, which are close to $5 trillion a year. As many people in this conference have said, the potential here is enormous. But while the promises are many, growth is only going to occur if there is a convincing business case. And making that case is going to be a very challenging proposition.

I recall when I was in school (and that was a while ago) the predictions of the checkless, cashless society. Well, I'm here to tell you that traditional currency still dominates our financial system. According to some recent estimates, over 80 percent of the retail purchases that take place in the U.S. economy each year are done with currency, and about 13 percent are consummated by checks. So everything else—debit, credit cards, travelers' checks, and the like—are really a very small fraction. Moreover, Internet volume is not likely to grow substantially until consumers are convinced encryption and digital signature technology is improved. These improvements must ensure, among other things, that electronic messages are secure from unauthorized manipulation and prying eyes, and that electronic transactions are nonrepudiable.

So what is the role of government in this evolutionary process? My part of government, the Treasury Department, is under a variety of conflicting pressures, and choosing the right course of action is no simple task. I think that patience and aggressive fact finding must prevail before we can begin the careful weighing of alternatives. Let me explain.

A number of people have raised various issues about the role of government in the Internet. In the banking area, I think four stand out: consumer protection, privacy, enforcement, and risk.

Consumer Protection

First, consumers enjoy many protections in the physical world that they will expect government to provide in the digital world. Now, electronic money comes in two forms—we would say electronic debits—transfers out of bank accounts and electronic cash, where the consumer actually carries around the means of payment. Consumer protections involving electronic debit transactions are pretty clear, but they are not entirely clear with respect to electronic cash. I think there's a real danger here that consumers may believe they have the same protections that they have in very familiar debit transactions, when a legal test may well prove they *don't* have those protections.

So questions arise such as:

- How much information do consumers need to make intelligent decisions about the use of e-cash products?

- Should there be limits on the amount of money that consumers can lose if there's a failure of an e-cash issuer, or if they lose their stored value card?

- Who is liable if the transaction fails to go through as everyone expects?

Privacy

Consumers are also interested in protecting their privacy. I think that there's a lot of simplification of a very complicated issue here. Consumer attitudes toward privacy are neither unequivocal nor unidimensional. Many of us have come to tolerate the notion that when we use a credit card, that information will be used in some kind of mass marketing campaign. But when we go into a bookstore and browse around, we pretty much assume that the bookstore owner isn't going to be looking over our shoulder. So how comfortable are we that on a web site, the web site provider can know every web site we touch? Or if we go into an online bookstore, that people can know exactly which books we looked at? So the question arises: Is there a role for government there?

Enforcement

There are a host of law enforcement issues as well. They include fraud, counterfeiting, money laundering, tax evasion. I think they're all pretty familiar, and without getting into details there is obviously a potential for these problems to arise in the electronic world.

The other issue we are looking at is the international dimension of e-money and banking. The payment system cannot function effectively internationally without monitoring by government agencies. It is not very clear exactly who's going to monitor this or how problems will be solved when we identify retail electronic financial frauds on an international scale.

Risk

Finally, I want to touch on bank examination, which is my neck of the woods. Banks are a common meeting ground for the effective and efficient resolution of many consumer, law enforcement, and international issues. Many of these fall into the area of what we call "operational risk." As you know, many banks are starting to create their own PC software. And as a regulator of banks, we're going to have to know what the problems are. Do these things really work as people expect? There are not many bank regulators and relatively few bankers that have a lot of experience in that business. We're going to have to figure out a way to solve that problem without imposing unnecessary burdens on the banks.

I think these illustrations suggest that in many respects, although not all, the challenges the Internet and associated technologies present to govern-

ment are quite familiar. However, the application of new technologies casts considerable doubt on the effectiveness of established and accepted solutions to age-old problems. For instance, most banking laws are rooted in some notion of geography. The Internet will make many of those rules moot. So we will have to rethink how we regulate this industry.

There are other pressures, as well. Government always faces pressure to respond quickly, to demonstrate that it's on top of the problem. But we know that bold intervention could have a chilling effect on the development and application of technological innovation, something that Michael [Fricklas] has raised as a legitimate concern. Further, in the rapidly changing area of electronic money and banking, the dimensions of the problem are not yet clearly defined, and there isn't any clear course of action that we can see. Products that are functionally similar on the surface can, in fact, raise very different legal and public policy questions.

So in my view, patience has got to be the watchword, at least in banking for now. But at the same time, patience cannot be an excuse for inaction. Government cannot afford the perception or the reality that waiting to see what happens is akin to advocating laxity. Government must be acutely attuned to new developments so that when it takes action, it can do so with a scalpel and not a meat ax.

OETTINGER: Thank you very much. Sharon Nelson.

NELSON: I'm very glad to be here. While I was preparing for this talk, looking over the roster of the very distinguished presenters for the conference, I thought, oh my gosh, I'm going to feel like a skunk at the garden party, being the regulator in the group. Now that I'm here and surrounded by such welcoming evidence of Seattle (like the coffee stand outside), I really feel quite at home. So rather than feeling like a skunk, the image that comes to mind is that of a raccoon, with all of you looking at that bold creature, trying to figure out what pesky business it's going to wreak on the party.

As a regulator for the last twelve years in the state of Washington, I have watched the evolution of what, heretofore, were considered natural monopolies into far more competitive environments. So I am here today not to praise traditional regulation, but to bury it. I'm definitely not proposing that we extend the telecom regulatory analogy to the Internet. Instead, I'm here as someone who has struggled with the thorny and tangled process of moving the highly regulated telephone industry into a more competitive environment, and I'm here looking for guidance. As I'll discuss later, how we deregulate traditional telcos will have a great deal of bearing on at least the immediate future of the Internet. And, fortuitously for us in the regulatory community, the Internet may offer some guidance on some of the decisions we're going to have to make in the next several months.

First, I'd like to admonish us all to avoid the trap of characterizing the Telecommunications Act of 1996 as deregulation. It ain't. Its very length should tell you that. The term "deregulation" is much too simplistic. It's not as if competition will simply develop if regulators just quickly step aside. We could do that, if you didn't care about the following:

- Whether captive residential and small business customers will pay rates that are fair.

- Whether the new conduit and content providers can interconnect efficiently with existing telephone networks.

- Whether the telephone companies will use their remaining network bottlenecks in an anticompetitive manner.

These are just some of the objectives that federal and state regulators are struggling with as we "deregulate." As was true of the deregulation of the transportation industries, we are finding in the states that the transition from a monopoly market to an effectively competitive one requires at least initially more, not less, regulation. But I am optimistic that if we all do our jobs right in the public and private sectors, the market will be the ultimate regulator.

Our first task under the Telecommunications Act of 1996 is to get a good interconnection policy for all sorts of providers at the local level. This is a new task that is assigned us by the Act. And I'd like to just digress for a minute with a short history of interconnection policy in the United States.

Telephone regulation emerged shortly before the end of the last century, when the expiration of Bell patents allowed new providers to enter the field. Surprisingly, about 3,000 systems sprang up between 1895 and 1902, financed privately, publicly, and cooperatively, all around the country. However, during this period, the old Bell system pressed every advantage it had to either forestall or eliminate its competition, including refusing to interconnect with unaffiliated companies. When Bell was threatened with antitrust action, Theodore Vail, the Bell president at the time, advocated the notion with success that the telephone system was a natural monopoly that should be regulated. To Vail, regulation was a fair price to pay for the security of protecting that monopoly.

What subsequently evolved was a form of regulation that rewarded telephone companies based on their level of investment and a set of a cross-subsidies, which further rewarded rural telephone companies for building networks to the outermost reaches of our country.

The upside of this history is that we have a ubiquitous and reliable national network in which more than 95 percent of all households are connected. The downside is that this form of regulation fostered the creation of a bureaucratic, rather complacent, and not very innovative management culture in the regulated telephone companies. In short, we have a fine system for hearing each other's voices, but an interactive seamless multimedia network is a long way a'coming.

Now, contrast that experience to the computer industry and the Internet. According to a recent *Forbes* report, the percentage of households with personal computers in our nation is around 35 to 40 percent, with a level of online Internet service penetration somewhere between 5 and 10 percent. That's not bad, given the relative time that personal computers and the Internet have been around. Telephones did not penetrate 40 percent of the nation's households until 1930, about 50 years after the invention of the phone. However, in terms of innovation and choice, the computer has vastly surpassed the telephone in its speed, capacity, and breadth of application. In short, we do not see any evidence of any type of market failure that would suggest the need for utility-style regulation of the Internet, computers, or their software applications.

With the accelerating convergence of computer technology and communications networks, however, the options for using telecommunications will continue to expand to the extent that no regulator will want to, much less be able to, control their deployment. Clearly, the future regulatory model should not be one of applying telephone regulation to every innovation that may look, act, feel, or smell like a phone. In my view, the recent petition filed by the American Carriers Telecommunications Association is just plain wrong. I think the comments that have been filed in the FCC docket all echo that sentiment. Instead of using a potential bypass technology to challenge and reform outdated regulatory arrangements, this petition seeks to extend those arrangements to cover voice communications over the Internet. Perhaps all of this reflects the old adage that "misery loves company."

In Washington state, we are blessed with a set of forward-thinking state laws, which have allowed us to adapt to the evolution of the telecom marketplace and to technological innovation. This has allowed us to adapt our forms of regulation to the actual market situation, including ceasing to regulate when monopolies erode. But today the problem is the same as it was when Theodore Vail ran the phone company. For example:

- We have to figure out a way to get competing new systems interconnected efficiently.

- We have to figure out how to price that interconnection.

- We have to figure out a way to ensure interoperability in a way that preserves what we have

and allows for flexibility to adapt to future innovation.

These questions are essential to the immediate future of the Internet. Even if you are lucky enough to have a choice about how your computer accesses the Internet, most users are still dependent on a local monopoly phone network to reach their online service provider. Last year, in a U.S. West rate case, we conducted a series of public hearings around the state to give consumers a chance to comment on the proposed rates and the company's services. We heard loud and clear from the Internet community: we heard from Internet service providers who are struggling to get T1 lines, and from consumers who are struggling to find out how in the world to get an ISDN line.

It's no coincidence that as the Internet grows, we're going to see this demand for broader band services. Companies like Intel, Hewlett-Packard, and Microsoft have all come to us, both formally and informally, to complain about the availability and cost of ISDN and high-speed dedicated lines in Washington state. Some of the first customers of Seattle's first alternative local phone company were Internet service providers. And my guess is that the biggest seller of ISDN service in this country today is not the telephone companies, but Microsoft, which has put enormous effort into making it easier for customers to order ISDN from their local telcos. These are indicators of the burgeoning unmet demand for advanced services that has the potential to keep driving network development.

I feel it is absolutely essential that this customer-driven demand should be our guide, rather than the various supply-side visions that have been advanced by telco or cable company executives, with all due respect to my co-panelist. That is why managing the transition to a competitive environment will have a profound effect on the Internet. It is more than just issues of content and censorship. It is also a matter of who is in control. If the supply side vision of building a top-down design network prevails, will the creative, independent, and occasionally cooperative chaos that we know as the Internet survive through merged monopolies (that is, the kind of cable-telco mergers we've seen)? Or is it possible to have an open, competitively developed telecommunication system that builds on the Internet experience, rather than destroying it?

The Internet community, with its experience of cooperatively managing a system of systems, has a lot to contribute to this debate. And there are a few things I'd really like to mention from the Internet history. One is the development of open, nonproprietary standards. I cannot conceive of how communications competition will operate seamlessly without such an open system. The Internet community can teach us state regulators about how to do that.

Customer-driven demand should be our guide, rather than supply-side visions that have been advanced by telco or cable company executives.

The second lesson we need to learn from you is how to price these interconnection arrangements appropriately. One of my staff economists said to me recently, "We have to find a way of getting away from the minutes-of-use regime, which has been the way we charge for phone services. It simply will not work in the new areas that the Internet offers us."

In the latest issue of *Wired*,[*] I was really interested in reading about the new growth theory, developed by Paul Romer from UC Berkeley. It is a description of how the whole dismal science of economics needs to be rethought in the context of the Internet. Romer's central tenet is that ideas create growth. To be sure, my engineers tell me that we priced and understood the economics of the old telephone network based on factors such as distance and usage. But the new technologies do not reflect those sorts of factors, so we must

find a different pricing paradigm for this new network of networks.

Questions & Answers

Q: *(For Michael Fricklas) 10,500 people [the number quoted as visiting the* Mission Impossible *site] aren't very many, in terms of a major studio release. And most of those people probably went to see the movie. Does your company not recognize the value of the free advertising you received?*

OETTINGER: And another question in a similar vein...

Q: *Research has shown that people read better off a book than off a screen. I still buy books that are available online. Are your fears of copyright infringement unfounded? Does not the* Mission Impossible *web site actually increase potential movie goers?*

FRICKLAS: To some extent, we do think that promotional use of this material helps us. In fact, if you go on the Internet to *http://www.paramount.com/*, you'll see that a fair amount of copyrighted material is available for downloading and interacting, in connection with the *Mission Impossible* site, for example. We do believe that there are promotional uses.

However, as copyright owners, we believe that those promotional uses should be under the control of the people who created the copyrights. That's not dissimilar from the way the copyright regime works today. In fact, the bundle of rights that go into making a movie or making a book are very highly negotiated with the individual creators of that work. We have different sets of rights, and what we actually put up on the Net are carefully negotiated with the various people with interests. Here's an example: Tom Cruise, the star of *Mission Impossible*, does not permit us to use his likeness except in circumstances in which he specifically approves. Having a regime where people, without any regard for copyright ownership, could willy-nilly place materials on

---

[*] Kelly, Kevin, "The Economics of Ideas," Issue 4.06, June 1996, p. 148.

the Net, obviously undermines our ability to control such matters.

Q: *Is there a danger of aiding criminal activity by making e-cash anonymous and ubiquitous?*

KAMIHACHI: Well, that's clearly the fear. For example, today, in money laundering, banks serve as a critical choke point for auditing transactions. There are some proposals to have e-money cards where the clearance would be entirely outside the banking system, so we could no longer use banks to trace those transactions. Another kind of concern the law enforcement authorities have is that today, if you take a lot of cash across the border, it's hard to hide, because this takes a lot of physical space. But if you can put it on a computer chip in a credit card–sized card, no problem.

However, the reality may be different. Europe is far ahead of the United States in the use of stored value cards. They're finding that actually, criminals don't want to use the stored value cards. One reason is because many stored value cards have load limits that are too small to be used in serious crime. But the other reason is, they're afraid that the government is going to secretly audit the cards. So the criminals would rather use cash.

The jury is still out. It's a logical fear, but we still have to wait and see how these systems develop.

Q: *What is the Comptroller of the Currency doing, if anything, to prevent the financial analog of the 1964 eastern blackout, which the speaker alleges created an electromagnetic pulse that would, under present circumstances, probably mess up a lot of transactions?*

KAMIHACHI: First of all, a lot of the big cash transfers are essentially wholesale transactions. That's where most of the money really passes in this country. The Federal Reserve supervises, and to a significant extent, runs that system. They have all kinds of people who worry about these transactions. At the OCC, we focus on the operations at the federally chartered banks, and make sure they have reasonable MIS systems. With e-money and banking we're talking about retail payment systems, and the problems involved are going to be fundamentally different from wholesale transactions. The dollar value of individual transactions

are going to be small. If something goes wrong, the bank's exposure is likely to be relatively small. At the same time, there are going to be a large number of transactions. So it's just a fundamentally different kind of problem.

So one of the things we do have to worry about is, if a person loses his money in the course of the transaction because of some computer failure, it's not going to make the bank fail, but that person will probably be a pretty mad customer. That's something we worry about, and with e-money, the protections aren't necessarily clear. Here is an area where the market incentives are really very closely aligned with the government, I think, because banks don't want to have unhappy customers any more than we do.

___: I'll just say this: I hope we're not going to let the market dictate this. If we do, we're going to be in very serious trouble.

NELSON: We find that as plain old command-and-control regulation gives way to more market mechanisms, other kinds of regulatory mechanisms have to be thought of. So for example, in the long distance business, with major outages in some huge interstate networks, the FCC created the Network Reliability Council. In the wake of transportation deregulation, safety agencies have to be given more authority to make sure that a basic level of security is in those systems.

KAMIHACHI: I don't want to come across as saying, "Oh, we'll leave it entirely to the market." But I do think that the bankers' incentives to conduct transactions accurately are the same incentives as the government's.

Q: *What role, if any, can Treasury take to regulate electronic cash issues based in other countries? If such an issue was found to be committing fraud on US citizens, what steps would Treasury take to address this problem?*

KAMIHACHI: That's the thing we're really worried about here now. How much the potential for that really exists, depends on what cards actually emerge. These things are in the very early stages. In fact, the experiments in this country are not very widespread and are in the pilot stages.

But what happens if somebody sets up an Internet server in Bora Bora, and is clearly engaged in fraud? We don't know whether we can actually go after that person. We don't even know which country's rules apply. We don't know where the transaction takes place, for the purposes of the law. So by the time we get the guy, we don't know whether we can take effective action. That's why we will need some form of international cooperation.*

Q: *Why should online service providers or Internet access providers be liable for content put up by users of the system? What did Viacom do when it discovered the* Star Trek *or the* Mission Impossible *site on the Net? And how do you propose for Internet service providers to be responsible for web home pages? Should they be strictly liable, or should they only be responsible when put on notice? If the latter, is it incumbent on the ISP [Internet Service Provider] to make its own decision on the validity of the copyright violation claim?*

FRICKLAS: Okay. Good questions. Given the caveat now that I'm speaking for myself and not for Viacom: I think there's a range of things that everyone understands in the nature of Internet service providers—the people who relate to content—that in some ways the copyright community hasn't really understood. And there are different answers, depending on where you stand in the chain.

There is no intention on anyone to impose copyright strict liability. "Strict liability," for those who aren't lawyers, means liability without fault. It means that if there is an infringement and it occurs on your facilities, that you're responsible. That's the law today for Internet service providers, for book publishers, and for everyone else. If I put out a book and that book contains an infringement in it, I'm liable for that. And if I acquired that content from someone else, I'm then allowed to go after whoever provided me with the content. That's the normal liability of publishers.

I think in the case of a common carrier, the chances are, the common carrier is not responsible. They're not a publisher of information. They're just carrying information. Clearly, a telephone company that sent a stream of bits that they didn't have any relation to, wouldn't be liable for a copyright infringement. The next step up would be someone who provides a server, a UUNET, a PSINET, someone like that, who's really doing nothing more than providing a gateway to the Internet. I also don't think that there's an intention that those people be responsible.

Where the area really gets contentious is when you talk about somebody like a commercial online service—America Online, Microsoft Network, CompuServe. Those people have edited information, information that they have worked on, that they have screened, that they have paid for, and, in a lot of cases, that they have set up links to. In those situations, we think they're acting a lot more like publishers, and under current law they would be responsible for making sure that those don't infringe. That's a logical way to set this up, because they have the relationship with the customer. They can say to their customer, "Hey, you misled us. You put up infringing information. We should be entitled to recover." Generally, the commercial online providers have been very helpful to us.

As far as the question about these sites [web home pages], I don't know the particular answers. Normally we contact the online service provider. The online service provider contacts their customer (often, we don't know who the customer is). That customer will then take the site down. In some cases, they won't take the site down and the online service provider will turn them off. We've gotten great cooperation from the online service providers, and it hasn't been a real issue.

Q: *If substantial segments of the population are rendered obsolete or superfluous due to insufficient literacy skills, or insufficient income to afford online services—once such services become essential or necessary to participate*

---

* For more about this subject Tony Oettinger recommends the book *Governing the Global Economy* by Ethan Kapstein.

effectively in society, should the government continue to be a service provider of last resort to information have nots by developing a second redundant Internet? For example, FTS2000 [one of the intra-governmental communications networks run by the General Services Administration] could be upgraded into a broadband optical fiber network to serve the information poor with email, public education, and access to public information in all formats, video, text, and voice.

NELSON: The new Telcom Act of 1996 worries about the "have, have not" problems, and asks eight regulators (three FCC regulators, four state regulators, and a representative of the consumer advocate community) to come up with a new form of "universal service" (the code word), to try to ameliorate the spectre of a society composed of information "haves" and information "have nots." It, in fact, says that somehow a fund will be created to provide access to schools, libraries, and rural telemedicine projects by what's called the Federal-State Joint Board on Universal Service.

I fear that this is the greatest new gold rush. As soon as I was appointed to this Joint Board, I got called by school directors in the State of Washington saying, "Now, is this a new block grant for us?" And I'm trying to tell people, "The way it will be created will be a tax on some other service that you pay as a householder." It's gotten so that people think of access to the Internet and access to computers as a panacea for all of our social problems. I heard a social service delivery person say she wanted a computer for every homeless person. And I said, "Now, where will that homeless person keep that computer?"

So it's something we need to worry about. But I'm hoping that this marketplace is capable of handling an economy of ideas—as I said, the Paul Romer article is very interesting. This is the marketplace of abundance. And the marketplace is delivering these products to those who want them, with a very beautifully declining cost curve. We will be struggling with these issues at the Federal State Joint Board. We're supposed to have some recommendations about how to handle some of these issues by November 1996.

In the meantime, we have lifeline programs in place, link-up programs, that sort of thing, so that people at least have a basic telephone. As I said, we've got 95 percent of our homes wired. But when you get into distinct subgroups, minority groups, the poor, obviously, they don't have phones in those percentages.

FRICKLAS: I, for one, can't resist pointing out that I think every homeless person should have a home page.

About the Speakers

ANTHONY G. OETTINGER is Professor of Information Resources Policy and Chairman of the Program on Information Resources Policy. He is on the Board of Visitors of the Defense Intelligence College, belongs to the Council on Foreign Relations, and is a Trustee of the Charles Babbage Foundation. In the White House, he was a consultant to the President's Foreign Intelligence Advisory Board (1981–90), the National Security Council (1975–81), and the Office of Science and Technology (1961–73). He chaired the Massachusetts Cable Commission (1975–79), being on it from its start in 1972. He founded the Computer Science and Engineering Board of the National Academy of Sciences and chaired it from 1967 to 1973.

MICHAEL D. FRICKLAS joined Viacom as Vice President, Deputy General Counsel/Corporate in 1993 and became Senior Vice President, Deputy General Counsel and a member of Viacom's operations Committee in 1994. In that capacity, he is responsible for day to day management of Viacom's 160-lawyer law department. Previously, he spent three years as Vice President, General Counsel and Secretary at Minorco (U.S.A.) Inc., and was an associate at Shearman & Sterling, where he specialized in corporate finance and mergers and acquisitions. Earlier, Mr. Fricklas was an associate at Ware & Freidenrich, a California-based firm, where he specialized in intellectual property, corporate, and securities law, representing high technology companies.

JAMES D. KAMIHACHI is the Deputy Comptroller for Economic and Policy Analysis. His department assesses the impact of OCC policies and regulations on national banks; analyzes the implications of major developments affecting the industry; monitors the financial health of the banking industry; develops quantitative measures of risks in bank portfolios; and conducts economic research on banking issues. He reports to Konrad Alt, Senior Deputy Comptroller for Economic Analysis and Public Affairs and Chief of Staff. Before joining the OCC, Mr. Kamihachi served in the Office of Information and Regulatory Affairs at the Office of Management and Budget (OMB) as Senior Advisor to the Administrator.

SHARON L. NELSON was appointed Chairman of the Washington Utilities and Transportation Commission on February 11, 1985 and reappointed to a second term on January 2, 1991. Her current term expires January 1, 1997. Prior to joining the WUTC, her experience included teaching history and anthropology in secondary schools, serving as staff counsel to the U.S. Senate Commerce Committee, and serving as legislative counsel to the Consumers Union of the United States. She has also been a lawyer in private practice, and has served as staff coordinator for the Washington State Legislature's Joint Select Committee on Telecommunications.

Standards

By Anna Aleksandrowicz

One of the people who doesn't believe Microsoft and Bill Gates should have complete control of the Internet expressed his conviction yesterday during a discussion of who should set the standards that govern how we use the Internet.

Speaking at a panel on the future of Internet standards, Fred Baker, current Chairman of a public-private education task force on Internet standards (IETF), emphasized the need for companies like Microsoft, Sun Microsystems, and Novell to talk and agree upon a one size fits all approach to standards. That conversation, he said, would avoid the all too common use of proprietary standards.

"I'm really getting teed off about this," Baker said, referring to the fact that in the last year alone, Microsoft and Ascent have set up five proprietary standards, going against what he said was the IETF emphasis on user involvement, rapid prototyping, and early deployment testing.

Standards on the Internet come down to a question of how one computer box talks to another. Baker, a Senior Software Engineer at Cisco Systems, Inc., said that when everyone agrees to adopt a standard, everyone wins. It provides a reason to implement the standard because it works, is a marketing focus for the company, a tool for network citizen, and a solution to a problem.

For the vendor, a standard is the reason why we should buy their specific box, so setting vendor-initiated, proprietary standards makes sense for the individual company, if not for the overall Internet community. According to Martin Sirbu, a Professor of Engineering and Public Policy at Carnegie Mellon University, a company's tendency to set its own standards is natural. "In the competitive marketplace, firms try to create a monopoly of power," Sirbu said. "One of the motivations for firms to agree on standards is to prevent one from imposing" on everyone else. According to Sirbu, a standard, therefore, needs to be "equally objectionable to all parties."

Internet standards differ from the standards that have been used until now because they develop in a much less formalized process. According to Sirbu, Internet standards have developed in "rapid prototyping," which emphasizes systems building, testing the systems against each other, then building the actual standard.

But success has changed all this, according to Sirbu. With many more people using the Internet, its new commercial importance, and the existence of an already-installed base, the process of setting standards will have to proceed more slowly as it goes forward.

In empty space, according to Sirbu, it was much easier to innovate, creating concepts like HTML and the Apple desktop, but innovation is much harder in the crowded fields we have today, such as routing algorithms.

Yet, going forward is still the operative word, and both Baker and Sirbu pointed out the need to keep the process of setting Internet standards an open one.

"The Internet gives new meaning to standards, [making them] exciting and interactive," Sirbu said. "It is important to understand, to think of, standards as a verb, as a standards process, or ongoing dialogue." Proprietary standards, by contrast, are a one-way street, where the company, whether it is Microsoft or Sun Microsystems, sets the standards unilaterally.

"The way forward, as we think about standards," Baker said, "is to emphasize innovation, accept initiation and comment from vendors, and emphasize open involvement, including users and competing vendors."

Public Policy
May 29, 1996

The Paradigm of Interoperability

Standards Setting for the Internet

MODERATOR: Brian Kahin
PANELISTS: Fred Baker
                   Marvin Sirbu

KAHIN: I'm very glad you're all here. Standard setting for the Internet is, of course, a very hot topic. Who would have dreamt 15 years ago that standards could possibly be a hot topic? In fact, we actually have a new word for it: "interoperability." It's one of the many "inter"s that make this an exciting area: Internet, interactive, international, and so on.

The Internet, in fact, has given new meaning to standards. It has made standards exciting, where the action is. Standards, in fact, are driving the infrastructure, and that's why the Internet has moved so fast in such a short time. In this session we are going to focus on the standards process itself. But I want to say a little bit that puts it in context.

One of the things that is important to understand, I think, is not to think of standards so much as a set of documents that emerge out of a terribly long and boring international process after many, many years, but to think of standards instead as a verb, like *standards development* or *standards processes*—an ongoing dialogue among different parts of different industries about what is going to be common technology.

By the same token, some of the traditional concepts within standards are broken down. I used to have this distinction between *de jure* (that's standards of right) and *de facto* (standards as a matter of fact). That used to be fairly clearcut, although that's no longer the case. Standards may be more or less *de facto*, and they may be more or less *de jure*. One of the issues has been the status of the Internet standards, the standards the Internet Engineering Task Force [IETF] creates. Are they *de jure*? Technically, they're not, because the Internet Society is not an official international standards body. And the old way of looking at it was that only products of the ITU [International Telecommunications Union] or ISO [International Organization of Standardization] could be actually called standards. Everything else was called specifications.

Another distinction that has broken down is the distinction between what is open and what is closed. It turns out there are various degrees of what is open. Microsoft says, "We publish our standards. Therefore, they're open." Other people take a somewhat different view. The Computer Systems Policy Project said standards are open if they are published and widely available on nondiscriminatory terms, and can only be changed with advance notice and public process—therefore cutting out Microsoft's standards. Sun, as you heard yesterday, has a rather different view. Sun says "open" means nonproprietary. Most of the rest of the computer industry disagrees with that, but Sun has made a very strong case that open standards should be nonproprietary. And we'll see if, in the case of Java, they put their money where their mouth is.

The distinction between proprietary and nonproprietary breaks down, too. At the "Intellectual Property Online" session that just concluded, one question that came up was, to what extent can you protect standards through different forms of intellectual property? And a number are used: copyright is perhaps not as effective as it was once thought to be, patents are important issues there, and trademarks can be used to control a standards process. Simply having a first mover advantage can give you effective control over standards.

In the Internet we see a merging of two themes in standards activity. One is the demand for open systems that arose out of corporate users in the 1980s, and increasingly among all users as they became aware of the problems of being locked into a particular manufacturer's standard. The other is the origins of the Internet in the government and research community, where great value was placed on sharing, being able to use a common code, common specifications. And in fact, the Internet was created and built as a way of sharing resources across the country. So we have both those factors pushing towards openness. In this standards-driven infrastructure we see that traditional strategies of proprietary client/server systems, as Scott McNealy was saying yesterday, are dropping by the wayside.

What does this mean in terms of intellectual property? This is a different intellectual property argument than you heard in the "Intellectual Property" session. But in some respects, it's similar. Does the fact that the business models are migrating toward this open environment mean that intellectual property is becoming less important? If you talk to the intellectual property community—and as a lawyer who specializes in intellectual property, I know that community, although I do not always share its views—you will hear again and again that intellectual property is becoming more important. But maybe this is something that comes and goes. Maybe there has been a shift in the technological environment in which users are more powerful with respect to publishers than they used to be, or that open systems are more attractive in the marketplace than they used to be, or more important as a business strategy than they used to be. So maybe this is something that comes full circle.

Java is being given to the Internet. You also heard yesterday that QuickTime was being given to the Internet—from Apple, who is way at the other end of the spectrum from Sun. Is that really an issue of corporate philanthropy, is it long-term corporate strategy, or something else again?

So let me now turn the session over to **MARVIN SIRBU**, a Professor of Public Policy and Engineering at Carnegie Mellon, Director of the Information Networking Institute.

SIRBU: I thought I would begin by giving some perspective to the nature of standards and the nature of the standards-making process, talk about different processes that have been used over the last several decades in relation to communications standards, and make some forecasts about how that process is likely to evolve with the explosive growth of the Internet.

The Nature of Standards

When we look at the nature of standards, you have to appreciate that the first person who makes a product is essentially setting a standard. That is, a device that works is a standard because everything that works the same way is exactly like that device because it's the only one. Most inventors don't think about that when they're creating products. They don't think, "Gee, I'm going to do this in a way that everybody's going to copy and use for the next two decades."

We often get into situations where the initial versions of products, as conceived by the inventors, get used far beyond the proportions they originally anticipated. In the early years of the Internet, those who focused on research networking communications were very upset about the fact that many people wanted to use the Internet for production purposes. It prevented the researchers from experimenting with and changing the protocol, though they weren't interested in freezing it in a particular configuration. Because it worked, however, people wanted to use it and continue to exploit it. We have many situations of that kind, where an early version of an idea becomes popular so quickly that we get stuck with the design.

Standards Processes

One can make a distinction between what I call "peer-to-peer standards," where you have two like systems that are trying to communicate (for example, two fax machines or two videoconferencing systems) and "interface standards" (such as a terminal talking to a modem, or a disk drive communicating with a PC). So there's a continuing debate in the standards community over how big a set of functions to try and get agreement on, versus the time it's likely to take to reach standardization of those.

A similar tradeoff debate occurs over the issue of how much to nail down in the standard versus how much to leave to the implementers. I remember going to a conference a dozen years ago, in which somebody observed that the standards for Xerox's network architecture was about this thick and the standards for TCP/IP were this thick, and the standards for OSI were this thick. Now, the assertion of this particular speaker was that the Xerox standards documents, which were only this thick, were the better set of documents because you didn't have to spend so much time reading it. But the fact was that everybody who implemented the Xerox documents did it differently. And so while they were great for interworking within a single vendor's system (so 3Com used it within their network architecture, and Xerox used it within theirs, and so on), when you tried to do interoperability between companies, you found out that they'd interpreted the documents differently. And while the OSI documents might have been twice as thick, there was a lot less likelihood that you would interpret them differently in implementing them. So again, there's this tradeoff between specificity and interoperability. One of the challenges has always been to get the right level of specificity while still leaving room for continuing innovation.

The third comment I want to make about the standards process is that almost always, at the end of producing the standards document, you're only about halfway through. The reason for that is because the standards document, in order to include the functionality everybody wants, often has so many options that no product vendor really wants to implement all of them. If he did, it would take a long time for the product to reach market. And then there's a process of deciding which of the many options in the standard you actually implement in practice.

A trick that standards developers sometimes adopt in order to reach agreement is, they say, "This is left for further study." Or they say, "This is for engineering implementation decisions." So often it's the case that two people reading the same document will implement things that don't interwork the first time. This has led to a need for testing or conformance testing procedures and protocols. The standard really isn't set until you've gone through a process of ensuring that implementations actually interwork with each other.

Now, we've seen a variety of different processes used to attempt to set standards. We've had organizations like the International Organization for Standardization, which is nearly 100 years old, the International Telecommunications Union, which is more than 100 years old, that have been involved in setting standards in communications for quite a long time. Over the years, they had developed very formalized processes that were very top-down:

- First you decide on a work item.

- Then you develop a services description.

- Then you develop a protocol document.

All kinds of formal procedures. Then when the document is issued, people would start to develop products.

The Internet has developed in a very different style with the Internet Engineering Task Force, the set of committees that developed standards for use in the Internet. If the first style can be called the "waterfall model of development," where you do requirements and design and implementation and testing, the Internet style can be likened to what in software is called "rapid prototyping." That is, you build a system, you see if it works, you interwork with other systems, you then figure out what needed improvements to make, and you do another iteration with new features.

So in the time that the formal Open Systems Interconnection process was trying to develop a standard for network management, the Internet Society, starting from some initial documents developed by the OSI, went through Simple Network Management Protocol 1, then 1.5, then 2, before the OSI group had finally finished their version 1. It is this style of standards development that has been described as "rough consensus and running code," which has, I think, enabled the Internet to take precedence over a process that had formal backing from a number of governments, and more support through international organizations than that of the Open Systems Interconnection. The emphasis was on building systems, testing them against each other, and making sure they worked before progressing something up to the area of a standard.

Future Directions

That process, which has worked very well for a number of years, is beginning to change. And it's changing under the weight of success. The number of people who attend Internet Engineering Task Force meetings has increased exponentially over the last several years.

They're also facing a new problem: they have an installed base. It's easy when you're inventing the first time. You've got a green field to work with. You can do whatever seems best. But once you have an installed base, you're faced with the difficult challenge of remaining backward-compatible. One only has to look at the gyrations that Microsoft went through, introducing Windows 95 and trying to remain backward-compatible with all that DOS 2.0 software that was out there, to recognize that backwards compatibility is very difficult to accomplish. And I think the effect of that requirement will inevitably slow down the progress.

In addition, the Internet is commercially important. And because it's commercially important, meetings are no longer limited to academics, government people, or national laboratory people who may have been somewhat disinterested; we now have very intense participation by multibillion dollar firms whose livelihood depends very much on their ability to stay on top of the process, implement products in a timely way, and to control their direction. I think we're seeing the process shift to where the role of vendors, particularly those vendors with important market share, is increasingly vital to the success of any standards evolution.

In the core of the network, for example, vendors such as Cisco or Bay Networks dominate the products that are sold for routing. And if they

don't endorse a change to a routing protocol, that change won't happen—too much of the network runs on their products for the standards to evolve without their consent. So at the same time that we've seen greater participation, we've also seen some concentration of power among a small number of firms who are the dominant suppliers of equipment, and it is they who determine evolution of standards, at least where their equipment is concerned.

So where is there room for continued innovation and vitality? Clearly, in areas where it remains a green field. As remarked in a previous session, we're at about release 0.9 of the Internet, not really even 1.0. That is, we ain't seen nothin' yet! To that extent, as we've seen just in the last two years with protocols like HTML or HTTP, a small company like Netscape [was] can drive the standard and the evolution of that protocol rapidly, because of the absence of entrenched equipment and installed system base. So we will continue to see innovation, largely in areas of new applications and new functionality. We'll see it very rapidly and with important roles by small firms. But the core protocols of the network—the migration from version 4 to version 6 of IP [Internet Protocol]—will be dominated increasingly by a small number of companies who are the major suppliers of the core equipment that has to implement these protocols.

KAHIN: That's great. We're closing in on the heart of the matter here. Our last panelist, **FRED BAKER,** is an engineer at Cisco Systems, one of those small groups of companies Marvin just mentioned, where he works on congestion control in multimedia. He is the current Chair of the Internet Engineering Task Force.

BAKER: I want to go over some of the areas that Marvin just covered, and ruminate on the direction we're going to need to go forward in developing standards.

But before we get into that, I think we need to work on this word "standard." I'm reminded of when I first went to college. I wanted to challenge out of a calculus course. I went up to the professor, and he asked me some questions. He said, for example, "What is an integral?" And I thought real hard, and said, "Well, it's the area under this curve." And he said, "Oh, no, no, no, no." And I thought about some other answers when finally he said, "An integral is a number. You're working too hard."

Well, what *is* a standard? Microsoft, I understand, says it's something that is publicly documented. Sun says it's something that is publicly owned. I think the standard is something much simpler than that. A standard, very simply, is something that we all agree to implement. And we all have reasons for agreeing to implement that.

At Cisco, we want standards because they work, because it's a marketing focus for our company. We're a router vendor, a switch vendor, so we're going to be looking very hard at router and switch things. We want something that will allow us to interoperate with Bay Networks and 3Com and whoever else. If you're Sun Microsystems, you're probably going to be very interested in how M stations can work together, so you're going to be interested in how TCP works. If you're Netscape, you want some way of displaying web pages so that everybody can read them. And by the way, you want some better way so that they come buy yours. It's marketing focus for the companies that are doing it.

From the perspective of people out in the trenches, it's a tool. A standard is nothing more than a tool. If we all know how to write a web page, we can all create web pages and share them with each other and look at them and say, "Gee, that's a neat web page. Why don't you put something useful on it?" It's a tool, and a tool we can all use.

It's a solution to a problem. When TCP was first developed, it was a solution to the problem, how can two systems know they're exchanging data effectively? And by the way, how can they do it over widely varying speeds of links, without having to worry about knowing the speeds of those links? When we first developed IP to solve the problem, how do we know where a message is going and where it came from? And how do we know what security parameters and other things

apply to it? It's a solution to a problem. And from a vendor's special perspective, it's a reason you need to buy my box: I support *foo bar*, and by the way, I do it better than any other vendor.

So what is a standard? It's a lot of things, and it depends on your perspective. Fundamentally I think it's something we all agree to implement.

Now, there are a number of ways that standards are made:

- They come from vendors.

- They come from users.

- They come from research.

The traditional ISO and ITU processes have followed this model pretty rigorously. Somebody comes out and says, "If we're going to do compression across an async line, what we really need is some kind of synchronous substrate that is on that thing, and then we run some kind of compression algorithm that may include lookups and tables." So we have a way of generating those tables and a way of getting stuff out the other end. Somebody puts a stamp on it and says, yes, that's V.42 bis, and now everybody knows what they can do, and they go do it.

Now, that standard came originally from IBM, Hewlett-Packard, and Unix, who all have patents that, if you go implement V.42 bis, you have to pay them. They got together and implemented it. They made some improvements on it over a period of time. And a bunch of people came out and implemented it. And now you can get it in your favorite PC or Mac or modem, everybody can get V.42 bis compression.

Many of the IETF standards also basically followed this model, with a few more iterations. OSPF [Open Shortest Path First], for example, Proteon, had a fundamental problem, and the problem was called Cisco. Cisco had a routing protocol that some people really liked and some people didn't. And it was a competitive problem for Proteon. Proteon decided they wanted to come up with a better solution to routing. By the way, there were some major problems in routing architectures in the world at the time. (People like to talk about RIP [Routing Info Protocol]. I'll leave that one alone. There were other, better approaches in the research community that they were looking at.) They had some experience with the SPF [Shortest Path First] algorithm. So they said, "Well, let's go do this Dykstra algorithm, this SPF algorithm, and that will give us a number of selling features. It will give us better reaction to problems in the network. And it will give us a way to sell against Cisco."

So Proteon started working on that. And some of the people in the IETF got wind of the fact, and said, "No, no, no. Don't do this as a proprietary protocol. What we'd like you to do is bring that into the standards community, where we can all talk about it."

And they did. So they came up with a protocol which I refer to as a "bucket of bolts," but it works. And now a large number of vendors have implemented it. I went to one interoperability test where we had 23 vendors in the room, all doing strange things with networks and making things fail and come back up, and following the changes and the topology around.

So some standards are vendor-initiated. They come basically because the vendor has a problem. The vendor sees a need in the user community, has competitive pressures that it needs to deal with, so the vendor wants to develop a product and put it in the marketplace.

Standards also come from the user community. And the user community in the Internet is, generally speaking, the network providers. The example I give here, Classless Internet Domain Routing, CIDR (we call it "cider"), actually came from BarNet, from a fellow named Vince Fuller, who was concerned about problems with the size of these routing tables. He took the subnet architecture that was already ambient in the Internet, and said, "Imagine just for fun that we got bigger subnets that were actually bigger than a network number." He called them "supernets." The idea got kicked around in the community, and we finally said, "Let's forget about class. Why don't we just have networks of whatever size you

need?" Now all this started with a user who had a need, who kicked around some ideas and developed an approach, and then went about banging on vendors' doors to go implement it.

Standards also come from research, often by academics, but not necessarily. This is often a matter of somebody finding an interesting problem to write a Ph.D. thesis about. Never mind whether it's actually ever going to be useful. They play around with a number of ideas, and some approach finally looks useful. And then a vendor might say, "That might actually solve a problem for me." And they implement it.

In the example of ISIS, one could argue that it was a proprietary protocol of Digital Equipment Corporation written by Radia Perlman. One could also argue that it came directly out of mathematical research in the '50s and '60s, a pretty direct outgrowth of Dykstra's papers in the early '70s. They were looking at graph theory and at the problems of routing in networks. Radia basically took this stuff out of the research community and put it to work in networks.

Another example is the protocol called RSVP [Resource Reservation Protocol], which is used for resource reservation in the Internet, or *may* be used some day, if I ever get my code out. That one basically came from MIT and from ISI and from the Stanford, Palo Alto Research Center. Different researchers got together to look at an interesting idea: they might be able to convince vendors to do something more than plunk out messages, one after the other, in lockstep order. And they thought, "What problems could we solve? What interesting things could we get into?" Several people got their doctorates out of that. And lo and behold, now some of that research is finding very interesting use in the Internet, and has some potential for different applications in the future.

So standards come from vendors, they come from users, they come from research. Sometimes—I can think of five events this year—they come from some vendor who defines something, and wings it out and says, "Here is the way you will talk to Windows 95 when you're on a point-to-point line." He uses the standards process as a way to publish his standard.

The example I gave was Novell IPX [Internet Packet Exchange] LAN [Local Area Network]. And that was literally the statement they made. We had a proposal in development in the PPP [Point-to-Point Protocol] working group, of how one might run IPX over a point-to-point line, when Novell said, "No, we are declaring a proprietary protocol. We're going to define it, publish it, and this is the way thou shalt do it." Now there are two approaches. One of them is Novell's and one of them is the public one.

One can accept the fact that one standards body uses one process, another standards body uses another process. The fact is that we're all guilty of all the sins of all the others; the question is largely one of degree. And that's why I have been very careful to grab one from ISO and one from the IETF, because we're all guilty. The one comment I'll make is that vendor bodies (the ITU and the ISO) and the forums—generic, which tend to be vendor bodies—tend to not have a lot of user input, not a lot of research input, whereas user input is a strength of the IETF. Apart from that, we basically all run those kinds of processes.

What makes IETF processes different? Marvin [Sirbu] used the words "rapid prototyping": that's an important part. What we're interested in, in IETF standards, is something that works. We really don't care much what it looks like. It can be ungainly as all get out. We like it to work, so we try things out, find out what works and what doesn't. And when we find things that work but are obnoxious in one way or another, we find something else that works which is perhaps less obnoxious.

Another attribute we try to have is user involvement. In fact, on the Internet Engineering Task Force, or on the ISG, we have people who run networks for a living, that are at the top of the structure, approving the things and saying, "Yes, that actually really does meet my needs." We try to get user involvement and user signoff, to be assured that the protocol is doing what needs to

be done. And we try to get early deployment testing.

The one thing that we really don't do—and recently we've made the State Department rather angry about it—is we don't come to some national body and say, "Please vote on this." We really don't care what the national bodies think about it. If they don't like it, they don't have to use it. We notice that all of the discussions they have on our subjects are using our protocols.

We really don't approve of the proprietary standards, the places where people come out and say, "This is the way thou shalt do it." The funny thing is, they happen anyway, and they're a reality. We need to find a way to make them work, because often proprietary standards are what moves various areas forward.

In the case of what I call the "HTML wars" at CERN [Conseil Europeén pour la Recherche Nucléaire], they originally developed HTML and came out with a fundamental specification for building a web page. And the people at NCSA [National Center for Supercomputing Applications] went off and built Mosaic. Then Netscape developed great market share by doing things that anybody using a good word processor in the last 20 years thought web pages should do, like center text: really basic, typical things. They put these capabilities into their browser, and lo and behold, people said, "Gee, I can build a web page that way." And now you see Netscape-optimized pages everywhere.

Just this last week, *Mac User* had an article on what they called web boards. It said that Microsoft's Internet Explorer is niftier because it has some other tweaks they really like. Often, innovation is the way things progress. Innovation is basically somebody coming out and saying, "This is the way you will do it. I have the marketing muscle to make that happen."

Another example of that is what we call "Internet tunneling." Andy Valencia came to the PPP working group and said, "We have a product we're starting to deploy, which looks an awful lot like leased lines—similar to the CompuServe model—where you can dial up with a local provider and use some kind of backbone infrastructure to get back to the plant." CompuServe has historically used X.25 switches and that kind of thing. Cisco proposed to use the Internet for the same kind of behavior.

At just about the same time, we had something mailed to the RFC [Request for Comments] editor from Microsoft, that said, by the way, here's exactly the same function, many of the same features, and done in a different way. It said, "This is the way thou shalt do it if you want to talk to Windows 95."

> *We're going to have to go get these vendors and beat them on the head and say, "Guys, go talk. Please come up with one approach. And by the way, solve the same problem."*

Not too long ago, we were discussing this episode with the two vendors, and discovered that Ascend had done the same thing. They had something else that combined Internet tunneling and mobility, which they mailed off to the RFC editor, asking, "Please publish this. This is the way it shall be done."

We're going to have to go get these vendors and beat them on the head and say, "Guys, go talk. Please come up with one approach. And by the way, solve the same problem."

There's quite a bit of pressure to go around our existing processes. And I'm going to be very blunt—I can think of a lot of vendors that have done what Ascend and Microsoft have been doing. They've done it five times this year. I'm getting a little bit teed off, quite frankly. I wish that they would play the game with the rest of us, who are trying hard to develop an entire marketplace for all of us to play in. And I get a little bit

miffed when people announce: "This is the way it shall be done." That doesn't work all that well.

On the other hand forums—the frame relay forum, the ATM forums—have worked well. Several vendors got together in the frame relay forum, built switches and made it go fast, and came out and put together a technology. The router and switch vendors started jumping on that, and interoperating with these things. Now, the forum got its technology out quickly, it built a marketplace, and it's been a very useful tool. I applaud them for that. The down side of it is, as you can read in newspapers, it didn't work. And it took an awful lot of effort on everybody's part to go sweep up the pieces and make them come together.

The frame relay forum has a problem now that it's kind of a self-perpetuating enterprise. It doesn't really have a need to exist any more, because frame relay is out there; the standards are set. We're basically all doing it. But now we've got this group of people that have meetings and get together and talk about things, and go around from place to place to place. And they need something to talk about at the next meeting.

The ATM [Asynchronous Transfer Mode] forum is at a different point in the curve, but there are similarities. They have done well in getting ATM defined, getting ATM out there, getting switches in place that some say work. The downside is a lot of hype. I refer to ATM as hype-intensive networking, otherwise known as a "data link with an attitude."[*]

I was just last month at Washington State University, talking with John Turner, who has developed a set of chips for running ATM at 1.2 and 2.4 gigabit. He wanted to sell his chips to my company and asked, "Would you please develop switches that use these chips and make really fast routers?" That sounded like a good idea. I wanted to talk with him a little bit further about that. I said, "Now, what happens when I put three of these in a box and a whole lot of traffic

---

[*] See the session "Global and Long Term Impact of ATM" for more information about this topic.

comes in from *A* and *B* and is trying to go out to *C*? What kind of buffering do you support?" He said, "Well, at these speeds, we know that queues don't form, so I know that 256 cells is all that I need." I shook my head and walked out of the room.

The ATM have pushed this myth that you don't form queues at that rate. I say that you develop deeper ones, if anything. The quality of services [QOS] that ATM has built its reputation on, just aren't there. The emperor's got no clothes.

In version 2 of the signalling protocol, which is what is primarily deployed now, there are some very basic things that are not fully implemented by the switches. The switches are just now thinking about round-robin by virtual channel. That is defined in version 3 of the protocol, which was agreed on last year and is in development by most of the vendors. And the vendors have already figured out that there's something more to do after that, so they're busily building version 4. Well, gee, if what we've got out there is version 2 and we're just starting to think about deploying version 3, why are we even defining version 4? Maybe we should just get that out there. So the processes there haven't worked as well as we'd have liked.

You'll note that until now I haven't mentioned ISO and ITU. It's not because I think they're irrelevant. It's because they have their place. And although in the past there has been a great deal of animosity between the IETF and the ISO and the ITU, that's largely a thing of the past. I don't see anybody running out saying we have to implement TP4 in the near future. But they have their place, and we can at least talk with them now and iron out issues, which is fine.

As we think about standards and standards processes what we really want to emphasize is *innovation*. We want to make sure that people have a way to go out and build marketplaces, solve problems, and agree to implement something, and agree that something else shouldn't be implemented because it doesn't work. We need to involve people from vendor communities, from research and users. We need all of those inputs,

because all of those people have problems that need to be solved.

We need to emphasize *open involvement*. And by open involvement, I don't mean publishing the document and I don't mean making it nonproprietary. What I mean is, everybody being able to make a comment and to have that result in a change to the specification. And that must include all of the people I've just mentioned.

We need to emphasize *prototype development*—my pet peeve with Microsoft and Sun. That's not something that we can just say and make it so. That's something that each of us needs to be involved in, to take an active part in making it work. That, by the way, is the reason I'm doing the job that I do, because I see the need to come together and make it work. So it's really up to all of us.

Questions & Answers

Q: *What does Netscape's dominance in web standard development portend for the future of the software industry? Is it just a fact of today's competitive marketplace that they'll have their moment in the sun and then someone else can come along and unseat them?*

SIRBU: I think there are a number of lessons that we can draw from Netscape. Standards have the property that installed base is very important. Imagine, for example, we go back 15 years when Beta and VHS are competing for market share. And you're trying to decide whether you should buy a Beta system or a VHS system. So you say, "Well, there are a few more people with VHS, so it will be a little bit easier to rent videos and trade tapes with my friends. I guess I'll choose VHS as well." And after a number of people have made that decision, suddenly VHS has 90 percent of the users. There's a rapid tipping phenomenon that happens with standards, where the larger the installed base, the more attractive the technology and the more reinforcement you get.

It's very difficult to unseat that dominance of a particular technology. Notice, I'm talking about a dominance of a technology, not about a firm.

The way that is unseated can be with a technology that is applied in a very different area and grows to be significant. Now you have two competing powerful technologies, and it's not clear if one will emerge or some synthesis will emerge.

So we've seen the growth in the Internet of a whole group of firms different than those who dominated telecommunications equipment and standards. People who make telephone switches are not the same people who make Internet routers. And we've had a whole new group of companies come up around a different technology. But now that it's so big, and people are talking about carrying telephony over the Internet, the switch manufacturers like Northern and Lucent Technologies are concerned. It will be interesting to see what the conflict of some rather large firms will yield.

In the case of Netscape, they came in in a vacuum and rapidly gained market share. They understand the importance of gaining market share—giving it away for free in order to get that installed base. Very well understood. (Probably first made clear by Apple with the Macintosh.)

So these dynamic effects of creating a rapidly installed base, and finding an area where there's an untapped market—where you're not displacing somebody so much as creating a new appearance—these are all ways to get your day in the sun. But the long term is much more uncertain. In the very case of Netscape, I'm wondering what's going to happen after three or four years of Microsoft giving away Internet Explorer with every copy of Windows 95, what effect that's going to have on the relative dominance of Netscape and Microsoft. So the story's not all told yet.

KAHIN: It's worth pointing out that the strategy of giving it away to gain market share is a lot easier to implement in software than in hardware.

Q: *When we're talking about giving products away, I'm wondering if there's a distinction between giving it away on the user side and giving it away on the manufacturer's side. I thought giving it away meant on the individual user's side. Otherwise, where's the economic benefit?*

KAHIN: My understanding was both sides.

Q: *How are they going to make money?*

SIRBU: I'm not sure. They may make money from the "halo effect," from people saying "Sun is a really top flight firm." Or they may make money from the effect of, "we're going to have better tools for writing Java programs." So if we've given away the technology for running them, to both software vendors and box vendors, then we'll make money with the tools for creating the programs that run in Java.

KAHIN: Even if you do pursue that strategy of giving it away on the manufacturing side, there are still some ways to maintain a competitive advantage. For example, you can still maintain control of the standard, even if you're licensing the software for free. You have the knowledge inside your company of where that standard is going. So that gives you some lead time in the products that build on that standard, that other companies don't have.

BAKER: Another thing. Imagine just for fun that Sun was to put a Java interpreter in microcode. So a Sun workstation would now become the very box to run Java on. They can make money on hardware.

KAHIN: There's an advantage to companies that appear to give away more than they actually are. Think of the Lotus case. Lotus did not go around telling users, back in the early '50s, that "We're going to lock you into this interface." That didn't come out until they started suing the clones, and finally Borland. Right? You don't make your intentions clear. And that's part of the business strategy.

Q: *Will the IETF have more and more difficulty dealing with proprietary standards?*

BAKER: The reality is that all vendors have what we call "value adds." They're the reason you buy my box as opposed to his box. This has always been true. What the standards cover is how the boxes talk to each other. But what I do within my box to make that run better can really improve the behavior of it and provide you with a feature that you otherwise might not get.

Let me give you an example. In the IETF, we have PPP. In the IEEE [Institute of Electrical and Electronics Engineering] community, we've defined the way one speaks on an Ethernet. And in the ANSI [American National Standards Institute] community, we've described the way one speaks on a FIDI. But none of those have dealt very much with queuing. Well, there are things that the router can do that will make life very bad for *n* stations talking across an Internet. And there are things that the router can do with queuing that will make life very good for those stations, that can make the network much more predictable. If I put some kind of fair queuing algorithm in my box, which is not in somebody else's box, your network is more predictable; therefore you will run my software as opposed to his software.

Value-adds have always been a part of being a vendor. But the standards cover how we talk to each other—what Marvin called "peer-to-peer" standards.

SIRBU: What you actually see is, the standards bodies will define a set of standards like this. Vendor A will build a box that does this. Vendor B will build a box that does this. This is where they really talk to each other using the standard. There may be an area where they talk to each other outside of the standard. And there will also be lots of value added, as Fred was saying, of functions that only vendor B has or only vendor A has, which they're trying to use to increase sales of their particular system. Part of the job of the standards is to continually try and enlarge this, and enlarge the overlap area of commonality.

BAKER: I don't see any reason to believe that. The way the standards processes have worked in telephony and television is a vendor-driven model, where the vendors get together and say, "These are the products that I know how to build." So

they define some way to make radio stations talk with radios or TVs or whatever, and do that all on a very vendor-driven model.

Now, the standards that relate directly to running telephony over the Internet (telephony being not limited to voice but to video and other things as well), have specifically come out of the research community. They're related to defining formats for carrying compressed voice and compressed video on the Net. Standards for defining what kinds of queuing services we're talking about—not defining the queuing algorithm but defining its behavior—so that we can select among different vendors' algorithms and get a consistent behavior. Reserving resources based on that, it's really with some beating from the vendors on the research community that it's even coming out of the IETF. I don't see any reason to believe that we need the same standards model in order to achieve a result.

SIRBU: I think there will be some convergence, but it results largely from the growth in the scale and commercial importance of the Internet. Some of the features of the way telecom standards are developed are a result of the size of that industry and the power of various players. What's particularly interesting if you look at telecommunications standards is the interplay between the service providers, who are the buyers of equipment, and the manufacturers (like Lucent and Northern and Digital Switch), who are the vendors of equipment. It is a process that was very much driven by the service providers. They, after all, are paying the bills to the equipment manufacturers, and they have a lot of say over what gets developed.

There's been lots of talk about a shakeout in the Internet services provider industry, that the small mom and pop ISPs [Internet Service Providers] are going to disappear in favor of a number of national or potentially even international providers, such as AT&T or MCI. When that happens, the power of those service providers to demand certain kinds of capabilities from the equipment vendors will be substantially increased. And it will begin to more resemble the kinds of dialogue we see between the carriers and the equipment providers in the telecommunications industry.

About the Speakers

BRIAN KAHIN directs the Information Infrastructure Project in the Science, Technology and Public Policy Program at the Kennedy School. He is also General Counsel for the Interactive Multimedia Association. He is the Editor of *Building Information Infrastructure* (McGraw-Hill, 1992) and co-editor of *Public Access to the Internet* (with James Keller; MIT Press, 1995); *Standards Development and Information Infrastructure* (with Janet Abbate; MIT Press, 1995); *National Information Infrastructure Initiatives* (with Ernest Wilson; MIT Press, 1996); and *Borders in Cyberspace* (with Charles Nesson; MIT Press, 1997). Mr. Kahin serves on the U.S. Advisory Committee on International Communications and Information Policy.

FRED BAKER has worked in the telecommunications industry since 1978, building statistical multiplexors, terminal servers, bridges, and routers. At Cisco Systems, where he is a Senior Software Engineer, his primary interest area is the manage-

ment of congestion for best effort and real-time traffic. He contributes to both ITU and IETF standards, and to such industry consortia as WIN-SOCK II and the ATM Forum. In the IETF, he has contributed to Network Management, Routing, PPP and Frame Relay, the Integrated Services architecture, and the RSVP congestion management protocol. He currently serves as the IETF Chair, as well as a technical contributor.

MARVIN SIRBU holds a joint appointment as Professor in Engineering and Public Policy, the Graduate School of Industrial Administration, and Electrical and Computer Engineering at Carnegie Mellon University. Professor Sirbu's interests are in telecommunications and information technology, policy, and economics. In 1989 he founded the Information Networking Institute at CMU, which is concerned with interdisciplinary research and education at the intersection of telecommunications, computing, business, and policy studies. Recent research activities have focused on electronic commerce, the economics of electronic publishing, compatibility standards in communications and computers, pricing of new telecommunications services, and new technologies for the local loop.

HARVARD NEWS

CONFERENCE ON THE INTERNET AND SOCIETY

May 29-31, 1996   Cambridge, MA

Fear of Institutional Control Haunts Discussions

By Ken Gewertz

The image of Victor Frankenstein wringing his hands in anguish as the monster he created wreaks havoc through the countryside haunts discussions about institutional control of the Internet.

To some, the villagers with their torches and pitchforks seem to provide the answer, if only they could get organized and agree on what they want to do. To others, it is the fearsome and unconquerable monster that holds the greatest promise, provided it can learn to regulate its own behavior.

All would agree, however, that the birth of the Internet is an explosive and unprecedented event of uncertain outcome having more in common with Mary Shelley's mythic fantasy than with most technological innovations of the past.

Even Jeffrey Rayport, moderator of a panel discussion, "Institutional Structure for the Internet: Who Will Control It?" is the first to admit that the question is essentially a rhetorical one. "Obviously, no one entity will exercise control over this vast, decentralized electronic network, but as the Internet grows larger and assumes greater importance to businesses, as well as to non-profits, government, and others, there will be an increasing demand for standardization, if not regulation in the traditional sense."

Panelist Mike O'Dell, Vice President and Chief Scientist for UUNET Technologies, Inc., a major Internet access provider, said in a phone interview last week that what would-be regulators must remember is that the Internet was originally designed for maximum survivability, and that this quality implies an inherent resistance to control.

"Remember that the whole point of this technology is that it borders on being a living thing. It's self-organizing, it's adaptive, it recovers from failures, and it heals itself. I don't think it can be stopped in any fundamental way, so the question is, how much are you going to be able to mold evolution?"

O'Dell sees the Internet as an explosive technological revolution and worries that there are some fundamental limits to what one can manage.

"There certainly are some infrastructure issues that we could do better, and I think there are some proposals around for proceeding on that and making all that better, but most of them consist of surprisingly simple solutions," he said.

As for the larger, more open-ended control issues, "Competition, market forces—that's the most effective large-scale manager. Let nature take its course, which is what it's going to do anyway. The question is, do you want to stand in front of the train or not? It's your choice."

Tony Rutkowski, Vice President for Internet Business Development at General Magic, Inc., sympathizes more with the villagers' need to exert some control over the monster.

"With the Internet's newfound importance as both a multibillion dollar market and as Global Information Infrastructure, there is a need for responsible bodies with the constituencies, skills, and processes to deal with emerging issues and controversies," he said.

For the most part, Rutkowski added, institutions are being created to meet these emerging needs, and old ones are evolving. "These emerging institutions include standards organizations like the WWW or Intelligent Agents Consortium, as well as bodies to deal with public policy and legal matters like the Internet Law and Policy Forum. There is, however, an emerging controversy concerning the transition of control of basic Internet administrative functions."

Recounting the Internet's history, Rutkowski points out that because of its beginnings as a DARPA (Defense Advanced Research Projects Agency) research project, every significant aspect of the Internet's deployment and use was decided by those with the authority within the project.

But even as the Internet grew and evolved into a major market and morphed as an underpinning to the World Wide Web, some remaining control was maintained over such areas as top-level domain naming practices and administration, overall global IP address allocations, Western Hemisphere registrations, and IETF standards activity administration.

"The question now arises as to how this status quo control should be transformed into a stable, ongoing international administrative regime for the Internet, and what that regime should be like."

Rutkowski's recommendation is that the transition process be accomplished openly, that it should be accessible to all affected parties, and that it should meet all business, legal, and public policy requirements appropriate for a global information infrastructure. He suggests that a viable solution may lie in fashioning a World Internet Alliance as a global organization of Internet organizations.

"But the ultimate answer on the control issue is that highly heterogeneous, distributed, and autonomous global environments are inherently difficult to deal with, and probably represents a new species of Global Commons," he added.

Public Policy
May 31, 1996

Institutional Structure for the Internet
Who Will Control It?

MODERATOR: Jeffrey F. Rayport
PANELISTS: Paul Callahan
Mike O'Dell
Tony Rutkowski

RAYPORT: We have a very interesting and very exciting panel to share with you this morning. We are looking at an issue that is obviously on many people's minds: If the Internet is the kind of viable and robust commercial space and space for political and social interactions, what kind of order and what kind of governance, if any, will be suitable to the Internet space? And where will that governance or imposition of order come from, if it is to come from anywhere? This involves a whole variety of questions, which I know that my colleagues here are going to address. One of those questions is, is there an Internet *per se*, or are there, in fact, many Internets? We also hear people in corporate life talk as often about Intranets as they talk about Internets.

This governance issue rather centrally involves the following questions:

• Assignment of domain names.

• Security encryption.

• The form digital money may take.

• Governance and public policy issues in general.

• The whole realm of public policy with which this particular track of the "Internet and Society" conference is concerned.

Let me introduce the panelists starting with **TONY RUTKOWSKI**, who joins us from General Magic Cor-

poration. Next is **MIKE O'DELL**, Chief Scientist at UUNET, the largest of the Internet access providers in this country. And **PAUL CALLAHAN** comes to use from Forrester Research. I'll give you more detail about these speakers in a moment. But we have, I think, an exciting opportunity here—with some rather radically contrasting views about what is possible in this Internet space.

I spent a little bit of time wandering around the Web last night, trying to see whether anyone had much to say about all this. And one of the issues that seems to be on everyone's mind these days is, of course, protection of our computing environments, protection not only from hackers but from viruses that may run amuck throughout our systems, few of which are standalone any more. I was stunned to find that a whole rash of viruses related to public policy are, in fact, traveling across the Internet. I don't know if you are all aware of this fact, but we are facing a veritable epidemic.

One of these viruses was described as the "government economist virus," and apparently can be characterized as "nothing works, but all your diagnostic software says everything is fine." There is another one that is referred to as the "federal bureaucrat virus." It apparently divides your hard disk into hundreds of little units, each of which does practically nothing, but all of which claim to be the most important part of your computer. My personal favorite was the "Congressional virus." Apparently, you'll know it because your computer screen locks up, and the screen splits erratically, with a message appearing on each half blaming the other side for the problem. And this just goes on and on. The other Congressional virus we've seen runs every program on the hard drive simultaneously, but doesn't allow the user to accomplish anything. And then, of course, there's one that's grown up in Boston, the "Paul Revere virus." It warns you of impending hard disk errors: one if by LAN, two if by C-prompt. But my absolute favorite and the last one here is simply the "Elvis virus." Apparently, your PC will get fat, slow, and lazy. It will then self-destruct only to resurface at shopping malls and service stations across rural America! This is what I learned on the World Wide Web last night.

Let me now ask Tony Rutkowski to share his views about how the Elvis virus and other problems will be handled. Tony has had a rather extraordinary career involving the Federal Communications Commission, the Internet Society, Sprint. He spent some time in local municipal politics as a councilman, and is known as one of the real gurus in terms of ruling life on the Internet. Tony?

RUTKOWSKI: One of the real perennial problems at the outset is, what is the Internet, or Intranets, or for that matter, everything else associated with it? I think the fundamental point is that these are all abstractions, actually. They're highly distributed, they're bottom-up, they're heterogeneous. I've got a class C network that I run in my house. A number of parts of the Internet literally are in different people's rooms in our house. We've got a web server. All of these things are part of the Internet. So one has to intrinsically ask at the outset, "Just what kind of potential governance—if we can even speak in those terms—could one use for what is really a very ubiquitous, almost fractal-like infrastructure?"

On the other hand, I'd like to point out that there's really a number of components—I like to call them institutional components—that have been associated with the Internet for many years, that in part have enabled this. I like to divide them conveniently into business, governmental, administrative, standards, and professional.

On the business side, business has been involved in the Internet in one way or another almost from the outset. There have been norms in groups that have been put together by institutional homes within the business community. I'm fond of pointing out that when the technology emerged from the DARPA [Defense Advanced Research Projects Agency] environment circa the mid '80s, almost immediately it began to be used in what are now called "Intranets." A lot of this began to be discussed and introduced, and the whole paradigm moved along in the context of InterOp[erability]. It didn't take very long before

Internet service providers began going after that market, building their own backbones. In fact, UUNET here is actually one of the very first, if not *the* first, to have done that. A variety of industry groups have arisen to deal with industry-related problems: the Commercial Internet Exchange Association in the early '90s, and in the last year, the Internet Law and Policy Forum.

On the governmental side, there are a couple of different tracks. One that is often overlooked is the fact that the FCC [Federal Communications Commission] and the ITU [International Telecommunications Union] actually laid the framework in many respects for the Internet to emerge. They said this was really not a space in which government should play any kind of a regulatory or significant hands-on role; that it should just, for the most part, enable Internet and Internet-like things to happen. And that's by and large the regime we have now, pretty much worldwide.

On the DARPA side, of course, DARPA and the science agencies and their counterparts around the world like CERN [Conseil Européen pour la Recherche Nucléaire], which gave birth to the World Wide Web, were all government initiatives or institutions that caused the Internet to happen.

On the administrative side today, we still have DARPA and the Federal Networking Council playing fairly heavy hands-on roles, in terms of continuing to fund some of these activities. And a lot of the dialogue that will probably be followed here, that you'll see percolating up to a policy over the next year, has to do with how you transition out of that environment.

On the standards side, again, there was originally the DARPA-supported IETF [Internet Engineering Task Force]. What's happened, remarkably, in just the last couple of years of maturation—and because the Internet is this foundation for so many applications and specialized standards groups—you've got the World Wide Web Consortium [W3C], which is actually based at both MIT and CERN in France. You also have an Internet Mail Consortium, and just a whole variety of different industry-led consortia groups.

On the professional side, you've had the ACM [Association for Computing Machinery]; the Electronic Frontier Foundation [EFF]; the Internet Society; the Center for Democracy and Technology; the World Wide Web Society—all groups for individuals. So this is really a grouping and a timeline associated with all the institutional infrastructure associated with the Internet.

(Perhaps this is a little bit too detailed, but I've actually broken up and characterized each of those groups. This is actually on the World Wide Web, if you go to *http://www.wia.org/*. There's a section at the bottom that's a pointer to this list, which then allows you to use the URLs, so you can go to any one of these organizations. I've included all the industry organizations, governmental, administrative organizations, and standards organizations in that kind of order, so they're all fleshed out.)

I'd like to just touch on what we want to accomplish here, which might be a point of departure and certainly a thread through subsequent presentations and discussions. I would argue that we want to maintain the Internet, Intranets, World Wide Web, etc., as open, global, competitive platforms for development, growth, and use. That's a norm, if you will, that I think everyone could agree to; whatever we do, we should encourage this.

The second point is to allow innovations and new markets to be easily and effectively introduced, which seems to be one of the things the Internet as a platform is remarkably suited to. I spent half my life out in Silicon Valley, and it is absolutely unbelievable how, almost every day, there's a half a dozen new startups producing some new product or component for the Internet or World Wide Web.

And last, I think we want to encourage industry-driven rather than government-driven institutions and solutions to perceived needs and problems. I think, if we can do that, we'll probably have something that not only comports well with this kind of fractal communications medium we've created, but that will allow it to remain highly dynamic. Thank you very much.

RAYPORT: Tony, thank you for your comments.

We are now going to turn to Mike O'Dell, who, as Tony mentioned, has been part of a firm that has been one of the real leaders in providing Internet access, and more recently, commercial Internet access. Therefore, Mike is an ideal person to start telling us about the governance issue from the technology infrastructure point of view. He is Chief Scientist at UUNET. Prior to that, he was at Bellcore for a number of years. He began messing around with Internet protocol networks as early as 1981, when I think he built his first one right in his own home, long before many of us were concerned about this platform.

O'DELL: Thank you. I'm going to give you a somewhat focused view, based on the issues as seen from the trenches, because I wake up and go to bed worrying about keeping it all working. There are a couple of ideas that are central to understanding how this all works, and why it keeps working.

In the spirit of recycling, now that the Cold War is over, we have a new home for the phrase "mutually assured destruction." The Internet is the world's largest—I add the word "constructive"—collaborative effort. (You could describe wars as collaborative, but they're not very interesting from that standpoint.) In some sense, all great works are collaborative. It's a group of people that decide to work together in one way or another. And while the folks from the Harvard Law School might take issue with this, a contract is really a record of an agreement to cooperate so that you can remind each other that you agreed to be nice about something at some point. In some sense, you can't force people to succeed; you can merely try to convince them that it's in their interest.

All the large Internet operators understand one important notion, which is central to this "mutually assured destruction" idea, and it's that our customers pay for global connectivity. They don't pay to talk to just our customers, they pay to talk to everyone who's out there. I think Metcalf's Law is one of the most succinct descriptions of what's going on here: The value of a network parallels the square of the population served. While you can argue about tinkering with the polynomial, I think it certainly captures the spirit of what's going on. Once you realize that, the corollary is that the off-Net traffic for any large network is one minus market share. If one is 100 percent of all the networks on the Internet, and you have a certain percent of market share, then basically, the assumption is that most of the destinations people want to reach are, in fact, somewhere else. So the off-Net traffic is one minus market share. What that means is, nobody can own enough of it to exercise any sort of bizarre control thing. So you're really forced to cooperate in some very fundamental ways, because everyone's customers are paying them to talk to everyone else's customers. This gets back to customers and what they're paying you for.

I also point out that there is no global PTT [Postal, Telegraph, and Telephone]* required to make the phone system work. Basically, everybody realized that it was in their best interest to reach some consensus about how to make this thing interoperate. And that's why you can basically make phone calls from lots of places. The same kinds of things operate in the context of the Internet. This thinking is central to the engineering and planning that goes on in large operators.

But again, in a lot of the discussions I hear, people say, "Well, what if somebody does something really bizarre?" If someone does something sufficiently bizarre, like tries to isolate their customers to just their network, they will quickly wither and die because that's not what people pay you for. AlterNet customers do not pay to talk to other AlterNet customers. They expect to do that, but that's only a very small piece of a very large Ven diagram.

I'm fixated on the title a little bit, which is this notion of control. And I think the interesting question gets down to, do you want control or do you want leadership? Do you want control or do you want stewardship? That's an interesting idea.

There are some intellectual resources you have to worry about—the DNS [Domain Name System] name space being one, and the IP [Internet protocol] V4 address space being another. In terms of thinking about this, I would recommend that people use the force link. The technology we've invented is largely self-organizing. That's why it is so incredibly powerful. It's because it exhibits all the self-preservation instincts of a living organism. It finds its friends, they find each other, and suddenly you have connectivity. That's why you can build these Internet things out of amazingly simple pieces that work.

What's important down here at the bottom is, currently we have humans doing resource allocation for computers, in the form of these registries. And when you think of it in those terms, it's just got to be wrong. So we have to fix that. The registries have to go away. There are some technical solutions, at least a couple of things on the table to allow distributed DNS registration, where we can have multiple registrars without having to chop up the name space at the TLDs [Top Level Domains]. The root's name servers—that's a leadership issue. If all the large operators will have to run one, fine; it's self-interest. Something else that I've been spending a tremendous amount of time worrying about lately, in terms of IPV6, is basically how to tweak things so that the address space becomes self-organizing. The notion of having to do something silly like hand out tokens to number networks, that's just wrong. Because again, you have a human doing the bookkeeping for a computer, and that's a recipe for down-scaling. So that's an important thing I'm working on there.

Some of the other problems, however, are not technical. They do reflect an inability of the non-technical infrastructure to cope with the change, although the current track seems to be toward less regulation, rather than more. A good example is the trademark I-prop issue domain name. Is a domain name a trademark thing? Well, we didn't cause the problem. It's been there all

---

* This is often used to refer to a monopolistic telephone service provider outside the U.S.

along. The Internet is just a catalyst. What we did that basically brought this to the fore is, we created the first truly global name space, where the collisions were inevitable. The traditional notion in trademark law is that if the business areas are sufficiently distinct, then you won't run into each other and it won't matter. Well, we committed the horrible sin of basically flattening that. And now you basically can't pretend it will go away. And whether this is national or across international boundaries doesn't matter: the name space is global.

The technologist can't solve it because it's not a technical problem. And besides, our arms are too short to box with God. I think the real job here is for the policy mechanics in concert with the technologists, so we can have something that produces running code. This is a reference to Dave Clark's credo of, "We don't believe things presidents are voting; we believe in rough consensus and running code." But the collaboration is real important here, because lots of people can imagine things that can't be implemented. So it's critical to have the implementers involved.

This is an important notion: Control does not imply good stewardship. Just because you're in control doesn't mean you'll do a good job. Control does not require trust. Trust cannot be demanded. Leadership can earn trust. Good leadership *will* earn the trust. And the consent of the governed can grant stewardship. And in some sense, the long history of the IETF has been leading by example. Basically, the one who shows up with running code and has real experience is the one whose opinion counts, simply because he has something to base it on. It's easy to make things that work on the whiteboard, but then when you put the bits in the box, you have a very humbling experience.

The last piece is that leadership has obligations and responsibilities: to protect the shared achievements, to promote the continuing achievements, to contribute directly and generously. That means running root name servers, running large name servers. (The name cache at UUNET—I guess we have about 17,000 zones at this point, secondary for all kinds of folks.) And to be a good stew-

ard. This sort of moral imperative is not very popular these days, in a bottom line-driven world. But at the end of the day, when you realize that since it is a collaborative effort, and you must keep the trust of the people you're involved with, I don't think there's an option.

RAYPORT: Mike, thank you very much. We are clearly moving into some issues that we're going to need to debate as a group in a few minutes. Is any kind of command-and-control approach suitable or even possible in an environment or space like the Internet? Is power and influence, in the form of leadership and stewardship (as Mike suggested), the model that is likely to emerge as the only viable model, as well as perhaps the only dominant model? And what role will enlightened self-interest (as the economists like to call it) play?

I think our next speaker, Paul Callahan, has some pretty strong points of view about that. Paul is the Senior Analyst at Forrester Research, which many of you know as the blue chip provider of information about Internet and electronic commerce businesses in the country right now. Paul is somebody I've known for a good while. I think only two and a half years ago, Paul was trying to convince his colleagues at Forrester that, in fact, the Internet was an area of commercial activity worth writing about. They, of course, thought he was absolutely out of his mind. A few of us sympathized with him. And now, I guess poetic justice has come home to roost, to mix several metaphors inelegantly. (But I think we can do that: I'm from the Business School!)

Paul, like many people in the businesses related to this new field, has had a fascinating career. Much of his expertise in Internet issues stems from the fact that he had an early career as a commercial fisherman off the coast of New England. Paul, your thoughts about the Internet.

CALLAHAN: Thanks, Jeffrey. So who will control it? I figured the important thing to do here with this question, since the entire panel was going to be asked to answer it, was to answer it at least once. My feeling is in fact that no one should control it. I do agree, I guess, with Mike [O'Dell], that there's an issue around stewardship here. And in my opinion, this is very much a free market situation. We are a long, long way past the origins of the Internet with government involvement. The way Internets (plural) are constructed worldwide has very little to do with government agencies.

I'm going to talk a little bit about how these things are constructed. For those of you who think of the telephone network as an extremely reliable worldwide network, you might want to think about how it is governed. Probably the most important governing feature of this telephone network is the management of phone numbers. And one of the biggest issues coming up around the Internet going forward, as Mike alluded to, was the management of domain name—the DNS space—as well as the IPV4 (version 4) address space. Our belief is that critical to the growth of the Internet is the adoption of what has been known as IPng, IP next generation, now known as IP version 6 or IPV6. We think that the Internet will fall flat on its face without IPV6, not because corporate users will need it, but because the carriers will need it, because companies like UUNET will need it.

Now, let me also drill into some of these issues, because there are a number of myths around the Internet, the first of which is that it is one network. It is *not* one network, not any more than the worldwide telephone network is one network. In fact, there's a site that you should take a look at on a daily or weekly basis, called The List [*http://thelist.com*]. The last time I checked this, three months ago, there were not 2,712 Internet service providers worldwide; there were only 1,895. And when I checked this in November of 1995, there were only 1,480. So you can see that there is not one Internet, though many of these people, many of these concerns, many of these companies are resellers of other people's Internet services, like UUNET or Sprint, for example, which is a huge reseller. They are nevertheless Internets. So that's the first myth.

The second myth is that the Internet, as it was in the beginning, is just a bunch of routers hung together with leased lines. Nothing could be further from the truth. Let's take a look, in fact, at how UUNET and many other service providers build their network. Routers are part of the network, but in fact, the management core of all these Internets is, in fact, switched. It is high performance switches, either ATM [Asynchronous Transfer Mode] or frame relay switches or a combination of both. Routers are, in fact, performing a peripheral function, because you can't manage circuits with a router. You can't trace calls with a router. You can't really manage a network of the scale of these Internets with routers. You need switches, either virtual circuits or circuits. So you're going to find that as these Internets are built going forward, they are managed and operated with traditional telecom equipment.

I'd like to discuss what a typical POP, a typical Point of Presence, looks like at UUNET, at PSI, and at Netcom, because they all use basically the same architectures. There are T1 lines coming in from the customer, aggregated at a cascade 9000 switch, shunted up to a CISCO 7000 at 45 megabits, back down again to another switch, and then out to the core switching fabric of the network, operating at 45 megabits nationwide. The router is doing what it does best, which is looking at policy issues, not managing circuits.

In addition, the way these Internets are interconnected is changing. Right now, one of the ways that Internets—these almost 3,000 Internets—are interconnected is through these points that you see named here in the U.S. And these are very hefty interconnection points using LAN technology; using, in fact, switched FDDI [Fiber Distributed Data Interface], uncontested 100 megabit straight pipe to each one of the providers.

But even this is going away, because even this is not enough. This kind of multilateral interconnection ensures that you can get anywhere in the network. But what if you have hefty traffic? What if you're Sprint and you have a hell of a lot of traffic between you and MCI? What do you do? You set up bilateral connections, which are the way the Internet is going to evolve. Instead of these interconnection points (which are useful for ubiquity), you're going to see a lot of direct linkages from carrier to carrier on an as-needed basis for bandwidth. So what is going to happen to the Internet as it evolves technically is, it's going to be a very large, high bandwidth, mesh network.

Now, who is going to regulate this mesh network? Who is going to tell Sprint they cannot connect directly to MCI at any speed they want? Nobody. That is the way the network is going to evolve. And that is a very healthy growth phenomenon, in my opinion.

So the answer, I believe, is that no one should regulate this network. And I hope that we get some lively discussion out of this.

Questions & Answers

Q: *Who in fact funds the existing Internet today? If there are capacity problems, who will build out the capacity? And if the Internet is the existing backbone of all of the commercial and social and political activity we've been talking about at this conference, how do we know it's going to be there in the future?*

CALLAHAN: I think that, for the first time in many years in the networking business, I'm seeing the business side of the house driving the need for the Internet. It's not technology for whiz bang technology's sake. Let me give you an example.

When a company like Millipore, that has 40 divisions worldwide, decides that their strategy is going to be to connect any employee with any partner or customer, any way they want, the reason they are choosing that philosophy is basically because they believe, if they can connect to their business partners easier and quicker than anybody else, they're going to lock them in, and they're going to prevent other people from partnering with them. They're going to prevent other people, because their partners are going to say, "Millipore is so great to work with, it's so easy to work with their people, inside their network and at the edge of it, that I couldn't possibly give up that relationship." And the only way you're going to accomplish that is with the Internet. So there is the business side of the house, beating on MIS to get them connected to their partners.

Q: *Who's going to guarantee that the routers, the switches, the backbones, the fundamental fabric of the Internet is still going to be out there? Who's paying for this? Who guarantees its future?*

O'DELL: Who guarantees the future of any public infrastructure? By and large, that answer is increasingly, "No one." It's certainly not true with the telephone network. It's not true with broadcasting networks.

Q: *There are PTTs that run this kind of infrastructure in every other country in the world. Why are we assuming that the commercial sector is going to guarantee its viability in the U.S.?*

O'DELL: The answer, I think, is straightforward. I spend a lot of my time talking to those PTTs, because they want to talk to us. And the reason they talk to us is real simple: we're profitable, and they aren't. More and more, the folks where they live are getting tired of paying them to not do a very good job. And the message is going out that you will, in fact, figure out some way to have a clue.

So my customers pay for it. And they keep paying me for it. And we keep raising the bar on what we have to deliver. As long as they keep paying, it will still be there. That's straightforward. That's how any business survives. Nobody has a divine right to succeed.

CALLAHAN: You know, you raise a very interesting point, that this is generally telecom deregulation-focused. But if you look back, six years ago, if you laid down a pipe, your own fiber optic cable between two buildings in Australia—let's say the two buildings were 50 feet apart—you had to pay Telecom Australia for the use of the cable that you put in the ground, on a monthly basis. That's no more. Telecom Australia now has competition. Things are changing worldwide. And if you look at this from a security point of view, if you look at holdouts like Singapore and France, and their attitudes toward security (secure transactions or encryption crossing their border) that's only going to hurt them in the long run. They're going to have to realize the implications of that and live with them.

RUTKOWSKI: I'd point out that half the Internet infrastructure is actually outside the United States. And with very few exceptions, that's essentially privately owned, or at worst, research and academic institution owned and operated infrastructure. So the paradigm still persists around the world, basically, to have a sort of bottom-up, private sector-driven Internet.

The other factor that's worth pointing out is that 112 nations plus in the GATT accord now, under WTO, basically committed themselves that this should be an open, competitive environment, the whole realm of enhanced networks, of which the Internet infrastructure is a part. So there is not only the *de facto* that's the way it is today, but in terms of where it is likely to go in the future, there is a commitment that can be built upon, that assures that it will not be a closed, monopolistic environment in countries around the world.

Q: *But who has built this thing? Who's paid for the switches? Who's paid for the trunk lines? Who's paid for the routers? (We all know it came to exist with the 1965 DARPA involvement, but who's building this thing today? And why is it still there, even though government has stepped out of the equation?)*

O'DELL: Well, like I say, my stockholders and our customers build my piece. Sprint and MCI both made major, major capital investments in their infrastructure. UUNET was the first commercial Internet operator. And that was all funded, frankly, from money that we got from the UUCP service.

CALLAHAN: MFS Datanet just paid a considerable sum of money for the infrastructure that UUNET built. The routers, switches, and leased lines that they put together to build this network. They weren't on drugs. This is a viable business. And I'm sure that MFS, if you dig really deep into their strategy, will admit that this is their future. And every other carrier in this business sees this as their future, as well.

Let me tell you another story about making money. One of the tiny, tiny little Internets that's out there today is a place called Cape Internet. I called them on the phone one day, just to see who was there and what they were all about. I talked to some guy in his kitchen, who started this Internet service provider, and I asked him to tell me his story." He said, "Well, I started with one modem in August, and in November I had 600 customers. It was only because the reseller I was dealing with gave up on NYNEX in trying to run lines out onto Cape Cod that I was in business. And boy, we're really happy." So obviously, this guy is making money from installing equipment and attaching himself to the Internet.

So what's the story here? This is a business. This is not a government-funded experiment any more.

RUTKOWSKI: What is the Internet? There's 100,000 plus networks, part of the Internet. There's several hundred thousand intranets. There are 10 million plus computer hosts that constitute the Internet. There's some number of N times 10 million more than are in intranets. That's reality.

Who owns that infrastructure? Well, by and large, it's people. I mean, I own a chunk in my house. There's five machines and a network that are part of the Internet, that I own. In fact, I would argue that most of the infrastructure of the Internet, in terms of what it's on, is probably on Ethernet, which that man several rows up here actually helped create. So he was part of making the Internet infrastructure happen, as well. When you look at the cost component, it's really distributed across literally millions of people and institutions.

RAYPORT: Tony, let me see if I can follow up with you. If I understand you gentlemen correctly, the position that we seem to be taking up here is that the Internet is a bunch of privately owned machines, say, 100 million personal computers that belong to individuals, something like 100,000 networks that belong to institutions (universities, large corporations), and the lines that connect them are either leased access lines that are run by PTTs and telephone operating companies, or they are lines that are run by companies like UUNET and PSI, that actually, as Paul says, make a good business out of providing that connectivity.

O'DELL: And we buy those lines from the phone company.

RAYPORT: So let's move from that to the question of, given that we've got a network that is unprecedented—unlike the interstate highway system, unlike the phone companies, unlike the networks that cable television operators run—this is one in which ownership is not centralized. It's hugely decentralized. It truly seems to be a grassroots, bottom-up environment. Does there need to be some kind of public policy, whether it's standards protocols, rules, ethics, Netiquette, etc., that should be imposed on that free market situation?

> *The Internet is very, very much like the physical world. And we keep applying a lot of nonsensical rules to it that don't match our current experience. The physical world is a dangerous place. Have you forgotten?*

RUTKOWSKI: By the way, the complexity nightmare is even much worse than that, because we've just been talking about the lower level of transport. Remember, we've got web infrastructure on top of this. We've got all kinds of server infrastructures that are even more distributed and more diffuse, that are very much part of the Internet. In fact, most people today actually deal with the World Wide Web, which is yet another abstraction layer that's very diffuse across this whole infrastructure.

RAYPORT: So part of our problem is that we're trying to define the Internet the way we defined ownership and control of conventional infrastructures before it, which have been a very different model from the one that's grown up here.

RUTKOWSKI: Right. But to get to the second part of your question, there are and will continue to be institutions that will attend to making it happen, to facilitating it, to allowing this collaboration to occur. The institutional infrastructure that exists and that needs to be perpetuated really is a collaborative infrastructure, as opposed to a governance infrastructure of any kind. And also, to some extent, I think there's a myth that somehow legal norms don't apply. Our existing laws very much apply to activities that are conducted on the Internet. So that's not going away. It's just that the whole notion of who, at the operational level, regulates this or controls this, is a broken notion.

But let me give you another example, because there are laws that apply to the network that most people don't know about. Maybe some of you remember when AT&T announced, about six months ago, that when you use their universal MasterCard or Visa card on the Internet, that they would guarantee that you could only lose $50, just like the physical world. And weren't they magnanimous for doing that? Well, you know, that was complete bunk—which is polite translation for something else. In fact, the law already covers anybody right now using a credit card on the Internet. *It is the law.* If you go and enter your MasterCard of Visa or American Express card number via the Internet, and somebody steals that number and misuses it, you are still only liable for $50. It's the law. It has nothing to do whether it's the Internet or the physical world.

I maintain that we are really, really deranged about the way we think about the Internet at this point. It is very, very much like the physical world. And we keep applying a lot of nonsensical rules to it that don't match our current experience. The physical world is a dangerous place. Have you forgotten?

Q: *Someone said that you're not going to worry about people taking control of the Internet because it just can't happen. So are the fears about a company like Microsoft taking over just people getting caught up in a hype? Or is there any substance to those kinds of fears?*

RAYPORT: What's to prevent consolidation, whether it's Bill Gates or the local phone companies? If that happens, we could see consolidation of ownership of this very free and open network.

CALLAHAN: I'd like to respond to that. One of the great things about this particular technology is that it changes some of the rules of the game. It led to the creation of a company called Netscape that is really giving Microsoft a run for its money.

The thing that really changed the game for them was the existence of the Internet, because when they sell their product (Netscape) against Microsoft, they have a product that has 90 plus percent margins, because there are no shrink-wrap boxes, no cellophane, no disks, no CDs, no manuals to stock. When they sell 100,000 copies of Navigator to GE, the bits go over the wire and they send them a bill.

So suddenly a new distribution channel has appeared, in the form of the Internet. I've sat at my desk over the past two months and downloaded six different versions of Navigator and Internet Explorer from Microsoft. And my MIS guy hasn't a clue that that happened—the vendors are going directly to the users.

So there are some changes here, and I believe that Microsoft's monopoly is being seriously challenged. It's the Internet that has allowed Netscape to do that. And I think there will be other challengers, as well.

RUTKOWSKI: One of the remarkable attributes of the Internet, too, is its ability to create new applications, new developments. So there are going to be markets for all kinds of new domains constantly opening up. In fact, you might even ask why a small software company from Silicon Valley is interested in this. It's because we focus on what we imagine—in fact, fully expect—are going to be two of the next biggest emerging marketplaces that are going to be Internet-founded: personal Internet communicators and intelligent agents on the Internet, that are going to provide platforms like the World Wide Web provides, for all kinds of new applications. I think you're going to see a constant emergence of new marketplaces: this is not a static environment.

Q: *What is the panel's reaction to the Telecommunications Act of 1996, with its decency provisions for content on the Internet? Is this a good thing or a bad thing? Or is more of this type of legislation inevitable?** *

CALLAHAN: Well, it's a social issue. It appears that that particular portion of the Telecommunications Act will be challenged in court. And it may, in fact, be struck. I'm not a legal expert by any means, but it looks to me like a mismatch, in terms of the government trying to control a situation that is technical, with social implications. But I think that pornography is a problem in the real world, in the physical world. It's again a situation of fearing the workings of the technology itself, and somehow turning things topsy-turvy.

RAYPORT: Meaning, if the First Amendment is valid in the physical world, it ought to be valid in the space of the Internet?

CALLAHAN: Yes.

RUTKOWSKI: I was one of the testifiers on the Hill on this matter. I think the Telecommunications Act was perhaps a political rather than social phenomenon. It caused things like PICS [Platform for Internet Content Selection] development activity, which was a technical response by the industry. And I think the provisions in the Act are probably not going to survive a judicial challenge.

RAYPORT: We're essentially saying that it's the free market that will continue to build out the infrastructure. We're essentially saying that principles like the First Amendment are going to regulate content rather than things like the Decency Act portion of the telecommunications legislation. What about those details like assigning domain names? Who is going to handle that, in the absence of an explicit government role?

RUTKOWSKI: I think there are some significant liability issues that are associated with that. But I think the solution ultimately ought to be an industry one, with the liability issues covered. And there

---

* The Communications Decency Act (CDA), a provision of the Telecommunications Act, was shot down by a three-judge court in June, 1996. However, on December 6, 1996, the U.S. Supreme Court agreed to hear the government's appeal for the legal challenge to the CDA. The case is expected to be heard in March, 1997. See *http://www.cdt.org/* for more details.

are pre-existing models for that even in the telecommunications industry, where for example the FCC says, you, industry alliance, actually take care of the problem, and we'll provide the cover, if you will. That's one possible solution.

There are probably other roles for government that have been played, and that will probably continued to be played, that are useful along the line of sort of a leadership role. One is getting everyone using the technology. And using it doesn't mean just passively accessing this stuff. I mean, this is technology that enables you to put up your own content. So to get people thinking creatively and innovatively, and actually publishing information on the network.

The notion of universal access is not dead. It's just different. One useful role the government can play would be to enable people who don't possess the economic means to gain access. It just needs to be done in a market-oriented way.

RAYPORT: This has been, obviously, a complicated discussion, an interplay between a complex technology infrastructure and a complex public policy problem. It's probably worth remembering that we spend a lot of time wrangling in Washington every day, trying to figure out how to deal with governance issues in the physical world. It would be a radical misconception to think that they would be any less complex in the information space of the Internet.

About the Speakers

JEFFREY F. RAYPORT is an Assistant Professor of Business Administration in the Service Management Interest Group at the Harvard Business School. His research focuses on the impact of new information technologies on service management and marketing strategies for information-based product and service firms. As a consultant, Dr. Rayport has worked with corporations in North and South America, Europe, and Japan and the Pacific Rim, on helping companies develop new product/service strategies related to information

technology deployment. His writing has appeared in a variety of publications, including *Fortune* magazine, *Harvard Business Review*, *McKinsey Quarterly*, the *Boston Globe*, and the *Los Angeles Times*.

PAUL CALLAHAN leads Forrester's research efforts in corporate Intranet and public Internet technologies. He analyzes the emerging trends in World Wide Web architectures and high-bandwidth networks for carriers and corporations. Before becoming Group Director, Paul played a major role as Director and Senior Analyst in the Network Strategy Service. While Senior Analyst, Paul developed great insight into the information technology industry's analysis of the evolution of cable TV, wireless, videoconferencing, and video-over-LAN technologies. Putting a stake in the ground that ATM, contrary to industry thinking, would remain a niche technology is just one of Paul's most influential ideas. In 1992, he was one of the first analysts in the industry to predict that Ethernet LAN switching would stymie ATM and extend the life of traditional LANs.

MIKE O'DELL is Vice President of Research and Development at UUNET Technologies, Inc., one of the national-scale IP network operators in the US. Prior to joining UUNET, he was at Bell Communications Research in Morristown, NJ. Way back in 1980, he was site liaison for ARPAnet IMP-34 at the Lawrence Berkeley Laboratory. While at LBL, he collaborated on the RAND VAX/NFE for ARPAnet NCP, did research on the real-world behavior of token rings, and ran one of the first VAXes to go production with TCP/IP even before The Great TCP Conversion. He has been kicking around the Unix world longer than he cares to contemplate. He is former Vice President of the USENIX Association and is Co-Director of the Operations Requirements Area of the IETF and the Internet Engineering Steering Group.

Currently Vice President for Internet Business Development at the leading-edge Silicon Valley mobile agent/personal communicator software developer General Magic, Inc., **TONY RUTKOWSKI** is responsible for developing the company's Internet-related business strategies, opportunities, product positioning, and Federal Systems division. Mr. Rutkowski is a highly visible and well-known global leader, official, lecturer, and author in both the Internet and telecom worlds, with a career spanning 30 years of diverse positions in the business, public, and education sectors.

NII
By Ying Chan

Citizens could become less informed as they switch from newsprint to virtual news on the Net. Instead of holding hands in the Net community, their political life could become more lonely and atomized. And while universal access to the Net is a desirable goal, it is unlikely to happen because of the heavy government subsidy required.

Amidst the hype and promises of the digital age, Richard Zeckhauser, Professor of Political Economy at the Kennedy School of Government, Harvard University, sounded these cautionary notes at a panel discussion on the role of the Internet in the country's information structure.

"We have to recognize that access to the new technology is dependent on your educational background," said Zeckhauser. "There will always be the technological elite."

Because of the cost involved, "information will be sold at a price" he said.

The television revolution has prompted more societal bonding, as when it brought the realities of the Vietnam War into every American's living room. "The Internet may lead to diminished communications with others," he said.

Flashing the *Los Angeles Times's* customized personal news page on a huge screen, Zeckhauser warned that the online format could deprive readers of the "peripheral information" they would pick up while reading a paper of atoms instead of bits.

The electronic format gives readers ten choices for the news they want. After a reader checks off a few sports and entertainment items, little room is left for news items.

Industry representatives were more upbeat.

George Conrades, President, CEO, and Chairman of the Boston-based BBN Corporation, echoed the sense of optimism shared by many at the conference: "The open protocols of the Net are giving thousands of companies, and millions of people, around the world access to the same opportunities.... and to each other."

"It is the technology itself...high speed, high bandwidth digital networks, over which we can share all kinds of information...across all kind of platforms," said Conrades. "The Internet is attracting more intellectual and financial capital than any technology in history."

If experts are still gazing into crystal balls for the future of cyberspace, they are more certain of how far Netizens have come along.

And for the technologically chosen, the future can only be better.

Howard Frank, Director of Information Technology Office, Advanced Research Projects Agency, told the hushed audience that as the Net becomes more incorporated into the country's information structure—the multifarious ways citizens receive information, the Net will become more "the average" as a technology. It will cease to be an experiment in collaborative engineering or a mechanism for rapid testing of standards. But it will continue to stimulate application development, promote application access, and facilitate information dissemination, he said.

Public Policy
May 29, 1996

The Place of the Internet in National and Global Information Infrastructure

MODERATOR: Lewis Branscomb
PANELISTS: George Conrades
Joseph Duffey
Howard Frank
Richard Zeckhauser

BRANSCOMB: It's a pleasure to moderate this session in the public policy track which looks at the Internet in the context of some much broader questions. It is indeed a little strange to have as broad a conference as this is on the subject of the Internet. There are a lot of people who, at least until 18 months ago, would entertain a serious argument about whether the Internet—which, after all, was developed as a vehicle by scientists and engineers, largely for their own use—might be considered a prototype or an experiment: one that lacks characteristics needed to sustain the backbone running the word's information activities, and therefore might be viewed as something transitory. I think that view has changed dramatically and relatively recently. But it is a fact, as Ambassador Dougan just pointed out, that there's a much bigger world of information infrastructure out there, most of which is still analog, much of which (the parts of it that are not part of the Internet) carry the biggest investments and generate the most cash. And that huge amount of leverage of capital investment, corporate interest, and consumer participation has yet to play its hand out in the evolution of the Internet.

By way of getting started, let me just put a couple of definitions of information infrastructure on the table. It's clear that national information infrastructure is a big collection of activities, public and private. It includes both content-based activities, like print publishers, record companies, and the like, as well as telecommunicators, access providers, computer companies, and so on. It already exists. It's not something we're waiting to build. Nevertheless, it is and always will be in flux.

Let me give you two quotations from *The Unpredictable Certainty*, published by the National Research Council in 1996. But I'm going to call your attention to the second of these two quotes, from Mike Roberts of Educom:

> Beware falling victim to the tendency in Washington to add coats to every available coat hook. The National Information Infrastructure cannot possibly be the sum of all our expectations for a better society, based on improved communications of electronic information. Even if someone were capable of articulating the vision of that scope, none of the rest of us would grant him or her the power to execute it. What we can have is a system of electronic communications and information resources based on computing technology.

> Despite efforts by many to promote ideological visions of what the system can do for society, the system is fundamentally amoral. Much of its development has been and will continue to be based on technological Darwinism.

Where did we hear about that?

Now, we're going to be dealing with public policy issues, so let me just make one observation about the role of the federal government before I introduce one of the more admirable specimens of people who work in our federal government. First of all, the government certainly doesn't run the Internet. As a matter of fact, if it did, you'd have to ask, who in the government is in charge? Well, the President does have a National Information Infrastructure task force. It was chaired very ably by the late Secretary of Commerce. It still exists, of course, but it was largely not a measure for running anything. It was a device for finding out what the heck was going on, because the government was into the activities of the NII all over the place, in all kinds of ways.

But ever since the little altercation we all enjoyed between Mr. Allen of AT&T and the Vice President during the transition (before the President assumed office), in which the Vice President mistakenly allowed the Information Superhighway metaphor to give him the idea that the government was going to build it (as indeed his father authored the bill causing the Feds to build the cement highways). Ever since, the Feds have played a complex and vital but largely passive role. And here are some of the dimensions.

One of the most important dimensions is, of course, the federal government's support for the research, not just the technical research (though that mostly), but also policy analysis, economic analysis, and other studies. And that research owes its origins right back to the beginning of the first glimmer of the idea of the Internet, namely the ARPAnet and the Advanced Research Projects Agency in the Department of Defense. Dr. HOWARD FRANK, our principal speaker, is Director of ARPA's Information Technology Office [ITO]. He manages a $350 million annual budget, aimed at advancing the frontiers of information technology. I can tell you that so long as ARPA and its companion agency NSF [National Science Foundation] stay out in front of the industry—and typically, they stay a long way out in front—they open up opportunities. These opportunities allow different segments of the industry to acquire a vision of the technologically possible, to which they can match market conviction and create competitive opportunity that, in fact, greatly accelerates the amount of competition and the rate of progress.

Before becoming director of the ITO, Howard Frank was Director of the Computing Systems Technology Office, which is now part of that function, and earlier was Special Assistant to the director of ARPA for information infrastructure technology. He has made major contributions to the most advanced capabilities in the Department of Defense's information networks. For purposes of public policy, it's important to appreciate the role he has played as Chair of the Technology Policy Working Group, familiarly known by its acronym TPWG, of the President's Information Infrastructure task force. It was that working group that sponsored the National Research Council to work on the project that led to *The Unpredictable Certainty*.

Howard had a significant private sector career as the founder, chairman, and CEO of several companies in the information industry before he came into government, and therefore is immune to the accusation levied against many of our best civil servants that they've never met a payroll. Indeed, he probably finds meeting his current payroll harder than he did when he was the CEO of those companies. Howard Frank.

FRANK: Thank you very much. But Lew is too modest. He chaired the group that developed the "Unpredictable Certainty Report," which, without Lew, wouldn't have existed. It was a fabulous job. When he called and asked me to come here, I had to say yes, even before knowing the topic, because I owe him a lot. (Incidentally it's the first time anybody's ever called me a specimen. But yesterday I had to testify before some staffers from the Senate Appropriations Committee. And that was exactly the right word.)

One of the things you learn to do, both in the commercial world and in government, if you're going to be successful, is to answer the question. So when Lew gave me the topic, I said, let me actually think about it, as opposed to adapting a canned speech. To answer the question, I thought I would first address the question, "what is infrastructure?" It's an oft-used, oft-abused word.

In my mind, infrastructure is "stuff." And by its very definition, it is *average* stuff. For instance, if I made the statement, "This audience is average," I would have no idea whether that's true or not, but if I make the statement, "The world is average," I know that's exactly true by definition. So what I'm going to do is think about infrastructure and the things that go into infrastructure in three groups:

1. Very advanced experimental stuff, which may or may not work (most of the time, it doesn't).

2. Advanced capabilities, which come out once the experimental stuff has been proven to work a little bit.

3. Infrastructure, which, as time moves on, is where the advanced capabilities end up when they become average.

So let me talk first about some of the properties of these different groups. Starting with *advanced experimental stuff*, you're usually trying to do one thing: get some sort of "ultra" performance. For example, when ARPAnet was first introduced, ultra performance meant 50-kilobit communication lines, the ability to send information across the country in half a second, and actually having good error control. Now, that sounds trivial today, but compare this to what human beings could do with teletype (10 or 30 characters a second), and with the state of communication lines, where the average is about 2400 bits per second. At that time, a significant debate was going on about whether we could transmit at 4800 or 9600 bits per second through a telephone line. So at one time, ultra performance was very minimal, but still, that's ultimately where the experimental stuff focuses.

Then when you get *advanced capabilities* you get higher performance, but you start worrying about connectivity. It's not very useful to have an advanced system that only operates in a laboratory. You have to get it out to a campus or a city or a local region. For example, we have an advanced network that circles the Washington area. It's 2.5 gigabits in speed. We have a dozen or so nodes connected to it, and local area networks attached to those. Each of those nodes operates at 622 megabits per second. You could barely buy that in the commercial world. But you certainly couldn't buy it across the country with the guarantee that it was up most of the time, it was available, and it worked with anything else.

So when a capability becomes advanced, you start worrying about keeping it up a lot (as opposed to during the duration of the experiment), making it work with other things, and seeing that it could be expanded from the local or modest sized region of the experiment to a larger scope. And ultimately, it penetrates into *infrastructure*, with luck. Infrastructure has different properties:

- You worry about coverage.

- You worry about reliability.

- You worry about availability.

- You worry about low cost. (It's not going to be infrastructure if its cost is not low. Obviously, "low" is a relative number, low with respect to whatever the infrastructure is at the time.)

- You worry about ease of use.

I'm going to use these criteria to address what I think the Internet is, in terms of its role in infrastructure, and where it might go.

But first, let me give you a few examples of what I think (my own opinion) today's environment looks like. Up at the top, in the experimental world, we have gigabit test beds. They tend to run like the one around the Washington area, at 2.5 to 10 gigabits per second. (We do have one in New Jersey that's looking to get up to 100 gigabits per second. We have one in California that's a similar size.) There are a variety of private test beds: at Sarnoff Laboratories, at Harvard, at MIT. You can find them around the country. And there are things like high definition TV, which have been built in the laboratories but really have not yet been built in any significant way across the country.

Then, if you look at advanced capabilities, you have a technology, which we hope will become infrastructure relatively soon, called ATM, which stands for *asynchronous transfer mode*. Though we might expect that to be the infrastructure of the early 21st century, right now, it's an advanced capability.

And what is infrastructure? It's all the familiar things: telephone networks, television broadcasting, cable television, and so on.

The Internet is sort of in the middle. In my mind, it's not quite infrastructure yet, because if you go back to those criteria (which I will in a moment), you'll see that it doesn't meet most of them. But it's no longer an advanced capability, because it's gone beyond the parameters of an advanced capability. So it's sort of migrating downward into infrastructure. And—if you remember what I said about infrastructure or the intelligence of the world—ultimately, it's got to become average. Now, that doesn't mean that the average can't go up. But ultimately, it will become average. And that's going to be one of my themes: Where is the Internet going, and what does "average" mean?

Lew said it, but let me repeat that Internet is not alone. There's obviously a vast economic enterprise in the information world: broadcast, cable, evolving in-home networks, a huge variety of private nets (which may even be built on the same technology as Internet but have their own special capabilities), and evolving ATM networks. And this entire mix is starting to come together.

But the real secret of an Internet success in penetration into the infrastructure is *interoperability*, making all these things work together. And that's not here yet. For example, in my own mind, the real breakthrough for Internet technology will come when it's interoperable with the next generation of broadcast digital TV. If you remember, the last parameter I had for infrastructure was ease of use. If you think about Internet and ease of use today, and think about the percentage of people who are able to use the Internet, you get a tiny fraction of the world's population. And then if you compare that with ease of use of the television set or a telephone, you discover that Internet is not easy to use at all. In fact, it's a very complex phenomenon.

So the real challenge is interoperability. And Internet alone, or the technologies around Internet, can't drive that. The technologies of the rest of the infrastructure also have to converge. This will require:

- Digital displays in the home.

- Convergence in the set-top box.

- A continuation of cable modem experiments and a restructuring of the cable plants in the United States.

- The integration of the asynchronous transfer mode [ATM] technology and the Internet technology, because the ATM technology is a technology of the 21st century telephone company.

- A series of standards technology developments, which will make all this work together in a reasonable way.

So we've got a long way to go in this challenge.

Let me go back to Lew's question, What is the future of Internet? Two stark alternatives were posed: evolve to the dominant service type in the digital world or not. If not, what attributes will likely survive? I'd like to address that specifically.

First of all, this list describes what I think the role of Internet is. It's not a trivial one.

- An advanced communications infrastructure.

- A mechanism for rapid testing and introduction of standards.

- An experiment in collaborative engineering.

- A market generator for advanced private networks.

- An applications access medium.

- An advanced design environment.

- An applications stimulator.

- An enabler/stimulator for a social communications revolution.

It's not completely understood yet or in fact completely defined. When the Internet was developed, it really did provide an advanced communications infrastructure. In the days when it was called ARPAnet, it provided reliable communications between machines and people, long before there were any alternatives. It was a different model for computers and communications to speak together. And that happened. It also then provided, as part of that advanced communication infrastructure, mechanisms for large numbers of networks to talk together.

The Internet also provided a means for the rapid testing and introduction of standards and new technologies and protocols into the network world. If you look at the world of standards before Internet, it was a decades-long process where elaborate standards committees worked to find consensus. Sometimes it took years, many years, to come up with new ways of doing things. Then quite often, after the standards were developed, it was discovered that the marketplace had gone in a completely different direction. The Internet found a new way of developing standards, which was to first put things into the field and test them to see what worked, and then, by group interaction, develop standards that actually could be demonstrated.

The Internet was also an experiment in collaborative engineering. I remember trying to write a paper collaboratively in the early 1970s, using ARPAnet technology. And the local switching center within the local telephone company was not adequate to transmit bits into the ARPAnet. But people found, as time went on, that you could actually collaborate, use applications for collaboration, on top of this communications technology. And in fact, we discovered that it was easier to engineer things with groups of people interacting at distances, in this new environment, than it was sometimes to engineer things with groups of people operating in the same building.

The Internet also then became a market generator for private networks. If you look down the hall, for example, there's Bay Networks, who are demonstrating some of their equipment. There's a vast technology that is Internet technology, which has generated thousands and thousands of networks not connected to the Internet but which use identical technology that dominates today's world of private networks.

The Internet also became a way for applications to access a new medium. If you put up an application now, millions or tens of millions of people can have access to that application, virtually instantaneously (if they can find it)—a completely different model of distribution to large numbers of people.

The Internet also became an information dissemination medium. In fact, I have a screen saver on one of my machines that was installed three days

ago, which has a public stock market ticker, news, and information, and so on. And it's there all the time. That's a completely different model than we've ever had before, in terms of distribution of information.

The Internet is now becoming an advanced design environment. If you look at the Web and the web technology that resulted from the Internet, the next generation of design is being built upon those technologies in a way that is very different than the last generation of design.

The Internet is also now acting as an applications simulator; that is, new applications that exist only because of this very mechanism we built are now coming to the fore very, very quickly. Search applications and intelligent agents and brokers and knowledge mediators and the like couldn't have existed without this new medium.

And finally—and I think most important—the Internet is an enabler-stimulator for a new kind of social revolution based on communication. In this regard, we have no idea where it's going to take us because there's still a long way to go.

Now let me give you my take on where we are for Internet to really make it all the way down into the commercial world. As you can see in Figure 1, one star means poor, two stars mean fair, three stars means good, and four stars mean excellent. And these were the criteria I had for moving into infrastructure.

Internet Commercialization

High Performance	★ ★
Connectivity	★ ★ ★ ★
Uptime	★
Interoperability	★ ★
Scalability	★ ★
Coverage	★ ★ ★
Reliability	★
Availability	★
Low Cost	★ ★
Ease of Use	★

★ *Poor*   ★ ★ *Fair*   ★ ★ ★ *Good*   ★ ★ ★ ★ *Excellent*

Figure 1

High performance? "High" is always a relative term, but if you're a researcher using the Internet, you would say Internet now doesn't even get one star, because we've discovered a new thing. Internet is no longer an advanced technology.

Connectivity? I give it the full four stars. You can virtually reach anyplace in the world.

Uptime? Well, I was being generous. One star. Why? It's not because you can't get communication lines up time but because you can't get to the applications which sit on servers which are advertised to be there, because most of the time there's no infrastructure for the maintenance of the servers holding the information in the Internet. The Internet has gone from the communications media to the information media. And as an information medium, it has virtually no uptime whatsoever. It doesn't meet any standard of commercial reasonableness.

Interoperability? I give it two stars. Why two? Again, I think I'm being generous. About two years ago, I was on a panel talking about interoperability, and I said, "Virtually nothing in this world is interoperable with anything else." And one of the other speakers on the panel was the president of the Internet Society, who said, "Everything is interoperable with everything." And I said, "No, you really don't understand what I mean. Being able to send a bit from one place to another place and read it on a terminal doesn't mean that it's interoperable. It's the content of the information that counts." And from that perspective, interoperability is down at zero stars. But from the perspective of the fact that our networks can talk together, I give it two. So using the original goal for interoperability in the Internet as defined by ARPAnet, it might even get a three. But we really have a very long way to go.

Scalability? What do I mean by scalability? The ability to take a small thing, make it medium, then make it big, without breaking. The Internet has held together, but the rapid growth of the Internet and the rates we've seen over the last few years can break the entire model over the next few years. And the technologies that need to go into it have not yet been developed to make it work as it balloons: instead of 100 million nodes, 500 million nodes, or a billion or two nodes. Note that by a billion nodes, I don't mean a third of the population of earth. Every device we may develop may be a node on the Internet, and that kind of scalability is an unsolved technical problem.

Coverage? Pretty neat.

Reliability? Pretty bad.

Availability? Pretty bad.

Low cost? Very good.

Ease of use? Again, I'm being generous. One star, because after all, if you do try, you can get through.

So here are the two bottom lines, starting with what I think is going to survive. The Internet will continue to be a major driver for the generation of technology for private advanced networks. I think it will continue to be the leading access and dissemination medium, at least for the next decade or so. I think we have yet to see the full promise as an advanced design environment or as an applications stimulator. And I think the real stimulation of the social revolution based on the new communication model is yet before us.

Finally, here's what I think drops by the wayside. The first one is, in a sense, trivial, because it is a necessity, if the Internet is going to become infrastructure. It can no longer be an advanced communications infrastructure. It has to be average. So the fact that the Internet becomes average is both good and bad. But that means we need another advanced infrastructure to be behind it. And in fact, the technologies in the laboratories right now, and the technologies being planned, have the potential for being the next generation of advanced experimental networks.

There was an experiment that took place roughly nine months ago in San Diego, at a conference called Supercomputing '95. For the first time ever, for one week, a system called the I-way (Information way) existed. In that one-week period of time, it was the most powerful distributed computational system ever built on earth. It involved dozens of large scale computers distributed around the country. It involved very high speed communications. And it involved the interaction of those two things with new ways of interacting with machines, using virtual reality caves and other advanced interactive mechanisms. Then it was taken apart because it was only an experiment.

I took part in a demonstration where the person giving the demonstration said, as a picture of a map was coming up very slowly, "You should have been here this morning, because it came up then with lightning speed. This morning we were on the I-way, now we're on the Internet." So this next generation of advanced communications infrastructure, which is possibly a decade or 15 years away, is out there waiting to be invented.

I think also what falls by the wayside is the mechanism to test and introduce standards in a rapid, novel way. To my mind, that has to break down as it becomes commercialized.

Finally, the experiment and collaborative engineering that was the creation of the ARPAnet and the Internet, I think, is virtually over, if not completely dead. It was created in a world where we assumed certain things: a benign environment, that there weren't good guys and bad guys, only good guys. Information security was not an issue. That collegial world is gone.

So with that, I'll turn the floor back over to Lew.

BRANSCOMB: Thank you very much. I like your criterion for what constitutes infrastructure. I hadn't heard it before. It reminds me of the fact that once, when I was a child, I was giving my mother a hard time for some injustice she had perpetrated on the children, accusing us of something we hadn't done. She listened to me complain for a while, and she turned around and shook her hand in my face, and she said, "You shut up. Your parents are not perfect. But you should realize that half of the kids in the world have below-average parents." I thought about that a long time.

GEORGE CONRADES is chairman and CEO of what we know here in Boston as Bolt, Beranek and Newman. I guess it now goes by the high flying name of BBN, thereby allowing locals to confuse it with the well known primary boarding school in Cambridge. But Bolt Beranek and Newman was there when it all began, right there with ARPA, because they were an important implementer of the critical hardware units that were used in the early ARPAnet, and they've been very much involved in internetworking ever since, and indeed still are.

George joined Bolt, Beranek and Newman only two years ago. He had a 30-year career with IBM, where I certainly enjoyed his collegial relationship very, very much. He not only ran U.S. operations, but importantly, he ran the IBM Asia Pacific Group in Tokyo. Since joining BBN, he's focused on growing the company's presence in the commercial Internet market, maintaining strong ties to government customers. And I'm sure that's a world market and not just a domestic one.

CONRADES: I'm delighted to be here, and to be part of this impressive conference and this distinguished panel. Let me begin by congratulating Lewis for his work in chairing the NII steering committee, and for the comprehensive report that they've produced. I'd also like to recognize and thank Howard Frank for his insightful analysis of that report, and for focusing our attention on the key issues.

Let me offer the liberal arts view of the Internet. I'm reminded of another technology that existed, that was developed over a century ago, the electric motor. I wonder if anyone at Harvard back then thought of convening a conference on the subject. The motor, as you know, revolutionized industry, and by extension, significantly transformed much of society. Let me rephrase that. It really wasn't the motor that did that; it was the countless individuals and organizations who successfully exploited the mechanism to create power, generate power, manufacture goods, move people and products around the globe.

Now, thanks to their efforts, the electric motor has become what we call a ubiquitous technology. It's everywhere from vacuum cleaners to automobiles to trains to washing machines. And at the same time, it seems to be nowhere. It's so seamlessly integrated into our systems and our processes that we simply forget that it exists. I think that's what Howard [Frank] communicated so well. It's become average.

In the future, I think that will be true of the Internet and I don't think we're going to have to wait another century before that happens. But the speed at which the Internet becomes ubiquitous will rely, for now, on two essential forces:

- *The technology itself:* high speed, high bandwidth digital networks over which we can share all kinds of information—text, graphics, sounds, and moving images—across all kinds of platforms. Ultimately, I believe we will have a universal data dial tone that connects people, organizations, and institutions around the world.

- *The diverse communities* that have been set loose by the recent Telecommunications Act. These folks from the telephone, television, publishing, computing, even the utility industries think they are all in the same business now—communications. And all of them are targeting the Internet. In the coming months, it's going to be exciting to watch them jockey to position themselves through mergers, acquisitions, and strategic alliances to control at least part of the system. Or at least, they'll try.

Certainly, the technological challenges are formidable. But I think all of those criteria—and Howard gave us a great list—are being met at a remarkable rate. Various companies are working hard to build safer, faster, more reliable, stable networks, while scores of others are developing applications and services to make the networks even more productive and ultimately easier to use.

At BBN, we've spent over 25 years helping the government maintain the highest standards for secure and reliable internetworking services. Certainly, ARPA has been critical to that work. Now we're playing a central role in helping to transform and upgrade the Internet as an essential tool. In BBN's case, it's a tool for business-to-business use, and ultimately to enable electronic commerce. In fact, the market for Internet-related products and services appears to be growing faster than the early emerging markets for any previous communications technology—including the personal computer.

On the other hand, the cultural differences that separate the new Internet players will probably take longer to resolve. They remind me of the fabled blind men encountering the elephant. Many of them can only imagine the Internet in the context of the platform from which they came. Some are beginning to understand how text, audio, video, graphics, and objects can be coded into digital bits. But most of them still don't see how that transformation is turning the process of communication inside out. Today, it's the receiver who not only determines the rules of engagement but also determines the value of information. And it's the sender who has to respond appropriately. Consequently, many communications firms today lack a coherent vision for the Internet's future or an appreciation of its past.

As Howard pointed out, from its very beginning, the Internet has been a grassroots effort. Its original intent was to connect heterogeneous computers, using a common language. And those early user groups developed spontaneously. First it was the government researchers, and then the academics. Eventually, the computerphiles began to take advantage of networked computing.

But since then, the Internet has continued to change and to grow. And of course, in the last few years, with the introduction of the World Wide Web and the retirement of the NSF [National Science Foundation] backbone, there's been a tremendous spurt in commercialization. So today, business people and professionals, politicians, and ordinary citizens are all looking for better ways to connect with one another.

I think it's these new users coming on board now, particularly in business, who are forming a third and perhaps even more powerful force. Like the individuals and the organizations who incorporated the electric motor within a myriad of other devices, they're using the Internet now to build new applications and to redesign entire business processes. Even traditional competitors have begun using internetworking capability to do business together. The international petroleum industry is building a shared ATM network, which supports IP [Internet Protocol], to exchange vast amounts of geological and commercial information. In Detroit, the Big Three auto makers are pooling resources—IT resources and personnel—to provide network access to thousands of suppliers nationwide.

Yet these and countless other examples that are springing up are just the tip of an economic and social iceberg, I believe. Because right now, the Internet is attracting more intellect and more capital than any other technological evolution in history. As Howard articulated so well, the open protocols of the Net are really giving thousands of companies, millions of people around the world, access to the same opportunities and to one another. And that makes every node on the Internet a potential source of new ideas, individual and collective, that keep igniting innovation. That really is the power of this medium. And there is no other like it. It's a medium that's one-to-many, many-to-one, and one-to-one, all at the same time.

Not only are these innovations enabling us to create new technologies to further enhance reliability, speed, and security—all of which are being worked on at the most amazing pace—they are also allowing us to extract the still untapped potential of existing technologies like copper and cable. (I don't know how many of you here are on the Continental Cablevision trial. BBN and Continental Cable have about 200 families in Newton and Cambridge using high speed, two-way cable access to the Internet. And it's going very well.)

Now, as these organizations and individuals use the Net and incorporate it into their offers into the marketplace, they're making it possible to use this information infrastructure to deliver better health care, to support financial transactions, to educate adults and children, and to accomplish

tasks that we really have yet to imagine. All of this is part of the inevitable progress toward making the Internet a ubiquitous technology.

Today, we read a lot about how companies are trying to marry the bandwidth of the Internet to the horsepower of the silicon chip to create a smaller, simpler Internet appliance. If they succeed, I think that will just be a starting point. For tomorrow, I believe we'll be able to seamlessly integrate the Net into our homes, our offices, our schools, and not just through appliances but in the walls, in the furniture. We'll even attach it to our bodies as wearable devices, in the form of watches or vests or sensors. And I think when that happens, someone will convene a conference about the Internet, and no one will come because it will be such a familiar part of our tools and our processes, we'll just simply forget that it exists. Thank you so much.

BRANSCOMB: Our next speaker has taken a federal agency (not a technical agency), namely, the United States Information Agency [USIA], and has enthusiastically embraced this technology and used it to reach audiences all around the world, thereby testing both the ability of an agency affiliated with the State Department to be an effective user of this technology, but importantly, testing the cultural compatibility of the medium with the message.

JOSEPH DUFFEY was appointed by President Clinton and confirmed by the Senate as the Director of USIA in April of 1993. He previously served as Assistant Secretary of State and as chairman of the National Endowment for the Humanities under both Carter and Reagan. We in Massachusetts remember him as Chancellor of the University of Massachusetts at Amherst, and as President of the University of Massachusetts system during the 1980s. I'm proud to say that he's a former fellow of the Institute of Politics at our John F. Kennedy School of Government. He and I, in a part-time eleemosynary assignment, tried to help the state of Massachusetts encourage its economy through collaboration between the higher education institutions, the private sector, and the state government. He holds all kinds of honorary degrees and distinctions, which I will not go into in order to avoid stealing any more of his time.

DUFFEY: Consider an irony. The Internet is at present inciting an information revolution that is the essence of freedom and capitalism. But the fact is that this breakthrough in technology came as the result of massive government intervention in the free market system. It was not, in the initial instance, the result of market driven investment. The technology that made the Internet possible was the result of unrestrained spending by the federal government over a number of years, in technological innovation.

The Cold War is over and some observers today claim that traditional diplomacy, government to government relations which have remained much the same since the Congress of Vienna, has pretty much run its course. They point to a new interconnectedness between publics around the globe, to new international networks of communication that challenge many of our long held assumptions about international relations.

I first came to the Boston area for graduate study in the early 1950s. That was the time when great changes were taking place in the Roman Catholic church. I remember talking with a number of young men studying for the priesthood during that time who were going through a kind of vocational identity crisis. On the one hand the church was shifting from centuries of celebrating the mass in Latin to a new liturgy in the English language. And at the same time lay people were beginning to stand up and speak from the pulpits. What I heard from young priests in training then can now be heard from confused and puzzled diplomats today. They ask, "What's going on?" and "What role do we play in this new time?"

The instruments and the assumptions of traditional diplomacy are slow to change. One of our senior ambassadors recently sent a cable to colleagues at the Department of State, pleading for access to the Internet and for computers capable of handling such access. She was being asked to forward copies of official statements from U.N. member governments to Washington for distribution to U.S. posts overseas. But this ambassador

had discovered that those documents were already on the Internet, unbeknownst to her colleagues in Washington. They could be read by her colleagues at the State Department much faster if only they had computers capable of Internet access.

At USIA, we began three years ago to try to understand and adapt to this new era, its challenges, and its opportunities for a new era in diplomacy, and for the efficiencies and savings required in the new federal economy. I believe we have, by will and effort over the past several years, made USIA an example of one attempt to change bureaucratic culture and understand the meaning and potential of these new technologies.

Some of my colleagues who have worked on this project are here with me today. It was more difficult just three years ago when we began to use the Internet in our efforts at public diplomacy than it is today in terms of acceptance by the public and those who write about diplomacy in the nation's press. But in many diplomatic quarters in Washington the scene is rapidly changing. Today the U.S. is hardly in the lead in adapting to new technologies in our diplomatic activities around the world. Several other nations have gone even further.

The United States Information Agency was established with essentially two objectives which define its mission. The mission of the USIA is to seek to initiate and sustain informed dialogue and understanding between peoples and institutions in the United States and their counterparts around the globe. This is distinct from official government channels of recognition, collaboration, negotiation, and sometimes confrontation, which have always characterized traditional diplomatic activity. The USIA works to increase more accurate understanding by foreign publics of this sometimes enigmatic and complex society in which we live. It is often difficult for observers from abroad to understand our society because our government is based on a balance of powers and checks and balances.

USIA also works to increase sympathetic, or at least accurate, understanding of America and of our institutions around the globe.

This work ranges then from supplying supplemental information overseas about aspects of American life and policy that are not covered—and probably never will be—by traditional commercial news networks, even in a global information era. One aspect of our work, which is probably more familiar to many of you, has to do with exchange programs like the Fullbright Program.

We are trying to move beyond the Cold War consciousness with which my generation has lived most of our adult life. We don't yet know the full implications of the end of that era. We have yet to find compelling new paradigms for this new time, a time without a name, a "time between the times." But this we do know: this new technology, like new technologies before it—but in an infinitely more expansive way—is changing the structure and nature of international relations in our time.

As President Vaclav Havel said when he spoke at the Harvard commencement last year, the changes in the nature of boundaries and the nature of nationalism itself are creating a whole range of new instabilities. Those of you who were at the commencement may remember President Havel talking about a "great skin of global information" which is covering the globe. But he spoke as well of the seething differences and distinctions just beneath the surface of sameness, which today create so much chaos in parts of the world.

As we seek to diffuse, manage, and contain that chaos, information technologies are useful tools. But they are no substitute for wisdom, judgment, and a proper sense of our place. For in the great scheme of history and nature, of which we are surely a part, we are creatures more of choice and will than fate and destiny.

BRANSCOMB: Our anchor panelist is **RICHARD ZECK-HAUSER**, who is Frank D. Ramsay Professor of Political Economy at the John F. Kennedy School of Government. Dick was one of the small number of founding faculty members of the new version of the Kennedy School that followed on Don Price's Graduate School of Public Management. He is a fellow of the Association for Public Policy in Management, the Econometrics Society, and the American Academy of Arts and Sciences. He is also the author of many papers and books. His most recent book, *Wise Choices: Games, Decisions, and Negotiations,* is, I suspect, very appropriate to much of this debate. Finally, if you find yourself stuck in an airline lounge with three other people, and one of them is Dick Zeckhauser, and he quietly suggests passing the time with a bridge game, at a dollar a point, don't.

ZECKHAUSER: Thank you, Lew. I will address myself to the underpinnings of the social revolution Howard Frank told us about. My remarks address two areas: politics and economics.

The conference volume outlines three central questions for our session:

- How will the Internet evolve?

- Which of its most valuable attributes will survive?

- How is the public interest affected?

Before addressing these questions, I want to issue two cautions: First, people are greatly overconfident of their ability to predict. In more formal language, they assess probability distributions too tightly. Say you ask someone how many cellular telephones there will be in the United States in the year 2010, and ask him to be sophisticated and respond with a probability distribution. That distribution will not nearly be as wide as it should

In fact, we do an experiment in my class where we first warn students about narrow distributions, and then ask them to assess distributions for a variety of quantities. We might ask them about 1995 wheat production, or some current capacity measure for the Internet. Their subjective distributions are much too tight. Let us label as their surprise points the first and ninety-ninth percentiles of their subjective distributions. A good assessor finds that the true values are outside their surprise points about two percent of the time. Despite my warnings, my students, who are trained in decision analysis, are surprised about thirty-five percent of the time. If we were to undertake this calibration experiment right now, you too would assess distributions too tightly. Thus, when predicting any quantities, the first caution is, do not be too confident of your predictions.

The second caution relates to technologies. In the past we've tried to predict the development and effect of various technologies with a very mixed record of success. George [Conrades] talked to us a bit earlier about machines of 100 years ago. We could talk about more recent inventions as well. Television is one of the preeminent new technologies of the 20th century. It was first widely presented to public audiences at the 1939 World's Fair. The general response in newspapers around the country, by people who were talking on the radio and so forth, was that this technology would not make it in a big way.

On the other hand, we do not always underestimate technologies. When I was a boy all sorts of people claimed that we would have nuclear-powered cars in 20 years. Well, it's now 50 years later, and we still don't have them, and I would not be amazed if they do not show up in the next 50 years either. HDTV, High Definition TeleVision, has been another disappointment. I was at Sony's lab in Japan perhaps 15 years ago. There was a magnificent large HDTV screen, and I was told that HDTV would be coming to everybody's home in a short period of time. Well, it hasn't, at least not to the homes that I visit. So the second caution is, Be humble about our abilities to predict the development of technologies.

Let me now throw caution to the winds, as I address the extraordinary potential of the Internet to affect our political system. Most commentators believe that network television has had a profound effect on the American political system. Some think the effect is good, some think it's bad, but there is general agreement that it has been profound. Now we have cable television. It has probably not yet experienced its full development, as network television has. And the Internet, as Howard told us, is just beginning to penetrate society.

How will the Internet and cable TV affect *political society*? I see three very different possibilities.

1. *They could individualize politics.* Basically, each of us would operate alone, not as part of an organized group.

2. *They could have a pluralistic effect*, where society is balkanized, splitting into groups like environmentalists, the Christian Coalition, and people with interests in particular foreign policies. So we split according to tribalistic types of concerns. Some may think such groupings are positive; some may think they're negative; some may think that they are the very basis of the American political system.

3. *We may get societal bonding.* This is predominantly what the enthusiasts of the Internet's consequences for politics expect, that it will promote greater discourse. It will make it much easier for us to talk to people who aren't like us. Most of us in this room correspond regularly over the Internet with people overseas. That's an opportunity we didn't really have a decade ago.

I would argue that although network television has had many detrimental effects, it has been beneficial in providing society with a common set of experiences. By making the news omnipresent, it introduced many of us to common sets of issues, issues we couldn't get away from. I think the best example is the Vietnamese war. You may have had a different view of the war than I did, but no one could escape that war.

I believe cable television may have a more pluralistic effect. I tune into a few of the 30-odd (in some places, 100) channels available without satellite dishes. They are the ones that I happen to particularly like. Whether one's passion is Fox, MTV, or CNN, one is linked with others with like interests.

I have a concern—though I may be wrong—that the Internet may individualize politics. For example, if you subscribe to the *L.A. Times* Internet news service, you get to choose ten topics. Suppose I take a little bit of leisure, a little bit of sports, and a little bit of business. When I choose from the general topics and regional news, I might choose Massachusetts, and perhaps Asia and the Pacific, and I'd skip the others—law, medicine, military affairs. I've already chosen half my topics, and I've left recreational activities aside. So I'm not going to see lots of information I currently do see in a paper newspaper.

Now, I would bet that about 85 percent of the people in this room read a newspaper every day. (If I ask my students in the School of Government—and say they're going to be quizzed on it, because otherwise they might dissemble, "How many of you read a newspaper every day?" the answer, alas, is about 15 percent.) When you read a newspaper, you see more information than you seek. As I'm turning my way to the Sports section, I learn about Bosnia; I learn about environmental movements; I learn about children who perish in fires. That's useful. It's important to have people learn about their society.

Let me turn to how politicians use the Internet, which at present is primitive. Every major politician has a home page. They use it, basically, as a form of broadcasting. It's cheaper than buying television or radio time, but it's not particularly sophisticated.

Consider now the evolution of political action in our society in general, and how technological change affects it. We're all familiar with the notion of grassroots. This is a pluralistic, almost spontaneous thing. The people of North Cambridge decide that they don't want the new plant built next door to them; they organize at coffee klatches and respond. But technology is changing all that. Now we have situations with telephone banks that call at dinner time to request support, perhaps asking that constituents phone their representatives to support or oppose a measure. This is a sort of development beyond the grassroots. People talk about "astroturf," the technologically advanced equivalent of grassroots. It's very helpful in promoting a concentrated interest. In contrast to grassroots organizing, the participants need not be geographically compact.

The cigarette companies have been quite effective in employing astroturf approaches. Their rep-

resentative calls you on the phone and says, "I'd like to talk to you about the new tax that the federal government is thinking of putting on cigarettes. Are you a smoker?" And you respond, "Yes, I am." He says, "Well, they're proposing to make you pay an extra $1.25 per pack. How do you feel about that?" You say, "That's outrageous. How can they possibly do that to me?" The cigarette representative says, "How about this? Let me provide you with some information," and he also solicits some information for push polls (polls designed to get a particular result). Finally, he says, "If you're really mad, I can patch you through to your Congressman right now." And the cigarette company pays for your call to your Congressman. The Congressman says, "Oh my God, 75 people have called me about the cigarette tax." But all of these techniques are child's play in comparison to what will come.

I have a concern... that the Internet may individualize politics.

I predict the development of what I will label "cyberturf." It will be much, much cheaper than having somebody call and talk to you on the phone. Cyberturf will be a mechanism whereby various causes will be able to send thousands of messages to Congressmen, each individualized as its sender wishes, but with guidance from the solicitor. And that will have a very significant effect on how politics is conducted.

In the future, will we have something more like an electronic town meeting (which might be what many people in this room would like)? Or will cyberturf be an intensification of astroturf, so that well-organized, concentrated interests have much more of an influence on politics than they do today? Or will there be—and this is my prediction—a tremendous loss of information because of information overload? No legislator will be able to get much information from his or her community. The other prediction I would make, hedged to reflect my own views about the accuracy of predictions, is that politicians will move toward "narrow-casting," finding specific groups of individuals who will support them on particular issues. Some politicians are already doing this.

Let me speak, briefly, about three economics questions.

Will the current information-for-free environment of the Internet prevail?

I think the answer is no. Corporations are betting vast amounts of money that it will not. Even magazines that have been free on the Internet—one went under in the past week or so—aren't oriented that way. There was a long article in the *New Yorker* recently about how *Slate,* Microsoft's magazine, will charge money. The *L.A. Times* newspaper is planning to charge for its services, as is the *Wall Street Journal.* Online services like America Online are valued at many, many billions of dollars. So, many people obviously believe that Internet services will *not* be free over the long run. Advertising will provide some of the revenues. But as we all know, advertising is an inefficient medium for paying for its accompanying information. With advancing technology, moreover, people will probably get better at screening out advertising. So it's quite likely that information that is costly to acquire will be sold at a price in a wide range of circumstances.

Will vast rents be shuttled from one party to another?

I believe so. Corporate executives all think that the Internet will help them go from $100 million worth of sales to $300 million worth of sales, or $1 billion in profits to $5 billion worth of profits. But some firms will get hurt very severely, because they are now reaping very substantial rents or profits from yesterday's technology.

Think about telephone services. I make twice as many long distance contacts as I did five years ago, and I pay half the cost, because mostly I'm sending messages over the Internet kindly provided by the gentlemen sitting next to me. So email (which is far short of online telephony) has replaced phone services for me. Fortunately for the telephone companies, there aren't very many

of me. But over time, will we have online telephony as a major component of voice communications? Maybe, maybe not; but if we do, vast assets will be stranded. In the electrical utility industry, tens of billions of dollars have been stranded—lost, really—in the United States and other countries, owing to electricity deregulation. This will seem like small potatoes in comparison to the rents that are going to get shifted around on the Internet. And, if they are shifted, that will have vast political consequences.

Pricing will be a key component of Internet economics. There's a real question as to whether the price of the services I now get for free will go up dramatically or not. Will capacity stay ahead of demand? If capacity expands more swiftly than demand, prices will remain low. If it doesn't, they will escalate rapidly.

Can we deal with distributional issues effectively?

Unfortunately, I think the answer is no. With extensive cross-subsidy, we may have what people are generally after, which is universal access. We may have cheap terminals and cheap use for basic services, so that will satisfy people. But since the Internet is far harder to use than a telephone, many commentators will be less concerned with widespread access than with widespread use. Unfortunately, even 10 or 15 years from today, a large fraction of our society may be unable to benefit notably from using the Internet. Knowledge rather than resources is likely to be the binding constraint. The information-deprived, I believe, will always be with us.

Thank you very much.

About the Speakers

Lewis M. Branscomb is Aetna Professor of Public Policy and Corporate Management at the John F. Kennedy School of Government of Harvard University, where he directs the school's Science, Technology, and Public Policy program in the Center for Science and International Affairs. Formerly a Research Physicist at the U.S. National Bureau of Standards (now the National Institute for Standards and Technology), Dr. Branscomb was appointed Director of NBS by President Nixon. In 1972 he was named Vice President and Chief Scientist of IBM Corporation; while an IBM executive, he was appointed by President Carter to the National Science Board, where he served as Chairman from 1980 to 1984.

GEORGE H. CONRADES has been President and Chief Executive Officer of BBN Corporation, based in Cambridge, Massachusetts, since January 1994; he became Chairman in November 1995. The core of BBN's business is to provide Internet access and value-added services to more than 2000 mid- to large-size businesses and organizations. Since joining BBN, Mr. Conrades has concentrated on growing the company's presence in commercial markets while maintaining strong ties to its government customers. Mr. Conrades is a former Senior Vice President of IBM. During his 30 years with IBM, he oversaw the creation of Integrated Systems Solutions Corporation, established IBM's Asia/Pacific Group, and served as General Manager for IBM's AS/400 and Personal Systems divisions.

JOSEPH DUFFEY was named by President Bill Clinton as Director of the United States Information Agency on April 15, 1993. His appointment was confirmed by the United States Senate on May 24, 1993. Dr. Duffey previously served as President of The American University in Washington, D.C., and was Assistant Secretary of State for Educational and Cultural Affairs and Chairman of the National Endowment for the Humanities under Presidents Jimmy Carter and Ronald Reagan. Dr. Duffey holds 14 honorary degrees from American colleges and universities and in 1993 was awarded the honorary Doctor of Letters by Ritsemaken University in Japan.

HOWARD FRANK is the Director of DARPA's Information Technology Office (ITO) where he manages a $350 million annual budget aimed at advancing the frontiers of information technology. Dr. Frank is responsible for DARPA's research in advanced computing, communications, software and intelligent systems with programs ranging from language systems and human computer interaction to scalable high performance computing, networking, security, and microsystems. Dr. Frank helped found the DARPA/Disa Joint Program Office, and was DARPA's representative on the White House's National Science and Technology Council's Committee on Information and Technology.

RICHARD ZECKHAUSER is Frank P. Ramsey Professor of Political Economy at the John F. Kennedy School of Government, Harvard University. His entire academic career has been at Harvard. Often working with others, Professor Zeckhauser has authored more than 150 articles, two books and eight edited books. His most recent edited books are *Strategy and Choice* (1991), and *Wise Choices: Games, Decisions, and Negotiations* (1996). His current research involves examining the potential for a market for evaluations of Internet messages, and of ways to build trust in Internet business transactions.

CHAIR: CHARLES R. NESSON
Weld Professor of Law
Harvard Law School

Law

INTELLECTUAL PROPERTY ONLINE

MODERATOR: Terry Fisher
PANELISTS: James Boyle
Henry Gutman
David Nimmer

CONTENT CONTROL ON THE INTERNET

MODERATOR: Charles R. Nesson
PANELISTS: Jan Constantine
Mike Godwin
George Vradenburg

DIGITAL CONVERGENCE AND VERTICAL INTEGRATION

MODERATOR: Reinier Kraakman
PANELISTS: Steve Weiswasser
Gary Reback
Joel Klein

HARVARD

CONFERENCE ON THE INTERNET AND SOCIETY

May 29-31, 1996   Cambridge, MA

NEWS

Panelists Debate Protecting Online Property

By Ken Gewertz

Does the Internet stimulate creativity or threaten it?

The answer depends on whether you're looking at the Net as a toolbox for creating and disseminating new forms of art and information, or as a lawless frontier in which intellectual property rights have become unenforceable or inapplicable.

"The question remains, where will the content come from? Who's going to create it, and why? True, not everyone works for money, but you still have to provide protection and incentives for those who do," said Henry Gutman, a participant in the panel on "Intellectual Property Online."

An attorney with the firm of Simpson, Thacher & Bartlett, Gutman criticized the "romantic vision" of the Internet that contends that intellectual property rights no longer apply, that in the new world of cyberspace, everything will be free.

"The fact is that somebody somewhere is spending time and money to create content. How do you protect that person's expectation of profit? How do you deal with the book you've spent ten years creating, or the software program that a company may have spent millions of dollars to create?"

Gutman said that it was necessary to make a distinction between legal rights and business strategy. Legal rights clearly have to be protected, but what form business on the Internet will take is still open to question.

As a first step in solving the legal issues, Gutman said that the federal White Paper "Intellectual Property and the National Information Infrastructure," produced by Assistant Secretary of Commerce and Commissioner of Patents and Trademarks Bruce Lehman, (originally scheduled to be a member of this panel) provided a modest beginning.

"You don't have to throw out the existing law, but you have to clarify," he said. "I think the courts can provide incentives within the existing law and that they are capable of wrapping their minds around the new technology."

Jamie Boyle, a Law Professor at American University Law School, took a different perspective.

"There are two ways to fail at the game of intellectual property," he said. "You can set the level too low, which means there's not enough incentive. Or you can set it too high, which cuts future creators off from the raw material they need to create new works."

Boyle was critical of the government's white paper, particularly of its assumption that "the Internet is basically a giant copying machine."

The white paper's answer to the problem of unauthorized copying on the Net is "to jack up the level of protection to compensate for the revenue you might lose," Boyle said.

Thus, he said, the white paper defines the principle of fair use very narrowly, limiting the extent to which one can quote or sample a work for journalistic or creative purposes. It also defines the loading of a work into RAM as a form of copying, which could mean that simply viewing a document on a computer screen might be seen as a form of copyright infringement.

Such an approach is wrong, Boyle said, because "we only want to give as much protection as we need to insure the maximum production of new works." Beyond that, the effect is to stifle creativity.

For example, when VCRs were introduced, Hollywood "howled" that the new technology would destroy the movie business and tried to get Congress and the Supreme Court to impose strict controls. But instead, what happened? Video rentals saved Hollywood by producing a huge new market.

Instead of imposing strict copyright controls on the Internet, Boyle said, "We need to leave the existing copyright law alone and just wait until the cyberdust settles."

David Nimmer, a partner with Irell & Manella and the author of *Nimmer on Copyright*, said that he has begun to question "the myth of the Internet," the notion that all forms of communication must inevitably mutate into digital form.

"I no longer believe that we face the migration of all forms of authorship to the Internet. It may be that people will still want to go to a darkened theatre to watch a movie or go to a store and look through rows of CDs, or pile the family into the car and go rent a video."

Along with this change in perspective has come a more relaxed attitude toward the question of copyright law and the Internet. Nimmer said that five years ago, the possibility of effortless, widespread copying via the Internet seemed to pose a tremendous threat to existing copyright law. But since that time, his opinion has changed. He characterized his present position as being approximately midway between the two former panelists.

Nimmer said that he did not share Boyle's alarm on the subject of the federal white paper, calling the document "unremarkable." But he agreed with Boyle's contention that it was too early to enact legislation.

"We don't yet have the wisdom to know what the future will bring," he said.

Law

May 29, 1996

Intellectual Property Online

MODERATOR: Terry Fisher
PANELISTS: James Boyle
                   Henry Gutman
                   David Nimmer

Editor's Note: Because of a bomb scare immediately prior, this session was not taped. The following text is a transcription of the Session Notes by Online Moderators Lori Lesser and Sousan Arafeh.

Professor **TERRY FISHER** began the session by sketching out a few issues in the debate over intellectual property [IP] online, such as how copyright, trademark, and patent systems should be modified to adapt to the challenges the Internet system poses:

What kinds of creations to cover? "Creative works" are covered by copyright law, but not databases. Much of the valuable information on the Internet, however, is in databases. Do we expand copyright protection to databases? Or, for material for which we do not need incentives to place it on the Internet, should we withdraw IP rights?

Legal protection of collective products. The Internet allows for many different strangers to collaborate; we are seeing increasingly collaborative ventures in creative works. Should these ventures be protected? How?

Legal protection for derivative works. When derivative works are used in combination with a primary work, which author governs the rights— that of the derivative work or the primary work?

Browsing rights. Do we allow people to sample for free, or do we let the market decide, in

which case publishers will distribute free samples when they want to do so?

Fair use. There is a zone of permissible use of copyrighted works, for educational and critical use and the like. Should we maintain this system or modify it? Should we develop an entirely new system?.

Liability of intermediaries. Bulletin board operators and any operators that serve as conduits for downloading and transmittal of information may be liable for copyright infringement.

Trademark problems. Distinguish goods from different sources. What laws should govern marketing?

International IP rights. When materials are posted on a bulletin board and downloaded in another nation, whose laws govern? Do we need a more international system than TRIPS [agreement on trade-related aspects of intellectual property rights (1994)]?

Contracts and licenses. With the growing amount of material on the Internet, market forces will prompt the proliferation of licenses; people will demand agreements that their work will not be forwarded or that they will receive fees.

HENRY GUTMAN confirmed Bill Gates' observation that the Internet is indeed a new method of distribution. The question is, who will produce the content to be distributed? On the Information Superhighway, who builds the cars and creates the reason to get on the highway, and who says where you want to go?

"Some say that IP rights are not relevant on the Internet," Gutman said. "Bill Gates mentioned the romantic vision where there are no lawsuits and everything is free for the taking. But we still need to ask, who will create the content, and why? We need an incentive and reward system."

Gutman said that IP rights are becoming more relevant in the information age and these issues are making more of an impact in our economic life. "The problem we all confront," Gutman said, "is how do we draw the lines?"—especially when the Internet poses the greatest threat to property rights since xerography.

Gutman observed the need for incentives to creators. "I am not suggesting that all that is creative is done for money. There are artists and scholars who do their work for love…but the professors at Harvard have a source of income from Harvard. Its not done purely for charity." Gutman commented that it has been the premise of IP laws, with roots in the U.S. Constitution, that Congress wants to create laws and incentives for original works of authorship. "Most of the things we appreciate on the Internet, someone spent time and money to create with the expectation of profit," Gutman said. "How do we protect the expectation of profit in a world where the production of the first video creates a problem online and instant worldwide distribution? How do we deal with a book you spent 10 years creating and want to sell when the first copy is downloaded worldwide? Or software you spent a billion dollars to create? How do we protect this?"

Gutman then noted the important distinction between one's legal IP rights and one's business strategy for maximizing profit from them. The legal rights are clear, he noted, that an author is entitled to a copyright and an inventor is entitled to a patent. These rights must be preserved on the Internet. What is less clear, Gutman added, is what works as a business strategy, and what laws should govern this. Whether to have an IP right, and whether one can appreciate such a right without having it be part of your business plan are two entirely different questions.

Gutman cited long time Internet privatization critic [and former Grateful Dead lyricist] John Perry Barlow [*http://www.eff.org/~barlow/*], encouraging "bootleg" recordings of the band's concerts and applauding this free approach to content as a strategy for profitability.

Gutman noted the multiple models to describe future Internet access:

Advertiser-driven. Will Internet content be advertiser-supported like broadcast television?

Subscriptions. Users will not be charged per-view, but for unlimited access over a period of time.

Metered use. Similar to the phone companies for long distance calls.

Give up on IP rights. Esther Dyson, publisher of Release 1.0 and prominent commentator on the topic, has argued for Internet "giveaways" of material. She believes that enforcement is hopeless, and competition lies in services rather than content.

Regardless of what model is used, Gutman noted, we will still need protection. He added that a legislative solution is in the works, and briefly summarized these legislative proposals. One proposed change, he noted, involves the transmission of content online, and whether that should constitute a "distribution" and thus an invasion of an authors rights, a.k.a. copyright infringement. Other new provisions are addressed to efforts people might make to frustrate copyright owners security measures regarding their creative works. While the legislative proposals are not perfect, Gutman noted, "they are not that radical." One question is the liability of online service providers, he said, adding: "Those folks are justifiably concerned about the issue." Another question is browsing. One does not have to pay to browse in a bookstore since reading is not a use restricted to the author, Gutman noted.

Gutman concluded, "I think we can address the incentive issue within the fabric of the existing law. I hope that courts can wrap time-honored doctrine around the new technologies."

JAMES BOYLE began his address by asking for a show of hands of the non-lawyers, who dominated attendance at the session. He first described some of the current proposals to regulate copyright on the Net: the Clinton Administration's White Paper, and the Congressional bills H.R. 2441 and S. 1284, which implement its proposals. Then he discussed some of the ways that policy makers think about intellectual property on the Internet.

Boyle started by reviewing the underpinnings of intellectual property: "Intellectual property—in the American tradition—is largely about encouraging the arts and sciences," Boyle said. "It is not about rewarding people for working hard; it is not intended to give creators a dependable annuity...it is about encouraging creators to produce new works within a set of rules that will cause the arts and sciences to flourish." Given this framework, Boyle noted that setting the proper level of IP protection is a complex balance; like the feedback mechanisms in simulation development games such as SimCity, intellectual property rights will fail to achieve their goals if they are set too *low*, but also if they are set too *high*.

"If the level of IP protection is too low, you get many negative effects—authors do not get royalties and drug companies lack the money for research and development," Boyle noted. In contrast, if IP protection is too severe, "you cut future creators out from the raw materials they use to create new works," he added. For example, could Bill Gates have created MS-DOS if BASIC and CP/M had been proprietary systems protected by an expansive intellectual property regime? Intellectual property regimes supply incentives, but they can also deprive future creators of the "bricks" they need to build with. IP laws require a balance, Boyle stated, just like the feedback in the simulation game—where too little road-building will stifle economic development but too much will cause pollution and taxpayer flight. "Intellectual property protection is not a straight line graph."

Having described the basic philosophy of intellectual property, Boyle turned to the current legislative proposals. These proposals come in two parts:

- A White Paper* that purports to say what copyright law is now.

- The recent bills in Congress proposing a set of changes to the White Paper's version of the status quo.

"The interesting thing," Boyle said, "is that the heart of the controversy is about a White Paper that purports simply to describe what the law is now. The bills are actually more modest in the transformations they recommend (even though I don't agree with them)." He noted that many lawyers and scholars have argued that the White Paper is wrong in its description of current IP law. A "footnote-crunching debate" about what the law really is might be boring to a non-legal audience, Boyle said, but to some extent the question is moot in the current context, because "whether we agree on the accuracy of the White Papers *description* of the laws, and I argue elsewhere that the White Paper is extremely inaccurate, we surely still have to evaluate whether these rules are *good* for the Net. I believe they are not."†

The White Paper's basic philosophy is two-fold, Boyle argued. First, content will drive the Internet—a point with which Boyle agrees. Second, the Internet is basically "a giant photocopying machine" that multiplies both "illicit and licit copying." "The White Paper seems to be premised on the belief that if you have more copying, there will be more rip-off, so you need to jack up the copyright protection for authors in order to compensate them for the declining revenues." The White Paper achieves this increase in copyright protection for the Internet based on the following account of current law:

- A narrow definition of the "fair use" exception in copyright ("fair use" is a defense to infringement whereby certain educational, journalistic and other uses of copyrighted material are excused from liability) for copying.

- An expanded definition of "copying" on the Internet, whereby even loading material into RAM counts as a copy, though such "copy" is transitory and fleeting. Under such definition,

---

* "Intellectual Property and the National Information Infrastructure (The "White Paper"): The Report on the Working Group on Intellectual Property Right," September 1995. See *http://www.uspto.gov/web/offices/com/doc/ipnii/*.

† See James Boyle' criticism of the White Paper, "Overregulating the Internet," at *http://roscoe.law.harvard.edu/courses/techseminar96/course/sessions/whitepaper/boyle.htm*l.

browsing, not just downloading, could be an infringement.

- The imposition of strict liability (liability regardless of fault, knowledge, or negligence) upon online service providers for copyright infringement done by their subscribers.

Boyle noted that the White Paper had other features—for example it promotes a program for educating even pre-school children in a particular view of intellectual property. Boyle agreed that kids should know that it is wrong to steal but found the proposed education to "smack humorously of *1984* or *Brave New World*. It fails to recognize that the question of how extensive intellectual property rights are, and what effect they have on free speech. It's a little more complicated and subtle than teaching the 'what's mine is mine/what's thine is thine' dichotomy in order to prevent fighting over a sibling's toys."

The statutes that build on these recommendations, Boyle said, seem to be such that every distribution would be considered an infringement—a user's transmission of material would equal "distribution," which requires permission under the copyright laws. In addition, one would incur civil liability by creating a device that interferes with an author's copy protection system. This has aroused fears that one could be sued for making a device to crack open a program's protective system, even though the device was created for the legitimate goal of "decompiling" the program in order to make it interoperable with other programs.

Boyle said of the new IP bills: "They dramatically expand copyright liability and I think that is a bad idea." He repeated his general thesis about copyright laws needing to strike a proper balance between the provisions of incentives, and the protection of the public domain, and argued that these proposals ignore or undervalue the latter. Then he turned to his second theme—the "structural malfunctions in the way we think about copyright on the Net" evidenced by the current proposals to regulate the Net:

- First, Boyle argued that these proposals show that it is always easier to imagine an infringing use of new technology than to imagine a ways in which the technology will lower costs and offer new markets. Consequently we tend to the ways that the Internet will lead to widespread copying of their software rather than thinking about the ways in which it might also allow them make money through different strategies or gain a greater return from a lower investment. Boyle argued that this seems to happen with every new technology. For example, when VCRs came on the market, Hollywood and the TV industry wanted them taxed to compensate for lost revenues caused by home taping of protected material. The issue even went to the Supreme Court in the Sony Betamax case.

- Second, Boyle said, these proposals show that we undervalue the importance of the public domain—for example the use of the "fair use" defense to copyright infringement in providing building blocks for future creators. In current law, something has to be "original" to receive copyright protection. But focusing on the term "original," we inevitably underestimate the extent to which the work we are protecting depended on material in the public domain, because it seems that the original creator is creating out of thin air. "We undervalue the giants on whose shoulders we stand," Boyle said. (Note: An abbreviation in copyright law reflects this can see farther than the giant alone.)

- Third, Boyle argued that these proposals show the difficulty that copyright has in dealing with the distributed architecture of the Net. Copyright premises liability largely on copying. "But on the Net transmission *means* the generation of lots of temporary unstable copies. That's what transmission is." So there is reason to worry about too much copyright protection on the Internet because it means that we are locking ourselves into a certain perception of the Net as a "copyright problem"—particularly if we define "copying" in the way the White Paper does.

- Fourth, Boyle argued that the reaction to these proposals shows that we don't yet have a politics of intellectual property. For example, "duck hunters, bird watchers, and tree-huggers" now recognize their common interest in protecting "the environment." It took a long time to show that common interest under apparent differences. We need a similar concept and a similar movement among all of those who have an interest in protecting the public domain — ranging from teachers to rap artists and biographers to software developers. "I hope we see a democratic politics of Intellectual property protection. IP is now big business and big money and it can't be left to lawyers. It implicates too many values and it is so important in the world economy. We can't just have it dealt with by a small group of people."

"Let the cyberdust settle," he said. "We do not want to adopt the White Paper now, or we will destroy the kind of balance needed to ensure a flourishing SimCity."

DAVID NIMMER began his address by noting that he was speaking on this subject five years ago, "calling attention to the gathering storm clouds, the advent of lawlessness" in IP rights. Today, the "Twister" is here, and now he offers the opposite perspective: "Maybe the revolution on whose cusp we sit is not going to come upon us."

Nimmer noted that the Internet debunks a lot of myths—for instance, one can't give away products and make money: Netscape, Yahoo!, and Java are all examples. Another myth is "the inevitability and invincibility" of the Internet itself.

Nimmer used the Information Superhighway analogy and set up three lanes on it to describe Internet content:

- The left, fast lane for tractor-trailer trucks representing vast compilations of data.

- The right shoulder for three- to four-page Usenet postings and email messages whizzing by on two and three wheels.

- What is missing is the center lane of cars— those people who do not watch Pocahontas or read Tolstoy on the Internet.

Nimmer asks, "Why? Because the technology isn't there? Because people do not want to?" There is no set answer yet. But we do know that all works of authorship will not inevitably migrate to the Internet. People will still want to go to a darkened theater and put their kids in a car and burn gasoline to go to a video store. Maybe people like flipping through the boxes in the store and asking their favorite clerk for a movie recommendation. In the future, "authors" may be thousands of strangers collaborating, or maybe Shakespeare still has an audience, and people still desire the linear view of one authors perspective on a story over time.

Nimmer stated that he found the White Paper, "unremarkable and framed in government bureaucratese." He agreed with it that making a copy in RAM counts as an impermissible "copy." For example, if Nimmer sent a copy of material to Professor Fisher and Mr. Gutman and 500 copies proliferated from the one licensed copy, that would implicate copyright protection. Yet, Nimmer disagreed with the legislative proposals in the White Paper stating that they are still "too early." He noted, "We have no data points to know the proper course for the laws yet."

"The Internet is still in beta-testing," Nimmer said. "We are not yet in Internet 1.0." Nimmer said he disagreed with Gutman that simple rules can still guide courts down the right paths. He noted that there are 1909 laws that were lucid for years, but are often misinterpreted now. As of now, he added, we have only three court decisions on this topic by district (lower) courts, and thus just three data points on the laws directing more authority by appellate courts (whose decisions have more authority) is needed, he said. At least 20 cases or so.

As to the point that browsing on the Internet is always permissible, Nimmer noted that reading a book in a bookstore is not a matter of IP law but is a business plan that allows us to peruse before purchasing. There is no inherent right to browse in current law. Regarding reading books in bookstores, Nimmer stated, "I am sure that if I went to B. Dalton every day and stayed from 8 a.m. to 6 p.m. and read books cover to cover, I would be escorted out." He noted that publishers can put "shrinkwrap" on their books if they want to; however, they refrain of their own volition. Therefore, while there is no "right" of a user to browse, it may be to soon to state changes in this area. "The booksellers of the future may say that anyone gets 30 minutes free to browse, or one chapter, and then we charge." He noted that the movie studios allow free, brief movie "trailers" to appear on television to promote sales, while hotel rooms give the first 10 minutes of a movie for free, and then allow viewers to pay or discontinue watching. It could be the same with the Internet, Nimmer noted. "So I do not see the link between browsing and the changes being proposed."

Finally, as to "fair use," Nimmer noted that even if Congress was sufficiently unwise so as to implement tomorrow the changes recommended by the White Paper, it would not change directly the concept of "fair use," because fair use is not directly implicated by the proposals. The Copyright Office began registering computer software in 1964, but no one could foresee the growth in the software industry. Years later, the Ninth Circuit (the Court covering California and several Pacific states) stated in the Sega case that it was "fair use" and therefore permissible to decompile your competitor's elements to your own product to make the two interoperable. Such an application of fair use to computer software could not have been predicted until we got to the middle of the road in terms of software development. Therefore, Nimmer notes, we should wait and reconvene on the precise legislation for the Net.

Questions & Answers

Q: *Are we to sit tight and wait for the market, or technological innovation to decide these issues? For example, the new wave-meter chip can administer the use of content at the client level, like a vending machine, and* voluntary collective licensing agencies abound, such as ASCAP and BMI.

GUTMAN: This goes to the distinction between legal rights and a business plan to exploit them. There are certainly plausible ways to give revenue to the creator without unduly hampering the right to take advantage of the new distribution mechanism. Some software on the Internet is not free until you give a credit card number to the service, and there are other such mechanisms. What the White Paper is trying to do, in addressing transmission and finding it equivalent to distribution, is trying to eliminate one mistake the courts could make by adding clarity.

We do not need to remake the copyright laws, but I am not convinced that the courts can decide the issues well either. A technological solution like the wave-meter chip is one possible solution [*http://www.wavesys.com/*].

Q: *Databases seem like the semis on the Superhighway and are radically underprotected. Should we expand or create* sui generis *(brand new) protection for databases or should we leave things alone as Boyle says? Should a sui generis system be retrospective and cover existing ones? What about various international agreements on this issue?*

NIMMER: If you will accept the concept of the three "lanes" on the Superhighway, we need to shed the notion that one copyright law can govern all lanes and aspects. Maybe we need three rules: one for the Usenet and email, one for the average user, and one for vast compilations. I subscribe to the view that we need a different set of laws for compilations. The Supreme Court in the 1991 Feist case found that the most objective and useful information was outside the realm of federal copyright protection, but that state law could protect it.[*]

Congress could also protect databases under the Commerce Clause (a clause in the U.S. Constitution providing that Congress can enact laws that affect commerce between states), not just the

---

[*] In Feist, the court held that copyright law did not protect the White Pages of the phone book, that alphabetical listings or names were not sufficiently original and creative to merit federal copyright protection.

Copyright Clause (the clause in the U.S. Constitution providing that Congress can enact laws to protect databases. The roots of this protection are not new. In the 1918 case *INS v. AP*, the Supreme Court held that state unfair competition laws were the proper vehicle to forbid one wire service agency from copying the facts from the news stories of its competitor, despite the fact that federal copyright law did not apply. [The federal copyright laws protect one's particular expression of factual information but not the underlying facts, leaving a loophole by which news agencies can steal factual information from one another.]

The discussion of protecting databases under various international agreements is "too technical" for purposes of the session.

Q: *What amount of latitude should we give to Internet users? The first-sale doctrine prohibits an author from controlling the final destination of the creative work after its first sale. What about browsing? What does it mean to legislate a browsing right?*

BOYLE: One of the results of the White Paper would be to abolish or severely limit the first-sale doctrine. [The first-sale doctrine allows you to buy a copyrighted book at B. Dalton and then give that same copy to a friend as a birthday gift. It does not allow you to photocopy the entire book so that two copies exist.] We should give only the intellectual property rights we need to give. If certain products would be on the Internet anyway without increasing copyright protections, then the copyright law should stay the same or go down. You shouldn't get the IP protection unless there is market failure. IP rights should not be just "automatic rights" and then you add them to your business/profit strategy.

Fair use and the fair use exception for education depends on the context of other rights given on the Internet. There is a strong argument for depositories and libraries to have stand-alone terminals where people can access protected material on the Internet, but cannot transmit it.

RAM storage should not be a "copy" of protected material. First, it is not stable or permanent. Second, as a functional matter, we do not need to give copyright owners the right to control RAM copies. One's business strategy is based on one's legal rights. If the *New York Times* could control its facts, it would have a different business strategy. [As noted earlier, federal copyright laws do not protect raw facts but a journalist's particular expression of them in a story.]

NIMMER: I would advance entirely the opposite view. If the Internet produces ample works, if there is enough shareware on there, then we should accord copyright protection to those works because they would already have an audience willing to pay a tariff to get them.

GUTMAN: The current legal system for copyright has worked well for 200 years. The U.S. software and movie industries are the envy of the world. Rather than tinker with the system now and risk losing it, we should wait, because we can always fix it when we have more market information.

BOYLE: I agree, but that's not what we are doing, because the White Paper would change the law.

About the Speakers

WILLIAM FISHER received his B.A. from Amherst College and his J.D. and Ph.D. from Harvard. After completing his education, he served as a law clerk for Judge Harry T. Edwards and Justice Thurgood Marshall. He joined the faculty of Harvard Law School in 1984, where he is now Professor of Law and Director of the Harvard Legal History Program. He has written extensively in the fields of intellectual property law and American Legal History.

HENRY B. GUTMAN is a partner in the New York office of Simpson Thacher & Bartlett, where he heads the intellectual property group. Mr. Gutman graduated with honors from the University of Pennsylvania (A.B. 1972) and the Harvard Law School (J.D. 1975). Since 1985, Mr. Gutman has served as lead counsel for Lotus Development Corporation in a number of major cases, including *Lotus v. Paperback Software*, *SAPC v. Lotus*, *REFAC v. Lotus*, and, most recently, *Lotus* *v. Borland*, which he argued for Lotus in the U.S. Supreme Court. Mr. Gutman is a frequent lecturer on intellectual property and computer litigation subjects.

JAMES BOYLE is Professor of Law at American University in Washington D.C., where he has taught since 1982. He has also taught at Harvard Law School, Duke Law School, Boston University Law School and the University of Pennsylvania Law School. Mr. Boyle is a graduate of Glasgow University and Harvard Law School. Recently, Mr. Boyle has been working on the legal issues posed by the information society. His news articles on the subject have been published in the *New York Times*, The *Washington Times*, and *Insight Magazine*. His book *Shamans, Software and Spleens: Law and the Construction of the Information Society* was published by Harvard University Press in May 1996.

DAVID NIMMER[*] is Of Counsel to Irell & Manella in Los Angeles, California. Since 1985, he has assumed responsibilities from his father, the late Professor Melville B. Nimmer of UCLA Law School, for updating and revising *Nimmer on Copyright*, the standard reference treatise in the field, routinely cited by U.S. and foreign courts at all levels in copyright litigation. Apart from his treatise, Mr. Nimmer authors numerous law review articles on domestic and international copyright issues and lectures widely in the copyright area. In addition to writing and lecturing, Mr. Nimmer represents clients in the entertainment, publishing, and high technology fields.

---

[*] See *http://www.bender.com/nimmer.htm* for a transcript of David Nimmer's speech from the conference "Copyright Issues in Cyberspace," held on June 6, 1996, in New York City.

HARVARD NEWS

CONFERENCE ON THE INTERNET AND SOCIETY

May 29-31, 1996   Cambridge, MA

Censorship: Difficult, Even if You Think It's a Good Idea

By Lori Valigra

The idea of the U.S. government censoring Internet content riles free speech defenders, but even lawyers backing alternative ratings systems are tongue-tied on basics such as how to define "indecency."

"The First Amendment does not protect perjury, threats, or obscenity," noted Mike Godwin, counsel for the Electronic Frontier Foundation. "But indecency does not follow these rules. Print material can be 'indecent' even if it is not judged obscene."

The Internet poses some unique problems for would-be censors. Although it is an interactive medium, today's state-of-the-art cyberporn is mostly explicit, static photographs.

Unlike the strong First Amendment protection afforded text and movies, which can be deemed artistic by virtue of their context, still photos lack context and have the least free speech protection, said Charles Nesson, the provocative Harvard Law School professor who led a panel at Harvard's Conference on "The Internet and Society" on censoring indecent Net content.

The panel of lawyers protested the recent passage of the Communications Decency Act, which imposes up to a two-year jail term on the use of any interactive service making sexual or excretory content available to anyone under age 18.

"It seems very strange and draconian and hard to justify under the First Amendment," said God-win. "The real question is what the government can regulate under the First Amendment."

"The Supreme Court has not said the government has general authority to regulate indecent materials, but materials deemed harmful to minors is a different matter," Godwin said.

Regulating beyond national borders is another issue. Even if the U.S. government could rid American web sites of material it deemed improper, Americans still could access foreign web sites.

There is "no way" the Communications Decency Act can be effective, said Nesson, because it is difficult to patrol the Net. "It's in the nature of the Net that there is no center, and for law enforcement this presents a problem," he said. "And it seems that the people passing laws about the Internet are not really knowledgeable about it, and that poses problems."

But alternative efforts aimed at self-policing content have been met with skepticism by Congress, said George Vradenburg, a partner at Latham and Watkins in Los Angeles.

Vradenburg is behind an industry effort to create software called Platform for Internet Content Selection (PICS) that parents could buy, and then pick and choose what information their children can access on the Web.

"The problem with the PICS system is its complexity. It is very hard to be comprehensive and accurate with this because of the rapid growth of web sites," he said.

While contending that PICS should reduce the political aspect of censorship on the Net because it puts screening in the hands of parents rather than government, he admitted he has found little support from Congress.

NewsAmerica Corp. General Counsel Jan Constantine worries about what the Communications Decency Act will do to commercial online service providers like Prodigy, which her company owns.

"There will be a backlash to commercial online service providers because while content may not be obscene, it may be deemed unpatently offensive by some people," said Constantine, who called the Communications Decency Act abhorrent.

She said the solution is not to punish online service providers, which generally opt to delete potentially offensive material rather than face jail or lose business. She agreed with Nesson that online service companies are sensitive to making money, so when they are in doubt about content, they take it out.

Law

May 30, 1996

Content Control on the Internet

MODERATOR: Charles R. Nesson
PANELISTS: Jan Constantine
Mike Godwin
George Vradenburg

NESSON: Our subject here this afternoon is "Content Control on the Net." That's a fancy way of talking about censorship. Although there is a range of subjects we can include under the net of censorship, the stuff that's really driving the subject is sex and violence. So let's talk about censorship, sex, and violence.

The *Financial Times* columnist Tim Jackson formulated what he calls "Jackson's Law of Technology." Jackson's first law: If pornographers are among the early adopters of a new technology, it has definite commercial possibilities. Jackson's second law: If there is a public backlash against pornographic use of the new technology, its future is assured.

The background of this subject, in legal terms, takes a bit of focus. I want to give you a little bit of background. Then I'd like to address a question to each of the three panelists, and have them respond so you get a sense of where they are. And then we will take questions.

The question of obscenity is not one that comes intuitively to people. It has been a subject with which the Supreme Court has struggled over the course of years, and is now pretty much defined by the doctrine of a case called *Miller v. California,* a case in the '70s, which sets out a test for obscenity. I want to articulate that test for you, and then

briefly explore it. Here is the Miller test of obscenity. It's got three parts to it, three prongs:

1. Whether the average person applying contemporary community standards would find that the work, taken as a whole, appeals to the prurient interest.

2. Whether the work depicts or describes in a patently offensive way sexual conduct specifically defined by the applicable state law.

3. Whether the work, taken as a whole, lacks serious literary, artistic, political, or scientific value.

Now, there's no definition, no concrete standard for measuring value, no less serious value. The best that some judges have been able to do has been typified by Justice Stewart, who said, "I know it when I see it."[*] And that's about as far as he was able to get. Local community standards apply to the first two of these prongs but not to the third; that is, the artistic merit is judged by a national standard. And that has been the governing standard.

Now, what does that mean where the rubber hits the road? As far as determining what materials are actually considered obscene, you can take a few starting points. First, printed works, text, are generally given the widest First Amendment protection. And although it's theoretically possible for text to be judged legally obscene, it's damn difficult. You have to stretch very hard to find text that will be declared obscene. Similarly (and to some extent, surprisingly), pornographic movies are usually held to be not obscene. That's because they meet the artistic value prong of the Miller test. Even the smallest semblance of plot or character can grant the most pornographic of films some form of artistic value. Still photographs of sexually explicit activities receive the least amount of protection, because they lack the redeeming context. Isolated shots of highly charged sexual materials do not, by themselves, come off as part of any story, but are readily seen as the reduction of focus to the sex act itself, and

[*] *Jacobellis v. Ohio*

therefore are much easier targets of obscenity prosecution.

So we hit a kind of a puzzle. Here I am, Mr. or Mrs. America, with my darling impressionable children. I know that the stuff in the XXX side of the video store is obscene. I don't care what anybody tries to tell me, I know it's obscene. I know it, even if the courts say otherwise. The courts, in fact, call it indecent rather than obscene. And indecent materials can be regulated in terms of harmfulness to children. Indecency has traditionally been regulated over broadcast media, on a theory that the broadcast media represent a scarce resource that justifies some government regulation. That's why you don't see indecent materials, at least before ten o'clock at night. And relatively recently, a new kind of rationale has been increasingly thought about for purposes of broadcast, which is the degree of pervasiveness of the medium into the home.

So here I am, Mr. and Mrs. America, and this new medium of the Internet presents itself. It's something I don't really understand. My kids understand it. It is coming into the home, and it is surrounded with an aura of pornography. *Time* magazine does big cover stories about it. I listen at cocktail parties and hear how easy it is for kids to jump into it. And my Congress responds to me and passes the Communications Decency Act.★

MIKE GODWIN, who is lawyer for the Electronic Frontier Foundation and a deep student of First Amendment, has been following and participating in the challenge to the CDA that's taking place currently in Philadelphia. Mike Godwin, tell me why our Congress shouldn't be able to keep indecency off the Net.

GODWIN: The real question is, what can the government regulate under the First Amendment? The First Amendment says "Congress shall make no law." It's incorporated as against the states by the Fourteenth Amendment. But what is the contour of that freedom? What is its shape? What does it cover? We know the First Amendment is not an absolute. Even the so-called First Amendment absolutists on the Supreme Court always knew that there were things that could, in fact, be regulated or restricted by government action, speech that could be regulated or restricted by government action, copyright infringement. Certainly, perjury is speech that can be regulated; threats, and of course, obscenity. Ever since the Roth case in the '50s, it's been clear that obscenity has no First Amendment protection.

But what about speech that's not any of these things? That's what is at stake in the Communications Decency Act case, because the Communications Decency Act criminalizes the sending of so-called indecent material to a minor, or the act of displaying in a way that's available to a minor, patently offensive material. Both of these kinds of material are not obscene. In other words, they don't have to flunk the obscenity test.

NESSON: Mike, can I just intrude? The XXX stuff in the video store—obscene or not?

GODWIN: What community are we in? We're in Cambridge, so I say no. If we were in Boston, I might change it. It turns out that the obscenity test is a local community standards test. You judge it really by what the local jury says. That's a fact determination by the jury. Whether it has serious value is ultimately a legal determination by the courts.

But indecency doesn't even follow any of that stuff. There is some talk about community standards in the indecency cases involving broadcast, but it turns out, when you ask the FCC, "What do you mean by this?" they say, "We mean the national community of broadcast viewers." Well, some community. Right? The courts have granted the FCC, the federal government, authority to regulate broadcasting. And it's partly justified by scarcity and partly by pervasiveness. We also, by the way, have a new theory, which is called an antitrust market dysfunction theory,

---

★ The Communications Decency Act (CDA), a provision of the Telecommunications Act, was shot down by a three-judge court in June, 1996. However, on December 6, 1996, the U.S. Supreme Court agreed to hear the government's appeal for the legal challenge to the CDA. The case is expected to be heard in March, 1997. See *http://www.cdt.org* for more details.

which I know the economists among you will love.

But the fact is, the scope of the Communications Decency Act is far broader not only than obscenity but even than pornography. Some of you may remember that the key case setting out indecency as a separate category involved the George Carlin comedy routine involving the seven words you couldn't say on television. Well, it turned out, you can't say them on radio either. That was what was determined by the Supreme Court in the FCC case. But that material wasn't pornographic. I mean, nobody listens to George Carlin and becomes sexually aroused.

NESSON: I don't know about "nobody."

> *The material on the Net that we want to see remain legal is material that is already legal in Wordsworth at Harvard Square, it's already legal in the libraries, it's already legal in Barnes & Noble in any city in the country.*

GODWIN: I think that the real issue is, the material that is being defended, the material on the Net that we want to see remain legal, is material that is already legal in Wordsworth at Harvard Square, it's already legal in the libraries, it's already legal in Barnes & Noble in any city in the country. So the question you have to keep asking is, under what Constitutional justification can you say that material that is perfectly legal in any bookstore in the country, perfectly legal, by the way, in any movie house in the country, becomes illegal because it's on the Internet?

NESSON: Can I be Mr. and Mrs. America again?

GODWIN: Which one are you?

NESSON: Either one. Pick your prong. I don't care. It's okay with me to have that XXX stuff down in the video store, because my kid can't get at it unless he goes through somebody at the counter. And he's not going to get past the guy at the counter. It's a different proposition for me to have that XXX stuff coming through the Internet, into my home. And yes, I know it's all still pictures on the Internet right now, but I've been to this conference where I hear that, hey, bandwidth is opening up and multimedia video, ta da, and pretty soon it's going to be interactive.

GODWIN: You know, I did an experiment. I'm an empiricist in these matters. And I did an experiment—I went to Powell's Bookstore in Oregon, in Portland. It's a big bookstore. And I just said, you know, I'm going to see just how much sexually explicit material is available here, that can be seen by a child without anybody watching. It turns out that the material relating to explicit depictions of sexuality—there are sexual self-help manuals, and some of it's erotica—it's actually all right there. It's not even on the top shelf. It's on the bottom shelf! So even people who are seven or six or five can access it. Some of this stuff has pictures…right there in the bookstore.

And I'm thinking we don't normally expect the bookstore operator to prowl around even the most remote stack to make sure that the minor isn't browsing that book. It may be hard for a minor to buy a copy of *Tropic of Cancer,* or to buy a copy of Madonna's *Sex,* but they can look at it in the bookstore. (Well, Madonna's *Sex,* no. It had that wrapping.) You know what I'm saying.

In fact, if they like Judith Krantz, one of the things we know is that print material can easily be indecent, even if it's hard to find it obscene. And Judith Krantz very helpfully italicizes the sexual passages in her novels, so you can just flip through and spot it immediately. And that material was easily available, not just to 7-year olds or 10-year olds, but of course to 17-year olds, who are hard to distinguish from 18-year olds.

NESSON: So what's your point?

GODWIN: Under the Communications Decency Act, if you show indecent material, nonpornographic material, material that may not even appeal to the prurient interest, but that does qualify as indecent, to anyone who's under 18—and that includes freshmen at Harvard, at least a lot of them—if you use a computer to do it, you go to jail for two years. And that seems very strange, very draconian, and very hard to justify under the First Amendment.

NESSON: Thank you. **JAN CONSTANTINE** is the current General Counsel for NewsAmerica publishing. That includes *TV Guide,* Harper Collins, Fox, Delphi Internet provider. She has been working since 1993 with Delphi Computer Service. She's now working with iGuide, a very popular free web site that contains *TV Guide* online and other material from News Corp. and from Fox. She's very well qualified to speak from the position of the online providers.

Jan, let's just suppose Mike is successful in some way, in his challenge, and that we address the question of control of content not so much from the point of view of making it illegal for me to put something up, which has enormous enforcement problems, but from the point of view of a government—perhaps not just the U.S. government, since this actually is a global problem—a government that's worried about how it's actually going to enforce. Now, it's in the nature of the Net that there's no center, and it's in the nature of law enforcement that if you don't have a center, you've got an enforcement problem. Why isn't it inevitable in the architecture of law enforcement when it marries the Internet, that law has got to go after the online providers and make them the closest thing we have to centers on the Internet, responsible for content? The idea being, there's no other entity, there's no other way for government to get a handle on anyone who has the power to do anything about the problems they're concerned with. Why doesn't that lead inevitably to the online provider being a target for law enforcement?

CONSTANTINE: The best quote I've heard in a long time, having been a lawyer for an online service provider, was when I tried to find out from my techies whether we could block allegedly obscene and perhaps indecent and possibly patently offen-

sive materials in the Usenet newsgroups we had on our host computer, to the U.K. The manager there was concerned that he was going to be arrested under the obscenity law in the U.K., which essentially gave criminal fines and imprisonment to any person who, whether for gain or not, publishes an obscene article. This is the U.K. obscenity statute. And I was told that the Internet defines censorship as damage, and then reroutes around it. Therefore, technologically speaking (at least when I asked that question in 1994), there was no way, other than blocking an entire newsgroup, to actually block content from outside the border.

So essentially, I think what Professor Nesson is saying is: If the online service provider is in a jurisdiction (and it doesn't have to be the United States; it can be Singapore; it can be Saudi Arabia; it can be France) that enables the government entity to go after that online service provider for any content located in any other jurisdiction, whether it be legal in that jurisdiction or not, then, by going after the party within their jurisdiction, that eradicates the problem because somehow that user will not get access to this offensive material in that jurisdiction.

But it doesn't work that way. What will happen is, they will sign on with an Internet access provider, or an AT&T, or an MCI, and they will be able to get access to that material deemed offensive in that jurisdiction through some other means of communication. Therefore, the online service provider, who is supposed to be there and make everything user-friendly and encourage children to go onto kids' areas that are specifically groomed for that purpose, will indeed go out of business, and will not want to incur the risk, both criminally and financially, of lawsuits on the copyright side (which we're not talking about now), as a reaction to this kind of heavy-handed governmental regulation.

I took the liberty of going on the Internet and finding out what kind of legislation was out there. China has issued a new regulation aimed at dissuading citizens from engaging in any of these prohibited activities; they want to control what goes through computers in their country by having the government take over all the computers. Under the statute, everything must go through a centralized government computer before it goes onto the Internet.

France, apparently, went to a local cybercafé and closed it down because a book by Mitterand's physician about his cancer fight, which had been banned, was on the Internet.

The prosecutors in Germany got to CompuServe, my colleagues, and basically said, "We find these 200 Usenet newsgroups to be indecent, and we want you to shut them off from being received by the 140,000 subscribers in Germany." All CompuServe could do at that point was shutdown these 200 newsgroups from their three or four million subscribers *all over the world,* in jurisdictions where they wouldn't be considered to be illegal, indecent, obscene, or offensive.

AOL was also involved recently with the Germans when they had on their system (and accessible to the AOL subscribers in Germany) a neo-Nazi text from a Canadian server, which was perfectly legal in Canada. But AOL was told, "We don't want our German AOL subscribers to have access to it."

It doesn't work. It will never work. The Internet will find ways around it, and the people you're worried about, the minors and the children, are the ones who are going to be hacking their way around it anyway.

NESSON: Wait. What do you mean, it doesn't work? It worked for Germany. It worked great with CompuServe. I know. I went up on the University of Massachusetts site and a few others. And if you were super duper industrious, you could find it. But the fact is, from Germany's point of view and from China's and Singapore's, why isn't it working? They're going after the online providers. They are doing the best they can, and CompuServe did take it off.

CONSTANTINE: Well, I wouldn't have taken it off. I would have recommended to the people in Germany, if I were CompuServe's general counsel, not to take it off, and get a cry raised internationally about the unfairness of taking it off at that time. The CompuServe general counsel was concerned that some of its people were going to be sent to jail and actually have to serve a jail term.

NESSON: You say, "Hey, let them go to jail. Goodbye and God bless you!"

CONSTANTINE: I would have. I would have said that. And I'll tell you why. I owe you, by full disclosure, my background. I served as a prosecutor. When I was in the Eastern District of New York, one of my more pleasant jobs was to be on the committee that looked at all the pornography that came into the airports, to decide whether it violated the community standard in New York. And by God, not one of them did, because it was New York! So I know pornography. (Judge Thomas and I watched a lot of those films.)

GODWIN: We have a similar standard in the Bay Area.

CONSTANTINE: I'm a media lawyer, and I'm obviously a kneejerk First Amendment supporter, because I think that's what differentiates this country from other countries. So the Communications Decency Act, to me, is abhorrent, and I'll be glad to talk about that during the question time.

I also am an avid reader of fiction and nonfiction. I am a devout TV viewer (mostly of Fox, because that's my employer) and an occasional traveler in cyberspace, because I advise my clients so I must be in there as much as possible. I can't type at all. And I have three children, ages 9, 15, and 18. So I've seen it all, been there, done that. And I'm not concerned about what's out there in the Internet.

I believe the solution is not government-regulated content control by either an online service provider who decides that they're risking fines and criminal prosecution by allowing certain things to be on their system. And I'm telling you right now, given my experience, the online service providers are risk-averse. They are going to err on the side of taking things off, whether or not it's offensive or indecent or obscene or anything, because they want to avoid being hassled.

They have a low profit margin. We're in the board room now, not in the courtroom or the classroom, I respectfully submit. And these companies are going to be pushed economically out of business, and there will only be access providers out there who will not give you pretty road maps to the good stuff. And then, where will the Internet be? It will just be a place where only pornography lives. And nobody will want to put compelling content out there, because they'll all be afraid of regulation or possible criminal fines.

NESSON: Let me just see if I get the logic of it right. What you're saying is that as an Internet provider, you're very sensitive to margins. And so when in doubt, you take it out. That's your basic rule.

CONSTANTINE: I'm not saying it's a policy of any of my companies, but I've seen it. And that's what happens. It's a reality.

NESSON: And the next step is, you think you go out of business for doing that?

CONSTANTINE: No. What I'm saying is—and it's happened. And if you listened to Bill Gates, I'm sure he said this, too. The proprietary services (CompuServe, AOL, Prodigy) are all going out into the Internet now. CompuServe just announced last week that it was scrapping its proprietary system. It will be there but as a secondary platform, and open standard on the Internet is the way to go. So everybody is providing Internet access, and everybody is focusing on the Internet, because there is content out there that is very compelling, and people want access to it. Nobody's going to go to an online service and pay money if they can go to AT&T and MCI, and it's just a small increment to their phone bill unless there is a *real* reason to use a proprietary platform. So they have to go out there and join the club.

I think that because there is free stuff on the Internet and because these online service providers are now not going to be making money on subscriber fees, because those fees are going down

and down and down to meet the Internet competition, the fees will be on advertising and on other means of supporting some of the incredible capital-intensive costs that are incurred in running this media. So I think that by singling out the online service providers, who actually are acting responsibly already—probably too responsibly, in my view, because they're risk-averse—and allowing people who put illegal or infringing content on the system to not be prosecuted because it's more difficult to find them perhaps, or because they're in another jurisdiction, and why bother? You can just get the distributor. Why deal with the content creator? It's a very bad development for technology and the Internet.

And George is going to be talking about the technological solutions, which I think are far better than the legal and other solutions that are now being proposed.

NESSON: Thank you, Jan. **GEORGE VRADENBURG** was General Counsel for CBS. He was part of the team that defended CBS and *60 Minutes* against the defamation suit brought by General Westmoreland. After that, he became Executive Vice President at Fox, and he is now the co-chair of the Entertainment, Sports, and Media Practice group at Latham and Watkins in Los Angeles. He is wonderfully qualified to bring a Hollywood entertainment law perspective to the problems we're talking about.

George, the industry response here has basically been to try and develop a system of user control, the development of the PICS [Platform for Internet Content Selection] standard,[*] which perhaps you will describe. It is a standard that depends on self rating. It means we're going to have a rated Internet. It's a strategy that takes the thought behind the V-chip and seeks, in a sense, to expand it and extend it to the Internet. Would you give us the perspective of Hollywood, or maybe a little bit broader, on whether this actually can work? Can you have a user control system, or a rating system that will actually accomplish effective content control with enough mus-

---

[*] For more information on PICS, see the World Wide Consortium (W3C) page at *http://www.w3.org/pub/WWW/PICS/*.

cle to it, so the Mr. and Mrs. America I represent are actually going to be politically satisfied? And when we come to daughter of the CDA, if we get that far, we won't be just trying to repass the first one.

VRADENBURG: Let me contrast the V-chip solution and the PICS solution, for a moment. I tried these arguments on Congress, in terms of why the V-chip system wouldn't work, and I didn't succeed there. I think I've got a better audience, at least in intelligence and sophistication, here.

Let me start with the V-chip, because by describing why I don't think it will work, I'll describe why I think the PICS approach on the Internet has a good deal more promise. I think the V-chip solution is a closed system. It is, in fact, of limited utility, and it will be of limited utility to the parents of America. And thus, I don't think it's going to work and indeed, it has some dangers that I'll describe. The PICS system, by contrast, I think, is open and flexible and does have a good deal of promise. But it's going to need some industry support.

The V-chip has two components. By January of 1997, the broadcast and cable industry is supposed to come up with a voluntary rating system satisfactory to the government (hence, one questions whether it's voluntary), which will set some ratings for all of the stuff on cable and broadcast TV, and will incorporate those ratings in the electronic signals they send out. Then, by January of 1998, you'll start seeing TV sets that will respond to that rating system and permit a parent in the home, the prototypical single parent with 14 kids and four jobs, who will be employing this system, to block out the programs with ratings that parent finds unsatisfactory.

Now, obviously, this system is closed. It's going to have a single set of ratings. It's going to be adopted by the industry with the approval of the government. And it's going to have a technology inside the TV set that will respond only to that rating system. Broadcasters and cable-casters had argued for an open system, basically, to adopt some intelligence inside the TV set that will allow a parent to block out any kind of program-

ming, limit the kinds of usage you want to make, but don't impose a rating system on top of that. The government concluded—not persuaded by these arguments—that in fact, it was too difficult a system to use; that in fact, parents wouldn't use a system that was open and that allowed them a great deal of discretion; consequently, Congress imposed upon the industry a rating system.

Now, what's wrong with a rating system, at least this rating system? Let me describe, just for the sake of argument, three approaches to it. The statute contemplates that the program will be rated either with a V, an S, or an O—for Violence, Sex, and Other indecent material that should be made available or disclosed to a parent before they expose it to their kids. Now, obviously, if you rate something with a V, an S, or "Other indecency," you've got absolutely no context. You don't know what the quality is. You don't know what the character of the programming is. You don't know the difference in a V system between *Schindler's List* and *Texas Chain Saw Massacre*. And S, you couldn't distinguish between a *Friends* episode, with sex between two of the lead characters, and *Debbie Does Dallas*. Or with the "Other indecency," who knows what that means? Does it mean that you've got to rate the lesbian kiss episode of *Roseanne*, the masturbation episode of *Seinfeld*? One doesn't know what it means. But you don't know whether, in fact, you would agree with the rating that's going to be imposed by the industry.

Another approach would be simply to rate by age, which may very well be the approach the industry takes, notwithstanding the suggestion in the statute to the contrary. "This programming is suitable for all ages. This programming is suitable for all ages over 12. This programming is suitable for all ages over 18." Now, that approach at least gives you some semblance of an approach, but your kids could be different ages. What if I don't mind my kid watching certain sexual content or innuendo, but they happen to be within the age category that, in fact, some broadcaster or the industry has decided is appropriate for a different age category? You don't have much descriptive content as to exactly what it is that is supposed to be unsuitable for your kid. So you don't know whether or not to use that particular classification.

Another classification would be by category of product. Talk shows. There are some awfully bizarre behaviors described on talk shows, but is it sexual? Is it violent? Is it otherwise indecent? Who knows? Is it for particular age groups? Who knows? But you know that talk show stuff has just got to come off. So many think that product category is a better classification to use: talk shows, soap operas, news, sports—something like that.

You can see, if you start getting into these categories and classifications, there are any number of ways to classify this system. If you try to mix and match all of them, you get such a complex system that probably the V-chip will never be able to handle it and parents will not be able to make sense of it. On the other hand, if you just pick one of those kinds of approaches to classification, you're not giving enough information to any particular parent to be able to decide what that particular parent wants. So the problem is, you have such a vast array of programming on cable television and on broadcast television, and such a wide mix of parental reactions to what their kids ought to see, that no single classification is going to be very satisfactory or very useful to parents. So the V-chip is going to be of limited utility.

On the other hand, once you start classifying this stuff, then programmers will have to start building to the classifications. So all of a sudden, programmers will have to start avoiding the V or the S or the "Other indecency," and you might knock off of TV something that's perfectly great and valid, *NYPD Blue* might get a V, which would be a black mark, and obviously, it would force it out, either because advertisers won't support it, or some set of parents might block it out for their kids. And you'll start to get distortions in the programming pattern. So it's a limited utility system, and it's got some dangers.

Now, the PICS system basically says, here is a standardized approach that you can install—here, to the computer software industry, is a set of standards and platforms to which you can write any

kind of program selection categories you want. (Jan can come in and write a computer program that basically says, these are the web sites to avoid if you want to avoid sexual content. Mike can come in and say, this is a set of program selections based upon certain other criteria, like, "They collect marketing information on you; watch out.") You can write a variety of selection criteria into the different programming software, so that in fact, any parent can go out in the marketplace and buy a set of software that will rate programs and classify web sites based on different kinds of selection criteria. This would give a parent a wide variety of choices among the extraordinary amount of information on the web, to make the choice. This is now more useful to parents, and probably, therefore, more used by parents. And at the same time, it doesn't have the sort of dangerous problem of trying to get people to program to particular cubbyholes, because in fact there are so many different cubbies that they can offer up anything they want and appeal to whatever niche they want.

Now, the problem I see with the PICS system is one of complexity. There can be so many choices that parents really don't know what to choose from. The other problem is, obviously, it's very difficult to be comprehensive and honest about this; comprehensive, because there are so many web sites, and they keep multiplying. And then to have an accurate classification system to make sure you've really picked out or knocked out everything you're representing to a particular consumer of your selection software. Because how do you really search all those present and future web sites?

So it seems to me that the PICS system is both more useful, certainly more friendly in terms of program diversity, but it's going to need a good deal of support from the industry to try and figure out how to make it useful to consumers.

Now, Congress didn't buy any of this, Charlie.

CONSTANTINE: The courts will.

VRADENBURG: You hope the courts will. The problem with the courts is that, notwithstanding

Mike's argument, the courts have found that there is a class of programming that's not obscene and is short of everything that describes or depicts sexual conduct or activities. There's something called "indecency," that the government is permitted to regulate in the interests of kids. And the government supposedly has a compelling interest to do this. As long as it uses the least restrictive alternative to get at it, they will.

One of the things that the courts have not yet permitted to be taken into account in assessing this thing is whether there are marketplace solutions that will allow parents to make the supervisory decisions here. The government has an independent interest itself in protecting the psychological and physical well-being of minors. It's not just an interest in assisting parents to make those selections; the government has its *independent* interest.

So even though PICS may be out there—even though PICS may be 100 percent effective in terms of parental satisfaction—the government has an independent interest. PICS has a very good political argument, which, if it is in widespread use, should diminish the political motivation, the political force behind any censorship on the Net. And that's why I think PICS is so useful, because the CDA will get struck down and PICS becomes more widely used and useful and perceived to be so, and there's a strong political argument for why the government ought not to get into it.

GODWIN: I think George and I probably disagree about how to read one of the key cases in this area, which is *Sable Communications v. FCC.* It's a dial-a-porn case. In 1989, the Supreme Court upheld a ban on obscene material on dial-a-porn services, but struck down a ban on *indecent* material on dial-a-porn services.

NESSON: I'm Mr. and Mrs. America. I don't want my kid to be able to go to the phone and dial the 1-900 number and get through to hot sex. And I want the government to do something abut it. They did something about it, but the court stopped them from excluding indecent phone sex.

GODWIN: That's right; they didn't stop them from regulating it. But that's a separate issue from the one I wanted to raise with regard to George's comment. And that's that indecency, until now, has always been defined in terms of what it's not—it's not obscene—it doesn't have to appeal to the prurient interest. It's never defined in terms of what it is, except by the FCC, those (as we like to say) outside the beltway, those unelected bureaucrats inside the beltway. Nobody knows precisely what it means or what the test is.

There is some discussion of indecency in *Sable Communications,* but what the Supreme Court has never said—and I challenge anyone to prove me wrong on this—the Supreme Court has never said that the government has general authority to regulate so-called indecent content.

Harmful-to-minors content is somewhat different. You'll hear the phrase "harmful to minors," and you even see it in *Sable,* but that seems to be a separate category, a narrower category of material that is sexually explicit.

VRADENBURG: Both in *Pacifica* and *Sable,* the court recognized the ability of government to regulate access of minors to indecency. It has been sustained, so long as it does so in the least restrictive means available. The Supreme Court will strike down, I think, any blanket restriction of indecent material where adults can't get access to it.

NESSON: Let me just intrude here with a piece of information. The key provision of the Communications Decency Act that is being challenged—and there's actually a question as to whether we have a total ban or a least restrictive ban—the one that is most problematic is: "Whoever uses any interactive computer service to display, in a manner available to a person under 18 years of age, any communication that in context depicts or describes in terms patently offensive, as measured by contemporary community standards, sexual or excretory activities or organs, shall be fined or imprisoned not more than two years, or both." So it's any action that makes available to somebody under 18, which sounds like it's putting up in any open space on the Web something that meets this description.

GODWIN: Or Usenet or a mailing list.

VRADENBURG: Subject to a series of defenses.

CONSTANTINE: Could I talk about these defenses for one minute? In the way of full disclosure, I have to admit that I was actually involved in drafting some of the CDA's defense provisions. Now, I don't want this to leave this room, but at the time we were told by our lobbyist of the Interactive Services Association (a trade association to which all the online service providers belong), that this was inevitable. It was going to happen, and the best thing to do is try to work with the staff of the various Congressional representatives that were shoving it down the throats of the people, because it was an election year and everybody was afraid to vote against it. So we were asked to actually develop some language with respect to the defenses to make it more palatable for the online service providers to accept.

One of the things that we tried to do was fashion a defense that would limit our liability to anything that was on our system (on the proprietary platform); but as far as the Internet is concerned, to say that "as long as we didn't have any editorial control"—and that was the language that has since been deleted—we wouldn't be responsible. So the dilemma under the current language, which talks about "if you knowingly transmit for an online service provider" is the following.

Everybody knows that there are Usenet newsgroups on the Internet called things like *alt.binary.pictures.sex.bestiality*, or *alt.sex.pederasty*. They're out there, and we've seen them, and other people have seen them as well. No one will admit to it, but somehow they're very popular. If we know they're out there, as an online service provider, and yet we allow access to them through our service—and I won't get into the caching/mirroring distinction, but essentially, they're on our servers. They're not through some gateway out in the Internet, because we want

people to have quick response time and we don't want to have to go searching for them every second, because they're very popular. Does that mean, by virtue of the fact that they're out there and people access them, that we knowingly make them available?

So regardless of our attempts to insulate ourselves with these defenses, the defenses are very unartfully drafted, and leave absolutely no certainty with respect to the online service providers, or for that matter, Internet access providers, of any kind of assistance in thwarting a prosecution under the Act, because there is no way you can exist with language so vague and imprecise that would enable you to even attempt to comply with the statute in the first place.

So we've come a long way from primitive blocking software to the PICS software. But really, we, the online service provider community, always said Prodigy was wrong in trying to do the "right" thing.★ The defenses in the CDA recognized that they were trying to do the right thing. There's a good faith or good samaritan defense, which basically says, if you implement this kind of software (and there is other software, other than PICS, like SurfWatch, NannyNet, and CyberPatrol in place now), you will not be held liable either for civil and criminal attempts, as long as you're doing this in good faith.

GODWIN: Let me say very briefly that the leading case in deciding this issue about Internet service providers and everyone else is a case called *Smith v. California,* an obscenity case from the late 1950s. And the principle there was that you can't just assume that a bookstore owner knows all the content and is knowingly distributing obscene material. And that has been extended to libel by *New York Times v. Sullivan.*

Now, it's not the case that bookstores never make editorial decisions; they make editorial decisions all the time. In fact, you would think it was crazy if a mystery bookstore that refused to carry science fiction were suddenly more liable to a

---

★ Prodigy attempted to block certain four-letter words on their service.

libel lawsuit than anyone else. That would just be a crazy outcome.

NESSON: So your point in a sense is, we're really right at the beginning of judicial consideration of this problem.

GODWIN: That's right.

Questions & Answers

Q: *My name is José. I'm a practicing attorney/law professor in Puerto Rico. Back to the issue of enforcement, isn't this the same argument as whether or not public international law is possible because there is nobody to enforce it? Yet, some sort of enforcement is possible or was possible at some point.*

NESSON: Well, I'll tell you a version of that question that is of interest to me. The Communications Decency Act that's under consideration here is evaluated as a balance. There's a recognition that protected speech for adults is actually burdened by the statute. And the question is, is that balance justified by the benefit it brings in accomplishing the objective, which is supposedly to protect children?

When you go to the Internet and you start looking for pornographic material, what you find is that there is a load of pornographic material there, and a load of it that comes from outside the United States. So that this statute, if it were completely effective in cleaning up all Internet sites that originated in the United States, would still leave the situation as one where somebody under 18 goes to AltaVista and plugs in "sex adult" hotlink, they're going to get inundated with hotlinks and inundated with pornography.

So one could clearly make the argument that there is no way this statute can be effective in accomplishing its purpose. And if that's true, then there's no way the balance that justifies the imposition on protected speech comes out in favor of the Act.

Is that a decent argument? Is that a winner or is it just academics?

VRADENBURG: Academics, because I don't think the United States government will ever be held by the Supreme Court to be disabled from trying to protect its citizens in some fashion. Illegal activity outside the United States that can be accessed inside the U.S. can be prohibited. I mean, we've got everything from drug smuggling to whatever, which, in fact, is difficult in terms of enforcing the law. Even in the First Amendment context, I think, as long as this thing is sustainable on its own foot inside the United States, it's not going to defeat that argument that, in fact, you can still get access to this material outside.

GODWIN: My two-word answer is "Manuel Noriega."

NESSON: Translate that for us, would you?

GODWIN: It turns out that the United States government reserves the right to go outside the country and prosecute people who commit some element of a crime inside the country, or a crime that has an effect inside the country. It's a little bit imperialistic, according to some of us, but nevertheless that's what we do.

NESSON: A little bit imperialistic? What are we going to do? Send the Marines to Finland?

GODWIN: Stranger things have happened.

CONSTANTINE: I would just add two words. I think it would be compelling for someone to use that argument that you've just given, to say it's not the least restrictive method. I would say that the government has the right to do it, however unsuccessful, but that a court would be very sympathetic to that argument that, once they eradicate everything in the United States, the Internet will still be able to reroute and find it in Finland. Therefore, why should you do this? It's not the least restrictive. Put PICS in the hands of the parents. Then you really are doing something that's meaningful.

GODWIN: Right. Part of the "least restrictive" means test, constitutionally, is whether the means are effective. That may sound like an academic argument, but actually it's a very fact-bound argument. So if you can adduce evidence in a case to show that the government is saying the least restrictive means to accomplish its legitimate goals are not, in fact, effective, that sinks it just as much as anything else would.

NESSON: Steven McGeady [Intel keynote speaker].

McGEADY: An Iranian court requested the extradition of Madonna and Michael Jackson from the United States for violations of Islamic law. It was treated as a humorous story. About six months after that, another couple, a California bulletin board service operator was extradited from California to Tennessee, tried, found guilty, and I think was put in jail for violating Tennessee's community standards by running a bulletin board service in California.

Now, I want to sort of turn that previous discussion on its head and ask, how do you define, or how do you create community standards? Each of you sort of bandied that word or that phrase about, in the discussion of how we regulate indecency, as opposed to obscenity. Are there such things any more as community standards? Do communities have a legitimate right to regulate pornography?

GODWIN: Those are two separate questions. The reason I'm going to answer this or take a lead on this is that I worked on Thomas' case, so I know something about the case in detail. The Electronic Frontier Foundation filed an amicus brief on the issue of community standards, and I've actually written in *Reason* magazine and elsewhere about the fact that we may be coming to the end of where "community standards" talk is meaningful legally. It used to be that communities were primarily geographic. One of the things that we've discovered about this online world is that people form communities of interest that have nothing to do with geography. And in fact, those are the communities that mean most to people, at least, to a lot of people who are online.

Now, the courts are not going to ever recognize this while I think any current jurist is alive. It's the nature of things. As Thomas Kuhn says in *The Structure of Scientific Revolutions,* the principal way that paradigms shift is that all the old guys die. Right? And then the new people who have grown up with the new technology or whatever, recognize the new paradigm. In fact, it seems to be that we're having a paradigm shift. And although the obscenity law in this country, for all the people who think "community standards" or "reasonable man" or "prurient interests" are vague, obscenity law in this country has been relatively stable—remarkably so—since 1973, when the Supreme Court handed down *Miller v. California.* I think we're now heading into the end of that era of stability.

There's one other issue. And that is what I think of as a criminal law due process issue, which is, can you commit this crime while you're asleep, while you're not even near the computer that's transmitting the stuff? In fact, what happens when someone downloads an image from a BBS or an FTP site is not, in a very fundamental way, like a traditional pornography vendor putting something in the mail or sending something through UPS. In the latter case, you have an intentional act. In the former case, what you have doesn't quite, in my view as someone who does criminal law, amount to the kind of intent necessary for criminal liability. So that's a separate issue.

CONSTANTINE: I'd just like to add a footnote. When the *Thomas* conviction came out, I told my CEO of the Delphi online service that all of this Usenet newsgroup stuff would be obscene for any subscriber in Tennessee, and he might consider thinking about taking it off the Net because he might be subject to criminal fines and, in fact, a jail term. Before this, we were operating under the *Cubby v. CompuServe* model, which essentially said, as long as you don't touch it and have any editorial control over what goes on your system, then, according to the Southern District of New York, you wouldn't be liable. Here, by monitoring or looking behind the names of these newsgroups and deciding what was obscene under this *Miller* three-prong test, you would risk liability on the one hand; but the conundrum was, if you didn't take off some of this stuff residing on your server, you might be sitting next to the Thomases in some Tennessee jail.

So what we did was, we decided we didn't want to do anything that the competition wasn't doing.

VRADENBURG: Heaven forbid!

CONSTANTINE: That would be terrible. We'd lose subscribers. We had about 120, and I think AOL had tipped three million by that time. And all of our subscribers liked all of these Usenet newsgroups. The ten most popular were all within the *alt.binary.pictures.bestiality* category. So what we did was tiptoe around the issue. We had all of these Q&As ready if the press came to us. And we took off three groups that were really disgusting, even in my eyes. And we waited and waited. And then I asked Customer Service, "Have you had any complaints?" She said, "Some people called who said, 'Why did you delete some of these groups?' But when we asked them which groups were deleted, none of them were brave enough to admit that they ever participated in any of these groups." So it was really a nonevent.

But the *Thomas* conviction was enough to get my CEO, who is a purist, to say, "Wait a minute. I'm really nervous about some of this stuff that's out there on the Internet. I may have to do something about it."

If the CDA is indeed deemed to be Constitutional, which I hope it's not, there is going to be a backlash on the commercial online service providers. They're going to have to really think about their access to some of this questionable material. It may not be obscene, but there is definitely stuff that could be deemed to be patently offensive by somebody.

VRADENBURG: In the ratings world, there are 36 or more countries that have ratings systems, only three of which have nongovernmental rating systems: the United States for the MPAA, Germany—interestingly enough, because of the Second World War history (the current rating scheme there is nongovernmental)—and Japan. The rest of the ratings boards around the world are government established. And by and large, they actually restrict access to material that is rated in certain fashions. In many of those countries, sacrilegious material is one of the standards by which they will classify the material and thus ban it.

I think it is a fascinating question in the future about what kind of international standards might begin to evolve in this area. One looks at the existing state of the world, and you look at someplace like Sweden or the United States on the one hand, to the Muslim countries in the Middle East, and you say there's quite a disparity. The only sort of thing in international treaties in this area is a general consensus about free flow of information. But that generally was thought, I think, to deal with political information and people's right to know. But it's written very broadly, so that the text provides some degree of assurance of the free flow of information out there. And the question is, in fact, for members of the U.N. or other parties to these treaties, if in fact they begin to restrict material because of its religious or political content, whether there is some mechanism (to go back to this gentleman's prior question) in the international world in which one can begin to establish at least some standards for preventing nations from precluding the free flow of information around the world.

Q: *Will PICS make it easier for countries to exclude whole categories of information from their people's purview?*

VRADENBURG: Certainly, users will be able to exclude material from any Web site.

Q: *Does Singapore require that every computer carry a given piece of software with a form of CyberPatrol?*

VRADENBURG: Yes, but then, that wouldn't be the PICS system. The PICS system is basically designed to allow the user to select the range of things that they want to pick out of the Internet. The problem of PICS, as a practical matter, is, how does a software maker who is trying to preclude sacrilegious content (if you're sitting in Saudi Arabia) really search out the web sites of the world for sacrilegious programming?

Q: *My name is David Wolf. Is there a difference between parental control over religion, politics, types of* *education, and any other type of content—let's say, obscenity or indecency? If it's an inherent right and responsibility of parenting to guide, filter, and encourage development, how are they (and we know who "they" are) holding the Internet to a somewhat different and, on the surface, paternalistic method of enforcement?*

VRADENBURG: Well, this argument first arose in the broadcast context, because in fact, in the broadcasters' challenge to the criminal provisions of indecency over broadcasting, which have been there for 60 years, and the FCC's decision, barring the broadcasting of indecent programming, the broadcasters raised this issue and demonstrated that there was a parent actually present to supervise kids' viewing about 96 percent of the time; that varies during the course of a day, of course. And the broadcasters argued that you shouldn't really ban indecent programming on the air during those times of the day, when in virtually all the cases, there's a parent there to supervise. And the court basically said, government is not limited to regulating indecent programming and kids' access to indecent programming, based upon trying to support parental supervision.

I agree with you. I think this is a job for parents, and this has been traditionally a job for parents. In other contexts, whether it be family formation or adoption cases, parental rights have been considered paramount, and indeed, in some sense of the word, a Constitutionally protected right in other contexts. In this context, at least in the broadcasting environment (and now, the government argues, in other environments), the government has an independent interest, above and beyond assisting parents in protecting the psychological and physical well-being of kids. Some cases suggest that the government has an independent, compelling interest in protecting the ethical and moral upbringing of kids.

GODWIN: I have to say something here. I'm not disagreeing with anyone; I'm just saying that this question came up in the final argument of the Communications Decency Act challenges in Philadelphia. There was this great moment in the courtroom, when Judge Dalzell raised this hypothetical for the government attorneys. He said,

"Look." He held a copy of the *Philadelphia Inquirer* in his hand, indicating the full page one photo of a battlefield execution of a soldier in, I think, Bosnia. Judge Dalzell questioned the government attorney as to a hypothetical newspaper decency act: "Suppose that Congress were worried about the dangers to children posed by violent newspaper images," Dalzell said. And suppose that Congress, recognizing that it couldn't constitutionally ban such images altogether, or even from the front page of the newspaper, were to say, "Look, in the newspaper decency act, you can have it on the front page but you must print it below the fold." Would such a law be constitutional?

And the government attorney had to concede that, by everything we know, it wouldn't. So at least as regards the print medium, the government does not have kind of a general authority—

NESSON: You say it would be constitutional, or it would be unconstitutional?

GODWIN: He said it would *not* be constitutional. And you have the government conceding that at least as regards the print medium, the government's authority stops, even when the care of children is at least ostensibly the rationale.

Having said that, this is America, and we're weirder about sex than we are about other stuff. And the fact is, arguments that may not be compelling as regards violence, even though I personally think violence is worse than sex for children. The fact is, we tend to give the government more scope to regulate sexual content than other kinds of content. That's our social response.

NESSON: Let me just say that one of the phenomena that strikes me as very real is that people passing the laws about the Internet are really not very knowledgeable about it. And that has produced some serious problems. That seems to be a problem that will be replicated in other jurisdictions beyond the United States, as they come to confront problems of regulation. And in some sense, the best thing that I think could happen with our Communications Decency Act is that it turn out to have served as a kind of cooling off period. I'd love it to be declared unconstitutional, myself. I'd love there to be a period before the Congress goes back and starts to think once again about this problem. It's been my experience that the more people are acquainted with the Net, the more they come to understand it and respect it. And we'll get better, more sensitive legislation out of it.

About the Speakers

CHARLES NESSON is the William F. Weld Professor of Law at Harvard Law School, and the co-director of the school's Center for Law and Information Technology.

JAN FRIEDMAN CONSTANTINE is the Senior Vice President and General Counsel of NewsAmerica Publishing Incorporated, and the Senior Vice President of the News Corporation Limited. She is responsible for legal affairs for U.S. operations in areas of litigation, intellectual property, mergers and acquisitions, corporate financings, bankruptcy, antitrust and trade regulation, labor, and employment. Her client companies include *TV Guide*, the *New York Post*, and Delphi Internet Services. Ms. Constantine lectures on topics relating to copyright, libel, employment, antitrust, and bankruptcy, and is a regular participant on panels relating to cyberspace and Internet legal matters.

MIKE GODWIN is Staff Counsel for the Electronic Frontier Foundation, where he informs users of electronic networks about their legal rights and responsibilities, instructs criminal lawyers and law-enforcement personnel about computer civil-liberties issues, and conducts seminars about civil liberties in electronic communication for a wide range of groups. Godwin published articles for print and electronic publications on topics such as electronic searches and seizures, the First Amendment and electronic publications, and the application of international law to computer communications. Godwin has written articles about social and legal issues on the electronic frontier that have appeared in the *Whole Earth Review*, *The Quill*, *Index on Censorship*, *Internet World*, *Wired*, HotWired, and *Playboy*.

GEORGE VRADENBURG is a partner at the Los Angeles office of Latham & Watkins, where he is co-chair of the firm's Entertainment and Media Industry Practice Group. Mr. Vradenburg has extensive transactional, litigation, and regulatory expertise in various sectors of the entertainment industry. His experience as aggressive and creative legal counsel at two networks—as Senior Vice President and General Counsel at CBS and as Executive Vice President of Fox Inc.—adds invaluable industry insight to the firm's entertainment and media practice. Mr. Vradenburg is a frequent speaker on technical, trade, and social issues of communications and entertainment.

Law

May 31, 1996

Digital Convergence and Vertical Integration

MODERATOR: Reinier Kraakman

PANELISTS: Joel Klein
Gary Reback
Steve Weiswasser

KRAAKMAN: I am the moderator today of our ambitious topic, "Digital Convergence and Vertical Integration," which could also have been titled "Competition in the Information-Based Industries." When I first heard our title, I was reminded of the cover of an issue of *Wired* from several years ago, from a time when the phrase "Information Superhighway" was still fresh and not quite as embarrassing as it might be today. Bell Atlantic, the large phone company, and TCI, the cable giant, were involved in a merger dance, with plans, in their own words, to become "Information Superhighway Pioneers." The spirit of the moment—the super-heated hopes and fears of the time—were captured by putting the head of Bell Atlantic's CEO on the body of a sword-wielding Conan the Barbarian on that *Wired* cover. Pretty terrifying, except it made no economic sense. The deal fell through. And Ray Smith, the head of Bell Atlantic, was unceremoniously returned to his own body and to the distinctly less primordial and mythical business of serving phone customers.

In any case it's pretty clear now that the broadband future, in which all information—video, voice, and data—travels down a single wire, is still a long way off. Nevertheless, the process of digital convergence has begun, even if the end is still a way off. What we're going to try to do today is to peer into the future, to get some sense

of the business strategies the major players are likely to adopt, by extrapolating from the strategies they've already pursued. As lawyers, we're not just concerned with business strategy, we're also concerned with how business strategy is or is not likely to—or ought to—be constrained by the law, specifically the antitrust law.

Many of you are not lawyers, but that's okay. For our purposes, the goal of antitrust law is simple enough. It's to ensure that firms don't engage in anticompetitive behavior: behavior that harms the consumer by "artificially" limiting competition in the market.

Our goal is to answer the following questions:

- What strategies are the major players likely to adopt?

- How might these strategies be significant for the Internet?

- When might these strategies come into conflict with the policies of antitrust law?

STEVE WEISWASSER is going to tell us about some of the business strategies cable television companies have used, what they are, why they work, and why the government has seen fit to regulate. Steve is well qualified to do all of this because of the variety of his experience as a communications lawyer for Wilmer Cutler in D.C., as a Senior Executive at Capital Cities/ABC, and now as CEO of Americast, an alliance of three Baby Bells, GTE, and Disney. Americast, as many of you know, aims to compete against the cable companies to distribute television programming.

Next is **GARY REBACK**, head of the technology practice at Wilson, Sonsini in Silicon Valley, the venture capital firm. He wrote the white paper that led to blocking Microsoft's acquisition of Intuit, and won the *Lotus v. Borland* case in the Supreme Court earlier this year. His undergraduate degree is from Yale and his law degree is from Stanford.

Our last guest is **JOEL KLEIN**, currently Principal Deputy Assistant Attorney General for Antitrust in the U.S. Department of Justice. He has served as Deputy Counsel to President Clinton, and was a former partner in Klein, Farr, Smith, and Toronto, in Washington, D.C., where he specialized in appellate practice. I've asked Joel to help synthesize Gary's and Steve's observations, to compare the two industries they're going to tell us about, locate the similarities and differences, and come up with a grand synthesis of their comments here.

Steve, you run a company that hopes to sell cable programming in competition with the cable giants. What can you tell us about the competitive concerns that arise, when real or potential new entries try to challenge the existing cable monopolies?

WEISWASSER: Americast is a new venture that in many ways can be regarded as a start-up company, but one with the advantages that come from fairly wealthy parents. Bell South, Southwestern Bell, Ameritech, GTE, and Walt Disney each put up 20 percent of a half-billion dollars over the next five years, develop a content package to compete in the multi-channel distribution world. We can't just point to cable as the source of our problems, as everybody knows. There is direct broadcast satellite (DBS). There's digital Multichannel Multipoint Distribution Service [MMDS]. There is the potential that broadcasters themselves will get second channels that will be digitized and capable of providing multiple services, and so forth.

Our venture is one of two. The second one TeleTV, is the child of Michael Ovitz—then of Creative Artists Agency, now of the Disney Company—a form of convergence of its own), and NYNEX, Bell Atlantic, and PacTel [Pacific Telesis]. PacTel is about to be bought by Southwestern Bell, so now one of the partners of the other ventures is being bought by one of my partners, and nobody quite knows what that's going to produce. Again, another form of digital convergence. There is clearly the potential that the two ventures will work together.

We were born, each of us, out of a vision as naive as the one that suggested that Ray Smith was a dragon slayer: that the telephone companies were going to build out massive wire-based systems and produce converged content—every-

thing from telephony to interactive software to interactive Internet-based content to new forms of interactive broadband television—all by the end of the decade.

I'm here to tell you that isn't going to happen. It is a much slower process. The cost of the wire builds that people were envisioning are far greater than anybody anticipated. The speed with which the telephone companies can rewire or will rewire, and marry their telephony with video, is considerably reduced. The speed with which the cable industry—which five years ago and then three years ago was said to be poised to get into the telephone business—will add significant telephony to its video offerings, has been significantly reduced because of the vast costs associated with that effort.

Our strategy today as a startup venture (albeit one with deep pockets), is ultimately to create a balanced wired and wireless system. We may use DBS, digital MMDS cable and wired services together, and Internet access (which we will package to create Internet content) to offer a range of services to our customers. These services will not, in fact, be converged with telephony, but may well be bundled with it. So this will be part of a marketing plan rather than part of a technology plan. The casualty for a while will be some of the more esoteric notions of interactive communications and interactive content. The speed with which people are prepared to absorb that kind of content in a broadband environment remains open to question.

I find myself left with the need to create a business, to get to market with a product, and to create a national brand (in this case, Americast), with fairly traditional television offerings. I'm going to be in the television business, the cable television business, whether I'm delivering it by wire or wireless. I'm going to be in the business of delivering multichannel content. And to do that the first order of business must be to offer our customers content that is familiar to them, that is similar to what they can get from their cable television operator. I should add that to compete effectively, we ultimately have to do a good deal more than that.

But the *sine qua non*, the first step in the pitch to people must be, "You won't lose anything by coming to us." And that means I have to be able to offer what is familiar. In my judgment, people will not switch from cable television or enter the digital world without getting familiar names— HBO and CNN and ESPN—as well as all the other traditional content packages, like the ABC or NBC local affiliates.

The question becomes, "How do you get the essential first level of content from the competitor in your market whom you're trying to beat?" By and large, we will be competing against TCI, Time Warner, and a variety of other companies who are fully vertically integrated in the content and distribution business. I am acutely aware that as a startup venture trying to compete with them, I have very little leverage to obtaining the content I need. As a result, we have spent an enormous amount of time in the last year simply amassing content that is already grist for the cable TV mill. Our success in this arena is due, to a large extent, to the Cable Act, which creates a right of access to our competitors' content. Most of the vertically integrated cable program services would not have been available to us if not for the fact that government mandates that vertically integrated cable companies make that content available to competitors. Even with the act, it has taken us a considerable amount of time to amass the content. There's always an argument, there's always an excuse, always a reason. And delay is always in the interest of the incumbent.

I would say (taking care to avoid getting in the middle of current governmental conflicts), we have not had the same problems with Time Warner and Turner, for example, that we've had with a number of the other program services. Turner was the first company to make its content available to us, and Time Warner was close behind, although we have had some issues with HBO.

From the perspective of the cable program service, the obvious reality is that it is almost confiscatory to require that the people who develop the service be required to make it available to competitors. On the other hand, in order for the government to meet its goal of breaking up the extraordinary dominance by the cable industry in most markets, and thus providing a competitive market in the media industry, requires that the content be freed up.

Just yesterday, Liberty Cable, a small, wireless cable operator in New York City (which I think has amassed, after ten years of street-to-street combat with Time Warner Cable, three percent of Manhattan cable homes) felt compelled to challenge the Time Warner-Turner merger through an antitrust suit, on the grounds that Time Warner had withheld content. And whether the problem that exists in New York is one of unavailability of content or the inadequacy of wireless cable as a technology, I won't judge. But it is extraordinary, given the relative quality of Time Warner Cable in Manhattan, that any competitor could not amass more than three percent of the cable homes. There are complexities because there are obviously a great number of apartment units, involved. And it is also clear that Time Warner has gone to some lengths to aggressively put down that competition. It will be an interesting case.

Notwithstanding our size, or the fact that our partner, Disney, itself now controls four or five basic cable program services and has the capacity to deny these services to our competitors, the bottom line is this: we had significant difficulty in signing up any number of these services, which are the *sine qua non* for our operation.

I think this provides a good starting point for further discussions.

KRAAKMAN: Let's jump industries and turn to Gary's experiences with the Internet.

REBACK: I would like to talk about Steve [Weiswasser's] comments in light of the software side of the industry. Specifically, I'll mention three antitrust-related issues:

- The issue of the relevant market for the companies I work for, which is commonly called the intranet.

- Network economics.

- Bad acts. You'll understand what I mean, once I get a little further.

Now, let me try to put everything in perspective so that you can converge Steve's comments with mine. First, we have the software industry; there is the Internet that is the subject of this conference; and finally many companies have what is known as a private Internet protocol network, an intranet. Your intranet might be accessed through a browser, for instance, a Netscape or Microsoft browser, on your desktop, running on top of, say, Windows. And your company (or in this case, Harvard), has a server. It might be a Unix server, or an NT server. It allows people within the intranet, using the Internet backbone, to communicate with each other. There's a firewall around the server so that no one can get inside it or tamper with it. Yet people on the inside, using their browser, can go out on the Net. That server, that construct, is generally known in industry as the "enterprise." The general assumption in these industries is that he who controls the enterprise will, in time, control everything else.

You've heard discussion of set-top boxes from people like Scott McNealy and Larry Tesler. You've heard Bill Gates say they'll never go anywhere. You hear the Sun people talking about pagers, cable companies. That's the business-to-home market that includes Java applets—a very interesting nascent market, which exhibits some of the same kind of problems of vertical integration and competition you see in my markets.

I want to focus on the intranets, because I've had difficulty communicating with the government about what we see as problems here. That's because we're speaking about two different markets. Some people conceptualize the Internet as one broad market and wonder how it can be monopolized. But the truth is, there is also the intranet market. And that's really where the action is, for Netscape, Microsoft, Sun, and so forth.

To compare and contrast the two types of markets, I'm going to refer to some web pages. The first is from Zona Research Publishing, *PC Week,*

I think. You can get it off the Zona web site [*http://www.zona.on.ca/*]. It shows that over the next two years, the investment in intranets will be four times the size of the investments in the Internet. That's where the growth is, where the competition is, what the action is all about.

As I said, you get into the Internet and use your intranets through a browser. There's a lot of discussion about what a browser is. A browser is a client and it works with a server. And, unlike the desktop, the notion of an application program just working on a desktop makes no sense in intranet or Internet types of environment, because an application has to run both on the browser and on the server. So, if you had a large share of the browser market and tried to implement some changes there, but the changes weren't recognized by any server, they wouldn't be implemented. They wouldn't be visible or accessible to the user. So when we think about who controls these markets, how they will be controlled, and how vertically integrated companies want to control all this, we have to think about both sides of the equation.

Another example from the Zona web site shows the results of some recent polling they've done. It shows that although Netscape has a significant lead in the number of browsers used in the intranets in the business environment, that lead is transitory and fragile—Netscape has about 44 percent to Microsoft's 17 percent—but, 75 to 80 percent of the operating systems they run on are Windows 95, Windows 3.x, or Windows NT: *75 to 80 percent.* And he who controls the operating system can obviously control the browser, because Microsoft has announced they're going to bundle the browser straight into the operating system.

In corporate environments, there isn't a lock-in yet in terms of browsers. Although Netscape has the lead today, the MIS directors of corporations haven't fixed on a single browser. So, if you were thinking just of the browser as an application, you would ask, "Is there any market power in the browser market?" I'd say the answer is no. If you were looking more globally, because of the client/server nature of this market, you would say the power and the investment would be on the server side.

This is the Forrester Research home page [*http://www.forrester.com/*]. You can see, looking forward, that the investment and the revenue from browsers will be about ten percent of servers. So to succeed here, if you want to be on the intranet side of the pipeline (as opposed to the side of the Internet pipeline where Steve [Weiswasser] is), you want to control the server market.

Note that the tools used to build applications will also be three times the size of the browser market. I know many of you observed, early this year, Microsoft's acquisition of Vermeer, a tools company that did $400,000 of business last year. Microsoft paid $100 million for them. Why would they do that? Because they have a lot of money and they just want to waste it? No, no. Because they see this is where the growth is.

There has been a lot of discussion here across the Net as to what's going on. Bill Gates says he stays up nights worrying about his share of the browser market. If that's the case, why would he worry? What is there to worry about? I've talked about the browser as an application, and I've argued it's really not. I've talked about the browser as an effective promo for the server, which is the way you might think of it. But most fundamentally, one might think about the browser as a new operating system, because applications are being built on the browser. Therefore, the great concern of Microsoft is that the browser might come to replace Windows.

Another example is from the c|net web page [*http://www.cnet.com/*]. It's a very interesting interview with Steve Balmer, one of the top executives, who talks about Netscape Navigator as a threat to Windows. The reporter says, "While the rivalry between Netscape and Microsoft has been portrayed as the heated battle of browsers, the two companies are engaged in a more fundamental high stakes struggle, pitting Navigator against Windows, not the Internet Explorer."

That's why we have such a big fight going on here. That's why Microsoft is investing every-thing they're investing in this. That's why they consider it a threat. It attacks their very fundamental franchise, the product line from which they get all the juice. And Microsoft makes no bones about what their goal is in this respect, and what their concerns are.

If you liked it from Balmer, you'll love it from Gates. This is Bill Gates' discussion (which I think you can find on the Microsoft web page [*http://www.microsoft.com/*]) of Netscape's strategy. But the notion is, over time, Netscape will add memory management, file systems, security, scheduling, graphics; everything else in Windows that applications require.

The point is, there is now a battle between operating systems. There's the desktop OS that's owned by Microsoft, virtually 100 percent. There's the operating system, the browser with its server, that's still a somewhat open market. It's not clear who's going to control it.

How will it be controlled? That depends on network economics, a branch of economics called "increasing returns economics." In this month's issue of *Forbes* magazine, there is a very interesting article about increasing returns economics. In this month's issue of *Fortune* magazine there's a very interesting article on increasing returns economics. In this month's issue of *The Economist* there's a very interesting article on increasing returns economics and the role it plays in these markets. Basically, these markets run to standard. They work off common protocols, whereas in other markets there's a shared industry. Somebody has 30 percent, somebody has 40 percent, somebody has 20 percent. Generally not the case. As in VHS and Beta, one standard comes to dominate the market. Who controls that standard?

If you can get your standard out in the lead and advance your technology, you can come to control that standard. Right now, in the Internet it's an open standard, but eventually, it will be controlled by some group or other. The market will tip in your direction, and then it will run hard to standard, and you'll be able to essentially blow away the rest of the competition because everybody will be on your standard.

Which brings me to the issue of bad acts. *How do you get to control the standard?*

The allegations we've made in the Intuit White Paper and in other forums are that Microsoft, through its domination of the desktop, is attempting to retard entry by the browser people into this market, making it difficult for them to compete by doing a number of things: by engaging in predatory pricing, they give their browser away. Not only do they give their browser away; they give a discount on the operating system to OEMs [Original Equipment Manufacturers]. They tie the browser to the operating system. We'll get to the point where they even embed protocols. The point is that they use their market power in one market to try to dominate another market, the intranet market.

Microsoft, through its domination of the desktop, is attempting to retard entry by the browser people into this market.

If you want to read a detailed description of the kinds of things that are going on, you might go to James Gleick's article in the *New York Times Magazine*.

Another place I'd send you is the Justice Department's web page [*http://www.usdoj.gov/*]. Earlier this year, Carl Shapiro, Chief Economist of the Justice Department this past year, made a very interesting speech, that didn't get a lot of publicity. In that speech he alludes to a hypothetical software company, U-soft. (Those of us in the industry make a micron [μ] like a U, so the way we would write "Microsoft" is micron, or U, soft. So one might guess to whom Carl's referring.) He hypothesizes a number of very bad acts, and speculates what the Justice Department might do if those bad acts were executed. And interestingly enough, each and every one of those acts is being done. So we'll see what happens.

The other interesting thing about Carl's speech is that network economics is generally thought of as all of a piece, which is only a recent development. Until very recently, there were a number of camps among network economists. There was one camp that's typified by Carl Shapiro, that believed that running to standard was more or less benign; in other words, that these industries run to standard, and advance by being around a standard, and therefore, perhaps we ought to give the bearer just a little something, a little monopoly for owning the standard.

Then there's another group, typified by Joe Farrell, chief economist of the SEC (Securities and Exchange Commission) whom I'll call the "bad acts guys." They use words like "predation," and they say, if somebody owns a standard, they will choke you and choke you and choke you to death with that standard, unless the government does something about it.

So where does the government come out on this? Only time will tell. But I think we're in for some very interesting times. Very recently, Bill Gates made a speech in which he indicated, along with other alleged bad acts, he's going to embed HTTP in the operating system, the same way Microsoft embedded TCP/IP in the browser. Once they did that, there was no more innovation around TCP/IP. If you take HTTP and embed it into the operating system, it's going to be much more difficult for Netscape and others to continue to advance the protocol. And Microsoft would then try to move everybody onto its operating system development track once every three years, instead of advancing this very innovative track of browser and server development every six months.

If that were to happen, it would be very interesting to see what the government would do about it. But it all boils down to a point Steve made regarding the difficulty in competing with a vertically integrated company. The point here is that in the cable market, access was mandated. If Microsoft owns the desktop and the desktop is the way you get into the intranet, then should access be mandated in that market as well? I think that's the fundamental question we're going to be facing.

KRAAKMAN: Now I'd like to ask Joel Klein to bring the two industries together, and comment on how the practices referred to bear on the wave of mergers we're seeing.

KLEIN: I must say, trying to synthesize these two speakers is a little bit like herding cats. It's an impossible task. Having said that, let me take a step back and tell you the way we think about these problems and pick up some of the strands. I would like to give you an over arching view of the way we in the Justice Department's Antitrust Division look at the common themes in both presentations.

I think the problem each speaker is addressing is one of essentiality. What I mean by that is, take the simple hypothetical: If, in order to bring a widget to market to the ultimate consumer, you need access to aluminum—that's an essential ingredient in making widgets, shall we say—and if I own all the aluminum in the world, nobody can make widgets but me, if I don't want to sell aluminum. This is what Gary [Reback] is concerned about, forced access. Steve [Weiswasser] is concerned about content. Essentially, they're both talking about a problem of essentiality.

Steve has a method of distribution but, because of historical events, he needs content. And somebody else has the content. Not surprisingly, the multisystems cable operators, who, for a whole variety of historical reasons based on the way the industry developed, got over 90 percent of multichannel distribution. And so they quite sensibly built up their programming. Steve has a new method of distribution, but even if he had the most advanced, most high tech, clearest way of distributing at the cheapest price, it's useless if he doesn't have content. So that's the problem he teased out.

Gary sees the same problem in the computer industry; a somewhat different paradigm, but essentially the same problem. What he's worried about is, Microsoft basically has control of the operating system. And at some level, all the other products or many of the other products—have to basically tee off the operating system.

Again, take a simple hypothetical. You can have the greatest spreadsheet in the world today. It just could be better than Lotus, better than Borland, better than anything in the market. But if it doesn't run off the Microsoft operating system, who's going to buy it? It's useless to you. So basically, it must have a way to effectively run off of this input.

Now then, the question from our point of view gets complicated. The issue of essential inputs is something antitrust laws have looked at over the course of their one hundred year existence. We have a doctrine known as the "essential facility doctrine." It is invoked more in the journals than in the courts, in the sense that there is a certain historical antithesis in America to forced access. It's based on a combination of theories. In other words, I, Microsoft, develop an operating system. Other people want equal access. Or I, Time Warner, develop a massive stable of programming, and Steve wants equal access. But this problem of equal access and forced access has come up in a variety of contexts. Not so long ago, in a ski resort case, the Supreme Court ordered forced access in some narrow circumstances, where three out of four ski slopes in Aspen, Colorado, were owned by one company and a fourth was owned by another. And the fourth slope couldn't survive without being able to sell a ticket that gave you access to all four. The Supreme Court, on the facts of that case, forced access. It's a limited but not unimportant.

Now, the reason there is an antipathy, but by no means a bar, to forced access, goes to late 20th century views of property in America. When I was in law school, I remember Charlie Reich had this famous article in 1963, I believe, called "The New Property," describing an idea that was much more compatible with forced access. And indeed, the antitrust laws in the early '60s were more compatible with forced access than they are in the late 20th century. That's again in part a shift in paradigms about private property.

The corollary to that is about innovation, which goes back to what we looked at with intellectual property: if you don't have some protection for your property, the incentive to be able to make the kind of huge investments in R&D to introduce a new operating system, or to introduce a new drug, or to introduce a patented item, is going to diminish. The thinking goes, let somebody else develop the first one, and then try to bring an antitrust claim for forced access. You don't have to do the development. So these are the ingredients that go into the calculation— none of which means there shouldn't be forced access in appropriate circumstances. And that is the question we wrestle hardest with.

Gary rightfully makes our problem harder by citing cases which are not familiar in everyday parlance but have become critical in antitrust laws. And that is essentially the problem of network effects.

If you read poetry, you know the famous line from Frost:

> Something there is that doesn't love a wall.

In my business, something there is that doesn't like a monopolist. And network effects make it easier for people to gain monopolies. It may not be a question of bad acts; it may just be the inevitability of standardization in a market.

So what you worry about is that, in the old days, if I was building widgets and trying to get a monopoly, I had to do it one consumer at a time. But now, in the operating system business, at some point early in the process, you're going to hit a tipping point. That's what happened in the Beta/VHS face-off. At some point, the balance will tip. And then you have a monopoly, in effect, in a particular area. The problem then is not just that you have a tipping point, but a lock-in. The very factor that enabled you to tip will often lock you in and make it hard for a new entrant to undo you.

It's the same kind of problem in different degrees that Steve is facing. And he illustrates this with the Liberty–Time Warner situation in New York: when Liberty tries to penetrate the New York market even with post-merger TCI, the balance is already tipped. So from our point of view, that is a very serious concern. And that's why

Carl Shapiro, our Chief Economist, wrote the paper on network effects that Gary mentioned.

We have a situation in which we have two or three important problems to consider. One is, these are fast-moving markets. Therefore, if we're going to play, we've got to be prepared to play quickly, which often means preliminary injunctions. You've got to prepare your case, be ready to pull the trigger, convince the federal court judge to stop something in its tracks on the basis of a preliminary hearing. So that means, you have to have some sense of where the markets are going.

Now, one of the questions that's hard for me to anticipate is, what will the picture look like three to five years from now, in terms of operating system competition with Netscape, which is looking to take its browser beyond the browser market. The very numbers Gary referred to—the ten times the server to the browser figures— indicate that Netscape has read the same data its lawyer has and they're aware of these problems. So the question is, where is the real competition going to come? Again, the government will only jump in if it's reasonably certain that its actions will be beneficial, that we're not simply addressing yesterday's problems, which the market itself will sort out tomorrow. What you saw, which is different in Steve's industry from Gary's industry, is that the antitrust laws did not cure the problem of forced access to content. Congress cured that in the 1992 Cable Act.

Ironically, even with that cure, we brought a couple of forced access cases. These include the Prime Star case and the TCI/Liberty merger case, in which the effect of the Cable Act is imperfect. So, we have had to reinforce forced access to content through the use of consent decrees. If you violate one of our consent decrees, we can impose fines and imprisonment, whereas if you violate the Cable Act, you have to go through a lengthy Federal Communications Commission [FCC] proceeding. So at least in that respect, the remedy is not wholly efficacious. By and large, it is a Congressionally imposed remedy, rather than an antitrust remedy that Steve is looking at. And quite frankly, we are looking at the role of anti-trust in a similar circumstance, where you have network effects, essential ingredients, and potential market dominance and hegemony.

It may well be in the end that we will bring appropriate forced access cases. But anyone who studies this field will tell you that they are not the easiest cases in the current climate to bring or to win. There's some question of how far the anti-trust laws can go versus how far Congress can go on forced access.

The other area we are scrutinizing now in the Justice Department is whether, in industries dominated by these kinds of economic concerns: the route to monopoly is now a 100-yard dash, instead of a mile run. Gary's focus on bad acts is very important, but it's very hard to observe. Because in a 100-yard dash, if you jump start the race by half a second, that's sufficient to win. In a mile, if you jump start the race by half a second, you could win, but it's unlikely. On the other hand, half-second jump starts for officials in Washington may be hard to detect.

One of the things we're thinking about is whether there are prophylactic rules. What are conventional antitrust doctrines, in addition to essential facilities? Typically, you go to vertical relationships, and those are tying type doctrines, which Gary has talked about—what you bundle together in the operating system. We are looking at leveraging theories; that is, where you have dominance in one network market, and the small gain you get in the second market is a kind of leverage. For instance, Kodak has a camera; Kodak has film. It can, through its sprockets in the camera, control the film markets, if it chooses. We're trying to look at that kind of effect from the operating system into the application market and to the information services markets, and finally, to issues of exclusive dealing.

We have brought two major lawsuits against Microsoft. We blocked the Intuit merger, and along with the European Commission, we undid Microsoft's exclusive pricing and long-term contracts with OEM.

In antitrust law, this is a very exciting time. I will conclude with this. Because of the evolution from what we did to AT&T, to what Congress did in the 1992 Cable Act, to what Congress and the President did in the 1996 Telco Telecommunications Act, in the decades ahead, we will see many different ways to get content to the home. And while that doesn't deal with the intranet problem, it will deal with the Internet problem.

My prediction is that you will see an abundance of new content come online. The problem Steve faces in the short run is a threshold problem: how does he stay viable at a time when other people are running down the field? But in the long term, he knows—I think anybody who studies the industry knows—that content is going to evolve. Much more interactive content will be in demand and be developed. And indeed, the tests that the telemedia types have done with respect to conventional content on telemedia are not nearly as encouraging as they had originally hoped. So there will be whole new developments of content, all sorts of lines into the household.

And our job is to make sure that content is available to distributors—open and not bottlenecked, as it once was in the telephone business. That, I think, is one of the great challenges that face 21st century antitrust enforcers.

Questions & Answers

Q: *How will new technologies, such as voice over the Internet, affect the strategies of companies such as Americast?*

WEISWASSER: As a general proposition, anything that enhances the Internet and creates the capacity to accommodate better interactive services is an important step forward. Voice is part of what I want to see in the Internet. Americast, on the other hand, is much more interested in seeing full-motion video and improved speed of access before it worries about voice. That has to do with my content bias, because of my television background. Obviously, the voice issue is very important on the telephony side, but less important on the media side. That's a problem for my partners, not me.

Q: *What is the Justice Department doing to prevent AT&T, the 1,000 pound gorilla, from rising up the line, threatening to control it all?*

KLEIN: Right now we've got before us a couple of 500 pound gorillas. We've got the Bell Atlantic-NYNEX merger before us, which involves a lot of wire. Now, there's a classic example, paradoxically, of the problem for antitrust enforcers: here you have two so-called Baby Bells. And you're worried about AT&T. One theory is that these two Baby Bells merge, and they're a formidable alternative. Another theory is they merge and it exacerbates the problem. So those are the two competing theories you hear, that are now before us. The second thing that comes up all the time is, what are the alternatives to wires? If all these cable folks, who are very strong players, begin to distribute voice over coaxial, that may also have long-term market impacts.

Now, you say it ought to be the end users who ultimately decide the outcome. But I must tell you, in my business, we talk to a lot of end users and they don't all have the same views. So it's not an easy problem. But when it came to AT&T, some might say that it took the Justice Department a long time, but ultimately we did dismantle it, and effectively.

KRAAKMAN: Steve, want to jump in and protect the Justice Department here?

WEISWASSER: I wasn't involved in this at the time of the AT&T divestiture, but it seems very difficult to argue that the AT&T divestiture has not significantly enhanced competition in virtually every market in which AT&T has operated. Consider the long distance market, to start. I think you underestimate the capacity of the regional Bell companies to create significant competitive alternatives to AT&T. And I suspect that you (and you're not alone) overestimate the capacity of AT&T to dominate the markets that interest you, as a practical matter. Everybody worries about AT&T. Of course, all of my partners are AT&T progeny, or at least three are. They always

worry—one always worries about one's parent, in some ultimate psychological sense. But the fact is that there is potential for enormous competition, and while AT&T is a very significant competitor to be highly respected, it is by no means alone in any sphere of the business in which it operates. One example is, it lacks the line to people's houses right now, an extremely important part of the entire process in which you're interested.

REBACK: I'd like to add one comment. At the risk of publicly embarrassing Joel [Klein] by agreeing with him, in my industries the breakup of AT&T has led, for example, to the Internet. I mean, MCI developed the Internet; it built most of the backbone. MCI and Sprint developed pagers, other aspects of telephony. And interestingly enough, on the software side of the business, many people no longer see AT&T as the Great Satan. AT&T, after all, is now what we would call an "open systems" company. They have to be able to connect up. It was once that they were like IBM, for proprietary everything, because they had everything hooked vertically, straight up to your pocketbook. Now it's Microsoft that has that. So the poles have shifted, and you see very weird alliances. You have Microsoft and MCI, and you have Netscape and AT&T (although not on an exclusive basis).

I do sympathize with Joel on this problem. To me, it's very much an east coast kind of phenomenon, because out in the west, we worry about the telcos [telecommunications companies] a lot less than they seem to in Washington.

Q: *Can you comment on giving away free software as an anti-competitive practice?*

KLEIN: Clearly, if you give away something for free, it can be predatory. If you sell it below marginal cost, it's predatory. "Free" tends to be below margin of cost, so it can be predation. Even if that's all it's worth.

WEISWASSER: That's right, but that's a different point. It's my experience that people don't give away things for free for no reason. There are two problems. The first question is, what are its market impacts? If you try to stop it, you're taking something out of the market that people are getting for free. There is a certain inhospitable attitude toward the government doing that. So you have to make sure that the effects are really strangle holds. Second, the Supreme Court in the Brooke Group, as recently as two years ago, cast a very skeptical eye toward predatory pricing claims in general.

Gary [Reback] has a strong view on this, and this is the first time he's ever agreed with me in public that it didn't make me rethink my own position. So this is a new bond being formed. See, this is all legacy. Gary and I argued the Microsoft case in a D.C. circuit together. And I must say, he did a very effective job in a losing effort. It's not a question of the talents of the lawyer; it's just the merits of the case.

KRAAKMAN: That's particularly easy to say when you win!

KLEIN: Think about how many people give out free software—America Online, Prodigy, CompuServe—all of which is below cost when they give it out. So to give away something for free doesn't answer the question, but it certainly raises a potentially important question. Now Gary will answer it for you.

REBACK: I'd like to make a couple comments. Some of you may know the Brooke Group case. I disagree with Joel to some extent. The holding of the Brooke Group case is not clear, but a lot of the learned commentary following the case argues that if it had been presented as a "willful maintenance" case, instead of a market penetration case, the good guys—the plaintiffs—would have won; that is, the charge of giving away the product was not a means of squashing something in the new market, so much as it was of maintaining the monopoly in the old market. So, was giving away the browser in the new market a way of maintaining control of the desktop operating system, or was it a way of enhancing competition in the browser market? That's the question we keep putting to Joel. I maintain it's the former.

I also think you have to look hard at what's being given away, and where. Netscape, for example, on the home side of this four-block diagram, gives stuff away to students, to charitable organizations and the like, but not on the business side, where the server sits. Microsoft now proposes not only to give the browser software away on the business side, on the intranet (where I would say the cognizable antitrust market is), but also to give the server away in that market. And to me, that presents a very different set of circumstances, circumstances that fall within Joel's definition of predation, as opposed to enhancing competition.

REBACK: It's a very interesting and important question. It requires some pretty sophisticated economic modeling to try to decide whether the consumer welfare is enhanced or not. But I would agree strongly that if somebody has a lock on the operating system and that's the important gateway in, then when they give something away for free, they are not engaged in benign conduct. They're engaged in conduct that maintains that monopoly and is intended to extend it to the next market.

KLEIN: Yes, it can be. Whether it can be different, for example, from Microsoft or from Netscape, depends on a variety of issues: market power screens, economic analysis. Whether it is or not is a fact-specific determination. And as Gary well knows, those inquiries are currently underway, so I can't say anything more about that.

Q: *Given the happy results of the AT&T breakup, does the Justice Department foresee any problem about the recombination of the Baby Bells and the formation of joint ventures like Americast?*

KLEIN: We will surely take a hard look at these issues, which are some of the most challenging antitrust issues. If you look at most merger analysis (I mean horizontal merger analysis), we have the 1992 guidelines. There's a conventional way of thinking about the problems. You can argue about what the product market is, what the substitutes are. You can argue about the geographic market, and so forth. But it's a conventional, straightforward way of thinking about problems. Everything we're now looking at and talking about is comparable to something that has been developed in the last four to five years; innovation market thinking. We have two people in different markets. Normally, why would you worry about that? It's only because you're trying to anticipate a change in the world.

Now, fortunately, we're going to have the best economists and best lawyers in the country help us sort it. But I do think, when the sun sets (much like the Time Warner-Turner thing), it will be widely watched, and there will be some criticism no matter what you do, because you're making predictive judgments on very fast-moving markets with important consequences.

WEISWASSER: I think it would be very difficult to argue that the venture of the kind I've got, or that comes out of the other group of telcos, is in any sense an antitrust problem. First of all, we're too small. Second, look at the array of competitors against whom we have to compete, and at the size of the market. And look at the opportunity for competition. Think about who is likely to break into the cable or multi-channel distribution market and compete, and how it's going to happen. This is probably the only way it could happen. These are probably the only people who could do it. And none of them can do it alone.

I have a disadvantage right now. My venture basically reaches about 65 percent of the homes in the United States and I'm competing against people who are producing content for 100 percent of these homes. I have to solve that problem. One way to do that is combine the two ventures, although that is, again, a matter out of my control.

But the idea that somehow these ventures are themselves potentially anti-competitive, because of the size of the partners involved, is very difficult for me to see.

KLEIN: When we talk about Steve's business, it's the only time we don't put quotes around the word "baby" when we talk about Baby Bells. With him, he's got a baby operation.

Q: *Assuming that both sides (Time Warner and Microsoft) have merit, how would you preserve their competitive advantage, protect their interests, in the*

same way that you're looking for forced access or opening up standards?

WEISWASSER: We're not proposing that they *give* content to us, first of all. Take Time Warner, for example. I want to compete against TCI in Chicago. I need Time Warner programming to compete against TCI. But it is not in Time Warner's interest for me to succeed in Chicago—not so much because it's trying to protect TCI, but because it's simply not in Time Warner's interest for me to succeed, period. Yet it will sell the program to TCI. Why wouldn't it sell to me? I'm not asking for the content to be sold below market. I'm merely saying, if you're going to sell it to third parties, I want to be able to buy it at market.

REBACK: I have a different set of concerns and, therefore, a different answer. I have to disagree in part with your premises. Since you gave me the underlying premise, though I'll take it from there. (The government charged—and Microsoft consented to the notion—that they maintained their installed base through illegal means. So once you start there, you automatically reach a different result.)

But let's start from the proposition that it was benign. I learned about antitrust from Bill Baxter, who brought the Chicago school to Washington. And one of the things he taught me was that the remedy for monopolization should be the ticker tape parade. Once you achieve this great result you're talking about, we give you a ticker tape parade down Wall Street, and then we break you up. Why do we do that? Because competition produces the best products at the lowest prices.

So the answer to your question might be, we have to ask not what's best for Microsoft; we have to ask what's best for the consumer welfare. And those two things might not be the same.

About the Speakers

REINIER KRAAKMAN is Professor of Law at Harvard Law School, where he teaches corporate law and corporate finance. He participates in the New

Foundations Working Group and is a past chair of the American Association of Law Schools Section on Business Organizations. Reinier Kraakman has co-authored several articles on corporate governance and on the law of takeovers, including most recently a proposal for the election of professional directors by institutional investors. He has also consulted on corporate governance topics and written extensively about liability sales and the corporate structure.

STEPHEN A. WEISWASSER is President and Chief Executive Officer of Americast, a joint venture of Ameritech, BellSouth, GTE, SBC Corporation, and the Walt Disney Company, where he is responsible for providing programming services and other content for distribution by these telephone companies. Formerly, Mr. Weiswasser served as a Senior Vice President of Capital Cities/ABC, as President of the Capital Cities/ABC Multimedia Group, where he was responsible for centralizing and expanding the company's activities in new and emerging technologies, and prior to that, as Executive Vice President of ABC News. He is married to Andrea Timko and has four children.

GARY REBACK is a partner in the law firm of Wilson, Sonsini, Goodrich & Rosati, where he is head of that firm's high technology group. Mr. Reback authored the widely read "White Paper," successfully opposing Microsoft's acquisition of Intuit, and was counsel for the anonymous amici, opposing the Justice Department's consent decree with Microsoft in *United States v. Microsoft*. He also represented Hasbro in its successful defense of Mattel's hostile takeover attempt and is currently representing Lexis-Nexis in the proposed acquisition of West Publishing by Thomson.

JOEL I. KLEIN is currently Principal Deputy Assistant Attorney General for Antitrust in the U.S. State Department of Justice. From 1993 to 1995 he served as Deputy Counsel to President Clinton, and before that he was a partner with Klein, Farr, Smith & Taranto, where he specialized in appellate practice. Mr. Klein has argued ten cases before the Supreme Court and numerous others before the various federal courts of appeals. He has published numerous articles in scholarly as well as popular journals, and has served as an Adjunct and Visiting Professor at Georgetown Law School.

CHAIR: JOHN J. SVIOKLA
Associate Professor of Business Administration
Harvard Business School

Business

CUSTOMER RELATIONSHIPS

MODERATOR: F. Warren McFarlan
PANELISTS: Robert Elmore
                 Mark Jeffrey
                 Les Ottolenghi

THE NEW ECONOMICS

MODERATOR: John J. Sviokla
PANELISTS: Kathy Biro
                 Tim Brady
                 Jack Donegan
                 Stephen Kahane
                 Christine Maxwell

COMMUNITY AND MARKET FORMATION

MODERATOR: Jeffrey Rayport
PANELISTS: Nick Grouf
                 Haig Hovaness
                 Lincoln Millstein
                 Angelo Santinelli

HARVARD NEWS

CONFERENCE ON THE INTERNET AND SOCIETY

May 29-31, 1996   Cambridge, MA

Brands on Web Still Pose Potential Risks

By Lori Valigra

It's an undisciplined, volatile, and fickle world, one that defies control and demographics. It's not a place corporate America would typically go to establish or embellish a brand name.

But the fast-moving world of cyberspace can make almost instant heroes out of those brave enough to venture through its portal with an innovative web site.

"Technology shapes brands in this marketplace, not media messages," Les Ottolenghi, a Holiday Inn executive, told a near-capacity crowd at Sanders Theater yesterday. "Certain interactive technologies can be used to build brand value."

For Ottolenghi, brand awareness is built around a well-designed home page. Visitors to the company's web site [*http://www.holiday-inn.com/*] can take a virtual tour of any Holiday Inn, anywhere, any time of day. They can visit rooms, look at health facilities, see the quickest route in from the airport, and book a room.

Ottolenghi, Director of Emerging Technologies for the hotel chain, quickly discovered a cyberspace truism: Internet cruisers demand information quickly, all day, every day. And the more information and services they get, the more they want.

So Holiday Inn added incentives to keep its fickle audience, such as letting customers redeem frequent service points or buy goods.

The payoff has been big, Ottolenghi said. Holiday Inn's two web sites, established in 1995, are pulling in 11,000 reservations a month. A $158,000 investment to build the sites has added more than $10 million to Holiday Inn's annual revenues of $1 billion.

Ottolenghi and others said corporations must adjust to thinking about "space" rather than a "place" for their products or services, because potential buyers are not limited by a physical store shelf.

"If a brand is not associated with online values, it can be diminished," Ottolenghi said.

In a sense, the enormity of information on the Internet makes brands more important, although a strong brand does not automatically guarantee success if it is not targeted to an online audience.

"You are sort of up for reevaluation on the Internet," said Mark Jeffrey, Director of Time Warner's Palace Group.

The Palace is a meta-world created by Time-Warner, a combination of a chat room, virtual reality space, multi-user dungeon [MUD], and puppet show that aims to engage visitors long enough to gain brand recognition for vendors at the site.

Jeffrey foresees more such chatroom corporate web sites where customers can give feedback to corporations, making sales more of a two-way street.

"Unlike the Web, where people are always traveling but never arriving, chat rooms retain people and keep them coming back," Jeffrey said.

One corporation that became an early innovator in such brand marketing was the Saturn Corp. subsidiary of General Motors Corp. Saturn sells cars mostly by customer recommendations, and it set up a web site where customers can add comments [*http://www.saturncars.com/*].

"They are taking a bit of a risk," said Jeffrey, "but people are using chat-based information to extend their brands into cyberspace."

There *is* the risk of getting negative comments. But that is part of the still ill-defined social and legal structure of cyberspace.

A more pressing threat to brands, ironically, is new technologies such as "intelligent agents," which can seek specific information on the Web. "An intelligent agent can take consumers off our web site and to a site where they can make hotel reservations," said Ottolenghi. And that web site may bump Holiday Inn off the map.

Business

May 29, 1996

Customer Relationships
What Happens to Brands?

MODERATOR: F. Warren McFarlan
PANELISTS: Robert Elmore
Mark Jeffrey
Les Ottolenghi

McFARLAN: Our first speaker is **ROBERT ELMORE** of Arthur Andersen's Business Consulting practice. Our second speaker is **MARK JEFFREY** from Online Ventures, a part of Time Warner. Our third is **LES OTTOLENGHI**, Director of Emerging Technologies, Interactive Strategies, and New Media, Holiday Inn. You can see that we have a great deal of battlefield experience in this very new, emerging area. Let's turn to our panelists now. So let me introduce Robert Elmore.

ELMORE: Thanks, Warren, I'm really glad to be here with you today. I have been dealing with these issues for many years, but please know that I come less as an expert than as a practitioner, and also know I probably have more questions than I have answers. With that in mind, I would like to start by sharing three stories.

My first story starts 35 years ago, when I was trained by Scott Paper to sell facial tissues and other products to the small Mom and Pop stores in the Boston area. If you grew up in the '50s and '60s, one word would immediately come to mind when you heard "facial tissues." Does anybody remember that term? Yes, that's right, Kleenex. While Scott Paper called their product "Scotties," I learned very early that there was no point in my trying to compete with Kimberly-Clark's brand image of Kleenex. Scott did get some brand carry over from its towels, so people at least believed that Scotties were of equal quality to Kleenex.

Out of necessity, I chose to compete at the level of convenience. My goal was to make it easy (more convenient) for the customers to get Scotties versus Kleenex. I would go in with my satchel of paper goods and, dressed as best I could, wet behind the ears even with all the training that Scott Paper had given me, rearrange the space to get twice or three times as much space as Kimberly-Clark, to show off my product, Scotties.

That was a very long time ago in my business life, but I certainly received a wonderful initiation into the ABCs of branding. You have to first establish awareness, next, buy-in from the consumer, and finally, their commitment to buy. I think *a*wareness, *b*uy-in, and *c*ommitment apply as much today as they ever did. When we translate these ABCs to current thinking, especially when working on the Internet, it is very important to recognize how easy it is to change the commitment to buy. I changed my browser after two brief exposures to Netscape, and felt no loyalty to my favorite browser of the past. That is how fickle commitment can be today.

Many of you have heard the story of the pig and the chicken, as they walked down a dusty Nebraska road, and saw a restaurant sign, "Ham and Eggs for Breakfast." The chicken observed how good it felt "to make such an important contribution to that breakfast." But then the pig rather glumly brought the conversation to a halt when he observed that the chicken's contribution was "nothing like the commitment he had to make."

So when we talk about brand image, my first message is about *commitment*. It is relatively easy to make someone aware and even get their buy-in at an intellectual level, but if they're not committed we really haven't been effective with our "branding" dollar. To obtain commitment, we must be the very best at what we do. When you are the very best, you begin to build true brand identity. Today it is much easier to gain access to the best through the Internet. The playing field has been leveled, and now companies big and small will compete on value delivered.

My second experience with branding came 27 years later, after spending the majority of my career helping Andersen Consulting build its business. I shifted my focus to help Arthur Andersen transform its business into the knowledge era. I found the ABCs being applied in a very different context at Arthur Andersen, where the goal was to broaden their image from accountants and auditors who facilitate the trade of goods and services in the traditional marketplace to a firm that also applied its skills and competencies in marketspace. (John Sviokla and Jeffrey Rayport, Harvard Business School professors, first coined the word *marketspace* in 1994.[*]) If this is a new term for you, think of marketspace as electronic commerce and trading conducted in a virtual way through the Internet.

In its early days, "T accounts" formed the fundamental paradigm and frame of reference for the way Arthur Andersen conducted its business. Today, less than 25 percent of the market capitalization of our clients is represented by the transactions that formally flow through these T accounts. So we must ask the obvious question: how do you account for and audit the other three-quarters of our clients' market capitalization that does not show on the record books?

As the market creates new valuations in the knowledge era, the accounting progression must create new models for giving opinions about these evaluations. This begs a new question. If we change our methods, will Andersen's brand carry over to help maintain and build market share in the new economy? And before we can answer the question of a brand carry over, we have to be very clear about our intention for the brand. All professionals have an interest in branding trust and integrity, but each practitioner must do something special to distinguish itself from competitors. Arthur Andersen has historically chosen the role of being a "thought leader" in our profession.

Some of you may remember the role Arthur Andersen played in the '50s and '60s, when we lobbied for more uniform application of accounting principles in published financial reports. While this was often frustrating for our competitors, we prevailed and were successful in changing the way the principles were developed and reported by the accounting profession. I personally believe that much of our growth over these years, from being one of the smallest to being one of the largest global firms, results from our "thought leadership" and the image we established as an aggressive firm that thought and talked straight to anyone who cared to listen.

As we release our new understanding of the Information Age accounting and new ways of understanding and measuring values in the knowledge era, one hopes the brand leadership in the progression will drive us to new levels of growth.

This is not to say that accounting firms are not providing value today. We are. Clients enjoy a two- to three-percent reduction in their cost of capital when their books are audited by one of the Big Six accounting firms. That represents over $50 billion in savings to U.S. companies, which is far in excess of the amounts we bill them.

In summary, the Arthur Andersen story is about how we continue to do what we have been doing and, at the same time, develop a new paradigm for accounting and valuation in the market and maintain our image of "thought leadership" in the profession.

As we think about the future, all of the old rules of brands, such as ABC and consistent quality, will still apply. But we must also think of new qualities, such as time. It is as important that you not waste consumer time when on the Internet as it is to provide quality content. Netscape caught my attention for this reason. Ease of finding and working with information is going to be a major part of brand identity in the future...and this is just the tip of the iceberg. In addition to quality of product and quality of time, brands must respond to a shifting set of buyer values. Brian Hall has published a good book on this subject

---

[*] John Sviokla moderated the session "The New Economics: How Will Value Be Created and Extracted?" Jeffrey Rayport moderated the session "Institutional Structure for the Internet: Who Will Control It?"

about values and the valuing process. Rather than concentrate on Maslow's list of deficiency needs—food, shelter, and so on—Hall points to the complement of these needs which Maslow called our "belief needs." (This may be too intense for a ten-minute presentation.) But there are new techniques for eliciting values, directly from the customer, that can then be incorporated not only in the way you deliver your product and service to the customer, but in the way you brand it as well.

Some of you may recall Professor Knowell's comments yesterday when he talked about how Harvard introduced the Internet on campus over 19 months ago, and the exponential curve that has been experienced (almost a gold rush, to use Gates's words) using the Internet. He concluded that there's only one thing the customer wants, and that is "more." Today you can establish a good brand by saving people time: they want more time. They are going to want more quality and more value. The list is sure to expand.

As I waited in line to get into this hall, an attendee behind me was asked by a fellow participant if his expectations were being met. He answered, "I have very high expectations and so far they've marginally been met, but I do not expect over these four days to have all my expectations met. The big thing I want is to learn, and I would expect that I would learn at Harvard." He went on to say that there are a lot of people who come to sessions like this with an "ax to grind," i.e., something to sell. Harvard, in lending its brand image to this conference, is indirectly declaring that the focus here is on learning, not selling. That's why we come here, drawn by a powerful brand to a place where we expect to learn. I hope that learning does occur for you here. But consider the risk to Harvard if it does not. And consider the challenge of providing a consistent high quality learning environment with such an eclectic group of speakers, or should I say "teachers." We are talking here about intellectual capital, and it is clear that the rules for managing brand in an economy that is conducted in place and space are going to change in the future.

Thirty-five years ago I might have been found stirring up the space on your local grocer's paper shelves. Today, my goal was to stir up the space in your mind. There is a place there for brand identity, but recognize that the rules for branding have changed and that anyone—even the smallest player—has a chance to displace the very largest of competitors.

McFARLAN: Robert, thank you very much. Allow me to introduce our next speaker, Mark Jeffrey.

JEFFREY: It's an honor to be here. I'm with a part of Time Warner called the Palace Group. What we do is something that is a combination chat room, a MUD [multi-user dungeon] or MOO [multi-user object-oriented dungeon], virtual reality, Color Forms, and a puppet show—it's all those things blended together. Basically, I am here because I want you to understand the angle from which I approach the brand issue.

First of all, I'd like to talk a bit about a couple of web pages that I think are really great examples of extending the brand awareness of that product or that company into web space.

When we talk about brands, what exactly are we trying to do when we put up a web page in cyberspace? I think most of the time the answer to that question is we're trying to promote our company or our product, but I don't think that's always the case. I think some of the more successful pages have offered a service—an example is Federal Express, which lets you actually track your packages online [*http://www.fedex.com/*].

Another great example of a company which has been very successful extending their brand on their web page is Saturn. If any of you check out the Saturn web page [*http://www.saturncars.com/*], you won't just find an online brochure talking about Saturn cars: you'll actually find a lot of buyers' comments that are sort of homey and fit the image Saturn portrays in its print and television advertisements. What you'll find is that they've co-opted the users. They've gained the help of the actual users and people who come to that site to help to sell their cars.

There's another side of this: part of Saturn's whole advertising campaign is to get other people to buy cars based on the personal recommendations of other people who have bought Saturn cars. So to some extent, it works because it's Saturn. However, Saturn has also taken a bit of a risk by allowing other people to add new material and content to their web site. And this is something that relates very well to the Palace.

The Palace architecture is a client/server architecture which allows you to enter what *Wired* is now calling *metaworlds*. These are virtual spaces that share a lot of characteristics of chat rooms but are very graphical.

Users [on the Web] will be able to talk back a lot more, and they will have to become a part of your brand extension.

A number of people are now using chat rooms and chat-based applications to extend their brands into cyberspace. Some examples are Fox, Sony Pictures, MTV, Capital Records—a whole bunch of brand names you'd recognize. Now why are they doing this? In part, it's because chat rooms—unlike a lot of the Web, where you're always traveling and never arriving—tend to create retention. In other words, people will come back to chat rooms, whereas they may go to a web page once and never return. So chat rooms are starting to spring up now in order to hold a visitor's attention and keep people coming back to those sites.

Before I get into that too deeply, let me talk about another brand that I actually helped to build on the Internet, *TV Guide*. *TV Guide* started off with the premise of taking their core business and extending it into cyberspace, on a web page, but they weren't really sure which direction they wanted to take.

There were two camps. One camp said, "Well, what does *TV Guide* do for television? *TV Guide* gives you the listings for everything in this medium. It's the ultimate guide to everything that's on television." So the logical extension of *TV Guide*'s brand into cyberspace would be to model itself on Yahoo!, which later became known as a search engine; in other words, take that same core idea that worked on TV and extend it into cyberspace by doing the same thing.

Then the other camp said, "No, really we're about TV, and what we should do is put up web pages that relate to television and don't extend our brand in that other direction." And this was very early on, a long time before the search engines really gained recognition. (This is the year [1996] the search engines have exploded. So this was perhaps a year and a half ago.) They finally decided to go the television route and missed, in my opinion, a more logical extension of their brand and a bigger opportunity, as evidenced by the explosion of the search engines we're seeing today.

Let me show you now what the Palace looks like [see *http://www.thepalace.com/*]. I think the Web is going to become more like this, in that users will be able to talk back a lot more, and they will have to become a part of your brand extension. It will be different from the way it is today—taking your content, or content that someone produces for you, and putting it up on the Web. It's going to be a mixture of your content and the context for other people to respond and interact and actually become a part of the web site.

This echoes what Steve Jobs [founder of Apple] said in a recent issue of *Wired*. He pointed out that this trend of upload—in other words, more users actually adding to the content—is only going to increase. And the line between what we today call the client and the server is going to blur and eventually disappear. Clients and servers will be exactly the same thing on the Internet. That means there will be less blast of information from a lot of web sites, and you'll get something closer to what you see in the Saturn web site.

There will be a lot more user-produced content on professionally produced web sites. The Palace is an example, because the users can talk back to you.

McFARLAN: Les.

OTTOLENGHI: When I think about the Internet and society, I think back 20 years ago, when I grew up during the 1970s and I think about how many things have changed. Back then, John Travolta was a big box office star. Jimmy Carter was going around the world settling global peace. The Beatles were making a comeback, and the Internet was an emerging technology, ready to reshape our society. Things have really changed, haven't they?

All joking aside, I things really *have* changed. Especially in commerce and in business. To me, the differences between interactive markets and physical markets are vast. Nonetheless, one common aspect exists: for each company, product, and set of consumers, brand value has a different meaning. It is clear that no one interactive strategy or any brand fits all situations. However, it may be possible to experience or to discern a way to plan, implement, and develop strategy for a specific brand in markets like the Internet.

With that said, let me tell you the story of Holiday Inn's experience, and what happens to consumer brands on the Internet. In 1995, Holiday Inn launched two web sites; one for the Holiday Inn brand of hotels and another for the Crown Plaza brand. Holiday Inn was the first and is still the only hotel chain to offer real-time online reservation bookings. In the first six months of operation, the economic results of our web sites were 11,000 reservation bookings per month, with over 75 percent of all visitors to the site checking for room availability.

Marketing results for the first six months revealed some successful marketing techniques and tactics in establishing consumer brand value. Based on our Internet user surveys, we have determined the following:

Brand awareness is built around good informational design. The launching of sites with an easy-to-access and attractive interface build a sense of friendliness and quality about the Holiday Inn brands in the minds of over 80 percent of our site users.

The layout of the Holiday Inn home page [http://www.holiday-inn.com/] is mostly graphics and very little text. We've created a theme of a hotel bureau, in which icons represent the various kinds of information you can find on our site. For instance, if you want to learn more about the Holiday Inn brand of hotels, you can go to an ice bucket, a familiar icon within the hotel environment. And you can learn about our different brands by clicking on little cups which represent each brand. You can also learn about summer promotions by clicking on a suntan lotion bottle, or go to a worldwide directory to get a directory of our hotels.

Concurrent product placement and price information induces brand sells. Through the combination of a product, a marketing message, and information about our hotels, Holiday Inn established a sense of superior convenience about the Holiday Inn brand with nearly 100 percent of all web site visitors. We not only put in our marketing message, we allowed people to go in and book reservations online. That is, we presented our product as well as our message. We put the two in the same context and allowed the users to easily navigate and find a hotel by using graphical information.

New and additional services boost brand loyalty. For 72 percent of our Priority Club members (our affinity marketing group), the ability to check and redeem their frequency points online was considered valuable. And when surveyed, they responded that the experience made them more likely to stay and use Holiday Inn hotels in their next leisure or business trip. In other words, incentives, rewards, and patronage were all possible in one environment when we went out onto the Internet.

Experiential and fun activities help broaden brand appeal. Over 85 percent of site visitors surveyed who used our two fun and experiential environments or offerings said they enjoyed the experience so much, they felt that Holiday Inn provided superior value. One of these activities is VR tours—actual virtual reality representations—of our hotels. You can move back and forth in this space, up and down, or you can actually zoom in and walk inside the hotel. Of course, you can also look in rooms as well as take a look at what facilities are offered throughout the hotel.

Our other experience and fun activity is a travel game called Travel Buff, based upon the popular board game sold through WALMart, Toys "R" Us, and Kmart throughout the world. The game is the most popular adult board game sold, and in our efforts to market the game, we actually included a web browser inside each box. Through this marketing effort, we had an additional 200,000 visitors to our web site in the month of December [1995]. The game is a basic trivia game about travel in which multiple choice questions are asked, and answers are given.

Press and publicity generates new customer relationships and potential positive brand impact. Holiday Inn received more press attention and had more press articles written about its Internet offerings than any other event in the company's history by a two-to-one margin. This includes the sale of Holiday Inn to Bass PLC of England, in 1991, and the introduction of four new hotel brands in 1994. Moreover, not one press release was produced until one month after the Internet launches.

Each Holiday Inn web site has had the distinction of being named to the top five percent of the Internet. And in August of 1995, both were rated by Meckler Media and *Information Week* among the top ten percent of all commercial Internet web sites. As a result, Holiday Inn web site visitors continued to grow by 40 percent each month in the first six months.

So, in its first attempt at consumer branding on the Internet, Holiday Inn met with some success. Holiday Inn discovered that in an interactive market like the Internet, certain interactive technologies can be used to build brand value. Unfortunately, change is swift. The technologies and applications we used at first to succeed have changed. And in a broader sense, technological change is in fact redefining the marketplace of the Internet itself.

For example, intelligent agents, metaworlds, and drag-and-drop web pages all threaten to preempt our best efforts at brand marketing. So the question arises: what do we do now? How do we preserve brand in the Internet world? We know it's an interactive world, but how do we approach the customer? Which technologies should we use? Within the context of these questions, an attempt has been made to put some parameters and intelligent choices around brand marketing efforts. The task, it was decided, was to try and define the basic elements of the Internet marketspace, virtual or real.

Consequently, marketing strategies or tactics might focus on the marketspace traits and reveal basic consumer behaviors. The result is a strategic, conceptual model. Specifically, the model identifies four broad categories of technology which define the Internet. The four technology categories are:

- A digital device
- Program intersoftware
- Data and media
- Connectivity

For the Internet to function, a specific technology from each category must be present. That is, only when a *digital device* like a Mac laptop includes *software* like a Netscape browser with a *media message* like email and *connectivity* like a dial-up PPP account can interactivity and the Internet exist.

Commercial value on the Internet is only produced when corresponding business systems connect with the same interactive characteristics on the Net. That is, a digital device must be connected to another digital device at a business in order for commerce to occur. At the consumer level the Internet can be defined by an interactive television, a PDA [Personal Digital Assistant], a kiosk, or a computer. Integrated with Windows 95, 96, 97, or a browser, a video game, CNN [Cable News Network] online, or a SimCity. And connected with fiber optics, satellite communications, or wireless transmissions.

Regardless of the exact technology, the four broad interactive technology categories still apply. Thus marketing efforts can be aimed at one or more of the technology categories. Consumer behavior is therefore influenced in some way. Of course, consumers use the Internet to do a lot more than buy goods and services—they also play sports, send postcards, make dates, find lost pets, learn about flowers, and on and on.

But with each of these activities, there is an opportunity to associate a brand-related message. So sponsorship or development of digital devices, software, media, or connectivity when it enhances consumer response, is more certain to derive brand value than just sticking a web page somewhere on the Net and hoping people will find it. This approach is even more powerful when the activity is the direct selling of a company's brand to the consumer.

For instance, Holiday Inn's use of the model has led it to develop an electronic business card or super email function for its travel guests. Identifying technologies which improve manipulation, communication, and sharing of information on the Internet, Holiday Inn has developed something called "Attaché" to help its clients send postcards, meet friends, shop, or do more business with Holiday Inn.

Let me demonstrate Attaché for you. The objectives of Attaché are to:

- Foster goodwill about our programs.

- Expand our marketing research.

- Reinforce our brand image.

- Increase visits to the web site.

- Add money or some other financial value to Holiday Inn.

As a technology, it's a new media marketing opportunity. It's branded multimedia delivery in an electronic package which applies text, graphics, audio, and video. Attaché can be personalized for each user.

Information can be dropped, or inserted, within Attaché. Any kind of information: pictures, virtual reality tours, messages—whatever you like, as well as web linkages. It gives users the ability to go straight to Holiday Inn's home page from within the Attaché application.

In terms of developing brand value, the situation might work like this. Our Priority or Affinity Club gives a member a copy of Attaché—a piece of software—on a floppy disk. Second, he or she opens Attaché and automatically links to register on our web site, using connectivity to get to us. This member registers by providing us with some personal information and, in return, receives his or her own personalized version of Attaché. He or she starts working it on his computer, adds personal files or media messages, and then communicates to a colleague, who wants a copy too.

In the process, his colleague automatically links to our web site and purchases her own Attaché.

Holiday Inn has done nothing to sell a room, but it has facilitated communication, manipulation, and sharing of information. It has also provided basic values for the consumer online and linked them to us to do more business. Obviously, Attaché can be used for marketing and sales promotions such as the following:

- Marketing research

- Web site promotion

- Direct mail marketing

- Digital business cards

- Interactive envelopes

In other words, a host of old and new methods of brand marketing.

With regard to the model I've presented, I must state three caveats:

1. The model does not try to predict exact consumer behavior and extract brand value ratings on the Internet (although we are in the process of conducting that research). What we have found are four basic behaviors which we believe define the use of technology on the Net. Those four basic values are the ability to *control information* with a digital device, *manipulate information* with software, *communicate a* *message* through media, and then *share the information* communicated.

2. Each of the four elements described are more potent collectively than any one is by itself. Within each, there is an opportunity for product, service, promotion, placement, and price, which ultimately yield brand value.

3. The level of success of a specific marketing tactic within each of the four elements may be dependent upon a reciprocal business system.

In conclusion, and in an attempt to answer the question, "What happens to consumer brands on the Internet?" I find three things.

First, the Internet is an interactive world, not a media world. Technology shapes brands in this marketplace, not media messages. Brands must therefore transform themselves to adapt to these new markets. That is, Holiday Inn must offer reservations online. We must offer a metaworld like a cyberhotel to become the hosts or the hospitality kings of the Internet.

Second, brands must become adaptive to at least one of the four consumer technology usages I demonstrated. Web pages are good, but operating system icons and satellite broadcast deliver real punch.

And third, brands must experiment to become technologies themselves. They, in essence, must be able to offer themselves in the form of an Attaché and deliver the exact brand value they've always offered to their consumers.

Of course it should be said that no brand has to go it alone. Good advisors, strategists, technology partners, host sites, media companies, and metaworlds can all help. But once a brand has found its starting place in the interactive Internet, it's important for those who know the brands and who produce it to understand how it might be enhanced and succeed.

Finally, a brief personal observation on what I believe is the most crucial aspect of brand success on the Internet. That is business vision. I have a favorite quotation posted on my desk that says,

'In most organizations, the future does not have a lobbying group."

Well, I firmly believe those who lobby with vision and with spirit are more likely to succeed in times when the basic values of a company are threatened.

Advocate, solicit, preach, and learn. Put your ears to the ground and hear the change that technology brings. Truly get close to the bits and bytes, for innovation of these harbingers are the path we will all follow. On this, too, I speak from experience. And that is yet another story.

Questions & Answers

Q: *Robert, are you suggesting that the Internet for brands is creating a monopoly world?*

ELMORE: That's a good question. Since the Internet is an inclusive place, or should I say space, people have the opportunity to be the best they can be. And, in this setting, monopolies will have a much harder time putting good people down.

Q: *Aren't brands just an artifact of an information-poor civilization? Won't they vanish as product selection, information, and tools expand dramatically on the Net?*

OTTOLENGHI: Well, brands, as they're articulated in the physical world, build a certain sense of trust or security about the quality of a product. It may not be completely known to a consumer what they're buying unless it has a brand associated with it. Those don't necessarily immediately translate into a sort of perfect information world—I think that was the underlying assumption in that question in the sense that, on the Internet, you supposedly can see all and know all; therefore, what's the purpose of the brand and that trust value?

There are different sets of consumer values online; that was where I was trying to head in my presentation. You not only have values of knowing a product or getting more information about a product, but you have the values of what you do when you're on the Internet: manipulation, control, sharing, and communication of information. If a brand is not associated with those online values, it can be diminished. However, if it *is* associated with those online values, then it has, in a sense, given value to the consumer in a brand value.

JEFFREY: Brands are by no means dead on the Internet. There really is a lot of stuff out there and I think brands will become more important as time goes on. You're going to find some sources of information that will be trustworthy if you haven't already. I think it's the enormity of the information that makes brands even more important in some respects.

On the other hand, our experience with the Palace has also shown that brands, as they exist today, don't necessarily guarantee the same kind of success in the new environment. For example, we have two Palace servers up right now. One Fox Television put up and another one was put up by two guys in their basement running a web site called Cybertown.

Now Cybertown immediately took off. There are approximately 30 people at any given time on that site. The Fox site has between five and ten and sometimes it's empty. I think, in part, with respect to metaworlds, it's because the Fox brand doesn't carry the same weight that Cybertown did when it first came up—it wasn't applicable in the same way. So I think brands will continue to be important, but as they exist today, they don't necessarily translate. You're sort of up for reevaluation on the Internet.

ELMORE: I would just add a couple of things. Number one, when it comes to brand, we will see an immense amount of confusion as we move from the old paradigm of mass communications and advertising hype to more selective personalized communication by choice. People will try to establish brand by the old paradigm without really understanding their purpose. Les talked about vision. I absolutely agree that understanding purpose and vision are key to establishing brand. And if that brand doesn't align with vision and purpose, you're going to get trapped, perhaps without even knowing it.

Finally, brand always comes back to trust and, as we go forward, we're going to learn together, we're going to innovate with our customers as a whole new way of doing business. And if you don't have trust between your people and your customers, then you're not going to win the new game of the 21st century. In a word, brand is all about trust.

Q: *Have you found your customers have a different set of expectations for your product and services offered via the Internet versus your regular distribution channel? Do you have any evidence of that?*

OTTOLENGHI: Oh, absolutely. That is the key element. I mean, they expect us to provide them convenience and time savings and the ability, 24 hours a day, 7 days a week, 365 days a year, to be able to come in and find where it is they want to stay and book that reservation. They also want to know more about their travel process. That is, where is it they're going to get off the plane and get to a cab and get a map of the city and buy tickets to go to a show if they're on a trip for leisure. Or if they're a businessperson, what's the quickest route to their business appointments.

We're seeing that we have to integrate not only our Internet information, but some other intranet-type information with our commercial travel agent partners. So yes, absolutely. Our brand has to be represented in a much different way when it goes onto the Internet.

JEFFREY: I can only tell you about what we've seen with the Palace. Like all Internet products, I don't think you're going to find my story's going to be very different. People expect very quick responses to their purchase. It's like shareware: you get a version that works 90 percent of the time, and for the remaining 10 percent you pay $20. You call an 800 number and give your credit card number over the phone.

The thing that's different here is instead of four to six weeks for delivery, people expect the thing, the unlocked good, to be sitting in their email box in under an hour. So it's definitely a different set of expectations with respect to delivering information as a product.

ELMORE: We will continue to bill by the hour in the traditional context of service delivery. But ultimately, as more work is performed through the Internet, we must understand how and where we create value. It will not matter if you are a lawyer or a professional in the hospitality industry. If you don't know where that value is and you don't have a vision of how value is provided, you're going to have a hard time relating the cost of your services to the value you help create. Then, we must all learn to bill for that value in new and different ways.

MCFARLAN: So it's more than just information. In other words, instead of being an information deliverer, you've got to be an information value adder somehow; you've got to put embedded intelligence in what you give to them.

Q: *Les, your site is very interesting and fun. Did you develop it yourself, and if so, what software did you use to develop it, and how much did you invest to build the web sites?*

OTTOLENGHI: Yes, we did develop it ourselves. It was originally a "skunkworks" project dreamed up by myself and the first person I hired on my staff. And then we actually had 35 people within the organization assigned to us, both in technology and marketing, to fully develop it and launch the sites. The technologies, like the Travel Buff video game, were developed by us. We utilized everything from QuickTime VR from Apple to Macromedia's Director in order to present this type of multimedia information.

Then we did the basic things, like the web page construction, using the best toolsets available.

Our basic costs for launch. We were able to reuse a lot of our technology assets. So I believe the latest estimates on doing a transactional-based web site for a company are somewhere in the $800 to $900,000 range. We did it for approximately $158,000.

Q: *Customer service has become an increasingly important aspect of many company brands. How does the Internet reconcile that with the fact that lots of customers still want to deal with live customer service reps?*

ELMORE: A great question. And I see the answer lying in how we personalize our dialog. In a funny way I think we are all going to operate as real-time concierges with video connections! There is a limit to how much you can do through email. You're going to see this notion of concierges gaining momentum. First, it will be in live voice and then it will be videos as the new technologies are introduced. John Sviokla and Jeff Rayport's article on marketspace in *Harvard Business Review*[*] gives us a good framework for analyzing this question. They really did a wonderful job differentiating between place and space in that article.

Q: *Since posting information on the Internet is free for many people, we may, in the future, see our customers posting web sites—presenting, favorably or unfavorably, our brands. How should companies deal with this?*

JEFFREY: Well, I think with respect to Palace, you can customize what you look like.

As far as what happens when someone presents it unfavorably, I think that the legal jury is out on this. I don't think that we have all of the answers yet. However, within the context of The Palace, I would say that it's really not any different. Whatever it ends up being, it won't be any different than free speech.

We make a tool, so we really haven't taken a stance on this one way or the other. In the same way, I don't think you'd find Netscape responsible for somebody putting up a web page that had content you disagreed with. I think that we fall sort of in the same boat. I think that we're going to have to wait until the legal opinion comes in before you have any sort of actionable recourse.

OTTOLENGHI: I believe our opinion on it is that this is a natural result of interactivity. We do agree that there are some legal definitions that still have to be made and those are going to come out over a long period of time. But those will probably be

---

[*] Rayport, J.F. and J.J. Sviokla, "Managing in the Marketspace," *Harvard Business Review*, November/December 1994.

rather lengthy discourse. That is, they'll also be costly discourse. This is an interactive world, and we want to kick that crutch out from under the people who are disgruntled with us—give them the opportunity to come to us and work their grievances out on our terms.

So we are actually going to offer the ability to facilitate the discussion about our brand, how you like it, what you don't like. We're going to create an environment for that very purpose so that it isn't something that is a rogue web site or some other person's opinion posted throughout the Internet. We'll make it an environment in which everyone can participate, make those kinds of statements, and hopefully see a response in short order. Then we can credit or discredit any of the allegations or assumptions that are made.

McFarlan: I want to thank the three of you for a really outstanding set of ideas. It's hard for me to believe that we're only two and a half years down the road in this.

Somebody asked me, "Are there a clear set of messages from this session from which I can take concrete business action?" What I'd take away from this session myself is that this is a very fast moving, very volatile new field of endeavor. As Les described, you are sort of reinventing all along the way. We're still working our way through this unstable, fragile period.

About the Speakers

F. Warren McFarlan is Senior Associate Dean and Director of External Relations at Harvard Business School. He teaches in the Advanced Management Program: International Senior Managers Program, and is Chairman of Delivering Information Services Program. Professor McFarlan's newest book, *Corporate Information Systems Management: The Issues Facing Senior Executives* (fourth edition), co-authored with Professors Lynda M. Applegate and James L. McKenney, appeared in 1996. "How to Manage an IT Outsourcing Alliance" appeared in the Winter 1995 issue of the

Sloan Management Review. He also served a three-year term as Senior Editor of the *MIS Quarterly* (1986–1988).

In his 34-year career as a business consultant, **Robert L. Elmore** has served both large and small clients in a wide variety of industries: first as an auditor; then as a systems consultant, and finally as managing partner of the Business Systems Consulting practice of Arthur Andersen. Mr. Elmore presently operates as an independent consultant helping organizations plan for and enable transformational business strategies spurring growth and profitability. He has authored numerous articles in leading industry journals that focus on the executive's use of information technology, cost accounting, and project management techniques, and the use of new groupware technologies.

Mark Jeffrey headed the original Time Warner team that created virtual world of The Palace. Through his efforts, The Palace was recently spun off into its own independent company whose investment partners include Intel, Time Warner, and Softbank. Prior to joining The Palace Group, Mr. Jeffrey headed the 20th Century Fox office of Delphi Internet's entertainment unit, creating the very first web site for a TV network (fX cable network). He also managed online service and web production for 20th Century Fox Film, Fox Broadcasting Corporation, TV Guide Online, fX Networks, Fox Interactive, Fox Video, and Infiniti Broadcasting radio station KROQ-FM.

Les Ottolenghi is currently Vice President, Strategy, Planning & Interactive Technologies at Carlson Company. Previously he was the Director of Emerging Technologies at Holiday Inn Worldwide. At Holiday Inn, his responsibilities included research, trial implementation, and evaluation of Internet and interactive television technologies for the worldwide hotel chain. Most recently, Mr. Ottolenghi launched two web sites for Holiday Inn, including the first Internet-based online reservations system, and the first use of virtual reality technologies over a network. The Holiday Inn web sites hold the record for the largest commercial launch in Internet history.

HARVARD NEWS

CONFERENCE ON THE INTERNET AND SOCIETY

May 29-31, 1996   Cambridge, MA

No Easy Answers for Business on the Internet

By Tom Ashbrook

They called the session "The New Economics," but all the audience really wanted to know was: who is going to make money on the Internet, and how are they going to make it?

Beneath all the high-minded contemplation of social impact, new paradigms, and techno-evolution, the heart of the Net buzz is still the digital gold rush. But there were no simple answers yesterday to the question of how value will be created in and extracted from the digital realm.

Panelists ranked customer service as a key area in which the Internet will add value. One-to-one marketing and the trade in specialized information were also highlighted as promising areas. But at this point, many companies jumping into an Internet presence are driven as much by fear as opportunity or understanding, panelists said. Thinly conceived web sites serve as little more than "brochure-ware." And new business models have yet to fully gel.

"The problem with the Internet is that nobody knows who's selling razors and who's selling blades," said Harvard Business School professor John Sviokla, moderator of the session.

In the short term, advertising-based services are practically the only operations pulling direct revenues from the Internet, noted Tim Brady, Director of Production at Yahoo!, the Sunnyvale-based Net search phenomenon. More revenue streams are expected to emerge, said panelists, but all will require more development of consumer trust, real value, online product branding, and corporate understanding of the logic of the Net.

Trust remains a key unresolved issue, starting with consumer reluctance to commit credit card numbers to the Net. Many firms are working on improving the security of online commerce.

Panelist John Donegan, of First Virtual, a developer of Internet payment systems, argued yesterday that part of the solution must also lie in lowering expectations of perfect digital security.

"People are beginning to understand that there is a certain level of risk in doing business on the Net, and accept it as they do in the rest of life," said Donegan.

Trust of content is also a key issue. Information providers on the Net will have to engender trust that they are independent, unbiased, and willing to direct customers wherever they need to go, even if that means sending them to a competitor's site, said Yahoo!'s Brady. Then they have to have to deliver real value.

"Your competitors are a click away," said Brady. "If you don't deliver a competitive product, your customer is gone."

Even providing good information may not be enough for much longer, said Christine Maxwell of the McKinley Group, provider of the Magellan search engine.

"The shelf life of information property is getting shorter and shorter," said Maxwell. The profitable way ahead, she said, lies in distributing information for free, in order to sell related services and relationships for profit.

The effort to create value beyond the information trade turns quickly to marketing, and the deepening of relationships with consumers of many kinds of products.

"Like all gold rushes, it looks like the only people who have a prayer of making money are the ones making picks and shovels," said Kathleen Biro, president of Strategic Interactive Group in Boston. "But marketing and serving customers are where the real money is."

Internet marketing "is not about mass communication," said Biro. "It's definitely not about hits or clicks. It's about delivering on the promise of direct customer contact."

Biro's firm is a wholly owned subsidiary of Bronner Slosberg Humphrey, one of the world's largest direct marketing and response companies. She is now working to take that experience into the Internet realm with clients like IBM, AT&T, Kraft Foods, and L.L. Bean.

"The advertising community got caught flat-footed," said Biro. "It looked to them like it was just geeks on the Net, then lots of geeks. Now we're hitting the big magic place, which is upscale families with children. And you've got to think in terms not of mass marketing, but of putting specific customers into motion."

L.L. Bean now finds that 60 percent of its affluent customer base has personal computers and is "Net-enabled." By September the woodsy mail order company will offer direct ordering over the Net.

Stephen Kahane, president of Datamedic Clinical Systems in Waltham, said the managed care push in health care creates a ripe target for Internet services, as firms offer up-to-date medical protocols and track health care delivery online. But privacy concerns remain a brake on full development of the industry's Internet potential. Consumers want medical privacy, doctors don't like to be closely tracked, and health care providers are wary of systems that open them to constant scrutiny.

And so it went: lots of nuance and new logic, few easy answers, and plenty of hunger to know what lies ahead.

"Which industry will be eviscerated first and why?" came a late question from the audience. Old information providers, came the answer. Of course.

Business

May 29, 1996

The New Economics
How Will Value Be Created and Extracted?

MODERATOR: John J. Sviokla
PANELISTS: Kathy Biro
Tim Brady
Jack Donegan
Stephen Kahane
Christine Maxwell

SVIOKLA: Welcome to "The New Economics: How Will Value Be Created and Extracted." My name is John Sviokla. I'm an Associate Professor at the Harvard Business School and it's a pleasure to have you all here at our conference on the Internet and society. The issue of the Internet and society is something very much on the mind of the university and also of the Harvard Business School. We are currently in the middle of a considerable investment and research to understand the use of the Internet and its impact on education and our economics. And we think that it's going to be fundamental to the way that knowledge is created and distributed.

Today we have five representatives on our panel who worry about this same issue in very different domains.

Dr. **STEPHEN KAHANE** is a medical doctor with a Master's degree in computer science. Stephen is the founder and CEO of Datamedic Clinical Systems. Datamedic deals with how to get health care professionals, in particular, doctors, to use technology. Because, as Steve has informed me, 80 percent of health care costs comes from the pen of the doctor. If we can influence that point of con-

tact, Steve believes, we can make quite a difference in the way that health care is provided.

KATHY BIRO is the founding President of Strategic Interactive Group, a wholly owned subsidiary of Bronner Slosberg Humphrey, one of largest direct marketing companies in the world. Kathy's job is, as I understand it, is to take what we have learned in domains such as direct mail and apply it interactively to customers. This new interactive medium has the power to extract information and create a new kind of value proposition for the customer.

We have a course about electronic commerce at the Harvard Business School called "Managing in the Marketspace" that I created with a colleague, Jeffrey Rayport.* **TIM BRADY** was one of the first students in that course, and was the third employee of Yahoo! Inc. Yahoo! is the largest and most popular Internet index at the moment, and the only company that I know of that has a market capitalization that's 333 times revenue. They have quite a race to run, lots of interest from consumers, and a lot of value to add here as we talk about the new economics.

Dr. **JACK DONEGAN** spent 36 years in the Navy and served, among other assignments, as Program Manager for the Strategic Defense System and Commanding Officer of the Naval Research Laboratory. His 36-year career was not, as he put it, as a seagoing officer, but rather as an engineer and scientist in the domain of technology—it was his job to understand how to use that technology in the Navy. Currently, Jack is the Vice President for Operations for First Virtual Holdings, which is concerned with how to get money from a seller to a buyer in a robust manner, and how to ensure the customers' trust.

CHRISTINE MAXWELL is one of the four founders of the McKinley Group, best known for their Magellan Index, one of the top five indices on the Web. Their claim to fame, in terms of their value proposition, is editorial content—rating sites, and the ability to deliver a value-added index for their

---

* Jeffrey Rayport moderated the Public Policy session "Institutional Structure for the Internet: Who Will Control It?" and the Business session "Community and Market Formation: Where Will Business Occur?"

customer base. I have a warm spot in my heart for Christine, because before she was a successful entrepreneur, she was an elementary school teacher.

I've asked our participants to include remarks on these three fundamental issues on economics in the Internet:

Trust. How do we create trust for consumer-to-business or business-to-business relationships?

Economics. What will be the fundamental changes in economics, especially of the businesses they are competing in?

Price cutting. What do we think will happen to price?

Some people think the use of the Internet will, in fact, allow people to raise price, to have more extracted value from customers through value-added services. Other people, myself included, think we will see a phenomenon in the Internet of price cutting and incredible price pressure that we haven't seen since Sam Walton came into the retail business.

Steve Kahane will start us off.

KAHANE: Despite being a physician/computer scientist, I am a nice guy, so bear with me here. I'd like to talk briefly about the health care information system industry. If it weren't for the Internet, we might be the hottest industry around. If you look at the five top health care information system companies in the public market over the past two years, you'd find that their market value has quadrupled. And this is very significant.

Now, despite that quadrupling in market value, the health care information system industry is actually quite small: probably under $10 billion. When you think about the fact that we spend about a trillion dollars as a nation on health care, that represents a very small percentage on actual information processes in that industry. That is changing, and it's changing not because technology is getting better. That's part of the reason, but it's really changing because of fundamental changes in the health care industry. These changes include the way physicians and hospitals

are reimbursed, the lay public's level of interest and sophistication regarding quality measurements, report-carding, and, in terms of quality, how different managed care companies and different providers compare.

As a resident at Johns Hopkins, I saw the profound power of these types of changes on the behavior of physicians. I was a resident there when DRGs [Diagnostic Related Groups] hit, and all of a sudden I went from being patted on the back for keeping my beds full and ordering more tests, to getting patients in and out and ordering fewer tests. DRG is a prospective payment system, based on an average hospital stay for a given procedure: physicians and hospitals are paid a set amount of money to take care of their patients. In order to survive, it is their job to manage costs and resources accordingly. So changes like this are driving the health care information system industry.

When you look at those costs, it's immediately apparent that about 80 percent of them, over 80 cents on the dollar, is going to pay for services the physician decides to order. If you're truly going to manage care, you need to be "in that physician's face," supporting cost-effective decision making and beginning to influence the process. I think the health care information system industry is moving rapidly toward trying to address those issues and is frantically trying to apply new technology to make that hurdle. The Internet can, and is beginning to, play a role in that arena.

The health care information system industry is quite broad. So when I was asked to talk about the Internet's role, I wasn't sure whether to focus on the consumer's side of health care, the provider's side, or the payer's side. In fact, the Internet is having an impact on all three areas within the health care system. The role it's playing is in terms of platform independence.

The Apple Macintosh, for instance, has a fairly significant penetration in the health care arena, which demonstrates that we do have heterogeneity of client systems. The Internet provides a way for health care information system vendors and others—consumer health care information system companies—to provide products and services in a platform-independent way. The availability of lightweight clients provides many benefits, such as reducing the costs associated with implementing systems, enabling ubiquitous wiring on the Internet, providing for low-cost publishing, timely access to knowledge, and so forth.

Now, for the first time ever, you can go out on the Internet and look at up-to-date protocols on how to manage heart attacks, how to manage different types of cancer, and things of that sort. In the past, that was a challenge to keep up with.

[In] a digital gold rush... the only people who have a prayer of making money are the ones who are manufacturing the picks and shovels and making up the maps as they go.

Of the three topics John asked us to speak about, I'm going to start with trust. Trust is a huge issue in health care in several different ways:

Security. When one of our users at a prominent Harvard hospital gets a test result or a note on our system from another clinician, he or she has to be assured it has not been tampered with. A single bit twiddled can make a big difference: they have to know that no one has messed with that data.

Privacy and confidentiality. There are three components associated with this:

- Privacy in terms of patient data.

- Privacy in terms of physician practice data (physicians don't like the idea of a big brother hovering out there, watching and monitoring everything they're doing).

- Privacy from an institutional standpoint. If we were to go speak with folks at MGH [Massachusetts General Hospital] or Beth Israel, I don't think any CEO of a promi-

nent health care organization is comfortable with the idea that anyone could tap into and view practice patterns on their physicians or their institutions.

- Intellectual property. The Mayo Clinics of the world believe that they can take the Agency for Health Care Services Research and make those protocols more valuable. That's something they own and should be able to use to their benefit: predictability in terms of response time. (Okay, physician users are not going to wait three seconds for this, ten seconds for that.) You who have used the Internet know that predictability is not there yet. But again, industry will deal with that.

Economic change. I believe that the real pressure is going to be in price cutting, new ways for marketing, a more level playing field for new companies, and improved market access—in other words, new ways to get to your consumer directly. This can have a profound impact on health care in general. In terms of pricing and power shift, I think these economic changes move power to the smaller organizations and open up amazing opportunities for smaller groups, both in terms of publishing and in gaining access to providers and consumers for transaction support.

BIRO: Because we're working with a lot of world-class players as diverse as L.L. Bean, AT&T, IBM, Kraft Foods, American Express, and Eastman Kodak, we are privileged to have a bird's-eye view of what these blue-chip clients are doing on the Internet to explore electronic commerce and emerging business models. It's clear that the future role of the Internet for these companies will be very different from what we're seeing today.

Here at Harvard we've heard a number of speakers talk about the "digital gold rush." Like all gold rushes, the only people who look like they have a prayer of making money are the ones who are manufacturing the picks and shovels and making up the maps as they go. I'm reminded of the end of that documentary on the Donner Pass.

The moral of the story was, "Don't take no short-cuts, and hurry along as fast ye can." And that's kind of what's happening here. Everyone is chasing their tails to be part of this high technology phenomenon.

But if this industry is going to fulfill its promise, we're going to have to quickly adapt our thinking to the point where we're no longer focusing on the technology of picks and shovels but focusing instead on the business of marketing and serving real customers. Because this is where the gold really lies, where the bulk of routine transactions and relationship building with customers is built and nurtured digitally. When this occurs, the Internet will no longer be a passing fad but will realize its full potential as the new space for an emerging digital economy.

What are the features of this new digital economy? The first is that it's digital, not physical. It's about doing business without walls. Imagine that in this new world, there's nothing between you and your customer—your unique intellectual capital, your goods and services—and what you provide. In this digital world, the limitations of your overworked sales force or "feet on the street," the productivity page goals you have per square inch in your catalog, your retail distribution problems—all that stuff disappears. The customer is suddenly "in your face."

And if the customer is in your face, the central question becomes, who are you anyway? Now that you're no longer encumbered by the physical limitations of how you do business today, what is it they can discover about your unique point of difference in the marketplace? For example, we're working with IBM in the personal computing area, and their web site now is essentially "brochureware" [http://www.ibm.com/]. What they have to do is evolve to a point where they can leverage the Web to establish new types of relationships with customers and really showcase the brain power behind the brand. Because that's the IBM point of difference.

The Web then becomes a window into the IBM point of difference, its true value added, and it's frankly the only window they have left to tell their story. Certainly with L.L. Bean (http://www.llbean.com/), the window is their unique intellectual capital of outdoor expertise and heritage. And again, it is a story they cannot tell through traditional channels.

The second thing about this digital economy is that it's about direct marketing, not mass communications. Now there's lot about advertising and emerging models on the Internet. But if you're really in the business of selling ad space on the Internet, it's not an easy sell. I personally get about 15 calls a day from would-be ad sales reps. For most major advertisers, the current Web phenomenon still isn't hitting their radar screen. They are still looking for a reach and frequency game.

We believe the promise of the Net lies not in its role as a mass communications vehicle but in its promise to transform the way we market to customers, one customer at a time. It's definitely not about hits or clicks, it's about delivering on the promise of real-time marketing. The economics of a direct response view of the Net is really based on the value of putting individuals in motion. What is the economic value of the customer behavior we're trying to induce? How much is it going to cost to get it? It's a matter of leveraging, or linking, our web-based activities to actual customer databases so that we can establish an ongoing dialogue with customers in a cost-effective manner.

The good thing is, in comparison to traditional communications vehicles, the economics of the Internet are incredibly attractive: ongoing customer contact over the Web is essentially free. The direct marketing power of the Internet is really not a matter of speculation anymore. While we all talk about the emerging digital economy, companies like L.L. Bean are quietly, conservatively proving the power of the Web as a cost-effective vehicle—in fact, the *most* cost-effective vehicle—at their disposal for quality customer acquisition.

What we're seeing is so encouraging that it's easy to imagine within the next few years they'll be spending half of what they spent today to get twice as many customers. And these customers will be more targeted: they will be younger, more active, they will have higher conversion rates, higher average order value, and they will have higher lifetime value. And this is happening right now. We've got the numbers to prove that.

In this digital world, speaking of L.L. Bean, branding is still important. We believe customers are not going to behave differently on the Web than they do with any other traditional channel of communications and distribution: they will gladly take anything for free from anybody. And that's a lot of what we're seeing on the Web today—people gladly taking things for free. They will actively do business, however, with those household names that they know and trust. Over time, what's going to happen is companies like AT&T and IBM and L.L. Bean and Kraft Foods will start to become more pervasive on the Web.

When that happens, when blue-chip companies truly exploit the Web, the digital economy will get that much-needed dose of legitimization, and the customer jitters problem is going to dissipate.

Some things won't change. In this digital economy, price is still a function of value. And getting on the Web with meaningful content or transactions or access to account information or self-help tools, or whatever it is, can be an expensive proposition. The expense is not necessarily physically putting the site up, it's coming up with the content in the first place. Without this commitment, you are doomed to what we're seeing on the Web today: 95 percent brochureware, delivering no value to anyone.

But how will companies capture the value for what they're providing in the form of compensation? First, we have to stop giving everything away and habituating the marketplace to expecting everything free.

Second, for most companies, capturing value has to do with linking the Internet activities to the core business of the organization, delivering real value to specific target groups, and measuring business impact across the board—its impact on traditional channels and distribution—just as you

would anything else you do from a marketing or business standpoint. And if you do this, the Web becomes one more tool to build and nurture customer relationships.

We are intrigued by reports that Ernst & Young, for example, is doing a "dial-a-consultant" service on the Web. Have you read about this? They target smaller enterprises who aren't going to pay their big fees, but they'll actually provide their consulting services through bulletin boards and email over the Web. This way they can get to a customer group they can't get to any other way, and at lower cost. Who knows if this is going to work. I mean, who's going to take these clients to lunch? But this is precisely the kind of thing that major companies are going to have to do to prove the power of the Internet to generate business.

Last, we need to realize that opportunities using the Net exist across the entire value chain. If you believe our premise that the most promising business model to emerge on the Net is some transmogrification of the business you are already in, then the critical next step is to evaluate and exploit specific opportunities across that entire value chain. And that means examining revenue growth and cost reduction opportunities across the marketing board, from sales to support to customer marketing, and of course customer services, which is where lots of companies now are realizing they can deliver a higher quality of service at lower cost.

So if you start to do this across the value chain, the next time you're asked that question, "How will we make money on the Internet?" the answer is, "It's no different from the way we make money today." It's about delivering material value for which certain very specific and targeted individuals will, in fact, pay a price. And it's about explicitly linking back to the core business of finding and nurturing customers, one relationship at a time.

BRADY: Before I touch on the issues of trust and the new economics, I'd first like to talk about the necessity of trust for a company like Yahoo! Yahoo! is a web site dedicated to helping users find information on the Internet for free. Yahoo! has five very strong competitors, all with very easy to use, easy to learn products. Those of you with Netscape browsers know very well that under the "Net Search" button sit five companies right next to each other. Our competitors are one click away. So the idea of trust, building brand loyalty, is paramount to Yahoo!'s success.

So how does Yahoo! build trust? We do it in four ways. First, we deliver a competitive product. It sounds pretty simple, but if you don't do that, you're not going to win. Again, your competitors are a click away and it takes users less than a second to go elsewhere. By a competitive product we mean a comprehensive, accurate, and easy to use product. The number of people coming onto the Net greatly outweighs the number of people already there. So ease of use is an extremely important issue.

Second, we build trust by focusing exclusively on user needs. We accomplish this by understanding the user. We have an organization of about 80 people, over half of whom spend eight to ten hours every day online—not writing software, not writing reviews about Internet sites, but living and looking at sites and truly understanding the medium. And we translate this understanding into a better product.

We further understand users' needs by reading their email. Yahoo! gets about 2,000 email messages every day. Because users can just type a sentence and hit "Send," a lot of users send their comments. That provides an extremely valuable source of information about our users and for improving our web site.

We also develop our product with the purpose of serving our users at almost any cost. For example, sometimes users can't find what they are looking for within Yahoo!. Instead of giving up on them, we point them to our competitors which are linked at the bottom of every Yahoo! search results page. This sends a very strong message to the user: "Hey, we're out for you. And, yes, we're running a business here, but we understand you're here to find information and we're going to do what it takes to get you to that piece of

information." As a result, our users go to Yahoo! to start their Internet search, because they know we're ultimately going to help them find what they're looking for.

Third, we build trust by being responsive to users. For the first eight months of the product's life, the two founders answered every email message. Users felt as though they had a stake in helping build Yahoo!—and they did. We've implemented many of the suggestions our users have fed us.

We can't answer every email message these days because we're getting about 2,000, but we answer well over 80 percent. And we go out of our way to respond personally, and not issue some canned message from an email robot. And on every single page of Yahoo! except the top page, there's a navigational bar with a button that says, "Write us."

Fourth, Yahoo! builds trust by perpetuating the perception of editorial independence and inclusiveness. In the early days of the company, Yahoo! got some very generous buyout offers from large companies. The founders didn't sell to these large companies because it would have fundamentally changed the way users perceived the Yahoo! product. Yahoo! is built solely for the purpose of helping users find what they want on the Web. If users perceived that Yahoo! had an alternative agenda, they might stop using the product. Remaining independent is important.

Inclusiveness is also critical. This means making sure all information is displayed and put into proper context. While we don't agree with a lot of what is on some web sites, we still feel it is important to include everything. You'll never find a Holocaust revisionist site without a Holocaust site right next to it. Providing this context and building trust with the user is important to us—our users are comfortable knowing that we don't "hide" information. The user is the filter.

Next, I'd like to discuss extracting value and the economics of the Web. I have a different perspective from Kathy's because Yahoo! gives its information away free. Yahoo!'s web site is supported by advertising. We are able to sustain a business by selling ads on the top of our web pages. Going forward, Yahoo! will continue to supply users with information for free.

The economics surrounding the "giving away" of information is critical to our future. We think it's going to shake out like this: information that has a broad appeal will remain free. If a large enough user base is interested in it, it will be supported by advertising. Sole suppliers and niche suppliers of information will be able sell their goods on a per piece or subscription basis.

Over time, however, as the ability to track and report and target advertising increases, the price of advertising will increase, as will the number of web users. So I expect to see an increase in the amount of information that will be advertising supported and accessed for free. In the end, however, what we'll find is a network TV/subscription TV model, where most of the things on the Web are free. But users looking for extremely specialized information will have to pay for it.

DONEGAN: I picked up a couple of witticisms at the Intellectual Property session earlier this morning. One of the speakers said, "I have enough trouble predicting the past, I don't try to predict the future." Maybe that's a good place to start this morning. I work for First Virtual Holdings; we're in the business of providing secure credit card transactions over the Internet. We do that through an email-based system that replaces your credit card number on the Internet with a Virtual PIN [Personal Identification Number]. We are very interested in the economic commerce question, but we are no better at predicting the future than anyone else.

There were two major conferences in Washington in May that bear on this area of trust and emerging economic growth. The first was the Software Publisher's Association Digital Commerce Conference, May 6 [1996], and the second was the American Bankers Association International Conference on Financing and Commerce in Cyberspace, May 8 [1996].

The speaker at both of these conferences was Eugene Ludwig, the Comptroller of the Currency. As the head of the Treasury Department's task force on Internet commerce, he noted that the Treasury's main interest in this area is focused on law enforcement, government financial operations and financial system stability. He emphasizes that the government looks upon Internet commerce as an emerging, very small operation, and they're not interested in pushing extensive regulation at this early point in the development of electronic commerce.

So when you hear a lot of this hype about how big things are and how fast they're moving, it's good to know that there are people in the world who think this whole thing is just getting started.

Ludwig points out the dichotomy between our current regulations, which are based on geography and political boundaries, and the nature of electronic commerce. He's not sure what to do about it but he feels there's time to work the issue. He points out, for example, that a consulting group made a recent prediction of Net commerce that 20 percent of U.S. household spending would be on the Net by the year 2005. Well, if you do the math, starting from that fact that roughly $350 million was spent in business last year, to get to 20 percent of the economy, you have to do 130 percent annual compound growth over the next decade. Should that happen, it would be nice for all of us in the business, but I don't really think it will.

Also at one of these conferences, we learned that the Federal Trade Commission [FTC] has formed a task force with the National Association of Attorneys General [NAAG] on Internet consumer protection. This morning you heard Bill Gates say that the FTC believes that scam artists are at work in cyberspace; the FTC is also concerned about Net advertising aimed at minors. These facts are certainly going to put a damper on electronic commerce.

The FTC has also taken a strong position on privacy. This bears directly on the issue of trust. They believe that consumer options must go beyond the traditional opt-in/opt-out approach, but they aren't coming up with any answers. As a matter of fact, they leave it to conferences like this one to come up with the answers.

The FTC's primary goal is to encourage industry self-regulation: in fact, they are holding a two-day conference in Washington on the 4th and 5th of June [1996] specifically on the subject of Internet consumer privacy. At the banking conference, the Federal Reserve's Governor Edward Kelly discussed the Fed's views. The major points he made were the following:

- Due to slow growth expectations of Net commerce, the Fed will not propose extensive regulations at this time.

- The Fed will not seek to introduce its own stored value card.

Nevertheless, the Fed is moving out. On May 21, 1996, the Board of Governors of the Federal Reserve approved a notice filed by Cardinal Bankshares of Lexington, Kentucky, through Security First Network Bank, to acquire Five Paces Software, Inc., of Atlanta. This acquisition will allow data-processing activities related to providing Internet banking and financial services.

This order is the first instance in which the Federal Reserve has specifically determined that engaging in activities designed to facilitate Internet banking services meets the "closely related and proper incident thereto" test for permissible activities of bank holding companies.

The Board's order also specifically takes note of the potential security risks of such activities and outlines the steps it expects banking organizations to take to mitigate these risks. The wording of this ruling shows a real appreciation of the development nature of electronic commerce.

The Board "carefully considered the possibility that, by helping to make banking services available over the Internet…the activities of Five Paces could expose financial institutions, their customers, information, and transactions to electronic interception, interference, or fraud" and recognized "that neither the software developed by Five Paces nor any other software product or security system can provide absolute protection against these risks."

The Board further stated, "the nature of these risks is not different, however, from those to which more traditional banking operations are exposed in other forms."

In its analysis, the Board declared that it "expects banking organizations considering whether to provide services over the Internet to analyze carefully the associated risks, and to evaluate carefully whether those risks are consistent with their policies relating to the security of customer information and other data."

The Board expects such analysis to mitigate the risk of unsound banking practices. The Board expects financial institutions, as part of such an evaluation, "to implement any modifications to their information security procedures and controls that appear to be necessary or appropriate in light of the risks associated with Internet-based services." Overall, the Board found that the proposed acquisition would enhance consumer convenience and generally satisfy the public interest factors.

This is a large part of where the issue of trust comes in. Our fundamental banking regulation and commerce system in this country operates on a level of assumed risk and trust across a broad level of exposure. Since the Board found that the proposed acquisition would enhance consumer convenience and generally satisfy the public interest, even the Fed is starting to say we should just go and do it. Perhaps the economic changes are really just a question of adapting the way we currently do business in this country in a wide set of other areas.

All of this seems to be pretty positive. Colin Crook, CitiBank's Chief Technology Officer, said at the bank conference that brand, combined with relationship, will be very important in cyber-commerce. He forecasted that if banks coordinate their efforts, e-check will be a highly effective payments mechanism, although he cautioned that e-cash will be subject to repeated attacks and counterfeiting.

(By the way, Tim's product Yahoo! really does work very well. Getting ready to come up to this conference, I had to catch the commuter train. I don't take it very often, and I'd forgotten the schedule. So I immediately clicked on Yahoo! Three more clicks and I was down to Virginia Railway Express. One more click and I had the schedule and made my train.)

First Virtual is in the business of trying to develop consumers' peace of mind and trust. One of the things we try to do is to raise your confidence about spending money on the Internet: we'll make sure you get your product from a reliable merchant, and that your credit card and other personal information is safe on the Net.

To sum up, trust seems to be a major focus here, with banking regulators and everybody else. The Internet payment systems and electronic cash are things that must be studied and dealt with. The real message here is that those of us in the emerging electronic industry need to work hard to find ways for people to incorporate the advantages of electronic commerce into their everyday lives. We need to work hard to discuss and resolve a broad range of issues that will determine how we deal with each other and with the consuming public. The government will be more likely to step in if commercial transaction volumes grow and if those of us in the community are unable to resolve issues such as standards and privacy.

SVIOKLA: Christine Maxwell is next.

MAXWELL: The first issue I'd like to address is trust. Trust is absolutely paramount, and is tied into knowing the source of what it is you're looking for on the Internet. Today when you go into the Internet you often don't know where the information comes from or how it got there. The background of the McKinley Group, which was formed in 1993, is fundamentally different from the backgrounds of its competition. And that has a lot to do with the tremendous differences in the way information is presented in the Magellan site [*http://www.mckinley.com/*].

From its inception as an Internet publishing company, our fundamental focus was on content. Of course, technology is vital as well. For us, content has always been king—international as well as domestic. At Magellan, we figure out how people look for information, where they go for that information, then we organize that information and present it in a way that allows them to find it quickly. This system has been a driving force in the way Magellan presents its content.

I've been involved in providing search services for people for many, many years. I ran an information brokerage company for 15 years. The art of looking for and finding information is truly an art and not a science. At Magellan our focus is on adding value to content, not just by going into the Internet resources, but by actually evaluating them, rating them, and helping people to decide which resource would be the most helpful to them.

The next important aspect is customer service. We are very, very affected by our customer interaction, and listen closely to what they are saying.

The editorial process, which has to work with technology, is essential to keep Magellan responsive to its audience. We have really leveraged our value-added content and editorial capacity, which comes down to the issues of brand loyalty and so on. We have major alliances with AT&T, Time Warner (which selected Magellan for its Pathfinder site), IBM, Netcom, and the Microsoft Network [MSN].

I'll talk for a moment about the economics of the Internet and where we believe things are headed. I think it's fundamental to look at what's happened to intellectual property: the shelf life of information is getting shorter. Essentially, because people can copy at will, there really is a need to change the intellectual property aspect and to enable publishers of content to provide advertising services such as support, aggregation, filtering, assembly and integration of content modules, and even training.

The best likely defense for content providers is to distribute intellectual property for free in order to sell services and relationships. The provider's task is really to figure out the following:

• What to charge for.

• What to give away for free.

- How to set up relationships.

- How to develop ancillary products and services to cover the cost of developing the content.

Next, let's talk about advertising. In the Magellan Directory, McKinley does major advertising, and this is a very important part of our revenue-driven model. As we go forward, however, the direct marketing aspect is certainly going to become important in this new one-to-one world. Increasingly, advertising will be tailored and of higher quality, because those with more money to spend will actually get better quality advertising. So while advertising is important, we're also going to see much more direct marketing in the future.

As a result of Magellan's editorial and publishing expertise, formed from over 25 years in the publishing business, we have a unique ability to recognize very strong intellectual capital, to bring it onto the Net, and to publish that content in a new way. In the future, it will become much easier to find very specific content than it is today.

How will we play a role in helping you find exactly what you need in the most efficient way? One answer is to improve the way indexing works. I think this is the golden age of indexing, just as it is the golden age of astronomy. And the more we work on that aspect, the better it will be for all of us.

Finally, I'd like to talk about pricing. Magellan is free today and I think that's very important: 90 percent of the people who use the Internet start with a directory service. So it's a critical gateway. We are getting millions of hits per day because of our position in Netscape's Directory page. Because of this, we have a major responsibility to make sure people can find what they're looking for free of charge. On the other hand, we do believe that people will be prepared to pay for value-added information as it becomes more accessible on the Net. Still, a large part of the content will remain free: the services that get appended will enable people to be paid for the value of their work.

This is a very exciting time where the Internet is in a state of transition. And Magellan is geared to listening to its audience and their request for *content*—not just in North America, but around the world.

SVIOKLA: Our panelists have covered a lot of ground, and I heard a number of different themes. One was this issue of trust at many levels: an individual's security, privacy, and brands. On the economics theme, there are shifting power relationships among providers, payers, channel members, and indices. And on the price theme, I was reminded of the old wag who said about the Internet, "It's a lot like when Gillette started the razor blade business: they gave the razors away and made money on the blades." The problem with the Internet is that nobody knows who's selling razors and who's selling blades.

Questions & Answers

Q: *I'm interested in what you would say about changing rates in telecommunications, and what implications it has for you in terms of your strategies.*

DONEGAN: Well, you can either lower the rate or you can raise enough money to pay the bill.

Right now, there's not enough money flowing through the system to pay the bill and so the rates look high. But if electronic commerce starts to go, then the ISPs [Internet Service Providers] and the businesses can pay the bills and the structure will go. In reality, it's not how much it costs today, it's where to get the money to upgrade the structure to get the bandwidth that Bill Gates was talking about this morning. That infrastructure construction is what really ought to be worrying us because right now the infrastructure of the Net is not growing anywhere as fast as the number of people in the population.

MAXWELL: I would like to make an additional comment that first of all, we do care about that issue. It's particularly an international problem because the price of access in Europe, for example, is incredibly high. It's like the difference between buying a gallon of gas in England and a gallon of gas here. It is beginning to come down in Europe and I think we will see it coming down here over time as well. But from our point of view, it remains important to continue providing free access to our content.

Q: *How quickly will which industries be affected? Which industry will be eliminated first and why?*

MAXWELL: I'd like to specifically to address that from the point of view of those who have been king of the information access heap for a long time. Until the advent of the Internet, the cutting edge of information gathering was the online vendors: Dialog, Lexis-Nexis, etc. It's been a very interesting time for them because these are large organizations who, up until now, never had to worry about what was going to happen to them—all the major corporations who needed access to information could pay for it. And they did so through the nose.

Today of course, as I said, running an information broker company the likes of Dialog was absolutely the key to finding information for people. Those are now the conventional tools in the toolbox of a research company; they're not the cutting edge. The Internet is now the cutting edge. Now you've got organizations who are really, really frightened, because each of their databases is beginning to come into the Internet. As a result, there are many issues at the moment. When you go and search a database through the Internet, you neither have the archival access going back many years nor the refinement of the way Boolean logic works in a dialog search.

This is an example where companies, who have absolutely had a field day for decades, now have to change their tune because they are no longer at the top of the heap.

SVIOKLA: Some of the companies between the crosshairs are the information providers who have been, if not usurious, aggressively pricing their products. These businesses, I think it's fair to say, draw off a little bit of cash flow. And you're saying that those people will be particularly vulnerable. Would you put somebody like a Bloomberg on the list in the financial services area?

MAXWELL: It's slightly different because it's in a closed system: if you can pay *x* thousand dollars, you can have a Bloomberg on your desk. But they do have a web site. You have some access.

Q: *Who is making money, and what are the dominant models for money making today in terms of the value extraction part? Is it simply a stock market game at this particular point where investors are buying options on the future?*

KAHANE: Within the health care field, I would say that more of the Internet move is towards controlling costs, reducing costs, improving customer intimacy, and things of that sort. I haven't seen a lot of revenue generation activity within the health care industry. I think it's more looking at ways to reduce costs.

Q: *What kinds of costs, do you think?*

KAHANE: I've heard it said that the health care industry is the largest spectator sport in the U.S. I mean, it's amazing how many folks get involved in simple transactions. Just think about when your doctor orders a prescription or gives you a prescription, all the players that get involved. At a certain level, that is highly inefficient. I alluded to ways to streamline that earlier—the role of the payer is really changing. Large medical groups are consolidating and growing today, and going directly to employers as opposed to going through a managed care organization like U.S. Healthcare.

I think the intermediaries are really pretty scared and looking at what role they will play in the future.

Q: *So it's more about cost reduction, especially around document and information handling and complex sets of relationships?*

BRADY: I'd just like to echo what Steve [Kahane] said. In terms of customer support, particularly in the technology industry where customer support is extremely important and there's a lot of it, being able to build a web site of information about your product saves an extremely large amount of money. I met with people at Cisco a while ago and they're saving millions just by posting basic information about their product, which they normally would have people answering phones for at $2.00 a minute. So in that sense, they definitely are making money, if you will, or not losing money.

Now in terms of people that are making money, I think in the short term the advertising-based sites on the Net right now are making money. That's about it.

Q: *We're hearing about information handling costs, customer service. How about on the advertising efficiency? Is that getting any better? Worse?*

MAXWELL: I think it's getting better. We are actually getting much better feedback from the advertisers that it's actually having an effect. They are getting sales or whatever they wanted from that.

SVIOKLA: Just to calibrate that can anyone in the audience estimate, how much of your car that you buy for $15,000 to 20,000 is advertising? About $1100 dollars of every car is advertising.

MAXWELL: Most of the sales that happen are *off* the Net, not *on* the Net at this time.

Q: *Is the overall cost of customer service going down?*

DONEGAN: Well, the problem is that half the people on the Internet weren't here a year ago, so you have an awful lot of new people being added all the time who, for the first time, go through a process of getting an online provider or getting into a transaction system or getting into a search system, and they require help. So the level of help that's being required is going up. The systems to provide help are becoming more efficient, so the cost of providing help is staying about even. But if the Internet continues to double every year, then those people who weren't on it a year ago wind up needing the help.

BIRO: There is also the issue of critical mass. How big is the through pipe? All you have to do is quickly run the numbers. Email costs you a lot less to service than does a live operator call. We've done that kind of analysis across all sorts of businesses from hardware to software, packaged

goods, and so on. The issue is that we don't yet have a critical mass of penetration. But still, we can reduce cost, one customer at a time, for those who are enabled. And over time, the number of customers impacted, and the associated costs savings, will grow. There's no question that through the Internet, you can deliver a higher quality of customer service at significantly lower cost.

But again, it's a direct response view of the world. It's the same issue on the revenue generation side. We know that advertising is more efficient and effective a customer at a time, for those who are impacted. And if you take that view on a marginal revenue base, as a marginal cost, it becomes very easy to justify these expenses.

Q: *Kathy, could you just give an order of magnitude in terms of the difference between the kind of service you get, say, on a phone versus over the Internet? The costs to the provider?*

BIRO: Well, it depends on how you do it, but if you provide self-help tools and tables and intelligent agents and wizards and so on, that's the area we're involved in with respect to IBM. Consider how much of the after-sale expense for a company like that is in ongoing technical support. All you've got to do is take that intellectual capital, repurpose it, have people sort through the information, and be able to help themselves arguably better than they can through a live operator. That's ten times less expensive than what they're doing today.

Q: *What kind of relationships are getting built? I know you answer email, but are you doing anything else?*

BRADY: Other than the email, last year we did a survey on our front page asking users to tell us about themselves, to help us with advertising. We asked them if they're interested in getting the "cool pics" of the week or being a data tester. So we have a long list of people helping us out, and we are very proactive in that aspect.

Q: *The question is, do you reconnect with them or is it a one-time event?*

BRADY: Absolutely. It's a dialogue for sure.

Q: *It seems like a powerful advertising medium, but why aren't businesses more aggressively moving into this medium as a means to advertise?*

BIRO: The advertising community is still dominated by a mass communications view of the world. That is, you look for large groups of people who vaguely resemble each other, and until it hits a critical mass in the millions, it really doesn't hit the radar screen of most advertisers. That's why the advertising community is being caught kind of flat-footed—the Internet phenomenon took them by surprise. It went from this group of geeks to a larger and larger group of geeks and suddenly we're hitting the "sweet spot," which is upscale families with children—what every company in America is going after.

But that's why you're not seeing all this money chasing the Net yet. People are still worried about how to market their own goods and services this way, and are waiting until the audience numbers are large enough to hit their radar screen.

The other interesting thing is that when you're talking about mass communications, though people do spend millions and millions, they have no idea what the impact on the business really is. Because mass communications is not measurable at all. So if I spend $50 million today and I kind of like my sales results, I may feel good afterwards, but I have no idea whether I would have gotten the same result with a different mix at half the expense.

Q: *Have you done calculations for existing businesses that have moved onto the Internet (such as L.L. Bean), as to what percentage of customers come to you over the Internet compared to your traditional services and traditional approaches?*

BIRO: Well, let me flip the question a little bit: what we've done with them is to look at the intersection of how many people are in fact enabled on the Web and what their current customer base looks like. L.L. Bean is perhaps anomalous because 60 percent of their base is PC/online-enabled, which is a very, very high number. Now, in terms of who's actually doing business, it's obviously small relative to the overall base. But remember, L.L. Bean doesn't even have direct ordering on the Web yet. They will by the end of this year. They've just announced that.

L.L. Bean does have individual web-specific SKUs so that if you hit the Web and then order, we can separately track how much of the business is being generated by the Web versus other SKUs. And again, what we're proving is that the Web is a much more cost-effective vehicle than traditional media: lower acquisition costs, higher conversion rates, and higher order value. How big that becomes is the question of, over time, how many people in aggregate we will succeed in putting in motion.

About the Speakers

JOHN J. SVIOKLA is an Associate Professor at the Harvard Business School. His current work focuses on electronic commerce and knowledge management. In particular, his work addresses how managers can effectively use the power of technology to create more value for customers and extract value though superior financial performance. Dr. Sviokla's other work focuses on marketing and knowledge management. In these realms he has authored or co-authored several publications, including "Seeking Customers and Keeping Customers," "Expert Systems and Their Impact on the Firm: A New View of XCON," "The Effect of Expert Systems Use on the Information Processing of the Firm" and "Putting Expert Systems to Work." Dr. Sviokla consults for large and small firms, and teaches in the Harvard Business School program.

KATHLEEN L. BIRO leads the Strategic Interactive Group, which assists clients in developing and executing Interactive Media strategy. Kathy has more than 17 years experience in marketing and new business development. Her marketing experience spans both traditional and evolving communications channels, with particular expertise in all forms of direct response and alternative electronic delivery. Her industry experience includes financial services, trade and professional publishing, resort marketing, catalog marketing, computer hardware, and online information services.

As the third employee at Yahoo!, **TIM BRADY** started up its marketing department. He now runs Yahoo!'s production efforts. Before Yahoo!, Tim spent three years with Motorola's Semiconductor Division in Tokyo, Japan as Product Marketing Manager of the 16-bit microcontroller product line. In this role, Tim managed the introduction of the product line into Japan, in charge of business development and product development. Tim holds a Masters degree in Business Administration from Harvard University and a B.S. in Electrical Engineering from Stanford University.

JOHN DONEGAN is an active consultant and lecturer on the influence of information technology on American society and business. Until recently his principal client was the San Diego Supercomputer Center. He is Vice President for Operations of First Virtual Holdings Inc., a San Diego corporation specializing in secure financial transactions on the Internet, and is President of his own company, John Donegan Associates, Inc. Dr. Donegan received a three-year appointment to the National Research Council of the National Academy of Sciences in 1994. He is also a member of the American Physical Society, the Naval Institute, and the American Society of Naval Engineers.

STEPHEN N. KAHANE, M.D., is President and CEO of Datamedic Corp., a leading health care information system company that provides electronic patient record and business systems solutions to the health system and physician office marketplace. Dr. Kahane is a Johns Hopkins–trained physician and computer scientist and has been in the health care information systems business since 1983. Dr. Kahane was co-founder of Clinical Information Advantages, Inc. CIAI developed electronic patient record products that integrate new technologies such as state-of-the-art graphic user interfaces, pen-tablet, speech recognition, relational database, and knowledge base technologies to address the requirements of the health care professional and the health care institution. Datamedic acquired CIAI in 1992.

Net Marketing Gives Power to Consumers

By Margie Kelley

If you surf the Net, you are a target—a potential consumer—of every merchant in the virtual marketplace. The problem for business, according to experts on Internet marketing, is that you are a moving target at best and you can shoot back.

"It's a double-edged sword," said panelist Angelo Santinelli, Vice President of Marketing at Shiva Corporation. "While the Web can give a company a larger image to advertise, the velocity and voice that the buyer now has is larger. Take chat groups. Buyers go there and they can say good things but they can also say terrible things about you and your products."

To respond to this power shift, Santinelli said that Shiva, which produces remote access servers and provides technical support services to telecommuters and remote users, is monitoring chat rooms to learn what consumers are saying about their products and services.

"This forces you to react much more quickly," he said. "In fact, we've had nine new product announcements in three months as a result."

But with the shift of power to the buyer comes a lot of responsibility. What will the rules be for this community? Do they police themselves or does the government need to be involved?

Recognizing the newfound power of the consumer online is about all that could be concluded from the hour-long panel discussion on communities and market formation. The jury is clearly still

out on how to effectively define virtual communities for efficient and profitable market transactions.

Figuring out what defines a community, relationship, or market on the Internet is difficult, according to panelist Lincoln Millstein, Vice President of New Media for the *Boston Globe*. Millstein used the *Globe*'s success in sales of classified advertising to illustrate this point.

"Today, classified ads are responsible for 35 to 40 percent of our revenues," Millstein said. "It's the most profitable part of our business. But in 1992, when I first signed onto America Online and discovered these chat rooms, I intuited a threat to our classified ads. It allowed consumers to communicate in a lightning-fast manner. I rang alarm bells at the paper."

The *Globe*'s response was to launch the city-wide web page, *http://www.boston.com/*, which includes 35 other Boston-based organizations. Since then, Millstein said he has discovered that chat rooms on the Internet are not really competing with his classified ads after all.

"I'm not convinced that now that consumers can talk to each other on the Internet that they necessarily want to do business with each other," he said. "The Internet is still chaotic."

"So what is it that makes up a community?" moderator Jeffrey Rayport, Assistant Professor of Business Administration at the Harvard Business School, asked the panel.

One approach to finding that answer—known as agency—has taken off in the last year for one hot company based here in Cambridge, called Agents, Inc. According to panelist Nick Grouf, its president, the company provides individual web users with a software "agent" that navigates the Web to find information of particular interest to each user. The information is based on an initial questionnaire that each user completes anonymously.

Beginning in 1995 with a database of 200 musical artists, Agents helped users discover music that their preferential profiles indicated they might like, even if they had never heard of that artist or type of music before. Now, according to Grouf, the music database contains 20,000 artists and Agents has 130,000 subscribers to the Firefly service (*http://www.ffly.com*).

"The agent can also hook people up with others who share the same tastes in music," he said.

"This technology lets us move away from geographically-based communities to taste-based communities. The agent finds those people whose opinions and taste match yours and which therefore you trust, and it's completely generic. It can be used for anything: books, restaurants, movies, hotels."

Grouf said the service does not destroy serendipity because users can still see all possibilities in any category. They would just receive them in an order that puts a priority on more preferred items.

Another key to the development of virtual communities is the emergence of secure and selective networking technology. According to panelist Haig Hovaness, Manager of Enabling Technologies for KPMG Peat Marwick, virtual private network technology, or VPN, will enhance virtual organizations by combining encryption with wide area networks and firewall technology.

"The thing to remember is that the World Wide Web is not a push environment." said Grouf. "It's a pull environment. The consumer pulls what it wants. If we don't pay attention to consumers' needs and rights, they will scare us in another direction altogether."

Business

May 30, 1996

Community and Market Formation

Where Will Business Occur?

MODERATOR: Jeffrey Rayport
PANELISTS: Nick Grouf
                  Haig Hovaness
                  Lincoln Millstein
                  Angelo Santinelli

RAYPORT: We are here to talk about community and market formation, and this is a panel all of us have looked forward to a great deal. Our keynote speaker this morning [Steven McGeady] talked about community and the kind of responsibilities we all take for building communities in this Internet space quite seriously. It seems to be the next big challenge many of us face, whether from public policy or (in our case) business perspectives.

We have a wonderful panel of individuals. So let me make some introductions. **ANGELO SANTINELLI**, Vice President for Marketing at Shiva Corporation; **HAIG HOVANESS**, Manager for the Enabling Technologies Practice at KPMG Peat Marwick; **LINCOLN MILLSTEIN**, Vice President in charge of New Media for the *Boston Globe;* and **NICK GROUF**, CEO of a company in Cambridge called Agents, Inc., that runs a site many of you may be familiar with, *firefly.com,* which does predictive modeling for people's music tastes.

I'd like to reintroduce Haig Hovaness, who as part of a practice group of six professionals at KPMG works with a number of major clients to figure out how to establish the technology infrastructure to help them make electronic communities a real part of their business.

HOVANESS: Good morning. It's an honor to be here, and I congratulate Harvard for having the foresight to create this conference. I think it's a very productive event that will contribute to the maturation and evolution of the Internet in many ways.

Today I'm going to talk about concrete Internet technology as well as more general issues. When I got up this morning, I thought about making some prefatory comments and an old essay I read as an undergraduate came to mind. It was an essay C.P. Snow wrote about the "two cultures," and it describes a phenomenon that I observed in yesterday's sessions. There seems to be a significant gap here between people who are hands-on practitioners, close to technologies, and people who are observers, perhaps alarmed and anxious observers. The word we hear a lot in these sessions is "concern." I would like in my comments to address that Internet culture gap and perhaps close it a little bit. Let's start with a description of the specific technology I'm going to talk about.

Virtual private network technology, abbreviated VPN, has just emerged in the Internet communications world. It is a secure data communications network implemented on the public Internet by means of data encryption. There are many good things associated with VPN. For instance:

It exploits the ubiquity of the Internet. Ubiquity is victory as Internet technology-based companies are coming to realize.

It's transparent to enabled nodes. Transparent, in this context, means that it operates automatically and unobtrusively.

Encryption technology has been available for a long time in the network world, but typically it would require complex measures on the part of the user to make it work. You'd have to download the right software, set it up, and agree with your counterpart on an encryption scheme. VPNs make most of this transparent. And, as I'll demonstrate later, that's a very convenient facility.

Of course, I don't have to explain the importance of security and authentication on the Internet. I'm representing a firm, KPMG Peat Marwick, that has deep roots in assurance and risk control.

We are very much interested in Internet technologies that the world of serious commerce can employ. I think some of you have the impression that the Internet is a wild and wooly scene where nothing is safe, nothing is secure. But in fact, the technologies have already been invented and are now commercially available to make the Internet highly secure and trustworthy for prime-time, serious business. And VPN technology is now increasingly available as a standard feature of Internet firewalls.

How does VPN work? The brick walls in Figure 1 represent Internet firewalls. These protect your in-house intranet users from unauthorized access from hackers and other intruders. What the firewall makers have discovered is that the firewall software could be made smart enough to selectively and dynamically encrypt and decrypt traffic, outbound and inbound, based on Internet destination and source addresses. Now if you think about where this takes us, it means that we can establish a secure channel with any counter party, be it an individual or an institution out there on the Internet. This enhanced firewall technology will do the encryption/decryption automatically.

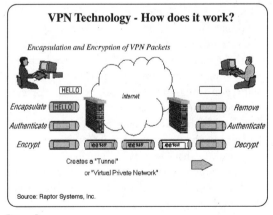

VPN Technology - How does it work?

Encapsulation and Encryption of VPN Packets

Encapsulate — HELLO
Authenticate
Encrypt

Remove
Authenticate
Decrypt

Creates a "Tunnel"
or "Virtual Private Network"

Source: Raptor Systems, Inc.

Figure 1

For example, if Professor Rayport and I decided to work on some joint project that involved sensitive information, the KPMG firewall and the Harvard Business School firewall could be "tuned" to each other to establish a secure channel for communication, establishing a virtual private network between our two organizations. This capability

addresses many security concerns about freewheeling use of the Internet.

VPN is a classic case of what I call technology fusion: when two component technologies, bound together, yield a new result of great utility. We see this happening more and more, and I think people need to start looking at the Internet in terms of an evolutionary model, an evolving technological ecosystem, where more and more new "life forms" will be emerging at an accelerating rate. To the end user, it doesn't really matter that it's a simple or compound technology that emerges from the Internet ecosystem; they just perceive it as a new feature.

What is the impact on the marketplace? VPN is going to promote virtual organizations. A book called *The Virtual Corporation,* published a few years ago, made a bit of a buzz that has since died down. But virtual organizations are going to be very widespread and heterogeneous, and they will become the vehicles for a lot of professional activity. There must be mechanisms for people outside the traditional corporate institutional world to do knowledge work. And VPN is a key enabling factor in facilitating that.

The knowledge services marketplace is going to become more efficient and there will be an increasing presence of freelance knowledge workers. Conversely, conventional institutions will have diminishing significance; we see a number of impacts resulting from one specific technology.

If you remember nothing else from my talk, please try to remember the image in Figure 2, because I think it's historically important. What you're looking at here is the perforation of the cell wall of an organization. If you look at the ellipse, the people inside this virtual private network function as a logically defined workgroup. They have complete secure communication amongst themselves. It's as though they had chartered a little company or organization for the duration they will be in collaboration.

My thesis is that these VPNs, these dynamically created workgroups, will become the dominant form of collaborative work on the network. And the traditional rigid boundary organizations will

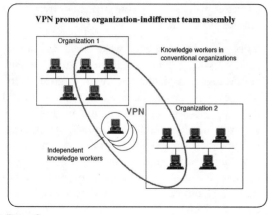

Figure 2

begin to fade in significance. They will be with us for a long time, but, increasingly, people will be putting together dream teams, ideal combinations of practitioners. And their collaboration and commerce will be facilitated by technologies like virtual private networks.

So what do we need to deploy VPN? A fundamental requirement is standards for secure key transmission and management. Many of these are under development and there needs to be some consensus about which ones to use. We also need rules and laws for virtual workgroups. There's an excellent article in *Harvard Business Review* this past month on the importance of rules and guidelines in supporting marketplace activity, that I recommend to you.[*]

We also need better interoperability and progress in access to authenticated credential and bonafide data. This last area is a new frontier. You don't hear much talk about it yet, but there must be some way of moving information on practitioner integrity, capability, background, and credentials out onto the Internet and away from the proprietary control of traditional institutions.

This is what a lot of institutions are selling, by the way. We consume the services of a KPMG, or Harvard, or Mayo Clinic, because of the assurance of quality implicit in the reputation or "brand name" of the institution, yet services are ultimately delivered by *individuals*. This disintermediation of service institutions is the most radical transforming potential of VPN technology. Accompanying the ebb of institutional dominance of knowledge work will be the decline of geographically defined organizations. It is an irony of this conference that we are sitting in perhaps the most prestigious geographically chartered institution in the U.S., discussing technologies that are leading to the diminution of the importance of geography as an organizational basis for institutions.

VPN exploitation will require a nonobstructive government role, and, ideally, some standards leadership from the Information Superhighway pavers in Washington. Unfortunately, the prospect of enlightened Federal Government involvement in secure Internet commerce is not a bright one at the moment.

Figure 3 shows Federal Government policy on data encryption on the Internet.[†] Just when we thought privacy was safe, when we thought Clipper [three] was a bad memory, the key escrow proposal has re-emerged from its lair in the National Security Agency. The latest paper from the executive branch shows that the Federal Government still wants control of escrowed encryption keys, a situation that has been compared with entrusting the town fathers with copies of keys to all the houses in the town. We can imagine the eagerness of individuals and corporations to commit the most sensitive information to communications that "security" agencies can intercept upon production of a court order. Until this issue is dealt with, we're going to have difficulty in fully exploiting VPN.

There are going to be winners and losers as virtual private network technology takes hold. I think participants in the knowledge services marketplace will do much better than the proprietors

---

[*] "The Real Value of On-Line Communicaties," by Arthur Armstrong and John Hagel III, appeared in the May-June 1996 issue of Harvard Business Review. *http://www.hbsp.harvard.edu/groups/hbr/mayjun96/96301.html.*

[†] As of the publication date, there has been no substantive change in the Clinton administration's insistence on key escrow.

Electronic Marketplace Transformation:
Clipper III: Just when you thought privacy was safe

Executive Office of the President
Office of Management and Budget
Washington, D.C. 20503
May 20, 1996

MEMORANDUM FOR INTERESTED PARTIES

SUBJECT: Draft Paper, "Enabling Privacy, Commerce, Security and Public
Safety in the Global Information Infrastructure"

✓ Key escrow required
✓ Escrow authorities to yield keys of third parties to government on demand
✓ Represented as necessary for promoting electronic commerce

Figure 3

of the marketplaces of old, because the value premium will move in their direction. Subject domain-based institutions are winners, geography-based institutions will tend to be losers. High value added intermediaries will do better. Multimode participants, people who interact in multiple ways with multiple corporate and individual forms, will do better. Flexible organizations will be better able to exploit VPN technology; rigid organizations will not fare as well. Knowledge traders will prosper; knowledge hoarders will find it more difficult to create value by attempting to preserve knowledge scarcity.

In summary, VPN technology will increase the liquidity and efficiency of the knowledge work marketplace. In effect, the workplace is going to become a marketplace. We are accustomed to thinking of them as separate paradigms, but if you can build collaborative groups dynamically, irrespective of organizational affiliation, knowledge work becomes more of a continuous marketplace phenomenon rather than a "job" situation. All this is made possible by the technology fusion of universal Internet addressing, firewalls, and encryption into the hybrid technology we call virtual private networks.

I believe that the obstacles to exploitation of Internet marketplace technologies are largely social and political, not technological. We need to build up our social capital on the Internet, and we need to regenerate some of the institutions that used to function well in tying together divergent strands in our society. I think the government has been damaged in the last few years in terms of its credibility as a trusted intermediary, and I think there is a vacuum now that other institutions, academic and professional, need to fill to rebuild that social capital.

I believe that as participants in the Internet better understand the political environment, they will become more effective in promoting their interests. I think they will come to understand that the answer to the Communications Decency Act is not explaining to Senator Exon what's wrong with the CDA; it's removing Senator Exon from office. And as people figure out how to do that—how to communicate with votes, the language politicians understand—we will make progress toward unlocking the full potential of the Internet's capabilities.

I hope I have illuminated VPN, and I think that our subsequent discussion will illustrate how various participants in the marketplace are trying to create collective value from new Internet technologies.

RAYPORT: Haig, thank you very much. When we all met for breakfast this morning and Haig walked into our august-looking faculty club on Quincy Street, he looked around and said, "Magnificent institution," and then said it would make a marvelous adult theme park. I thought that was a wonderful observation because at least he was from KPMG. If he'd been from Disney, I would have really been worried.

We turn next to a company keeping several of Haig's observations in mind. One is this notion that the kind of geographical business activity, like a conference or meeting like this, is something that may go by the wayside if the Internet environment can become robust. Or we will have the choice for those who want to congregate in physical, as opposed to virtual, communities. There is also this other notion that what we have today is the technology, and the reason we're all here is the fact that we've got a technology infrastructure that works in the Internet. The question is, what does it take to build communities there in which we can do business? Last is

Haig's other major point: it is the social capital, the political structure, that may be the thing that's lacking from this platform.

Let's turn to Angelo Santinelli, who comes to us from Shiva Corporation, which has grown at an astronomical rate. The last time I checked they had 150 people. This morning I see they're up to 644. They describe themselves as the "plumbers of Internets and intranets." With that august notion, let's hear about how these folks, the architects of many virtual communities, make this happen for their clients.

SANTINELLI: Thank you. When I describe our role at Shiva as "just sort of plumbers," my friends say, "Gee, I thought the Internet was a lot more sexy. You have Netscape and all these other attractive parts of it. How did you get into this business where you describe yourself as a plumber?"

I quickly remind them that during the California gold rush, the only people who really made money were the ones selling picks and shovels. The business that we're in is providing the infrastructure for not only Internets, but also intranets, a topic that has been written about a lot lately. And certainly, virtual private networking plays into that. The technology that we provide allows telecommuters, mobile workers, or small branch offices to tie directly into their private LAN.

This technology also ties together your private LAN to the public network so that you can access not only your private information at your corporation, but, as I do, by dialing into my company and gaining access to our intranet, you can go also outside of your company's firewall and get onto the Internet.

It has been very interesting to watch the market formation. Rather than talk about our company and its technology and what it does (because you can find that out for yourself on the Internet) I will talk a little bit about how the Internet, the Internet phenomena, and market formation has affected our business.

Watching this over time, one of the biggest things that I've noticed when talking about communities that form around the Internet is the "buying community." Our business happens to be involved with a buying community that doesn't like to talk to human beings; they like to talk electronically. This has affected the way we do business, the way we support our customers, moving more toward electronic support. One of the more interesting things it has affected, this community of buyers, is their power over the entire market that supplies this technology to them.

Information about your company and about our competitors and products is available for customers. They can do very quick price comparisons by going to our web page. This is also a double-edged sword. A small company can project a much larger image using a web page—they are able to go out there and really advertise their business worldwide and make their name known. The double-edged sword, though, is the velocity and the voice the buyer now has. One of the phenomena is that there are lots of chat groups out there that our community of buyers frequent. The double-edged sword is that some of them can say very pleasant things about you and some can say very terrible things about you, in this community of buyers. I'm interested in the effect that has had, now that I've had some time to reflect on this and the feedback from monitoring all of these groups. We now have people in a marketing department who spend a good deal of their time monitoring the Internet and chat sessions to find out what people are saying about us and about our competitors.

The good side is that we can find out what kind of features people need, what kind of features our competitors aren't using, and apply some of that information in our product development process. The other side of it is that information travels so fast over the Internet, throughout this community, that it forces you as a business to react to that much more quickly. You can't have long product cycles. Reflecting on our business, I think again about how we made nine product announcements in three months. Much of that was in reaction to issues out there, either by our competitors or in response to peoples' needs for more features.

So around this community of the Internet, and the communities that are forming, one of the biggest things I've seen again is a shift to the buyer. With that shift comes a lot of responsibility. Some of the issues I hope we can talk about today include the following:

- What is the responsibility?

- What are those rules that some of these communities must start to adhere to?

- How do those rules get formed?

- How are those rules enforced?

- Does the community police itself?

- Or do entities like the government need to get involved in policing us?

RAYPORT: Angelo, thank you; we appreciate those comments. We turn next to one of the companies that's been on the leading edge of making use of and orchestrating electronic communities in our own home town: the *Boston Globe.* Many of you who have an interest in Boston and many of us who live here spend a lot of time with the web site [*http://www.boston.com/*], to figure out all kinds of things—from searching what we thought was in the newspaper three days ago to finding out what's going to be on movie screens tonight.

In thinking about these notions that Angelo has highlighted for us, one aspect of electronic communities, Internet communities, is the shift in power between customers and the companies that serve them. Between the demand side and the supply side, which some think of as the value chain, is a very profound notion: the idea that product development processes would be driven more and more by customers as a function of how robust those customer communities become on the Internet. It suggests very different ways of managing our businesses.

Lincoln Millstein has been at the center of that at the *Boston Globe,* trying to figure out how to reinvent that portfolio of information services we normally think of as a product, as a newspaper, in a platform that demands it be delivered as an online information service. Lincoln has been at the *Bos-* *ton Globe* for 13 years. He's spent time running just about every part of that paper: the metro desk, the business desk, and most recently, the features part of the paper. He is now focusing on electronic delivery of news. Lincoln.

MILLSTEIN: Thank you very much. I represent one of those geographic-based institutions. So I guess, by definition, that makes me an alarmed observer. This [the *Boston Globe*] is the product I represent. It holds about 1.4 megabytes of data everyday. As you can see, it's got a traditional but fairly friendly user interface. It's eminently portable. There's a search function, called an index, on the front page here. And it's retrievable. If I want to save this article that I read here, I just retrieve it and I store it.

What's remarkable about this product is that almost half a million people every single day pay 50 cents for each one of these. And there isn't a single web site in this world that doesn't envy that kind of subscription base. In addition to that, because we have built such a critical mass of circulation, we've been very successful in selling advertising because we draw so many eyeballs. This is a fairly common economic model for publishing out there.

Around the end of World War II, however, in Boston, there were probably as many as ten daily newspapers. I'm just guessing. But the *Boston Traveler* existed, and the *Boston Post,* the *Boston Herald.* In those days, the *Boston Globe* was not the dominant paper. In fact, I think it ranked four or five in a field of probably a dozen competitors. But the Taylor family did something quite remarkable at the end of World War II, as millions of GIs came back home from the war. They intuited that these millions of GIs would also be millions of consumers who would want to buy houses, want to buy cars, who would want to raise families.

So the Taylors, as the good professor would say, took their value chain and added to it by selling little bitty ads to consumers where they could list houses for sale, cars for sale. All the other publishers in Boston laughed at the *Boston Globe.* "Why would you want to expend great resources selling little bitty ads when you can sell full-page ads to Filene's or Jordan Marsh?" they countered. So the *Boston Globe* went at it alone and became the only paper in this town. They really developed classified advertising as we know it today.

Today, classified advertising is the most profitable part of our business. It is the highest margin business because, instead of having one ad that you discount for Filene's because they're a high-volume user, you charge 400 people a higher rate to have little bitty ads. The totality of a page of classified is about double the income of a display ad.

For about 30 to 40 years after the war, we were rolling along swimmingly. Now fast forward to 1992: you just bought a computer and you just hooked onto something called America Online on your 9600 baud modem, and you hook it on and out pops this thing called a "chat room." In those days, there were only about 250,000 subscribers to America Online, of which I was one. And in those days, you got fed into "lobby" number two or three and you waited for a while until somebody else came into the lobby to chat with you. (Today I think there must be 100 lobbies.)

As soon as I saw that chat room, I intuited a threat to classified advertising. I saw, for the first time, a very fast medium that allowed consumers to communicate with other consumers in a lightening-fast, broad manner. Well, you don't have to be a genius to see how that can be a threat to your basic concept of classified advertising. I came back to the *Globe* (now I was on the news side), and started ringing alarm bells. Since I was one of the few people in the place who even knew what I was talking about, and as is quite common with these things, the response was, "It's okay, Millstein, you're the only one who understands it. Now you go out and find a way to solve this perceived problem."

So we created a new division and that new division last year launched something called *boston.com*. It's interesting that we picked the name *boston.com* and not *globe.com*. We had to overcome a lot of our own biases about being a dominant information provider in our own market and understand that the Internet is a wide open platform. Instead of just transporting the newspaper online, we decided to be an aggregate of content that involves Boston. So we invited partners, or content providers, to join *boston.com*—today, we have about 35 partners who provide content that makes *boston.com* a robust service, drawing eyeballs.

Returning to the original economic model of publishing, the whole purpose of drawing those eyeballs is to sell advertising. Selling classified advertising online is a different ball game, now that I'm on the other side. And I am very much more sanguine about the ability of this product to survive than I was back in 1992.

I think the Internet and this new medium have a way to go to understand the difference between community, audience, and the marketplace.

I think there's a huge difference between community and audience and marketplace. Now you're an audience here, you all came here for a common reason. But that doesn't make you a community. And just because you're a community, just because you're in a chat room on America Online, does not make you a marketplace. The more we try to sell classified advertising online, the clearer this is to me. I think that I'm a lot less alarmist about the future of our traditional media than I was in 1992 because I think the Internet and this new medium have a way to go to understand the difference between community, audience, and the marketplace.

Communities and chat rooms do not necessarily want to be an audience of classified advertising, nor do they necessarily want to be a marketplace for classified advertising. One thing we know how to do at the *Boston Globe* is to aggregate content, and we know how to push it linearly to an audience. Now that the audiences can interact with one another, I'm not convinced that audiences necessarily wants to do business with one another. And that, to me, is a very hopeful sign for traditional media.

That is not to say that I don't see the new medium as a huge threat to traditional media; I do. But as the Web continues to explode and as it continues to be chaotic, it plays into the hands of traditional aggregators of content like us. Because the one thing we know how to do is provide order to a world that's becoming more chaotic.

RAYPORT: Thank you very much for those comments. In listening to this, it is a profound reminder of the fact that one can, in the physical world, find countless "communities of people"; that is, lots of warm human bodies in an enclosed space. And some of them are in fact commercially useful and some are not. I certainly learned my first lesson about what makes up a commercial community when I was about nine years old and attended a "Star Trek" convention for the first time. I think of that bunch of Trekkies, about 5,000 of them, in Cobi Arena in Detroit as my first leap into this world of virtual communities.

But one of the things that made them an interesting community from a business standpoint had very little to do with our shared interest, other than our willingness to buy Tribbles and other small plush animals that related to the television series. So one of the issues we clearly need to take up in the discussion that will follow, as Lincoln mentioned, involves community. What is it that makes a community? And what is it that makes a community that's of interest to business?

Well, perhaps our next speaker can contribute some insight to this. Nick Grouf is President and CEO of a company that germinated as an idea in the Media Lab at MIT under the direction of Patty Maes. Agents, Inc. has used some sophisticated neural networking to start getting ahead of the kinds of fire power we're hearing about from Shiva Corporation and from the *Boston Globe* to help customers figure out what their preferences are likely to be before they actually have them. If you could do that for every category of goods and services in your life, you would either find your life greatly simplified or you'd be buying things all the time.

But Agents, Inc., is pioneering that area. Nick, tell us about it.

GROUF: Thank you very much. It really is an honor to be here. I was a student here at this university a year ago, so it says something about the trajectory of the Internet and the sort of opportunities that it can create. Our company, Agents, Inc., was founded about a year ago by myself and Professor Patty Maes and a number of her fellow researchers at the MIT Media Lab. What we're doing is commercializing a set of technologies called *collaborative filtering,* or *agenting.*

The research on this work goes back about four or five years when Patty and our chief scientist, Max Metro, were looking at agents for email. The most important mail would be sifted to the top and the least important mail, for you as an individual, might be pushed down to the bottom or off to the side. It's the sort of tool I think we all could find useful. But they found was that training these agents took an inordinate amount of time. So, they thought, what if these agents could talk to each other, really communicate with each other, teach other?

Here's a classic example: a piece of mail comes to me from Nicholas Negroponte who runs the Media Lab. Having never received a piece of mail from Nicholas before, my agent goes out into the community and says, "Hey, help me out. I don't know what to do with this." And some people say, "Oh, this is Nicholas Negroponte. Very, very important." And others say, "Well, Nicholas, I wouldn't worry about him." My agent makes a decision and says, "Nicholas, he's important, I'm going to put his mail at the top." When I come to read my email and I see Nicholas' piece of mail, and if I simply read it and move on, I'm reinforcing that behavior. I'm saying to my agent, "You did the right thing."

If instead I come back and I say, "Well Nicholas, he's a great guy but I don't need to hear from him right away," the agent says, "Okay, in situations like this, I'm going to start discounting the opinions of the people who told me to put this at the top of the list. And the people who said I should put this down at the bottom of the list,

I'm going to start taking them a little more seriously." In effect, the agent is trying to find the community that best fits me, and it's really a community of shared interests and tastes.

Based on that original work, another member of the founding team of our company said, "That's cool, but let's look at a larger information space: say, all the musical artists and albums in the world." So he first launched a system called "Ringo" that quickly had its name changed to "Homer." Homer went live in December 1994/January 1995 with 200 artists in the database [see *http://www.firefly.com/*]. Its promise to a user was that it could discover music you might not have heard before and introduce it to you.

In effect, instead of having to wade through thousands of titles in a music store, you could have your own shelf of the five things most interesting to you. What you saw might be very different from what your brother, neighbor, or anybody else saw. The database started with 200 artists in it. Users, in a handful of months, quickly increased that to over 20,000. The technology not only allowed you to find music that you would be interested in, but it worked to find a community of *people* who shared your tastes and preferences. We call these people your "nearest neighbors."

So you could go into the system and not only find out about Led Zeppelin, but perhaps find someone to have coffee with on a Saturday afternoon, or people to chat with in a virtual space.

While that work was going on, another founder named Yezdi Lashkari [founder and VP of Firefly] said, "All right, musical artists and albums is a big information space. But let's look at something even larger and even less manageable, the Web itself." He developed a system called "Webhound." Webhound did three very interesting things:

1. It was a personal *hot list generator*. The system could say, "These are the five sites you'll be most interested in checking out today." And the five it showed me might be very different from the five it showed Jeffrey.

2. The system was a *personal filter*. You'd go to a search engine like Lycos or Infoseek or Yahoo! today and say, "Give me documents on flat panel displays." And the system spits back 500 to 1,000 documents. Then you're compelled to go through them, one by one, to find the document most relevant to you. With this system, the agent could actually say, "Hey, Nick, these are the ten documents you're going to find most interesting." And the ten, again, that I saw might be very different from the ten that you saw.

3. The system is a very powerful *similarities generator*. You can say to the system, "I've been doing research and I found this document interesting. Show me others like it." And, again, the system can extrapolate what "like" means to me as opposed to you as opposed to anyone else. A simple example might be that two of us say, "Here's the Apple Computer home page. Show us other documents like this." I might see the documents for computer hardware companies, he might see the documents for computer software companies.

Based on that work, we decided there was a tremendous opportunity here. The Internet, as we've said before, is really a move away from the notion of geographic communities toward communities that might be more case-based. In the world that we live in, there is a universe of people we know. Within the context of that universe, there's a small subset of people that we know whose tastes and opinions we actually trust. You know, my grandmother will tell me to see all sorts of movies, but I rarely take her advice. I take other people's advice quite seriously, on the other hand.

This system allows your agent to go out and actually find those people you can trust. And it does so across a huge and disparate geographic space. It can find people you've never met before—it leverages their opinions and experiences, in effect, raising your intelligence to the power of n, when n equals the number of other people in that community.

The interesting thing about these algorithms is that they're completely generic. So they're applicable for music, books, movies, travel, or looking for a restaurant or a hotel. Not only can it find a restaurant for me here in Boston, but it can find a restaurant for me in Cincinnati, a place I've never been. Again, it accomplishes this by finding a community of people whose advice I can trust. You can apply it to things like doctors in the context of an HMO. An example: I want to get a pediatrician with good bedside manner for my three-year-old, and the agent can go out and find that for me. So the technology is very compelling.

The system went live in January 1996, and within about three months, there were about 130,000 people with agents. The next application for the company is obviously to roll out tools so that anybody with a web site with an important or a large piece of information, can share that sort of technology with their users. It gives them the ability to effectively talk back in the face of information overload, find just the things that are most relevant to them, and do it in a way that leaves room for serendipity.

One of the other technologies that came out of this work is something we call *active agenting,* or *active collaborative filtering.* Not only can I say, "Agent, what five things would you recommend to me?" but I can say to the system, "Peter Lynch seems to know a bit about stocks. What five stocks would he recommend to me?" And again, the system will know that there might be a difference between what he recommends to me and what he recommends to Jeffrey [Rayport] or anybody else.

Another interesting thing that comes from this technology is that you begin collecting some very interesting data. Preference information has been the holy grail for marketers for decades. The problem has been this: how do you create an incentive that will be sufficiently compelling for a consumer? We all get those preference cards in the mail—I don't know what you do, but I toss them in the circular file. With an agent, the more I tell my agent, the smarter it gets. But also, the more other people use their agents, the smarter

that entire community becomes. So you can create a knowledge base for that community and then prune it based on your personal interests.

The last thing you can do with the technology is to apply it not only in an Internet environment but in what Angelo [Santinelli] was talking about, in intranet environments. So within your organization, you might have a strategic planning group, or perhaps you run an investment bank. Somebody's gone to look for a document on, say, remote FCC filing. With this technology, you can leverage the experience of the ten other people who might have done that before, and effectively learn from them, so your experience of searching for that document or looking at a piece of news might be more relevant.

RAYPORT: Nick, thank you very much. These comments, taken altogether, suggest those challenges that business strategists have in navigating this very rapidly evolving landscape. The notion of being able to get this far inside a customer's head—and in a bunch of customers' heads—and make the knowledge utility, not only of the network but of the users of the network available to other users, is extraordinary.

The thing that strikes me from your comments, Nick, is this notion that many of the people who do web site development of the kind that Lincoln Millstein has been involved in, wonder how you take what is popularly perceived as a cold machine environment of a network and turn it into something that's warm and human and compelling and full of personality. Clearly, this kind of access to people's minds, opinions, tastes, and judgments is one of the ways we're going to get there.

It reminded me a little bit of the head of Sony, Nobuyuki Idei, who was quoted in the business press, recently, talking about the top goal of that company to develop a new generation of consumer electronics. The interface of the future, the access to this network world, he suggested, will be more in the nature of a "warm animal." And when you see some of the things that the Sony folks are playing with in their R&D labs, they *do* look like warm animals inside this world of the screen that all of us are here to explore.

Questions & Answers

RAYPORT: Let me see if I can put a first question to the panel and let me frame it in terms of thinking about the types of communities. We've heard everything from the infrastructure of how these things get built to the ways they do and don't work as markets, to what we think may be some of the new frontiers in terms of the uses of electronic communities for business.

But in a recent *Harvard Business Review* article, our colleagues, John Hagel (who heads up the multimedia practice at McKensie) and one of his partners talk about four types of communities in which businesses have achieved some measure of commercial success. Let me run these communities by the four of you and let's discuss which of these we, as a community, ought to be betting on.

The first one they describe as a community was based in transactions. The *transactions community* contains most of the web retailers that don't allow chat forums to take place on their webs. Virtual Vineyards is one of them. Sells wine. You can send them email, you can hear from their master Peter Granoff, who's referred to as the "Cork Dork" in that site. And the Cork Dork will, in fact, write back and tell you all about wine and answer questions. The Trekkie convention I went to was a transaction community. We didn't talk to each other, we just bought products and got signatures from Leonard Nimoy.

The second type of community that they define is one of interests. We heard about *interest communities* from Angelo, in terms of what Shiva is enabling for their corporate clients across intranets. Obviously Agents is becoming a community of interest. Motley Fool in America Online is a community of interest: people with shared interests, who primarily want to show up and talk to one another.

The third type is one that really, arguably, began all this: *fantasy communities,* where we can grab an avatar or play a game, whether it's Doom, Dragon, or any number of things, and live out some kind of fantasy in the virtual world that would be difficult and socially unacceptable to live out in the real world.

The final community is one of relationships. *Relationships communities* are something like the one that we're going to form online related to this conference. Where we all want to start a long term dialog with one another around a common interest. The AARP has created some of the most robust communities based on relationships among retired people. So let me ask our panel:

Q: *What should we be betting on? Are all of these [communities] going to be present in one form or another in the future where businesses find ways to make money?*

HOVANESS: What's novel about the computer? The key breakthrough in the digital computer was its general purpose architecture. Von Neumann wrote a paper on a general purpose computer at Princeton, and everyone said, "Wow! You can put the instructions and the data in the same space." They immediately ran out and started making what we call general purpose digital computers. Why are we so keen on segmenting, stratifying, and classifying target areas within the Internet? Why don't we consider the remarkable fluidity and low inertia of the Internet and start thinking about a model of constantly evolving relationships and communities?

It is reminiscent of old fashioned broadcast and print advertising strategies. We're segmenting and slicing the marketplace. What if the big amplifying value of the Internet is its ability to tailor itself to our particular needs and track our evolutions as individuals? We should begin to think in terms of fluid, evolving communities and individually determined market phenomena rather than rigid classes and categories.

Q: *So in other words, it's going to be driven on the buyer side, not the supplier side? And therefore it will constantly evolve as people shift affiliations?*

HOVANESS: Right. It will be like tracking an ecosystem with short duration evolutionary eras, where you may have many stable forms evolving, maturing, then fading away, to be replaced by new "life forms." The future will belong to people who can swiftly identify emergent Internet marketplace phenomena, add economic value, and then move onto the next evolving phenomenon.

Q: *Statistics indicate that 80 percent of a person's activities involve their local community; these are activities like communications, transactions, social involvements. Given this overwhelming statistic, do we really believe that the Internet can influence us in moving us away from geographically based community activity?*

MILLSTEIN: I think it's going to go both ways. Yes, it will move us away from geographically based institutions. But on the other hand, it will move some people toward geographically based organizations. Take the category of auto classifieds. People on the North Shore of Boston do not drive to the South Shore of Boston to buy a car. That is just a human phenomenon, behavior, that's not going to change regardless of what the Internet does. And there's the marketplace. You want to capture that geographic area known as the South Shore and try to sell cars there.

RAYPORT: But Lincoln, if I were looking for a '66 Ford—

MILLSTEIN: Classic cars are different. That's a different market. If you're looking for a '66 Mustang, you'd drive to Peru to get it.

Q: *Why is one market geographically based and the other one information-based?*

MILLSTEIN: I have no idea. But people aren't going to drive to Peru to buy a Ford Taurus. I think there are a slew of other locally based, geographical, meaningful organizations that will evolve on the Internet. If somebody in my family just developed a serious illness, I'd use the Internet to learn all about that illness. But when it comes to looking for a physician to treat that person, that's a local, regional application.

RAYPORT: Therefore, for some types of markets, we have a geographically based community. For other types of markets it's horizontal.

MILLSTEIN: It's going to accentuate both ends, I think.

___: I have to agree with Lincoln [Millstein]. I think that if you just look at the last nine months of the Internet, it has sort of reinvented itself and it will probably reinvent itself again in the next nine months. The first phenomena that we have seen is these groups of interests, to sometimes forming relationships or splinter groups on a wide geographic basis. But with things like *boston.com* coming online, you're starting to see an equal interest in the geographic focus and the power of the Internet geographically.

I find *boston.com* very useful because of my travel schedule; most of the time I'm not here. I'm out of the country or somewhere else other than Boston. I try to be home on the weekends and I want to do something with my family. And where do I go? I go to *boston.com* to find out what's happening in the community because I don't have the ability to buy that paper when I'm somewhere else. So I do think it's going to grow both ways.

We are now seeing heightened interest in communities, starting in the educational communities, and locally with cable modems coming online now. You'll start to see the infrastructure getting in place for smaller geographies to expand their use of the Internet.

RAYPORT: I think you raised an interesting point. You talked about being able to be a member of the Boston community when you're somewhere else. About 80 percent of our time is spent on geographically centered activities. It's largely a function of convenience. That's the world that we live in. If I don't have access to information on the California car market, I'll never know about that '66 Mustang. If indeed I do have access to it, that sort of changes the environment I'm behaving in.

MILLSTEIN: It's very interesting that we're trying to build businesses where the audience hasn't hit critical mass yet. All of us are guessing where that will end up. Right now, only five percent of the population has even seen the World Wide Web. Only ten percent of the population has even been online. We can't make a business out of those kinds of numbers. Whether that number will someday be 25 percent or 75 percent, like VCR penetration, is a very critical question. Because 25 percent and 75 percent are two very different markets. (By the way, I own a Ford Taurus and the quality is job one.)

HOVANESS: I disagree with Lincoln a little bit. We can extrapolate pretty reliably from people who are well-positioned on the Internet. There are the fortunate amongst us who have high bandwidth access to the Internet, and are highly educated, with a lot of disposable income. They are the precursors of what's going to happen with the rest of the population.

Another way we can look into the future is to do something that is always fun: we can study the wealthy. We are all going to be wealthy with information. And you know the wealthy enjoy community—they enjoy lots of communities. It's not unusual for a wealthy person to have three or five different homes. But the wealthy participate in communities with precision and efficiency. When they go to a community, they reap the best, the richest things about it because they have a schedule and often events come to them. And when they arrive in Palm Springs or wherever, they reap the fullest measure of advantage from being in that community. And then they're off to Paris or to Monaco. So I think the Internet can help us enjoy community enormously, but with much greater precision and efficiency.

I would also suggest that another reason we are doing local activities 80 percent of the time is because we're driving around looking for that peculiar item that we can't quite locate. So I think that we can extrapolate and there's no necessary conflict between joining a community and the Internet-amplified lifestyle.

RAYPORT: Maybe there's an important point to underline. Recent statistics suggest that American households, and this is all 100 million of them on average, spend eight hours every day watching television. So you can argue that the eight hours the household spends watching television is a geo-

graphically defined activity. But the question is, where are their minds?

Their minds are traveling in the space, I would argue, that we're talking about. And to that point, let me bring up another question for the panel, which asks us to think about some of the moral, social, and political implications of what we're describing up here. Since we're all talking about it so blithely, I guess we have a responsibility to do this.

Q: *Moving from business politics, do you see these communities as empowering individual citizens and citizen networks, not just customers and customer networks? Are we moving toward direct democracy rule by the masses away from representative republican?*

HOVANESS: I can comment on that. I've done some thinking along those lines. It's arguable that if the founders and framers were looking at the Internet today, they would say, "Oh, you've got to convene another convention immediately because you can't go continue with a Constitution based on carriage travel and pen-and-ink correspondence. Now you've got to change everything." One of the things they might suggest changing is the representation ratio. Maybe if you can email your local rep, there should be 3,000 people in Congress instead of a few hundred.

Another possibility is shadow governments, where small groups of citizens break off one particular piece of government's machinery and aid that activity and follow it very, very closely. There are people who follow the government closely today—they wear Gucci loafers and are called lobbyists. If, in your living room, you have access to all the information and all the apparatus of government, you and your neighbors can focus on a particular issue or particular subsection of the Department of Agriculture and make them accountable, make them perform.

So I think there are enormous political dynamics coming out of the Internet that have yet to be explored. And they come down to what I would call "precision government": universal electronic access to detailed information about government structure and legislative action, the kind of information that's mainly in the hands of lobbyists today. When the entire electorate has that kind of information, and especially when the politically active segment—three to five percent—of the electorate have that information, you're going to see a very beneficial impact.

Q: *You described a community of buyers as people who shop electronically and do not talk to or communicate with another human in the process. So the question here is, what makes such a collection of consumers a community? Where is the relationship? Where is the connection? Is this the future of digital culture?*

HOVANESS: I can give a counter-example to that. My son is a collector of Star Wars memorabilia. He was looking for a particular back issue of some Star Wars publication. So we got on Usenet looking for Star Wars collectors. And sure enough, there's a newsgroup out there for collectors of little figures, books, pamphlets, whatever. At first, we just looked for general "for-sale" ads. And then we hit a very interesting for-sale ad. It was posted by a student at Princeton who was auctioning off his Star Wars collection. This, to me, was a beautiful microcosm of the protean potential of the Internet.

In this one email message, he laid down the ground rules, the framework, and protocol for a miniature auction. And then in an exchange of dozens of messages over the next five days, he auctioned off a large part of his collection very efficiently. There was an excitement and interaction in this process. My son and I had a bidding strategy against the other auction participants. And at the very end, we got the thing we were chasing with a $1 increase to our bid. So these Internet-mediated interactions can be very fruitful and enjoyable and they can take many unexpected forms.

Usenet, by the way, is not a high-tech environment. It's just plain ASCII text messages bouncing back and forth. But again, in this marvelous ecosystem of the Internet, all of these new marketplace phenomena are starting to take shape. What if there was a framework and protocol for

generic auctions within the Internet that everyone could rely on? If one person can do it with one message, how much more could we accomplish collectively if we built up the social capital of the Internet?

___: There's no question that the new medium is going to have a definite impact. But take another category like real estate. You know, real estate agents and brokers all over the country are shaking in their boots because of this medium. It has the potential of cutting out the middle person— people in California can sell a house to somebody in Boston. I can put my house online, including photographs.

I don't know how many of you have sold houses—I've sold about a half dozen in my lifetime and I tried to sell one on my own as a consumer. It was a total nightmare. It was stressful. And I don't like real estate agents particularly, but I have come to appreciate the important role they play in that transaction. They add value to the process and the Internet is not going to remove that value because most of you who have sold homes, I guarantee, don't want to confront the buyer. You want the middle person to handle that stressful transaction. I see a lot of businesses that appear to be threatened. I think the Internet is going to help accelerate business for them once they learn how to use it. So I'm not convinced that a lot of traditional businesses are going to change all that much.

RAYPORT: There are a few final questions that seem to represent what is on a lot of people's minds: the kind of dark side of leveraging a community.

Q: *What happens if a predatory agent accesses the extensive knowledge base that cooperative agents assemble? And is there something about this community that could turn against us? Will we narrow ourselves into the bunch of decisions and preferences that we've expressed in the past rather than exploring new things in the future?*

GROUF: One of these things is what we term (in-house) the "country club effect." The notion that everybody gets put into a small little community that gets tighter and tighter, narrower and narrower, and people are more and more similar. The technology is *not* about limiting your access. It's about creating an *n*-dimensional taste space: placing you as an individual in your unique position in that taste space and then presenting the universe of products, services, and people to you from that unique perspective.

There's nothing that prevents you from navigating to the opposite end of the spectrum or anywhere in between. So hopefully what it doesn't do is limit your interests, but actually expand them. But it also finds ways that can save you time. The word "agent" sometimes has very negative implications. Symbiotically speaking, the word agent actually means nothing because there are so many different definitions for it.

RAYPORT: At this point, let me ask each of the panelists to share any parting thoughts with us. Angelo, can we start with you?

SANTINELLI: I just wanted to come back to that one last question about communities, and whether buying communities replace the middle person involved. I have to decide with Lincoln on this. I just don't think it happens. I think about our own business, where a lot of people are saying the Internet will actually replace the distribution channel or the value-added reseller. "Value-added" is the key there. People don't want, in all types of products, to go out and buy that product over the Internet. What they want to do is get their information quickly and conveniently. But they always want somebody else to add value and do the work.

So I don't think that the Internet is going to replace a lot of jobs. I actually think it's going to increase the speed of information flow and decision making and it's probably going to create more jobs.

HOVANESS: I'd like to close by just underlining, if I haven't done so already, the notion of increasing social capital on the Internet. There's a book out about democracy in Italy: a Professor Putnam[*] spent a decade studying why Northern Italy

works better in many respects than Southern Italy. And the answer is the difference in the invisible infrastructure Putnam calls "social capital." It's the difference, in the south, between a narrow village mentality dominated by superstition and the Mafia, as opposed to an atmosphere of public trust and thriving public institutions in the north. We need to think about the social health of the Internet and consider if we are going to be in a collection of small villages governed by superstition and fear or if we going to be a big, thriving, progressive, prosperous community. The difference will be determined by the amount of social capital built on the Internet.

Unfortunately, many institutions currently in disrepute are major generators of precious social capital. Silicon Valley start-ups and million dollar IPOs are not going to bring us social capital. We've got to build that for ourselves and preserve it through sound political institutions that reflect the richness of possibilities of the Internet.

MILLSTEIN: There's no question that this medium has the ability to segment markets. But we need to keep in mind that American businesses don't necessarily want to reach only highly segmented markets. You don't really grow if you just reach that segmented market. The market businesses love the marginal buyer who makes our profits. If I sold Toro lawnmowers, I would love to sell lawnmowers to people who don't have yards.

GROUF: Fundamentally, I think it's important to remember that the Web is going to displace very little. Very little changed with the introduction of radio as far as the way people spent their time. You know, people thought that radio was going to be displaced by television, television would be displaced by cable and the Web. But we tend to find more and more room in our lives, despite how frightening that all seems.

The second thing that I think is important to remember is that the Web is not a "push" environment. It's not the same as pushing products onto a consumer. It's a "pull" environment

---

[*] Putnam, Robert, *Making Democracy Work: Civic Traditions in Modern Italy*, Princeton: Princeton University Press, 1993.

where the consumers are actually going to pull the information, the services, the products that they're interested in.

If we don't pay attention to the consumer's needs and rights, we will all be kidding ourselves. They will steer us in a different direction.

RAYPORT: These final comments from my colleagues remind me a little of a novel that some of you may be familiar with. Nick, I'm sure you read it in your infancy, but it came out in 1992, and it's called *Snow Crash.*[*] It's a science fiction story in which people have not left behind the physical world. They still live in it, they still run profitable businesses. But it's been taken over by the Mafia. The primary occupation of people who work in the physical world is that of couriers who deliver packets. People drive cars around and deliver pizzas in less than 30 minutes.

The high culture of the civilization exists in what he calls the "metaverse." Some of us call it the marketspace, some call it cyberspace. But it is a world that functions very efficiently because of many of the things our panel is calling for: etiquette standards, protocols, ethics, rules, laws, and an understanding of how it is that we behave in that world.

The only thought I would like to leave all of us with is that of the many, many panels that we all will be attending over the course of this conference, many of them obviously will become obsolete as we solve various technological problems, as we build certain types of networks, as we figure out how to design better and better web sites for the Internet.

I suspect that if we had this conference five years from now, we could very easily, and with a great deal of confidence, schedule another panel on community and the role it plays in our lives, either in politics or social lives or in business. We would still be answering many of these questions about how to structure the world that we're all slowly gravitating into, as we continue to live in

the physical world on the Internet. Thank you to Angelo, Haig, Lincoln, and Nick.

About the Speakers

JEFFREY F. RAYPORT is an Assistant Professor of Business Administration in the Service Management Interest Group at the Harvard Business School. His research focuses on the impact of new information technologies on service management and marketing strategies for information-based product and service firms. As a consultant, Dr. Rayport has worked with corporations in North and South America, Europe, and Japan and the Pacific Rim, on helping companies develop new product/service strategies related to information technology deployment. His writing has appeared in a variety of publications, including *Fortune Magazine*, *Harvard Business Review*, *McKinsey Quarterly*, the Federal Reserve Bank of Boston's *Regional Review*, the *Boston Globe*, and the *Los Angeles Times*.

HAIG HOVANESS is a Manger in KPMG Peat Marwick's Information, Communications, and Entertainment (ICE) Technology Consulting Practice in New York City. He has over 18 years of diverse information systems experience. Before joining KPMG Peat Marwick, Mr. Hovaness held systems positions at PaineWebber, Random House, and Citicorp. Mr. Hovaness has been a featured columnist for *Corporate Computing* magazine, and has published articles in other journals. He is an active participant in research and discussions on the commercial future of the Internet. Mr. Hovaness is a member of the Association for Computing Machinery (ACM) and the Electronic Frontier Foundation (EFF).

As Vice President of Marketing, **ANGELO SANTINELLI** is responsible for Worldwide Marketing at Shiva Corporation. In this role, Santinelli heads up product marketing, product management, marketing communications, and business development for Shiva. Mr. Santinelli came to Shiva from The

---

[*] Stephenson, Neal. *Snow Crash*, Pasadena: Salem Press, 1992.

Boston Consulting Group, where he managed engagements in both the high technology and consumer goods/retail practice groups for five years. In this role, Santinelli worked extensively in the areas of fast product development, marketing strategy and process re-engineering. Previously, Santinelli was an Account Marketing Representative for IBM.

NICHOLAS A. GROUF is a founder and the Chief Executive Officer and President at Firefly Network, Inc. Nick's professional experience includes an associate position at Goldman, Sachs in its Mergers and Acquisitions department, where he focused on communications and technology clients. In addition, Nick worked for two years as a business analyst at McKinsey & Company, where he worked primarily for broadcast, media and telecommunications clients.

LINCOLN MILLSTEIN is Vice President for New Media for the *Boston Globe*, where he is directly responsible for the Boston Globe Electronic Publishing division and its principal product, *boston.com*, the much-acclaimed web site of the *Boston Globe* newspaper. Millstein is a 13-year veteran of the *Globe* newsroom, where he held a variety of editing assignments, including Business Editor, City Editor, Cultural Editor and Managing Editor for Features. He came to the *Boston Globe* from the *Hartford Courant* where he was Business Editor. He graduated from the University of Connecticut and then attended Stanford Graduate School of Business as a National Endowment for the Humanities Fellow.

Panels

Who Owns the Internet?

MODERATOR: Lawrence K. Grossman

PANELISTS: Anne Branscomb
Peter Fowler
Kathryn Montgomery
Russell Neuman

Cultural Imperialism on the Net

MODERATOR: Arthur R. Miller

PANELISTS: Izumi Aizu
Jacques Attali
Karanja Gakio
Nathan Gardels
Douglas Rushkoff
Anne-Marie Slaughter
Xiaoyong Wu

New Organizational Forms

MODERATOR: Lynda Applegate

PANELISTS: Robert Hiebeler
Jack Phillips
Jed Smith

Wrap-Up Session

MODERATOR: Mark F. Bregman

PANELISTS: Lewis Branscomb
Arthur Miller
Paul Severino

Who Owns the Net?

By David Bank

Don't worry, be happy.

Russell Neuman, who is leaving Tufts University to join Harvard's Shorenstein Center on the Press, Politics, and Public Policy, said yesterday that the Internet itself will solve problems such as universal access, obscenity, and interoperability without government intervention.

"Lawyers and public interest activists worry too much," Neuman said on a panel brought together to answer the question, "Who Owns the Internet?"

Neuman was in the minority on a panel whose other members suggested that government might have a role in harnessing the power of technology for disadvantaged communities and countries, protecting children from manipulation by online advertisers, providing resources for public spaces on the Internet, and clarifying copyright protections online.

The issue of the proper role for government in the face of new technology has been a major theme running through Harvard's Conference on the Internet and Society.

"I don't think we have a major problem here," Neuman said. "Correctives are built in. I don't think we need to be concerned."

Neuman said an economic property of networks themselves—the value of any network increases as more people get connected to it—provided a driving force for spreading the benefits of information technology to all. He said concerns that the network might fragment because of a welter of competing standards were being met with easily distributed software that creates common interfaces between incompatible systems.

And he said that the tendency to spread information itself would guarantee that even the unwired remain informed of issues of public importance.

"Poorer communities are not going to have access as soon, their equipment will be slower," he said. "But it's hard to put a brake on public affairs news that's important and of interest.... The nature of the Net, and the nature of information, means that while not [everyone] may have a high resolution display at home, the information will get out."

Other panelists insisted that problems were emerging that called for collective government action. Kathryn Montgomery, President of the Center for Media Education, said online advertisers were targeting children and blurring the line between entertainment and advertising. The Federal Trade Commission is planning public hearings on the issue next month.

"Children are regarded as the lucrative 'cyber-tot' category," Montgomery said. She said children are being asked to fill out online questionnaires with marketing information and have been solicited with personalized email from characters like Snap, Crackle, and Pop. She said advertisers recognize that children enter a "flow state" while online that makes them particularly receptive to advertising.

"While commercialization of the Internet is in its early stages, it is important to have [a] public debate and ask how services for children are evolving. We believe there should be rules of the game," she said. "My hope is that we can leave an electronic legacy in place that will value children not just as consumers but as citizens."

Peter Fowler, an official with the Department of Commerce, said a recent conference in South Africa to discuss the global information infrastructure had challenged the notion that the free market alone would equitably distribute the benefits of the information economy. Fowler noted there are more telephones in Manhattan than there are in all of Africa.

"Technology is increasing the gap between the developed countries and the developing countries, not diminishing it," Fowler said. "The fear is that gap is going to become insurmountable." While computer technology in the United States is beginning to become almost as commonplace as indoor plumbing, Fowler said, in much of the world, "they wouldn't know the World Wide Web if it came up to bite them."

"How is technology going to be harnessed to help the vast population of the earth in terms of economic and social development?" he said. "Or do we just go ahead and develop our own cyber-world?"

Anne Branscomb, author of *Who Owns Information*, said ownership and control of the Internet was distributed between network providers, software producers, advertisers, Webmasters, and users, making central control impossible as well as undesirable. She said software features such as "bozo filters" and "cancelbots," as well as the organic rules of conduct known as "netiquette" were beginning to evolve into a new form of self-organization. She cited as an example collective measures to limit "spamming," the widespread distribution of unsolicited email advertising.

"Many of us hope that the users will exert control and turn the Internet into a genuine vehicle for worldwide democracy," Branscomb said. "Can cyber-democracy work? Can benign anarchy become the norm?"

Panel

May 29, 1996

Who Owns the Internet?

MODERATOR: Lawrence K. Grossman
PANELISTS: Anne Branscomb
Peter Fowler
Kathryn Montgomery
Russell Neuman

GROSSMAN: Our panel is charged with what I regard as a Mission Impossible, to respond to the question, "Who owns the Internet?" The Internet itself is merely an ephemeral set of ones and zeros, and the question is, can anybody own it? Is it even a material question? One might say this is much like the public owning the airwaves during the era of radio and television, though as far as the public is concerned, it was CBS, NBC, and ABC that owned broadcasting.

In any event, to respond to this challenging, perhaps awesome, question, we have four panelists. **ANNE BRANSCOMB** is the author of the seminal book, *Who Owns Information?;*[*] a research affiliate of Harvard's program on information resources; a distinguished communications scholar; and cited by *Boston Magazine*, I was fascinated to see, as a cyber-Brahmin.

PETER FOWLER is an attorney adviser, official of the Office of Legislative and International Affairs of the U.S. Patent and Trademark Office, Department of Commerce. And we'll find out who has the trademarks and patents on the Internet as a means, perhaps, of defining who, if anybody, owns it.

KATHRYN MONTGOMERY is the President and founder of the Center for Media Education, which has the role of educating the public and policy leaders about key media issues. An advocate for children, who may be the real owners of the Internet (if my own family is any model—every time I run into problems with the Internet I call my 14-year-old granddaughter or 10-year-old grandson, who have nothing but disdain for the simplicity of my questions).

RUSSELL NEUMAN, formerly Director of the Edward R. Murrow Center at the Fletcher School of Law and Diplomacy at Tufts, is now about to join the Kennedy School at Harvard as Assistant Director of the Shorenstein Center on the Press, Politics, and Public Policy. And he's also the author of an impressive book, *The Future of the Mass Audience.*[†]

Is "Who owns the Internet?" even a material question? The two answers I've heard are, in fact, polar opposites. On the one hand, we talk about the Internet as an institution of functional anarchy—uncontrolled and uncontrollable. Everyone becomes a media mogul. What everyone owns perhaps no one owns. When everyone is in charge, is anyone in charge?

The other side of that coin is the plausible argument that the Internet is following, in an uncanny kind of a way, the path of the development of radio. Radio began like the Internet in many ways. Promoted by the Defense Department (at the time it was the Navy) to find a way to communicate between ships, radio was taken up at first by interested, ordinary people who found it a neat new way to communicate across long distances. So many were doing that in radio's early days that it was described as total anarchy. In the 1920s, the airwaves were simply filled with individual public communications, so many voices.

At that time, nobody knew how to make radio pay, but it was enormously popular. In the beginning, it was thought that perhaps the way to make it pay would be to sell radio sets. Now, to get people on the Internet, we're selling software

---

[*] Branscomb, Anne, *Who Owns Information: From Privacy to Public Access*, Basic Books, 1994.

[†] Neuman, Russell, *The Future of the Mass Audience*, Cambridge University Press, 1991.

and access paths. And when people finally did figure out how to make radio pay, William Paley of CBS testified before Congress, opposing an amendment by Senator Wagner of New York, suggesting that some of the channels ought to be owned for public service purposes, by universities, religious groups, co-ops, and labor unions. Paley said you don't have to worry about having time on radio for public service programs. There was so much time, there was so much capacity, CBS would never use more than a third of its time for commercial purposes.

The question is, is the past prologue, or is the Internet taking us down a new and unprecedented path? And to start, I'll ask Anne Branscomb. Who owns the Internet, Anne?

BRANSCOMB: When I discovered that the topic I was to address was "Who owns the Internet?" I thought, this is going to be a very short presentation. The answer is very simple: either nobody owns the Internet or everybody owns the Internet or something in between. And since nobody really knows, I decided that we should start, as a lawyer does, with definitions. First, what is the Internet? It is a protocol for committing lots of disparate computer networks with different operating systems, speaking different computer languages, to converse with each other. Stated simply, it is the death of distance.

Next, we have to define "ownership." In simple terms, it means that what is mine is not yours, what is ours is not theirs, and what is private is not public. It is a right to control, manipulate, monitor, exclude, include, patrol, or govern. More than just something of value that you can purchase or sell, it is a legal right to assert sovereignty if you're a nation-state, or to assert autonomy if you are an individual or an organized group.

I thought we would be better off addressing questions like who owned the Internet in the past rather than who owns the Internet today, or who might own the Internet in the future, and whether or not it really matters to us whether anybody owns the Internet.

Now, who are the candidates that we can assess? Originally, the Internet was a child of the defense establishment, evolving from the ARPAnet, a research project of the Department of Defense, intended to facilitate the sharing of centralized computing facilities by research contractors. Later it was administered by the National Science Foundation as a network to aide all research scientists in more generalized, nonproprietary research. It's now in the process of being turned over to the private sector.

The Internet is used primarily by an English-speaking global population which is keyboard competent. Its architecture rests largely in the hands of researchers who design the network software. Access to it is controlled largely by those who own the gateways—the telecommunications common carriers, the information service providers, the Internet access providers, and the managers of private networks.

There are many in the Net world who consider that all of us who own computers and have modems really ought to control our own destinies in cyberspace. But that leaves out a whole lot of people, as Ambassador Dougan told us, all over the world. Most inhabitants of the globe have no computers, no modems, or the competence to use them, or even a telephone line to connect them to the Internet. In fact, most people don't have the hard cash to buy these capabilities even if they were available locally.

Now there's no problem identifying who the original Internet users were. They were 95 percent males, virtually all in their early professional years; many in jobs designing or using computers for professional work. At a conference held by the National Conference of Lawyers and Scientists a couple of years ago, some of the participants came up with these two definitions:

- Worldwide, Highly Intelligent, Technological Elite

- Western, Homogeneous, Imperialistic, Telecommuting Entrepreneurs

These both translate to the same acronym, WHITE.

Today's Internet population, which is estimated at some 37 million in North America, is a little more varied now, with about one-third females, but still largely limited to professionals and commercial establishments in the rest of the world.

Now, the most obvious candidates for ownership in the future are some of the major software companies, led by the most obvious and most pervasive, Microsoft, which provides 75 percent of the operating systems and controls how PC computers behave. Apple Computer, whose software many devoted users consider far more versatile and useful, seems to be losing market share: down to 7.8 percent, although Larry Tesler said yesterday that about 21 percent of those have access to the Internet. There are of course other candidates. Sun Microsystems with its Java applets and a strong software and hardware position in the server market runs second to Microsoft. Netscape—its Navigator captures about 84 percent of the browser market—may be in the running. But there are others perhaps yet to make their entrance and find the racetrack to vie for dominance. But control of the software determines what we can do with our computers and our modems, and how easily we can manipulate them. Unless we are confident programmers ourselves, we're simply at the mercy of those who design for us.

Another set of candidates are those professionals who can, in fact, manipulate the software to control behavior they deem unacceptable. Many of them, the computer gurus and wizards, have designed special software such as filters for screening out undesirable message content or "bozo" files for deleting messages of undesirable communicants. They have "cancelbots" to delete a set of similar messages from the electronic bitstream or even "toading" undesirables. (That's like in a fairy tale, turning them into a frog by banishing them from these virtual communities.)

There are also steps taken by the managers of university systems and commercial information service providers to set forth rules of acceptable conduct or contracts with subscribers that proscribe certain behavior, and give the managers of these systems the right to exclude those who do not comply.

Clearly, technical access to the common carriers or access providers is a well-recognized bottleneck. If one has an account with a university or works for a major corporation, high-speed broadband access is provided on the company local area network or intranet to facilitate accomplishing the job for which one is hired. Others must contract directly with AT&T, or with America Online, Netcom, Sprynet, or one of the hundreds of others. And in many cases, they use very poorly conditioned lines for data access. How these suppliers of either raw information transport or information content design their systems will determine what users can do within the Net world.

The next most likely candidates for ownership and control of the Internet are the advertisers. You've heard about the power of brand names in previous sessions.[*] Commercial domain names on the Internet are now up to 89 percent as of May 14 [1996]. Most of these companies are interested in advertising their wares. The World Wide Web is a very dandy place for advertising products and services that can be delivered elsewhere. The tourist and computer software industries are good examples.

But an individual's time is limited and viewers will flock to the most attractive web sites. So let me tell you about a few. You will find many very familiar corporate names on the Web, like IBM or Eastman Kodak, which is giving away these beautiful images in the expectation that you will buy more film. Others, like Time Warner's Pathfinder and Hotwired, are trying to break new ground and find new paths to your pocketbooks. Even the popular searcher, Yahoo!, is now supported by advertising.

And it's true that a tiny entrepreneur in a small town in Georgia can gain access to the global

---

[*] See the session entitled "Customer Relationships: What Happens to Brands, in the Business track."

market, if it can be found in the morass of information circling the globe on the Web. And a tiny monastery can bolster its income by having its monks design web pages, the new scriptorium of the Information Age.

But the skill and financial resources of the owner of the web page can make a real difference in whom it attracts. Compare, for example, the home page of the commercially sponsored Telluride, Colorado, Tourist Industry home page with that of a nonprofit, Telluride Infozone. I rest my case. Indeed, many of the most aggressive advertisers are not-for-profit institutions.

Last year marked the point at which users worldwide discovered that the Internet was being used to access images that many cultures found objectionable. So long as the Internet was used primarily by similar members of the research tribes, little outside governance disturbed the natives. But now that "cyberporn," hate messages, and inflammatory content are beginning to creep out into the real world, the "cybercops" are coming into these lawless frontiers of cyberspace and attempting to tame the natives.

Many of us hope that the owners of the computers themselves—now at about 100 million worldwide, still a tiny fraction of the 5 billion world population—will assert control over the Internet and turn it into a genuine vehicle for electronic, democratic governance.

The users themselves, the Netizens of these cyber-communities, as we call them, have developed their own devices for self-government. Netiquette requires that newcomers read the FAQs, or Frequently Asked Questions, before entering a new discussion group. And software has been designed to give users more control over their own online environment with such filtering devices as Netsurf and Net Nanny. But many of us, as Larry [Grossman] has pointed out, admit that our children and our grandchildren are far more competent at manipulating the software than we are.

The expansion of email post boxes and Usenet groups has provoked the wrath of the Netizens.

They take steps to stem the tide of commercial messages by flaming the miscreants. And oftentimes, they merely migrate from cyber-communities where the environment is undesirable or the natives unfriendly. In several of the MUDs [multi-user dungeons], serious attempts have been made by the participants to devise democratic procedures and sanctions embodying new processing. But can sovereign democracy work or can a benign anarchy become the norm?

We who are Net users are beginning to understand that we must prevent the unwelcome intrusions that the information economy has in store for us, especially if we want to maintain some autonomy over our own private spaces. Some of us indeed love the unsolicited catalogues that arrive at our door, and others cringe at the wasted paper or trees that go into the trash. But unsolicited mail in electronic traffic is more troublesome than in the postal service.

It uses up electronic space, it interferes with the flow of meaning of threads of conversation in discussion groups, and generally wreaks havoc with the efficient use of the system. Isn't the Web a perfect place to search for something, using one of the many search tools to find exactly what we want? Can we not devise a methodology to offer more autonomy over email boxes, either by agreement of system managers or even the good sense of corporate and advertising executives who really don't want to offend their customers? It shouldn't be necessary to enact prohibitions that would be effective only within a specific jurisdiction rather than everywhere in the Net world.

Now, transaction-generated information is even more troubling than unsolicited advertising. Last Christmas, I gave an elderly aunt a puzzle, one puzzle, and this managed to get me onto a distribution for catalogues of nothing but puzzles. This example is pretty benign, yet it's troubling. It might have been different had I been purchasing a drug for AIDS, for example, because it means that the computers somewhere are recording my every movement in the real world. Moreover, someone, namely DejaNews, is tracking everything you post in the Usenet groups.

Indeed, one of the major threats of the Internet is that everything you purchase, every trip you make, everything you say, everything you may do, may end up in an amazingly accurate dossier about you: your personal preferences, your lifestyle, and your political preferences. It is not so much "Big Brother, the Government" that is the threat today, so much as "Big Brother, Big Business." Your web tracks are very revealing. What can we maintain as secret, and can we retain the privilege of participating responsibly in the Net world while remaining personally anonymous?

If we are to maintain more autonomy over personal information about ourselves, then we, ourselves, must take steps to preserve the protocols, to design the rules, and/or enact the legislation to protect what we consider valuable information, assets. Of course many people, especially those who describe themselves as having a web presence, want to distribute as much information about themselves, their writings, and their activities, as possible. And isn't that what the Web is really good for? To share the information that really does want to be free.

But how much control do we have over our web presence? Suppose that your name is Ronald McDonald. Clearly that would be of considerable interest to the chain that has trademarked that name for its services. Even worse, suppose your name is John Doe or Joe Smith or Bob Jones. How do we accommodate personal identity in a Net world that can circulate information at the speed of light to over five billion humans? According to Auth's View, now that we've passed the Telecommunications Bill, the free-for-all among the telephone, computer, electronics, publishing, and entertainment conglomerates will mean a future with no limits.

But he asks, "What about my limits?" What about the limits of the human mind to cope with the fast moving pace of the Net world, with its Java applets, its browsers and searchers that can locate, in a matter of seconds, many thousands of sites where the information you think you want is located?

Can anybody truly own this conglomeration? Fortunately, not everybody wants to own the Internet, but I suspect that many of you in the audience will want to try.

GROSSMAN: Actually, from Anne's remarks, I realized that the question may not be *who* owns the Internet. The real question is, does the Internet own *us*? Peter, from your perspective, who owns the Internet?

FOWLER: My first reaction to the question was also either everybody owns it or nobody owns it, or perhaps Bill Gates will own it. But it's sort of a misleading question. I think it really poses the wrong question, like who owns the airwaves or who owns the interstate highway system. We all sort of do, but we don't really believe we do.

I think it's more like asking who owns the earth's navigable waters. Because in a way, I think the Internet and cyberspace is a lot like what our seafaring ancestors faced when they went out sailing —they saw water as a way to get places, to conduct commerce, to discover far-off lands, to bring back spices and slaves. And in the process they created maritime and admiralty laws, rules of the seas, and regularly battled pirates. It sounds like what a lot of people in the Internet, and certainly those in government and industry, are trying to do today, which is create the rules of the highway or the rules of the Internet and cyberspace.

Part of my duties with the Department of Commerce and the Patent and Trademark Office is to facilitate the "Conference on Fair Use," which was established to provide a discussion forum as a voluntary process to develop guidelines for fair use in its various forms, and library and educational uses of copyrighted material under the copyright law. That process has been going on for about two years. At the very beginning, many of the parties involved—whether from publishing or audiovisual fields, from libraries or educational institutions—took very different, opposing views, and many of them felt that they could not actually agree on what constituted fair use of copyrighted materials in a digital environment.

For a government process, it has been incredibly instructive, educational, and productive, actually.

Over the two years, 20 months or so, that it has been going on, they're very close to actually agreeing on a number of different voluntary guidelines as to how to operate, how to respect fair use as a component of not only the Internet but just of dealing in a digital environment. Which then brings us to the issue of laws.

There are many within cyberspace, if you will, who have argued for years that no one owns cyberspace, no one owns the Internet, that it's an open area, that is anarchy, it's chaos, it's every person for him- or herself, and whoever can get by does so. That's the way netiquette will govern, the thinking goes. We don't need laws. But I think that's probably not true. In fact—this may sound like heresy—there's nothing that unique about cyberspace. It is not the unreality, it's the current reality we're dealing with.

It involves the same types of rules, the same types of human transactions—whether it's in licensing, in contracting, providing content, duplicating it, distributing it—that goes on currently. It's just a major technological advance because it basically provides for global disk duplication and distribution of content, as well as worldwide transactions with a modem and a few clicks. So the Internet it not some kind of otherworldly outland that is totally ungovernable. It's governed by laws just like everyplace else.

The challenge, of course, is dealing with it in a technologically different way, because the environment destroys any concept of territoriality, on which most of the intellectual property laws and other laws are based. Those laws are not irrelevant, we simply have to adapt them for the new cyber-environment. So the medium of the Internet is not a reason to chuck all the systems of laws that we've developed; it's actually a reason to develop a way to adapt the laws.

One of the most interesting things about the Internet, the industries constantly spawning, and the new commercial uses of it, is that it has proven itself to be incredibly adaptable to what humans beings want to do—communicate, sell, advertise—all the things they've been doing for thousands, if not hundreds, of years. Copyright

law, for example, provides a good framework for dealing with protecting intellectual laws into content within the Internet. And frankly, without that content, the Internet would consist of a lot of email, a lot of public domain material, government publications and information, directories, and indexes, and not much interesting content.

In fact, the lack of clarity within the copyright law as to the application of copyright protection to a digital environment has been one of the drawbacks to the explosive expansion of the Internet and the World Wide Web over the last year or two. That's being addressed in Congress currently with the NII legislation, which would clarify aspects of copyright protection and transmission rights, etc., as well as a major stumbling block—the liability of online service providers for copyright infringement.

But most of those using the Internet do so to accomplish something. They want to communicate, they want to sell, they want to advertise, they want to use it to create new business sources and revenue and new ways to do things. That brings into play patent laws, trademark laws, copyright laws. Patents to protect the hardware involved; trademark laws to protect the advertising; copyright laws to protect the content. And the challenge is to create new ways to protect intellectual property in a global environment.

That means getting away from territory concepts about protection. Because when the teenager in South Africa can download from a database in Canada and send the results to a friend in Argentina, concepts about territoriality and the applicability of certain copyright laws or trademark laws to one country or another lose any real meaning. The current efforts within the World Intellectual Property Organization to address these types of issues, and to coordinate copyright laws in particular to adapt to a digital environment, will go a long way to answer the question not only of who owns the Internet, but also who protects it. Thank you.

MONTGOMERY: Larry Grossman's opening remarks about the beginnings of radio remind me of an experience that I had about 15 years ago, when I was teaching a course at UCLA entitled "New Media Technologies." I invited a guest speaker who had been a reporter for one of the trade publications, a man in his seventies. His opening remark was, "So you're studying the new media technologies. Well, I've been studying new media technologies for 50 years." He put it in a perspective that I always remind myself of, that becomes more meaningful as I get older. It's particularly important when we're writing and talking about the emerging new media that we remember that nothing we say can really be set in stone, and many of the changes that have taken place in the last couple of years with this new medium have surprised a lot of people.

Two years ago, for example, there was a lot of talk about the so-called 500-channel cable universe, which doesn't seem to have materialized. At that time, if people had talked much about the World Wide Web, most folks would have thought it was some kind of international spy ring. And now we have seen all of these things have changed dramatically. It's precisely the unpredictable, dynamic changes that are part of the excitement and challenge of dealing with these new media.

I believe we are in an historical moment for this emerging new media system, shifting from its early beginnings as a research and communication tool that was the domain of government, the research community, and the many computer users around the country, to a privatized, commercialized, mass media. This transition brings about enormous potential for a flowering of diverse, innovative services. But it also raises a number of important issues, many of which are being discussed at this conference.

Our Center for Media Education is working on a number of these issues, and I brought copies of our publication *Infoactive* with me. Today, I want to focus on the commercialization of the Web and, particularly, on its impact on children (an issue I've been working closely on for the last year or so). The Center for Media Education released a report in April [1996] that was the result of our investigation of emerging online commercial services targeted at children.

As most of you know, the growth of advertising and marketing on the Web has been very dramatic. Advertising is likely to become a dominant revenue source. What is critically important to us is that the emergence of this online medium is happening at the same time that the children's market has been growing very dramatically. In 1995, children under 12 spent $14 billion on consumer goods; teenagers, another $67 billion. Together, they influenced $160 billion of their parents' annual spending. And their increasing value as a target market is happening at precisely the time that new services for this emerging interactive medium are being developed.

Children are regarded as the lucrative "cybertot" category. They are, as most of us know, early users of online services, and more facile with it than a lot of us adults. My child is only three, so she hasn't yet introduced me to all of her knowledge. But she probably will be zooming ahead of me very soon.

What concerns us is that advertising and marketing are not just being used to support content but, in many ways, are actually shaping the content as well as the design and structure of the new services. And we are particularly concerned about the blurring of advertising and information; the "infomercialization" of the Web. Advertisers are carefully studying how children interact with online services. The fact is that children easily enter the flow state when they go online. As one advertiser said, "This is a perfect environment for advertising."

So interactive branded environments are being created where children are encouraged to interact with product spokes-characters and to develop relationships with them. In our study, children were receiving unsolicited email—personalized email—from Snap, Crackle, and Pop and other online product characters. At this point, that's the first trickle of the kind of interaction being developed for this medium. But if we can imagine, as real-time audio, video, and other technologies come to the Web, these could be animated characters with which children will be developing relationships.

Our question is, will this commercial culture be dominant and the most appealing part of this online environment for children? Obviously, another concern, which Anne [Branscomb] raised, is the concern about privacy. We're concerned that marketers could transform the Internet into a kind of one-way mirror that will use the "clickstream" and navigational data to create personal profiles of us as targets for one-to-one marketing. Again, this is a particular concern about children.

In our research, we found that a number of web sites were asking children to fill out surveys and play games and answer questionnaires to provide detailed information about themselves. I'm sure they didn't realize what it was being used for, nor did their parents. We recognize that while commercialization of the Internet is still in its early, unpredictable stages, it is important to have a public debate now about how the services, particularly for children, are evolving.

We also believe in the need for safeguards. Currently there are no set rules about how you advertise to children. We believe there should be rules of the game. We have petitioned the Federal Trade Commission, which is holding a hearing next week on privacy in the Internet, with a special session on children.

I think this kind of public debate is particularly important if the online media surpass television as the dominant medium in children's lives, which is very likely. More important, we need a broader debate about the impact of the emerging online commercial culture on our civic discourse. My hope is that we can leave an electronic legacy that will value children, not just as consumers, but also as citizens. Thanks.

Grossman: Thank you, Kathryn. Russ?

Neuman: When Bill Kovach asks the question, "Who owns the Internet?" he's not asking who's going to make money and what new stock offering we should invest in. He's asking the question, "Who *controls* the Internet?" and is there cause for concern about gaps in public policy as the tech-

nology quickly outpaces our capacity to address these concerns.

Perhaps you're already weary at the end of the day from talking and thinking about the Internet. So I'm going to talk about three other things: a cow pasture in England; a fireplug in Baltimore; and Boothill Avenue, here in the impoverished urban ghetto of Boston. And when I'm finished, there might be some relevance to the original question.

> *While commercialization of the Internet is still in its early, unpredictable stages, it is important to have a public debate now about how the services, particularly for children, are evolving.*

First, a cow pasture in England. I'm talking about a policy issue. My question is, do these metaphors for public policy apply and make sense and cause concern in the case of the Internet? The cow pasture is the commons; public policy concern is the presumed tragedy of the commons. Let me very briefly run through it. The notion is, if everybody has their cattle on their own private land but there is a commons that's shared by the villagers in the area, the commons gets overgrazed because you've got control over your own private ground.

On the commons, you get your cattle out there first and then just overgraze it. And then, because there's nothing left but sand and dirt, you come back and use your own resources, your *private* resources. So the question is, does the tragedy of the commons—if we've got a mixture of private and public networks—lead to rich people using their private networks and an impoverished disconnected public network withering away while people move to private networks? Is that a cause for concern?

Next, the fireplug in Baltimore. There was a major fire in Baltimore. The suburban fire companies came in to lend a hand but couldn't connect their hoses: the thread on the Baltimore hydrant wasn't the same as that of the suburban fire department's hose. The lack of government-enforced standards resulted in a tragedy, and serves as a metaphor for proprietary standards in the world of the Internet.

Last, the notion of the impoverished and minority communities. Will there be electronic redlining? Is the issue of universal service and universal access a clarion call for government and/or federal reaction to make sure that information and access services are made available through policy, legal, or some kind of redistributive economic taxation technique, to make sure that the public as a whole is involved in public affairs debates?

My answer in all three cases is, I don't think we've got a major problem. I think correctives are built in. I'm not terribly concerned. I might find myself at some distance from my fellow panelists here, so let's find out.

Number one, tragedy of the commons. The issue that keeps this metaphor from applying in my analysis from the network of networks that we now call the Internet, is this issue from economics—network externalities. The term "network externality" is a basic logic that says, your network access is worth more if you have more people connected to it; thus, the underlying brilliance of the architecture of TCP/IP and the Internet itself. The value of the Net increases as more people become connected to it. Therefore, the kind of logic of overusing the resource of the common won't apply in this case; the metaphor fails.

The fireplug. We've seen a growth of open standards. It could have worked otherwise but there is an increasing growth of open standards and a realization that it's actually pretty easy. You don't need to actually rebuild all those fireplugs, you just need an interface device. In an increasingly software-driven world, the capacity to generate and download as an applet or interface device—something that takes the information fire hose

from one community and make it accessible to another—solves the problem a lot quicker, more easily, and at a lot lower cost.

So I don't think the need for federally enforced standards is likely to be the problem drawing on the classic fireplug example that it is.

Finally, universal service. In fact, the 1996 Telecommunications Act has a long discussion and will empower the committee to think hard and put forth a proposal for a definition. That's the charge in the law to this commission: to define what universal service and universal access mean in a digital, Internet world.

I think it's true that the poorer communities are not going to have access as soon, and their equipment is going to be slower and their motivations might be significantly different. But what you come into is economies of scale. I think you'll find that the well-to-do and the already upper class connected are going to see it sooner and with more convenience. They'll have their computers in the home. I think you'll find a rollout and a resale, so that the pay-for-view movie, the premium cable channel, and maybe the first run motion picture may not be accessible, but at some delay, the information or the entertainment gets out.

In the case of news, there might be a premium access newsletter, where first you get the news electronically faxed to you, and then it shows up in a less expensive daily metropolitan newspaper. It's hard to put a brake on public affairs news that's relevant and of interest. So although there may be a delay, I don't think the inequities of access (which will be the most sharply drawn at the outset) should be a cause for major policy intervention. I don't think, as some have proposed, that we need information stamps modeled on food stamps to make sure our poorer citizens have access.

I think the nature of the Net and the nature of the character of information means that, although they may not have a wide-screen, high-definition display in their home, the information *will* be in the public domain. So I don't think it's a cause for concern. I wouldn't ignore these issues, I'd keep tracking them. I'd want to make sure that the law and the practice and proprietary control didn't get out of hand. But as I look at it today, my concern is not great. So I conclude, don't worry, be happy. Thank you.

Questions & Answers

GROSSMAN: We have two models in media history. One, the print model in which everything goes and it's every person for him- or herself with no restrictions, no laws, and no requirements except for certain copyright and libel restrictions. And we have the electronic model, which does have a history of regulation, restrictions, and government requirements.

We've heard three calls for various degrees of restrictions and requirements imposed on the Internet, either by government or by government and industry put together. And we've heard one great optimist, who says let everything alone and it will work out itself. Anybody want to amplify where you are in that public policy debate?

BRANSCOMB: I guess I would like to take on Russ Neuman. I thought Russ Neuman was really going to tackle the question of where the public space is in which people come together to resolve issues of the larger communities? One of the major difficulties with the cybercommunities is that everybody can find someone that's more or less another pea in the same pod, and they can all go off in their little space and communicate with each other.

I think as we develop these commercial sites and cybercommunities, there is less and less gathering in large communities to make important public decisions. That's why I was a little disappointed that Russ didn't tackle the problem of where the public space is on the Internet. I think he used the metaphor of the public domain perhaps in a way I would not have done. I think the public domain more nearly resembles Peter [Fowler's] interests—that is, what goes into the public domain, what remains proprietary, who manages and maintains quality control, and who archives

all that information that's on the Web, that's allegedly in the public domain? It gets overgrazed and nobody cares about it. Nobody has a proprietary interest in managing the public domain.

I've heard lots of librarians anguish over this, and I think this is a question that we really ought to address.

FOWLER: I was also a little surprised when Russ said, "Smile, be happy." The Telecommunications Minister of the recent South African Conference on the Information Society in Developing Countries ended his introductory address by envisioning the day in which every man, woman, and child in South Africa would get up in the morning and say, "I'm glad to be alive in this information age." In response, a lot of people said, "That day is either a long way away or this guy is very disconnected." Because first of all, there are very, very few laptops in South Africa, let alone the rest of Africa. And the gap expressed by many of the developing countries at that G7 meeting was growing, not diminishing.

Technology is making the gap between the developed countries and the developing countries of the world even greater. One statistic kind of stuck in my mind in Johannesburg—there's more telephones in Manhattan than there are on the entire African continent. And 65 percent of those telephones are in South Africa, and the other 25 percent are in Egypt, with the rest scattered among 50 other countries.

So there is the fear there that we are beginning to take this technology for granted, just like indoor plumbing, while in the rest of the world, 90 percent of the population wouldn't know what the World Wide Web was if it came up and bit them. So I'm concerned that the following policy issue gets discussed, both by developing and developed countries: how can technology help the vast majority of the Earth's population in social, cultural, and economic development?

Or does the gap just grow? Do we develop our own cyberworld, much like in the society in the novel *Fahrenheit 451*, where everybody becomes socially isolated from each other? Will future generations say, "They had so much at their fingertips, in terms of 500 channels of interactive soap operas and communications and entertainment, that they really didn't need anyone else—even though they had this appearance of an expanded community." I think this is an international policy discussion that is just beginning to be launched.

MONTGOMERY: Domestically, the universal access issue remains a very, very important policy issue, and one that we have, with the Telecommunications Act, made some progress in working on. But a great deal more will need to be done, and I'm particularly concerned about universal access for children. We are at a time when more and more children are falling into poverty, and the gap could be widened. Children will need access to these new media as an essential connection to daily life in this country—not only at school, but also at home. I really worry a great deal that we could lose a generation of children during this transition period who are not adequately connected to the national information infrastructure.

Q: *Does the common carrier document have relevance on the Internet? Should those along the "pipes" be barred from providing content? Also, should those who are commercially exploiting the Internet have any role in paying for non-commercial societal needs such as education, civic information, free political time, and so on, on the Internet? Are there any models that we should apply here? Or is it no holds barred?*

NEUMAN: Let me start with a personal observation: lawyers and public interest advocates worry too much. Let's find an exciting new business and tax it and find new restrictions for it. Let's try to make sure the restrictions and taxes keep up with the growth of the new business. Here we've got a new technology in which the cost of a computer's basically been pretty stable. It's something like $2,000 to $2,500 for the last five to ten years. And that's because the power of that computer, and its storage capacity, and its video processing capacity, have doubled every year.

So once you get to a viable network computer device and hopefully run it off other video screens in the household, you've got something

that's going to be pretty damn cheap. The cost of a compact disc player, a personal stereo, or a boombox. Not an inaccessible, very expensive, computer-like access device. We'll move from a centrally controlled series of one-way systems, like broadcasting or newspapers, to a two-way system that puts control in the hands of the individuals so they can go to the public space(s) they want to.

Q: *Commercial providers expect to charge for access to their services and resources. Why not have a similar economic model to mediate access to our resources, our time, by charging advertisers for email access to our private email boxes?*

BRANSCOMB: Actually, that's exactly what the commercial sites are beginning to do. Last fall I went to an Internet conference here in Boston and I went to the IBM booth. They were going to give away a free T-shirt if you would just tell them your name and address, what kind of computer you used, and all the software you had. And I thought, "Ah ha. Do I really want that T-shirt?" If you look at what's happening, the entrepreneurs are beginning to say, "I'm going to give you something of value if you will just disclose everything about yourself, so I'll know how to serve you better."

And actually, if you're dealing with a trusted intermediary, you may want to disclose a lot of information, because you can be better served by the computer, by people who know your interests, and you won't get bothered by all the things you don't want. I think there's a wonderful entrepreneurial opportunity for someone on the Internet to set up the sort of site that manages all your personal information and gives it only to those people that you really want to deal with. I think the commercial interests themselves are seeing that this is a marketing opportunity.

Q: *But is there a way for us to charge if we're going to give away information about ourselves, or if we're going to let information come into our own mailboxes?*

BRANSCOMB: Well, this is what this intermediary is going to do. If you want to know everything about me, go pay 25 cents or something to this guy who I'm willing to give the information to.

GROSSMAN: It's going to be like junk mail. You can get put on the list of the Postal Service to block junk mail from being delivered to your mailbox.

BRANSCOMB: I tried to get the junk mail out of my post office box and the Postmaster says, "I'm sorry, but legally I have to put it in there."

NEUMAN: For someone out there that's a software developer, that sounds like the perfect opportunity to develop some kind of commercial service that will block junk mail from your email.

GROSSMAN: Call it a V-chip.

MONTGOMERY: I think there will be a need for all kinds of innovative remedies as people feel more and more intrusions of their privacy. But right now, the default is that your privacy is invaded unless you do something to try to keep that from happening. A better model might be one where you would opt into a system where you're giving up information. When comes to kids, clearly kids are being offered all kinds of free gifts and incentives to give up information when they don't even realize that's what they're doing.

We would like to see some mechanism whereby parents are part of that process. Because the way it works now, the medium really bypasses the parents in many ways. The way the services are being designed, they intend to do that.

Q: *How does the anonymity on the Internet, e.g., Usenet, affect the various proprietary interests online?*

BRANSCOMB: Well, I guess I'll have to tackle that one since I've written a lot about anonymity. I think it is the most serious problem we have on the Internet. There's a tremendous clash between those who feel that they have a right to anonymity and those who feel that you cannot have a responsible community without some legal liability flowing to those who behave unacceptably. I think we have to sort out what purpose this is for. Pseudonymity is important and can be protected; there are all sorts of good things about being able to do something without being recognized. And people like to try on different personalities and play around in the MUDs [multi-user dungeons] and the MOOs [multi-user object-

oriented dungeons]: it's important for a whistle-blower not to be identified. Likewise, journalists protect their sources.

But usually somebody knows who the person is. Even with the "Federalist Papers," which a lot of lawyers claimed to be anonymous, somebody knew who wrote them. On the Internet, if you go through three or four anonymous remailers, you can really have an anonymous message that is technically almost impossible to identify. We don't have a consensus in this area yet, but I think it's extremely important to sort out where you're going to require some identification when real harm has occurred.

NEUMAN: Anne, would you propose that we outlaw remailers?

BRANSCOMB: I would require that remailers keep the identity so that it can be obtained under a court order.

Q: *Do you anticipate a movement to shut down the Internet for children, similar to recent efforts to shut off the television? And what formats would you anticipate as to how to do it? (Isn't it interesting how we're getting into all the same issues that have afflicted us on the so-called old-fashioned world?)*

MONTGOMERY: Well, first of all, I want to say that I am not a supporter of the "turn off the TV movement." I really believe that the important thing is to try to harness the power of these electronic media as positive forces in children's lives. We've been the group that's been leading the effort to get the Federal Communications Commission to strengthen the rules on the Children's Television Act to encourage more educational programming so that we can see some positive uses there. In terms of the Internet, I believe there are a lot of wonderful sites being developed for kids. We want to see more of that and we believe very strongly in access for children.

We also are not in any way trying to get rid of advertising to children on the Internet. All we want are some fair rules of the game; we want to work with industry to talk about how to do that. The most important thing now, when these new services are being designed, is that we have some kind of framework in place about how far you go, what's appropriate, and what isn't appropriate for kids. We need that debate now, to encourage more services to be developed that will really respect children.

Q: *In this technological revolutionary setting, who will be able to keep up? How many of the current have-nots will be able to master this technology? (In fact, how many panelists will be able to master that technology?) As the entry level skill and knowledge increase, how can the mass of average citizens be given reasonable access to the Net or the national information infrastructure? And a contrasting question: are we the only ones hypnotized by the Internet? Maybe the Third World is better off.*

BRANSCOMB: I think, for "the great unwashed," we will need a much simpler environment in which most of the intelligence is back somewhere on a server that they don't have to see and don't have to manage. That doesn't mean that people who are sophisticated users shouldn't have all that power on their desks. But I think we're a long way from universal service and access with the complicated software that we're producing in each program. And you know, you reload something and it does away with something else you thought you understood. So you keep getting into more and more levels of complexity. I don't think we can expect very many people to cope with that.

Q: *Universal access was never posited as a public policy goal for telephones, radio, broadcast TV, or cable TV. But why should it be for the Internet? Don't we have something to learn from the development of these other media, which were also once new and revolutionary and, incidentally, quite exclusive?*

MONTGOMERY: Universal access has been a policy goal for telephones. In terms of the Internet and the new interactive media, as I've said before, I think we've not yet had a medium that has been as essential as this one may be for access to education, health information, and all of the other needs in our society. I think it is a very important policy goal to ensure that we don't have built in inequities to the system.

NEUMAN: Where does the term "universal access" as a public policy goal come from? Is it from the Constitution or some major public policy issues from the Civil War? No, it comes out of a deal between Theodore Vail, then President of AT&T, and Kingsbury. It's known as the "Kingsbury Commitment of 1913." Vail said, "I don't want the competition because our patents for the Bell System have run out. Let's cut a deal: I'll do my best to get universal service if you protect me from competition." It was a deal. It's come to be and it's reflected in the 1934 Communications Act because people said that's an appropriate role.

We don't want to romanticize this, though, and we should take a close look at the history. It was because of the tremendous techno-success of what was initially not a guaranteed public service. It was a new experiment and nobody knew if it was going to work or not. It was the telephone and telegraph. The feds took a look at it and said, "No, we think this is a business that could be better developed by private concerns." And perhaps it was. So I'm not sure that we need to romanticize these issues.

Is there an area for public sector institutions to address these issues? I think, indeed, that is true. I think public kiosks, a very aggressive use of computers, access in libraries, in schools, and other public civic spaces makes a lot of sense. So let's involve the public sector in these debates, but let's not over-romanticize evolved public goals like universal service.

GROSSMAN: Oh, so you're not a purist in that. Let me push that a little further. In the political session panel today ["Life and Politics on the Net"], it was suggested, and I certainly agree with it, that online voting, online registration are going to come. In Oregon, we have mail-in ballots and the next point is going to be keypad ballots because the postal system is obviously becoming old-fashioned. Then, if to exercise citizenship, everybody requires a keypad ballot and if online becomes central to that, it will make a big difference in terms of how you treat, as a public policy matter, this question of universal access. It's basically the entertainment media that we didn't have to address this issue for. However, when it came to electricity and telephones, deal or no deal, it was considered to be something quite different.

BRANSCOMB: Clearly, if the computer becomes a ballot box, then you're going to need lots of public ballot boxes around the town that people can get ease of access to. But I don't see why that won't happen in the same way that public telephones are ubiquitous.

NEUMAN: I'd have a concern there. I'm not for universal access to the Internet, much the same way I'm not sure that I'd automatically expect to get an electronic ballot in the mail unless I ask for one. It raises, I guess, the other side of the coin. I'm very much in favor of people participating in democracy and voting, but I can respect that some people, for whatever reasons, don't want to vote. Are we creating a system whereby we push a policy of universal access; do we expect everybody to use it?

You know, the *World Book Encyclopedia*, years and years ago, was a great resource and probably every home should have one. But, on the other hand, there was no government mandate that every family had to buy a World Book Encyclopedia to read.

MONTGOMERY: But we do have public libraries.

NEUMAN: That's right. There should be lots of ways, if people want to access the Internet, that they can do so.

Q: *Are we looking at a successor to the FCC, in effect, with the Exon Bill particularly, as we get the first foot in the door to federal regulation of the Internet?*

MONTGOMERY: I do believe that the Communications Decency Act is far, far too broad and that it's completely inappropriate to have that kind of law that really outlaws constitutionally protected speech. We do believe, however, that there will be some need for safeguards in the areas of privacy and marketing, some of which can be achieved through self-regulation. There is a role for the federal government to play in fostering debate about that and in encouraging guidelines that will really be meaningful, particularly in the area of deceptive advertising and privacy.

NEUMAN: Let me pick up, if I might, on that. There's something calls PICS [Platform for Internet Content Selection], which is a programmatic development of the World Wide Web Consortium down at MIT [see *http://www.w3.org*]. Their notion was, instead of coming up with a V-chip-like definition such as, "This is violent, this is sexually explicit," and simply cutting off, in a form of electronic censorship, certain types of labeled speech or graphics or narrative entertainment, the PICS system says, "You pick a judge." It might be a conservative Christian church judge group or a literary club, but there can be hundreds, thousands of judges, that code and interpret the Net.

It leaves this decision up to the communities, plural, to make those judgements. You can put filters onto the flow in your computer that are derived from independent parents, citizens, and groups that reflect your concerns about what you do and do not want, junk mail, and sexually explicit material, coming into your home. I think the "Let a thousand servers bloom" philosophy makes a lot more sense than getting back to the old model of mass media censorship.

BRANSCOMB: I agree that the software screening services may be very, very effective tools for parents to use. But I just want to draw a distinction between what I've been focusing on and what PICS, Net Nanny, and the other services have been designed for. A lot of them were developed in response to the pending legislation which became law, the Exon Amendment. The idea is to protect children from content out there on the Web that you may not want them to have access to. We're looking really at the services that are being designed for children and will be targeted at children, and asking for rules for doing that in a fair way.

About the Speakers

LAWRENCE K. GROSSMAN is author of *The Electronic Republic, Reshaping Democracy in the Information Age*, and former President of NBC News and

PBS. Mr. Grossman occupied the Frank Stanton First Amendment Chair at the Kennedy School of Government.

ANNE BRANSCOMB is a communications and computer lawyer, author of *Who Owns Information?* and President of the Raven Group. Mrs. Branscomb has written extensively in both popular magazines and professional journals about the emerging law of cyberspaces and the impact of information technology on the law. Currently she is serving on the Advisory Council of Privacy & American Business, on the editorial advisory board of Transnational Data and Information Law, as trustee of the Telluride Institute, and adviser to the Telluride Infozone. She has also served on numerous other corporate and nonprofit organizations.

PETER N. FOWLER is an Attorney-Advisor in the Office of Legislative and International Affairs, U.S. Patent and Trademark Office, Department of Commerce in Washington, D.C., where he works on such domestic policy matters as the Conference on Fair Use, the Copyright Awareness Campaign, and the National Information Infrastructure legislation. He also monitors national and regional copyright policy and developments in Latin America, the Caribbean, the Middle East, Africa, and Southeast Asia. Prior to government service, Mr. Fowler was a partner in the San Francisco law firm of Lilienthal & Fowler.

KATHRYN C. MONTGOMERY, PH.D., is co-founder and President of the Center for Media Education, a Washington, D.C.-based public interest organization dedicated to educating the public and policymakers about critical media issues. The Center's project, Action for Children in Cyberspace, is a research public education, and policy initiative focused on the needs of children in the new interactive media environment. The Center also publishes *InfoActive*, which covers communications technology and policy developments for the nonprofit and child advocacy communities. Dr. Montgomery is the author of *Target: Prime Time. Advocacy Groups & the Struggle Over Entertainment Television* (Oxford University Press, 1989).

RUSS NEUMAN joined the Shorenstein Center of the Kennedy School in July, 1996, as Lombard Professor, Visiting and as a Senior Fellow at the Center. He is also a Research Associate with the Research Program on Communications Policy and the Media Laboratory at MIT Professor Neuman's current research focuses on the impact of the advanced telecommunications and the economics and policy of new media technologies. His books include *The Future of the Mass Audience* (Cambridge University Press, 1991), *The Telecommunications Revolution* (Routledge, 1992), *Common Knowledge: News and the Construction of Political Meaning* (University of Chicago Press, 1992), and *The Gordian Knot: Political Gridlock on the Information Highway* (MIT Press, 1997).

HARVARD NEWS

CONFERENCE ON THE INTERNET AND SOCIETY

May 29-31, 1996   Cambridge, MA

Cultural Imperialism on the Net: Policymakers from Around the World Express Concern over U.S. Role

By Miriam Herschlag

The French have taken to the barricades, certain that an Anglocentric World Wide Web is poised to bulldoze their culture into oblivion.

Singapore fears its national values will drown in a tidal wave of individualism and promiscuity. And the Chinese government is threatening to yank the plug on the Internet, viewing unfettered electronic communication as a weapon of subversion in the hands of dissidents.

In Europe, Asia, Africa, and truly around the globe, concern is mounting over America's overwhelming influence in cyberspace.

In arguments that sometimes show traces of paranoia and sometimes ring true, policymakers from around the world are charging the United States with "cultural imperialism."

Douglas Rushkoff, a prolific technology writer, (*http://www.users.interport.net/~rushkoff*) has little patience for the chorus of international complaint.

"The underlying force threatening the paranoid enemies of so-called American Imperialism is progress itself," says Rushkoff. "If progress looks American, that's not America's fault."

But English is clearly the dominant language on the Internet, accounting for some 90 percent of all information posted. This especially rankles the French, who treasure their language as a bastion of cultural heritage. French purists have, in fact, been fighting a losing battle for years against such viral influences as the Big Mac, Hollywood movies, and New York slang. The problem is even more daunting for Japan with its multiple alphabets and holistic language forms.

The concerns haven't fallen entirely on deaf ears. Netscape browsers and support services are already available in French, with Japanese on the way. German, Hebrew, Italian, and Russian are also fairly well represented on the Net, with translation programs available for some 75 languages.

While language may be the most obvious problem, some countries are also wary of the sheer quantity of content generated by the American infotainment machine. That massive bulk is a force that "Jihad vs. McWorld" author Benjamin R. Barber [*http://intlrel.soc.hawaii.edu/paac/programs/globalism*] says can "absorb and deconstruct and then reassemble the soul." In this context, some countries feel freedom of expression is a luxury they can't afford.

Singapore, for example, has imposed restraints on sites with political and religious content. It also requires all local Internet access providers to be registered and to screen out "objectionable" content. The country's Minister for Information and the Arts, George Yeo, defends the censorship moves as merely a symbolic way to maintain awareness of what is socially acceptable.

"The fact that we sin every day is not a reason to abolish the Ten Commandments," he told *New Perspectives Quarterly* [*http://www.enews.com/magazines/npq/*] last fall. "Indeed, it is precisely because we sin every day that we need the Ten Commandments."

While the devil may be in the message, the medium itself promises economic salvation. Singapore plans to wire nearly all its households by the year 2000, apparently convinced that widespread access will ensure its place in the global economy.

Japan is also searching for its footing on the Net. Its leaders are less concerned about the gush of Western ideas than more agitated over the U.S. lead in establishing market standards.

Their hesitation in jumping aboard a predetermined information infrastructure has made some local Internet advocates impatient. Izumi Aizu, Research Director of the Institute for HyperNetwork Society of Japan has been bringing his Internet expertise to not only help launch Tokyo executives into cyber-commerce but to organize a grassroots political movement for an entire prefecture with 1.25 million people spread over thousands of square miles.

Aizu, a scheduled speaker on the "Cultural Imperialism" panel, sees the Net as a tool for both national and local empowerment. His view is shared by Douglas Coupland who, in a talk reported in the *Ontarian* [*http://tdg.uoguelph.ca/~ontarion/back_issues/../118/issue4/5894.html*], warned, "it is absolutely necessary that developing countries have a voice in Internet development at a global level. As the Third World continues to be marginalized in the growth of information technologies, the Net will become another source of cultural imperialism perpetuated by the privileged First World."

The world's unwired regions, however, include not only societies who are unable to afford the technology but those who fear it. Namibia tried to quash Net use, and China has tried to force local computer networks to use only approved links. It appears what they really fear is the Net's suitability for mobilizing protest movements. They may claim they are protecting their citizens from unwanted Western influence, but as Rushkoff puts it, "The Internet is no more American than electricity."

Panel
May 31, 1996

Cultural Imperialism on the Net

MODERATOR: Arthur R. Miller
PANELISTS: Jacques Attali
                 Izumi Aizu
                 Karanja Gakio
                 Nathan Gardels
                 Douglas Rushkoff
                 Anne-Marie Slaughter
                 Xiaoyong Wu

MILLER: My name is Arthur Miller. I teach law here at the Harvard Law School. We have assembled a panel to talk about the cultural clash on the Internet. You should understand that we prepared valiantly for this session. We spent at least 30 seconds shaking hands. So what happens up here is completely spontaneous. The only preparation is the enormous experience these people bring to the subject.

Now, in the spirit of improvisation, I'll ask the panelists to introduce themselves.

AIZU: As you see, my name begins with "A" so I'm usually the first. I have been doing this kind of networking for about ten years. I was highly impressed that, finally, here you are talking about Internet and society. We do the kind of social side of the analysis or study about network society in Tokyo and in another city called Oita. I work for two institutions: one is global, the Center for Global Communications; the other is called Institute for HyperNetwork Society, whatever that means. But I am not a specialist. I didn't go to college or university at all. I am a generalist. I like people. I don't like information. I love communications. That's it.

GAKIO: I run the technical operations of Africa Online, a company I founded along with my friends a couple of years ago to provide Internet access in underserved areas of the world. In particular, we focus on sub-Saharan Africa.

GARDELS: I am the editor of the Global Service of the *Los Angeles Times* syndicate, the largest feature and commentary service in the world. We have 30 million readers in 20 languages, through papers from the *Sunday Times* of London to *Le Monde* to *Yamiri Shinbun*. We transmit in English around the world, which is a subject I want to talk about, language on the Net. We have been very interested in the Net at the newspaper syndicates because one day it will put us out of business. So we're following developments very closely and have some observations about that. I also publish a journal called *New Perspectives Quarterly*, which looks at some of these issues of the media in a little more depth than is possible in a newspaper, and a little more sophisticated than I've seen in especially many places on the Net.

RUSHKOFF: I'm a native of the datasphere. I've written five books, including *Cyberia, Media Virus,* and *Playing the Future,* that prove beyond the shadow of a doubt that technology is just an expression of popular cultural will. I develop content for TCI's forthcoming interactive television channel. And I think everything's going to be okay.

SLAUGHTER: I'm a law professor here at the Harvard Law School, where I managed to spend three years avoiding being on the other end of Arthur Miller's searching questions. But that's not going to be true this morning. I am studying the desirability and the feasibility of developing a worldwide network of lawyers called "Lawyers Without Borders," which would focus on providing public interest services to developing countries.

MILLER: There's a piece of cultural imperialism. Right? Exporting the American legal system. Terrific, Anne-Marie.

WU: I have two hats on myself. One is that I work for a brand new television company in Hong Kong called Phoenix Satellite Television, a joint venture between some Chinese companies and Star TV. Our main target is to penetrate into the

China market with entertainment television programs. My other hat is that I am Chinese and have been working as a journalist for more than a dozen years in China. And my only knowledge of Internet is that I've been using it for about 50 hours, maximum. (My son is having a lot of fun downloading games like Doom.) That's about the only experience I have with Internet, but I do have a personal interest in the service and what impact it will have on China.

ATTALI: I am Professor of Economics at the University of Paris. Among other things, I have been Chief of Staff for the President of the French Republic for ten years. I now head a company specializing in international finance in Paris. I have published more than 25 books, including books on the information society, and I am working on something to link to the Internet.

MILLER: So you see we have four continents represented in our panel. That's not bad for a conference on the World Wide Web. Let's say for the moment that I'm from Mars; the proverbial "man from Mars," looking down at this society. Perhaps those of us from Mars, unhappy with Mars, want to come to this planet to live here, to assimilate, to vote Republican. And I have literally dropped in to this conference. And understand that Bill Gates talked a few days ago about the clash of cultures on the Internet being one of the great, great issues before the Internet. And I pick up this little newspaper and see this headline, "Cultural Imperialism," words that weren't included in my study of world history on Mars— Imperialism was an 18th century word. Nathan, what the hell are these people talking about?

GARDELS: I've never been asked to speak for the Martians before, but I'll give it a try. There was an article in the *New York Times*, a few months ago about a Russian guy complaining that everything on the Net was English. This was cultural imperialism. How can we have access to the Net if it's only in English? I think that's not really an issue. I think there is an aspect of the Net which involves a clash of civilizations, but I don't think it's an issue of imperialism. In fact, I think the Net is anti-imperialist.

In my view, there is no question that America dominates the meta-world of images, information, and icons. These days, everywhere you look is a Cindy Crawford or a Pocohontas staring out at you like statues of Lenin in the old Soviet Union. Or Madonna and Michael Jackson of the Muzak of the world disorder: everywhere you go, you hear the music. That's cultural imperialism, perhaps.

But the Net is not. The Net is anti-imperialist because it allows you to communicate with whomever you want. It's not a one-way communication; it's a means to be unmediated. So in that sense, I think the Net itself is implicitly anti-imperialist. And in this country as well, I think that is acknowledged by people like Newt Gingrich. (You mentioned the Republicans.) On Mars, we even know about Newt Gingrich.

MILLER: Hardly an imperialist type.

GARDELS: We should not forget that one of the reasons Newt Gingrich or cultural conservatives like George Gilder are so fond of the Net is because they believe it's the means of revolt against the media class dominated by the Hollywood glitterati and the mass broadcast elites of the East Coast.

Second, English is not some kind of oppressive Esperanto. I think English is a translation machine; a conductor of global information flows. It's the global lingo. It's true, at the moment it *does* marginalize other languages or puts them in their own domain. For example, some people say French will be the Latin of the 21st century because English is marginalizing it. That would be true, except for Zaïre and the other French colonies that will be populated by the most French speakers in the next century.

But I agree with Georgiou, the Information Minister of Singapore, who believes the world will not go Anglo-Saxon; that every culture will develop its own analogies in cyberspace. I see this already in the newspaper syndication business. It's true, we bring in a lot of articles that we translate from other languages, from Serbo-Croatian or Russian or Italian, into English. We transmit them again in English, to be translated back again into other languages.

MILLER: Nathan, if I get this straight, you think this is a big non-issue.

GARDELS: I'm getting to where the issue is. This is my second point. The English is a non-issue. The third issue is an issue. And that's an issue of this clash of civilizations. I think the Net is inherently anti-authoritarian because it is unmediated, and it is a liberating technology, if you will. But societies need to be governed, not liberated. And I think that there is a cultural clash, not as Sam Huntington said, between all those elements (that's another issue)—Islam and the West, for example—but there is a cultural clash of civilizations, I think, between the soft city and the real city, between cyberspace and a place where people need to be governed, and there needs to be appropriate social authority. I think that's a very big issue, and you see the debate taking place, very sophisticated and very richly, in places like Singapore, perhaps more than you do in this country.

So I do think there's an issue there. But as for the Net being imperialist, no, I think the Net is anti-imperialist.

MILLER: Now, Jacques, equal time. You're a man of the world. You're the ultimate sophisticated French person. But somewhere in Paris, there must be someone who is worrying about the French language. Certainly, plenty of them exist up in Montreal.

ATTALI: Yes, you're right. But I wouldn't say that the Internet is the core of the problem, because as you know, the Internet is really a very marginal element of what we may call cultural imperialism. It takes place in media, in politics, in diplomacy, but not the Internet. Who knows about the Internet in the world? I would say one to five million people out of five *billion*, which is nothing. Therefore, we are talking about an issue which for the moment, is really marginal.

It's true that language is really a problem, and is a problem on the Internet, because it's true that 80 percent of what is available on the Internet is in English. Even in France, where the Internet is beginning to pick up, it's beginning to be a prob-

lem because people are linked to English-speaking networks. Although we have our own network in France, "Minitel," which was quite a success, it is a dead end because it's impossible to link it to the system at large.

But to come back to the questions that Nathan raised, I would say I believe that the language is really a problem. It's a problem because we certainly may see English becoming the dominant language for a while. My bet is that it won't be true for the future. I think that English is the Latin of the 21st century, because if you look at the world 50 years from now, no more than 20 percent of the world will speak English. Chinese, of course, and other languages, will be more widely spoken than English.

> *I think the Net is inherently anti-authoritarian because it is unmediated, and it is a liberating technology, if you will. But societies need to be governed, not liberated.*

I think one of the most interesting decisions this year was CNN's decision to begin Spanish-language broadcasts, because I do believe that the business community will understand that if they want access to the worldwide market, they have to develop their products in languages other than English. If I weren't in the business community, I would be interested in working in automatic translation on the Net, which I think will be absolutely vital in the future.

I also believe that cultural imperialism on the Net will be very important as a device, as a tool—even as a diplomatic tool, because in the future the Net will be a place to develop leaks, false news, rumors, diplomatic strategies that are totally new. It will be interesting to study before it's too late.

SLAUGHTER: Jacques, it's interesting that you mention diplomatic links, because it's my observation that when French was the international diplomatic language there was no complaint about cultural imperialism. It was just assumed that French was the language to best express nuance and subtle shades of meaning. It was the perfect language for international communication. But now, since English has supplanted French, now we need to worry. I would argue that even though we have multiple languages—

ATTALI: I wouldn't worry at all if English had the exact status that French had in the 18th century, to be spoken only among the diplomats, and not to be the language of the general communities.

SLAUGHTER: But it was the language of international communication, which at that time was much more limited to diplomats. Now we live in a world in which you do not need to be a diplomat to travel the world, either virtually or literally.

ATTALI: This is not the point. The point is the question of knowing, if we go toward a universe where only one language will be spoken and one language will represent the structure of the mind of everybody—because the Net is not only a language, it's also a way of thinking. And this way of thinking is linked to English. I do believe that it's not in the interest of the American community, not of the English-speaking community, to go toward a world of uniformity.

SLAUGHTER: It's my observation that the real global language is not English; it's bad English. It's English spoken in many, many different ways, in ways that do, in fact, reflect different cultures.

ATTALI: That's why it is in our common interest not for everybody to speak bad English, but for everybody to speak his own language.

AIZU: Well, I ask how many of you are bilingual? Raise your hands, please. And how many of you are bicultural?

MILLER: What does "bicultural" mean?

AIZU: I don't know.

MILLER: Izumi, you'd better not ask the third question.

AIZU: I will give the answer. The point is, I don't think in Japan or in China or in Singapore or even in France, that people are dominated by English, even if they are using the Internet, say, five hours a day. On the Net, most of the communication and conversations among the local people are exchanged in the local language. If needed, we could find some other language, a common language. If I could speak Chinese, I would like to do that. (I studied it once. My daughter is now trying to learn French on top of English.) What's the problem? I don't understand.

GAKIO: I would like to say this whole debate between English and French is all very interesting, but if I'm sitting in Nairobi trying to communicate with my cousins who live outside of the city, our languages, because of the past 78 years of history, have definitely been marginalized. The question is, are our languages going to get enough of an opportunity on the Internet to express themselves and to find these communities of interest so they can continue to grow? Definitely, as the use of English has spread, I think it will be the language that we ultimately end up with 100 years from now. English will be quite different than the idea of English we have now.

MILLER: What do you worry about? Not you individually, but the people in Africa, where you are trying to operate Africa Online. Do they worry about this thing, "cultural imperialism?" Do they see the Internet as destructive to their culture?

GAKIO: I think it depends on who you ask. There is a segment of society that actually cherishes getting all the new ideas and infusions from outside cultures. It also has a lot to do with the seductiveness, particularly of Western culture.

MILLER: Is this the Madonna factor?

GAKIO: Yes, yes. Precisely. Exactly. But then, there are other people who want to rein in these foreign influences. In a way, this whole Internet debate is actually (I'd have to agree with Jacques)—quite marginal in Africa because some of the problems we're facing are much more serious than this. It's more a question of survival, really. And one of the challenges for us now is to try to make sure that even as you provide new capabilities, access to new resources—whether they're in English or in French, or whatever language—we don't create conditions which further separate the elite and everybody else.

RUSHKOFF: Ironically, one of the beauties of the Internet today is that it forces its users to realize that they are part of this elite; that we are part of the .01 percent of the world's population that is online. Originally, I suppose we felt inspired to get the Third World online. That was the new frontier: to go to Africa, or any developing nation, and get their populations online so they could take part in the global renaissance to which Internet denizens aspired. The Internet exposed elite cultures to the fact that there is a whole world out there, and they wanted to wire it all up. Faced with the enormity and, in some ways, the inappropriateness of this task, the goal has changed. I think there's a growing sense of how disconnected from the rest of the world we've been all along. The Internet has only made it more concrete. I would think the real challenge for us now is not really to bring the rest of the world online but rather, for those of us who are privileged enough to be online and have finally realized there *is* such a thing as a global culture, to go offline and experience what the rest of the world has been going through.

SLAUGHTER: The real problem is not cultural imperialism, but rather a problem of two cultures. There are more telephone lines in Hong Kong than there are on the entire African continent. That is a problem. We are talking about a major divide between those who are privileged and online, and the rest of the world. And even if those of us who are online occasionally go out into the rest of the world there is still a huge problem.

RUSHKOFF: I'm not talking about taking a bus trip in Nairobi in order to pay your dues to the Third World. What I'm saying is, before the Internet, I think most people, certainly most kids, didn't realize there was another 99 percent of the world with which they were completely out of touch. We really believed the television we watched, and the insular American media world we were

in, was the whole world. *Cosby* was reality. And I believe, because we can feel on the Internet how much is truly out of reach, that now there is a new imperative for the First World elite to find out what's going on and to deal with it.

MILLER: It's very interesting that early in his remarks, Nathan spoke glowingly about Internet.

GARDELS: How else can a Martian speak?

MILLER: *I'm* the Martian. You're the journalist. You're the lowest form of animal life. Listen, you spoke about the Internet being the great equalizer, in terms of informational opportunity. But Karanja speaks of the Internet as a potential tool of the elite, thereby widening the existing gulf within cultures and between cultures.

GARDELS: If a Martian asked me to describe the planet 50 years from now, I would say (as has been said in so many words by Bill Mitchell at MIT, or Manuel Costels at Berkeley, in the Urban Planning School), you have a kind of *Bladerunner* situation: where you have these tall towers, with acid rain dripping, and on the top you have people connected on the Net through your networks, speaking some mix of English, and down below, you have all kinds of people who are disconnected. You have the rise of the mega-city, the global city, which is connected, but the social communication within the societies is broken. So at once you have the rise of the mega-city and the collapse of urban civilization.

I think you could certainly see that kind of a gap growing, where you have a second-class citizenship, where a lot of people are connected in a global city. Even though it's dispersed geographically, they're all in the same nonspace.

But the point I was making—I don't think I said it was the equalizer—is that the Net allows for unmediated communication, allows for an escape from "cultural imperialism," from the mass broadcast, it's top-down culprits. The Net, in that sense, is a tool, because you can speak to anyone without permission. You can speak unmediated. That was the point I was making.

MILLER: Xiaoyong, with your experience in China, I would think you might have a different view of what the Chinese think of cultural imperialism via the Net.

WU: First of all, I don't worry too much about the so-called cultural imperialism over the Internet. My prediction is that the Internet will eventually become somewhat fragmented. China at the moment is building its own network. Its slogan is to use the Internet to show the outside world what China is doing and, through the Internet, to learn about what others are doing.

To go back to the language issue, I think, the major concern is cultural identity or national identity. In China, it doesn't seem to be a problem because everybody has strong confidence in their own culture. They learn English with the understanding that it will be another language tool to understand other cultures. But I'm not so sure about the smaller nations. I guess the imposition of the English or French language during the colonial days was very much linked to imperialist behavior. In that sense, I guess it could be a worry to some smaller countries, if you have to learn the English language to get on the Net. But in China, we'll eventually see quite a number of sites in Chinese language. It's already happening in Taiwan and Hong Kong. And people in China log onto the Net, mainly looking for information in the Chinese language.

MILLER: But following Tiananmen (which you know so well because you reported from Tiananmen), there has been pressure in China to control the use of the Internet in terms of political ideology. Now, that's another form of cultural imperialism. We've talked about the Madonna factor, the language factor, but China seems to be wanting to keep the Internet free of political ideology.

WU: That's correct. The government has a very self-contradictory policy at the moment. On the one hand, it wants to continue to control the flow of information. On the other hand, China has a very dynamic economy which demands the free flow of information. Therefore, we see a very ridiculous policy, including a ban on issuing information about China's finance or economy

from any source other than the Xinhua News Agency.

However, the economy does require a lot of free flow. So I think the policy of control is doomed to fail. We will see a day when China will have freedom of speech and freedom of information. And the tools the government has to control the flow of information in any case are very limited and ineffective.

Nevertheless, the government does realize that China must get into the so-called Information Superhighway. In the ninth five-year plan, which is effective toward the end of this century, the government accords the information industry top priority. As for how to control it, I don't think they have any effective means to do that.

MILLER: We tend to think (at least some people in the West tend to think) that China has been uniquely successful in controlling information flow within its borders. Why do you think it's ineffective?

WU: I don't think it's effective at all. Take Canon, for example. The fax machine played a major part in getting information out of China and into China. And we in the television business are trying to provide information through satellite to Chinese homes. I think we are quite successful. The government denies it, but we have about 32 million households capable of receiving the signal from Star TV (now it's called Phoenix TV). Information is available, but the government control is also limited by the fact that it controls only the government media organizations. And there are other means to get information. The Internet is certainly one of those. So in China's case, I think the Internet does more good than bad. It provides a channel through which people can get information they wouldn't otherwise get.

MILLER: Didn't Murdoch agree not to show BBC [British Broadcasting Corporation] on the channel because the government objected?

WU: Yes, Murdoch tried to appease the Chinese government by cutting off the BBC World Service and other gestures. But getting to China is very difficult because of government control.

And the government is really scared because they know, once the information flows freely, the people will begin to understand that they are living in a big lie.

RUSHKOFF: Right. Which is why, as a last-ditch attempt to control the flow of information, academics and governments come up with terms like "cultural imperialism," which is just social pessimism rehashed by people who want us to believe that if the population of the world gains control of what we think and say, we're going to run amuck, rape and pillage each other, and move toward some sort of Nazi tyranny.

SLAUGHTER: But it *is* cultural imperialism. It's a culture I happen to agree with. I'm born in it and support it. But if you're right, if the provision of information over the Internet creates a *de facto* norm of freedom of information and that will change the political systems, that's a culture of pluralism and of tolerance and of freedom of expression. That's one culture, the traditional Western culture. And it will be imposed on non-Western peoples.

RUSHKOFF: I believe that's the natural evolution of the human species that the Martian is observing on our planet.

SLAUGHTER: That's imperialist!

MILLER: Oh! We are in the presence of a divinity here! This is eternal truth, Doug?

RUSHKOFF: No, it's what I observe: that we have a civilization that's attempting to restore contact, that's attempting to find some cohesiveness. There is a longing, I would argue, in almost every individual here, to reconnect with the rest of what's going on. And that's what's happening globally.

MILLER: Have you spoken to the Amish lately, or the Hasidics in Brooklyn, for this eternal truth?

RUSHKOFF: I think that in fundamentalist footholds you'll find, whether it's the militia of Montana or the Ayatollah, people fighting information technology because it's allowing this very natural, freeform, liquid relationship between human beings to take place.

MILLER: And the job for those of us who have eternal truth is to steamroller those people into submission.

RUSHKOFF: No, we don't have to do a thing. It's going to happen by itself. Just as biology evolves so will we.

GAKIO: I disagree. I don't think there's any free flow of information exchange going on here. I think a lot of it is dependent on economic realities. If I go to a village in Samburu in northern Kenya and see somebody wearing a Bull's T-shirt, there's something incongruous there.

RUSHKOFF: Incongruous, yes. It's hybridized. And if we become a planet of mocha-skinned, Chinese-speaking people, there is something incongruous about that, too. But that seems to be the nature of intercourse.

SLAUGHTER: But people all over the world are trying to reassert their culture, precisely against that kind of homogenization. The Chinese culture was around thousands of years ago while we were running around in skins. They don't need instruction from us, and they fear the submergence of their distinctive traditions.

RUSHKOFF: That's because people cannot conceive of a global organism that respects the individuality of each member or each culture. They can't look at biological models like the coral reef, where each tiny little microorganism on 300 miles of reef has more effect on the networked whole, not less. If you put five women in a house together, their menstrual cycles will synchronize. That doesn't deny the individuality of each member, but there is a certain coordination that naturally occurs.

ATTALI: A dimension we have not touched for the moment is the economic element. At the beginning, the Net, as with all new technologies, had the effect of decentralizing and creating competitiveness, which has been the case for telecommunications technology at all different stages of progress. But if we see what happened with Microsoft and other competing industries, we may say that perhaps the cultural imperialism comes not from governments or from any kind of ideology but from industry, which will organize through competition and through monopoly, to channel their own views on the system.

The point I think is very difficult to understand is that it's clear that the Net is decentralized, fragmented, is everything associated with the creation of a pure market, as the economists of the 19th century would have dreamed. But what is the next stage? Is the Web going to be, through the economic concentration and the necessary capital, swallowed by a company like Microsoft, which will not only have its own agenda in terms of technology, but in terms of products as well? Will we see a merger between Disney and Microsoft? And what kind of products will be on the Net as a result? I think this is the real issue, the consequences and the possibility of imperialism. This is not the case for the moment but it may be the question of the next decade.

AIZU: Microsoft didn't really pioneer the Internet at all. They came late. And the dominant share of the browsers now is not Microsoft. It's Netscape, a tiny little company. Do you blame Netscape for dominating or monopolizing the market? I don't think so. It's so dynamic. It changes very quickly, so I'm not too worried about that side.

But I must say there are certain people in Japan who also worry about English domination on the Internet, the techno-domination by nontech, middle-aged people, even young people. As Nathan said, there might be some separation between those who can afford to have computers or the Net and those who can't, but I don't think that's a problem of the Net itself. It's a larger issue. One aspect is the economy.

Two years ago, in Beijing, I went to a seminar called "Internet and Business." And more than 300 people came. Don't just pay attention to the government policy there, pay attention to the way the people are thinking. They are trying to connect to the rest of the world, they see what's going on, and they are saying what they want to do. That's more important.

I am working on projects with the lesser developed Asian countries who need the Internet connection, and we are trying to help them. The point is, we need to address the economic issues by using all the available tools. Tools by themselves are not the problem, the problem is the people or the society who are using the tools. So we should separate those.

But I don't really believe too much in the decentralizing nature of the Net, or the utopian kind of optimism for it. But again, what's important is the people who use the Net. The Net itself is changing. I see some of the mass media—more one-way flow of information—coming to the Net. And so it doesn't really guarantee any "natural" success or "natural" solution. It sometimes creates more problems.

MILLER: Izumi, yours is a nation with a great set of cultural traditions, social traditions, artistic—

AIZU: So are the French and Chinese.

MILLER: Yes, but I'm talking to you for the moment. I know you're a great enthusiast for the Net, but are there people in Japan who worry that the great Japanese art forms of literature, poetry, and woodblock printing, for example, may be submerged and lost because the Net will simply drown out those art forms?

AIZU: Not many. If you look at some of the Japanese web sites, there is all the Japanese woodblock printing or all sorts of cultural things you can display. And this seemingly minor culture now has a place where it can exhibit, that the mass media or the mass economy cannot pay attention to. Even individuals can do that. And for that reason, I don't think it's a problem.

The problem we now have is, where should we steer Japanese society or our culture? Fifty years after the war, we have had fairly successful economic development. And now we are seeing the beginning of the problem, the social crisis. The real crisis perhaps comes later. So now the Ministry of Education in Japan decided to hook up all the elementary schools to the Net and start to teach English in the elementary schools. I doubt if it will be effective, but that aside, we're concerned about how we position Japan as a whole, in the global context. I think other countries may share the same problem. It's not the Net.

MILLER: But Jacques, there is movement in your country to create quotas in terms of air time devoted to different—

ATTALI: No. We have, as I said, vast experience of something close to the Net, called Minitel, which has been used for more than 20 years now, and which is very efficient. By the way, to use it, you need to read, which is better than just looking at images on TV. Therefore, the Net is interesting because it pushed people to go back to reading.

RUSHKOFF: I used Minitel when I was in Paris, but it seemed most of it was advertisement for prostitutes and escorts.

ATTALI: I'm sure you got good experts to advise you where to find it, but it's not the only use. But to answer your question, we use quotas for fostering the French movie industry. And actually, the quota is a success so we plan to continue and expand it to the European level.

MILLER: Can I ask you whether those quotas are cultural or economically driven?

ATTALI: They are culturally driven. But of course, as the media is an industry, you cannot foster cultural goals without paying heed to the financial means required. But this is not at all the issue for the Net. The Net is amazingly marginal and it's not an issue at all. We are talking as if the Net were the instrument of imperialism. It is not. What is an instrument of imperialism is the fact that people don't read fairy tales any more. They only know fairy tales from movies. They know *Notre Dame de Paris* through the cartoons! That's what cultural imperialism really is, not the fact that through the Net you can reach a different library or reach different people.

So, I don't believe that in the next year or so, or even decade, the Net will be an instrument of imperialism, except if some people use it as a technology for political goals. And I do believe that this will happen; that someone will use it as Hitler used radio in the '30s. That doesn't mean that radio should be cursed. But someone will use it as an instrument of imperialism. This for sure. In the future the Net may be an instrument of imperialism if it continues to develop what I would call the new kind of elite, an elite of people who are always plugged in, wherever they are in the world. It's a kind of nomadic elite of a new world. The new elite will be plugged in everywhere, always informed and always in charge.

MILLER: This laptop is the new secret handshake?

ATTALI: This is the new instrument of a new nomad. Certainly, yes.

GARDELS: I think this distinction between the image media, the broadcast media, and the Net is an important one. Going back to the China question, I do agree with the way some Asian leaders see it.

I have this wonderful quote from Li Kuan Yu that I can't resist reading. He says, "The top three to five percent of society can handle this free-for-all, this clash of ideas on the Net. If you do this with a whole mass, if you do this with a whole society," he says, "you'll have a mess." In this vein "let them have the Internet." How many Singaporans will be exposed to all these ideas, including some crazy ones, which they hope they won't absorb? Five percent? Okay. That's intellectual stimulation that . . . provides an edge for the whole society. But to have day to day images of violence and raw sex on the picture tube, the whole society exposed to it, will ruin the whole community. That's the cultural imperialism.

So I think there's a distinction there, and it's not lost on those in Asia, particularly those who are trying to figure out with which part of the West they want to integrate, and which part they don't.

MILLER: This is interesting. You have experience with Singapore, I am told. We have China. We have Japan. Is Singapore more likely to be successful in engineering control mechanisms to preserve its—

GARDELS: Social engineering?

MILLER: Yes, social engineering—then China, because of its vast land mass and population? Is Singapore unique? It's just a city-state.

GARDELS: Correct me if I'm wrong, but the ideal of Chinese planners is to have 500 or 600 Singapores around China in the next century.

Wu: You mean, they have advisors from Singapore?

Gardels: Singapore is doing a Potemkin Singapore.

Gardels: Like Suchou. But in the ideal mind, by the middle of the next century, Asia has got to cope with 50 cities with 20 million people each. And you're going to have a *Bladerunner* or a Singapore type of situation: either an ordered society or a completely chaotic one such as Bombay, or even Shanghai. So, my view is that a lot of the Asian leaders look toward the Singapore model.

Now we were talking on the Net last night, whether Singapore could be successful. The problem is, once you build structures, once you build buildings, once you build something to last, it ages: you're moving mesh. A mistake could well be planning itself to be an information hub, but information doesn't stay at a physical hub. Information moves in a mesh. So it's a bit of a trading hub. An information hub, doubtful.

Aizu: Singapore is a very artificial city, and it's dangerous for vast China to model after. But I don't think that's the primary issue. I think the point is that, yes, cultural imperialism (whatever that means) can be dangerous if people are fooled to believe. And there is some role for the Americans; for example. Don't pretend that you're innocent. Sometimes what you are subconsciously or unconsciously doing may affect the other side of the world. Even within your country, there are some problems happening anyway. And I think it will depend on how you are using [the Net]—it's not automatically solved. That's what I would like to repeat. Many problems will unfold around the Net, beyond cultural imperialism: the individual crash, flaming, invading others' privacy, and things like that, which are very difficult to trace on the Net.

Slaughter: We haven't talked much about cross-fertilization. We have been focusing on the imperialism side. But it's certainly true the Net can also link up cultures in ways that result in mutually beneficial cross-fertilization rather than hybridization. For instance, there's a network of public interest lawyers devoted to using law to protect the environment. It's called E-Law. It's

an Internet conference, which works not by email sent to the U.S. and U.S. information forwarded to different countries but by a South African lawyer asking a question and from a Sri Lankan lawyer, from a Hungarian lawyer, from a Chinese lawyer. The result is a compendium of the different ways in which different cultures, different legal systems are using law to protect the environment. This is the dimension of the Internet that is the antithesis of cultural imperialism.

Miller: Do you think that's a plus?

Slaughter: I think that's a plus.

Miller: All these lawyers talking to each other?

Slaughter: Yes.

Miller: That may be Jacques's elite of the 21st century.

Attali: Yes. It's just an assumption, but I don't say that critically. An elite will be needed, but this elite will be the structure of a new imperialism. It will not be an imperialism of a nation but an imperialism of a new group would be internationally minded by structure. And the Net will certainly be a tool. Actually, I said they would be nomads. They will form a virtual tribe of a new elite. And we have seen that kind of virtual tribe of lawyers, which is an interesting example.

Rushkoff: A particular alarm goes off in my head, though, when I hear someone describing a nomadic tribe of people not directly connected but somehow involved in a conspiracy to run things—

Attali: No, I didn't say "conspiracy."

Rushkoff: It sounds to me much like the way people described the original Jewish merchants, also nomadic people with a sense of connection to one another—apart from geography as they first migrated to Europe. And I think we have to ask whether, if there are this ten million or eight million people on laptop computers, talking to each other on cellular devices, are they doing something that's good for culture or not? Are they just sucking out all the money and making everybody suffer? Or are they looking for ways to build roads and get water to people who don't have it?

ATTALI: That's why I say—

RUSHKOFF: Just because they are talking among themselves doesn't necessarily mean that they're—

ATTALI: There was no negative connotation in what I said. Just an analysis of the situation.

SLAUGHTER: That was the reference to lawyers.

MILLER: It's just the natural paranoia.

ATTALI: Guilt complex.

MILLER: Well, I just wonder. Karanja, the nations in the area you focus on have developing cultures. I mean "developing" in the sense of coming to market. The cultures have existed for centuries. They may be thinking of commercialization of those cultures, whether it's film or theater or music or literature. Does anyone worry about the fact that the inundation of the Madonna culture or the McDonald's culture or the American or French movie culture will somehow inhibit the indigenous cultures from being able to flower, grow, come to market, and compete internationally?

GAKIO: That's definitely a concern. But sometimes I feel that many of us have basically shrugged our shoulders and said, "What can you do?" I mean, it's really an issue of economic and commercial viability. We are a microcosm of the world at large, so the same issues we're talking about of getting culturally overrun on a global scale occur on the regional level as well.

In Kenya there was an incredible national debate over whether the influx of pop music from Zaïre was going to end up killing off indigenously developed music. A ferocious debate. So we're definitely worried about that.

But again, it's a question of access to the medium. For us at Africa Online, we're trying to come up with ways to provide as broad a level of access as possible and also to encourage participation in the creation of tools—the tools for creating content, the tools for participating in this new universe.

MILLER: Playing the role of devil's advocate (or Martian advocate), if a culture—whether it's a nation-state or a city-state—wants to see its culture flourish—whether it's artistic or ideological, or religious culture—is there anything inherently wrong with that culture setting barriers to avoid the inundation, to provide a sort of fertilizer to allow its own culture to flourish? Doug, would you find that reprehensible in your view of the world?

RUSHKOFF: I don't find it necessarily reprehensible, but I think when they decide some day to let those boundaries go, they might end up in a very weakened position as they attempt to compete in the cultural marketplace. So I would think the real danger is, if you don't have a Golden Age—when you have your Inquisition and lock yourself away—you're going to come out looking pretty weak. I was thinking, if I were a French citizen and there were quotas on the movies coming in, and I knew that there were these protected French movies, it would turn my entire French cinematic experience into PBS. There is nothing wrong with PBS, but there's that "this is good for you" feeling about it. And you lose a certain zest and a certain life. And I think this will inhibit their chance to compete.

ATTALI: It's easier to fight something that you caricature. This is not at all the case. France is not at all putting quotas on films entering France. (In France you can see more than 80 percent of American movies, which I think is too much, by the way, as a quota.) The quotas are intended to push the main TV networks to finance the production of movies. And I think it's good to push the movie media industry to finance the movie industry, because it helps to find a compulsory way of financing culture. The market is not strong enough to finance culture. All economic theories demonstrate that the market will never find a good way of financing culture. Therefore, someone else (call it quotas or anything you like) will have to push toward financing culture. We have found this is working very well, and I do advise other countries to do the same. I do believe, even from an American point of view, that it is in the interest of the American market to create diversity, because an industry will die from uniformity. And I don't think it is in the interest of the American movie industry to do that.

MILLER: There was an interesting outburst from some agitated member of the audience. Is culture simply the marketplace?

RUSHKOFF: Well, I think culture is a gene pool.

MILLER: And you're going to homogenize it?

RUSHKOFF: No. That's the whole point. Unless you actually kill a species of people, their genes don't go away, and neither do their cultural genes. They mix their recessive qualities. Things come back.

____: I speak four languages, and there are things that I can still not translate.

RUSHKOFF: Right. And if it's impossible to translate things—I think that's precisely why you don't have a Spanish-speaking panelist here, because it's language, culture, cultural imperialism.

____: We talked about CNN now being broadcast in Spanish.

ATTALI: And Julio Iglesias in English.

MILLER: Wait a second. What is your point?

____: The point is that I have struggled not with cultural imperialism, I have struggled to make the translation. And I cannot do it. The words do not work.

MILLER: Is your point that there is no way to communicate effectively; that the use of a single language on the Internet is doomed to failure because the nuances simply do not come across?

____: Let me give an example. The people who speak several languages relate to each other in a different way than people that speak only one language relate. I see it: the people who speak several languages can do things that the people that speak only one language cannot do. That's the reality.

RUSHKOFF: Right. So you see an argument here for a mono-linguistic future—that this is our agenda. I don't think anyone here has said that, but that is a perception: an inability to imagine anything else.

____: And it's English-driven. Make no mistake. I'm not accusing you of anything. I received most of my formal education in English, and when I go back to Spanish, I cannot even speak in my own language. I only know it in English.

SLAUGHTER: I'm not arguing that English should be the only language. I'm only arguing that the fact that many different nations can learn English is a good thing. It allows, for instance, a Japanese factory operating in Prague to communicate with Czech workers. Now, the language they're speaking may not sound a lot like what we think of as English, but it's a common language that facilitates communication. It's certainly not the only form of communication. There is a need for multiple languages at the same time. But if everybody simply operates in different languages, there's no communication.

GARDELS: That's precisely why other languages will survive—until experience becomes generic. Then it will be English. And that's another issue.

MILLER: He is suggesting we'll all be dead by then.

____: Another kind of imperialism which I associate with English, is the domination of the business vocabulary in addressing the Internet. If "cultural imperialist" means you look for markets everywhere, if the Internet is seen almost exclusively as a marketplace, and to hear this whole four-day conversation as almost entirely a conversation of business...perhaps what's going on isn't about business at all. Maybe it centers more on words like "community" or notions of the extension of man and the extension of the mind. Confining it to a marketplace conversation, talking about marketplace implications, leaves me feeling so completely unheard and left out—it just took everything I had to stand up and speak.

GAKIO: For me, the key language issue is whether the Internet will provide an opportunity for my language to be heard. But of course, for my language to be heard, I must have somebody to speak to. If I can't identify a person to speak to, my language isn't really going to survive. In fact, a question for me is, if you came from Mars and you visited Earth through the Net today, you would not see my language there. You wouldn't even notice my culture.

I also think that a lot of this discussion about markets and so on is mostly the hype that's driven by meta-corporations that are staking pieces of territory for the future. What we want is for those whose languages can't be heard, to jump in and make an opportunity to do something about it.

AIZU: I agree on one hand that this conference is more or less dominated by business and this marketing terminology, but don't misunderstand. Many activities on the Net now center around community areas or nonprofit, and there are a lot more of these areas than you may think. There was a Community Network Conference that took place two weeks ago in Taos, New Mexico. But there are many activities beyond the market mechanisms, that we sometimes call Intelplace (nothing to do with the Intel Corporation, by the way). People can exchange knowledge or thinking in their own words, or mutual words, even write people living in the other side of the world, at very low or nominal cost. So you don't really have to rely on too much of the existing media or existing structure of the economic framework. So in some of the developing countries, people are now jumping in to use the Net, not only to absorb the knowledge or information from the advanced countries but to share their *own* with others. *That's* the significance of the Net, I think.

MILLER: As the man from Mars, let me offer a couple of observations and see your reaction. In this conference called "Internet and Society":

- Karanja is worried about the fact that the Martian, seeing Earth through the Net, will not see his culture.

- Our friend from the audience is worried that in time the Net will become so dominated by business and marketplace concerns that the coin of the Internet will simply be commerce.

- Jacques is concerned that the French language may not survive.

- Doug speaks about homogenization.

Should we be talking about the Internet and society? Or is it just hopeless even to think we should be talking about Internets and societies, or that the Internet is not the province of business or of English?

ATTALI: I'm sorry. I'm not frightened by the danger of English. I believe, on the contrary, that English will be threatened by the Internet and by the future.

GAKIO: Yes, yes. But the point is the same.

ATTALI: No, it's not the same.

MILLER: The point is well put by these two people, that Karanja's culture may disappear if the world is viewed through an Internet that is monolithic, and that the world, in all its dimensions, becomes weaker if the currency of the Internet is simply marketplace and commerce. The ultimate imperialism is the notion that the Internet should somehow be monolithic.

SLAUGHTER: But I think that misses the point. I'm going to sound like Doug for a minute because I actually think that to talk about Internets and societies misses, indeed denies, what is perhaps the great hope of the Internet. When we think of "Internets" rather than "the Internet," we think of multiple computer networks. This doesn't have nearly the same resonance as the notion of an Internet that represents a united world that celebrates diversity and plurality.

MILLER: But how do you preserve the diversity? When I travel in the United States, I can talk to a Georgian, I can talk to you, I can go to Amish country. I can go to Miami and be in Cuba, in effect. I can go to the Hasidic community in Brooklyn. And somehow, we've preserved the—

RUSHKOFF: But saying that diversity needs to be preserved, diversity needs to be protected, seems to me to assume that there is this one thing that's actually the best or most powerful, and that if we don't contain it, it will rise and just conquer up everything else. The fact is, there is no one thing that's the best, which is why we don't have to worry about preserving things. Things can preserve themselves.

MILLER: That's not what I heard from Anne-Marie. She's worried.

RUSHKOFF: No, she's worried about the way people are talking about the Internet. What happened is, the cart got in front of the horse. People started doing this cyberspace thing and then all these big companies said: "Oh my! Look at all these people doing this! How are we going to make money from that?" And they're trying to get in front of it to make a profit. The fact of the matter is, it's the human will; it's the human hunger for inter-connectedness that is driving the Internet. And a bunch of companies are figuring out ways—or trying to—to put toll booths on that.

SLAUGHTER: Well put. Very well put.

ATTALI: I don't think that's the main point. I think the main question is, will we, through the Inter-net, develop the capacity for creation? The Inter-net for the moment, as far as I know, is just a way of channeling information. I don't know any spe-cific art which has been created for the Internet or in Internet. And I do believe that creation is the core of producing culture and the core of fighting against cultural imperialism. Then the main question is, what will be the political and economic as well as technological means devel-oped to foster creation, artistic and cultural cre-ation, through the Net? Whoever can develop new techniques of creating, or perhaps new works of art, through the Net will be adding something to world diversity. I don't think com-munication is enough. Creation is the core of cul-ture.

RUSHKOFF: This reminds me of a comment (to go back to the market). Edith Croisson who's now the EEC [European Economic Community] Commissioner for Industry, commented that Americans focus on infrastructure when they think about the Net or cyberspace. Europeans focus on content. And it parallels a critique of Jacques de Lore of American society, which is that it's a market society and that's the problem. Everything is subject to the imperatives of the competitive global marketplace. So it's not simply this conference that is overwhelmed by business discussion, it's the U.S. market society.

Now, Europeans are the only ones that talk this way. The Chinese talk nationalism but I've never seen a market society like the Chinese. I mean, it is the most raw market society I have experi-enced in my life. They're going to be throwing the toll booths up there all over the place. And only Jacques Attali and Edith Croisson will be there trying to stop them.

____: I think some sort of imperialism affects the nature of our society itself. But if we just let this technology grow and evolve and develop, and not figure out how we're going to make a buck from it, I think it will be a great enabler and facili-tator of communication.

MILLER: Are you optimistic?

____: Sure. For the people who are worried about different languages...when you go to *AltaVista* and use the search service, we don't search on an English word but on a company name or a person's name. We get references all over the world in English, German, French. So you now have more of an incentive as a student to learn those languages. In the United States we live in a very homogenous linguistic environ-ment. We never learned another language, whereas Europeans have had the advantage of having heard and spoken them all the time. And I think this is likely to help motivate U.S. grade schools and high schools to teach other languages.

SLAUGHTER: Yes. And indeed, our own words can take on multiple meanings through that exact pro-cess. In Prague, "defenestration" means to exit the Windows program.

____: Do you think the Internet itself is one of the most outstanding creative events of our gener-ation?

ATTALI: I don't consider the Internet a work of art. I consider it a tool.

MILLER: But don't you acknowledge its creativity?

ATTALI: No.

MILLER: There are creative tools. The paintbrush is a creative tool.

JACQUES ATTALI: Yes, it is promising, but I don't know if it's a work of art. But it is promising.

____: There is a lot of new media art going on online.

SLAUGHTER: It's also changing the way we think about art and the way we make art. I would disagree with Jacques that it doesn't spawn new forms of creativity.

ATTALI: I didn't say that. I say the influence of the Internet on culture will be mainly through creation *in* the Internet, not by the Internet itself.

SLAUGHTER: No, but I'm answering exactly that point, which is that the Internet—the mode of technology, the decentralization, the multiple perspectives that are possible through the Internet—changes the way we think and the way we create because it really changes the way we visualize things.

MILLER: Is it possible that we will see the Net create its own culture?

ATTALI: I think so. What does "culture" mean? My answer is that the Net will help people go back to nomadism in terms of culture, which is culture of movement, not linked to a territory and to roots but linked mainly to ideas, to virtual tribes. And get rid of fighting for borders, for territory and for identity, which is linked to something concrete, literal, and fight for something which is linked to ideas.

MILLER: Now the questioner, having inserted the knife, twists it a bit and says, Is it possible that the Net, to the extent it does create culture, has moved from barbarism to decadence without passing through civilization? And that the real challenge is, how do you avoid the bankruptcy of the online culture?

RUSHKOFF: The way to avoid it is to contribute to it.

MILLER: The decadence?

RUSHKOFF: No. The way to avoid its being bankrupt is to invest something in it.

ATTALI: More creativity. Usually, a civilization, as far as I know, is created in something like 1000

years, or at least 100 years. I don't know if the Net is in place long enough to say that it has been through all the different stages.

MILLER: Is that a plea for patience?

ATTALI: Well, yes. Certainly, yes.

GARDELS: Four thousand years.

MILLER: Four thousand years ago we did have Socrates and Eschewals and folk like that.

RUSHKOFF: Today they're on the Net.

GARDELS: I think this point about culture is a point I tried to make in the beginning. I think it *is* a nomadic culture. It's a civilization really, not a culture. It's not rooted in place. Salmon Rushdie writes in *Satanic Verses* about the 747, the jumbo jet. All these immigrants are going, leaving their past, going to a new place; everything is thrown up in the air. When you throw everything up in the air, everything gets all mixed up. So what you have is hybrid characters and people with no place. The Net is like that. It's a vast nonplace of migrants of the mind, kind of floating out there. And that's very different than a rooted civilization in a territorial authority. And I think there will be big conflicts, as I said before, between those two, because as we talked about Li Kuan Yu and others, you want to judge what's going on in cyberspace by what rules?

There's the famous story of the guy in Memphis who downloaded pornography from San Francisco and was sued in Memphis, but he couldn't be sued in San Francisco because the laws were different. You're going to see a lot more of that happening, and I think that will shape the culture and the ethos of that civilization.

MILLER: On that note our time's expired.

____: The panel is missing the point.

MILLER: All panels do.

SLAUGHTER: That's a nice way to end.

MILLER: All right. I've got to get back to Mars, where the gene pool is pure. My thanks to the panel.

About the Speakers

ARTHUR R. MILLER is the Bruce Bromley Professor of Law at Harvard Law School, where he has taught since 1971. Among lawyers he is nationally known for his work on court procedure, a subject on which he has authored or co-authored more than 25 books. The general public, however, knows him for his work in the field of the right of privacy. His book *The Assault on Privacy: Computers, Data Banks, and Dossiers* (1971) has been extremely influential. Since July, 1980, Professor Miller has been appearing on ABC's *Good Morning America* as the program's legal editor. He also comments regularly on legal topics for Boston Channel 5's noontime news, and he is the host of the weekly *In Context* program on the Courtroom Television Network.

IZUMI AIZU has a rich experience in inter-cultural communications in the field of international advertising and marketing, public relations, and technical writing. He was one of the founders of Institute for Networking Design, a think-tank for online communications specializing in computer conferencing. He served as secretary general of Networking Forum, an annual conference of PC networking in Japan, and has been member of numerous study groups on computer networks and the Internet. Mr. Aizu is interested in forming global culture through the Net and linking people to people through heart-to-heart communications in cyberspace as well as in the real world.

KARANJA GAKIO, originally from Eldoret, Kenya, is cofounder and Vice President of Technical Operations for Africa Online, Inc. Mr. Gakio also cofounded Karisi Communications, Inc., a company which inaugurated quality electronic mail and web services in Kenya. In 1996, following a merger with an African cellular provider, Karisi Communications was renamed Africa Online, Inc. and acquired a continent-wide mandate. Today, the company is part of Prodigy, Inc., and is the largest Internet service provider in East Africa.

NATHAN GARDELS has been Editor of *New Perspective Quarterly* since it began publishing in 1985 and editor of the Global Viewpoint service of the Los Angeles Times Syndicate since 1989. He has written widely for such American publications as *The Wall Street Journal, Los Angeles Times, New York Times, Washington Post, Harper's, U.S. News & World Report*, and the *New York Review of Books*. He has also written for many foreign publications. From 1983 to 1985, Gardels was Executive Director of the Institute for National Strategy. He has also been a member of the Council on Foreign Relations for many years. From 1979 to 1983, he was key adviser to the Governor of California on economic affairs, with an emphasis on public investment, trade issues, the Pacific Basin, and Mexico.

DOUGLAS RUSHKOFF is an author who moonlights as a social theorist, television producer, journalist, and software developer. He's probably best known for his book, *Cyberia: Life in the Trenches of Hyperspace* (Harper, San Francisco 1994), a celebration and exploration of the original, fledgling cyber and rave communities. His bestseller *Media Virus! Hidden Agendas in Popular Culture* (Ballantine, 1994) is a slightly wily deconstruction of the American mediaspace and the memes passing through it. His latest book, *Playing the Future* (HarperCollins, June 1996) explores the culture of the "screenagers" for their insights on thriving in an increasingly chaotic age.

ANNE-MARIE SLAUGHTER, formerly Anne-Marie Burley, is Professor of Law at Harvard Law School. She has participated in the litigation of a number of international cases, representing countries including Nicaragua, the Philippines, Egypt, and the Marshall Islands. Her teaching and research interests focus on civil procedure, international litigation, and particularly the application of international relations theory to both public and private international law. Many of her writings in this area have focused on the distinctive legal relations among liberal democracies. She is currently working with a group of students at Harvard Law School on establishing Lawyers Without Borders.

XIAOYONG WU is the Assistant CEO of Phoenix Satellite Television Company Ltd. in Hong Kong. He began his career as a journalist when he was assigned to work for Radio Beijing English Service. He subsequently became program producer, reporter, political and diplomatic correspondent, news editor, announcer, talk show host, news director and English Service deputy director at Radio Beijing. On June 4, 1989, as a result of reporting on the massacre of innocent people by martial law troops in Beijing, he was jailed by the Chinese government for 13 months, and was released. Mr. Wu completed the Nieman Journalism program at Harvard University in 1995, when he joined the Phoenix project.

Panel

May 30, 1996

New Organizational Forms

MODERATOR:　　Lynda Applegate
PANELISTS:　　Robert Hiebeler
　　　　　　　　Jack Phillips
　　　　　　　　Jed Smith

APPLEGATE: Good afternoon. The focus of our panel this afternoon is new organizational forms. We're going to be thinking and talking about the impact of the Internet on organizations in the 1990s, looking at the current state, looking toward the future, and basically talking about different issues in that area.

The first panel member is **ROBERT HIEBELER**, who is a senior partner at Arthur Andersen, in charge of their global best practices initiative. In that large, global knowledge-based organization, he's been working with and worrying about how we can use technology to help support the transfer of knowledge, communication, and coordination within a large global firm. Currently they are using CD-ROM and other forms of technology, and are shifting to the use of the Internet. He consults with companies on the use of best practices in process reengineering and in thinking about the issues that companies are now facing.

Our next speaker is **JACK PHILLIPS**. Jack is Vice President of Sales and Marketing of a company called Internet Securities, one of the most exciting Internet entrepreneurial ventures I've heard about. I've been very fascinated by the rise and growth of this firm. Jack's background is in publishing (for McGraw Hill) and the media, both primarily in financial services. He's done a lot of international work and that plays in very well to the kind of Internet venture he's started. He'll be talking about the impact of technology in organiza-

tions as a channel for distributing products and services, and some of the information arbitrage opportunities.

JED SMITH, our last panel member, has founded another fascinating entrepreneurial venture that's a little different than Jack's, but is moving in somewhat the same area. Jed was the co-founder of Cybersmith Café here in Harvard Square and has opened two new locations this past year in White Plains [NY] and in Quincy Market. Jed will talk about the impact of the Internet as a method of delivering products and services, as well as a method for coordinating and communicating within a very rapidly growing organization.

Before we get started, I'd like to spend a few minutes teeing up some of the ideas we'll be talking about. The focus of my work at Harvard Business School has been in the area of general management, working with companies and doing research on the impact of technology on organizations and the restructuring of organizations in the 1990s. I've actually been working with some companies for over ten years, looking at the kinds of changes they're trying to go through.

You've all heard about it: downsizing, delayering, teams, trying to push decision authority, empowerment (the "e" word), and so on. I hear a very consistent message from both large and small companies as they think about the organization they're trying to create in the'90s. What they say to me, in the words of Jack Welch and GE (a company I've been working with for a number of years), is, "I'm trying to create a company that has all the power, resources, and reach of a large firm with the hunger, the agility, the spirit, and the fire of a small one."

Is there a way to define a new kind of organization that somehow brings together the benefits of "the body of a big company with the soul of a small one"? Our three panelists are basically going to talk about that, about the need to have both global scope and scale. Small companies are growing extremely rapidly and are trying to integrate far-flung operations to achieve a common look and feel, a common organizational design. And large firms, like Arthur Andersen, are trying to somehow coordinate and manage all of the initiatives and the knowledge and the expertise of a far-flung series of consultants located all over the globe. Can we somehow bring those together?

We don't have any good traditional organizational design theory that tells us about this. We've heard about matrices and *ad hoc* processes in different kinds of organizations from the '60s and '70s, but we always heard that trying to do that caused a tremendous amount of confusion, a tremendous amount of cost, duplication, and difficulty in coordinating these different kinds of resources. So the model itself was not stable, was not a model companies could move toward very easily. So the question becomes, what's different in the '90s? What makes us think that we can do this now when we couldn't do it before?

Enter information technology. What's interesting here is that the information infrastructure of the firm—the information and communication infrastructure, the technology platform that delivers it, the challenges of managing the information—has paralleled the challenges of trying to manage the organizational form itself. Organizations are information processing systems. In the past, what kept companies from being able to get to that quadrant, to form that question mark in an efficient and productive way, is that they did not have the information processing capacity, the ability to coordinate and integrate vertically and laterally, to make those models work effectively in a large firm that was also trying to operate quickly and dynamically.

So what we're seeing is the progression of information technology infrastructure from the hierarchies of the '60s, which were ideally suited to the hierarchical organizations of the day, to the entrepreneurial-style local area networks which are ideally suited to small scale rapid response and transfer of information, to the more distributed information infrastructures we have today. Client/server and now Internet-based, global, ubiquitous platforms are, for the first time in history, beginning to provide the capabilities for information processing to match the organization's requirements for that information.

Today we're seeing firms that, for the first time, are beginning to satisfy the information processing requirements. What's interesting is that in the '60s we had people trying to create those organizational models, matrices, "ad hocracies," etc., but the need to do so was limited to some very specialized industries. You saw the aerospace industry, some of the computer industry, some of the other kinds of industries where you might find people struggling with the model, but it wasn't widespread.

What I find more interesting today is the confluence of the capabilities for processing information coming together with the demand for being able to solve these organizational initiatives, so that more and more industries, more and more companies, can increase their ability to comprehend, assess, and process information. But for many industries, many companies, the cat is in the maze—they are struggling very hard to work out the details and to find ways to harness the power of the information platform to be able to satisfy the informational demands of their organizational model.

Our panelists will take it from here and talk about how their firms are attempting to bring together organizational and informational kinds of activities to satisfy the challenges that they face.

HIEBELER: Thank you, Lynda. I hadn't heard Jack Welch's comments about taking advantage of the strength and resources of a large company, and yet achieve the hunger, spirit, and fire of a small company. I will talk about how we, as a large organization, are trying to have the soul of a small company, the kind that Jack Welch is talking about.

I'll first set this up by describing our organizational structure. Think of Arthur Andersen in terms of two major business units. We have Arthur Andersen as a business unit, primarily accounting, audit, tax, and certain business consulting services for our clients. And we have Andersen Consulting, which deals with information systems and systems integration consulting on a worldwide basis. In total, we're about $8.5 billion in revenue, with 80,000 professionals located in over 360 offices worldwide. We have a vast network of people who are working with clients on a daily basis.

I'd like to talk about three facts I think you need to keep in your mind as you think about our large organization.

1. We are organized in engagement teams that provide services to clients at the client location. Many times, these teams will change as frequently as weekly, or it may be the same team for over three years. So we are organized by teams.

2. Most of the knowledge and expertise in our organization is in the heads of our partners and managers dispersed around the world.

3. The average age of our 80,000 professionals is 26.

So if you think of these three facts, you can appreciate the need to leverage knowledge down to our young professionals dispersed all over the world, organized in teams. This is the basic model that we have as an organization, both with Arthur Andersen and Andersen Consulting.

My comments come from a perspective as partner in charge of Global Best Practices within the Arthur Andersen business unit. I also serve as the Chairman of our Knowledge Strategy Team, a team of partners and managers in Arthur Andersen that focuses on using knowledge for a competitive advantage, using technology to enable the knowledge-sharing processes. If you think of the whole knowledge era imperative, you must think of the discrete elements of process, people, technology, leadership, and how they must work together to leverage knowledge.

I want to cover these points in my remarks:

• What Global Best Practices is all about.

• Some of our knowledge-sharing systems within Arthur Andersen.

• Our Internet strategies.

• How this impacts our organizational structure.

Global Best Practices

Global Best Practices is a worldwide initiative that started about four years ago and is designed to capture best practices information about how key business processes are performed around the world, and to share that information with our 45,000 professionals within Arthur Andersen. The whole process of working with process experts from around the world, as well as packaging best practices information, has been a dynamic learning experience over the last four years, and we've developed a proprietary knowledge base in the process.

We obtain best practices information from many sources: we do secondary research, we tap into our process experts, we do benchmarking studies, etc. When I talk about processes, I'm talking about finance processes, customer service processes, supply chain management processes—basic business processes. We've taken a strong "process view," without regard to industry, to obtain the most creativity. Over the last four years, we have tapped into 500 or 600 process experts, focused on about 70 business processes, and have created a knowledge base on CD-ROM of about 20,000 pages of material.

So it's been a very divergent and convergent process of searching out what's out there in best practices, capturing it, bringing it in, and putting it on CD-ROM. Best Practices, in essence, describes the best way to execute a business process. The "best companies" information is really case studies; stories about how companies achieved excellence: engagement experience, studies, articles, and the other information listed support best practices by process. These are the packaged knowledge objects we've captured through a process of working with people around the world.

Knowledge-Sharing Systems

I would call Global Practices an example of a "packaged knowledge" system. I want to talk about packaged knowledge, and the interplay of packaged knowledge versus communication networks. Figure 1 shows the different kinds of knowledge systems that we have in Arthur Andersen. On the left is what we call packaged knowledge. I consider Global Best Practices to be an example of 20,000 pages of packaged knowledge, put on a CD-ROM, and made available to anyone around the world. So it's knowledge that people can "tap into."

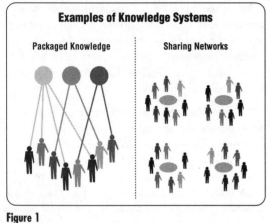

Examples of Knowledge Systems

Packaged Knowledge   Sharing Networks

Figure 1

We also have service line packaged knowledge, such as a Consultant's Advisor for our business consultants and something called the Audit Resource and Reference Disk (ARRD). The ARRD disc has all of our reference material for the audit practice on a 125,000 page CD-ROM that people can tap into to get the latest accounting pronouncements from the FASB, the SEC, and so forth. So these are three examples of packaged knowledge. In packaged knowledge systems, we've gone through a rigorous process of capturing and codifying knowledge for the firm. And while the content is from all over the world, it is packaged and made available centrally.

The other kind of knowledge systems you see in Figure 1 that we have are sharing networks. What I show on the right of this figure is a group of "communities of practice." We have something called "AA Online," which is a Lotus Notes–based system (like an intranet within Lotus Notes), which is organized around communities of practice. "Communities of practice" are groups of professionals who are experiencing the same issues, processes, skills, etc. For example,

each professional may participate in several communities of practice. He/she may be an auditor in the telecommunications industry. Therefore, he/she might participate in the worldwide audit community network and the worldwide telecommunications network. This figure depicts four communities of practic; there are about 50 of them in our system in Lotus Notes worldwide. We also have various industry team communities as formal communities of practice.

Our professionals use these virtual electronic communities to share ideas, and to communicate, around issues facing people doing like-tasks in the community. The way that we have woven these systems together, I think, gets to the issue of how different packaged knowledge systems and how different divergent knowledge sharing networks can work together by community.

On top of each of these sharing network systems are Knowledge Managers. There is usually one Knowledge Manager for each community, worldwide. Their key role is to "monitor the traffic" on these sharing networks as well as discerning and anticipating trends, and more importantly, packaging information that has great leveragable value and sending it over to various packaged knowledge systems.

We operate using both packaged knowledge and these sharing networks, with a network of knowledge managers monitoring them, packaging up information that has value. I believe that you need to have both kinds of knowledge systems in place to take advantage of the learning that happens in communities, as well as the high value of packaging information.

In terms of Internet strategies, we started off with our Arthur Andersen home page [*http://www.arthur.andersen.com*]. In fact, everything at Arthur Andersen goes through this single home page. It's designed to be, in essence, our worldwide "storefront." Our home page consists of about 2,000 pages and provides information about who we are and what we do. It is our "stake in the ground" for expansion to other Internet strategies.

Now we have a number of strategies going forward. We will publish information that we think adds value to broad communities. We will provide an interactive experience to our visitors through our diagnostic assessment tools. We will engage people in dialogue on key issues, and allow that to be directed to, and have conversation with, leaders who are process experts from around the world.

Some of our other guiding principles and strategies include how to evoke a positive experience by visiting our site, getting a sense of who we are, what kinds of issues that we're talking about, etc. We've already gone through a process through Global Best Practices, of identifying process experts around the world. This has allowed us to position them to leverage their knowledge, not only within our organization, but in the public as well.

Right now we're researching extending our home page and our Internet activities in order to identify people who have needs, and hook them up with people within the firm who can help them. We are also focusing on leading issues of the day, describing some of the best practices, and helping people get energized to move towards those best practices.

One of the things that's key to the Internet experience is understanding the way that people become engaged in the medium. Figure 2 shows the steps of engagement: initial awareness, education, diagnostic, assessment, implementing and achieving change. In our firm, as we talk to clients, we are delivering professional services that help an organization change. But with the capabilities of technology and using the Internet, we have new opportunities to realize these goals by delivering "learning products."

If you think about delivering learning products as pre-conditioning someone for change, using diagnostic tools is all about getting them engaged in change. The purpose of a diagnostic tool is to disturb you! But disturb in a *positive way*. To get you energized for change—to be dissatisfied with the current condition—to seek a better solution.

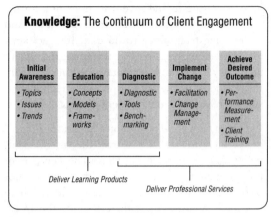

Figure 2

So, in summary, we have opportunities in the new Internet to do some of things in the early awareness stages of identifying leading topics, providing education and frameworks on these topics, and then providing diagnostic tools to engage people in change. In fact, our diagnostic tools are some of our most active web pages.

We believe the impact of the Internet on our organization is large, and it's going to get larger. The Internet will allow us to bring people together, not only connecting our people internally, but also connecting us with our clients. This is a huge advantage because we have so many clients and they have many different technology platforms. The Internet will allow us to connect our experts with their clients' questions. We are very excited about these opportunities. Thank you very much.

PHILLIPS: Bob [Hiebeler] started out by saying they're an $8.5 billion company. Big, trying to look small. That's a problem I would love to have. We, on the other hand employ 60 people, we're two years old, and we have under $1 million of revenue. Let me take a minute, not to sell our company, but to tell you a little about what we're trying to do.

We're in the aggregation and information arbitrage business. We cover emerging financial markets around the world, such as Russia, China, Poland, and Hungary. All we're really trying to do is take this kind of information from over here, aggregate it, and give it to users in a format they can use over here on their desktop. And we're using technology to do that. It's very simple. The arbitrage comes in the sense that we're taking what we think is undervalued information, we're adding something to it with technology, and we're selling it on a subscriber basis.

Our company is called Internet Securities [*http://www.securities.com/*]. We're over the Internet, but we're also on a direct-dial basis. The key part of our business is not advertising-driven (we're not Yahoo!); we are a pure content provider. There is a lot of confusion out there because the Internet is thought of as a consumer medium. But we're a business-to-business, frankly an intranet service. We provide information which we've taken a lot of time to gather and aggregate, and we sell it to a high-level business user who appreciates getting frontline information—getting publications that many of you probably haven't even heard of—from China and Russia.

Our users want the frontline information, and they pay a lot for it. So delivery is our business. Aggregation is our business and technology enables us to do that very well.

What does the Internet enable us to do on the product development side? I think that's probably most important for us. Imagine us, we have offices in about eight different markets and we have a technical hub in Pittsburgh, Pennsylvania. We're collecting data in places like Warsaw. On the Internet we're able to effectively, simultaneously, create a product that we're selling to users in New York and back in Warsaw. This is a product of business information, this is company information, this is news, this is macroeconomic information, but it's all in one place. So people in Warsaw are saying, "I'd rather look at your aggregated product than walk to the corner newsstand and buy all the publications." For those local markets, that's brand new. For the Western markets, getting all of this without having to use this kind of company is very simple but it is ground-breaking. People are going crazy for it.

So the technology is our product. The technology enables us to deliver our product. Today you see a lot of products in development that start from within a company. We started with the Internet as our product when we decided to get into the content business. Then we moved backwards and created some internal distribution products that have worked very well.. But my message today is the product that we sell isn't the technology. We're publishers.

Organizationally, we're no different than what I think *Business Week* does everyday. They gather data and they deliver it to you in paper form. We deliver it in a much faster and (we think) in a much more concise form. That's all we really do. When a client sees this product, they love it and they say, "Wow! You've got all these great tools: I can cut and paste this information, I can save it to my hard drive, and I can do all these great things with technology. I can get it over the Internet and I'll pay you a nominal fee for it!" But ultimately the technology is not a panacea; it's not as much of a hype as it seems out there. Now of course we put the word "Internet" in our name because there is a hype. But at the end of the day, customers still demand the beef, they demand what's important.

It's important to think about what technology does inside our business as it aids our product. Again I come back to *Business Week* or any traditional publisher. They've got two sides of their business: the editorial side—gathering a lot of information from far flung markets—then they have a sales side. We're no different. Our editorial staff is all over the world. But the way we use the intranet and intranet technology as a way to communicate is really important for us.

I have a group in Warsaw that's gathering data and throwing it onto our product, which people in New York and Warsaw see. Our ability to communicate quickly, by email or by our Y-talk system enables that. But can we do away with face-to-face meetings? Have we done away with client visits? No. So internally, technology is important. But again, it doesn't solve all our problems. We still get all of our country leaders together and we talk to them and we find out about the major issues.

I suppose that's a pretty standard conclusion. I think Lynda [Applegate] started out by saying we were a great Internet entrepreneurial company. I think we are, but we're still publishers. And we can't get ahead of ourselves with the technology.

The most important question for me is this: are we going to be able, in this environment, to defend our position as a intermediary between content providers and people who desire that content? I think that we will continue to use the technology to our advantage to deliver our products over the Internet or through direct dial, and that will help us internally. But I think that the environment is moving so quickly that unless we just basically beat our competition, in our case, to better data sources, higher quality data sources, we're not going to win. Our competitors will beat us if we don't get the raw materials.

It's not the actual computer or the wires behind it, but it's the people that make it all significant.

A lot of people ask us if this virtual corporation is working. "Is it really working for you? Are you able to be completely without phone, without visits? Can you create a product? Can you sell it?" Sure, maybe one out of ten customers comes to us over the Internet and we never talk to them. They call us and say, "We like your product, we want to know more about Russia, we want to know more about Poland, we want to know more about the Czech Republic." And we can do it entirely without talking. But that's one out of ten.

Lynda started out by talking about high tech, high touch. We are low touch. We have to still touch our customer. I'll end with an email that I got this morning, actually I guess it was yesterday afternoon, from our management team. It referred to the biggest question that's facing our team now: which city are we going to choose for the management team to meet in? So even though we're 60 people in 27 markets and we're just going great, we all say we need to be together. Thanks.

SMITH: I'm Jed Smith and I hope Cybersmith [*http://www.cybersmith.com/*] is a name you know. Our first café/technology arcade is across the yard, in Harvard Square.

As you've heard in the past few days, "This is a big paradigm shift—a revolution!" that's going on here. This is exciting, and it's changing the way we've worked. It's changing the way we communicate. It's changing the way we organize. I want to bring the discussion back a little bit, and talk about how this shift changes the organizational structure within Cybersmith—bring it back to the desktop, bring it back to people who are really behind all of these machines.

I guess if I had a philosophical view, of which you've heard many in the last few days, it is this: the computer has changed from this ugly box that just sits on your desktop—it calculates for you, automates your tasks, it's a tool—to part of the new communities that are forming. There are people behind those machines and it's the people that make it important. It's not the actual computer or the wires behind it, but it's the people that make it all significant.

Cybersmith is based on that concept. There's a quote from Lao Tzu that I always go back to.

I hear and I forget. I see, I remember. I do and I understand.

Cybersmith is about doing. Cybersmith is a retail location with 45 computer stations. The general concept is that people feel left out. Though they hear about it—there are talking heads like myself and articles written about it constantly—the general public is left out of the new technology. But what better way to understand new technologies than to do, than to try it out, firsthand. We've created locations, retail stores (the first one was in Harvard Square as Lynda mentioned), where people can try out the latest advances in information technology, experience them, hands-on, and then bring it home, if they wish.

In polling the world for which technologies had hit a critical mass, we chose virtual reality, the World Wide Web or Internet stations, consumer online services, CD-ROM and multimedia software, and games systems. These are the different pieces of the puzzle that we have viewed that make up technology as it's hitting the home at this point. And we're showing them off in one store, in one location where people can try them out. I expect that these technologies will merge. The three-dimensional capabilities of virtual reality, the connecting and networking capabilities of the Internet, the multimedia capabilities of CD-ROM, and the graphical capabilities of some of the games systems, which are leading the way in graphics right now, will merge over the next five to ten years.

That's exciting for me, although it's a little bit scary. Cybersmith will be a very different location in five to ten years. We always need to change, we need to learn, uncover new technologies, and bring them in. That is exciting and scary.

Just a little pitch about who's behind Cybersmith. We have Nicholas Negroponte, who is an investor; Michael Porter, from Harvard Business School; and George Soros. We have some retail entrepreneurs: Ray Ozzie of Lotus Notes and Jeff Parker (who's also an investor in Internet Securities). We have a great team and we're poised for our national rollout at this point. We're opening up five stores this year. In addition to the ones in Boston and New York, we're opening in Seattle, San Francisco, L.A., Chicago.

The niche I see Cybersmith providing is an interim step in this move from the marketplace to the marketspace. As John Sviokla and Jeffrey Rayport have been talking about at Harvard Business School,[*] there's a shift in commerce from the bricks and mortar of store to Internet commerce that we're seeing emerge across the country—the old model being the consumer going through a distributor or a retailer, and the distributor or

retailer purchasing from a manufacturer. Clearly, there's a new model emerging, where customers are going directly to the manufacturer; and that is one of the most obvious and new applications of the Internet: cutting out the middle-man, cutting out the interim step.

I see Cybersmith as a step in that direction. What we are doing is providing a learning curve, an educational component for the general public to try new technology, to experience it and learn about it, and then purchase it either through the Internet at our store—which we would call a thousand stores within a store—or from their home and on their desktops. But what better way than to see it hands-on, rather than having to go out and buy your $3,000 computer or application from CompUSA without trying it first.

What has turned out, which was a bit of a surprise for me, is that we have been developing very strong technology alliances. Technology companies see Cybersmith as a unique way to market and showcase their product. Rather than a magazine ad or a direct marketing piece, MCI sees our 10,000 customers a month as a perfect avenue for them to show off their Internet access capabilities. Compaq has donated all of the computers for the next eight stores we are opening in exchange for that exposure and advertising. The same with Digital, Marathon Line. And my impression is that will be a growing part of our business model.

Within Cybersmith, we're using some pretty interesting technology tools and Internet-related, organizational, informational sharing structures. We have a digital cash system. Each customer that comes in gets a cybercard. They pay cash, $10 or $20, for that card and when they swipe it through the card reader, it gives them access to the computers and to the experiences in our stores. What is interesting is that we are then able to track that demographic data to understand which web sites they're hitting, which CD-

---

[*] John Sviokla moderated the session "The New Economics: How Will Business Be Created and Extracted." Jeffrey Rayport moderated the sessions "Community and Market Formation: Where Will Business Occur," and "Institutional Structure for the Internet: Who Will Control It."

ROMs they're trying, what experiences they're seek. So we have full utilization information in our stores so we know which ones to change.

We also have tremendous demographic information that, at this point, is very difficult to get over the Internet. People are not willing to give their name and address and full information over the Internet. I guess the anonymity is part of the excitement at this point.

I would call the second application that we have an intranet. We're using Netscape as our POS system. People swipe their cybercard in when they log in, and it's one of the first, if not *the* first, retail companies in the country to use the Internet to track this data. Therefore, we do not need to worry about platform-specific issues (whether it's in Macintosh or a Pentium-based or a Sun computer), we can port that over with our Internet application and bring it easily to the home office.

Finally, when I first thought about organizational structures and what this panel would be talking about, what first came to my mind were virtual offices and virtual companies and outsourcing. For Cybersmith, that's really not for us. I'm a believer, as our stores represent, that people are what make it happen. We're trying to bring the physical community back together rather than just you in your basement or on your desktop in this new virtual community and chat room. We're bringing the people in the physical community back together.

I think that's true in our corporate offices as well; if we were to distribute our marketing capabilities in San Francisco and our technology team in Boston and our operations team in New York, we would not be a functional organization. Especially in a company our size. For us to compete, we need the teams, we need the presence of our organization in person and together. That's something I believe strongly at this point. It also relates to outsourcing, which is an important thing for larger corporations, as you've heard from General Motors and General Electric. But for a small, emerging, growing company, that's something

that is not appropriate for us at this point. Thank you very much.

Questions & Answers

Q: *Two days ago Bill Gates said that part of the problem with achieving virtual communities, virtual office, virtual work kinds of design is that the technologies are not quite there yet to achieve that virtual kind of presence. The ability to do the very high level multimedia and high touch kinds of communication over the Internet or over networks right now is limited. For those who thought that it was not possible to achieve virtual organizations at the present time, is that due to the limitation of the technology or is it due to some other factor that hasn't been discussed?*

SMITH: I guess my quick impression is that there are technology applications that are available right now that can do it. There's tremendous video conferencing coming out of Intel and Picturtel. And there's also CU-SeeMe video conferencing on the Internet, which is somewhat available and will be less expensive as it moves on. That's a valuable tool that will help people and organizations communicating on a certain level. But there's nothing better, nothing more worthwhile than bumping into someone in the hall, exchanging a thought, taking it a step further—impromptu meetings that are less formal and structured, but that just happen in a normal work business environment. In my mind, the technology it will get better, but there's nothing better than saying, "Hey, what do you think?"

PHILLIPS: Jed commented on the sort of employee-to-employee talking. We also think about it from us to the customer. And I think the customers also want to be able to pick up the phone or even have an office visit and say, "I can't change the color on my screen. I know you provide content, but help me with something very basic." I don't know—if they can't even do that, videoconferencing might be in the future at some point.

HIEBELER: Speaking from a large organization, it's hard to have people bumping into each other in the hall, so we try to achieve that experience electronically. I agree with Bill Gates' comment on being able to "replicate the feeling" of being able to bump into somebody. We have had good experiences with Lotus Notes but it's limited in its benefits. It's good for posing a question, or for moving packaged knowledge around, it's good for leveraging packaged knowledge, but it's not good for packaging the kind of experience that you're talking about. So until we achieve that experience, which we can't totally do, that is going to be a challenge, certainly for us.

We try to structure our "get together" social sessions. For example, we use our St. Charles learning center as a place to get to know fellow professionals and have deeper dialogue. In essence, have the social contact that can't occur electronically.

A quick, additional comment is that there's a lot of fear in the general public that technology and computers are replacing books, teachers, libraries, and people. I disagree with that completely and I think many of us here do. I see technology as *enhancing* the teacher's capability for teaching, enhancing the value and learning that you get from a book, and enhancing what you get from a library. It's the same in virtual offices and virtual corporations. The computer can enhance an organizational structure, but I hope it will not replace the actual physical interaction that goes on.

APPLEGATE: Several years ago, I was involved in a fairly extensive research project that looked at the impact of technology on group communication and group process. We looked at both group communication and coordination across networks, and some of the technologies that are now being developed within electronic meeting room kinds of environments, to see what impact the technology would have on face-to-face group communication.

But at that time, one of the more interesting findings was that technology tends to enhance a process. So if you automate or you add technology to a bad process, the process gets worse. Technology really needs to be looked within the total kind of group dynamics, group process, group structure, and you have to think more clearly about the interaction of the technology on that process as you move forward.

Second, as technology enhanced the amount of information available, whether textual information, data, or graphics, the possibility for information overloading increased simultaneously. I found it interesting that the information overload tended to be an important phase in learning how to use that information to make decisions: over time, in the process of experiencing overload, decision makers would get together, make sense of the information, imbue more meaning into it, imbue more structure, and ultimately would learn more about the activities, the decisions, etc.

I think the same things will happen as we move to richer kinds of communication media. There will be the need to learn how to use that technology to support processes, and we'll have to really think about changing processes and communication and coordination as we integrate the kind of technologies we're putting in place.

You can't just flop it down and expect that people will all of a sudden form a community. But I do also agree that we're moving. As the technology gets richer, people are learning more and more to communicate across networks. We just have to continue research in kinds of practice in this area to make it better.

Q: *How do [the people at Cybersmith] help people off the street? What tools and techniques do they use?*

SMITH: By now you can probably predict my answer. We use people to do that. They're called "technosmiths." We've set up two things. First, we have a team of technosmiths that can help guide anyone that comes in off the street. Their mission is to make your experience as easy and accessible as possible. Second, we've created interfaces for accessing different technologies that are as easy as possible. Point and click. You don't have to load the software, you don't have to deal with the hard drive and memory issues, you don't have to deal with anything. We're showcasing the end experience, we're showcasing the potential, we're showcasing what will happen as opposed to all the aggravation that may be involved in the setting up process that most of us experience.

Q: *Reengineering has had a tremendous impact on some organizations. As businesses adopt process-oriented models which change the relationship between managers and staff, could you comment on the development of competency groups or communities of practice models that are emerging, specifically around terms of performance measures, HR, etc.?*

HIEBELER: I think the two words I picked up on here are "competency groups" and "communities of practice" and I think they're both evolving. In Arthur Andersen we see that individuals have competencies in different areas of expertise. And so competency groups, whether they are finance organization or business risk or performance measures or basic content, provide a power that you can tap into.

Communities of practice is a larger arena. You have a local "community of practice" of people that are in the same environment that you're in in terms of geographic location. You have industry communities, people that have the common community of industry issues and concerns. Then service line communities. For example, doing an audit, doing tax work, doing consulting. People that have the same kinds of experiences when they get up and go to work everyday. So the aspect of "communities of practice" is very important and developing systems that support that activity.

Q: *Arthur Andersen is sponsoring a K–12 school: how does that fit in with the kinds of things that we've talked about today?*

HIEBELER: It does fit in strategically with the issue of developing *capability*. If you talk about what this is all about, especially the knowledge economy, it's really to develop an individual's capability. So it's kind of extending that basic strategy to the educational process. How we develop people's capability, looking at experimental ways of understanding how people learn, how they relate in a community, from the social aspect, and how they develop their personalities, and also how they develop a rich learning process. They're focusing on developing outstanding learning capabilities as opposed to the content of what they're learning. If we want to develop those capabilities, we've got to go to the educational system in the beginning, because that's where it's all going to be developing.

Q: *Is Cybersmith making any money or does it operate more like a foundation?*

SMITH: Luckily, we do have to develop the technology, we do not pull together the content. We can rely on the brilliance of the incredible amount of money that's being invested by venture capital companies into high tech companies around the country. We just put together what other people have invested in and showcase them. The business model that we have and the reason why we are making a lot of money is that we're selling time and time is not very expensive. When you have computers donated by Compaq and phone lines donated by MCI, our cost of goods sold are extremely low and our profit margins are incredibly high. So yes, the rollout is not a virtual rollout, it's real.

APPLEGATE: A famous author, philosopher once said, "What's past is prologue." And we've had, over the number of years now, been developing and evolving our concepts of information.

One of the things though that I've been struck by as I've worked with a number of different types of organizations is that as we moved into the future, we are not abandoning what we've learned in the past. And in fact, it's very important to recognize that we are building off of all of the knowledge that we gained about organizations, about communities, about the way we manage an organization, about the way we structure an organization, about the way we define the authority levels in organizations, about the way we coordinate and communicate. And the information technology has always been a tremendous support to being able to develop these systems, these organizations, the communication systems, etc. But they have never supplanted the systems, the processes, and the people that all come together to create what we call an organization.

About the Speakers

LYNDA M. APPLEGATE is an MBA Cohort Chair and a Professor at the Harvard Business School, teaching courses in general management, management information systems, and organization design. Dr. Applegate's research and recent publications focus on the role of information technology in transforming market structures and the organizations that compete within them. Recent articles on this topic have been published in *Harvard Business Review*, *Management Information Systems Quarterly*, *Journal of Organizational Computing*, and *Journal of Operations Research*. She is the author of a custom-published book, *Managing in an Information Age*.

ROBERT J. HIEBELER is partner-in-charge of Arthur Andersen's Global Best Practices Initiative, which seeks to capture best practices information from around the world in selected business processes. He is a recognized expert in benchmarking and best practices and has specialized expertise in financial processes. Mr. Hiebeler recently completed a three-part video series with Harvard Business School of Management Productions on "Outside-the-Box" benchmarking for process improvement, and has written numerous articles on benchmarking and best practices for publications such as the *New York Times*, *CFO Magazine*, *Industry Week*, and *Management Review*.

JACK PHILLIPS now serves as Vice President of Product Marketing for Internet Securities, Inc. Mr. Phillips joined ISI after holding positions in information publishing at McGraw-Hill. Before finishing a graduate degree at the Harvard Business School, Mr. Phillips pursued a career in Investment Banking, initially at Morgan Stanley, then later with the Long-Term Credit Bank of Japan in Tokyo.

JED SMITH is co-founder and Senior Vice President of Cybersmith, a retail chain showing off the latest advances in information technology, based in Cambridge, MA. Cybersmith has been featured in the *New York Times*, *Newsweek*, *USA TODAY*, and the front page of the *Boston Globe*. At Cybersmith Jed has negotiated strategic partnerships with Compaq, Oracle, Digital Equipment Corporation, Microsoft, and Bolt, Beranek & Newman. Jed serves on the Board of Directors of the Cambridge Center for Adult Education. He is also working closely with professors at MIT to help integrate new technologies into the educational system.

Panel

May 31, 1996

Wrap-Up Session

MODERATOR: Mark F. Bregman
PANELISTS: Lewis Branscomb
                   Arthur Miller
                   Paul Severino

BREGMAN: I found this conference fascinating and I think probably every one of us has learned something here. We have a very tough task in this last panel, which is to pull together, synthesize, and leave you with some of the key issues from this conference. I'd like to introduce our illustrious panel. **PAUL SEVERINO** is the founder and Chairman of Bay Networks. Bay Networks was formed from the merger of Synoptics Communications and Wellfleet Communications in 1984 and is the world leader in the Internetworking market, particularly in building the infrastructure for the Internet. He also is distinguished and represented on this panel because he was the co-founder of a company called Inter-LAN, the first company to bring to market some of the Ethernet adapters for mini- and microcomputers. So he's been with LANs and the Internet from the very early days.

LEWIS BRANSCOMB, who has been up here before,[*] is the Inda Professor of Public Policy and Corporate Management as well Director of the Science, Technology, and Public Policy Program at the Kennedy School. He holds a Ph.D. in physics from Harvard. My experience with Professor Branscomb goes back to IBM, where from 1972 to 1986 he was Vice President and Chief Scientist. I first interacted with him when I came to IBM in 1984. He's been involved as an advisor to the government in scientific policy for many years and has a broad background in this area.

Our third panel member is Professor **ARTHUR MILLER**, Bruce Bromley Professor of Law at the Harvard Law School, where he's taught since 1971. He has a law degree from Harvard and is known among the law community for his work on court procedure (although I don't expect most of the nonlegal community to recognize him for that). What he *is* known for and what uniquely qualifies him here is that he has done a lot of work in the area of the right to privacy, particularly how it interacts with some of the new information technologies, including the Internet.

So I'll ask each of our panelists to give us their view of what all of this means. Paul?

SEVERINO: Thank you. One thing I'll say is that, having been involved in this industry since 1981, this is the most unique panel I've ever seen.

I'm coming at this from the view of a company that sees an opportunity to make profits. And although profit-making is not the most popular agenda item here today, I think it's an important one. What's happened on the Net up until now, and its future direction, is wrapped up in companies that are providing technology, products, services, networks, or network services to the customer.

When we started in this business neither my friend Bob Metcalf, who was my competitor back then, nor I imagined that in 15 or so years, this would be a technology and a paradigm that would literally change the concept of how we communicate in the world environment. We were doing some pretty basic things, making high–speed connections between computers. And I thank Bob every day for inventing the Ethernet. It certainly has given us all a great opportunity to play in this business. But we were doing some very basic things.

What grew out of that was a paradigm shift in how all of us think about how we're going to communicate, live our lives, and get information in the future. And this is having a tremendous

---

[*] Lewis Branscomb moderated the session "The Place of the Internet in National and Global Information Infrastructure."

effect on the companies who are primarily in this industry.

You can break those companies into three areas:

- Companies like mine that provide equipment that is utilized in the Internet.

- Those that provide communications services: companies like UUNET, PSINet, AT&T, MCI, Sprint, British Telecom.

- Those who provide content.

If you look at those three sets of industries, those three separate areas, what's happening is a massive consolidation, a massive change in their structure, based primarily on this paradigm shift. In the equipment supplier industry, before this paradigm shift, most of us interested in starting data communications companies thought we were hugely successful to build a $100 million business that had maybe a $300–$400 million market cap.

In today's world, my company, Bay Networks, is well on the way in this fiscal year to achieving revenues of over $2 billion, with an $8 billion market cap. And one of our competitors, a very big player in the Internet infrastructure, has about a $28 billion market cap. That's allowed us to think seriously about where we want to be a few years from now, given this paradigm shift. It has allowed us to take that market cap and invest it into technologies and companies to build these mega-companies that will provide a lot of the capability and services across the board—not only to the Internet community but to corporations who are building what you've heard around here as the intranet. The corporations that are building the intranet have been doing it for a while. It just got a new name primarily because of Web technology. But before the Internet really exploded, our business primarily sold to corporations, building their own (what we used to call) "enterprise" networks.

So there is a tremendous consolidation of bigger companies buying smaller companies. There's consolidation of bigger companies merging to get mass or to get channel or to get customer service capabilities. And now there's the concept of smaller companies merging to catch up to the bigger companies. Wall Street loves it. The venture capitalists love it. It's really starting to happen in a big way.

If you look at communications services, the environment there is going to be even more dynamic over the next few years. The telephone companies, the cable companies, are all going to compete with each other, they're all in each other's businesses. No one wants to let go of any of the areas. And on the content side you see exactly the same thing: Disney, Time Warner, buying up other content providers.

One of the interesting factors is that all of the innovation and technology—this whole Internet environment—has been built by entrepreneurial companies, entrepreneurial people. And suddenly, in order to move this forward, we're trying to build these big companies. I think that's going to be a really tough issue, because it deeply affects how we proceed to innovate. Wall Street is basically telling us to keep growing at 10 or 15 percent per quarter. And when you get up to these levels, that becomes difficult to do. And if you don't grow at 10 or 15 percent per quarter, your market caps go down by a factor of 40 or 50 percent. That affects your ability to compete and buy companies. So I think it's going to be an interesting business development.

At the same time, you've got the Internet infrastructure that's under tremendous pressure to change and continue to grow. Primarily because there are more users going on the Net, Web growth is just incredible, and new multimedia applications are going to start hitting the Net.

A friend of mine is starting a company to do what he calls "Netphone." We're starting to look at Web pages with multimedia clips in them. We're going to see video clips coming over the Net very, very shortly. All of that is driving the need for a lot more bandwidth in the backbone of the Net, and a concept that doesn't exist today in the Internet, is called quality of service. If I expect to put video on this network or plan to have a videoconference from one end to the other or put voice on this network, I have to guarantee a certain level of bandwidth across my connections. If I don't get that, you won't be very satisfied with the quality of video. None of those issues are dealt with at all in today's Internet. Then if you add other elements, like security, you start to see the complexity of what's going on here.

In the bandwidth area, for example, there are two areas that are important: access and backbone. Access has to do with what you receive, for example, when you sign up at home. The problem is that to get at the services you want—primarily a telephone line with a 28.8 modem—is really not going to make it. So there's a lot of work going on in the area of higher performance access to individual users in the home. We're talking about access that goes from 28.8 kilobytes to 1, 2, 3, 4 megabytes per second: a very significant change.

That will happen in one of two ways, both of which face a number of challenges:

Through the cable companies. Cable companies are counting on a technology called "cable modems." It's a technology that's been around a long time but its price points have never been where they should be, according to the cable companies. Because the cable companies are forcing the vendors to lower prices, the vendors in that area will be looking at such thin margins that the amount of R&D they can spend in that technology will be very limited. So there are many challenges for them to get that kind of bandwidth to you.

Through the phone companies. Telephone companies have a technology today that would make a lot of us a lot happier if they would just deliver it to us. It's called ISDN. So now they're talking about going over the top of ISDN to these new technologies, which will deliver higher bandwidth to the home, yet we can't even get ISDN connections. If you live in Massachusetts, it's almost impossible to call NYNEX and get an ISDN connection easily. It might take four or five months.

Next is the backbone technology. The backbones are trying to get bandwidth up by a factor of a hundred, or a thousand, from where they are today. There are two technologies that are fighting it out in that space. Some ISPs [Internet Service Providers] want to go with an ATM [Asynchronous Transfer Mode] technology; some ISPs want to go with what we call "superrouters." Though standards are emerging in both places, they're not done yet. So there's just a tremendous amount of challenge involved in getting the Net to where it needs to be to make all this come together.

I think the future is going to be very interesting. There will be some very large companies that are kind of growing up, and they'll get there. There will be a lot of intranet building by companies to get the kind of services they want. The Internet will probably follow rather than lead, because the companies can invest and put the resources back into those kinds of services. So there will be a lot of these intranets that are connected to the Internet. And I think we'll continue to look at ISPs developing in the areas of new services or advanced services they can sell at a premium price to consumers to achieve higher profitability.

So it's a huge opportunity, a huge marketplace, and, from a company point of view, a great opportunity. Socially, the Net is an open net and Web sites are open environments, and individuals can do what they want. This network is not built with a common standard, where one place controls the whole thing; it allows for communities of interest. I think that's going to be where diversity really flourishes—the technology allows for diversity to occur. Thank you.

BRANSCOMB: When Scott McNealy was here, he remembered that the last time he was in Sanders Theater, he was sleeping through Classics lectures up there in the rafters. Last time I performed in Sanders Theater was in 1951 at the Freshmen's Smoker, singing with Tom Lehrer.

Well this has been a good experience too. This conference on "The Internet and Society" finally got around to "society" this morning, and I found it very stimulating. I want to thank the participants for giving us at Harvard an opportunity we haven't had before, which is to take all of the university's work in this area, and try to organize an event that would give us a chance to see how the pieces fit together.

We've been trying to do that a bit academically. The Kennedy School and the Business School have been teaching a course together on Internet-related matters. Next year, we are boldly going to try that with three schools teaching it together, with the Law School joining in.

It's not often that a university tries to struggle with a contemporary, fast moving issue to which most of the intellectual tools of our trades are not really very applicable. We are grappling here with an issue that calls perhaps more for judgment than it does analysis.

I want to make a few comments. First, to borrow from A. Conan Doyle about the dogs that didn't bark, I didn't hear anything in any of the meetings about "the search for the killer app." Why? Because we've only got one of two cultures here, with some exceptions. Mostly we have computer-oriented, computer thinking people. We didn't have the classic telephone company folks. And they have big problems, as my compatriot just pointed out. The telephone companies estimate something like $1,000 a home in capital investment to wire them with hybrid fiber coax. The cable companies estimate about half that. But that's a lot of money.

And if the telephone companies are going to put all their money up front to build that carriage infrastructure, they need the confidence that there's a stream of revenue to pay back that capital. They traditionally looked for a common denominator application—one that everybody wants—to leverage the network externalities and guarantee the sources of finance. They must ensure that the revenue will be there long enough to depreciate the plant at the long depreciation times the regulators have foisted off on them over the years. So the telephone companies worry about whether there's a profit margin sufficient to protect it against the risks if indeed there isn't the "killer application."

As the competition increases and prices move toward marginal costs, some of them say the only way they can recover that cost is by vertically integrating with the provision of content. And when they do that, they may find it attractive to capture a group of client customers for their proprietary content with a proprietary distribution offering. We may see, then, a trend away from what otherwise today looks like a commitment to interoperability.

The computer-based culture is basically optimistic. It assumes people buy computers because they'll do something useful—something they've never imagined. And there's conviction in the computer-minded parts of the industry that you can reach this audience without the killer app. Tens of thousands of niche markets and niche applications can drive the growth. So I want to sound a note of caution. Keeping the infrastructure up with the rate of innovation is going to be a big job if the rate of innovation itself doesn't slow down.

That brings me to the issue of the pace of change. Bill Gates whipped out the number "20 years" as the time needed to realize a lot of the things he talked about. An interesting point was recently made that people enable the technology, rather than the technology that enables people. If you think about that, you realize that you can concurrently experience extraordinarily rapid change while, in some sense, nothing is changing at all.

So what changes rapidly? Well, clearly the technological capability—the potential—is changing very rapidly. A demonstration of all the kinds of applications we can see, those are flowering with enormous rates. So the vision indeed changes rapidly. But certain things may be a little slower than we'd like to think. Let me start with the business aspects. The realization of new business structures, which generate enough revenue with sufficient certainty, must motivate the investment of billions of dollars of infrastructure to give adequate network interoperability in the end user bandwidth. As Marvin Sirbu[*] pointed out the other day, "God would never have made the world in seven days if he had to cope with a huge installed base."

The second thing that will move more slowly than we might expect are information services. Some service areas that have the power to bring money to this market may demand more investment than the money consumers will spend on these information services. Take the field of medicine, for example. Until the medical community adopts standard data formats and standard definitions, and other ways of automating this huge amount of complex information, the ability to fully use the Internet will be limited.

Finally, and this is purely a guess, perhaps the slowest thing will be the inevitable political transformations once communities no longer think of themselves as defined by geography.

I said that the pace of change might be frustrating if the rate of innovation continues. But maybe it won't. And here I want to hark back to something Howard Frank said.[†] I just swiped one of Howard Frank's foils. When asked to speak about the relationship between the Internet and information infrastructure, he said, "Well, what's infrastructure? Infrastructure is when the technology we all use becomes average, becomes commonplace, universally available, inexpensive, and the like." So he decided he would rate the Internet on this scorecard. As he gave the Internet fair to poor ratings, he said, "I think I've been overly generous in almost every category."

He worries about the fact that when the Internet actually has good scores on these elements, it may no longer be the kind of testbed and incubator for radical market and technology innovations it has been. At least, he says, it will surely slow down. As businesses mature, I suspect some of them, the dominant ones, will ensure that the innovation rate slows down in order to protect

their interests. And they will have lots of lawyers to help them.

Where will the radical future innovation come from? Well, he says he visualizes that DARPA and the NSF, the two principal agencies that drove the technological creativity, carried out in universities and small companies, are going to do the trick again. They're already experimenting with terabyte, switched networks. This will be a research environment, not a real–world commercial environment, and out of that will come a whole new set of dreams and visions which, in another generation, can be commercialized.

Well, are they right? If not, are we going to see the Internet gradually change, paced by capital investment, by consumer adaptations to business offerings, by legal resolution of rights and intellectual property, privacy, and security? Or will the Internet, which really is many nets, contain within it islands of innovation where, because of interoperability, the market still rewards the ability to test the new idea against a potentially huge audience without the commitment to the levels of quality, service, and standards that will dominate?

I think the answer is that this whole process will require a very careful and complex relationship between the public and private sectors. For one thing, we have talked a lot about who owns the Internet, who controls it. The dominant theme among all us computer-minded folks is, for God's sake, keep the government out and let free enterprise take care of it. Don't worry, be happy.

But in point of fact, the way we have defined our domain names was by segregating the world institutionally into *.coms*, *.edus*, *.orgs*, etc. And those have been issued by Americans. In the rest of the world, those domain names have a two-letter last element, representing the initials of the country: *.KR* for Korea, *.AU* for Australia, etc. If a domain name of particular commercial interest might cost a quarter million dollars to buy, how

---

[*] Marvin Sirbu participated in the session "The Paradigm of Interoperability: Standards-Setting for the Internet," in the Public Policy track.

[†] See the session "The Place of the Internet in National and Global Information Infrastructure," in the Public Policy track.

long do you think the other 126 nations of the earth are going to sit still while American institutions dole out *.com* names, which are worldwide business franchises?

If we're going to keep this out of the hands of governments, who are indeed deregulating their telephone systems around the world, the American Internet community must reach out aggressively to nongovernmental entities in other parts of the world, bring them into the process of in the way in which we create domain names, and resolve issues that otherwise slow down the rate of progress.

BREGMAN: Thank you. Professor Miller.

MILLER: I'm thinking about the 14th and 15th century. I'm thinking about the Vikings and Vespucci and Magellan and Columbus, about a world in which people like that could hop into their flimsy boats and just sail off in uncharted waters. It was a world of open environment. It was a world of individualization. I'm thinking of Lindbergh, who gets into a small plane on a tar strip in Long Island in 1927 and says, "I think I'll go to Paris." And he does. Late yesterday afternoon, I was sitting in a very small plane, not much bigger than Lindbergh's, in a place so south in Texas it was south of San Antonio. We were on a tar strip—no other human beings, just the pilot and myself.

I had to go to San Antonio. We took off like Lindbergh into uncharted waters, open environment. The age of individualization persisted, I thought. And I innocently asked the pilot, "Does anybody know we're around?" And he said, "Watch this." He flipped a switch and a display came on and he says, "We're now being monitored by a satellite and the satellite is telling me that we are so many miles from San Antonio, flying at such and such a speed, and we will arrive in so many minutes. And the satellite is telling Houston Air Traffic Control exactly where we are and Houston Control will tell us exactly how to get to San Antonio."

And I said to myself, "Uncharted waters, hell. Open environment, hell. Individualization, hell."

Now what's changed and why am I telling you this? The truth is, however we cherish the open environment, the individualization of the Internet, and the ability of any person on the planet to communicate with any other person on the planet, it is, in the long run, a bit of a kind mirror. In the years since Magellan and Columbus, we have developed the law of the sea. After all, we have to tell ships whether they are to pass on the left or the right. We have developed the law of commerce so that we can wire transfer money from Cambridge to Geneva.

> *The wonderful anarchy, individualization, unregulated environment of the Internet cannot persevere forever.*

We have developed the law of the sky. We have even developed the law of outer space. And in one of the great oxymorons of our time, we are in the Hague at the moment developing the law of war. Now it is my duty to inform you that we will have to develop the law of the Internet. The wonderful anarchy, individualization, unregulated environment of the Internet cannot persevere forever. We already see the tensions. They've been touched on in the days you have spent here and in your own experiences. I just draw from my own experience in terms of what I teach.

Communities, whether they be Tennessee or China or Singapore, have, for whatever reasons they may choose to find worthy, decided that there are reasons to establish barriers, inhibitions, restraints, on certain kinds of messages. I sat recently in Geneva, giving a lecture for the World Intellectual Property Organization and one of the people over lunch said to me, "I'm an Iranian. I'm an *Iranian*. It simply is inconceivable in this world of technology that we will permit signals to come into Iran that are fundamentally inconsistent with our religious beliefs."

So first of all, people will create barriers to what will be granted access. They will be porous barriers, but they will be barriers. There will also conversely be an attempt by communities, again whether it's Tennessee or Singapore or Germany, to reach out to punish those who seek to send impermissible messages to that community, whether those messages be ideological or arelious or pornographic or anti-semitic. Questions will arise among communities: What legal barriers or constraints can I impose on the messages coming in, and what power do I have to reach out to punish impermissible message senders?

Second, intellectual property, IP. Is the Internet a free market? It's a free market of ideas, but is it a free market in the sense that anything I find on the Net is free for the taking? Some people think the answer is yes. We will have to think about that legally. We will have to think about that in terms of the potential deleterious effects of that kind of free market thinking on notions of creativity and incentive theory for creativity. We will have to think about that in terms of commerce and the permissibility of that kind of free market.

Third. In 1971, I wrote this book called *The Assault on Privacy: Computers, Databanks, and Dossiers*. This is probably the only extant copy of it. In 1971—think about it—there was no Net, there were no chips. I was remarking how technology historically has been a study of blessing and blasphemy. There has never been a technology that has not been blessing and blasphemy, whether it's fire, the internal combustion engine, or the computer.

In this book I said that there may come a day when, if I fell ill in Paris, a local doctor could use my patient birth number to retrieve my medical history and drug reactions from a global medical databank, and instantly provide me with the needed medical treatment. Then I go on at nauseating length, pointing out that the same valuable information that so wonderfully might save my life 8,000 miles from home, would, if totally unregulated, provide a womb-to-tomb dossier of me that could be manipulated by nefarious interests, for ideological or commercial ends.

Is the ability to market one-on-one from retailer to consumer an unvarnished blessing? Or is it potentially a mode of privacy intrusion and manipulation? I give you these three illustrations simply to say that some day, maybe not tomorrow or next week or a year from now, we will have to sit down and figure out the rules for the Internet road. Do we pass on the left or do we pass on the right? We *will* have to regulate to some degree. It will be a task done in fits and starts that boggles the mind, because it will have to be done on a global policy-making basis.

BRANSCOMB: What are the rules of the road? Not only is the question critical to everybody in this room and one of the great challenges of the future, but another question—who is it that formulates the rules of the road—is a question of equal dimension. Who is it going to be? Is it going to be the technologists? I am sure I insult you when I say that word with dripping invective. Is it going to be the Luddites? Frankly, some of my best friends are Luddites. Is it going to be those evil bureaucrats we generically refer to as The Government, who Lew does not want to see into the tent?

Experience shows that you can go a long way with prescient self-regulation. If you do not engage in prescient self-regulation that is when, by default, one of these three groups tends to take over. And increasingly, in a complex environment, it tends to be the government.

So to me, challenge Number One is to have the foresight to understand that a modicum of regulation is necessary and to begin its formulation. The second great challenge is not to abdicate this responsibility to people whose policy formulation may prove to be counterproductive for those of us who want to live in the 21st century.

BREGMAN: Thank you very much. I think it's interesting that we're finishing on a note of caution and I think that's responsible. But I'm very optimistic by nature, and I think that companies like mine and Paul's will find ways to profitably continue to use this Internet to help others achieve their ambitions, whether they're social or intellectual, economic or artistic. And contrary perhaps to the comments from a previous panel, I personally don't feel that this is the beginning of the end brought on by the Internet. But it is, unfortunately, the end of the beginning brought on by this conference.

I would like to thank Harvard University for sponsoring this exchange. I would like to especially thank all of the participants for making this conference as rich as it has been. And I'd like to personally thank Professor Kung for his enormous contribution of energy to make this happen.

About the Speakers

Mark F. Bregman was appointed to the position of General Manager, IBM RS/6000 Division in January 1995. He joined IBM T.J. Watson Research Center in 1984 as a Post–Doctoral Fellow in the Physical Sciences Department. In 1991, Dr. Bregman was named Director of Advanced Technology Development in the Yasu Technology Application Laboratory, Japan, and in 1992, was named Director, Component Technology Manufacturing and Development, Asia Pacific Technical Operations, Yasu, Japan. In 1993, Dr. Bregman was Research Division Vice President of Technical Plans and Controls, and in 1994 Dr. Bregman was named Vice President, Systems, Technology and Science for the IBM Research Division. In 1995, he was named Technical Assistant to the IBM Chairman.

Dr. Lewis M. Branscomb is Aetna Professor of Public Policy and Corporate Management at the John F. Kennedy School of Government of Harvard University, where he directs the school's Science, Technology, and Public Policy program in the Center for Science and International Affairs. Formerly a research physicist at the U.S. National Bureau of Standards (now the National Institute for Standards and Technology), Dr. Branscomb was appointed Director of NBS by President Nixon. In 1972 he was named Vice President and Chief Scientist of IBM Corporation; while an IBM executive, he was appointed by President Carter to the National Science Board, where he served as chariman from 1980 to 1984.

Arthur R. Miller is the Bruce Bromley Professor of Law at Harvard Law School, where he has taught since 1971. Among lawyers he is nationally known for his work on court procedure, a subject on which he has authored or co-authored more than 25 books. The general public, however, knows him for his work in the field of the right of privacy. His book *The Assault on Privacy: Computers, Data Banks, and Dossiers* (1971) has been extremely influential. Since July, 1980, Professor Miller has been appearing on ABC's *Good Morning America* as the program's legal editor. He also comments regularly on legal topics for Boston Channel 5's noontime news, and he is the host of the weekly In *Context* program on the Courtroom Television Network.

Paul Severino co-founded Wellfleet (which merged with SynOptics to become Bay Networks) in June of 1986 to address the growing need for high performance, multiprotocol routing, and bridging within a campus or across the wide area. The company quickly became a leader in providing local and wide area solutions for enterprise-wide internetworking. Prior to founding Wellfleet, Mr. Severino was a founder and President of Interlan, Inc. until 1985, when the company was acquired by Micom Systems. He was also a co-founder of Data Translation, Inc., and held management positions at both Digital Equipment Corporation and Prime Computer. Mr. Severino presently serves as a Director on the boards of Data Translation, Inc., for the Computer Museum in Boston, Massachusetts, Bay Networks, and Massachusetts Technology Development Corporation (MTDC).

Name Index

Subject Index

More Titles from O'Reilly

World Wide Web Journal

Fourth International World Wide Web Conference Proceedings

A publication of O'Reilly & Associates and the World Wide Web Consortium (W3C)
Winter 1995/96
748 pages, ISBN 1-56592-169-0

The *World Wide Web Journal* provides timely, in-depth coverage of the W3C's technological developments, such as protocols for security, replication and caching, HTML and SGML, and content labeling. It also explores the broader issues of the Web with Web luminaries and articles on controversial legal issues such as censorship and intellectual property rights. Whether you follow Web developments for strategic planning, application programming, or Web page authoring and designing, you'll find the in-depth information you need here.

The *World Wide Web Journal* is published quarterly. This issue contains 57 refereed technical papers presented at the Fourth International World Wide Web Conference, held December 1995 in Boston, Massachusetts. It also includes the two best papers from regional conferences.

Key Specifications of the World Wide Web

A publication of O'Reilly & Associates and the World Wide Web Consortium (W3C)
Spring 1996
356 pages, ISBN 1-56592-190-9

The key specifications that describe the architecture of the World Wide Web and how it works are maintained online at the World Wide Web Consortium. This issue of the *World Wide Web Journal* collects these key papers in a single volume as an important reference for the Webmaster, application programmer, or technical manager.

In this valuable reference, you'll find the definitive specifications for the core technologies in the Web: Hypertext Markup Language (HTML), Hypertext Transfer Protocol (HTTP), and Uniform Resource Locators (URLs), plus the emerging standards for portable graphics (PNG), content selection (PICS), and style sheets (CSS).

The Web After Five Years

A publication of O'Reilly & Associates and the World Wide Web Consortium (W3C)
Summer 1996, 226 pp, ISBN 1-56592-210-7

As the Web explodes across the technology scene, it's increasingly difficult to keep track of myriad new protocols, standards, and applications. The *World Wide Web Journal* is your direct connection to the work of the World Wide Web Consortium.

This issue is a reflection on the web after five years. In an interview with Tim Berners-Lee, the inventor of the Web and Director of the W3C, we learn that the Web was built to be an interactive, intercreative, two-way medium from the beginning. At the opposite scale, as a mass medium, are urgent questions about the Web's size, character, and users. These issues are addressed in selections from the MIT/W3C Workshop on Web Demographics and Internet Survey Methodology, along with commerce-related papers selected from the Fifth International World Wide Web Conference, which took place from May 6–10 in Paris.

Building an Industrial Strength Web

A publication of O'Reilly & Associates and the World Wide Web Consortium (W3C)
Fall 1996, 244 pp, ISBN 1-56592-211-5

Issue 4 focuses on the infrastructure needed to create and maintain an "Industrial Strength Web," from network protocols to application design. Included are the first standard versions of core Web protocols: HTTP/1.1, Digest Authentica-tion, State Management (Cookies), and PICS. This issue also provides guides to the specs, highlighting new features, papers explaining modifications to 1.1 (sticky and compressed headers), extensibility, support for collaborative authoring, and using distributed objects.

Advancing HTML: Style and Substance

A publication of O'Reilly & Associates and the World Wide Web Consortium (W3C)
Winter 1996/97
254 pages, ISBN 1-56592-264-6

Issue 5 is a guide to the specifications and tools that buttress the user interface to the World Wide Web. It includes the latest HTML 3.2 and CSS1 specs, papers on gif animation, JavaScript, Web accessibility, usability engineering, multimedia design, and a report on Amaya.

O'REILLY™

TO ORDER: **800-998-9938** • *order@ora.com* • *http://www.ora.com/*

OUR PRODUCTS ARE AVAILABLE AT A BOOKSTORE OR SOFTWARE STORE NEAR YOU.

FOR INFORMATION: **800-998-9938** • **707-829-0515** • *info@ora.com*

Developing Web Content

Building Your Own WebSite

By Susan B. Peck & Stephen Arrants
1st Edition July 1996
514 pages, ISBN 1-56592-232-8

This is a hands-on reference for Windows® 95 and Windows NT™ desktop users who want to host their own site on the Web or on a corporate intranet. This step-by-step guide will have you creating live Web pages in minutes. You'll also learn how to connect your web to information in other Windows applications, such as word processing documents and databases. Packed with examples and tutorials on every aspect of Web management. Includes highly acclaimed WebSite™ 1.1—all the software you need for Web publishing.

Web Client Programming with Perl

By Clinton Wong
1st Edition Fall 1996
250 pages (est.), ISBN 1-56592-214-X

Web Client Programming with Perl teaches you how to extend scripting skills to the Web. This book teaches you the basics of how browsers communicate with servers and how to write your own customized Web clients to automate common tasks. It is intended for those who are motivated to develop software that offers a more flexible and dynamic response than a standard Web browser.

JavaScript: The Definitive Guide

By David Flanagan
1st Edition Winter 1997
700 pages (est.), ISBN 1-56592-234-4

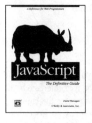

This definitive reference guide to JavaScript, the HTML extension that gives Web pages programming language capabilities, covers JavaScript as it is used in Netscape 3.0 and 2.0 and in Microsoft Internet Explorer 2.0. Learn how JavaScript really works (and when it doesn't). Use JavaScript to control Web browser behavior, add dynamically created text to Web pages, interact with users through HTML forms, and even control and interact with Java applets and Navigator plug-ins.

HTML: The Definitive Guide

By Chuck Musciano & Bill Kennedy
1st Edition April 1996
410 pages, ISBN 1-56592-175-5

A complete guide to creating documents on the World Wide Web. This book describes basic syntax and semantics and goes on to show you how to create beautiful, informative Web documents you'll be proud to display. The HTML 2.0 standard and Netscape extensions are fully explained.

Designing for the Web: Getting Started in a New Medium

By Jennifer Niederst with Edie Freedman
1st Edition April 1996
180 pages, ISBN 1-56592-165-8

Designing for the Web gives you the basics you need to hit the ground running. Although geared toward designers, it covers information and techniques useful to anyone who wants to put graphics online. It explains how to work with HTML documents from a designer's point of view, outlines special problems with presenting information online, and walks through incorporating images into Web pages, with emphasis on resolution and improving efficiency.

WebMaster in a Nutshell

By Stephen Spainhour & Valerie Quercia
1st Edition October 1996
378 pages, ISBN 1-56592-229-8

Web content providers and administrators have many sources of information, both in print and online. *WebMaster in a Nutshell* pulls it all together into one slim volume—for easy desktop access. This quick-reference covers HTML, CGI, Perl, HTTP, server configuration, and tools for Web administration.

O'REILLY™

TO ORDER: **800-998-9938** • **order@ora.com** • **http://www.ora.com/**
OUR PRODUCTS ARE AVAILABLE AT A BOOKSTORE OR SOFTWARE STORE NEAR YOU.
FOR INFORMATION: **800-998-9938** • **707-829-0515** • **info@ora.com**

Java Programming

Exploring Java

By Patrick Niemeyer & Joshua Peck
1st Edition May 1996
426 pages, ISBN 1-56592-184-4

Exploring Java introduces the basics of Java, the hot new object-oriented programming language for networked applications. The ability to create animated World Wide Web pages has sparked the rush to Java. But what has also made this new language so important is that it's truly portable. The code runs on any machine that provides a Java interpreter, be it Windows 95, Windows NT, the Macintosh, or any flavor of UNIX.

Java in a Nutshell

By David Flanagan
1st Edition February 1996
460 pages, ISBN 1-56592-183-6

Java in a Nutshell is a complete quick-reference guide to Java, the hot new programming language from Sun Microsystems. This comprehensive volume contains descriptions of all of the classes in the Java 1.0 API, with a definitive listing of all methods and variables. It also contains an accelerated introduction to Java for C and C++ programmers who want to learn the language *fast*.

Java Virtual Machine

By Troy Downing & Jon Meyer
1st Edition Winter 1997
380 pages (est.), ISBN 1-56592-194-1

This book is a comprehensive programming guide for the Java Virtual Machine (JVM). It gives readers a strong overview and reference of the JVM so that they may create their own implementations of the JVM or write their own compilers that create Java object code.

Java Language Reference

By Mark Grand
1st Edition January 1997
450 pages (est.), ISBN 1-56592-204-2

The *Java Language Reference* will be an indispensable tool for every Java programmer. Part of O'Reilly's new series on the Java language, this edition describes Java Version 1.0.2. It covers the syntax (presented in easy-to-understand railroad diagrams), object-oriented programming, exception handling, multithreaded programming, and differences between Java and C/C++.

Java Fundamental Classes Reference

By Mark Grand
1st Edition Winter 1997
330 pages (est.), ISBN 1-56592-241-7

The *Java Fundamental Classes Reference* provides complete reference documentation for the Java fundamental classes. These classes contain architecture-independent methods that serve as Java's gateway to the real world and provide access to resources such as the network, the windowing system, and the host filesystem.

Java AWT Reference

By John Zukowski
1st Edition Winter 1997
700 pages (est.), ISBN 1-56592-240-9

The *Java AWT Reference* provides complete reference documentation on the Abstract Windowing Toolkit (AWT), a large collection of classes for building graphical user interfaces in Java. Part of O'Reilly's new Java documentation series, this edition describes Version 1.0.2 of the Java Developer's Kit. The *Java AWT Reference* includes easy-to-use reference material on every AWT class and provides lots of sample code to help you learn by example.

Songline Guides

NetLearning: Why Teachers Use the Internet

By Ferdi Serim & Melissa Koch
1st Edition June 1996
304 pages, ISBN 1-56592-201-8

In this book educators and Internet users who've been exploring its potential for education share stories to help teachers use this medium to its fullest potential in their classrooms. The book offers advice on how to adapt, how to get what you want, and where to go for help. The goal: To invite educators online with the reassurance there will be people there to greet them. Includes CD-ROM with Internet software.

NetSuccess: How Real Estate Agents Use the Internet

By Scott Kersnar
1st Edition August 1996
214 pages, ISBN 1-56592-213-1

This book shows real estate agents how to harness Internet communications and marketing tools to enhance their careers and make the Internet work for them. Through agents' stories and "A day in the life"scenarios, readers learn what happens when technology is welcomed as a full working partner.

NetActivism: How Citizens Use the Internet

By Ed Schwartz
1st Edition September 1996
224 pages, ISBN 1-56592-160-7

Let a veteran political activist tell you how to use online networks to further your cause. Whether you are a community activist, a politician, a nonprofit staff person, or just someone who cares about your community, you will benefit from the insights this book offers on how to make the fastest-growing medium today work for you. Includes CD-ROM with Internet software and limited free online time.

Net Lessons: Web-based Projects for Your Classroom

By Laura Parker Roerden
1st Edition March 1997
300 pages (est.), ISBN 1-56592-291-3

Whe you use this book, you will inherit the advice, experience and project ideas of veteran Web users, teachers, and curriculum experts. This book includes:
• 100+ K-12 classroom lessons and ideas
• Standard lesson plan formats
• Assessment and goal-setting tools

NetResearch: Finding Information Online

By Daniel J. Barrett
1st Edition Winter 1997
240 pages (est.), ISBN 1-56592-245-X

Whatever your profession or avocation, NetResearch will show you how to locate the information in the constantly changing online world. Whether you're research statistics for a report, to find free software, or to locate an old college roommate, it pays to locate online information rapidly. But the Net is a very big, disorganized place, and it can be difficult to locate just the information you want, when you need it. In *NetResearch*, you'll learn effective search techniques that work with any Internet search programs. The author offers quizzes that allow you to practice your own research skills or that you can use as a teaching tool to help others. Covers the Internet, America Online, CompuServe, Microsoft Network, and Prodigy.

NetTravel: How Travelers Use the Internet

By Michael Shapiro
1st Edition Winter 1997
225 pages (est.), ISBN 1-56592-172-0

NetTravel is a virtual toolbox of advice for those travelers who want to tap into the rich vein of travel resources on the Internet. It is filled with personal accounts by travelers who've used the Net to plan their business trips, vacations, honeymoons, and explorations. Author and journalist Michael Shapiro gives readers all the tools they need to use the Net immediately to find and save money on airline tickets, accommodations, and car rentals. Includes CD-ROM with Internet software.

Net Law: How Lawyers Use the Internet

By Paul Jacobsen
1st Edition Winter 1997
254 pages (est.), ISBN 1-56592-258-1

From simple email to sophisticated online marketing, *Net Law* shows how the solo practitioner or the large law firm can turn the Net into an effective and efficient tool. Through stories from those who've set up pioneering legal Net sites, attorney Paul Jacobsen explains how lawyers can successfully integrate the Internet into their practices, sharing lessons "early adoptees" have learned. Includes CD-ROM with Internet software and limited free online time.

How to stay in touch with O'Reilly

1. Visit Our Award-Winning Web Site

http://www.ora.com/

★ "Top 100 Sites on the Web" —*PC Magazine*
★ "Top 5% Web sites" —*Point Communications*
★ "3-Star site" —*The McKinley Group*

Our web site contains a library of comprehensive product information (including book excerpts and tables of contents), downloadable software, background articles, interviews with technology leaders, links to relevant sites, book cover art, and more. File us in your Bookmarks or Hotlist!

2. Join Our Email Mailing Lists

New Product Releases

To receive automatic email with brief descriptions of all new O'Reilly products as they are released, send email to:
listproc@online.ora.com
Put the following information in the first line of your message (*not* in the Subject field):
subscribe ora-news "Your Name"of "Your Organization" (for example: subscribe ora-news Kris Webber of Fine Enterprises)

O'Reilly Events

If you'd also like us to send information about trade show events, special promotions, and other O'Reilly events, send email to:
listproc@online.ora.com
Put the following information in the first line of your message (*not* in the Subject field):
subscribe ora-events "Your Name" of "Your Organization"

3. Get Examples from Our Books via FTP

There are two ways to access an archive of example files from our books:

Regular FTP

• ftp to:
ftp.ora.com
(login: anonymous
password: your email address)
• Point your web browser to:
ftp://ftp.ora.com/

FTPMAIL

• Send an email message to:
ftpmail@online.ora.com
(Write "help" in the message body)

4. Visit Our Gopher Site

• Connect your gopher to:
gopher.ora.com

• Point your web browser to:
gopher://gopher.ora.com/

• Telnet to:
gopher.ora.com
login: gopher

5. Contact Us via Email

order@ora.com
To place a book or software order online. Good for North American and international customers.

subscriptions@ora.com
To place an order for any of our newsletters or periodicals.

books@ora.com
General questions about any of our books.

software@ora.com
For general questions and product information about our software. Check out O'Reilly Software Online at **http://software.ora.com/** for software and technical support information. Registered O'Reilly software users send your questions to: **website-support@ora.com**

cs@ora.com
For answers to problems regarding your order or our products.

booktech@ora.com
For book content technical questions or corrections.

proposals@ora.com
To submit new book or software proposals to our editors and product managers.

international@ora.com
For information about our international distributors or translation queries. For a list of our distributors outside of North America check out:
http://www.ora.com/www/order/country.html

O'Reilly & Associates, Inc.
101 Morris Street, Sebastopol, CA 95472 USA
TEL 707-829-0515 or 800-998-9938
(6 a.m. to 5 p.m. pst)
FAX 707-829-0104

O'REILLY™

Titles from O'Reilly

Please note that upcoming titles are displayed in italic.

WEB PROGRAMMING

Apache: The Definitive Guide
Building Your Own Website
CGI Programming for the World Wide Web
Designing for the Web
HTML: The Definitive Guide
JavaScript: The Definitive Guide, 2nd Ed.
Learning Perl
Programming Perl, 2nd Ed.
Mastering Regular Expressions
WebMaster in a Nutshell
Web Security & Commerce
Web Client Programming with Perl
World Wide Web Journal

USING THE INTERNET

Smileys
The Future Does Not Compute
The Whole Internet User's Guide & Catalog
The Whole Internet for Win 95
Using Email Effectively
Bandits on the Information Superhighway

JAVA SERIES

Exploring Java
Java AWT Reference
Java Fundamental Classes Reference
Java in a Nutshell
Java Language Reference
Java Network Programming
Java Threads
Java Virtual Machine

SOFTWARE

WebSite™ 1.1
WebSite Professional™
Building Your Own Web Conferences
WebBoard™
PolyForm™
Statisphere™

SONGLINE GUIDES

NetActivism
Net Law
NetLearning
Net Lessons
NetResearch
NetSuccess for Realtors
NetTravel

SYSTEM ADMINISTRATION

Building Internet Firewalls
Computer Crime: A Crimefighter's Handbook
Computer Security Basics
DNS and BIND, 2nd Ed.
Essential System Administration, 2nd Ed.
Getting Connected: The Internet at 56K and Up
Internet Server Administration with Windows NT
Linux Network Administrator's Guide
Managing Internet Information Services
Managing NFS and NIS
Networking Personal Computers with TCP/IP
Practical UNIX & Internet Security. 2nd Ed.
PGP: Pretty Good Privacy
sendmail, 2nd Ed.
sendmail Desktop Reference
System Performance Tuning
TCP/IP Network Administration
termcap & terminfo
Using & Managing UUCP
Volume 8: X Window System Administrator's Guide
Web Security & Commerce

UNIX

Exploring Expect
Learning VBScript
Learning GNU Emacs, 2nd Ed.
Learning the bash Shell
Learning the Korn Shell
Learning the UNIX Operating System
Learning the vi Editor
Linux in a Nutshell
Making TeX Work
Linux Multimedia Guide
Running Linux, 2nd Ed.
SCO UNIX in a Nutshell
sed & awk, 2nd Edition
Tcl/Tk Tools
UNIX in a Nutshell: System V Edition
UNIX Power Tools
Using csh & tsch
When You Can't Find Your UNIX System Administrator
Writing GNU Emacs Extensions

WEB REVIEW STUDIO SERIES

Gif Animation Studio
Shockwave Studio

WINDOWS

Dictionary of PC Hardware and Data Communications Terms
Inside the Windows 95 Registry
Inside the Windows 95 File System
Win95 & WinNT Annoyances
Windows NT File System Internals
Windows NT in a Nutshell

PROGRAMMING

Advanced Oracle PL/SQL Programming
Applying RCS and SCCS
C++: The Core Language
Checking C Programs with lint
DCE Security Programming
Distributing Applications Across DCE & Windows NT
Encyclopedia of Graphics File Formats, 2nd Ed.
Guide to Writing DCE Applications
lex & yacc
Managing Projects with make
Mastering Oracle Power Objects
Oracle Design: The Definitive Guide
Oracle Performance Tuning, 2nd Ed.
Oracle PL/SQL Programming
Porting UNIX Software
POSIX Programmer's Guide
POSIX.4: Programming for the Real World
Power Programming with RPC
Practical C Programming
Practical C++ Programming
Programming Python
Programming with curses
Programming with GNU Software
Pthreads Programming
Software Portability with imake, 2nd Ed.
Understanding DCE
Understanding Japanese Information Processing
UNIX Systems Programming for SVR4

BERKELEY 4.4 SOFTWARE DISTRIBUTION

4.4BSD System Manager's Manual
4.4BSD User's Reference Manual
4.4BSD User's Supplementary Documents
4.4BSD Programmer's Reference Manual
4.4BSD Programmer's Supplementary Documents
X Programming
Vol. 0: X Protocol Reference Manual
Vol. 1: Xlib Programming Manual
Vol. 2: Xlib Reference Manual
Vol. 3M: X Window System User's Guide, Motif Edition
Vol. 4M: X Toolkit Intrinsics Programming Manual, Motif Edition
Vol. 5: X Toolkit Intrinsics Reference Manual
Vol. 6A: Motif Programming Manual
Vol. 6B: Motif Reference Manual
Vol. 6C: Motif Tools
Vol. 8 : X Window System Administrator's Guide
Programmer's Supplement for Release 6
X User Tools
The X Window System in a Nutshell

CAREER & BUSINESS

Building a Successful Software Business
The Computer User's Survival Guide
Love Your Job!
Electronic Publishing on CD-ROM

TRAVEL

Travelers' Tales: Brazil
Travelers' Tales: Food
Travelers' Tales: France
Travelers' Tales: Gutsy Women
Travelers' Tales: India
Travelers' Tales: Mexico
Travelers' Tales: Paris
Travelers' Tales: San Francisco
Travelers' Tales: Spain
Travelers' Tales: Thailand
Travelers' Tales: A Woman's World

O'REILLY™

TO ORDER: **800-998-9938** • **order@ora.com** • **http://www.ora.com/**
OUR PRODUCTS ARE AVAILABLE AT A BOOKSTORE OR SOFTWARE STORE NEAR YOU.
FOR INFORMATION: **800-998-9938** • **707-829-0515** • **info@ora.com**

International Distributors

Europe, Middle East and Northern Africa (except France, Germany, Switzerland, & Austria)

INQUIRIES

International Thomson Publishing Europe
Berkshire House
168-173 High Holborn
London WC1V 7AA, United Kingdom
Telephone: 44-171-497-1422
Fax: 44-171-497-1426
Email: itpint@itps.co.uk

ORDERS

International Thomson Publishing Services, Ltd.
Cheriton House, North Way
Andover, Hampshire SP10 5BE,
United Kingdom
Telephone: 44-264-342-832
  (UK orders)
Telephone: 44-264-342-806
  (outside UK)
Fax: 44-264-364418 (UK orders)
Fax: 44-264-342761 (outside UK)
UK & Eire orders: itpuk@itps.co.uk
International orders: itpint@itps.co.uk

France

Editions Eyrolles
61 Bd Saint-Germain
75240 Paris Cedex 05
France
Telephone: 33 1 44 41 46 16
Fax: 33 1 44 41 11 44

Australia

WoodsLane Pty. Ltd.
7/5 Vuko Place, Warriewood NSW 2102
P.O. Box 935, Mona Vale NSW 2103
Australia
Telephone: 61-2-9970-5111
Fax: 61-2-9970-5002
Email: info@woodslane.com.au

Germany, Switzerland, and Austria

INQUIRIES

O'Reilly Verlag
Balthasarstr. 81
D-50670 Köln
Germany
Telephone: 49 221 97 31 60 0
Fax: 49 221 97 31 60 8
Email: anfragen@oreilly.de

ORDERS

International Thomson Publishing
Königswinterer Straße 418
53227 Bonn, Germany
Telephone: 49-228-97024 0
Fax: 49-228-441342
Email: order@oreilly.de

Asia (except Japan & India)

INQUIRIES

International Thomson Publishing Asia
60 Albert Street #15-01
Albert Complex
Singapore 189969
Telephone: 65-336-6411
Fax: 65-336-7411

ORDERS

Telephone: 65-336-6411
Fax: 65-334-1617
thomson@signet.com.sg

New Zealand

WoodsLane New Zealand Ltd.
21 Cooks Street (P.O. Box 575)
Wanganui, New Zealand
Telephone: 64-6-347-6543
Fax: 64-6-345-4840
Email: info@woodslane.com.au

Japan

O'Reilly Japan, Inc.
Kiyoshige Building 2F
12-Banchi, Sanei-cho
Shinjuku-ku
Tokyo 160 Japan
Telephone: 81-3-3356-5227
Fax: 81-3-3356-5261
Email: kenji@ora.com

India

Computer Bookshop (India) PVT. LTD.
190 Dr. D.N. Road, Fort
Bombay 400 001
India
Telephone: 91-22-207-0989
Fax: 91-22-262-3551
Email: cbsbom@giasbm01.vsnl.net.in

The Americas

O'Reilly & Associates, Inc.
101 Morris Street
Sebastopol, CA 95472 U.S.A.
Telephone: 707-829-0515
Telephone: 800-998-9938 (U.S. & Canada)
Fax: 707-829-0104
Email: order@ora.com

Southern Africa

International Thomson Publishing Southern Africa
Building 18, Constantia Park
240 Old Pretoria Road
P.O. Box 2459
Halfway House, 1685 South Africa
Telephone: 27-11-805-4819
Fax: 27-11-805-3648